MODERN
SCIENCE
AND
ANARCHY

Advance praise for *Modern Science and Anarchy*:

"Iain McKay's definitive version of *Modern Science and Anarchy* is another welcome product of his continuing effort to broaden our understanding of Kropotkin's ideas, recovering texts scattered and forgotten in the course of Kropotkin's transnational activism.... [T]his work offers Kropotkin's most concise exposition of the ideas that defined his life, focusing on anarchism's interactions with the defining scientific and political currents of modern European history, and staking a claim for anarchism as a vital, and intellectually sophisticated, component of this story." —Matthew S. Adams, author of *Kropotkin, Read, and the Intellectual History of British Anarchism*

"Finally...the definitive edition of Kropotkin's *Modern Science and Anarchy*. Here we have not only a mature restatement of Kropotkin's anarchist communism, but Kropotkin's own history of anarchist ideas and movements, a survey of libertarian and anarchist currents throughout human history.... But that is not all—the second half of the book, a series of essays selected by Kropotkin himself on the rise of capitalism and the state, contains some of Kropotkin's best work, including 'The State: Its Historic Role.' Iain McKay is to be commended for so carefully editing and annotating one of Kropotkin's most important books." —Robert Graham, author of *We Do Not Fear Anarchy—We Invoke It*

"This new, definitive edition of Kropotkin's *Modern Science and Anarchy* is an important addition to the literature on one of the most influential figures in the development of modern libertarian communism. Iain McKay's introduction is a model of scholarship and succeeds not only in contextualising and explaining Kropotkin's ideas, but also in addressing a number of misunderstandings and misrepresentations along the way. He also makes a convincing case for the book's continuing relevance for present-day radicals." —David Berry, author of *A History of the French Anarchist Movement, 1917 to 1945*

"This is a welcome new translation of a long neglected text by Peter Kropotkin. In the spirit of Kropotkin, the volume includes a highly knowledgeable and sympathetic—yet not uncritical—introduction by the editor, who also adds some clarifying footnotes to the original text.... This book will not only be of keen interest to specialists in science studies, political epistemology and the history of political ideas, but also to contemporary libertarian activists who will still find plenty of relevant, clearly explained material to engage with." —Benjamin Franks, author of *Rebel Alliances*

MODERN SCIENCE AND ANARCHY

PETER KROPOTKIN

EDITED BY IAIN MCKAY

Modern Science and Anarchy
Introduction and notes © 2018 Iain McKay
This edition © 2018 AK Press (Chico, Oakland, Edinburgh, Baltimore)

ISBN: 978-1-84935-274-1
E-ISBN: 978-1-84935-275-8
Library of Congress Control Number: 2017957076

AK Press
370 Ryan Ave. #100
Chico, CA 95973
USA
www.akpress.org
akpress@akpress.org

AK Press
33 Tower St.
Edinburgh EH6 7BN
Scotland
www.akuk.com
ak@akedin.demon.co.uk

The above addresses would be delighted to provide you with the latest AK Press distribution catalog, which features books, pamphlets, zines, and stylish apparel published and/or distributed by AK Press. Alternatively, visit our websites for the complete catalog, latest news, and secure ordering.

Cover illustration and design by Margaret Killjoy, birdsbeforethestorm.net
Printed in the USA on recycled paper

CONTENTS

Introduction

REALITY HAS A WELL-KNOWN
LIBERTARIAN BIAS

"[T]he State, with its hierarchy of functionaries and the
weight of its historical traditions, could only delay the
dawning of a new society freed from monopolies and
exploitation [...] what means can the State provide to abolish
this monopoly that the working class could not find in its
own strength and groups? [...] [W]hat advantages could the
State provide for abolishing these same privileges? Could
its governmental machine, developed for the creation and
upholding of these privileges, now be used to abolish them?
Would not the new function require new organs? And these
new organs would they not have to be created by the workers
themselves, in their unions, their federations, completely
outside the State?"
—*Peter Kropotkin*[1]

PETER KROPOTKIN (1842–1921) SHOULD BE WELL KNOWN TO MOST
readers of this book. Born into a Russian royal family, he rejected his

---

1   *La Science moderne et l'anarchie* (Paris: Stock, 1913), 91–2.

privileges to become an anarchist, a libertarian communist, struggling for the liberation of all from every shackle imposed upon the individual and society.[2]

Modern Science and Anarchy (*La Science Moderne et L'Anarchie*) was the last book by Kropotkin published during his lifetime. It marks the summation of forty years within the anarchist movement since he concluded that he was an anarchist after visiting Switzerland and joining the (First) International in 1872. Like his earliest books, such as *Words of a Rebel* and *The Conquest of Bread*, it is mostly made up of a series of articles originally published in anarchist newspapers (in this case, *Les Temps Nouveaux*). The exception is the first section, *Modern Science and Anarchy*, which was initially written as a pamphlet in Russian (in 1901) before being serialised and later expanded in *Les Temps Nouveaux* (in 1902–3 and 1911).[3]

As well as being an excellent summary of anarchist ideas and history and a useful restatement of the anarchist analysis of the State, this work also reminds us that Kropotkin's first love was science.[4] He was a well-respected geographer who made significant contributions to the understanding of the geography of Asia. Indeed, as well as the justly famous—and much reprinted—entry on anarchism, he contributed many entries on geography to the celebrated eleventh edition of the *Encyclopaedia Britannica*.[5] It also

---

2   Sadly, it is necessary to explain what we mean by "libertarian" as this term has been appropriated by the free-market capitalist right. Socialist use of libertarian dates from 1857 when it was first used as a synonym for "anarchist" by communist-anarchist Joseph Déjacque in an "Open Letter to Pierre-Joseph Proudhon" and in the following year as the title for his paper *Le Libertaire, Journal du Mouvement Social*. This usage became more commonplace in the 1880s and 1895 saw leading anarchists Sébastien Faure and Louise Michel publish *Le Libertaire* in France (Max Nettlau, *A Short History of Anarchism* [London: Freedom Press, 1995], 75–76, 145, 162). By the end of the 19th century libertarian was used as an alternative for anarchist internationally. The right-wing appropriation of the term dates from the 1950s and, in wider society, from the 1970s. Given that property is at its root and, significantly, property always trumps liberty in that ideology, I suggest a far more accurate term would be "propertarian" (See my "160 Years of Libertarian," *Anarcho-Syndicalist Review*. 71 [Fall 2017]). We will use the term *libertarian* in its original, correct, meaning as an alternative for anti-State socialist and *propertarian* for the right-wing liberals who have tried to steal the term from the left.

3   For details, see "*Modern Science and Anarchy*: A Publication History" below.

4   Kropotkin recounts his decision to forgo a career in geography in favour of life as a revolutionary in his autobiography (*Memoirs of Revolutionist* [Montreal/New York: Black Rose,1989], 223–4).

5   An obituary expressed regret that Kropotkin's "absorption" in his political views

marks an intersection between his political activism and what he did to earn a living—as he notes in the "Foreword" it reflects the research needed to produce the "Recent Science" column for leading British journal *The Nineteenth Century.*[6]

Modern Science and Anarchy is an ambitious work and covers a wide range of issues that are as relevant now as they were then—Where does anarchism come from? How will we create it? Can we use the State to introduce socialism? Does "human nature" make anarchism impossible? Will libertarian communism limit the free development of the individual? What is the relation of anarchism to other political theories such as liberalism?—and Kropotkin brings his usual clarity when answering these (and many other) questions.

It would be impossible to discuss all that Kropotkin addresses so here we sketch a few issues associated with his invocation of anarchy and science as well as correcting a few of the errors made in the work. We hope that these show how well the book has stood the test of time.[7]

* * *

Any book with a title that includes the words "Modern Science" is almost certainly going to be dated by the time it is published. This is the case with Kropotkin's work for the science he discusses reflects his research for the "Recent Science" column of *The Nineteenth Century* and so the situation in the ten years leading up to 1901 when the bulk of Part I, *Modern Science and Anarchy*, was first published. This raises an issue with Kropotkin's invoking of science to justify anarchism as his comrade and friend Errico Malatesta suggested:

"seriously diminished the services which otherwise he might have rendered to Geography." He "was a keen observer, with a well-trained intellect, familiar with all the sciences bearing on his subject" and his "contributions to geographical science are of the highest value." Kropotkin "had a singularly attractive personality, sympathetic nature, a warm but perhaps too tender heart, and a wide knowledge in literature, science, and art." (*The Geographical Journal* 57: 4 [April, 1921]: 316–319).

6   Kropotkin considered this as a matter of principle: "A socialist must always rely upon his own work for his living"(*Memoirs of Revolutionist*, 353–4).

7   This was not the first work in which Kropotkin links anarchism to science. In 1887, he wrote the article "The Scientific Basis of Anarchy" (*The Nineteenth Century*, February 1887). This was later revised and, along with its companion piece "The Coming Anarchy" (*The Nineteenth Century*, August 1887), published in 1891 as the pamphlet *Anarchist Communism: Its Basis and Principles*.

He affirmed himself in his conviction by maintaining that recent discoveries in all sciences, from astronomy to biology and sociology, concurred in demonstrating that Anarchy is the mode of organisation exacted by Nature's laws. One might have objected to him that, whatever conclusions might be drawn from contemporary science, it was certain that if new discoveries would destroy the present scientific belief, he, Kropotkin, would have remained an Anarchist in the teeth of logic.[8]

This is true, to an extent. Science, by its very nature, tends to upset conventional wisdom—including that of science itself. What was once a well-established position can be overturned by new evidence and a better theory. If you proclaim anarchy as a science because of research made up to a certain point then the danger is, as Malatesta suggests, new developments will make a mockery of your claims.

An obvious example of this—although one which is not entirely correct[9]—is provided by Marxism and its pretentions of being "scientific socialism" (a term first used, incidentally, by Pierre-Joseph Proudhon in the same work in which he proclaimed property is theft and himself an anarchist[10]). This claim is based primarily on the use of the then-latest word in economic analysis, namely the "Labour Theory of Value" advocated by David Ricardo and which can be traced back to Adam Smith. Yet in the two decades after Marx published the first volume of *Capital* in 1867, mainstream economics changed when what became known as neo-classical economics replaced this theory of value with one based on marginal utility.[11] Thus "the science" has

---

8   Errico Malatesta, "Peter Kropotkin: Recollections and Criticisms by one of his old friends," *The Method of Freedom: An Errico Malatesta Reader*, ed. Davide Turcato (Oakland/Edinburgh: AK Press, 2014), 517.

9   In this case "the science" actually reversed into a dead-end. Marginal utility theory replaced a dynamic theory of price formation rooted in production and time with a static one that ignored both. However, it did allow capitalism to be defended and so it flourished (with appropriate changes to ensure that key role—for example, the move from cardinal to ordinal utility when the former was used to defend redistribution of wealth via progressive taxation).

10   Pierre-Joseph Proudhon, "What is Property?," *Property is Theft! A Pierre-Joseph Proudhon Anthology*, ed. Iain McKay (Edinburgh/Oakland/Baltimore: AK Press, 2011), 133.

11   Various Marxists have suggested, but never proven, that neo-classical economics was a response to Marx's book. This not only ignores the earlier socialists, like Proudhon, who utilised classical economics to attack capitalism, it also ignores the awkward fact that Léon Walras, one of the founders of that economic theology, wrote a book

moved on, making Marxist economics appear quaint and old-fashioned and so, for many, easy to dismiss. It matters little that neo-classical economics is deeply flawed and far from an actual science.[12]

The same applies to anarchism. To take an example closer to Kropotkin, namely the idea of "group selection" which was popular in biology for many decades after the Second World War and to which Kropotkin, falsely, was linked via *Mutual Aid*. For some, the tendency was to suggest that Kropotkin's ideas were validated because "science" supported the notion that the unit of selection was the group. The rise of "gene-level" biology quickly undermined and replaced "group selection" theory and by the 1970s it had been placed, like so many other "truths" of science, in the history books (under "what were we thinking?").[13] If Kropotkin *had* advocated group selection, where would that have left his theories and his claims for the scientific validity of anarchy?

Luckily, such readings of Kropotkin were superficial—*Mutual Aid* does not suggest a "group selection" theory—but the danger remains. This can be seen from Kropotkin's support for Lamarckian "soft inheritance"—the idea that environmental factors promoted evolutionary change via a "use or lose" mechanism. He spent a considerable amount of time seeking to refute August Weismann's theories and time has shown that he was wrong.[14] Weismann is now recognised as one of the most important evolutionary theorists of all time and the idea of the Weismann barrier is central to the modern evolutionary synthesis. It does not matter that Kropotkin was summarising a common perspective in scientific circles of the time, the fact is that thanks to the discoveries associated with genetics in the 1930s we know that "soft inheritance" is incorrect.

If Kropotkin had based his ideas on mutual aid or anarchism on this "fact" of science, what would that mean for his politics? Kropotkin's Lamarckian tendencies (like Darwin's own[15]) are obviously dated in the

---

attacking Proudhon in 1860.

12   See Steve Keen's *Debunking Economics: the naked emperor dethroned* (London: Zed, 2011) for an excellent overview.

13   Saying that, "group selection" is undergoing a revival recently as, ironically, the gene-focused theories do not automatically exclude it. It should be noted that Darwin raised the possibility of group selection in his *The Descent of Man*.

14   Kropotkin discusses Weismann in "The Inheritance of Acquired Characters: Theoretical Difficulties," *The Nineteenth Century and After*, March 1912 (included in Peter Kropotkin, *Evolution and Environment* [New York: Black Rose, 1995]).

15   Kropotkin discusses Lamarckian tendencies of Darwin in his essay, "The Theory of Evolution and Mutual Aid," *The Nineteenth Century and Later*, January 1910 (this is included in Peter Kropotkin, *Evolution and Environment*).

light of modern genetics but they are not the basis for mutual aid. Indeed, if we can ignore the invocation of Lamarck we can easily see that Kropotkin's real aim reflects the still on-going "nature/nurture" debate. In addition, Lamarckian theories do have a place in analysing the development of social institutions and culture. This is reflected in Kropotkin's argument that while mutual aid represents an instinct, its expression varies considerably through human history. So while "soft inheritance" has been refuted, the discussion over nature and nurture remains.

Kropotkin was rightly worried that Weismann's arguments about heritability meant that an organism is unaffected by its environment. Yet genetic heritability, whether it is high or low, implies nothing about modifiability. This is deeply impacted by environment and so nature and nurture interact. The classic example is height which is strongly heritable (80 to 90 percent) but the average height can and does increase due to changes in diet. Similarly, intelligence (as measured by average IQ scores) is increasing across birth cohorts (for example, America saw an eighteen-point gain in average IQ from 1948 to 2002) and nurture plays its part (for example, adoption of a child from a poor family into a better-off one is associated with IQ gains of 12 to 18 points).

In short, a given genetic inheritance is not immune to decisive and permanent environmental impacts. Nurture—the environment—plays its role as Kropotkin stressed. If he had lived to see the genetics revolution of the 1930s we are sure that he would have admitted his errors (particularly in Lamarckian phraseology) and combated the naive assumption that heritable traits cannot be changed via environmental mechanisms. As Stephen Jay Gould suggested against those who argue that traits like aggression are genetic, "if some people are peaceful now, then aggression itself cannot be coded in our genes, only the potential for it. If innate only means possible, or even likely in certain environments, then everything we do is innate and the word has no meaning. Aggression is one expression of a generating rule that anticipates peacefulness in other common environments. The range of specific behaviours engendered by the rule is impressive and a fine testimony to flexibility as the hallmark of human behaviour."[16]

There is an irony worth mentioning in Kropotkin's heated critique of Weismann. While Kropotkin rightly rejects the simplistic Lamarckian position (as expressed by the notion that cutting off the tails of mice will result in a tailless mouse being born) the fact is that, given a Lamarckian "use or lose" mechanism, it would be possible—given sufficient repression, for example—to shatter the institutions and practices of mutual aid and so subsequent generations would grow up without this instinct. Mutual aid,

---

16   Stephen Jay Gould, *The Mismeasure of Man* (London: Penguin, 1997), 360.

then, is actually strengthened by "hard" inheritance: with a genetic basis, mutual aid instincts can *never* be lost in the short term. This far better fits Kropotkin's position on how mutual aid is the foundation upon which justice and morality is built.

* * *

Some confuse mutual aid with altruism. The biologist Steve Jones, for example, asserts that the "split between the anarchists and the capitalists reflected a fundamental clash of beliefs. Is humankind ruled by self-interest, or is altruism our true state? What is the lesson from [n]ature: mutual aid or inevitable strife?" For Jones, anarchists "see a benevolent message in the natural world," but the grim reality is that symbiosis "marks each stage in evolution, but the notion of mutual aid, a joint effort to a common end, has been superseded by a sterner view: that such arrangements began with simple exploitation." He does admit that many creatures "do appear to indulge in mutual aid" and that the "semblance of cooperation is all around." However, this is just appearance, for this is, in fact, based "not on mutual aid but on greed and mutual exploitation."[17]

The cultural presumptions and assumptions in suggesting that it is value-free science to describe animals and people working together in mutually beneficial ways as "mutual exploitation" while describing it as "mutual aid" is just non-scientific, emotional woolly-thinking should be all too obvious.[18]

Yet Kropotkin would hardly have disagreed. He was well aware that "strife" and "self-interest" in both the animal world and humanity existed—and that it drove mutual aid. "Life is struggle," he argued, "and in that struggle the fittest survive." He explicitly and repeatedly noted that *Mutual Aid* presented a one-sided perspective, that it was "a book on the law of mutual aid, viewed as one of the chief factors of evolution" and "not on *all* factors of evolution and their respective values." So sociability "is as much a law of nature as mutual struggle" and that, therefore, the question was who is the fittest, those who compete against each other or those who cooperate in the struggle against a harsh environment. He presented evidence that supported his view that "those animals which acquire habits of mutual aid

---

17   Steve Jones, *Coral: A Pessimist in Paradise* (London: Abacus, 2008), 116, 97, 98, 121.

18   That Jones clearly projects cultural biases onto nature can be seen when he states that economics "may help [us] to understand evolution" and the "laws of the market also help to explain systems in which proponents appear [...] to strive towards the same shared end." Moreover, sometimes "the market returns to Nature for advice" (Ibid., 120, 98).

are undoubtedly the fittest" because "life in societies is the most powerful weapon in the struggle for life, taken in its widest sense." Thus cooperation provides "more chances to survive" and animals and humans "find in association the best arms for the struggle for life: understood, of course, in its wide Darwinian sense."[19]

Kropotkin was well aware that the drive for cooperation rested on the "selfish" desire to survive. His argument was that mutual aid, rather than mutual struggle, between members of the same group or species was the best means of doing so. Indeed, he explicitly eschews the notion that "altruism" (in the common meaning of the word) is the basis of mutual aid: it is neither love nor sympathy as such that causes animals to assist one another, but rather a more hard-nosed recognition that it is in their own interests for survival to do so. And the evidence is that cooperation is extensive in nature—an awkward fact that seems to cause some naturalists no end of difficulty.

Then there is the central contradiction in Jones's account. He claims that for scientists "neither symbiosis nor the struggle for existence has much message for human affairs" before concluding a few pages later that anarchism has been "sidelined by the iron rules of greed that rule the globe."[20] This would be more convincing if he had not attacked political thinkers like Marx for drawing lessons for human society from nature. This is forgotten when he turns to Kropotkin. Then we have an assertion that the "iron rule of greed" is a universal law of nature. So, apparently, nature does have a "message for human affairs" after all and it just happens to coincide with the dominant economic system and the ideology of its ruling elite. Strange, though, that capitalism is such a recent development given its alleged genetic basis.[21]

Ironically, Jones suggests that "scientists have nothing to add to philosophy apart from facts," yet his comments about Kropotkin's life are consistently wrong. He talks of the fighting between the "adherents of Marx and Kropotkin" in the First International when, in reality, it was Bakunin who fought the former. We are informed that with "the apparent triumph of his ideas in the Bolshevik Revolution his Utopia was, it seemed, realised

---

19   Peter Kropotkin, *Mutual Aid: A Factor of Evolution* (London: Freedom Press, 2009) 70, 26, 32, 33, 68, 33, 229.

20   Jones, *Coral*, 98, 122.

21   Space precludes a discussion on how "selfish" genes do not equate to selfish individuals. In the introduction to the 30th anniversary edition of the *Selfish Gene* (Oxford: Oxford University Press, 2006) Richard Dawkins admits that he confused this in the first edition and indicates how "selfish" genes do not exclude the evolution of individuals who are cooperative and altruistic, quite the reverse. Kropotkin's position has been confirmed by modern, gene-focused, evolutionary theory.

and the Prince returned to Moscow. Within two years he was disappointed, and within three dead." Kropotkin returned to Russia *before* the October Revolution which suggests that Jones either is unaware Kropotkin died in 1921 or that both Russian Revolutions took place in 1917. The notion that Kropotkin would have expected his ideas to be implemented by Marxists is simply staggering: the Bolsheviks simply confirmed over four decades of argument against *State* socialism. Jones even talks about how "the Slavic experiment in mutualism that followed the Russian Revolution failed," so showing that it is not only Trotskyists who are ignorant of Lenin's stated desire to create State capitalism in Russia and his systematic campaign against cooperation in the workplace in favour of one-man management.[22]

* * *

Space precludes a detailed discussion of how mutual aid has become a staple of evolutionary theory.[23] As Stephen Jay Gould concluded "Kropotkin's basic argument is correct. Struggle does occur in many modes, and some lead to cooperation among members of a species as the best pathway to advantage for individuals." Yet while correctly noting that Kropotkin "did not deny the competitive form of struggle," Gould also suggested he "did commit a common conceptual error in failing to recognise that natural selection is an argument about advantages to individual organisms, however they may struggle" and "sometimes speaks of mutual aid as selected for the benefit of entire populations or species—a concept foreign to classic Darwinian logic (where organisms work, albeit unconsciously, for their own benefit in terms of genes passed to future generations)."[24]

Yet Gould also admits "Kropotkin also (and often) recognised that selection for mutual aid directly benefits each individual in its own struggle for personal success." This drains his (sympathetic) criticism of most of its force: for Kropotkin was well aware that the "result of struggle for existence may be cooperation rather than competition, but mutual aid must benefit individual organisms in Darwin's world of explanation" and so "did

---

22 Jones, *Coral*, 122, 96, 121. Maurice Brinton's "The Bolsheviks and Workers Control" is still the classic work on the Leninist imposition of state capitalism (Maurice Brinton, *For Workers' Power: The Selected Writings of Maurice Brinton* [Edinburgh/Oakland: AK Press, 2004], 293–378).

23 For a detailed discussion of *Mutual Aid* and modern scientific theory as well as refutation of the many myths associated with it, see my *Mutual Aid: An Introduction and Evaluation* 2nd Edition, (Edinburgh: AK Press, 2010).

24 Stephen Jay Gould, *Bully for Brontosaurus: Further Reflections in Natural History* (London: Penguin, 1991), 335–338.

include the orthodox solution as his primary justification for mutual aid."[25] In Kropotkin's words:

> [W]e may safely say that mutual aid is as much a law of animal life as mutual struggle, but that, as a factor of evolution, it most probably has a far greater importance, inasmuch as it favours the development of such habits and characters as insure the maintenance and further development of the species, together with the greatest amount of welfare and enjoyment of life for the individual, with the least waste of energy.[26]

For Kropotkin, cooperation was fundamentally of benefit to the individuals who practise it—not least because, as Darwin had already recognised, groups which "included the greatest number of the most sympathetic members, would flourish best, and rear the greatest number of offspring." Such practice "will have been increased through natural selection" for those who are constantly fighting and conspiring against each other will be at a disadvantage: "Selfish and contentious people will not cohere, and without coherence nothing can be effected."[27]

* * *

Kropotkin must be considered as the first post-Darwinian socialist. Yet as he explored in his posthumously published *Ethics* others had seen how humanity possessed a sense of fairness or justice, not least Proudhon.[28] So Marx's smug comment that "M. Proudhon does not know that all history is nothing but a continuous transformation of human nature"[29] simply shows his pre-Darwinian perspective. We are evolved creatures with an evolved "nature"—luckily, it is a nature that has evolved within groups and so is inherently sociable.[30] Indeed, Proudhon's position—that we have an innate

---

25   Gould, *Bully for Brontosaurus*, 338.

26   Peter Kropotkin, *Mutual Aid: A Factor of Evolution* (Montréal: Black Rose, 1996), 6.

27   Charles Darwin, *The Descent of Man, and Selection in Relation to Sex*, Part I (Princeton: Princeton University Press, 1981), 82, 162.

28   Kropotkin dedicates a chapter in *Ethics* to Proudhon's ideas. This is included in *Direct Struggle Against Capital: A Peter Kropotkin Anthology* (Edinburgh/Oakland/Baltimore: AK Press, 2014).

29   Karl Marx, "The Poverty of Philosophy," Karl Marx and Friedrich Engels *Marx-Engels Collected Works* (London: Lawrence & Wishart, 1976) 6: 192.

30   The work of Dutch primatologist Frans de Waal must be noted here: *The Age of*

sense of justice—has been confirmed by modern science (and this is an instinct we share with other social animals).[31]

So both the atrocious behaviour we deploy and the noble traits we praise are the product of evolution—as is the moral sentiment that allows us to judge whether specific actions are either. This does not mean that how this evolved nature expresses itself is fixed, far from it:

> Men's conceptions of morality are completely dependent upon the form that their social life assumed at a given time in a given locality. Whether it be based on the complete subjection to the central power—ecclesiastical or secular—on absolutism or on representative government, on centralisation or on the covenants of the free cities and village communes; whether economic life be based on the rule of capital or on the principle of the cooperative commonwealth—all this is reflected in the moral conceptions of men and in the moral teachings of the given epoch.[...] The ethics of every society reflects the established forms of its social life.[32]

This means "*Mutual Aid-Justice-Morality* are thus the consecutive steps of an ascending series." Morality "developed later than the others" and so was "an unstable feeling and the least imperative of the three." Mutual aid simply ensured "the ground is prepared for the further and the more general development of more refined relations."[33] Thus mutual aid was the basis of ethical behaviour (including altruism) but not identical to it, for it was—as Kropotkin repeatedly stressed—just one factor in evolution. In this he was reflecting a well-established position in mainstream Russian science of the time.[34]

Empathy: Nature's Lessons for a Kinder Society (New York: Crown, 2009); *Primates and Philosophers: How Morality Evolved* (Princeton: Princeton University Press, 2006); *Good Natured: The Origins of Right and Wrong in Humans and Other Animals* (Cambridge: Harvard University Press, 1996).

31   Richard Dawkins in *The God Delusion* (London: Bantam Press, 2006) has a useful discussion of "Does our moral sense have a Darwinian Origin?"

32   Peter Kropotkin, *Ethics: Origin and Development* (New York: B. Blom, 1968), 315–316.

33   Ibid., 30–31.

34   Daniel P. Todes, *Darwin without Malthus: the struggle for existence in Russian evolutionary thought* (New York/Oxford: Oxford University Press, 1989). Also see his "Darwin's Malthusian Metaphor and Russian Evolutionary Thought, 1859–1917," *Isis* 78: 294 (December 1987). As well as inspiring Gould to write "Kropotkin was no crackpot," this essential article was reprinted under the title "The Scientific Background

A close reading of Kropotkin's work shows that he was well aware of the need for reciprocal (hence *mutual*) interactions between animals. This means stopping anti-social behaviour and so stopping the few exploiting the cooperative behaviour of the many.[35] This applied to those in human society seeking to exploit or oppress others. Freedom—as history shows—needs to be defended:

> Provided that you yourself do not abdicate your freedom, provided that you yourself do not allow others to enslave you; and provided that to the violent and anti-social passions of this or that person you oppose your equally vigorous social passions, you have nothing to fear from liberty.[36]

Freedom does not mean the freedom to oppress, coerce and exploit others—and it says much about the nature of class society that many people think it does.

* * *

This short discussion of mutual aid should be sufficient to dispel a common fallacy about anarchism as expressed by Jonathan Wolff:

> If we are all naturally good, why has such an oppressive and corrupting state come into existence? The most obvious answer is that a few greedy [...] individuals [...] have managed to seize power. But [...] if such people existed before the state came into being, as they must have done on this theory, it cannot be the case that we are all naturally good.[37]

Yet anarchists have never suggested people are "naturally good" nor that the State is the only oppressive institution. Indeed, the subtitle of *Mutual Aid*—"A Factor of Evolution"—shows that if you cannot be bothered to read the book itself. Humans, like other animals, are both "naturally"

---

of Kropotkin's Mutual Aid" in the anarchist journal *The Raven: Anarchist Quarterly* 24 (1993).

35   Kropotkin, *Mutual Aid*, 38, 41, 59, 68–69.

36   Peter Kropotkin, "Anarchist Morality," *Anarchism: A Collection of Revolutionary Writings* (Mineola: Dover Press, 2002), 106. Also see, for example, Kropotkin, "The Permanence of society after the revolution," *Direct Struggle Against Capital*, 614.

37   Jonathan Wolff, *An Introduction to Political Philosophy* (Oxford: Oxford University Press, 2006), 33–34.

cooperative and "naturally" competitive and which of these tendencies is expressed or is predominant depends on numerous factors and specific circumstances.[38] Strangely Wolff prefaces his ruminations on anarchism with a quotation from Kropotkin—"No more laws! No more judges! Liberty, equality, and practical human sympathy are the only effectual barriers we can oppose to the anti-social instincts of certain amongst us"[39]—which actually refutes Wolff's own argument.[40]

As in *Mutual Aid*, Kropotkin in *Modern Science and Anarchy* presents an account of history marked by conflict between individuals and between classes which is much at odds with the standard view of anarchism. He was well aware that humans were capable of coercion and cooperation, conflict and caring, solidarity and selfishness. He sought a system where the varied potentialities that humans were capable of expressing were skewed toward cooperation—which benefits all—rather than toward the conflict of class society—which benefits the few. So the notion that Kropotkin idealised humans or primitive man is simply an invention:

> In the eighteenth century, under the influence of the first acquaintance with the savages of the Pacific Ocean, a tendency developed to idealise the savages, who lived "in a natural state," perhaps to counterbalance the philosophy of Hobbes and his followers, who pictured primitive men as a crowd of wild beasts ready to devour one another. Both these conceptions, however, proved erroneous, as we now know from many conscientious observers. The primitive man is not at all a paragon of virtue, and not at all a tiger-like beast. But he always lived and still lives in societies, like thousands of other creatures. In those societies he has developed not only

---

38   One Marxist critic recognises this. Paul Blackledge contrasts Marx's optimistic—but pre-Darwinian—perspective to anarchism's pessimistic one concerning "human nature" ("Freedom and Democracy," *Libertarian Socialism: Politics in Black and Red* [Basingstoke/New York: Palgrave Macmillan, 2012], Alex Prichard, Ruth Kinna, Saku Pinta, and Dave Berry [eds.]). However, the rest of his critique is deeply flawed and inaccurate as I discuss in "Libertarian Socialism: Beyond Anarchism and Marxism?," *Anarcho-Syndicalist Review* 62 (Summer 2014).

39   Peter Kropotkin, "Law and Authority," *Anarchism: A Collection of Revolutionary Writings*, 218.

40   Also see Matthew S. Adams, "Uniformity is Death: Human Nature, Variety, and Conflict in Kropotkin's Anarchism," in *Governing Diversities: Democracy, Diversity and Human Nature*, ed. Joanne Paul et al. (Cambridge: Cambridge Scholars Press, 2012), 150–168.

those social qualities that are inherent to all social animals, but, owing to the gift of speech and, consequently, to a more developed intelligence, he has still further developed his sociality, and with it he has evolved the rules of social life, which we call morality.[41]

If people are as bad as some philosophers like to proclaim, then it makes little sense to give such flawed creatures power over others. So if, as Wolff (wrongly) proclaims, anarchism is flawed because "to rely on the natural goodness of human beings to such an extent seems utopian in the extreme,"[42] then how do the ruling few escape from their genetic burden? Or are these—as Kropotkin mocks—somehow better than all other humans:

[W]hen we hear men saying that the Anarchists imagine men much better than they really are, we merely wonder how intelligent people can repeat that nonsense. Do we not say continually that the only means of rendering men less rapacious and egotistic, less ambitious and less slavish at the same time, is to eliminate those conditions which favour the growth of egotism and rapacity, of slavishness and ambition? The only difference between us and those who make the above objection is this: We do not, like them, exaggerate the inferior instincts of the masses, and do not complacently shut our eyes to the same bad instincts in the upper classes. We maintain that *both* rulers and ruled are spoiled by authority; *both* exploiters and exploited are spoiled by exploitation; while our opponents seem to admit that there is a kind of salt of the earth—the rulers, the employers, the leaders—who, happily enough, prevent those bad men—the ruled, the exploited, the led—from becoming still worse than they are.

There is the difference, and a very important one. *We* admit the imperfections of human nature, but we make no exception for the rulers. *They* make it, although sometimes unconsciously, and because we make no such exception, they say that we are dreamers, "unpractical men."[43]

Similarly, for those who proclaim that ethical behaviour is achieved against "human nature"—Kropotkin notes in *Modern Science and Anarchy*

---

41   Kropotkin, *Ethics*, 76.

42   Wolff, *An Introduction to Political Philosophy*, 34.

43   Kropotkin, "Are we good enough?," *Direct Struggle Against Capital*, 609.

that this was Thomas Huxley's position—then such a person "necessarily has to admit the existence of some other, extra-natural, or super-natural influence which inspires man with conceptions of 'supreme good'" which "nullifies" any "attempt at explaining evolution by the action of natural forces only."[44] Where we get the strength and ability to overcome our "nature" is never explained.

* * *

The obvious problem with basing your political ideas on empirical evidence is that it appears not to be able to take into account future developments or possibilities. This is not the case, as can be seen by Kropotkin continually stressing the *tendencies* within society that pointed beyond capitalism:

> As to the method followed by the anarchist thinker, it entirely differs from that followed by the utopists. The anarchist thinker does not resort to metaphysical conceptions (like 'natural rights,' the 'duties of the State,' and so on) to establish what are, in his opinion, the best conditions for realising the greatest happiness of humanity. He follows, on the contrary, the course traced by the modern philosophy of evolution. He studies human society as it is now and was in the past; and without either endowing humanity as a whole, or separate individuals, with superior qualities which they do not possess, he merely considers society as an aggregation of organisms trying to find out the best ways of combining the wants of the individual with those of cooperation for the welfare of the species. He studies society and tries to discover its *tendencies* past and present, its growing needs, intellectual and economic, and in his ideal he merely points out in which direction evolution goes. He distinguishes between the real wants and tendencies of human aggregations and the accidents (want of knowledge, migrations, wars, conquests) which have prevented these tendencies from being satisfied.[45]

In this he followed Proudhon's lead in *System of Economic Contradictions* in which the French anarchist argued that instead of contrasting visions of

---

44   Kropotkin, *Ethics*, 13.

45   Peter Kropotkin, "Anarchist Communism: Its Basis and Principles," *Anarchism and Anarchist-Communism* (London: Freedom Press, 1987), 24.

ideal communities to the grim reality of capitalism as did the utopian so-cialists (such as Fourier and Saint-Simon), we had to analyse the system and explore its contradictions in order to identify those elements which appear within it which express the future.

This means that there are tendencies within a system that are part-and-parcel of it, express its fundamental principles, and reinforce it as well as those tendencies which, although within it, are in opposition to it, express new principles, *and point beyond it*. Thus anarchy is consistent with de-velopments within capitalism—such as trade unions, cooperatives, etc.—which express new forms of social life and association in opposition to the wider system. The task of anarchists is to encourage these tendencies until such a time as we are strong enough to finally smash the State and capital-ism and replace them with a social organisation and system able to progress freely towards libertarian communism.

This is often forgotten when discussing anarchism. Stephen Pinker, for example, recounts how he was a teenage anarchist before "empirical" evi-dence showed him the error of his youthful ways:

> When law enforcement vanishes, all manner of violence breaks out: looting, settling old scores, ethnic cleansing, and petty warfare among gangs, warlords and mafias. This was obvious in the remnants of Yugoslavia, the Soviet Union, and parts of Africa in the 1990s, but can also hap-pen in countries with a long tradition of civility. As a young teenager in proudly peaceable Canada during the roman-tic 1960s, I was a true believer in Bakunin's Anarchism. I laughed off my parents' argument that if the government ever laid down its arms all hell would break loose. Our competing predictions were put to the test at 8:00 A.M. on October 17, 1969, when the Montreal police went on strike. By 11:20 A.M. the first bank was robbed. By noon most downtown stores had closed because of loot-ing. Within a few more hours, taxi drivers burned down the garage of a limousine service that had competed with them for airport customers, a rooftop sniper killed a pro-vincial police officer, rioters broke into several hotels and restaurants, and a doctor slew a burglar in his suburban home. By the end of the day, six banks had been robbed, a hundred shops had been looted, twelve fires had been set, forty carloads of storefront glass had been broken, and three million dollars in property damage had been inflict-ed, before city authorities had to call in the army and, of

course, the Mounties to restore order. This decisive empirical test left my politics in tatters (and offered a foretaste of
life as a scientist).[46]

It is hard to know where to start with this nonsense. While Pinker may
have been surprised, no anarchist would have been. After all, we have long
argued that people are shaped—corrupted—by hierarchical social relationships and inequalities of wealth and power.[47] Even if we assumed—which
anarchists do not—that people are inherently "good" and that it is institutions which corrupt them, the people of Montreal were living in a capitalist
and statist society and so corrupted by that system. This means that we
would expect anti-social behaviours—produced in the main by an unjust
system—to be expressed once the inadequate Statist means currently used
to contain them is taken away. Similarly, it was a society marked by inequality and it is unsurprising that people took the opportunity to grab
some of the wealth they had been excluded from. Indeed, a key postulate
of anarchism is that social wealth needs to expropriated during a social
revolution—but for the benefit of all rather than transferring it from one
individual to another as in looting.

More, the Hobbesian conclusions that Pinker draws from this "empirical test" are hardly consistent with the evidence as not everyone acted in
anti-social ways. Why the few are deemed to express "human nature" while
the many do not is rarely, if ever, explained. Similarly, these few—the likes
of warlords and the mafia—are exercising coercion and seeking to impose
their will on others. In other words, *they are acting as States.* These States-
in-embryo have not been as successful in legitimising their rule as the current rulers have but this should not make us forget that it is in these kinds
of acts—and the destruction of competitors—that the current State has
its origins.

Overall, the only surprising thing about this is not what happened but
that Pinker thought it wise to expose his ignorance of both anarchism and
the scientific method. For to be an "empirical test" the assumptions of anarchism need to be in place or approximated. In short, Pinker is like someone
who believes they have refuted the law of gravity by proclaiming a feather
and a brick do not fall at the same rate (and so ignoring the need for a vac-
uum to remove air resistance) or claims that evolution violates the Second

---

46   Steven Pinker, *The Blank Slate: The Modern Denial of Human Nature* (Putnam: Penguin,
      2002), 331.

47   "In a society based on exploitation and servitude," Kropotkin stressed, "human nature
      itself is degraded" and "authority and servility walk ever hand in hand" ("Anarchist
      Morality," *Anarchism: A collection of Revolutionary Writings*, 104, 81).

Law of Thermodynamics (and so ignoring that the Earth is not a closed system and the role of the Sun in providing energy).[48]

Anarchists have *never* argued that if you simply remove the State then everyone would be nice and good to each other. This is for two reasons. First, social problems are not simply caused by the State—the economic system produces its share, as do the hierarchies of sexism, racism, homophobia, and so forth. Second, social hierarchies have existed for centuries and will take time to overcome—both at a social level and within each individual. This can only be achieved by a process of self-liberation through struggle that both transforms the individual and builds the framework of the new society. This cannot and will not be achieved overnight—and even in the best circumstances anarchists would still expect *some* anti-social acts (such as settling old scores) to occur.

George Barrett long ago exposed the fallacy at the heart of Pinker's position in his excellent "Objections to Anarchism." First appearing in *Freedom* around the same time as Kropotkin's *The Modern State* serialisation, it is worth quoting in full:

> *Even if you could overthrow the Government tomorrow and establish Anarchism, the same system would soon grow up again.*
>
> This objection is quite true, except that we do not propose to overthrow the Government tomorrow. If I (or we as a group of anarchists) came to the conclusion that I was to be the liberator of humanity, and if by some means I could manage to blow up the King, the Houses of Lords and Commons, the police force, and, in a word, all persons and institutions which make up the Government—if I were successful in all this, and expected to see the people enjoying freedom ever afterwards as a result, then, no doubt, I should find myself greatly mistaken.
>
> The chief results of my action would be to arouse an immense indignation on the part of the majority of the people, and a reorganisation by them of all the forces of government.
>
> The reason why this method would fail is very easy to understand. It is because the strength of the Government rests not with itself, but with the people. A great tyrant may be a fool, and not a superman. His strength lies not in himself, but in the superstition of the people who think that it

---

48   See my "The God Delusion & Anarchism," *Anarcho-Syndicalist Review* 52 (Summer 2009) for more discussion, including the views of Bakunin whose anarchism Pinker claimed to be "a true believer" of.

is right to obey him. So long as that superstition exists it is useless for some liberator to cut off the head of tyranny; the people will create another, for they have grown accustomed to rely on something outside themselves.

Suppose, however, that the people develop, and become strong in their love of liberty, and self-reliant, then the foremost of its rebels will overthrow tyranny, and backed by the general sentiment of their age their action will never be undone. Tyranny will never be raised from the dead. A landmark in the progress of humanity will have been passed and put behind for ever.

So the Anarchist rebel when he strikes his blow at Governments understands that he is no liberator with a divine mission to free humanity, but he is a part of that humanity struggling onwards towards liberty.

If, then, by some external means an Anarchist Revolution could be, so to speak, supplied ready-made and thrust upon the people, it is true that they would reject it and rebuild the old society. If, on the other hand, the people develop their ideas of freedom, and then themselves get rid of the last stronghold of tyranny—the Government—then indeed the Revolution will be permanently accomplished.[49]

Or as Kropotkin succinctly put it: "A structure based on centuries of history cannot be destroyed with a few kilos of explosives."[50] As he elaborated elsewhere:

> [I]t was necessary to break up the old organisation, *shatter the State* and rebuild a new organisation from the very foundations of society—the liberated village commune, federalism, groupings from simple to complex, the free workers union. [...] To give full scope to socialism entails rebuilding from top to bottom a society dominated by the narrow individualism of the shopkeeper. [...] it is a question of completely reshaping all relationships, from those which exist today between every individual and his churchwarden or his station-master to those which exist between trades, hamlets, cities and regions. In every street,

---

49   George Barrett, "Objections to Anarchism," *The Raven: Anarchist Quarterly* 12 (1990), 355.

50   Martin A. Miller, *Kropotkin* (London: University of Chicago Press, 1976), 174.

in every hamlet, in every group of men gathered around a factory or along a section of the railway line, the creative, constructive and organisational spirit must be awakened in order to rebuild life—in the factory, in the village, in the store, in production and in distribution of supplies. All relations between individuals and great centres of population have to be made all over again."[51]

If Kropotkin thought that it was "ridiculous" for "this immense task, requiring the free expression of popular genius, to be carried out within the framework of the State and the pyramidal organisation which is the essence of the State" by voting for socialist politicians, we can only imagine what he would have said if someone had suggested a mere police strike was sufficient to produce an anarchist society![52] For if all it needed was that, it makes you wonder why anarchists—from Bakunin onwards—had spent so much time seeking to make propaganda, organise workers, unions, strikes, cooperatives, and so on.

In short, this "decisive empirical test" hardly contradicted anarchist politics for it did not pit what the theory actually argues against the facts, but rather a teenager's impressionistic notions of that theory. It is not "life as a scientist" to refute strawman arguments.

* * *

As Kropotkin makes clear in *Modern Science and Anarchy*, humanity has evolved institutions to manage interpersonal and social conflict throughout its history. Rather than see these institutions as being created by a select few (who somehow manage to rise above humanity's brutish nature), Kropotkin rightly argues they are the product of the many who seek a peaceful life and so organise to achieve it. This means creating various customs and organisations to stop and resolve the anti-social actions that are the first expressions of the few monopolising power and wealth. However, "instead of demanding that those social customs should be maintained through the authority of a few," anarchism "demands it from the continued action of all."[53]

That is why we see "mutual protection" and "defence of the territory" listed by Kropotkin as two of the purposes the federated groups of an anarchist society are created for—alongside production, consumption,

---

51   Kropotkin, "The State: Its Historic Role," *Direct Struggle Against Capital*, 257–258.

52   Ibid., 258.

53   Kropotkin, "Anarchism: Its Philosophy and Ideal," *Anarchism: A collection of Revolutionary Writings*, 137.

education, etc.[54] A police strike, by definition, would not allow enough time for such self-organisation to even start—particularly if we ignore, as Pinker does, the lack of preparatory social struggle needed to make anarchy viable. Our teenage Bakuninist would have been better proclaiming his ignorance of anarchist politics than their failure.[55]

If we apply the scientific method to Kropotkin's ideas (namely, gathering evidence on what he actually argued and basing conclusions on that evidence rather than assumptions about what he wrote), we quickly discover that most writers who dismiss them are by no means scientific. They simply destroy an invention of their own making.

While Kropotkin may have erred by proclaiming anarchy to be a branch of science, he was right to stress the importance of using the scientific method in both critiquing modern class society as well as building evidence for a better one. By so doing, we can expose the false assumptions inflicted upon anarchism by its critics, explain why they are wrong and how they do not accurately reflect the position that they are claiming to refute.

* * *

What we have said of anarchism also applies to the numerous attempts to invoke "science" to defend various aspects of the status quo—whether racism, sexism, economic inequalities, hierarchy, etc. We must not forget that every ruling class throughout history has required a justifying discourse or narrative. This has involved gods (or a god) to secure the right of rulers or make property (and its inequalities) sacred. For the past few centuries science—or the misuse of science—has also played this role as seen by the numerous "scientific" theories in support of inequality that regularly spring up (often thanks to well-funded think-tanks).

So Stephen Jay Gould was right to "criticise the myth that science is itself an objective enterprise, done properly only when scientists can shuck the constraints of their culture and view the world as it really is. [...]

---

54   Kropotkin, "Anarchism," *Direct Struggle Against Capital*, 163. Also see "The Permanence of Society after the Revolution" in *Direct Struggle Against Capital* and Peter Kropotkin, *Act for Yourselves!: Articles from Freedom 1886–1907* (London: Freedom Press, 1988).

55   Regardless of Lenin's claims in *The State and Revolution*, Kropotkin—like all revolutionary anarchists—recognised the necessity of defending a revolution by means of federations of workers' militias. This should not—as Lenin thought—be confused with a "new" State, for the State, as Kropotkin stresses in *Modern Science and Anarchy*, is a very specific kind of social organisation marked by centralisation and hierarchy (for further discussion, see section H.2.1 of *An Anarchist FAQ*, Vol. Two [Oakland, AK Press, 2012]).

Scientists needn't become explicit apologists for their class or culture in order to reflect these pervasive aspects of life." Recognising this obvious fact suggests that science "must be understood as a social phenomenon, a gutsy, human enterprise, not the work of robots programmed to collect pure information" and so science, "since people must do it, is a socially embedded activity." Even facts are "not pure and unsullied bits of information" as "culture also influences what we see and how we see it. Theories, moreover, are not inexorable inductions from facts. The most creative theories are often imaginative visions imposed upon facts; the source of imagination is also strongly cultural."

> [Science] cannot escape its curious dialectic. Embedded in surrounding culture, it can, nonetheless, be a powerful agent for questioning and even overturning assumptions that nurture it. [...] Scientists can struggle to identify the cultural assumptions of their trade and to ask how answers might be formulated under different assertions. Scientists can propose creative theories that force startled colleagues to confront unquestioned procedures.[56]

The same can be said of any branch of knowledge:

> To make good use of an economic theory, we must first sort out the relations of the propagandist and the scientific elements in it, then by checking with experience, see how far the scientific element appears convincing, and finally recombine it with our own political views. The purpose of studying economics is not to acquire a set of ready-made answers to economic questions, but to learn how to avoid being deceived by economists.[57]

Kropotkin's work must be seen in this light, as an attempt to refute, with hard evidence, the cultural assumptions at the heart of the science—particularly the Darwinism—of his day. As he put it:

> Besides, when some naturalists, doing honour to their bourgeois education, and pretending to be followers of the scientific method of Darwin, told us: "Crush whoever is weaker than yourself: such is the law of Nature!" it was easy for us

---

56   Stephen Jay Gould, *The Mismeasure of Man*, 53–55.

57   Joan Robinson, *Contributions to Modern Economics* (Oxford: Basil Blackwell, 1978), 75.

to prove, first, that this was *not* Darwin's conclusion, and, using the same scientific method, to show that these scientists were on the wrong path: that such a law does not exist, that Nature teaches us a very different lesson, and that their conclusions were in nowise scientific.[58]

As Kropotkin was aware, a lot of nonsense can be hidden by invoking pseudo-scientific jargon and masses of "analysed" data. Debunking this kind of work can be time consuming and even if successful may be limited in impact compared to the original claims. However, it needs to be done and that is where science and a good scientific education play their role.

* * *

Indeed, much of what passes as "science" amounts to little more than "just-so" stories in which middle-class individuals of Western capitalist societies are projected back to the dawn of recorded history, with varying degrees of plausibility. Whether it is "just-so" stories on the development of the State or private property, or to justify sexism or some other deplorable modern trait, this seems to be stock-in-trade for much of the scientific community.

The worst offenders are the so-called evolutionary psychologists who seek an evolutionary (i.e., genetic) basis for all human activities. That this is usually nonsense can be seen from the brave scientists who proclaimed to have proven that "girls prefer pink" on a genetic level because it would have aided our female hominin ancestors gathering berries.[59] Widely and uncritically reported by the media, the paper left much to be desired: the test used was not measuring discriminative ability but rather preference, not all berries are red when ripe nor were berries the sole food gathered and pink being considered a girl's colour is a relatively recent cultural phenomenon—a century before this study proclaimed preference for pink as being genetic in nature, it was considered as a boy's colour in the Western World.

Still, for some it is nice to think that people have roles and social positions determined "by nature."

* * *

One of the worst examples of this "just-so" story telling pretending to be "science" is seen in modern—neo-classical—economics. Yet the

---

58   Peter Kropotkin, *Modern Science and Anarchism*, (London: Freedom Press, 1912), 40.

59   Anya C. Hurlbert and Yazhu Ling, "Biological components of sex differences in color preference," *Current Biology* vol. 17 (21 August 2007), 16.

discussion of economics in *Modern Science and Anarchy* concentrates on classical economics and fails to discuss the neo-classical economics that steadily replaced it from the 1870s onwards. Perhaps this is understandable as neo-classical economics was even further from a science than its predecessor was.

Kropotkin's argument is that economics is not a science as can be seen when economists forget that their economic "laws" are premised on a given socio-economic situation. This means that rather than being universal "laws" they are describing what happens under capitalism. This is at best—at worse they are describing the conclusions of their models without the benefit of empirical evidence.

Kropotkin spends some time on the "labour theory of value" of classical economics but, sadly, this is incomplete, probably because it is primarily an attempt to discredit Marxism. While Ricardo thought that labour-value worked directly under capitalism, Marx argued that it worked indirectly and so prices did not equate to labour values. Marx spent a significant part of volume 3 of *Capital* on this aspect of his model of capitalism but in volume 1 he mentioned it, in passing, in a footnote:

> [T]he formation of capital must be possible even though the price and the value of a commodity be the same, for it cannot be explained by referring to any divergence between price and value. If prices actually differ from values, we must reduce the former to the latter. [...] How can we account for the origin of capital on the assumption that prices are regulated by the average price, i.e., ultimately by the value of commodities? I say "ultimately" because average prices do not directly coincide with the values of commodities as Adam Smith, Ricardo, and others believe.[60]

Volume 1 of *Capital* ignores the differences in capital between companies and assumes, at this level of abstraction, that prices are proportional to labour-values. Marx does this to show how labour can be exploited according to the postulates of classical economics itself. Sadly, not being a trained scientist he did not explicitly and clearly set out the simplifying assumptions in volume 1 (namely, equal capital investment and no market processes) which he used to do this. As such, Kropotkin was justified in noting its "unscientific character," how the theory of value "is not demonstrated

---

60   Karl Marx, *Capital: A Critique of Political Economy*, Vol. 1 (London: Penguin Books, 1976), 269.

scientifically but has to be taken on faith" and "its indulgence in scientific jargon."[61]

This meant that when volume 3 was posthumously published by Engels and reduced the level of abstraction by discussing "prices of production" within a market process involving industries with varying amounts of capital, many bourgeois critics of Marx argued that there was a contradiction between the first and third volume. As can be seen by his discussion, while Kropotkin had definitely read the first volume of *Capital*, he seems unaware of the contents of volumes 2 and 3. Yet he was hardly alone, as leading Marxist Rosa Luxemburg admitted in 1903: "for socialists in general, the third volume of *Capital* remains an unread book."[62] Most Marxists, like Kropotkin, had accepted volume 1 as the full analysis:

> The third volume of *Capital*, with its solution of the problem of the rate of profit (the basic problem of Marxist economics), did not appear till 1894. But in Germany, as in all other lands, agitation had been carried on with the aid of the unfinished material contained in the first volume; the Marxist doctrine had been popularized and had found acceptance upon the basis of this first volume alone; the success of the incomplete Marxist theory had been phenomenal; and no one had been aware that there was any gap in the teaching.[63]

So, in effect, volume 1 of *Capital* was the "first approximation" Kropotkin discusses in his "Foreword" while volume 3 is the next, more accurate, approximation. Sadly, Kropotkin's opposition to Marxism—while understandable given its negative impact on the labour movement—got in the way of a more sympathetic discussion.

* * *

The labour theory of value basically argues that the costs of production regulate a commodity's market price; that cost is the point around which prices fluctuate. It does not deny or ignore "supply and demand," but rather contends that before commodities can be sold they must be produced and

---

61   Peter Kropotkin, "Western Europe," *The Conquest of Bread and Other Writings* (Cambridge: Cambridge University Press, 1995), 220.

62   Rosa Luxemburg, "Stagnation and Progress of Marxism," *Rosa Luxemburg Speaks* (New York: Pathfinder Press, 1970), 109.

63   Ibid., 108.

this, the cost of production, regulates the market price which, over time, would approximate the price of production due to competition.

In and of itself, this is hardly a false model—although the notion that this price is proportional to the labour-time expended in producing a commodity is. The problem with Marx is, as Kropotkin suggests, his lack of scientific training. While trying to produce a "scientific socialism" (as shown by his use of actual empirical evidence at various points in volume 1 of *Capital*), he fails to clearly state his assumptions and confuses his abstraction ("value") with reality and seeks to equate all the value produced (in his model) with all the prices produced (in reality). A genuinely scientific account of value would recognise that exchange value is an abstraction that seeks to explain the dynamics of price formation.[64] In Marxist economics "value" exists and actual prices are governed by it. Paul Mattick indicates the confusion well:

> For Marx—as for the classical economists and for everyone else—only prices exist. As regards exchange relations, value, whether considered as of an objective or a subjective order, is not an empirically observable but an *explanatory* category. As such it does not cease to be a real phenomenon, but manifests itself not in its own terms but in terms of prices, precisely because capitalist society rests upon value relations. [...] Price must deviate from value to allow for the existence and expansion of capital. However, "deviation of price from value" is a somewhat unfortunate expression, because, mixing explanatory and empirical terms, it appears to refer to an empirically verifiable process, while observable reality contains no values but only market prices. Nevertheless, there is no way of avoiding the value-price duality, if we wish to understand why prices are what they are and why they change.[65]

Value is not "an empirically verifiable process" because it is an abstraction based on real processes to explain them. Labour, products and prices

---

64   In his 1853 work *Philosophie du Progrès*, Proudhon usefully summarised the law of value and its relationship to actual economic transactions (*Oeuvres Complètes de P-J Proudhon*, Vol. 20 [Bruxelles: Lacroix, 1868], 91–92). He never forgot that value is an abstraction and sought workers control over both their labour and its product rather than equate values, as so many—following Marx—wrongly assert.

65   Paul Mattick, *Marxism: Last Refugee for the Bourgeoisie?* (Armonk/London: M. E. Sharpe, Inc./Merlin Press, 1983), 25.

exist. Exchange value is an abstraction used to build a model of price dynamics, capitalist development, and to explain how labour is exploited within an apparently free economy.

This confusion can be seen from the so-called "transformation problem" first postulated in volume 3 of *Capital* when Marx tries to convert exchange values into prices.[66] In reality, this is a non-issue as it confuses a model used to simplify and so understand reality with reality itself. This is where Marx's lack of scientific training really becomes a hindrance and undermines what is, in many ways, a valid and powerful analysis of capitalism—built, without acknowledgement, upon a very similar analysis made earlier by Proudhon (and, ironically, mocked by Marx twenty years before the first volume of *Capital* was published).[67]

Undoubtedly, the quasi-scientific analysis of *Capital* explains the stagnation in Marxist economics that Luxemburg admitted: "The substance of that theory remains just where the two founders of scientific socialism left it."[68] The situation has hardly changed for most Marxist economists seem to spend their time analysing *Capital* rather than capitalism.

* * *

Kropotkin, it must be stressed, did not disagree that labour was exploited under capitalism and that workers did not receive the full-product of their labour. The empirical evidence is clear on this. The question is why this happens. Before Proudhon, most socialists had explained this by theories of "unequal exchange" between workers and capital. Proudhon placed exploitation within production and Marx extended this analysis. Every commodity has an exchange value and a use value. Workers sell their labour and they receive its exchange value—wages—and the boss receives its use value—its ability to produce more goods than paid in wages.[69]

---

66 It also becomes clear when trying to determine the exchange value of labour and its relation to real wages and the standard of living. The former cannot be determined and, in theory, it can rise or fall as the latter falls or rises.

67 See my "The Poverty of (Marx's) Philosophy," *Anarcho-Syndicalist Review* 70 (Summer 2017).

68 Luxemburg, *Rosa Luxemburg Speaks*, 107.

69 In other words, wages are not how much the workers produce but how much it costs to produce the workers. However, as Marx noted (echoing Smith and Ricardo), unlike other commodities, "the determination of the value of labour-power contains a historical and moral element." (*Capital* 1: 275) More, unlike other commodities, labour-power is embodied in people who can and do struggle and resist against how it is used, something Marx rarely acknowledged in his economic works (see Cornelius

Kropotkin, however, had little time for seeking to explain exploitation using "the basic principles of bourgeois political economy to attack its own conclusions in favour of capitalism."[70] Rather than producing (to use the sub-title of *Capital*) "a critique of political economy," Kropotkin sought an analysis of the capitalist economy. In practice, his analysis of how capital exploits labour is the same—private property means that workers have to sell their labour and their liberty to a boss who then makes them create as many goods as he wishes and keeps the product of their toil. It is this relationship of domination and subordination that allows the possibility of exploitation to occur. As such, his comment that the "evils of the present day are not caused by the capitalist appropriating for himself" surplus value but rather because workers "have to sell their labour force and their intelligence at a price" that makes surplus value "possible," is a distinction without a difference.[71]

∗ ∗ ∗

Over one hundred years after Kropotkin published this book, the task of creating an explicitly anarchist economics is not much more far advanced.[72] However, the same can be said of a genuinely scientific economics itself. Looking around at the various schools of economic analysis, we may suggest that Kropotkin would have been impressed by attempts of the Post Keynesian economists like Steve Keen to construct economics—in the sense of understanding capitalism—on a scientific basis and in the process show the weaknesses, limitations, and fallacies of neo-classical economics. He would also have been disappointed to see that they make little attempt to generalise from the facts of capitalism towards something other than a reformed capitalism.

So Kropotkin's critique of classical economics and its labour theory of

---

Castoriadis, *Political and Social Writings* trans. David Ames Curtis [Minneapolis: University of Minnesota Press, 1988] 2: 202–203, 242–251—a point made many decades before by French anarchist and syndicalist Émile Pouget, in *Direct Action* [London: Kate Sharpley Library, 2003], 9–10). So, unlike coal or a machine, the worker can influence both her wages (exchange value) and productivity (use value)— in other words, labour-power is fundamentally a "fictitious commodity" (to use Karl Polanyi's term) and can only be squeezed into the framework of classical economics by abstracting from (i.e., ignoring) the class struggle at the point of production.

70   Kropotkin, "Western Europe," *The Conquest of Bread*, 220.

71   Peter Kropotkin, *Modern Science and Anarchism*, 92.

72   A notable exception is the excellent *Debt: The First 5000 Years* (Brooklyn, N.Y.: Melville House Publishing, 2014) by anthropologist David Graeber.

value is flawed but does contain an important truth—empirical analysis is needed. He completely ignores the rise of neo-classical economics but this is understandable, for if classical economics tried to explain empirical reality, neo-classical economics simply sought to defend the capitalist status quo. Indeed, it can be considered as an intellectual construct designed to deny empirical reality in order to justify and rationalise its inequalities.[73]

* * *

Related to the Labour Theory of Value is Kropotkin's critique of Proudhon in which he wrongly proclaims that the mutualist advocated labour notes. In spite of stating that *System of Economic Contradictions* was a "work which, of course, lost none of its considerable merit on account of Marx's malignant pamphlet" *The Poverty of Philosophy*, he also states that Proudhon took up "Robert Owen's system of labour cheques representing hours of labour," thought the "values of all the commodities" should be "measured by the amount of labour necessary to produce them" and "all the exchanges between the producers could be carried on by means of a national bank, which would accept payment in labour cheques."[74] Yet it is from Marx's malignant pamphlet that this notion primarily derives, for Proudhon did not advocate pricing in labour notes:

> The idea of value socially constituted [...] serves to ex-
> plain [...] how, by a series of oscillations between supply
> and demand, the value of every product constantly seeks
> a level with cost and with the needs of consumption, and
> consequently tends to establish itself in a fixed and posi-
> tive manner.[75]

Proudhon argued that *"[p]roducts are bought only with products"* and "[i]n economic science, we have said after Adam Smith, the point of view from which all values are compared is labour; as for the unit of measure, that adopted in France is the FRANC." Rather than exchange notes that record hours worked, "the price stipulated and accepted for sold goods can become currency in the form of a bill of exchange."[76]

---

73   See section C of my *An Anarchist FAQ* volume 1 (Oakland: AK Press, 2008) for an introduction to this vast subject.

74   Kropotkin, *Direct Action Against Capital*, 214 n77, 183.

75   *Système des contradictions économiques ou Philosophie de la misère* (Paris: Guillaumin, 1846) I: 87.

76   *Système* I: 246, 67–68; *Système* II: 141.

This flows from Adam Smith's comment that the "produce of labour constitutes the natural recompense or wages of labour" and "labour be the real measure of the exchangeable value of all commodities,"[77] although Proudhon of course added that the "justice that Adam Smith would like to establish is impracticable in the regime of property." In *Modern Science and Anarchy*, Kropotkin does show he is a more astute reader of Proudhon than many, by recognising mutualism advocated common ownership of the means of production and land. For Proudhon, "the possession of these various instruments of production is already a monopoly" and "inequalities [are] created by these monopolies" and only socialisation ensures that "the work incorporated by each producer in their product be the only thing which is paid for when they come to exchange." Thus the "idea of socially constituted value, or proportionality products, serves to explain ... how social value continuously eliminates fictitious values, in other words, how industry brings about the socialisation of capital and property." Products would be individually owned and sold, with competition driving price down to labour costs for it was "the most energetic instrument for the constitution of value" and ensured a "reduction of general costs" for an "exact knowledge of value" can be "discovered only by competition, not at all by communistic institutions or by popular decree."[78]

The idea of "labour notes" was inflicted upon Proudhon's market socialism by Marx in his deeply dishonest and deliberately misleading *The Poverty of Philosophy*.[79] In Kropotkin's defence, once the notion of "labour notes" has been suggested it *can* be read into Proudhon's work—and many have done so. Nor should we discount the desire to show the unoriginality of Marxists from Marx onwards in advocating the notion.[80] That Kropotkin was repeating a commonplace myth about Proudhon is beside the point for it does not stop him being wrong.

∗ ∗ ∗

Anarchism—as a theory and a movement—started with Proudhon. Indeed, it would not be called anarchism without Proudhon's *What is Property?* and his influence on modern, revolutionary, anarchism is clear.

---

77   Adam Smith, *The Wealth of Nations* Volume I (Chicago: University of Chicago, 1976), 72, 35.

78   *Système* II: 525, 65; *Système* I: 87–88, 235, 189.

79   See my "Proudhon's Constituted Value and the Myth of Labour Notes," *Anarchist Studies* 25: 1 (Summer 2017).

80   See Marx's speculations on post-revolution economy in his *Critique of the Gotha Programme* (1891).

Kropotkin correctly places the birth of revolutionary anarchism in the International Workers' Association but his presentation may give the impression that anarchism as a political theory predates both this and Proudhon. A close reading shows that this is not the case. As he put it elsewhere:

> In the international labour movement Bakunin became the soul of the left wing of the great Working Men's Association, and he was the founder of modern Anarchism, or anti-State Socialism, of which he laid down the foundations upon his wide historical and philosophical knowledge.[81]

Ignoring the stressing of Bakunin's role—he became influential within the International mostly because he championed ideas already developing within it from reformist mutualism—Kropotkin was right to argue that modern anarchism was born in the labour movement and was part of the wider socialist movement. But what of anarchy before anarchism?

If anarchism—as Kropotkin stresses in *Modern Science and Anarchy*—is a combination of a scientific analysis of society and popular social movements then it would be strange indeed if anarchistic ideas and groups had not appeared before Proudhon described himself as an anarchist in 1840.[82] After all, class and hierarchy have been around for thousands of years and it would be hard to believe that during that period those subject to both had not questioned them—and sought to change their fate.

Kropotkin indicates that this is the case. Libertarian movements and ideas did develop before the rise of modern anarchism. Most obviously, he pointed to the popular movements and organisations of the Great French Revolution. The mass community assemblies created by the revolution were "practising what was described later on as Direct Self-Government" and so "the principles of anarchism [...] already dated from 1789, and that they had their origin, not in theoretic speculations, but in the *deeds* of the Great French Revolution." These bodies federated together to push the revolution

---

81   Peter Kropotkin, *Russian Literature: Ideals and Realities* (Montreal/New York: Black Rose Books, 1991), 299–300.

82   It should also go without saying that anarchism did not appear fully formed in 1840 when Proudhon published *What is Property?* Proudhon developed his ideas throughout his lifetime, particularly during the 1848 Revolution when his theoretical conclusions on the State and so forth were confirmed by its fate. Similarly, some of his ideas—such as his sexism—were in obvious contradiction to his stated principles and other anarchists rejected them. In short, while he laid the foundations of anarchism he was not without error and subsequent anarchists built upon and extended his ideas.

forward and "[b]y acting in this way—and the libertarians would no doubt do the same to-day—the districts of Paris laid the foundations of a new, free, social organisation."[83]

Yet it must not be forgotten that these thinkers and movements did not call themselves anarchist and played no role in the development of anarchism as a movement and theory.[84] As such, it would be anachronistic to label them as anarchist and far better to say they are anarchistic and part of a wider libertarian tradition which became fully conscious of itself (so to speak) in the nineteenth century with the rise of anarchism as an explicit theory and a movement.

So while William Godwin, like many others before Proudhon, had drawn anarchistic conclusions he did not actually influence the anarchist movement. His thought, like that of Max Stirner, was discovered in the 1890s by a well-defined social movement that retrospectively proclaimed them "anarchist." This explains Kropotkin's lack of discussion of Godwin's ideas beyond a short summary. He had no impact on the anarchist movement and its development—unlike the French Revolution, the labour movement, utopian socialism, and, above all else, Proudhon who first raised the characteristic ideas of anarchism (anti-State, anti-property, federalism, workers' self-management, communes, etc.) and which were taken up and expanded upon by Bakunin and then Kropotkin, amongst many others.

* * *

Overall, Kropotkin presents an accurate summation of Proudhon's mutualism. He recognises that the French anarchist was a reformist and advocated workers' associations to run socialised means of production.[85] What may be surprising for many revolutionary anarchists is how often Kropotkin references Proudhon in this book. He even goes so far as to quote his works, something he rarely if ever did with other influential anarchists (so in spite of the obvious influence and inspiration of Bakunin, Kropotkin never actually quotes his words). Elsewhere, he wrote that "the point of view of

---

83   Peter Kropotkin, *The Great French Revolution* (Montreal/New York: Black Rose Books, 1989), 183, 184, 186.

84   While Proudhon was the first person to embrace the term and apply it to their own ideas, it should be noted that the enemies of radical popular movements sometimes *did* label these "Anarchists." Kropotkin discusses one example during the French Revolution (see chapter XLI of *The Great French Revolution*).

85   This aspect of Proudhon's ideas is often ignored or denied. See my introduction to *Property is Theft!* or my article "Proudhon, Property and Possession," *Anarcho-Syndicalist Review* 66 (2016), 26–29.

Proudhon" was "the only one which, in my opinion, was really scientific."[86] He does, however, downplay the influence of mutualism within the First International[87] and on revolutionary anarchism (Bakunin considered his own ideas as "Proudhonism, greatly developed and taken to its ultimate conclusion"[88]). Kropotkin's only great error is in suggesting that Proudhon advocated labour notes.

However, some individualist anarchists also advocated pricing goods by time and as individualist anarchism—as Kropotkin noted—was influenced by Proudhon, he may have considered this advocacy as simply repeating the Frenchman rather than, as was the case, the direct influence of Robert Owen and his utopian experiments in America. Thus individualist anarchist Josiah Warren may have rejected Owen's communism after his experiences at New Harmony but he, like Stephen Pearl Andrews, advocated labour notes. Other individualist anarchists, like Tucker and Greene, did not.

* * *

This feeds into another issue with Kropotkin's account, namely his discussion of individualist anarchism. While very much part of the dominant libertarian communist tendency in anarchism, it seems fair to conclude he was not as well read on individualist anarchism.[89]

He takes Benjamin Tucker's linking of his mutualist ideas to Proudhon's mutualism at face value when, in fact, there are substantial differences between the two.[90] Most obviously, Tucker rejected Proudhon's position on socialisation of property and workers' associations and instead postulated the possibility of a non-exploitative form of wage-labour, so suggesting that he completely failed to understand Proudhon's theory of exploitation. Kropotkin, rightly, notes that Tucker's ideas are a combination of Proudhon's and Herbert Spencer's and argues that because they were based on individual ownership of the land they would inevitably result in the State being rebuilt.

As an overview, this is correct—as can be seen by Tucker's advocacy of private police, courts, prisons, and so forth (although he did think these

---

86   Peter Kropotkin, "Edward Bellamy," *Freedom* (July 1898).

87   For a discussion of Proudhon's influence, see my review "Workers Unite! The International 150 Years Later," *Anarcho-Syndicalist Review* 69 (Winter 2017).

88   Michael Bakunin, "The Paris Commune and the Idea of the State," *Bakunin on Anarchism*, ed. Sam Dolgoff (Montreal/New York: Black Rose Books, 1980), 263.

89   See section G of *An Anarchist FAQ* Volume Two for a more detailed discussion of the individualist current.

90   I sketch these in my introduction to *Property is Theft!*.

would become less needed as inequalities fell due to the end of non-labour incomes). However, Tucker's position on land was rooted in "occupancy and use" and so rejected capitalist rights on landownership—there would be no landlords in individualist anarchism, just workers living on and working the land. The problem arises when industry is considered for, as noted, Tucker had no issue with (non-exploitative) wage-labour arguing that it is a form of voluntary exchange. Yet his support for wage labour produces a massive contradiction with his "occupancy and use" perspective on land use. One letter to *Liberty* (by "Egoist") pointed this out:

> [I]f production is carried on in groups, as it now is, who is the legal occupier of the land? The employer, the manager, or the ensemble of those engaged in the cooperative work? The latter appearing the only rational answer.[91]

Tucker sadly did not address this part of the letter. Yet he defined the State as having two elements, namely "aggression" and "the assumption of sole authority over a given area and all within it." The "essence of government is control, or the attempt to control. He who attempts to control another is a governor, an aggressor, an invader" while "he who resists another's attempt to control is not an aggressor, an invader, a governor, but simply a defender, a protector."[92] Yet the employer assumes sole authority within the workplace and all within it in order to control both their labour and its product.

In short, the capitalist workplace is a mini-State, yet Tucker refused to see this. While defending strikers within capitalism (due to the capitalist State's interference in the economy in favour of capital), he was less sympathetic about labour protest in a future individualist society:

> Let Carnegie, Dana & Co. first see to it that every law in violation of equal liberty is removed from the statute-books. If, after that, any labourers shall interfere with the rights of their employers, or shall use force upon inoffensive 'scabs,' or shall attack their employers' watchmen, whether these be Pinkerton detectives, sheriff's deputies, or the State militia, I pledge myself that, as an Anarchist and in consequence of my Anarchistic faith, I will be among the first to volunteer

---

91   Benjamin Tucker, "The Distribution of Rent," *Instead of a Book, By a Man Too Busy to Write One* (New York: Haskell House Publishers, 1969), 340.

92   Ibid., "The Relation of the State to the Individual," 22–23.

as a member of a force to repress these disturbers of order, and, if necessary, sweep them from the earth.[93]

Given this, it is easy to see how correct Kropotkin was about the rise of a regime—albeit allegedly privatised rather than public—in which the few govern, exploit, and repress the many. This is a result of Tucker's lack of consistency over wage-labour and his dream that a non-exploitative form of it could exist while the worker sold her labour rather than its product. Even if non-exploitative wage-labour were possible (a big assumption!) it would still be based on authoritarian social relationships and these would need the machinery of a State to enforce and protect them.

This flows, as Kropotkin suggested, from the individual ownership of land—but as applied to industry rather than agriculture. Yet even with regard to the latter, the individualist position has its issues for any application of machinery would be limited in an "occupancy and use" regime. So either there would be an agricultural sector with low levels of investment or one marked, as in industry, with masters and servants. Similarly, coal and other mines would be impossible to exploit by one person and their family. Either associations are created or the owner hires workers—and "occupancy and use" becomes a joke.

Worse, Tucker's notion that wage-labour could be non-exploitative was wrong. He argued that under his system the demand for labour would be so high that workers would demand and receive as wages the full product of their labour. Yet this is optimistic for the whole point of the labour contract is that the worker agrees to labour to his master's orders and the product of his toil is owned—like that labour—by the employer. This, as Proudhon argued, allowed the boss to exploit the worker—for it occurs *after* the contract has been signed. Why would an employer hire someone if he were not to make a profit from so doing?[94] Thus wage-labour not only violates Tucker's own principle of "occupancy and use" but also ensures his hope that labour would get its full product would remain just that, a hope.

Other individualist anarchists—such as William Greene—had a better appreciation of the need for association and are far closer to Proudhon.[95] Tucker in this has more in common with liberalism than anarchism and,

---

93   Ibid., "The Lesson of Homestead," 455.

94   Carole Pateman's *The Sexual Contract* (Cambridge: Polity, 1988) provides a good overview of how the subordinate relationships generated by wage labour results in exploitation being possible. She also relates this to a wider critique of liberal ideology.

95   See Rudolf Rocker, *Pioneers of American Freedom: Origin of Liberal and Radical Thought in America* (Los Angeles: Rocker Publications Committee, 1949), 108–112.

indeed, individualist anarchism is the form of anarchism most influenced by—and closest to—liberalism. Yet his recognition that workers are exploited under capitalism plus his opposition to capitalist land ownership places him in the socialist camp, the camp he identified with.

* * *

As Kropotkin noted, the individualist anarchists of his time were influenced both by Proudhon and the radical liberal Herbert Spencer. Now a more-or-less forgotten figure, Spencer was at the time a well-known writer on science—he, not Darwin, coined the phrase "survival of the fittest"—as well as on politics, being a vocal anti-socialist who opposed State intervention in society beyond that needed to defend property.[96] Given this, it comes as no surprise that Kropotkin spent far more time discussing his ideas than Tucker's.[97]

Spencer's vocal opposition to State intervention led some to proclaim him an anarchist. As an example, in 1895 Russian Marxist Georgi Plechanoff— studiously ignoring the anarchist critique of the private property Spencer so loved as well as his support for a State—proclaimed Spencer as "nothing but a conservative Anarchist."[98] Someone should have told Spencer for in 1884 he explicitly rejected the suggestion:

> I entertain no such view as that of Proudhon—since I hold that within its proper limits governmental action is not simply legitimate but all-important. [...] Not only do I contend that the restraining power of the State over individuals, and bodies or classes of individuals, is requisite, but I have

---

96   See Stephen Jay Gould, "A Tale of Two Work Sites," *The Richness of Life: The Essential Stephen Jay Gould* (London: Vintage Books, 2007). Unsurprisingly, Spencer is often claimed by propertarians as being a precursor of their ideology.

97   For a good overview, see Matthew Adam's "Formulating an Anarchist Sociology: Peter Kropotkin's Reading of Herbert Spencer," *Journal of the History of Ideas*, 77:1 (2016). Kropotkin discusses Spencer in a chapter in *Modern Science and Anarchy*, in *Anarchist Communism: Its Basis and Principles* (his first major work in English) as well as devoting a chapter to him in *Ethics* (Chapter XII). He also wrote a lengthy obituary written at the time of his death (published in *Les Temps Nouveaux* as well as *Freedom* and included by Kropotkin as an appendix in this book) and a two-part "Co-operation: A Reply to Herbert Spencer" for *Freedom* in 1896–1897 (included as "Supplementary Material" in this edition).

98   Georgi Plechanoff, *Anarchism and Socialism* (Chicago: Charles H. Kerr & Company, 1909), 143.

contended that it should be exercised much more effectual-
ly, and carried out much further, than at present.[99]

And the function of the State? As Spencer put it in the early 1840s:

> What, then, do they want a government for? Not to regulate
> commerce; not to educate the people; not to teach religion;
> not to administer charity; not to make roads and railways;
> but simply to defend the natural rights of man—to protect
> person and property—to prevent the aggressions of the pow-
> erful upon the weak—in a word, to administer justice. This
> is the natural, the original, office of a government. It was not
> intended to do less: it ought not to be allowed to do more.[100]

Kropotkin exposed the fallacy of this claim: once the few have the bulk
of the land and other means of production then any attempt to challenge
or change this is classified as "aggressions" and the State acts to stop it. So
reducing the State to just the defender of property and the power that goes
with it is hardly anti-State and hardly anti-authoritarian:

> The modern Individualism initiated by Herbert Spencer
> is, like the critical theory of Proudhon, a powerful indict-
> ment against the dangers and wrongs of government, but
> its practical solution of the social problem is miserable—so
> miserable as to lead us to inquire if the talk of "No force"
> be merely an excuse for supporting landlord and capitalist
> domination.[101]

But, then, Plechanoff's work is a smear aiming to stop the Marxist faithful being tempted to read anarchist works. Still, Proudhon in 1851 had
already noted how liberals were sometimes confused with anarchists:

> [T]he disciples of Malthus and Say, who oppose with all
> their might any intervention of the State in matters com-
> mercial or industrial, do not fail to avail themselves at times
> of this seemingly liberal attitude, and to show themselves
> more revolutionary than the revolution. More than one

---

99   Herbert Spencer, "Specialised Administration," *The Man Versus the State with Six Essays on Government, Society and Freedom* (Indianapolis: Liberty *Classics*, 1981), 455.
100 Ibid., "The Proper Sphere of Government," 187
101 Kropotkin, "Communist-Anarchism," *Act for Yourselves*, 98.

honest searcher has been deceived thereby: they have not
seen that this inaction of Power in economic matters was the
foundation of government. What need should we have of a
political organisation, if power once permitted us to enjoy
economic order?[102]

In reality, they are "the chief focus of the counter-revolution" and
"seemed to exist only to protect and applaud the execrable work of the
monopolists of money and necessaries, deepening more and more the ob-
scurity of a science naturally difficult and full of complications."[103] This has
not changed since Proudhon wrote these words.

In *Modern Science and Anarchy*, Kropotkin notes that the bourgeoisie fought its battles against the absolutist State and sought to increase
freedom—in rhetoric, for all; in practice, for them. Thus the State may
have been opposed when it interfered with the property, power, and
privilege of the few but it was called upon when those were challenged
by the many:

> When a workman sells his labour to an employer, and knows
> perfectly well that some value of his produce will be unjustly
> taken by the employer; when he sells it without even the
> slightest guarantee of being employed so much as six con-
> secutive months—and he is compelled to do so because he
> and his family would otherwise starve next week—it is a
> sad mockery to call that a free contract. Modern economists
> may call it free, but the father of political economy—Adam
> Smith—was never guilty of such a misrepresentation. As long
> as three-quarters of humanity are compelled to enter into
> agreements of that description, force is, of course, necessary
> both to enforce the supposed agreements and to maintain
> such a state of things. Force—and a good deal of force—is
> necessary for preventing the labourers from taking posses-
> sion of what they consider unjustly appropriated by the few;
> and force is necessary for always bringing new "uncivilised
> nations" under the same conditions. The Spencerian no-
> force party perfectly well understand that; and while they
> advocate no force for changing the existing conditions, they
> advocate still more force than is now used for maintaining

---

102 Pierre-Joseph Proudhon, *General Idea of the Revolution* (London: Pluto Press,
1989), 225–226.

103 Ibid., 225.

them. As to anarchy, it is obviously as incompatible with plutocracy as with any other kind of -*cracy*.[104]

Thus Spencer "completely forgets the inability of the great mass of men to procure the necessities of life—an inability developed in our societies through the usurpation of power and through class legislation" and so "passed over lightly the fundamental facts [of] modern civilized societies" that the few "reap the benefits of the toil of propertyless men, compelled to sell their labour and themselves in order to maintain their children and household."[105]

In this he is typical of modern-day propertarians yet he was in advance of these because, at least in theory, he recognised the non-libertarian aspects of capitalism. Yes, as Kropotkin suggests, he defended the property-owners, "although in another passage he himself very sagely speaks against the usurpation of land in England by its present owners."[106] These comments explain, in part, why Kropotkin viewed Spencer sympathetically and are worth quoting:

> Equity, therefore, does not permit property in land. For if one portion of the earth's surface may justly become the possession of an individual, and may be held by him for his sole use and benefit, as a thing to which he has an exclusive right, then other portions of the earth's surface may be so held; and eventually the whole of the earth's surface may be so held; and our planet may thus lapse altogether into private hands. Observe now the dilemma to which this leads. Supposing the entire habitable globe to be so enclosed, it follows that if the landowners have a valid right to its surface, all who are not landowners, have no right at all to its surface. Hence, such can exist on the earth by sufferance only. They are all trespassers. Save by the permission of the lords of the soil, they can have no room for the soles of their feet. Nay, should the others think fit to deny them a resting-place, these landless men might equitably be expelled from the earth altogether. If, then, the assumption that land can be held as property, involves that the whole globe may become the private domain of a part of its inhabitants; and if, by consequence, the

---

104 Kropotkin, "Anarchist Communism: Its Basis and Principles," *Anarchism and Anarchist-Communism*, 52–53.

105 Kropotkin, *Ethics*, 320, 318–319.

106 Ibid., 320.

rest of its inhabitants can then exercise their faculties—can then exist even—only by consent of the landowners; it is manifest, that an exclusive possession of the soil necessitates an infringement of the law of equal freedom. For, men who cannot "live and move and have their being" without the leave of others, cannot be equally free with those others."[107]

Spencer rejected the idea that the land should be redistributed more fairly because future generations would "constitute a class [...] as having no right to a resting-place on earth—as living by the sufferance of their fellow men—as being practically serfs. And the existence of such a class is wholly at variance with the law of equal freedom." This produced a situation where "men born after a certain date are doomed to slavery." The landlord has the right "to impose just what regulations he might choose on its inhabitants" because they "are the only legitimate rulers of a country—that the people at large remain in it only by the landowners' permission, and ought consequently to submit to the landowners' rule, and respect whatever institutions the landowners set up." These conclusions can "only be repudiated by denying" that "the earth can become individual property." Thus "to deprive others of their rights to the use of the earth, is to commit a crime inferior only in wickedness to the crime of taking away their lives or personal liberties" and so it "is immediately deducible from the law of equal freedom. We see that the maintenance of this right necessarily forbids private property in land."[108]

The similarities with Proudhon's earlier critique of property are clear. Proudhon also applied this to industry and argued for the abolition of wage-labour by association. Spencer eventually did acknowledge this:

A wage-earner, while he voluntarily agrees to give so many hours work for so much pay, does not, during performance of his work, act in a purely voluntary way: he is coerced by the consciousness that discharge will follow if he idles, and is sometimes more manifestly coerced by an overlooker. [...] For so many hours daily he makes over his faculties to a master [...] for so much money, and is for the time owned by him [...]. He is temporarily in the position of a slave, and his overlooker stands in the position of a slave-driver.[109]

107 Herbert Spencer, *Social Statics: Or, The Conditions Essential to Human Happiness Specified, and the first of them developed* (London: John Chapman, 1851), 114–115.
108 Ibid., 120–122, 125.
109 Herbert Spencer, *Principles of Sociology*, vol. III (D. Appleton and Company: New

Given these comments, it is understandable that Kropotkin suggested that Spencer's ideas *could* be developed towards anarchist conclusions. The arguments for land socialisation logically apply to private ownership of workplaces (even by cooperatives) to ensure equal access and equal rights for new members. Only socialisation of industry along with land can secure liberty for all. Yet if we do so then we have moved far beyond liberalism and into socialism.

* * *

As is clear from *Modern Science and Anarchy*, anarchism is far more than just opposition to the State—it is against all forms of hierarchical organisation whether political, social, economic, or private. That is what makes anarchism a political theory and movement in its own right, with its own history and thinkers.

There are areas of overlap between anarchism and other political theories. The most obvious similarities are with other socialist theories like Marxism but there are some with liberalism.[110] Kropotkin explores this in his discussion of Herbert Spencer but it is clear that the assumptions of liberalism cannot lead to anarchist conclusions. That Spencer, at his best, could envision something beyond liberalism did not make him an anarchist even if he articulated, to some degree, libertarian ideals.

Spencer is far in advance of most propertarians who can neither envision anything other than wage-labour nor recognise the obvious unfreedom involved in it. Sadly, as Kropotkin notes, his practice was not in keeping with this analysis—he revised his early ideas to the right and happily supported various organisations seeking to secure the landlords in their property. Faced with a choice between liberty and property in the here-and-now, he consistently favoured the latter (even when reminded of his initial, irrefutable, position).[111] Yet to proclaim that *eventually*—once the masses have been educated—the evils of land ownership, wage-labour, and the State

---

York, 1897), 572–573.

110 Many Marxists, following Plechanoff, are keen to proclaim that anarchism has an essentially liberal core but this spurious assertion is based on nothing more than some superficial similarities between anarchist and liberal perspectives on (political) power.

111 For example, Spencer exchanged letters with Frederick Verinder, a leading advocate of land reform, on the subject of the former's change of heart in *The Daily Chronicle* between August and October, 1894. This was later reprinted as a pamphlet: *Mr. Herbert Spencer and the Land Restoration League: Correspondence Between Mr. Spencer and the General Secretary of the League, Mostly Reprinted from the* London Daily Chronicle, *August, September, and October 1894* (London: English Land Restoration League, 1894).

will be ended but in the meantime we will defend them all (within their proper sphere) does not make you an anarchist. Quite the reverse—it is not even a "philosophical" anarchism for it defends both private and public *archy* and so amounts to nothing: someone who postulates sometime in the distant future the end of chattel slavery would never be labelled a "philosophical abolitionist" particularly if he defends slavery and supports pro-slavery groups during his lifetime.

* * *

At least Spencer grasped to some degree the obvious contradictions in liberalism—unlike most classical liberals of the time and today's propertarian sects. While, in the abstract, he saw beyond the limits of liberalism and implicitly acknowledged the validity of the socialist critique of landownership and wage-labour, this did not make his ideas anarchist. Particularly when combined with practical politics that sought to bolster both for the foreseeable future. So if Spencer expounded some ideas in common with anarchists, he was nevertheless no more an anarchist than Marx who, likewise, had some ideas in common with anarchists and envisioned, in the future, a State-less socialist society.

As Kropotkin noted, this position does not actually reduce State action in society. As inequalities grow, so does the need to defend the few—it matters little if the police officers are from a private company or are "public servants."[112] The propertarians may cry power to the individual but in fact what they really mean is "power to the property-owners—and the State which protects them!" They seek to destroy all intermediate bodies—whether unions, local government, or whatever—by which individuals gain some means to counteract the power of property and the State. Ironically, their "anti-statism" actually boosts State power by systematically eliminating all social organisations that could limit its power. It leaves the individual alone against the might of the State machine—to which the owner appeals to help maintain their authority over those who use their property. This is why Kropotkin stresses in *The Modern State* and elsewhere that the State and capital are interwoven, with each supporting and aiding the other.

---

112 Indeed, in a very unequal society, the people at the top have to spend a lot of time and resources keeping the lower classes obedient and productive. There is "a significant statistical association between income inequality and the fraction of the labor force that is constituted by guard labor." So the more unequal the society, the more workers and resources are used to guard property and ensure obedience than actually produce goods. (Arjun Jayadev and Samuel Bowles, "Guard labor," *Journal of Development Economics* , vol 79 [2006]).

Being against certain (usually social) functions of the State is not "anti-State"—particularly when one is advocating State power as a defender of private property (and so private power). Being anti-State is necessary but not sufficient to be an anarchist due to the authoritarian relationships and organisations that property spawns. It is to Spencer's credit that he saw these relationships but it is to his enduring discredit that he acted in contradiction to these insights. This partly explains why he was quickly forgotten after his death as liberals increasingly saw this contradiction and sought State aid to mitigate the worst aspects of capitalism, defend society from the negative impact of free markets, and combat the inherent instability of the capitalist economy.[113] In addition to this, the capitalist class has always strengthened the State to bolster its position as it is the *bourgeois* State after all—something, as Kropotkin stresses in *The Modern State*, socialists and radicals singularly failed to recognise. These two movements—social reform and bolstering private power—sealed Spencer's fate far more than any internal ideological contradictions.

* * *

Kropotkin stresses that capital and State mutually support one another, and are interwoven. This can be seen from neo-liberalism. First imposed on the Chilean people by the dictatorship of General Pinochet, the elections of Thatcher and Reagan ensured that the 1980s saw a move away from the social-democratic consensus that had dominated the Western World since the end of World War Two.

Yet, as with Spencer, neo-liberalism has a reputation as being or seeking a capitalism based on a reduction in the role of the State. It is true that this ideology—inspired by the so-called "science" of neo-classical economics—has definitely rolled back aspects of State intervention, but this has been selective. As Tucker noted about Herbert Spencer:

> It seems as if he had forgotten the teachings of his earlier writings, and had become a champion of the capitalistic class. It will be noticed that in these later articles, amid his multitudinous illustrations (of which he is as prodigal as ever) of the evils of legislation, he in every instance cites some law passed, ostensibly at least, to protect labour, alleviate suffering, or promote the people's welfare. He demonstrates beyond dispute the lamentable failure in this direction. But

113 See Karl Polanyi's 1944 work, *The Great Transformation: The Political and Economic Origins of Our Time* (Boston: Beacon Press, 2001), for a good discussion of this process.

never once does he call attention to the far more deadly and deep-seated evils growing out of the innumerable laws creating privilege and sustaining monopoly. You must not protect the weak against the strong, he seems to say, but freely supply all the weapons needed by the strong to oppress the weak.[114]

The same can be said of neo-liberalism. While the rhetoric was for "free markets," the reality was the same as Kropotkin sketched over 100 years ago—particularly as regards organized labour. While "red-tape" was cut for capital, the rules, regulations and laws imposed on trade unions increased—encouraged by the ideological defenders of capitalism armed with their flawed analysis of the system, the mainstream economists. Indeed, the anti-union laws of the British Tories since 1979 restricting what workers can do and making it harder to strike and show solidarity echo Kropotkin's analysis in *Modern Science and Anarchy*. Needless to say, if you regulate strikes, if you regulate unions, you regulate the labour market—and as Adam Smith recognised: "Whenever the law has attempted to regulate the wages of workmen, it has always been rather to lower them than to raise them."[115]

That this is the case can be seen from the explosion of inequality since the imposition of neo-liberalism in the 1980s. Unions were weakened by means of State action (in line with neo-classical economics) and the link that had existed between wages and productivity broke (not in line with neo-classical economics). While productivity continued to grow, real wages stagnated (easy debt and partners entering the workforce allowed some improvement in family living standards). The gains of productivity flooded upwards as workers kept a smaller part of the wealth they produced in their own hands.

Thus, using British data, in 1950 the richest 1% of earners was rewarded with 12% of all income. By 1960 this had fallen to 9%; by 1970, 7%; and by 1980, 6% (and only 4% after taxes). By 1983 the income share of the best-off percentile was back up to 7%; by 1992 it was 10%; by 1997, 12%; by 2001, 13%; by 2005, 16%. In 1976, workers' share of the gross domestic product in the form of wages and salaries stood at 65.1%. By the end of 2016 that share was 49.5%. It is worse than that as this share includes exploding top management pay which has gone from around 10 times the average in the 1970s to 129 times in 2017: by mid-day on 4th of January in 2017, the average boss of a FTSE 100 company had earned as much as the

114 Tucker, "The Sin of Herbert Spencer," *Instead of A Book*, 370.

115 Adam Smith, *The Wealth of Nations*, 146.

average worker did in the whole year. For those who proclaim that this explosion in pay reflected improved company performance, study after study
showed little or no such link. Meanwhile, at the bottom low paid jobs have
grown relatively and absolutely as the floor that strong unions provided for
all workers was undermined.

This shows why Kropotkin was right to argue that unions are the "outcome" of the "popular resistance to the growing power of the few—the
capitalists in this case."[116]

All this is sometimes described as "market failure," but that is wrong—it
is precisely how capitalist markets *are meant to work*. Yet for neo-classical economics the only "failure" is that of our rationality in questioning
this outcome. This is a product of our evolved sense of fairness and hence
the pressing need for appropriate belief systems (such as provided by neo-
classical economics) to allow us to ignore it.

* * *

Interestingly, his call in *The Modern State* for economists to work out how
much labour the State gets from its subjects has to some degree been done—
by those associated with neo-liberalism. Thus the *Adam Smith Institute* likes
to proclaim "tax freedom" day each year when, it states, the average person
finally starts "working for themselves" rather than the State.[117] As to be
expected, the so-called think-tank is selective in its reading of *The Wealth
of Nations*, confusing, as Smith never did, wage-labour (toiling for a boss)
with "working for yourself":

> Nothing can be more absurd, however, than to imagine that
> men in general should work less when they work for them-
> selves, than when they work for other people. [...] The one
> enjoys the whole produce of his own industry; the other
> shares it with his master.[118]

The ideologues of neo-liberalism do not calculate "wage-labour freedom" day, namely the day when the average worker no longer "shares" the
product of their labour with bosses, landlords, bankers, shareholders. For

---

116 Kropotkin, *Modern Science and Anarchism*, 47.

117 As Proudhon noted, there "is no such liar as an average." (*Système* I: 156) Neither he
nor Kropotkin would not have been surprised that in 2014 the poorest 10% of British
households pay eight percentage points more of their income in all taxes than the richest—43% compared to 35%.

118 Adam Smith, *The Wealth of Nations*, 93.

obvious reasons, unlike Kropotkin, they fail to note how the riches of the few derive from the unpaid labour of the many.

* * *

As Kropotkin's discussed in *The Modern State*, the State has always intervened in the economy and society for the few. The notion that it should do so for the many is a relatively recent idea that arose once suffrage was expanded—few needed to be convinced that a Parliament elected by the wealthiest 5% of males would seek their interests first and foremost. Indeed, this was why Adam Smith argued for laissez-faire policies—to stop the wealthy few interfering to skew the economy even more in their favour (something conveniently forgotten by most of those who now invoke his name). So little has changed since Adam Smith:

> Whenever the legislature attempts to regulate the differences between masters and their workmen, its counsellors are always the masters [...]. When masters combine together in order to reduce the wages of their workmen, they commonly enter into a private bond or agreement, not to give more than a certain wage under a certain penalty. Were the workmen to enter into a contrary combination of the same kind, not to accept of a certain wage under a certain penalty, the law would punish them very severely; and if it dealt impartially, it would treat the masters in the same manner."[119]

Unsurprisingly, we see the advocates of labour-market "deregulation" (i.e., regulations to weaken unions) worry about the market power of organized labour while opposing suggestions to apply anti-monopoly laws to break up big companies. In fact, anti-union laws are almost always not recognised as interference in the market by the State. The same can be said of the defence of capitalist property rights, the privileges given to corporations (such as limited liability) and a host of other State interventions in favour of the wealthy.

Thus neo-liberalism shares the same features of the capitalism Kropotkin analysed in *The Modern State*—an instrument used by the few to secure and bolster their position. State intervention is only viewed as such when it favours the many.

Hence the privatisation of State industries at a low price or the use of public money to pay for goods or services by private companies previously

---

119 Ibid., 158–159.

provided by nationalised industries. Outsourcing is just the funnelling of public money to certain companies that prioritise paying dividends to shareholders over providing good quality and affordable services. Money previously used to pay unionised staff decent wages gets into the hands of companies employing people on the minimum wage with the surplus going to well-paid CEOs and shareholders. Similarly, the public subsidies to the allegedly "private" railway companies in the UK are far higher than the monies provided to nationalised British Rail—tax money is simply funnelled into the pockets of the shareholders while passengers get the most expensive, most over-crowded, and least reliable rail service of any comparable developed European nation.

Another example. The 2017 budget saw the Tory government announce £320 million for 140 new so-called "free schools" while the other 24,288 state-funded schools received £216 million extra for school maintenance. That is just under £9,000 for each state-funded school for three years compared to £2.3 million for every "free school." A simple gift to the few at the expense of the many, not to mention how the heads of "free schools" and "academies"—privately run schools which are funded and overseen by the Department for Education—could now decide to pay themselves huge salaries (as befitting their position).[120]

* * *

It is no coincidence that neo-liberal Britain is the most centralised State in Western Europe. Power rests in Westminster, itself increasingly marginalised by the executive—an elected dictatorship. Tom Crewe notes that of every £1 raised in taxation, 91 pence is controlled and allocated by central government. Yet before nationalisation and privatisation, there was municipalisation in which local councils "of differing political complexions in every part of the country bought out gas, water, electricity and tramway companies, on practical rather than ideological grounds." The first attack on municipal independence was nationalisation under the Labour government of 1945 to 1951 when "council-owned gas, water and electricity companies (and their profits) were transferred to central government control, depriving councils of a huge chunk of their independent income." Similarly,

---

120 Excessive CEO pay is not the only way academy trusts can divert money meant for pupils' education. One trust was established by a global edu-business that owns a copy-righted curriculum meaning that the Trust pays for its use and so £100 per pupil per year is transferred towards dividends. Then there are the numerous cases of influential individuals within academy trusts selling their goods or services, or the services of their relatives, to that trust.

the creation of the National Health Service led to the nationalisation of municipal hospitals. Then came Thatcher in the 1980s whose government "launched a sustained attack on the authority of local government" and the "destruction of local government as a potentially rivalrous state-within-a-state" (something, as Kropotkin stresses, the State cannot tolerate). Council housing was sold off to tenants at a reduced cost but councils were banned from using the income to build new housing. The net effect is clear:

> [I]t has only ensured that richer Britons are taxed less and poorer ones obliged to spend a much larger proportion of their income on goods they could once have gained for a fraction of the price. In 1981, rent for a council property absorbed less than 7 per cent of an average income; in 2015, for a private tenancy, the figure was 52 per cent (72 per cent in London), far higher than anywhere else in Europe.[121]

In 2016, the Commons communities and local government select committee found that forty percent of ex-council flats sold through Right to Buy are being rented out more expensively by private landlords. Almost a third of M.P.s were landlords, rising to nearly 40% for the Tories—the same Tories who voted down a law requiring landlords to make their homes fit for human habitation while, four years previously, they had voted to make squatting in residential buildings a criminal offence subject to arrest, fine, and imprisonment. Rather than allow local councils to build houses, the government spent £27 billion on housing benefit in 2014–15, tax money which goes straight into the landlord's pocket just to secure someone a home in the face of ever rising rents and house prices.

* * *

So rather than replace capitalism, nationalisation was a necessary step towards handing these concerns over to the capitalist and landlord class. This required both a commitment to capitalism and to a strong central State—as it had previously, the ruling class used the latter to bring the former into existence. And, of course, to destroy the various intermediate bodies within society which could challenge the power of the bosses, landlords, shareholders, politicians, and functionaries—particularly the trade union movement and local government (in Britain, for example, people had an unfortunate tendency to vote in local elections to protect themselves against Thatcherite

---

121 Tom Crewe, "The Strange Death of Municipal England," *London Review of Books* 38 (15 December 2016), 24.

social engineering). The word "localism" may be uttered but the practice is centralism—particularly to stop local people interfering with the activities of, say, fracking companies—for "[a]ttacks upon the central authorities, stripping these of their prerogatives, decentralisation, dispersing authority would have amounted to abandoning its affairs to the people and would have run the risk of a genuinely popular revolution. Which is why the bourgeoisie is out to strengthen the central government still further" and why the working class, "not about to abdicate their rights to the care of the few, will seek some new form of organisation that allows them to manage their affairs for themselves."[122]

Kropotkin pointed to municipalisation as one of the tendencies within capitalism that is anarchistic. It could be argued that for Kropotkin the local State was not really the State but this would be misunderstanding his argument. The municipalisation of services does not mean that he thought the local State could be used to free the working class (at best it could, like cooperatives, make social conditions better) but that it shows that local action could make a difference.[123] Local autonomy was a key feature of anarchism and if some improvements can be made today under the weight of representative forms as well as capital and the central State, then think what could be possible once both were abolished.

* * *

All this would not have surprised Kropotkin. Yet he was also aware of the problems associated with nationalisation. So rather than seek, as State socialists did, to add economic power to the political power of the (bourgeois) State, he suggested that such services like railways be handed over to the workers themselves—a position that Proudhon had advocated one half-century earlier.[124] As he suggested in a letter to Max Nettlau in 1912:

> The State phasis which we are traversing now seems to be unavoidable, but whatever its duration may be, it will never reach *now* the State Socialist conditions which were once imagined once upon a time by the social democratic and the Vidal school. Before they should come to that, there would be accomplished a complete change in the very forms of modern industrial production. I believe that, so far as we may see forward at this moment, it would be good tactics to

122 Kropotkin, "Representative Government," *Direct Struggle Against Capital*, 232, 228.
123 See the *Freedom* article "Municipal Socialism" reprinted in *Act for Yourselves!*.
124 Proudhon, *General Idea of the Revolution*, 151.

help the *Labour Unions* to enter into a temporary possession
of the industrial concerns, under the conditions of delivery
at certain established prices their products to given regions
of consumers. This would be perhaps an effective means to
check the State Nationalisation.[125]

The same should be argued for all State functions. So, for example,
would the British Tory government have been able to use the welfare State
as a punitive weapon during the 1984–5 Miners strike if the miners' unions
had managed welfare provision? Would the Tory government during the
austerity years of 2010 onwards been able to weaponise the benefits system
against claimants if that function had been in the hands of workers' unions
and cooperatives?

It matters *how* State functions are changed. Privatising nationalised industries simply changes the boss back from the bureaucrat to the capitalist—and anarchism is against both.[126] Some say that anarchists are being
illogical to oppose privatisation, neo-liberalism, or the imposition of austerity to "shrink the State" because we are, they proclaim, against the State. Yet
anarchism has never been just anti-State (surely "property is theft" shows
that?). We are against the State because it defends that property and theft,
so using economic crisis to impose austerity is nothing more than the State
acting as a weapon for the few against the many.[127]

Anarchists do not side with the State against its subjects. Rather we fight
with our fellow workers against attempts by governments to save capitalism
by pushing the costs of so doing onto the general population. This does
not mean we favour State welfare any more than any other State activity.

---

125 Quoted in Ruth Kinna, "Kropotkin's theory of the state: a transnational approach,"
   Reassessing the Transnational Turn: Scales of Analysis in Anarchist and Syndicalist Studies,
   ed. Constance Bantman and Bert Altena (Oakland: PM Press, 2017), 55.

126 See Vernon Richards ed., *Neither Nationalisation nor Privatisation: Selections from the
   Anarchist Journal Freedom 1945–1950* (London: Freedom Press, 1989).

127 In addition, there is the counter-productive nature of austerity. As even the most
   neo-classical Keynesian economist was aware, imposing austerity—like cutting wages—
   during a crisis would make that crisis worse and this is precisely what did happen in
   Greece, Spain, Britain, and other countries. Britain was unique in the sense that austerity was not imposed by the European Union and its central bank but was rather the
   choice of the Conservative government. In all causes, austerity made the crisis worse—as
   many, including anarchists, predicted (see my "Boomtime in Poundland: Has Austerity
   Worked?," *Anarcho-Syndicalist Review* 63 [Winter 2015]). Keynes may have sought to
   save capitalism, but to do that he needed to *understand* it. This is why he is worth reading,
   unlike most economists who simply eulogise and rationalise an unjust system.

Welfare, like the State itself, must be abolished *from below* by the many, not from above by the few seeking to increase their wealth and power—indeed, the much more extensive welfare State for the rich should be targeted long before anything else.

Such popular struggles against privatisation or austerity—against the decisions and actions of the State against its subjects, never forget—will build the confidence and organisations needed to *really* change things and to *really* reduce the authority of the State. Indeed, the UK anti-union laws show that our masters know this and know where our real power lies: not in Parliament but, as Kropotkin always stressed, in our workplaces and streets.

$$* * *$$

Kropotkin did not think that anarchy was inevitable.[128] That is why he spent a lot of time stressing the need for anarchists to involve themselves in social struggles and movements to make a libertarian social revolution possible.[129] So "since the times of the International Working Men's Association, the anarchists have always advised taking an active part in those workers' organisations which carry on the *direct* struggle of Labour against Capital and its protector—the State." This struggle, "better than any other indirect means, permits the worker to obtain some temporary improvements in the present conditions of work, while it opens his eyes to the evil that is done by Capitalism and the State that supports it, and wakes up his thoughts concerning the possibility of organising consumption, production, and exchange without the intervention of the capitalist and the State."[130]

It was in the First International that Bakunin correctly predicted that Marx's "dictatorship of the proletariat" would become a dictatorship *over* the proletariat while electioneering (the epitome of indirect means) would see any workers elected to legislative assemblies "become transplanted into a bourgeois environment" and "become converted into bourgeois" for

---

128 For a good overview, see Matthew Adams, "Kropotkin: Evolution, Revolutionary Change and the End of History," *Anarchist Studies* 19: 1 (Spring 2011).

129 The essential work on this is Caroline Cahm's excellent *Kropotkin and the Rise of Revolutionary Anarchism, 1872–1886* (Cambridge: Cambridge University Press, 1989). Also see works included in the section "The Workers' Movement and Class Struggle" of *Direct Struggle Against Capital*.

130 Kropotkin, *Modern Science and Anarchism*, 68–69. The links with Bakunin's ideas and syndicalism are obvious. The notion that syndicalism by advocating class struggle is influenced by Marxism cannot be sustained once an awareness of Bakunin's actual ideas is gained—see my "Another View: Syndicalism, Anarchism and Marxism," *Anarchist Studies* 20: 1 (Spring 2012).

"men do not make their positions; positions, contrariwise, make men."[131] Marxists denied this, with Plechanoff stating:

> The corrupting influence of the Parliamentary environment on working-class representatives is what the Anarchists have up to the present considered the strongest argument in their criticism of the political activity of Social-Democracy. We have seen what its *theoretical* value amounts to. And even a slight knowledge of the history of the German Socialist party will sufficiently show how in practical life the Anarchist apprehensions are answered.[132]

This was written in 1895 just as the debate between the reformists ("the Revisionists" or "Opportunists") and the orthodox Marxists broke out in both German and international Social Democracy on the death of Engels. The former wished to revise the rhetoric of the party to be more inline with its (reformist) practice, the latter wished to retain the rhetoric while pursuing the same tactics. The "Revisionists" may have lost various battles in terms of conference resolutions passed against them but they won the war because the rhetoric adjusted to the reality, as seen in 1914. Today, each one is—and has been for some time—reformist in both talk and action.

This transformation into (to use Kropotkin's words from 1899) a "party of semi-bourgeois—that is, radical but not socialist—peaceful progress, in other words, a reformist party" was because it had "moved away from a pure labour movement, in the sense of a direct struggle against capitalists by means of strikes, unions, and so forth. Strikes repelled them because they diverted the workers' forces from parliamentary agitation." Marxists "recognised the State and pyramidal methods of organisation" which "stifled the revolutionary spirit of the rank-and-file workers" while anarchists "recognised neither the State nor pyramidal organisation" and "rejecting a narrowly political struggle, inevitably became a more revolutionary party, both in theory and in practice."[133]

The Marxists did not capture the State, the State captured them. Still, being completely wrong—even when it was written—has not stopped Marxists recommending and reprinting Plechanoff's pamphlet to this day. Nor has it stopped the call to repeat the same tactics of "political action" in spite of the fate of the Social Democrats and then the Greens.[134]

---

131 Bakunin, "The Policy of the International," *Bakunin on Anarchism,* 171–172.

132 Plechanoff, *Anarchism and Socialism,* 99–100.

133 Kropotkin, *The Conquest of Bread,* 207–212.

134 This does not mean that social-democratic parties did not introduce significant—albeit

* * *

Malatesta also argued "the anarchist, if he were really an anarchist because of scientific convictions, would have to continually consult the latest bulletins of the Academy of Science in order to determine whether he can continue to be an anarchist."[135] However, his point seems too strong as Kropotkin, at bottom, simply stressed the need for anarchists to use the scientific method to build up their ideas. Thus our critique of the State is based not on feelings, but on a systematic analysis of how States developed as well as their role and practices. No State has ever existed, not even the so-called workers' state of the Bolsheviks, which did not create and maintain, perpetuate, and extend rule by the few, rule by a minority class.

Rather than just being against the State—as many proclaim, particularly Marxists—anarchists have always seen it in the context of class and as being interwoven with the economy. It is no neutral body but rather an instrument of class rule and structured accordingly. As Proudhon argued:

> And who benefits from this regime of unity? The people? No, the upper classes. [...] Unity [...] is quite simply a form of bourgeois exploitation under the protection of bayonets. Yes, political unity [...] is bourgeois: the positions which it creates, the intrigues which it causes, the influences which it cherishes, all that is bourgeois and goes to the bourgeois.[136]

The centralised, hierarchical, State is "the cornerstone of bourgeois despotism and exploitation."[137] It is no coincidence that "nothing resembles a monarchy more than a unitarian republic [*république unitaire*]."[138]

Kropotkin follows in this analysis, stressing how the State is a specific form of social organisation, a hierarchical, centralised and top-down one. This is why there are two sections in the book on the State: a historic overview and an analysis of the modern State. Both seek to explain what the State is and why Anarchists reject the idea of using it to transform society. The two are obviously related and are based on a class analysis of the State. In a nutshell, the State is an instrument by which minorities—minority classes—impose their rule onto the rest. As a result of

---

usually Statist and reversible—reforms but they were meant to *end* capitalism rather than make it nicer.

135 Malatesta, "Science and Social Reform," *The Method of Freedom*, 371.

136 Pierre-Joseph Proudhon, *La fédération et l'unité en Italie* (Paris: E. Dentu, 1862), 27–28.

137 Ibid., 33.

138 Pierre-Joseph Proudhon, *Du principe fédératif* (Paris: E. Dentu, 1862), 140.

this role it has evolved certain features without which it could not do it and so workers had to destroy and replace it with a new kind of social organisation more in line with the new tasks required by a people seeking its freedom.[139] This had to be based on the organisations created by the workers in their struggles against exploitation and oppression. In this he followed Bakunin:

> Workers, no longer count on anyone but yourselves [...] Abstain from all participation in bourgeois radicalism and organise outside of it the forces of the proletariat. The basis of that organisation is entirely given: the workshops and the federation of the workshops; the creation of funds for resistance, instruments of struggle against the bourgeoisie, and their federation not just nationally, but internationally. The creation of Chambers of Labour [...] the liquidation of the State and of bourgeois society [...] Anarchy, that is to say the true, the open popular revolution [...] organisation, from top to bottom and from the circumference to the centre.[140]

The "Chambers of Labour" were federations of local unions grouped by territory and Kropotkin likewise saw an anarchist society built from below by the workers themselves using their own organisations forged in the direct struggle against capital and the State:

> We see in the incapacity of the Statist socialist to understand the true historical problem of socialism a gross error of judgement [...]. To tell the workers that they will be able to introduce the socialist system *while retaining the machine of the State* and only changing the men in power; to prevent, instead of aiding, the mind of the workers progressing towards *the search for new forms of life* that would be *their*

---

139 Leading anarcho-Syndicalist Rudolf Rocker was very impressed with Kropotkin's evolutionary analysis of the State, using it to inform his discussion of the subject (*Anarcho-Syndicalism: Theory and Practice* [Edinburgh/Oakland: AK Press, 2004], 14–15). Likewise, his account of anarchism and its history follows that laid out in *Modern Science and Anarchy* and, as Kropotkin regularly did, links syndicalism with the libertarian tendencies in the First International (as did other syndicalists).

140 Peter Kropotkin, "Letter to Albert Richard," *Anarcho-Syndicalist Review* 62 (Summer 2014), 18 (originally from James Guillaume, *L'Internationale: Documents et Souvenirs (1864–1878)* [Paris: Société nouvelle de librairie et d'édition, 1905] I: 284–285).

own—that is in our eyes a historic mistake which borders on the criminal.[141]

Bakunin's vision of revolution predicted both syndicalism and the workers' councils of 1905 and 1917. Unsurprisingly then, it was Kropotkin and not Lenin who in 1905 saw the soviets as the means of both fighting and replacing the State as well as comparing them to the Paris Commune. Thus "the Council of workers [...] were appointed by the workers themselves—just like the insurrectional Commune of August 10, 1792."

> [The council] completely recalls [...] the Central Committee which preceded the Paris Commune in 1871 and it is certain that workers across the country must organise themselves on this model [...] these councils represent the revolutionary strength of the working class. ... Let no one come to proclaim to us that the workers of the Latin peoples, by preaching the general strike and direct action, were going down the wrong path. [...] A new force is thus constituted by the strike: the force of workers asserting themselves for the first time and putting in motion the lever of any revolution—direct action. [...] [The] urban workers [...] imitating the rebellious peasants [...] will likely be asked to put their hands on all that is necessary to live and produce. Then they can lay in the cities the initial foundations of the communist commune.[142]

The events of the 1917 Revolution show that Lenin's innovation of building a State upon workers organisations—namely, the soviets—simply confirmed the anarchist critique. This centralised regime quickly became alienated from the masses and produced a bureaucracy around it. To secure party rule, the Bolsheviks packed and disbanded soviets and repressed working class protest and strikes. Centralisation, as Kropotkin predicted, produced a new ruling minority. Applying the same organisational structures developed to secure minority rule simply changed who that minority was—replacing the capitalists and landlords by the Party elite

---

141 Kropotkin, *La Science moderne et l'anarchie*, 124–125.

142 Peter Kropotkin, "L'Action directe et la Grève générale en Russie," *Les Temps Nouveaux* (2 December 1905). This was also published as "The Revolution in Russia and the General Strike" in *Freedom* (November–December, 1905) under the alias "S" along with a letter signed by Kropotkin entitled "The Revolution in Russia" (this letter is included in *Direct Struggle Against Capital*).

and State bureaucracy.[143] Kropotkin was proved right—new functions need new organs.

* * *

As becomes clear from reading *Modern Science and Anarchy*, the suggestion by George Woodcock—repeated by many others—that Kropotkin became increasingly reformist from the early 1890s onwards cannot be supported. He remained a committed revolutionary and class warrior for almost the whole of his politically active life.[144]

We say "almost" for it would be remiss not to discuss events after the publication of this book for these undoubtedly explain why it has taken so long to be translated—indeed, the serialisation of *The Modern State* in *Freedom* ended mid-chapter in September 1914.

As is well known, with the outbreak of the First World War Kropotkin supported the Allies and, as a consequence, found himself completely isolated from the wider anarchist movement. This position came as a complete surprise to his comrades, particularly given the two chapters on war in *The Modern State* which were issued as pamphlets in both France (*La Guerre*, 1912) and Britain (*Wars and Capitalism*, 1914). These reflected the anarchist position Kropotkin had defended since joining the movement and so British anarchists continued to sell *Wars and Capitalism* while those around *Mother Earth* reprinted it due to it "embodying a logical and convincing refutation of his new position."[145] In Britain, his old friends and comrades Rudolf Rocker and Errico Malatesta refuted Kropotkin in the Yiddish and English-language press.[146] As an example:

> Allow me to say a few words on Kropotkin's article on anti-militarism published in your last issue. In my opinion, anti-militarism is the doctrine which affirms that military

---

143 See section H.6 of *An Anarchist FAQ*, Volume Two.

144 See my "Kropotkin, Woodcock and *Les Temps Nouveaux*," *Anarchist Studies* 23: 1 (Spring 2015).

145 Emma Goldman, *Living My Life* vol. 2 (New York: Dover Publications, Inc., 1970), 565; also see Alexander Berkman's "In Reply to Kropotkin," in *Anarchy! An Anthology of Emma Goldman's Mother Earth*, ed. Peter Glassgold (Washington: Counterpoint, 2001), 380–381.

146 Rudolf Rocker, *The London Years* (Nottingham/Oakland: Five Leaves Publications/ AK Press, 2005); Errico Malatesta, "The Anarchists Have Forgotten Their Principles" and "Pro-Government Anarchists," in *Freedom* (both are included in *The Method of Freedom*).

service is an abominable and murderous trade, and that a man ought never to consent to take up arms at the command of the masters, and never fight except for the Social Revolution.

Is this to misunderstand anti-militarism?

Kropotkin seems to have forgotten the antagonism of the classes, the necessity of economic emancipation, and all the Anarchist teachings; and says that an anti-militarist ought always to be ready, in case a war breaks out, to take arms in support of "the country that will be invaded;" which considering the impossibility, at least for the ordinary workman, of verifying in time who is the real aggressor, practically means that Kropotkin's "anti-militarist" ought always to obey the orders of his government. What remains after that of anti-militarism, and, indeed, of Anarchism too?

As a matter of fact, Kropotkin renounces anti-militarism because he thinks that the national questions must be solved before the social question. For us, national rivalries and hatreds are among the best means the masters have for perpetuating the slavery of the workers, and we must oppose them with all our strength. And so to the right of the small nationalities to preserve, if you like, their language and their customs, that is simply a question of liberty, and will have a real and final solution only when, the States being destroyed, every human group, nay, every individual, will have the right to associate with, and separate from, every other group.

It is very painful for me to oppose a beloved friend like Kropotkin, who has done so much for the cause of Anarchism. But for the very reason that Kropotkin is so much esteemed and loved by us all, it is necessary to make known that we do not follow him in his utterances on the war.

I know that this attitude of Kropotkin is not quite new, and that for more than ten years he has been preaching against the "German danger;" and I confess that we were in the wrong in not giving importance to his Franco-Russian patriotism, and in not foreseeing where his anti-German prejudices would land him. It was because we understood that he meant to invite the French workers to answer a possible German invasion by making a Social Revolution—that is, by taking possession of the French soil, and trying to induce the German workers to fraternise with them in the struggle against French and German oppressors. Certainly we should never have dreamt that Kropotkin could invite the workers to make common cause with governments and masters.

I hope he will see his error, and be again on the side of the workers against all the Governments and all the bourgeois: German, English, French, Russian, Belgian, etc.[147]

Comparing Malatesta's arguments to those in *The Modern State* we can easily see how far Kropotkin changed his position and why so many anarchists were surprised by it as well as why he was so quickly isolated by the movement.[148]

Needless to say, these facts are forgotten when Leninists discuss anarchism, perpetuating the myth that most anarchists followed Kropotkin in his support of the Allies.[149] In reality, the pro-war anarchists in spite of having "amongst them comrades whom we love and respect most" were "not numerous" and "almost all" anarchists "have remained faithful to their convictions."[150] Meanwhile, the vast majority of Marxists and Marxist parties supported their States and ruling classes in the conflict.

---

147 Errico Malatesta, *Freedom* (December 1914).

148 One Bay Area anarchist even went so far as to suggest "Kropotkin should have died before this war. Then he would have been held in grateful remembrance by future working classes." (Kenyon Zimmer, *Immigrants against the State: Yiddish and Italian Anarchism in America* [Urbana: University of Illinois Press, 2015], 135). While the damage and confusion Kropotkin's position produced—helped by the jingoistic press—made such extreme comments understandable, it must be said that his post-war output—such as the lessons of the Russian Revolution (namely, "Letter to the Workers of the Western World" and the post-face to the 1919 Russian edition of *Words of a Rebel*, both contained in *Direct Struggle Against Capital*) plus the unfinished *Ethics*—makes that too harsh.

149 This derives from Lenin's false assertion in *State and Revolution* about "the few anarchists" who "preserved a sense of honour and a conscience" by opposing the Imperialist War. (*Collected Works* [Moscow: Progress Publishers, 1964] 25: 470–471). Nor does Lenin mention that these few—which, sadly, included Kropotkin—had rejected Bakunin's position (turn the imperialist war into a revolution) in favour of Engels's defence of the fatherland while, ironically, Lenin went the opposite way. As regards Lenin's rejection of Engels' position, see "What Lenin Made of the Testament of Engels" by the ex-communist Bertram D. Wolfe (*Marxism: One Hundred Years in the Life of a Doctrine* [New York: The Dial Press, 1965]).

150 Malatesta, *The Method of Freedom*, 379, 385. Similarly, of the syndicalist unions only the CGT in France supported the war—unlike the vast the majority of Marxist parties and unions (significantly, the CGT was a member of the Marxist Second International).

Suffice to say, even the best of us can make mistakes and Kropotkin's love of France as embodying the revolutionary tradition from 1789 onwards played its part, as did his sympathies for national liberation movements and his fixation on France's defeat in the Franco-Prussian War and its negative impact on the labour movement by increasing Marxist influence within it.[151] Moreover, a trace of pro-French and anti-German sentiment can be seen in many of the articles on current affairs he had written for the anarchist press. All this—along with the absence of popular revolt in France against the war—undoubtedly played their part in making him forget the ideas he had spent nearly fifty years advocating.

Yet it would be a mistake—and a violation of the scientific method—to generalise from Kropotkin or his few supporters to conclusions about anarchism as such. Faced with the challenge of imperialist war, almost all anarchists met it by reasserting their Internationalist and class struggle principles while almost all Marxists failed. It is therefore unsurprising that Marxists have sought to build a myth by using Kropotkin to attack anarchism rather than the personal failings of an individual.

Kropotkin's repudiation of the principles of anarchism in 1914 saw him marginalised by the anarchist movement, which shows that his previous influence was due to how he articulated the ideas of anarchism. Once he stopped doing that, his previous contributions to the movement mattered little.[152] Yet these contributions should not be denied nor neglected as a result of the personal failings that were so horribly exposed in 1914.

* * *

Kropotkin's "lost" work is an important one whose themes are still as relevant as ever. Few these days even think of introducing socialism by means of the State—Social Democrats have become as blinkered by electioneering as Kropotkin indicated and can see no further than saving capitalism from itself. Fewer still are inspired by revolutionary Social Democracy—Leninism—after it simply confirmed the anarchist critique that State socialism would be little more than State capitalism and the dictatorship *over* the proletariat. Let all us socialists learn from the past rather than just seeking to repeat it.

So the need to base our politics on an analysis of society and its tendencies remains as true today as ever—as does the need to be able to debunk

---

151 See Jean Caroline Cahm, "Kropotkin and the Anarchist Movement," *Socialism and Nationalism*, ed. Eric Cahm and Vladimir Claude Fisera (Nottingham: Spokesman, 1978).

152 See my "Sages and movements: An incomplete Peter Kropotkin bibliography," *Anarchist Studies* 22: 1 (Spring 2014).

the pseudo-science used to defend inequality in all its many forms—and so *Modern Science and Anarchy* remains essential reading.

Regardless of the minor errors that crept into this work as would be expected, given its size, scope, and ambition, Kropotkin's final book is a fitting summation of his contribution to anarchism. It will be a fruitful read for even the most seasoned anarchist activist. As long as it is used as a source of inspiration for further analysis and action then its purpose will be served well.

MODERN SCIENCE AND ANARCHY
A PUBLICATION HISTORY

MODERN SCIENCE AND ANARCHY REFERS TO TWO WORKS—THE FIRST PART OF
the augmented 1913 edition and that work itself. The latter is a collection
of pieces published independently of the former but all were revised for the
1913 edition. Here we sketch the publication history of its various sections.

The "Foreword" was, unsurprisingly, written for the 1913 edition and
had not appeared elsewhere.

Section I, *Modern Science and Anarchy*, has had a varied publication history. Unusually for Kropotkin's works it was originally written in Russian in
1901 (but published in London) as part of his regular attempts to help and
influence the rising labour movement there toward anarchism and away from
Marxism.[153] This was serialised in *Les Temps Nouveaux* in 1902 and 1903,
with a French edition appearing later in 1903. That year also saw the first
English-language translation produced in America (another edition appeared
in 1908) while a German edition appeared in 1904. This edition did not have
the chapters on "Anarchy" ('L'Anarchie') and these first appeared serialised in

---

153 Other than *Modern Science and Anarchy*, very little of Kropotkin's Russian writings have
  been translated into English. *Direct Struggle Against Capital* includes four works—"Preface to Bakunin's *The Paris Commune and the Idea of the State*" as well as the three chapters
  written by Kropotkin for the pamphlet *The Russian Revolution and Anarchism*.

Les Temps Nouveaux in 1911.[154] They were included in the expanded English-language edition published by Freedom Press to mark Kropotkin's 70th birthday in 1912.[155] This was advertised as a "New and Revised Translation, with three additional chapters, and a useful and interesting Glossary." He further revised and expanded these chapters for the 1913 French edition.

	French	*English*
	"Les Origines de l'Anarchie," *Les Temps Nouveaux*, 18 October 1902	
II	"Mouvement intellectuel du XVIIIme siècle," *Les Temps Nouveaux*, 29 November 1902	
III	"La Réaction au commenecement du dix-neuvième siècle," *Les Temps Nouveaux*, 20 December 1902	
IV	"La Philosophie Positive de Comte," *Les Temps Nouveaux*, 24 January 1903	
V I	"Le Réveil des Années 1856–1862," *Les Temps Nouveaux*, 21 February 1903	*Modern Science and Anarchism* (Social Science Club, Philadelphia) 1903
VI	"La Philosophie synthétique de Spencer," *Les Temps Nouveaux*, 28 February 1903	
VII	"La Role de la Loi dans la sociéte," *Les Temps Nouveaux*, 2 May 1903	
VIII	"Position de l'anarchie dans la science moderne," *Les Temps Nouveaux*, 30 May 1903	
IX	"L'Idéal Anarchiste et les révolutions précédentes," *Les Temps Nouveaux*, 11 July 1903	

154 A footnote of the first instalment stated: "Our readers remember, perhaps, a series of my articles which were published in *Les Temps Nouveaux* in 1903 and which were part of a pamphlet *La Science Moderne et L'Anarchie*. Anarchy in this pamphlet was treated very briefly; I referred the reader to other works. Now, I fill this gap, and I give highlights of our ideas and their origins." ('L'Anarchie', *Les Temps Nouveaux*, 21 January 1911).

155 An abridged version of the new edition had been serialised in *Freedom* between October 1909 and May 1911. The most significant differences is that the sections of "Anarchism" are much shorter—sections X and XI in Freedom compared to X, XI and XII in the book—and so there are fourteen rather than fifteen sections.

X		Chapters X to XII
XI	"L'Anarchie," *Les Temps Nouveaux*, 21 January 1911 to 29 April 1911	("Anarchism") of *Modern Science and Anarchism* (Freedom Press, London), 1912
XII		
XIII		
XIV	"Quelques conclusions de l'anarchie," *Les Temps Nouveaux*, July 18 and 25 July 1903	*Modern Science and Anarchism* (Social Science Club, Philadelphia) 1903
XV	"Les Moyens d'action," *Les Temps Nouveaux*, 15 August 1903	
XVI	"Conclusions," *Les Temps Nouveaux*, 12 September 1903	

The revised and expanded 1912 edition was reprinted by Freedom Press in 1923 and was then included, in a very edited form, by Roger N. Baldwin in his 1927 anthology *Kropotkin's Revolutionary Pamphlets* (recently retitled as *Anarchism: A Collection of Revolutionary Writings*). It appears in full in *Environment and Evolution* (Montreal/New York: Black Rose, 1995) while extracts are included in *Direct Struggle Against Capital*.

Section II, *Communism and Anarchy*, is made up of two distinct texts. Part I was written in 1900 as an article ("Communisme et anarchie") for *Les Temps Nouveaux* (6 January 1900). Parts II–IV were initially produced as a talk (entitled *Communisme et anarchie*) for the *Congrès Ouvrier Révolutionnaire International* (*International Revolutionary Worker Congress*) held in Paris in September 1900. It was published in *Les Temps Nouveaux supplément littéraire* (No. 23–32: Rapports du Congrès antiparlementaire international de 1900 (Paris)) then as a pamphlet in 1903 (Publications des « Temps Nouveaux », No. 27). It was translated in *Freedom* (July and August 1901). Both parts were revised and expanded for inclusion in this book.

	French	English
I	"Communisme et anarchie," *Les Temps Nouveaux*, January 1900	
II	"Communisme et anarchie," *Les Temps Nouveaux*, supplément littéraire, no. 23, 29 September to 5 October 1900	"Communism and Anarchy," *Freedom*, July and August 1901.
III		
IV		

The *Freedom* translation is included in *Direct Struggle Against Capital*.

The *State: Its Historic Role* was written in 1896 as one of two lectures Kropotkin was asked to give in Paris by Jean Grave, the editor of *Les Temps Nouveaux*. It was serialised in *Les Temps Nouveaux* between December 1896 and July 1897 and was translated in *Freedom* between May 1897 and June 1898. It first appeared as a pamphlet in English (in 1898) and then in French (1906). It was slightly revised for inclusion in this book.

French	English
"L'Etat: son rôle historique," *Les Temps Nouveaux,* 19 December 1896 to 3 July 1897	"The State: Its Historic Role," *Freedom,* May 1897 to June 1898

A revised English translation was published by Freedom Press in 1946, 1969 and 1987. Its first and last sections were included in *Direct Struggle Against Capital*.

The first few sections of *The Modern State* appeared in *Les Temps Nouveaux* in 1900 before being translated over a decade later in *Freedom*. The two sections on war were serialised in 1912 (the English translation one year later used the book chapters as its basis rather than the original articles). The remaining sections (V to VII and X onwards) appear to have been written expressly for the book.

	French	English
I	"La Société actuelle son principe," *Les Temps Nouveaux,* 13 January 1900	"The Essential Principle of Modern Society," *Freedom,* November 1913
II	"Serfs de L'état," *Les Temps Nouveaux,* 3 February 1900	"Serfs of the State," *Freedom,* December 1913
III	"L'Impôt," *Les Temps Nouveaux,* 3 March 1900	"Taxation as a Means of Increasing the Power of the State," *Freedom,* January 1914
IV	"L'Impôt moyen d'enrichir les riches," *Les Temps Nouveaux,* 10 March 1900 and 17 March 1900; "A Propos de l'impôt," *Les Temps Nouveaux,* 24 March 1900	"Taxation a Means of Enriching the Rich," *Freedom,* February 1914 and March 1914
V	*La Science moderne et l'anarchie* (Paris : Stock, 1913)	"The Monopolies," *Freedom,* April 1914
VI	*La Science moderne et l'anarchie* (Paris : Stock, 1913)	"The Monopolies in the Nineteenth Century," *Freedom,* May 1914

VII	*La Science moderne et l'anarchie* (Paris : Stock, 1913)	"Monopolies in Constitutional England—In Germany— The Kings of our own time," *Freedom*, September 1914
VIII	"La Guerre," *Les Temps Nouveaux*, 2 March 1912; "La Guerre: La Haute Finance," *Les Temps Nouveaux*, 9 March 1912	"Modern Wars and Capitalism," *Freedom*, May to August 1913
IX	"La Guerre: La Guerre et l'Industrie," *Les Temps Nouveaux*, 16 March 1912 ; "La Guerre," *Les Temps Nouveaux*, 30 March 1912	
X	*La Science moderne et l'anarchie* (Paris : Stock, 1913)	
XI	*La Science moderne et l'anarchie* (Paris : Stock, 1913)	
XII	*La Science moderne et l'anarchie* (Paris : Stock, 1913)	
XIII	*La Science moderne et l'anarchie* (Paris : Stock, 1913)	
XIV	*La Science moderne et l'anarchie* (Paris : Stock, 1913)	

Extracts from the *Freedom* translation of parts I to VI are included in *Direct Struggle Against Capital* while the sections on War (VIII and IX) were issued as a pamphlet by Freedom Press in 1914 entitled *Wars and Capitalism*.

The glossary was added "by a friend" to the 1904 German edition and this was revised and expanded for the 1912 British edition before again being revised and expanded for the 1913 French edition.

The appendix on Herbert Spencer was originally written after his death in 1903 and appeared first in *Les Temps Nouveaux* (January to February, 1904) and then *Freedom* (February to September 1904).

French	*English*
"Herbert Spencer: Sa philosophie," *Les Temps Nouveaux*, 2 January to 13 February 1904	"Herbert Spencer," *Freedom*, February to September 1904

This obituary article has never been reprinted.

FURTHER READING

A GREAT MANY OF KROPOTKIN'S WORKS ARE AVAILABLE ONLINE. IN TERMS OF published works, George Woodcock edited Kropotkin's *Collected Works* shortly before his death in 1995.[156] In 11 volumes, it includes all his major writings as well as numerous important essays (although some are edited). This collection is by no means complete—it is missing the articles collated in *Act For Yourselves!* (Freedom Press, 1988), for example. It is also missing a very large number of articles in French and Russian anarchist papers which have never been translated as well as many in *Freedom* and other English language papers which have never appeared in book form. Many other editions of his most famous works—such as *The Conquest of Bread* and *Mutual Aid*—are also available.

Direct Struggle Against Capital: A Peter Kropotkin Anthology (AK Press, 2014) contains the most comprehensive selection of his writings. It includes extracts from all his books and numerous newspaper articles, pamphlets (some available in book form or in English for the first time). It also includes a lengthy introduction discussing all aspects of Kropotkin's ideas as well as a biographical sketch. A shorter collection of his pamphlets is

---

156 Published by Black Rose, it includes *The Conquest of Bread*; *Ethics*; *Fugitive Writings*; *Evolution and Environment*; *Fields, Factories and Workshops*; *In Russian and French Prisons*; *Great French Revolution*; *Memoirs of a Revolutionist*; *Mutual Aid*; *Russian Literature*; and *Words of a Rebel*.

available in *Anarchism: A Collection of Revolutionary Writings* (Dover Press, 2002). This was formerly published as *Kropotkin's Revolutionary Pamphlets* and contains much of his best short work, although most are abridged without indication of the edits.

Daniel Guérin's essential *No Gods, No Masters: An Anthology of Anarchism* (AK Press, 2005) has a section on Kropotkin, while volume 1 of Robert Graham's *Anarchism: A Documentary History of Libertarian Ideas* (Black Rose Books, 2005) has numerous extracts from his works.

In terms of Kropotkin's life story, the most obvious starting place must be his own autobiography, *Memoirs of a Revolutionist*, first published in English in 1899 and reprinted as part of his *Collected Works*. There are three biographies available. The one by George Woodcock and Ivan Avakumovic (*The Anarchist Prince: A Biographical Study of Peter Kropotkin*) has been republished as *Kropotkin: From Prince to Rebel* (Black Rose Books, 1989) as a supplement to the *Collected Works* project. As this dates from 1950, it should be supplemented by Martin A. Miller's biography *Kropotkin* (University of Chicago Press, 1976). *The Anarchist-geographer: An Introduction to the Life of Peter Kropotkin* (Genge, 2007) by Brian Morris is also a useful, if short, work on this subject. Caroline Cahm's *Kropotkin and the Rise of Revolutionary Anarchism, 1872–1886* (Cambridge University Press, 1989) is essential reading, as it covers the development of Kropotkin's communist-anarchist ideas when he was an active militant in the European anarchist movement.

For good introductions to Kropotkin's ideas by anarchists, *Evolution and Revolution: An Introduction to the Life and Thought of Peter Kropotkin* (Jura Books, 1996) by Graham Purchase and *Kropotkin: The Politics of Community* (Humanity Books, 2004) by Brian Morris should be consulted. Both cover his basic ideas and life, as well as indicating how modern research has confirmed the former.

NOTES ON THE TEXT

MOST OF THIS BOOK HAD ORIGINALLY APPEARED, IN SOME FORM, IN ENGLISH before. I have completely revised the existing translations and added any missing passages. Chapters without existing translations were translated by Nathalie Colibert. I have revised all the material and I accept responsibility for any errors.

We have decided to call the book *Modern Science and Anarchy* rather than *Modern Science and Anarchism* for two reasons. Firstly, Kropotkin used the word anarchy (*Anarchie*) rather than Anarchism (*Anarchisme*). Second, it will help identify which edition is which—*Modern Science and Anarchism* for English-language versions of 1903, 1908, and 1912 and *Modern Science and Anarchy* for this, the expanded 1913 edition.

We have tried to be consistent in translation (for example, "fonctionnaire" has usually been translated as "functionary" rather than "official" as it was felt this better expressed its bureaucratic nature). An exception is the word *Commune* which Kropotkin uses in five distinct related contexts:

1. The self-governing towns and cities of the Middle Ages;
2. The Municipality—the basic administrative unit of the modern French State;
3. The intentional communities advocated by the utopian socialists like Owen and Fourier and created by small groups of their

followers or, less often, by small groups of anarchists or other socialists;[157]

4. A territorial organisation created in the process of a popular revolution (for example, the Paris Commune of the Great French Revolution of 1871)

5. The basic (territorial) organisational unit of an anarchist society.

We have translated the term "commune" in line with these uses, retaining "commune" for the first, fourth and fifth usages (i.e., the commune of the Middle Ages, the revolutionary grouping and the future communes of an anarchist society[158]) while using "municipality" for the administrative body of the Modern State and "community" for intentional groups. The latter, we must note, also reflects Proudhon's critique of the Utopian Socialists whose various schemes he labelled "Community" (*La Communauté*).[159]

This work is in British English. Similarly, we must also note that Kropotkin often uses the term "England" and "English" to refer to "Britain" and "British." In this, he was reflecting current usage of the time but it is fair to note that this confusion is sadly still common—particularly amongst non-British people (and, to be fair, amongst many English people as well).

We have followed Kropotkin's capitalisation—hence "Anarchy" rather than "anarchy," "State" rather than "state" and so forth. We have done so to remain true to the original text and Kropotkin's intentions.

Finally, Kropotkin's language is dated and often reflects the prejudices of his time. So while committed to sexual equality, he uses the term "Man" to refer to humanity as a whole. Similarly, he uncritically uses terms like "savage" and "barbarian," reflecting the standard terminology of the time to classify human societies. However, he was well aware that the so-called

---

157 Or, more recently, the "communes" attempted in the 1960s and 1970s by people "dropping out" of mainstream society.

158 It *should* go without saying that the future anarchist commune is not a return to the Middle Ages however some Marxists—and some other commentators—have tried to link the two and assert Kropotkin (and anarchists in general) wished to return to an idealised vision of the Medieval Commune. Obviously, anarchist communes relate to the organisations created in revolution and was used precisely under the impact of the Paris Commune of 1871. For a discussion, see Kropotkin's essay "The Commune" in *Direct Struggle Against Capital*, 593–600.

159 Kropotkin, likewise, was critical of such intentional communities. For a good summary, see Matthew Adams, "Rejecting the American Model: Peter Kropotkin's Radical Communalism," *History of Political Thought* 35:1 (2014).

"civilised" nations have usually been far more "savage" and "barbaric," both internally and externally, than those societies they have arrogantly labelled so.[160] So while his language and terminology has dated, his evidence, arguments and conclusions have not.

---

160 As Kropotkin noted in *Mutual Aid*, a so-called "savage" would have been shocked by how the rich treated the poor—assuming that they survived the often genocidal imperialism inflicted on them by the "civilized": "I remember how vainly I tried to make some of my Tungus friends understand our civilization of individualism: they could not, and they resorted to the most fantastical suggestions" (*Mutual Aid*, 100).

ACKNOWLEDGEMENTS

As usual, I must thank the support and help of my long-suffering partner. Without her and her love, this work and my life would be much impoverished.

I must thank my comrade and friend Jim Tyson for providing me with the relevant copies of both *Comradeship* and *Labour Co-Partnership* and to the colleagues of Senate House Library for aiding him in that quest.

Finally, thanks to David Berry and Matthew Adams for their comments and suggestions on my introduction.

MODERN
SCIENCE
AND
ANARCHY

PETER KROPOTKIN

1913

PREFACE

WHEN WE ANALYSE ANY SOCIAL THEORY, WE SOON NOTICE THAT IT NOT ONLY represents a party programme and an ideal for the reconstruction of society, but that generally it is also related to some system of philosophy—of a general conception of Nature and human societies. This is the idea that I had already tried to highlight at two lectures on Anarchy,[1] where I showed the connections that exist between our ideas and the tendency, so well-marked at this time, in the natural sciences, to explain the great phenomena of Nature by the action of the infinitesimal—where we once saw only the action of the great mass—and in the social sciences, to recognise the rights of the individual, where we recognised until now only the interests of the State.

Now, in this book, I try to show that our conception of Anarchy represents a necessary consequence of the great general wakening of the natural sciences which took place during the nineteenth century. It is the study of this great wakening, as well as of the remarkable conquests made by science during the last ten or twelve years of the century that has just passed, that inspired me in this work.

---

1   Kropotkin was invited to take part in a series of lectures organised by Jean Grave, the editor of *Les Temps Nouveaux*, in Paris in March 1896. He planned to deliver two talks: *L'État. Son rôle historique* (*The State: Its Historic Role*) and *L'anarchie: sa philosophie, son ideal* (*Anarchy: Its Philosophy, its Ideal*). Neither was given as the police refused him entry into the country but both subsequently appeared as pamphlets. (Editor)

We know that the final years of the last century were marked by remarkable advances in the natural sciences, to which we owe the discovery of wireless telegraph, a series of previously unknown radiations, a group of inert gases refusing to enter into [any] chemical combinations, new elementary forms of living matter, and so on. And I was led to study in depth these new conquests of science.

In 1891, at the very time when these discoveries followed each other so quickly, the editor of the *Nineteenth Century*, Mr. James Knowles, proposed that I continue the series of articles on modern science in his review which until then had been produced by [Thomas Henry] Huxley, and that the great follower of Darwin found himself forced to abandon due to health reasons. One can understand how I hesitated to accept this offer. It was not elegant talks on scientific subjects that Huxley had produced, but articles that each dealt thoroughly with two or three great scientific questions of the day, and gave the reader, in a comprehensible style, a reasoned and critical analysis the discoveries concerning these questions. But Mr. Knowles insisted, and to facilitate my work the Royal Society sent me an invitation to attend its sessions. I finally accepted, and for ten years, from 1892, I wrote a series of articles, "Recent Science" for the *Nineteenth Century*, until a heart attack forced me to abandon this arduous work.

Led thus to seriously study the remarkable discoveries of these years, I came to a double conclusion. I saw on one hand, how—always thanks to the inductive method—new discoveries of an immense importance for the interpretation of Nature had come to be added to those which had marked the years 1856–1862, and how a deeper study of the great discoveries made by Mayer, Grove, Wurtz, Darwin and so many others around the middle of the century, while posing new questions of an immense philosophical significance, threw a new light on the previous discoveries, and opened new horizons to science. And where some scientists, too impatient, or too steeped perhaps in their initial education, wanted to see "a failure of science," I just saw a normal fact, very familiar to mathematicians, [namely] the passage of *a first approximation to the next.*

Continually, in fact, we see the astronomer, the physicist, demonstrate the existence of certain relationships that we call a "law of physics." After which, a mass of workers start to study in detail the applications of this law. But soon, as facts are accumulated by their research, these workers discover that the law they study is only a "first approximation": that the facts it is explaining are a lot more complicated than they seemed to be. So, to take one well-known example, "Kepler's laws" concerning the movements of the planets around the Sun are in this category. A meticulous study of the movements of the planets initially confirmed these laws. It proved that indeed the satellites of the Sun move roughly along ellipses, with the Sun occupying one of the foci. But it was also noticed that the ellipse was only a first approximation. In reality, the planets undergo various deviations in their progress along the ellipse. And when we studied these deviations, due to the action of the planets on each other, astronomers were able to arrive at a *second* and a *third approximation*, which corresponded better than the first to the real movements of the planets.

This is precisely what is happening right now in the natural sciences. After having made the great discoveries of the indestructability of matter, the unity of physical forces acting in animated as well as in inanimate matter, after having established the variability of species, and so on, the sciences that study in detail the implications of these discoveries are currently seeking the "second approximations" which will correspond with more perfection to the realities of the life of Nature.

The alleged "failures of science," currently exploited by fashionable philosophers, are nothing more than the search for the second and third approximations, to which science always devotes itself after each era of great discoveries.

So I will not dwell here discussing the works of some of these brilliant, but superficial, philosophers who are trying to take advantage of the inevitable pauses of the sciences to preach mystical intuition and discredit science in general in the eyes of those who are not able to verify these kinds of criticism. I would be forced to repeat here what is said in the text of this book on the abuses that metaphysicists make of the dialectical method. Besides it will suffice for me to refer the reader interested in these questions to the work of Mr. Hugh S.R. Elliot, *Modern Science and the Illusions of Professor Bergson*, recently published in England, with an excellent preface of Sir Ray Lankester (London, 1912, Longman and Green, editors).[2] In this book we can see by what arbitrary methods and pure dialectic, and by what virtuoso display of language, the favourite representative of this trend reaches his conclusions.

In addition, by studying the recent advances of the natural sciences and by recognising in each new discovery a new application of the inductive method, I saw at the same time how anarchist ideas, expressed by Godwin and Proudhon and developed by their successors, also *represented the application of this same method to the sciences that study the life of human societies*. I therefore tried to show, in the first part of this book, to what extent the development of the anarchist idea went hand in hand with the advances of

---

2   Kropotkin discusses the ideas of Henri-Louis Bergson (1859–1941) in "La croisade contre la science de M. Bergson" ["Mr. Bergson's Crusade Against Science"], *Les Temps Nouveaux*, (25 October 1913). In this critical review, he also recommends Elliot's book to his readers. (Editor)

the natural sciences. And I will try to show how and why the philosophy of Anarchy finds its completely obvious place in recent attempts to elaborate the synthetic philosophy, that is to say, the understanding of the universe in its entirety.

As for the second part of this book, which is a necessary complement to the first, I deal with the State. First I reproduce an essay on the historic role of the State, which was published as a pamphlet a few years ago;[3] and I have followed it by a study on the modern State, in the role of the creator of monopolies in favour of a minority of the privileged. I also study the role of wars in the accumulation of wealth in the hands of a privileged minority, and the parallel, necessary, impoverishment of the masses. By tackling this vast question of the State, creator of monopolies, I nevertheless had to restrict myself to indicating only its essential traits, and I did it all the more willingly as it is certain that someone will soon start this work, using the mass of recently published documents in France, in Germany and in the United States, and expose in full this monopolist role of the State, which every day becomes an increasingly dreadful public danger.

Finally, I indulged myself by putting at the end of this book, under the title of "Explanatory Notes," notes on the authors mentioned in this book and on a few terms of science. Seeing the number of authors mentioned in these pages—most not well known to my working class readers—I thought that these Notes would please the readers.

I hasten at the same time to express my deep gratitude to my friend, Dr. Max Nettlau, who was kind enough to help me with his vast knowledge of anarchist and socialist literature for the historical chapters of this book and the "Explanatory Notes."

Brighton, February 1913

---

3   *The State: Its Historic Role* was first serialised in *Les Temps Nouveaux* (between December 1896 and July 1897) before being published as a pamphlet in 1906. It was slightly revised by Kropotkin before inclusion in this work (Part III). (Editor)

I

MODERN SCIENCE AND ANARCHY

I

THE ORIGINS OF ANARCHY

ANARCHY DOES NOT DRAW ITS ORIGIN FROM ANY SCIENTIFIC RESEARCHES, or from any system of philosophy. Sociological sciences are still far from having acquired the same degree of accuracy as physics or chemistry. Even in the study of climate and weather [Meteorology], we are not yet able to predict a month or even a week beforehand what weather we are going to have; it would be foolish to pretend that in the social sciences, which deal with infinitely more complicated things than wind and rain, we could scientifically predict events. We must not forget either that scholars are but ordinary men and that the majority belong to the wealthy, and consequently share the prejudices of this class; many are even directly in the pay of the State. It is, therefore, quite evident that Anarchy does not come from universities.

Like Socialism in general, and like all other social movements, Anarchy was born amongst the people, and it will maintain its vitality and creative force only as long as it remains a movement of the people.

Historically, two currents have been in conflict in human society. On the one hand, the masses, the people, developed in the form of customs a multitude of institutions necessary to make social existence possible: to maintain peace, to settle quarrels, and to practise mutual aid in all circumstances that required combined effort. Tribal customs amongst savages, later the village communities, and, still later, the industrial guilds and the cities of the Middle Ages, which laid the first foundations of international law, all these institutions were developed, not by legislators, but by the creative spirit of the masses.

On the other hand, there have been magi, shamans, wizards, rain-makers, oracles, priests. These were the first teachers of a [rudimentary] knowledge of nature and the first founders of religions ([worshiping] the sun, the forces of Nature, ancestors, etc.) and the different rituals that were used to maintain the unity of tribal federations.

At that time, the first germs of the study of nature (astronomy, weather prediction, the study of illnesses) went hand in hand with various super-stitions, expressed by different rites and cults. The beginnings of all arts and crafts also had this origin in study and superstition and each had its mys-tical formulae that were provided only to the initiated, and were carefully concealed from the masses.

Alongside of these earliest representatives of science and religion, there were also men, like the bards, the *brehons* of Ireland, the *speakers of the law* of the Scandinavian peoples, etc. who were considered masters in the ways of customs and of the ancient traditions, which were to be used in the event of discord and disagreements. They kept the law in their memory (some-times through the use of symbols, which were the germs of writing) and in case of disagreements they acted as referees.

Finally, there were also the temporary chiefs of military bands, who were supposed to possess the secret magic for success in warfare; they also pos-sessed the secrets of poisoning weapons and other military secrets.

These three groups of men have always formed amongst themselves se-cret societies to keep and pass on (after a long and painful initiation period) the secrets of their social functions or their crafts; and if, at times, they fought each other, they always agreed in the long run; they joined together and supported each other in order to dominate the masses, to reduce them to obedience, to govern them—and to make the masses work for them.

It is evident that Anarchy represents the first of these two currents, that is to say, the creative, constructive force of the masses, who developed institu-tions of common law to defend themselves against the domineering minor-ity. It is also by the creative and constructive force of the people, aided by the whole strength of science and modern technology, that Anarchy now strives to set up the necessary institutions to guarantee the free develop-ment of society—in contrast to those who put their hope in laws made by ruling minorities and imposed on the masses by a rigorous discipline.

We can therefore say that in this sense there have always been anarchists and statists.

Moreover, we always find that [social] institutions, even the best of them—those that were originally built to maintain equality, peace and mutual aid—became petrified as they grew old. They lost their original purpose, they fell under the domination of an ambitious minority, and they end up becoming an obstacle to the further development of society. Then individuals, more or less isolated, rebel. But while some of these discontented, by rebelling against an institution that has become irksome, sought to modify it in the interests of all—and above all to overthrow the authority, foreign to the social institution (the tribe, the village commune, the guild, etc.)—others only sought to set themselves outside and above these institutions in order to dominate the other members of society and to grow rich at their expense.

All political, religious, economic reformers have belonged to the first of the two categories; and amongst them there have always been individuals who, without waiting for all their fellow citizens or even only a minority of them to be imbued with similar ideas, strove forward and rose against oppression—either in more or less numerous groups or alone if they had no following. We see revolutionaries in all periods of history.

However, these revolutionaries also had two different aspects. Some, while rebelling against the authority that had grown up within society, did not seek to destroy this authority but strove to seize it for themselves. Instead of an oppressive power, they sought to constitute a new one, which they would hold, and they promised—often in good faith—that the new authority would have the welfare of the people at heart, it would be their true representative—a promise that later on was inevitably forgotten or betrayed. Thus were constituted Imperial authority in the Rome of the Caesars, the authority of the [Catholic] Church in the first centuries of our era, dictatorial power in the cities of the Middle Ages during their period of decline, and so forth. The same current was used to establish royal authority in Europe at the end of the feudal period. Faith in an emperor "for the people"—a Caesar—is not dead, even today.

But alongside this authoritarian current, another current asserted itself in times when overhauling the established institutions was necessary. At all times, from ancient Greece to the present day, there were individuals and currents of thought and action that sought not to replace one authority by another but to destroy the authority which had been grafted onto popular institutions—without creating another to take its place. They proclaimed the sovereignty of both the individual and the people, and they sought to free popular institutions from authoritarian overgrowths; they worked to give back complete freedom to the collective spirit of the masses—so that the popular genius might once again freely rebuild institutions of mutual aid and mutual protection, in harmony with new needs and new conditions of existence. In the cites of ancient Greece, and especially in those of the Middle Ages (Florence, Pskov, etc.,) we find many examples of these kinds of conflicts.

We may therefore say that Jacobins and anarchists have always existed amongst reformers and revolutionaries.

Formidable popular movements, stamped with an anarchist character, took place several times in the past. Villages and cities rose against the principle of government—against the organs of the State, its courts, its laws—and they proclaimed the sovereignty of the rights of man. They denied all written law, and asserted that every man should govern himself according to his conscience. They thus tried to establish a new society, based on the principles of equality, complete freedom, and work. In the Christian movement in Judea, under Augustus—against the Roman law, the Roman State, and the morality, or rather the immorality, of that time—there was unquestionably considerable elements of Anarchy. Little by little this movement degenerated into a Church movement, fashioned after the Hebrew Church and Imperial Rome itself, which naturally killed all that Christianity possessed of anarchism at its outset, gave it Roman forms, and soon it became the principal support of authority, State, slavery, oppression. The first seeds of "opportunism" which were introduced into Christianity are already visible in the Gospels and the Acts of the Apostles—or, at least, in the versions of these writings that make up the *New Testament*.

Similarly, the Anabaptist movement of the sixteenth century, which inaugurated and brought about the Reformation, also had an anarchist basis. But crushed by those reformers who, under Luther's leadership, leagued with the princes against the rebellious peasants, the movement was suppressed by a great massacre of peasants and the "lower classes" of the towns. Then the right wing of the reformers degenerated little by little, until it became the compromise between its own conscience and the State which exists today under the name of Protestantism.

Therefore, to summarise,[1] Anarchy was born in the same critical and revolutionary protest which gave rise to socialism in general. However, one

---

1   The British 1912 edition adds the following before making the rest of the text into a new paragraph:

> Anarchism had its origin in the same creative, constructive activity
> of the masses which has worked out in times past all the social institutions of mankind—and in the revolts of both the individuals and
> the nations against the representatives of force, external to these social
> institutions, who had laid their hands upon these institutions and used

portion of the socialists, after having reached the negation of capital and of a society based on the enslavement of labour to capital, stopped there. They did not declare themselves against what constitutes the real strength of capital—the State and its principal supports: centralisation of authority, law (always made by the minority, for the profit of minorities), and [a form of] Justice whose chief aim is to protect authority and capital.

As for Anarchy, it does not exclude these institutions from its critique. It raises its sacrilegious arm not only against capital but also these henchmen of capitalism.

---

them for their own advantage. Those of the rebels whose aim was to restore to the creative genius of the masses the necessary freedom for its creative activity so that it works out the required new institutions, were imbued with the Anarchist spirit.

Any significant differences between the original English-language translations and the 1913 French edition will be indicated in footnotes. (Editor)

II

THE INTELLECTUAL MOVEMENT OF THE
EIGHTEENTH CENTURY

IF ANARCHY, LIKE ALL OTHER REVOLUTIONARY MOVEMENTS, WAS BORN amongst the people during the turmoil of struggle and not in a scholar's study, it is important, nevertheless, to know its position amongst the various currents of scientific and philosophical thought that exist at the present time. What is its attitude to these diverse currents? On which of them does it prefer to rely upon? Which method of research does it use to support its conclusions? In other words, to what school of Philosophy of Law does Anarchy belong? With what current of modern science does it show most affinity?

In view of the infatuation for metaphysical economics which we have recently seen in socialist circles, this question provides some interest. I will therefore try to answer it as briefly and simply as possible, avoiding all difficult terms where I can.[2]

---

2   At the end of the book can be found "Explanatory Notes" where the interpretation of various scientific terms are given in understandable language and the work of the various authors mentioned is summarised.

The intellectual movement of the nineteenth century originated from the works written by [Scottish,[3]] English, and French philosophers in the middle and end of the preceding century.

The awakening of thought which took place in those times stimulated these thinkers with the desire of encompassing *all* human knowledge in a general system—the system of Nature. Completely rejecting the scholasticism and metaphysics of the Middle Ages, they had the courage to conceive all Nature—the universe of stars, our solar system, our globe, the development of the plants, the animals, and the human societies on its surface—as a series of facts that can be studied in the same way as the natural sciences are.

Mainly taking advantage of the true *scientific* method—the inductive-deductive method—they undertook the study of all groups of facts presented to us by Nature, whether belonging to the world of stars or of animals, or to that of beliefs or human institutions, just in the same manner as a naturalist would study questions of physics.

They began by patiently recording facts, and when they ventured upon generalisations, they did so using induction. They made some hypotheses; but they attributed no more importance to these hypotheses than Darwin did to his hypothesis concerning the origin of new species by the struggle for existence, or that Mendéléeff gave to his "periodic law." They saw assumptions as providing a preliminary explanation [or working hypotheses] and facilitated the grouping of facts and their study; but they did not forget that these assumptions had to be confirmed by applying them to a multitude of facts and explained in a deductive way. They could become "laws" (*proved* generalisations) only after they had undergone this verification and the *causes* of the constant relations they express could be explained.

When the centre of the philosophical movement of the eighteenth century was transferred from England and Scotland to France, the French philosophers, with the feeling for system peculiar to them began to construct on general terms and on the same principles *all* human knowledge: historical and natural. They attempted to construct *generalised knowledge*—the *philosophy* of the universe and its life—upon a strictly scientific basis, rejecting all the metaphysical constructions of previous philosophers, and explained all phenomena by the action of those same physical (that is to say, mechanical) forces that sufficed them to explain the origin and the evolution of the terrestrial globe.

---

3   Kropotkin wrote English in the French edition but the 1912 British edition has Scottish. Given that Voltaire wrote that "we look to Scotland for all our ideas of civilisation," Scottish has been added for accuracy. (Editor)

It is said that when Napoleon I remarked to Laplace that in his *Exposition of the System of the Universe* the name of God was nowhere to be found, Laplace answered: "I nowhere felt the need of that hypothesis." But Laplace did better. He did not resort, either, to the grand *words* of metaphysics behind which generally hides incomprehension nor an obscure semi-understanding of phenomena and the inability to represent these in a concrete form, as measurable quantities. Laplace dispensed with metaphysics as well as with the hypothesis of a creator; and although his *Exposition of the System of the Universe* contains no mathematical formulas and was written in a style comprehensible to all educated readers, mathematicians could later express each separate thought of that work in mathematical equations—that is to say, as relations between measurable quantities: so exactly had Laplace thought out every detail of his work.

What Laplace did for celestial mechanics, the French philosophers of the eighteenth century had tried to do, within the limits of the knowledge of the time, for the study of the phenomena of life as well as for those of human understanding and feeling (psychology). They abandoned the metaphysical assertions found in their predecessors and which is encountered later in the German philosopher Kant.

It is known, indeed, that Kant sought to explain, for instance, the moral sentiment of man by saying that it is "a categorical imperative," and that such a maxim of conduct is obligatory "if we conceive it as a law susceptible of universal application." But every word in this definition substitutes something nebulous and incomprehensible ("imperative" and "categorical," "law," "universal"!) in the place of the material facts, known to us all, that he was meant to explain.

The French Encyclopaedists could not be satisfied with such "explanations" by "grand words." Like their English and Scottish predecessors, they could not—to explain whence man obtained his conception of good and evil—insert, as Goethe said, "a word where there is a lack of ideas." They studied this conception in man—as [Francis] Hutcheson had already done in 1725, and, later, Adam Smith in his best work, *The Theory of Moral Sentiments*—and they found that the moral sentiment of man derives its origin from the feeling of pity and of sympathy which we feel towards those who suffer. It comes from the capacity with which we are endowed of identifying ourselves with others—so that we almost feel physical pain when we see a child beaten in our presence, and this act revolts us.

Starting from this type of observation, and facts known to everyone, the Encyclopaedists arrived at wider generalisations. By this method they really *explained* moral sentiment, which is a complex fact, by simpler facts. But they never put, instead of known and *comprehensible facts, incomprehensible* and nebulous *words,* that explain absolutely nothing—like "categorical imperative" or "universal law."

The advantage of the method of the *Encyclopaedists* is obvious. Instead of "inspiration from on high," instead of an extra-human and supernatural origin for the moral sentiment, they said to man: "Here is the feeling of pity and sympathy, possessed by man since his origin, drawn from his very first observations of his fellow creatures, and perfected little by little by the experience of life in societies. From this feeling comes our moral sense."

We thus see that the thinkers of the eighteenth century did not change their method when they passed from the realm of stars to the realm of chemical reactions, or from the physical and chemical world to the life of plants and animals, or to the development of the economic and political forms of [human] society, the evolution of religions, and so on. The method remained the same. To all branches of science they applied the inductive method. And neither in the study of religions, nor in the analysis of the moral sense, nor in thought in general, did they find a single case where their method failed and where another method was necessary. Nowhere did they find themselves compelled to resort to metaphysical conceptions (God, immortal soul, life force, categorical imperative inspired by a superior being, etc.), or to some dialectic method—they attempted *to explain the entire universe and all phenomena in the same* NATURALIST *way.*

During those years of remarkable intellectual development, the Encyclopaedists built their monumental *Encyclopaedia.* Laplace published his *System of the Universe,* and Holbach his *System of Nature.* Lavoisier affirmed the indestructibility of matter and, consequently, of energy and movement. Lomonosov in Russia, inspired by Bayle, already at that time sketched his mechanical theory of heat; Lamarck explained the origin of the infinitely varied species of plants and animals by adaptation to their diverse surrounding environments; Diderot gave an explanation of moral sentiment, moral customs, primitive institutions and religions, without resorting to inspiration from on high; Rousseau endeavoured to explain the birth of political institutions as a consequence of a social contract—that is to say, by an act of human will. In short, there was not a single area which they did not study by means of facts, by the same scientific method of induction and deduction, verified by observation of facts and experiment.

Of course, more than one error was committed in that great and bold attempt. Where knowledge was lacking, sometimes hasty and erroneous assumptions were made. *But a new method had been applied to the whole of human knowledge* and thanks to this new method, the errors themselves were easily recognised and corrected later on. By this means the nineteenth century inherited a powerful instrument of research which enabled us to build our whole conception of the universe on a scientific basis, and to finally free it from the prejudices that obscured it, as well as those nebulous words which say nothing and which we formerly had the bad habit of introducing when we wished to avoid difficult questions.

III

THE REACTION AT THE BEGINNING OF THE NINETEENTH CENTURY

AFTER THE DEFEAT OF THE GREAT FRENCH REVOLUTION, EUROPE PASSED, as is known, through a period of general reaction: in the domains of politics, science and philosophy. The White Terror of the Bourbons [in France], the Holy Alliance concluded in 1815 between the monarchs of Austria, Germany, and Russia to combat liberal ideas, the mysticism and "pietism" in European High Society, and the State police everywhere, triumphed all down the line.

Yet the fundamental principles of the Revolution did not perish. The emancipation of the peasants and the town workers from the state of semi-serfdom which they had endured until then, equality before the law, and representative government—these three principles promulgated by the Revolution and carried by the [French] revolutionary armies all over Europe, as far as Poland, made their way in France as elsewhere. After the *Revolution,* which had announced [to the world] the great principles of liberty, equality and fraternity, began the slow *evolution*—that is to say, the slow transformation of institutions: the application to everyday life of the general principles proclaimed in France during 1789–1793. We note in passing that realisation by way of evolution of the principles announced during the preceding revolutionary upheaval could be recognised as a general law of the development of societies.

If the Church, the State, and even Science trampled under their feet the banner on which the Revolution had inscribed its motto: "Liberty, Equality, Fraternity"; if accommodation with what exists had then become the watchword, even in philosophy, the great principles of freedom nevertheless began to penetrate into life. True, the servile obligations of the peasants, as well as the Inquisition, that had been abolished in Italy and Spain by the armies of the Revolution, were re-established. But a death-blow had been dealt to these institutions: they will never recover.

The wave of liberation first reached western Germany; then it rolled as far as Prussia and Austria; it spread over the Iberian and Italian peninsulas; and, flowing eastwards, it arrived in Russia in 1861 and in the Balkans in 1878. Slavery disappeared in [North] America in 1863. At the same time, the idea of equality of all before the law and that of representative government also spread from west to east, and by the end of the century only Russia and Turkey remained under the yoke of autocracy—both, it is true, on their death-beds.[4]

There was more. On the dividing line between the eighteenth and nineteenth centuries, we already find the ideas of economic emancipation loudly advocated. Immediately after the overthrow of the monarchy by the people of Paris on August 10, 1792, and especially after the overthrow of the Girondins on June 2, 1793, there was in Paris and the provinces an outburst of communist feelings; and then we saw the revolutionary "sections" of the large cities and the municipalities of many small towns proceed in this direction in a large part of France.

Intelligent men of the people declared that Equality must cease to be an empty word: it must become a *fact*. And as the burden of the war that the Republic had to fight against "conspiring Kings" fell especially upon the poor, the people forced the Commissaries of the Convention to take some communist, egalitarian measures.

The Convention itself was forced [by the people] to take steps in the communist direction, and it took some measures tending towards "the abolition of poverty" and "levelling the fortunes." After the Girondists had been thrown out of the Government by the uprising of 31 May—2 June 1793,[5] the Convention was even forced to take actions that tended to nationalise not only the land, but also all the commerce of the nation [*le commerce national*], at least for essential items.

---

4   On this see the "Conclusion" of *The Great French Revolution*.

5   Kropotkin discusses this uprising and its importance in chapter XLVI of *The Great French Revolution*. (Editor)

This very profound movement lasted until July 1794, when the bourgeois reaction of the Girondists, combining with the Monarchists, gained the upper hand on the 9 Thermidor. But, despite its short duration, it gave to the nineteenth century its specific character: the communist and socialist tendency of its advanced elements.

So long as the movement of 1793–1794 lasted, it found its voice in popular speakers. But amongst the writers of the period there were none in France who could give a reasoned literary expression to these aspirations (which were called "Beyond Marat") in order to produce a lasting effect upon minds.

It was in England that William Godwin brought out in 1793 a truly remarkable work: *Enquiry Concerning Political Justice and its Influence on Morals and Happiness.* This work made him the first theoriser of socialism without government, that is to say, of anarchy; elsewhere Babeuf (under the influence, it would seem, of Buonarotti) emerged, in 1795, as the first theoriser of centralised socialism, of State socialism.

Later—developing the principles already put forth at the end of the previous century—came Fourier, Saint-Simon and Robert Owen—the three founders of modern socialism in its three principal schools; and later on, in the forties, we have Proudhon, who, without knowing Godwin's work, laid anew the foundations of anarchy.

The scientific basis of socialism in both its aspects, governmental and non-governmental, was thus elaborated from the beginning of the nineteenth century, with a wealth of development unknown, unfortunately, by our contemporaries. Modern socialism, which dates from the International [Workers' Association] has surpassed these founders on two points—undoubtedly very important—but on these two points alone. It has become revolutionary and it has broken with the notion of the "socialist and revolutionary Christ" which they loved to parade before 1848.

Modern socialism understood that to realise its aspirations social revolution is absolutely necessary—not in the sense in which we sometimes use the word "revolution" when speaking of the "industrial revolution" or a "revolution in science" but in its true, concrete sense: the general and swift reconstruction of the very foundations of society. Furthermore, modern socialism has ceased to mix its ideas with certain very trivial reforms of a sentimental order talked about by some Christian reformers. But this [last]—it must be highlighted—had already been done by Godwin, Fourier, and Robert Owen. As for officialdom, centralisation and the cult of authority and discipline—which humanity chiefly owes to theocracy and to imperial Roman law, the relics of a dark past as characterised very well by P. Lavrov—these are still fully retained by a host of modern socialists who, consequently, have not yet reached the level of their English and French predecessors.

It would be difficult to give here an adequate idea of the influence which reaction, having become supreme after the Great [French] Revolution, exercised upon the development of science.[6] It suffices to note [here] that what modern science is so proud of today was already indicated and often more than indicated—it was sometimes expressed in a definite scientific form—towards the end of the eighteenth century. The mechanical theory of heat; the indestructibility of movement (conservation of energy); the variability of species under the direct influence of surroundings; physiological psychology; the anthropological understanding of history, religions and legislation; the laws of development of thought—in short, the whole mechanical conception of nature as well as the synthetic philosophy (a philosophy that includes all physical, chemical, living and social phenomena as a single whole) were already sketched and partly elaborated in the eighteenth century.

But when the reaction had got the upper hand after the end of the Great [French] Revolution, they sought for fully half a century to suppress these discoveries. Reactionary scholars represented them as "unscientific." On the pretext of first studying "the facts" and amassing "the materials of science," scientific societies rejected any research which were not merely measurements—such as the elder Séguin's and, later on, Joule's determination of the mechanical equivalent of heat (the quantity of mechanical friction necessary to obtain a certain quantity of heat)—as soon as the scholars glimpsed some new principle! The Royal Society in England, which is the English Academy of Sciences,[7] even refused to print Joule's work on this subject, finding it "unscientific." And as for Grove's remarkable work on the unity of all physical forces—written in 1843—no attention was paid to it until 1856.

It is only by studying the history of science in the first half of the nineteenth century that we realise how deep was the darkness that enveloped Europe at that time.

The veil was suddenly rent in the late fifties, when people in the west experienced the beginning of the liberal movement that led to the uprising of Garibaldi, the liberation of Italy, the abolition of slavery in [the United

---

6   This is discussed in an English lecture "The Development of science during the Nineteenth Century" that I am preparing for publication. [This lecture was never published as far as we can determine—Editor]

7   *The President, Council, and Fellows of the Royal Society of London for Improving Natural Knowledge*, commonly known as the *Royal Society*, is a scholarly society for science and is possibly the oldest such society still in existence. It was founded in November 1660 and granted a royal charter by King Charles II as "The Royal Society." The French equivalent, *Académie des Sciences*, was founded in 1666 by Louis XIV at the suggestion of Jean-Baptiste Colbert (who served as the Minister of Finances of France from 1665 to 1683), to encourage and protect the spirit of French scientific research. (Editor)

States of] America, liberal reforms in England, etc. This same movement produced in Russia the abolition of serfdom and the knout, in philosophy it overturned the authority of Schelling and Hegel, and gave birth to the open rebellion against intellectual serfdom and abasement before any kind of authority which is known by the name of nihilism.

Now that we can trace the intellectual history of those years, it is obvious to us that it was the propaganda of republican and socialist ideas in the thirties and forties, and the Revolution of 1848, which helped science to rend the chains that restrained it.

Indeed, without going into details, it will be sufficient to note that Séguin (whose name has already been mentioned), Augustin Thierry (the historian who first laid the foundations of the study of the popular regime within the *communes* and the federalist ideas of the Middle Ages), Sismondi (the historian of the free cities in [Medieval] Italy) were students of Saint-Simon, one of the three founders of Socialism in the first half of the nineteenth century; Alfred R. Wallace, who discovered at the same time as Darwin the theory of origin of species through natural selection, was in his youth a convinced follower of Robert Owen; Auguste Comte was a Saint-Simonist; Ricardo, as well as Bentham, were [influenced by] Owenites[8]; and the materialists Carl Vogt and G. Lewes, as well as Grove, Mill, Herbert Spencer, and many others, experienced the influence of the English radical socialist movement of the thirties and forties. From this movement they drew their scientific courage.[9]

The appearance, in the short span of five or six years, 1856–1862, of the works of Grove, Joule, Berthelot, Helmholtz, Mendéléeff; of Darwin,

---

8   There is no evidence that either David Ricardo or Jeremy Bentham were followers of Robert Owen. However, when Owen arranged to have the other investors in the New Lanark Mills bought out by "men of like mind" to allow freer scope to his social activism, Bentham was one of new shareholders. As regards Ricardo, Owen was on friendly terms with the economist and in June 1819 Ricardo supported Owen's plan for farm colonies for the unemployed while later supporting a motion in Parliament on this (Frank Podmore, *Robert Owen: A Biography* [New York: Augustus M. Kelly, 1968], 94–96, 243, 263). It should also be noted that Owen had written *Mr. Owen's proposed arrangements for the distressed working classes, shown to be consistent with sound principles of political economy: in three letters addressed to David Ricardo*. In 1821, the third edition of Ricardo's *Principles of Economics and Taxation* included a new chapter entitled "On Machinery" which admitted that "the opinion entertained by the labouring class, that the employment of machinery is frequently detrimental to their interests, is not founded on prejudice and error, but is conformable to the correct principles of political economy." (Editor)

9   For all these names as well as those which follow, see the "Explanatory Notes" at the end of the book.

Claude Bernard, Spencer, Vogt and Moleschott; of Lyell on the origin of man; of Bain, Mill, and Burnouf—the sudden appearance of this work produced a complete revolution in the fundamental conceptions of scientists. Science was thus launched into new paths. Whole branches of knowledge were created with prodigious rapidity.

The science of life (biology), that of human institutions (anthropology and ethnology), that of understanding, will and passions (physical psychology), the history of law and of religions and so on were formed before our eyes, striking the mind by the boldness of their generalisations and the revolutionary character of their conclusions. What were in the previous century vague assumptions, often even intuitions, now presented themselves as proved by the scales and the microscope, verified by thousands of applications. Even the manner of writing completely changed and all the scientists that we have just mentioned returned to the simplicity, the exactness, and the beauty of style characteristic of the inductive method, and which those writers of the eighteenth century who had broken with metaphysics possessed so well.

It is definitely impossible to predict in which direction science will henceforth go. As long as scientists depend on the rich and governments, their science will inevitably bear that mark, and a stagnant period, like the one in the first half of the nineteenth century, can certainly be produced once more. But one thing is certain. In science, as it appears today, there is no need for the hypothesis which Laplace knew how to dispense with, nor the metaphysical "little words" which Goethe mocked. We can already read the book of Nature, which includes the development of organic life and of humanity, without resorting to a creator, a mystic "vital force," or an immortal soul, and without consulting the trilogy of Hegel, or hiding our ignorance behind any metaphysical symbols which we ourselves have endowed with real existence. *Mechanical* phenomena—becoming more and more complicated as we pass from physics to the facts of life, but always remaining mechanical—are sufficient to explain the whole of Nature and the organic, intellectual and social life we discover.

Without doubt much remains unknown, obscure and misunderstood by us in the universe; without doubt, we will always open new gaps in our knowledge as the old ones are filled. But we know no area in which it would be impossible to find an explanation of phenomena if we apply simple physical facts—[like] those that occur when two billiard balls meet, or when a stone falls; or the chemical facts that we see around us. These *mechanical* facts have been sufficient so far to explain the whole of Nature. Nowhere have they failed us: and we do not see the possibility of ever discovering an area in which mechanical facts would no longer suffice us. Nothing, thus far, makes us suspect its existence.

IV

COMTE'S POSITIVE PHILOSOPHY

IT IS OBVIOUS THAT AS SOON AS SCIENCE BEGAN TO ATTAIN SUCH RESULTS, IT was necessary to attempt the construction of *a synthetic philosophy* which would incorporate all these findings. Without wasting any more time on these products of their own imagination such as "substances," "the idea of the universe," or "the destination of life" and other symbolic expressions which philosophers used to entertain our fathers and grandfathers; and without appealing to *anthropomorphism*—that is, endowing human qualities and intentions to Nature and to physical forces—it was natural to seek to construct a philosophy that was *a systematic, unified and structured summary of all our knowledge*. Such a philosophy, gradually rising from the simple to the complex, would set out the fundamental principles of the life of the universe, and give us a key to comprehending the whole of nature. It would provide us, as a consequence, with a powerful instrument of research, which would help us to discover new relationships between various phenomena—that is to say, new natural laws—and inspire us at the same time with confidence in the accuracy of our conclusions, if they are contrary to the established current notions.

Several such attempts were made, in fact, during the nineteenth century, with those of August Comte and Herbert Spencer especially deserving our attention.

It is true that the necessity for a synthetic philosophy was already understood in the eighteenth century, by the Encyclopaedists, by Voltaire in his admirable *Philosophical Dictionary*, which still remains a monumental work, by Turgot, and, later, even more clearly by Saint-Simon. Then, in the first half of the nineteenth century, Auguste Comte undertook the same work, in a more scientific way, in response to recent advances in the natural sciences.

As regards mathematics and exact sciences in general, Comte fulfilled his task in a most admirable way. It is also generally recognised that he was perfectly right to introduce the science of life (biology) and [the science] of human societies (sociology) in the course [*cycle*] of positive sciences. And it is also known what a formidable influence Comte's positive philosophy exerted on most thinkers and scientists in the second half of the nineteenth century.

But why—asked the admirers of the great philosopher—why was Comte so weak when he undertook in his *Positive Politics*, the study of modern institutions and especially that of ethics, the science of moral concepts?

How could a vast and *positive* mind as his end up becoming the founder of *a religion* and a *cult,* as Comte did in his declining days?

Many of his students have tried to reconcile this religion and cult with his previous work and maintain against all evidence that the philosopher had followed the same method in both his works—his *Positive Philosophy* and *Positive Politics*. But two positive philosophers as important as J. S. Mill and Littré agree in not recognising the *Positive Politics* as part of Comte's philosophy. They see in it only the product of an already weakened intelligence.

Yet the contradiction between these two works of Comte—his *Philosophy* and his *Politics*—is extremely characteristic as it sheds light upon the most serious questions of our time.

When Comte had finished his *Course of Positive Philosophy* [in 1842] he had certainly to notice that his philosophy had not yet dealt with the essential question: the origin of the moral sentiment in man and the influence of that feeling on the life of man and his societies. Obviously, he had to indicate the origin of this feeling, to explain this influence by the same causes by which he had explained life in general; and he had to show why man feels the need to obey this feeling, or at least reckon with it.

It is most striking that Comte was on the right path—which was followed later by Darwin, when the great English naturalist tried to explain, in the *Descent of Man*, the origin of the moral sense. Comte wrote, indeed, in his *Positive Politics*, several admirable passages which show that sociability and mutual aid among animals and the ethical importance of this fact had not escaped his attention.[10]

---

10   I had not considered these passages when I wrote the first edition of this essay. It was a
      Positivist friend in Brazil who drew my attention to them, and he sent me a beautiful

But to draw out of these facts the necessary, *positivist* conclusions, biological knowledge was still insufficient at that time, and he himself lacked boldness. He removed *God*—the divinity of positive religions, which man must worship and pray to in order to remain moral—and in its stead he put *Humanity* with a capital letter. He ordered us to prostrate ourselves before and address our prayers to this new idol in order to develop in ourselves the moral element.

But once this was done, once it was recognised as necessary for man to worship some entity placed outside and above the individual, in order to keep the human animal on the path of duty—the rest followed of itself. The ritual of Comte's religion was naturally found in the rituals of ancient religions of the East.

In fact, Comte was inevitably bound to come to such a conclusion, as soon as he had not recognised that the moral sense of man, like sociability and society itself, was *of pre-human origin*: as soon as he did not recognise in it a further development of the sociability that can be seen in animals, fortified in man by his observation of nature and the life of human societies.

Comte had not understood that the moral sense of man is as much dependent upon his nature as his physical organisation is; that both are an inheritance derived from an extremely long development—of an evolution which lasted tens of thousands of years. Comte had noticed the feelings of sociability and mutual sympathy that exist amongst the animals; but, under the influence of the great zoologist Cuvier who was considered at the time as a supreme authority, he had not admitted what Buffon and Lamarck had already highlighted—the variability of species. He had not recognised the uninterrupted evolution from animal to man. Consequently, he could not see what Darwin understood: that the moral sense of man is nothing else but a further development of the instincts, habits of mutual aid that existed in all animal societies long before the first man-like creatures appeared on earth.

As a consequence, Comte could not realise, as we see today, that whatever the immoral acts of isolated individuals, the moral principle will necessarily live in humanity, in the form of instinct, as long as the human species does not enter a period of decline; that acts contrary to the morals derived from this source must *necessarily* produce a reaction from other men, just as a mechanical action produces a reaction in the physical world. And he did not realise that in this capacity to react against the anti-social acts of a

---

edition of the second great work of Comte, *Positive Politics*. I take this opportunity to express to him my warmest thanks. There are pages and pages, full of genius, in this work of Comte, as in *Positive Philosophy*; and to re-read them now, with all the knowledge accumulated during a life—at the invitation of a friend—was a profound pleasure.

few lies the *natural* force which *inevitably* maintains the moral sense and the sociable habits in human societies, as it maintains them in animal societies, without any intervention from outside; that this force is infinitely more powerful than the orders of any religion or any law-makers. But once Comte had not recognised this, he was bound to invent a new divinity— Humanity—and a new cult, so that this cult would always bring man back to the path of moral life.

Like Saint-Simon, like Fourier, he thus paid a tribute to his Christian education. Without admitting a struggle between the principle of Good and the principle of Evil (both evenly matched), and without man turning to the representative of the first principle to strengthen himself in the struggle against the representative of Evil—without this, Christianity cannot exist. And Comte, imbued with this Christian idea, returned to it as soon as he had to deal with the question of morality and the means of strengthening it in our feelings. The cult of Humanity was to be his instrument to keep man from the nefarious power of Evil.

V

THE AWAKENING IN THE YEARS 1856–1862

IF AUGUSTE COMTE HAD FAILED IN HIS STUDY OF HUMAN INSTITUTIONS, and above all in his study of the moral principle we must not forget that he wrote his *Positive Philosophy* and [*Positive*] *Politics* long before the years 1856–1862, which—as we have mentioned—suddenly widened the horizon of science and rapidly raised the level of the general understanding of every educated man.

The works on various branches of science which appeared in the course of those five or six years accomplished so complete a revolution in all our insights on nature, life in general and the life of human societies that you cannot find a similar revolution in the whole history of science for more than twenty centuries.

What the Encyclopaedists had only glimpsed, or rather foreseen, what the best minds of the nineteenth century had up until then found so difficult to disentangle, suddenly appeared with the full force of knowledge. Everything so completely and so well developed by the [application of] the inductive-deductive method of the natural sciences that every other method of research appeared incomplete, false, and pointless.

So let us stop for a moment on these results, the better to be able to appreciate the next attempt at a synthetic philosophy which was made by Herbert Spencer.

In the course of those six years, Grove, Clausius, Helmholtz, Joule and a whole phalanx of physicists and astronomers—including Kirchhoff, who, by his discovery of spectral chemical analysis, enabled us to identify the chemical composition of the stars, that is to say the suns most distant from us—broke the restrictions that had for half-a-century not allowed scientists to embark on far-reaching and bold material generalisations. And in a few years they proved and established *the unity of nature throughout the inorganic world*. It now became absolutely impossible to speak about mysterious "fluids"—caloric, electric, magnetic, or any other—which physicists had previously resorted to explain different physical forces. It was proved the mechanical movements of molecules—those which produce the waves of the sea, those that we find in the vibrations of a bell, or a metal blade—are sufficient to explain all physical phenomena: heat, light, sound, electricity, magnetism.

More than that. We learned to *measure* these invisible movements, these vibrations of molecules—to weigh, so to speak, their energy—in the same way we measure the energy of a falling stone, or a moving train. Physics thus became a branch of mechanics.

It was demonstrated, moreover, always during those years, that the celestial bodies most distant from us—even in the myriad suns which are visible in unfathomable quantity in the Milky Way—are composed of the very same simple chemical bodies, or elements, that we know on our Earth, that the very same vibrations of molecules occur there, with the same physical and chemical results, as on our planet. The very movements of the massive celestial bodies, the stars, which travel through space according to the laws of universal gravitation are only, in all probability, the resultant of all these vibrations that are transmitted for billions and trillions of myriametres[11] through the interstellar space of the universe.

These same caloric and electric vibrations suffice to explain all chemical phenomena. Chemistry is yet another chapter of molecular mechanics. And even plant and animal life in its myriad manifestations is only an exchange of molecules (or rather of atoms) in that vast series of chemical bodies, very complicated and consequently very unstable, which compose the living tissues of every animated being. Life is only a series of chemical decompositions and recompositions in very complex molecules: a series of "fermentations" due to chemical, inorganic ferments.

Moreover, at the same time it was grasped (to be better appreciated and proved in the years 1890–1900) how the life of cells in the nervous

---

11   The myriametre was the name for 10,000 metres. It is now obsolete and was not included amongst the prefixes when the International System of Units was introduced in 1960. (Editor)

system and their capacity to transmit every irritation to each other gave us a *mechanical* explanation for the transmission of irritations in plants as well as the mental life of animals. Following this research we can now, without leaving the domain of purely physiological observations, understand how images and impressions in general are engraved in our brain, how they act upon one another, and how they give rise to conceptions and ideas.

Today we are also able to comprehend "the association of ideas"—that is to say, how each new impression revives the impressions produced before. We grasp, accordingly, the mechanism even of thought.

Certainly, we are still extremely far from discovering *everything* in this direction; we are still at the first steps and an immensity remains for us to discover. Science, barely freed from the metaphysics which strangled it, is only entering the study of this immense domain—physical psychology. But a beginning has been made. A solid foundation has already been laid for further research. The old division into two absolutely separate domains which the German philosopher Kant tried to establish—the domain of phenomena which we explore "in time and space" (the physical realm), and the other, which could only be explored "in time" (the realm of mental phenomena)—this division disappears now. And as for the question that was asked one day by the Russian materialist Professor Sechenov: "What is psychology related to and how to study it?" the answer is already given: "To physiology, by the physiological method!" Indeed, recent research by physiologists has already thrown infinitely more light on the mechanism of thought, on the origin of impressions, their fixing in the memory and their transmission, than all the subtle discussions with which metaphysicians had entertained us hitherto.

So even in this stronghold which belonged to it without possible dispute, metaphysics is now vanquished. The domain of psychology is invaded by the natural sciences and by materialist philosophy, which has advanced our knowledge of the mechanism of thought in this branch [of science] with a previously unknown speed.

However, amongst the works that appeared during these five or six years, there was one which would overshadow all others. This was *The Origin of Species*, by Charles Darwin.

Buffon in the previous century, and Lamarck at the turn of the nineteenth, had already resolved to affirm that the different species of plants and animals we encounter on Earth do not represent immutable forms. They are variable and they vary continually under the influence of their surroundings. Does not the same family resemblance which is recognised amongst various species belonging to this or that group not prove, they asked, that these species descend from common ancestors? Thus, the various species of buttercup which we find in our meadows and our marshes must be the descendants of one and the same species of ancestor—descendants that diversified as a result of a series of changes and adaptations they have experienced in their varied circumstances of existence. Similarly, the current species of wolf, dog, jackal, fox, did not formerly exist; but in their stead there was a species of animals which in the course of ages gave birth to the wolves, the dogs, the jackals and the foxes. For the horse, donkey, zebra, etc. we already know perfectly well what the common ancestor is: we have found the bones in the [appropriate] geological strata.

But in the eighteenth century, you could not profess such heresies. For far less than that the tribunal of the Church had already threatened to prosecute Buffon, and he was forced to publish his recantation in his *Natural History*. The Church, at that time, was still very powerful, and the naturalist who dared to hold heresies disagreeable to the bishops was threatened with prison, torture, or the madhouse. That is why the "heretics" spoke with such prudence.

But now, after 1848, Darwin and Wallace dared to affirm the same heresy, and Darwin even had the courage to add that man also developed through a slow physiological evolution; that he derived his origin from a species of ape-like animals; that the "immortal spirit" and the "moral soul" of man had developed in the same way as the mind and social customs of a chimpanzee or an ant.

We know what thunderbolts were hurled by the Elders [of the Churches] at Darwin and especially at his courageous, learned and intelligent apostle Huxley, because he stressed those conclusions of Darwinism which most frightened the priests of all religions.

The struggle was terrible, but the Darwinists emerged victorious. And since then a new science—biology, *the science of life* in all its manifestations—has grown up before our eyes.

The work of Darwin provided at the same time a new method of investigation for understanding any kind of phenomena—in the life of physical matter, in that of organisms, and in that of societies. The idea of a *continuous development*, that is to say of *Evolution*, and a gradual adaptation of beings and societies to new conditions, as those change—this idea found a far wider application than explaining the origin of new species. When it was applied to the study of nature in general, as well as to the study of man, his abilities and his social institutions, it opened up new horizons and presented the opportunity to explain the most incomprehensible facts in the domain of all branches of knowledge. Based on this principle, so rich in consequences, it was possible to reconstruct, not only the history of organisms, but also the history of human institutions.

Biology, in the hands of Herbert Spencer, showed us how all the species of plants and animals inhabiting our globe could develop, starting from a few very simple organisms that populated the earth in the beginning; and Haeckel was able to trace the outline of a likely genealogical tree of the different classes of animals, man included. This was already [an] immense [contribution]. But it also became possible to lay the first solid scientific foundations of the history of human morals, customs, beliefs and institutions—which was absolutely lacking in the eighteenth century and to Auguste Comte. This history can now be written without resorting to the metaphysical formulas of Hegel, and without us wasting time with "innate ideas," the "substances" of Kant, or by revelation from above. We can reconstruct it, in short, with no need for those formulas which were the kiss of death to the spirit of research, and behind which, like [the sun] behind the clouds, the same ignorance was always hidden—always the same old superstition, the same blind faith.

Aided by the works of naturalists on the one hand, and, on the other, by the works of Henry Maine and his followers, who applied the same inductive method to the study of primitive institutions and the laws that draw their origin from them, the history of the development of human institutions could during the last fifty years be put on as firm a foundation as the history of the development of any species of plants or animals.

Without doubt, it would be unjust to forget the work already accomplished in the thirties of the nineteenth century by the school of Augustin Thierry in France, and that of Maurer and the "Germanists" in Germany, of which Kostomaroff, Byelaeff and many others were continuators in Russia. The methodology of evolution had certainly been applied previously, since the Encyclopaedists, to the study of customs and institutions, as well as languages. But it became possible to obtain accurate, *scientific*, results only after scientists learned to treat the accumulated facts of history just as the naturalist considers the gradual development of the organs of a plant or that of a new species.

In their time, metaphysical formulas no doubt had helped to make some approximate generalisations. They roused numbed thought, they shook it by their vague allusions to the unity of nature and its incessant life. At a time of reaction, as it was in the first decades of the nineteenth century, when the inductive generalisations of the Encyclopaedists and their English and Scottish predecessors were nearly forgotten, especially at a time when it needed moral courage to dare speak of the unity of physical and "spiritual" nature in the face of triumphant mysticism—and that courage was lacking amongst philosophers—the nebulous metaphysics of the Germans upheld at least the taste for generalisations.

But the generalisations of that time—established either by the dialectical method or a semi-conscious induction—were, for that very reason,

despairingly vague. The first were fundamentally based on very nave assertions, similar to those made by some Greeks in antiquity, when they asserted that planets must travel through space along circles, because the circle is
the most perfect of curves. The naivety of such assertions and the absence
of evidence were only concealed by the vagueness of the arguments and
[the use of] nebulous words, as well as by an obscure and grotesquely dense
style. As for the generalisations born from a semi-conscious induction, they
were always based upon an extremely limited amount of observations—like
these very broad and unsubstantiated generalisations of Weismann which
just recently caused a stir.[12] The induction being unconscious, the value of
these hypothetical conclusions can easily be exaggerated and represented as
indisputable *laws* while they were not, at bottom just guesses—hypotheses,
embryos of generalisations, which still needed to undergo elementary verification, comparing their results with the observed facts.

Finally, all these generalisations were expressed in a way so abstract and
obscure—such as the "thesis, antithesis, and synthesis" of Hegel—that they
left the fullest liberty to draw from them the most arbitrary practical conclusions. So that you could deduce (as was done) the revolutionary spirit of
Bakunin along with the Dresden Revolution, the revolutionary Jacobinism
of Marx, and the "approval of what exists," which led so many authors to
make "peace with reality"—that is to say, with autocracy.[13] Even today, it

---

12   When Kropotkin was writing, the full significance of Weismann's work was yet to be
appreciated while the role of genetics did not become dominant until over twenty
years later. As such, his comments must be considered part of the fierce debate raging
in scientific circles at the time. In terms of the evidence Kropotkin mentions, he is
referring to Weismann's experiments of removing the tails of white mice to see whether
as a result mice were born without a tail. Kropotkin noted that Darwin had already
dismissed the notion that removing an organ in successful generations would lead to
it eventually disappearing and so the experiment did not accurately reflect the views it
claimed to refute. Moreover, Kropotkin, influenced like Darwin by Lamarckian ideas,
was clearly concerned that it rules out the inheritance of acquired characteristics and
so ignored the impact of surroundings on the development of species and individuals
within species. Interestingly, recent work in plants and mammals on the role of the
environment on epigenetic modifications of DNA have led to the argument that inherited epigenetic variation is a kind of soft inheritance Weismann denied. Kropotkin discusses Weismann and his ideas more fully in "The Inheritance of Acquired Characters:
Theoretical Difficulties," *The Nineteenth Century and After*, March 1912 (included in
Peter Kropotkin, *Evolution and Environment*). (Editor)

13   A reference to Hegel's comment in *Elements of the Philosophy of Right* (1821) that
"what is rational is real: And what is real is rational." Right-wing Hegelians took this to
mean that existing social structures (namely, the aristocratic system then dominant in

suffices to mention the many economic errors into which [Marxist] socialists have lately fallen, as a consequence of their predilection for the dialectic
method and economic metaphysics, which they have resorted to instead
of applying themselves to the study of the actual facts of the economic life
of nations.

Germany) were rational while left-wing Hegelians took it to mean that they had to be
replaced by rational ones. (Editor)

VI

SPENCER'S SYNTHETIC PHILOSOPHY

ONCE THE STUDY OF ANTHROPOLOGY (THAT IS TO SAY, THE STUDY OF THE physiological evolution of man and the history of his religions and institutions) was conducted in the same way as the study of all other natural sciences, it became possible at last to understand the essential outlines of the history of mankind. And it became possible to separate it forever from the metaphysics which had hampered the study of history, just as the Biblical tradition had once prevented the study of geology.

One might have thought, therefore, that when Herbert Spencer undertook in his turn the development of a "Synthetic Philosophy" in the second half of the nineteenth century, he could have done so without falling into the errors found in Comte's *Positive Politics*. And yet, while Spencer's synthetic philosophy represented a great step forward (there is no place in this philosophy for religion or religious rite), in its sociological part it still contains errors just as serious as those in the positive politics.

The fact is that when Spencer came to the psychology of societies, he was not able remain faithful to his rigorously scientific method when studying this branch of knowledge and did not dare to accept the consequences to which this method would have brought him. Thus, for example, Spencer recognised that land should never be private property. The owner of the soil, profiting by his right to raise at will the rent charged for the land, has the power to prevent its farmers from extracting all that could be obtained from it through intensive cultivation; or else he may keep the land uncultivated, waiting until the price of his hectare of land goes up by virtue of the work that is done all around it.[14] Such a system—Spencer was quick to recognise—is harmful to society; it is full of dangers. But, whilst noting this evil with regard to the land, he did not venture to make the same arguments with regards other accumulated wealth—not even mines or docks, not to mention factories and mills.

Alternatively, he raised his voice against State interference in the life of society; he even gave to one of his works a title that represents a whole revolutionary programme: *The Man versus the State*. But little by little, under the pretext of defending the *protective* function of the State, he reconstructed the entire State—just like there exists today, imposing on it only a few timid limitations.

These contradictions and many others of the same kind can be explained, without doubt, by the fact that Spencer built the sociological part of his philosophy under the influence of the English radical movement,[15] long before he wrote the part on the natural sciences. In fact, he published his [*Social*] *Statics* in 1851, that is to say, at a time when the anthropological study of human institutions was still in its infancy. But, be that as it may, the result was that, like Comte, Spencer did not undertake the study of [human] institutions for their own sake, without preconceived ideas borrowed from a domain other than science. Furthermore, when it came to the philosophy of societies [sociology], Spencer began to use a new method, the most treacherous of all—the method of similarities (analogies), which he needless to say had not utilised for the study of physical facts. This method allowed him to justify a whole mass of preconceived ideas. And the result was that we still, to this day, do not have a synthetic philosophy built following the same method in its two aspects: the natural sciences and the sociological sciences.

It must also be said that Spencer was the least suitable man to study the primitive institutions of savages. In this respect he even exaggerated a

14   Kropotkin is referring to the increase in value of land and other resources due to improvements made in their surroundings by others. Owners, therefore, gained simply by owning property in areas made desirable by, say, the building of train stations, new shops, schools, housing, etc. See, for example, Chapter I ("Our Riches") of *The Conquest of Bread* [Oakland./Edinburgh: AK Press, 2007]. (Editor)

15   In this context, the term "radical" (from the Latin *radix* meaning root) refers to the classical liberals of early- to mid-nineteenth century who were proponents of a limited-State but also sought various progressive social reforms. So, in *Social Statics* for example, Spencer had like many liberals and democrats argued for votes for women and the nationalisation of the land to break the power of the aristocracy. Today, "radical" has a far wider meaning and generally refers to those seeking to go beyond liberalism. (Editor)

common failing in most of the English: that of not being able to understand the morals and customs of other nations. "We [English] are men of Roman law, while the Irish are a people of common law; that is why we do not understand each another,"—I was told once by James Knowles, a very intelligent and insightful man. But this inability to understand another civilisation than their own becomes even more apparent when it comes to those the English call "inferior races." This was the case with Spencer. He was absolutely incapable of understanding the savage with his respect for the tribe, or the hero of an Icelandic saga who considers "blood-revenge" as a duty, or the turbulent life, full of struggles and as a consequence full of progress, in the cities of the Middle Ages. The conceptions of Right which are encountered at those stages [of civilisation] were entirely foreign to Spencer. He saw naught there but savagery, barbarism, and cruelty and in that he definitely represented a retreat from Auguste Comte who had understood the importance of the Middle Ages in the progressive development of [human] institutions—an insight too often forgotten since then in France.

Furthermore—and this error was even more serious—Spencer, like Huxley and so many others, had understood "the struggle for existence" in an utterly incorrect manner. He depicted it, not only as a struggle between different species of animals (wolves preying upon hares, many species of birds living on insects, and so forth), but also as a relentless struggle for the means of existence and for a place on earth *within each species*, between all the individuals of the same species. However this last struggle certainly does not exist in the proportions that Spencer and many Darwinists imagined.

How far Darwin himself was responsible for this erroneous conception of the struggle for existence, we cannot discuss here.[16] But it is certain that when Darwin published *The Descent of Man*, twelve years after the appearance of *The Origin of Species*, he now understood the struggle for existence in a much broader and more metaphorical form than that of an endless struggle within each species. Thus he wrote in his second work that "the animal species which contain the greatest number of sympathetic individuals have the best chance of surviving and of leaving a numerous progeny"[17] and he even developed the

---

16   See *Mutual Aid: A Factor of Evolution* (Hachette). On how Darwin was led to change his views on the subject and increasingly admit the *direct action of surroundings* in the evolution of new species, see my articles on natural selection and direct action in *The Nineteenth Century [and After]*, July, November and December 1910 and March 1912. [These articles—"The Direct Action of Environment on Plants," "The Response of the Animals to their Environment" (in two parts), and "Inheritance of Acquired Characters: Theoretical Differences," respectively—can be found in Peter Kropotkin, *Evolution and Environment*—Editor]

17   Kropotkin is paraphrasing Darwin slightly: "In however complex a manner this feeling may

idea that the social instinct is, in every animal, a much stronger and much more permanent and active than the instinct of self-preservation. This is very different from what the "Darwinists" say to us.[18]

---

have originated, as it is one of high importance to all those animals which aid and defend one another, it will have been increased through natural selection; for those communities, which included the greatest number of the most sympathetic members, would flourish best, and rear the greatest number of offspring" (Charles Darwin, *The Descent of Man, and Selection in Relation to Sex* , Part I [Princeton: Princeton University Press, 1981], 82).

18   As many "Darwinists" say the same thing to us today, it is useful to quote Darwin's *The Descent of Man* on this matter:

"Many a man, or even boy, who never before risked his life for another, but in whom courage and sympathy were well developed, has, disregarding the instinct of self-preservation, instantaneously plunged into a torrent to save a drowning fellow-creature. In this case man is impelled by the same instinctive motive, which caused the heroic little American monkey, formerly described, to attack the great and dreaded baboon, to save his keeper. Such actions as the above appear to be the simple result of the greater strength of the social or maternal instincts than of any other instinct or motive; for they are performed too instantaneously for reflection, or for the sensation of pleasure or pain; though if prevented distress would be caused." (Part I: 87)

"As no man can practise the virtues necessary for the welfare of his tribe without self-sacrifice, self-command, and the power of endurance, these qualities have been at all times highly and most justly valued. [...] This conclusion agrees well with the belief that the so-called moral sense is aboriginally derived from the social instincts, for both relate at first exclusively to the community." (Part I: 95–97) "When two tribes of primeval man, living in the same country, came into competition, if (other circumstances being equal) the one tribe included a great number of courageous, sympathetic and faithful members, who were always ready to warn each other of danger, to aid and defend each other, this tribe would succeed better and conquer the other. [...] Selfish and contentious people will not cohere, and without coherence nothing can be effected." (Part I: 162)

"It must not be forgotten that although a high standard of morality gives but a slight or no advantage to each individual man and his children over the other men of the same tribe, yet that an advancement in the standard of morality and an increase in the number of well-endowed men will

In general, the chapters which Darwin devoted in his *Descent of Man* [on this subject] could have become a starting-point for development of a conception, exceedingly rich in consequences, on the nature and evolution of human societies (Goethe had already sensed it on the basis of one or two facts). But they went unnoticed. It was only in 1879, in a lecture given by the Russian zoologist [Karl] Kessler that we find a clear conception of the relations that exist in nature between the struggle for existence and mutual aid.[19] "For the *progressive* evolution of a species," he said, providing some examples, "*the law of mutual aid* has much more importance than the law of mutual struggle."[20]

A year later, Lanessan delivered a lecture, *La lutte pour l'existence et l'association pour la lutte* [*The Struggle for Existence and Association for Struggle*][21] and soon after that Büchner published his work *Love* in which he showed the importance of *sympathy* amongst animals for developing the first moral concepts; but by giving family love and compassion too prominent a position, he unnecessarily restricted his field of research.

It was easy for me to prove and develop in 1890, [in work later published] in *Mutual Aid*,[22] Kessler's idea and to extend it to man on the basis of accurate

---

certainly give an immense advantage to one tribe over another. There can be no doubt that a tribe including many members who, from possessing in a high degree the spirit of patriotism, fidelity, obedience, courage, and sympathy, were always ready to give aid to each other and to sacrifice themselves for the common good, would be victorious over most other tribes; and this would be natural selection." (Part I: 166)

These, and others like them, are the passages Kropotkin had in mind. (Editor)

19 For a summary of Kessler's argument, see Daniel P. Todes "Darwin's Malthusian Metaphor and Russian Evolutionary Thought, 1859–1917," *Isis* (December, 1987) 78: 4 (reprinted in 1993 as "The Scientific Background of Kropotkin's Mutual Aid," *The Raven* 6: 4). Also see his book *Darwin Without Malthus: The Struggle for Existence in Russian Evolutionary Thought* (New York: Oxford University Press, 1989). (Editor)

20 Kropotkin is paraphrasing, with added emphasis, from the published account of K. F. Kessler's talk: "O zakone vzaimnoi pomoshchi," *Trudy Sankt-Peterburgskogo Obshchestva Estestvoispytatelei*, 1880, 11(1), 135 (for a full quote, see *Mutual Aid: A Factor of Evolution* [London: Freedom Press, 2009], 34). (Editor)

21 Lanessan's lecture, which he delivered at a conference in Paris, was later published in 1881 as *Étude sur la doctrine de Darwin: la lutte pour l'existence et l'association pour la lutte* [*Study on the Doctrine of Darwin: The Struggle for Existence and Association for Struggle*]. (Editor)

22 Kropotkin produced the first of the articles that were later collated into *Mutual Aid: A Factor of Evolution* (1902) for the British journal *The Nineteenth Century* in 1890. These

observations of nature and modern research relating to the history of [human] institutions. Mutual aid is, in fact, not only the most effective weapon for every animal species in its struggle for existence against the hostile forces of nature and other enemy species, but it is also *the principal instrument of progressive evolution*. Even to the weakest animals it guarantees longevity (and consequently accumulation of experience), security for their offspring, and intellectual progress. This is why those animal species which most practise mutual aid not only survive better than the others, but they also occupy a higher position—in their own respective classes (of insects, birds, mammals [and so on])—by the superiority of their physical structure and their intelligence.

This fundamental fact of nature was not noticed by Spencer. He accepted as a principle which did not even need to be proven—as an axiom—the struggle for life within each species: the fight to the death, "by the tooth and claw," for each bite of food. Nature, "stained with the blood of the gladiators," as depicted by the English poet Tennyson, was his image of the animal world.[23] It was only in 1890, in an article for the *Nineteenth Century*,[24] that he began to understand to some extent the importance of mutual aid (or rather the sentiment of mutual sympathy) in the animal world, and began to gather facts and make observations in this direction. But until his death, primitive man always remained for him the ferocious beast of imagination which lives only by tearing "by tooth and claw" the last bit of food from its neighbours.[25]

It is evident that after having adopted as the foundation for his deductions such a false premise, Spencer could not build his synthetic philosophy without lapsing into a whole series of errors.

---

articles were as follows: "Mutual Aid Among Animals" (September, 1890); "Mutual Aid Among Animals" (November, 1890); "Mutual Aid Among Savages" (April, 1891); "Mutual Aid Among Barbarians" (January, 1892); "Mutual Aid In the Medieval City" (September, 1894); "Mutual Aid Amongst Modern Men" (January, 1896); "Mutual Aid Amongst Ourselves" (June, 1896). (Editor)

23 The expression comes from Tennyson's poem *In Memoriam A.H.H.* written in 1849 (Canto 56: "Tho' Nature, red in tooth and claw"). He did not invent the phase and his poem was published before Darwin made his theory public in 1859. However, the phrase was quickly adopted by others to summarise natural selection in the sense of a war of each against all for survival. The "gladiators" comment Kropotkin also mentions may be paraphrasing his poem *St. Telemachus* published in 1892. However, it may also be a reference to Thomas Henry Huxley's views. (Editor)

24 Herbert Spencer, "On Justice," *Nineteenth Century* (March, 1890) 27: 435–448. (Editor)

25 For example: "Cruelty rather than kindness is characteristic of the savage, and is in many cases a source of marked gratification to him" (Herbert Spencer, *The Principles of Ethics* [New York: D. Appleton and Company, 1895] 1: 185). (Editor)

VII

THE ROLE OF LAW IN SOCIETY

SPENCER WAS NOT, MOREOVER, THE ONLY ONE TO FALL INTO THESE ERRORS. Faithful to Hobbes, all the philosophy of the nineteenth century continued to consider primitives as a herd of wild beasts who lived in small isolated families and fought amongst themselves for food and for females—until a benevolent authority settled in their midst to impose peace. Even a naturalist like Huxley continued repeating this same fantastic assertion of Hobbes, and declared (in 1888) that in the beginning men lived by fighting "one against all" until, thanks to a few superior individuals, "the first society was founded" (see his article: *The Struggle for Existence: a Programme*[26]). So even a Darwinian scientist like Huxley had no idea that, far from having been created by man, society existed long before man, amongst animals. Such is the strength of an established prejudice.[27]

---

26   *Nineteenth Century* of 1888, reprinted in *Essais et Adresses.*

27   For some reason, the date of Huxley's article is wrong: as Kropotkin indicated in *Mutual Aid*, it was published in June 1888 in *The Nineteenth Century*. The date has been corrected. Huxley's argument was as bad as Kropotkin suggests:

> From the point of view of the moralist the animal world is on about the same level as a gladiator's show. The creatures are fairly well treated,

If we try to trace the history of this prejudice, it is easy to see that its origin lies in religion and churches. The secret societies of sorcerers, rain-makers, shamans, later the Assyrian and Egyptian priests, and later still, the Christian priests, have always sought to persuade men that "the world is steeped in sin";[28] that only the benevolent intervention of the shaman, sorcerer, saint, or priest prevents the power of evil from seizing man; that they alone can get a spiteful divinity not to engulf man by all sorts of evils, to punish him for his sins.

Early Christianity without doubt sought to weaken this prejudice with regard to the priest; but the Christian Church, based upon the very words of the Gospels concerning "the eternal fire," only strengthened it. The very idea of God the Son coming to die on earth to *redeem* the sins of humanity, again confirmed this way of thinking. And it is precisely this which later permitted the "Holy Inquisition" to subject its victims to the most atrocious tortures and to burn them on a slow fire: it thus offered them a chance to repent, to save them from eternal suffering. Besides, it was not only the

---

and set to fight—whereby the strongest, the swiftest, and the cunningest live to fight another day. The spectator has no need to turn his thumbs down, as no quarter is given [...] the weakest and stupidest went to the wall, while the toughest and shrewdest, those who were best fitted to cope with their circumstances, but not the best in any other sense, survived. Life was a continual free fight, and beyond the limited and temporary relations of the family, the Hobbesian war of each against all was the normal state of existence [...] The first men who substituted the state of mutual peace for that of mutual war, whatever the motive which impelled them to take that step, created society. But, in establishing peace, they obviously put a limit upon the struggle for existence. [...] The primitive savage, tutored by Istar [the Babylonian Goddess of love, war, fertility and sex], appropriated whatever took his fancy, and killed whomsoever opposed him, if he could [...] But the effort of ethical man to work toward a moral end by no means abolished, perhaps has hardly modified, the deep-seated organic impulses which impel the natural man to follow his non-moral course. (*Evolution and Ethics and Other Essays* [London: MacMillan and Co., 1895], 199–200, 204, 205.)

It was this article that motivated Kropotkin to produce the articles that later became *Mutual Aid*. Kropotkin discusses Huxley's essay in Chapter XI of *Ethics*, 282–287. (Editor)

28   A reference to "And we know that we are of God, and the whole world lieth in wickedness." (John 5:19, *King James Bible*). (Editor)

Roman Catholic Church which acted in this way: all Christian Churches, faithful to the same principle, vied with one another to invent new sufferings and new terrors to correct men mired in "vice." Even now, nine hundred and ninety-nine people out of a thousand still believe that natural accidents—droughts, earthquakes and contagious diseases—are sent from on high by a divinity to bring sinful humanity to the true path.

At the same time, the State in its schools and universities maintained, and continues to maintain, the same belief in the natural perversity of man. To prove the necessity for a power placed above society and which works to implant the moral element in society—by means of punishment for violations of "the moral law" (which is identified, by means of a little trick, with the written law); to convince men that this authority is necessary is a matter of life and death for the State. For if men began to doubt the necessity of strengthening moral principles by the strong hand of authority, they would soon lose faith in the high mission of their rulers.

In this way all our religious, historical, juridical, and social education is permeated with the idea that man, if he were abandoned to himself, would again become a ferocious beast. Without authority, [they say,] men would eat each other: nothing can be expected of that animal the "mob" but the war of each against all. This human horde would perish if above it there were not the elect: the priest, the legislator and the judge, with their helpers—the policeman and the executioner. They are the ones who prevent the battle of all against all, they who raise men to respect the law, teach them discipline, and lead them with a steady hand until such future times when nobler conceptions have grown in "hardened hearts," so making the whip, the scaffold and the prison less necessary than they are today.

We laugh at the king who, when he was driven into exile in 1848, declared: "My poor subjects! Without me they will perish!" We mock the English tradesman who is convinced that his countrymen descend from the lost tribe of Israel and, for this reason, it is their destiny to bestow good government on "inferior races."

But do we not find in all nations this same exaggerated self-appreciation amongst the vast majority of those with a little learning?

And yet the *scientific* study of the development of societies and institutions brings us to completely different views. It proves that the habits and customs humanity created for the sake of mutual aid, mutual defence, and peace in general, were developed precisely by the nameless "mob." And it was these customs that permitted man, as with animal species existing today, to survive in the struggle for existence. Science shows us that the so-called leaders, heroes, and legislators of humanity have added nothing during the course of history which was not [already] developed in society by customary law. The best of them have merely expressed, endorsed these institutions. But the great number of these so-called benefactors also strove to destroy those institutions of customary law which hindered the establishment of a personal authority either to recast those institutions for their own benefit or in the interest of their caste.

Already, since the ancient times lost in the darkness of the glacial period, men lived in societies.[29] And in these societies a whole series of rigorously observed customs and institutions were developed in order to make life in common possible. And later, throughout human evolution, this same creative power of the nameless multitude always worked out new forms of social life, of mutual aid, of guarantees of peace, as new conditions arose.

Furthermore, modern science clearly demonstrates that law, whatever its presumed origin—whether represented as being of divine origin or from the wisdom of a lawgiver—has never achieved anything other than to set, crystallise in a permanent form, or expand already existing customs. All the codes of antiquity were merely collections of customs and habits, carved or written in order to preserve them for future generations. But by doing that, as well as customs already in general use, the [legal] code always added some new rules made in the interest of rich minorities and armed warriors—rules which expressed the emerging practices of inequality and servitude, [rules] advantageous for these minorities.

"Thou shalt not kill," said for example the law of Moses; "thou shalt not steal, thou shalt not bear false witness [against thy neighbour]." But to these excellent rules of conduct it also added: "Thou shalt not covet thy neighbour's wife, nor his slave, nor his ass,"[30] and by that it legalised for a long time slavery and put woman at the same level as a slave or a beast of burden. "Love your neighbour," said Christianity later; but it hastened to add by the mouth of the Apostle Paul: "Slaves, obey your masters"[31] and

---

29   The last glacial period, popularly known as the Ice Age, is the most recent glacial period, which occurred from 110,000 to 12,000 years ago. This most recent glacial period is part of a larger pattern of glacial and interglacial periods known as the Quaternary glaciation (from around 2,588,000 years ago to present). We now know that modern humans evolved around 200,000 years ago in Africa and have always, like their hominid and ape ancestors, lived in groups. As such, Kropotkin's statement—reflecting the scientific knowledge of his time—remains valid. (Editor)

30   The sixth, eight, ninth and tenth of the Ten Commandants. The latter is actually states: "You shall not covet your neighbour's house; you shall not covet your neighbour's wife, nor his male servant, nor his female servant, nor his ox, nor his donkey, nor anything that is your neighbour's" (Exodus 20, *King James Bible*). (Editor)

31   Kropotkin is referring to one of the favourite passages of slave-owning Christians made by St. Paul: "Servants, be obedient to them that are *your* masters according to the flesh,

"No authority except from God"[32]—thereby *legitimising* and *deifying* the division [of society] into masters and slaves, and consecrating the authority of the scoundrels who then ruled in Rome.

Even the Gospels, while teaching the sublime idea of forgiveness which is the essence of Christianity nevertheless speak all the time of a vengeful God, and teach by this vengeance.

The same thing happened in the codes of the so-called "barbarians": the Gauls, the Lombards, the Alemanni, the Saxons, the Slavs, after the fall of the Roman Empire. These codes legitimised a custom, excellent no doubt, which was widespread at that time: that of paying *compensation* for wounds and murders instead of practising the law of retaliation (an eye for an eye, a tooth for a tooth, a wound for a wound, a life for a life) which was once commonplace. By so doing, the barbarian codes certainly represented an improvement on the law of talion,[33] which had [previously] reigned in the tribe. But at the same time they also established the division of free men into classes, which at that time was just beginning [within those tribes].

So much compensation, said these codes, for a slave (to be paid to his master); so much for a free man; and so much for a chieftain—in which case the compensation was so high that it signified lifelong slavery for the murderer. The original idea of these distinctions was, no doubt, that the family of a prince, killed in a brawl, lost much more than the family of an ordinary free man in the event of the death of its head of the family; conse- quently, the first had a right, according to the ideas of the time, to a higher compensation than the second. But in making this custom of the time a *law*, the code established by this very fact, permanently, a division of men into classes—and it established them so well that thus far we have not yet demolished them.

And that is seen in the legislation of all times, including our own: the oppression of preceding periods is always passed down by the law to

---

with fear and trembling, in singleness of your heart, as unto Christ" (Ephesians 6:5, *King James Bible*). While modern editions of the Bible translate "servants" as "slaves," it should be noted that employment relations were termed "master-servant" well into the nineteenth century, meaning that this injunction had a wider remit and at times included opposition to trade unions, strikes, and so on. (Editor)

32   "Let every soul be subject unto the higher powers. For there is no power but of God: the powers that be are ordained of God" (Romans 13:1, *King James Bible*). (Editor)

33   The law of Talion (Latin: *lex talionis*) was developed in early Babylonian law and was present in both Biblical and Roman law and is based on the notions that criminals should receive as punishment precisely those injuries and damages they had inflicted upon their victims. (Editor)

subsequent eras. The oppression of the Persian Empire was thus passed to Greece, that of Macedonia was passed to Rome; and the oppression and cruelty of the Roman Empire and the Eastern tyrannies were passed to the young barbarian States when they were in the process of formation, [as well as] to the Christian Church. By means of the law, the past fettered the future.

All the guarantees necessary for life in society, all the forms of social life in the tribe, the village community and the medieval city; all forms of relations between [different] tribes and, later [in the Middle Ages], city-republics, which subsequently served as the basis for international law, in short—all forms of mutual support and defence of the peace, including the tribunal and the jury, were developed by the creative genius of the nameless multitude. Whereas, all *laws,* from the oldest to the present, have always been composed of these two elements: one strengthened (and fixed) certain customary forms of life, recognised by all as useful; and the other was an addition—often just merely an insidious way of expressing a [long-established] custom—which had the purpose of establishing or strengthening the nascent authority of the lord, the soldier, the kinglet and the priest: to strengthen and sanctify this authority.

This is where we are led by the scientific study of the development of societies that has been carried out over the last forty years by a great number of conscientious scientists. It is true that very often the scientists themselves dare not draw conclusions as heretical as those we have just read. But the thoughtful reader of necessity reaches these [conclusions] by reading their works.

VIII

THE POSITION OF ANARCHY IN MODERN SCIENCE

WHAT POSITION, THEN, DOES ANARCHY OCCUPY IN THE GREAT INTELLECTUAL movement of the nineteenth century?

The answer to this question is already apparent in what was said in the preceding chapters. Anarchy is a conception of the universe based on the *mechanical* interpretation of phenomena[1] which embraces the whole of nature, including the life of societies. Its method is that of the natural sciences; and every scientific conclusion must be verified by this method. Its tendency is to build a synthetic philosophy which will include all the facts of Nature—including the life of human societies and their economic, political and moral problems—without, however, falling into the errors made by Comte and Spencer for the reasons already indicated.

It is evident that Anarchy must, for this very reason, necessarily give to all the questions posed by modern life other answers and take another attitude than all the political parties and, to some extent, the socialist parties which have not yet broken with old metaphysical fictions.

---

1   It would have been better to say *kinetic* but this expression is less known.

Of course, the development of a complete mechanical conception of Nature and human societies has hardly begun in its sociological part, which studies the life and evolution of societies. Nevertheless, the little that has been done already bears—sometimes even unconsciously—the character we have just indicated. In the philosophy of law, in the theory of morals, in political economy and in the study of the history of peoples and institutions, anarchists have already proved that they are not content with metaphysical conclusions and that they seek their conclusions on a naturalist basis.

They refuse to be imposed upon by the metaphysics of Hegel, Schelling and Kant, by the commentators on Roman and Canonical law, by learned professors of State law, or by the political economy of metaphysicians—and they seek to give a clear account of all the questions raised in these areas, based on a mass of work produced over the last forty or fifty years from the point of view of the naturalist.

Just as the metaphysical conceptions of the "Universal Spirit," "the Creative Force of Nature," "the Loving Attraction of Matter," "the Incarnation of the Idea," "the Aim of Nature and its Reason for Being," "the Unknowable," "Humanity" understood in the sense of a being inspired by the "Breath of the Spirit," and so on—just as these conceptions are abandoned today by materialist (mechanical, or rather kinetic) philosophy, and the embryos of generalisations hidden behind these words are translated into the concrete language of facts, we try to do likewise when we tackle the facts of social life.

When metaphysicians wish to persuade a naturalist that the intellectual and emotional life of man unfolds according to "the inherent laws of the Spirit," the naturalist shrugs his shoulders and continues his patient study of the phenomena of life, of intelligence, and of emotions in order to prove that all can be reduced to physical and chemical phenomena. He seeks to discover their natural laws.

Likewise when an anarchist is told that, according to Hegel, "every evolution represents a thesis, an antithesis and a synthesis" or else that "the aim of Law is to establish Justice, which represents a materialisation of the Supreme Idea," or even when asked what is, according to him, "the Purpose of Life?"—the anarchist, likewise, shrugs his shoulders and asks: "How is it possible, in the midst of the current development of the natural sciences, there still exist ancients who continue to believe in this 'palaver'? Backward beings who speak the language of the primitive savage when he 'anthropomorphised' nature and represented it as something that is governed by beings with human appearances?"

Anarchists do not let themselves be taxed by these "sonorous words" as they know that these phrases are always used to cover either ignorance—that is to say, incomplete investigation—or, which is far worse, superstition. This is why, when they are spoken to in this language, they move on without stopping; they continue their study of social conceptions and institutions, past and present, following the method of the naturalist. And they find, evidently, that the development of the life of societies is in reality infinitely more complex (and far more interesting for practical purposes) than we would be led to believe if it were judged according to these [metaphysical] expressions.

We have heard much lately of the dialectical method which the social democrats recommend to us for the development of the socialist ideal. But we completely reject this method which, moreover, is not accepted by anyone in the natural sciences. This "dialectic method" reminds the modern naturalist of something very antiquated—from a past-life and, thankfully, long since forgotten by science. None of the discoveries of the nineteenth century—in mechanics, astronomy, physics, chemistry, biology, psychology or anthropology—was made by the dialectical method. All were made by the inductive method—the only scientific method. And since man is a part of Nature, since his personal and social life is also a phenomena of nature—along with the growth of a flower, or the evolution of the social life of ants or bees—so there is no reason why we should, when we pass from the flower to man or from a village of beavers to a human city, abandon the method that had hitherto served us so well to search for another in the arsenal of metaphysics.

The inductive method which we employ in the natural sciences has so well proved its power that the nineteenth century was able to advance science more in a hundred years than had previously been done in two thousand years. And when, in the second half of the century, they began to apply it to the study of human societies nowhere did they hit a point where it was necessary to reject it, to return to the mediaeval scholasticism resuscitated by Hegel. There is more. When naturalists, paying tribute to their bourgeois education while claiming to base themselves on the scientific method of Darwinism, desired to teach us: "Crush whoever is weaker than you: such is the law of nature!" it was easy for us to prove, by the same scientific method, that these scientists were on the wrong path: that such a law does not exist; that nature teaches us something else and that their conclusions were not at all scientific. It is the same for the assertion that they would have us believe that inequality of fortunes is "a law of nature" and that capitalist exploitation represents the most advantageous form of social organisation. It is precisely the application of the method of the natural sciences which enabled us to prove that the so-called "laws" of bourgeois social science—including current political economy—are by no means laws but mere assertions or else assumptions that nobody has ever tried to verify.

One more word. Scientific research is only fruitful on condition that it has a particular *purpose*: to be undertaken with the intention of finding an answer to a clear, well posed question. And each investigation is even more fruitful the clearer we see the relations existing between the question that is posed and the fundamental lines of our general conception of the universe. The better it fits into this general conception, the easier is the solution.

Well, the question that Anarchy has posed could be expressed as follows: "*Which social forms best guarantee, in such a given society, and by extension, inhumanity in general, the greatest sum of happiness, and, consequently, the greatest sum of vitality?*" "Which forms of society allow this sum of happiness to grow and to develop in quantity and quality the best—that is to say, will enable this happiness to become more comprehensive and more general?" Which, it must be noted in passing, also gives us the formula of *progress*. The desire to help evolution in this direction determines the character of the social, scientific, artistic, etc. activity of the anarchist.

IX

THE ANARCHIST IDEAL AND PREVIOUS REVOLUTIONS

ANARCHY, AS WE HAVE ALREADY SAID, WAS BORN FROM THE INDICATIONS OF practical life.

Godwin, contemporary of the Great [French] Revolution of 1789–93, had seen with his own eyes how governmental authority, [although] created during the Revolution and by the Revolution, had in its turn become an obstacle to the development of the revolutionary movement. He was also aware of what was happening in England under cover of Parliament: the pillage of communal lands, the sale of profitable [official] positions, the hunting of the children of the poor and their removal from workhouses, by agents who traversed England for that purpose, to the factories of Lancashire where many perished; and so on. Godwin realised that a government, even if it were the Jacobin "One and Indivisible Republic," could never accomplish the necessary revolution—a communist social revolution; that even a revolutionary government, simply because it is the guardian of the State and the privileges every State has to defend, soon becomes a hindrance to the revolution. He understood and proclaimed this anarchist idea that, for the triumph of the revolution, men must first discard their faith in the Law, Authority, Unity, Order, Property, and other superstitions inherited from their slave past.

The second theorist of Anarchy who came after Godwin—Proudhon—lived through the failed Revolution of 1848. He, too, could see with his own eyes the crimes committed by the Republican government, and at the same time he became convinced of the impotence of statist socialism. Under the still fresh impression of what he had experienced during the movement of 1848, he wrote his *General Idea of the Revolution* in which he fearlessly proclaimed Anarchy and the abolition of the State.

Finally, in the International [Workers' Association] the anarchist conception also developed after a revolution, that is to say after the Paris Commune of 1871. The complete revolutionary impotence of the Council of the Commune although it contained, in very accurate proportions, representatives of all the revolutionary fractions of the time (Jacobins, Blanquists, and Internationalists) as well as the incapacity of the General Council of the International residing in London and its claim, as inept as it was injurious, to govern the Parisian movement by orders issued from England, both these lessons opened the eyes of a great number. They brought many members of the International, including Bakunin, to reflect on the evil of every kind of authority—even were it as freely elected as it was in the Commune and the Workers' International.

Some months later, the decision of the General Council of the International, taken at a clandestine conference convened in London in 1871, instead of an annual Congress, highlighted even more the drawbacks of a government in the International. According to this disastrous resolution the forces of the Association, which until then were joined together for an economic-revolutionary struggle—the direct struggle of the workers unions against the capitalism of the bosses—were going to get involved in an electoral, political, and Parliamentary movement, where they could only wither and be destroyed.

This decision led to the open rebellion of the Latin Federations [of the International]—Spanish, Italian, Jura, and, in part, Belgian—against the General Council in London; and from this revolt dates the anarchist movement which we see continuing today.

Thus the anarchist movement resumed each time under the impression of some great practical lesson. It originated in the teachings of life itself. But once underway, it also immediately sought to find its expression and its theoretical and scientific basis. Scientific, not in the sense of adopting an incomprehensible jargon, or clinging to ancient metaphysics, but in the sense of finding its basis in the natural sciences of the time, and becoming one of its subdivisions.

At the same time, the anarchists worked to develop their ideal.

No struggle can be successful if it remains unconscious—if it does not produce a concrete account of its actual aim. No destruction of what exists is possible without, during the struggles leading to the destruction and during the period of destruction itself, already visualising mentally what will take the place of what you want to destroy. You cannot even make a theoretical critique of what exists without already picturing in the mind a more or less clear image of what you would like to see in its place. Consciously or unconsciously, the *ideal*—the concept of well-being—always takes shape in the mind of whoever criticises existing institutions.

This is especially the case for men of action. To tell men: "First destroy capitalism, or autocracy, and then we shall see what we shall put in their place" is simply to deceive oneself and to deceive others. Never has a real force been created by deception. Indeed, even the person who speaks in such a way always has, nevertheless, some conception of what he would like to see instead of what he is attacking. Thus, amongst those working to destroy autocracy in Russia, some imagine a constitution in the English or German style emerging in the near future. Others dream of a republic, subject perhaps to the powerful dictatorship of their circle, or even a republic-monarchy as in France,[2] or a federative republic as in the United States. Others, finally, are already thinking about a still greater limitation of State power: greater freedom for cities, municipalities, workers' unions and all kinds of groups united together by federal links.

And anyone who attacks Capitalism always has a definite or merely vague idea of what they want to see in the place of existing bourgeois capitalism: State Capitalism, or some kind of State Communism, or else, finally, a federation of more of less communist associations for the production, exchange, and consumption of what they obtain from the soil or what they manufacture.

Each party has its own conception of the future. It has its ideal which enables it to judge all events occurring in the political and economic life of nations as well as to find its own means of action and best enable it to move towards its goal.

It is therefore natural that Anarchy, although born in every-day struggles, has also worked to develop its ideal and this ideal, this purpose, these aims soon separated the anarchists in their means of action from all political

---

2   Kropotkin is referring to the centralised, unitarian Republic of France which, as he notes in section X of *The State: Its Historic Role*, was marked by "the striking fact that the Third Republic, in spite of its republican form of government, has remained monarchist in essence," a republic "which remained monarchical." Thus the President was little better than an elected King. In this he echoed Proudhon who argued that "nothing resembles a monarchy more than a unitarian republic [*république unitaire*]" (*Du principe fédératif* [Paris: E. Dentu, 1862], 140). (Editor)

parties as well as, to a large extent, from the socialist parties which thought they could retain the ancient Roman and Canonical idea of the State and carry it into the future society of their dreams.

X

ANARCHY

Principles

ANARCHISTS, GUIDED BY VARIOUS HISTORICAL, POLITICAL, AND ECONOMIC considerations as well as the lessons of modern life have come, as we have discussed, to an understanding of society very different from that drawn by all political parties aiming to get themselves into power.

We stand for a society in which the relations between its members are regulated, not by laws—legacy of a past of oppression and barbarism—not by any authorities—whether they are elected or derive their power by right of inheritance—but by mutual agreements, freely made and always revocable, as well as [social] customs and habits, also freely accepted. These customs, how-ever, must not be petrified and crystallised by law or superstition; they must be continually developing, adjusting to new needs, the progress of knowledge and invention, and with the growth of a higher and higher social ideal.

So—no authority which imposes on others its will. No government of man by man. No stagnation [*immobilité*] in life: [but] a continual evo-lution—sometimes faster, sometimes slower—as in the life of Nature. Freedom of action left to the individual to develop all his natural abilities, of *his individuality*. In other words, no action *imposed* on the individual un-der threat of social punishment, whatever it may be, or by a supernatural, mystical, penalty: society asks nothing of the individual that he does not freely agree to undertake at a given moment. With this—complete equality of rights for all.

We thus acknowledge [the possibility of] a Society of equals, without constraint of any kind, and despite the lack of constraint, we do not fear that, in a society of equals, the anti-social acts of a few individuals would take threatening proportions. A society of free men would be able to avoid these better than our current societies which entrust the guarding of their social morality to police, spies, prisons—universities of crime—slave-driving guards, executioners and their suppliers. Above all it will be able to *prevent* anti-social acts.

It is obvious that so far no society has existed which practised these principles. But at all times, humanity has expressed a tendency towards their realisation. Each time that some portions of society succeeded for a certain time to overthrow the authorities which oppressed them, or to efface the inequalities which had established themselves (slavery, serfdom, autocracy, government by certain castes or classes); each time a new spark of freedom and equality soared out of society, the people, the oppressed, sought to put into practice, if only partially, the just stated principles.

We may say, therefore, that Anarchy is a certain ideal of society, which differs fundamentally from that which has been advocated hitherto by most philosophers, scientists and politicians, all of whom had the pretension to govern men and give them laws. It was never the ideal of the privileged but often it was the more or less conscious ideal of the masses.

However, it would be wrong to say that this ideal society is a *utopia,* because in everyday language we attach to the word "utopia" the notion of something that cannot be realised.

Fundamentally, the word "utopia" should be applied only to those conceptions of society that are based solely upon what the writer finds *desirable* from a *theoretical* point of view; never to those conceptions based on the *observation* of what is already developing in society. So one must place amongst the many utopias the Republic of Plato, the Universal Church dreamt of by the popes, the Napoleonic Empire, the dreams of Bismarck and Messianism of the poets who await the arrival, one day, of a saviour who will bring to the world grand ideas of renovation. But it would be wrong to apply the word "utopia" to predictions supported, like those of Anarchy, by *the study of tendencies already emerging in the evolution of society.* Here we leave utopian foretelling to enter the domain of science.

In our case, it is all the more wrong to speak of utopia, [for] the trends that have been indicated by us have already played an extremely important role in the history of civilisation since *it is they which gave birth to the Common Law, Law which dominated Europe from the fifth to the sixteenth century.* These tendencies now assert themselves again in civilised societies, after more than three centuries of experience of the State. It is on these observations, whose importance will not escape the historian of civilisation, that we base ourselves when we see in Anarchy a possible, realisable ideal.

We are told that it is without doubt an ideal far from its realisation. But to this we answer by recalling the end of the eighteenth century—at the time when the United States constituted itself—when it was regarded as an absurd idea to want to establish a society other than a monarchy on such a scale. And yet the republics of North and South America, along with France, proved that the "utopians" were not on the Republican side; they were amongst the monarchists.

The "utopians" were those who, guided only by their *desires*, did not want to take account the new *tendencies* which were emerging—those who attributed too much stability to the things of the past, without asking themselves whether they were not just the result of certain temporary historical conditions.

We have already mentioned at the beginning of this work that when we study the anarchist idea we find it has a double origin: on one side, criticism of hierarchical organisations and authoritarian conceptions in general; and, on the other side, the analysis of tendencies that are emerging in the progressive movements of humanity—in the past and especially in modern times.

Since the remotest times of the Stone-Age, men have realised the disadvantages that arose when they let some of them acquire personal authority, even if they were the most intelligent, the bravest, or the wisest. Also our ancestors worked from the earliest times to develop institutions that allowed them to fight against the establishment of such an authority. Their tribes, their clans, later the village commune and the guilds of the Middle Ages (guilds of good neighbours, of crafts and arts, of merchants, of hunters, etc.), and finally the free city of the twelfth to the sixteenth century are institutions that sprung up from the people—not the leaders—for resistance against the authority they saw being acquired either by foreign conquerors or by individuals within the clan, tribe or city.

The same popular tendency emerged in the religious movements of the masses across Europe during the Hussite uprising in Bohemia and the movement of the Anabaptists, who were the precursors of the Reformation.

Much later, in 1793–1794, the same current of thought and action emerged in the remarkably independent and constructive activity of the "Sections" of Paris and the great cities, as well as a large number of small communes. And later still we find the same tendency in the workers unions which were formed in England and France as soon as modern industry started to develop—despite the Draconian laws which prohibited these unions. Here again we find at work the same popular spirit trying to defend itself, this time against the capitalists.

Anarchist Ideas amongst the Ancients;
in the Middle Ages-Proudhon-Stirner

Popular movements of an anarchist character could not fail to find some echo in written literature.[3] Indeed, we already find anarchist ideas amongst the philosophers of antiquity, notably in Lao Tze in China and in some of the earliest Greek philosophers such as Aristippus and the Cynics; as well as Zeno and certain Stoics. However, since the anarchist spirit has its origin primarily in the masses and not within the small aristocracy of scholars and these felt little sympathy for these popular movements, intellectuals generally did not seek to clarify the underlying idea that inspired these movements. At all times, philosophers and scholars preferred to promote the governmental tendency and the spirit of hierarchical discipline. From the dawn of science, the art of governing was their preferred study and that is why it is not surprising that philosophers of the anarchist tendency were so rare.

However, the Greek Stoic Zeno was one. He preached free community without government, and opposed the governmental utopia—Plato's *Republic*. Zeno already indicated the instinct of sociability that nature, according to him, had developed in opposition to the selfish instinct of preservation of the individual. He foresaw a time when men would unite across borders and constitute "the Cosmos," the Universe—no longer needing laws, nor courts, nor temples, nor money to exchange their services between each other. Even his wording, it appears, resembles in a striking manner that used by anarchists today.[4]

The Bishop of Alba, Marco Girolamo Vida, affirmed in 1556 similar ideas against the State, its laws, and its "supreme injustice."[5] We also meet the same ideas amongst the Hussites (especially in Chelcicky during the fifteenth century) and the early Anabaptists and their precursors of the ninth century—the Rationalists in Armenia.

Rabelais, in the first half of the sixteenth century, Fénelon towards the end of the seventeenth century, and especially the Encyclopaedist Diderot at the second half of the eighteenth century, developed the same ideas,

---

3   Kropotkin goes into the Ancient Philosophers in a little more detail in his entry on "Anarchism" written for the eleventh edition of *The Encyclopaedia Britannica* (1910) to which readers were referred to in the 1912 British edition of *Modern Science and Anarchism*. This entry is included in most anthologies of his writings, including *Direct Struggle Against Capital*. (Editor)

4   See the work on Zeno by Professor G. Adler, *Geschichte des Sozialismus und Kommunismus von Plato bis zur Gegenwart*, t. I, 1899.

5   Dr. E. Nys, *Recherches sur l'histoire de l'économie politique*, (Paris: Fontemoing 1898), 222.

which found, as has just been mentioned, some practical applications during the Great [French] Revolution.

But it was the Englishman William Godwin who, in 1793, first expounded, in his *An Enquiry Concerning Political Justice*, the political and economic principles of Anarchy. He did not use the word *anarchy*, but he expressed very well its principles by attacking laws, proving the uselessness of the State, and saying that it is only with the abolition of the courts that we will succeed in establishing true *justice*—the only real foundation of any society. As regards property, he called for communism.[6]

Proudhon was the first to use the word Anarchy (no government) and to submit to severe criticism the vain efforts of men to give themselves a government which could prevent the powerful from dominating the weak and, at the same time, remain under the control of the governed.[7] The futile attempts made in France since 1793 to give itself a Constitution that fulfilled such an end and the failure of the Revolution of 1848 gave him abundant facts for this critique.

An enemy of all forms of State socialism, of which the communists of this time (the forties and fifties of the nineteenth century) represented only a fraction, Proudhon forcefully attacked all plans at revolution in this direction. And, taking as a basis the system of "labour notes" proposed by Robert Owen, he developed the concept of "mutualism" which would render any kind of political government unnecessary.

The exchange values of all goods can be measured, he said, by the amount of labour needed in society to produce each product, all exchanges would be made by means of a national bank that would accept payment in labour notes. A Clearing House, as do all banks today, would establish the daily balance of entries and payments to be made between all branches of the National Bank.

The services exchanged in this way amongst the various people would be *equivalents*. Moreover, the National Bank would be in a position to lend, not in money but in labour notes, the funds needed to the producer associations for production; and these loans would be interest-free,

---

6   We find this in the first edition, published in 1793 in two quarto volumes. In the second edition, published in 1796 in two octavo volumes, after the prosecutions that were conducted by the English government against the friends and Republican associates of Godwin, he removed his communist opinions and mitigated what he wrote against the state and against government.

7   Proudhon first proclaimed himself an anarchist in 1840 in *What is Property? An Inquiry into the Principle of Right and of Government* (see *Property is Theft!*, 133). (Editor)

since to cover administration costs it would be enough to pay *one* percent, or even less, annually on the amount loaned. Under these conditions of *interest-free loans*, capital would lose its pernicious character; it could no longer be used as an instrument of exploitation. Let us add that Proudhon provided ample details about his mutualism system to confirm its anti-government and anti-statist ideas. Proudhon probably did not know his English precursors; but the fact is that the mutualist portion of his programme had been already developed in England, in 1824, by William Thompson (who was a mutualist before becoming a communist) and the English followers of Thompson—John Gray (1825–1831), [Thomas] Hodgskin (1825–1832) and J. F. Bray (1839). Of course, these authors had not articulated Anarchy, as it was expressed by Proudhon and his successors, but it is very true—as noted by the English Professor Foxwell in his introduction to the English translation of the remarkable book by A. Menger, *The Right to the Whole Produce of Labour* (Vienne, 1886)—that a current of anarchist thought is felt in all of English socialism during those years.

In the United States, the same tendency was represented by Josiah Warren, who, after having taken part in Robert Owen's colony, "New Harmony," turned against communism and founded, in 1827, in Cincinnati a store where goods were exchanged on the basis of value measured by work-hours, that is to say of labour notes. Similar institutions existed until 1865 under the names of *Equity Stores, Equity Village,* and *House of Equity.*

The same ideas of exchange based on the measurement of value by the amount of work required to produce each article were spread in Germany, in 1843 and 1845, by Moses Hess and Karl Grün and in Switzerland by Wilhelm Marr, who thereby fought the authoritarian-communist teachings of Weitling (descendants, also, of the French Babouvists).

In addition, also in complete opposition to the authoritarian communism of Weitling which had found a great number of adherents amongst German workers, a German Hegelian Max Stirner (Johann Kaspar Schmidt was his real name) in 1845 published a book, *The Ego and His Own*, which was rediscovered, so to speak, a few years ago by J. H. MacKay and which caused quite a stir in our anarchist circles where it was considered a sort of manifesto of the individualist anarchists.[8]

Stirner's work is a revolt against government and against the new tyranny which would be imposed [upon humanity] if authoritarian-communism succeeded in being introduced. Reasoning like a true metaphysician of the school of Hegel, Stirner proclaimed the rehabilitation of

---

8   A French translation was published in 1890 by Stock; an English translation was published by B. R. Tucker, in New York, in 1907.

the "I" and the "Supremacy of the individual," and so comes to preach "A-moralism" (no morals) and "the Association of egoists."

However, it is obvious—as already highlighted by anarchist writers and recently again by the French professor V. Basch in his interesting work *L'individualisme anarchiste Max Stirner* [*Anarchist Individualism Max Stirner*] (Paris, 1904)—that this kind of individualism, by claiming "full development"—not for all members of society, but only for those that would be considered the most gifted, without thinking about the development of *all*—is merely a disguised return to the monopoly of education that exists today for the few "nobles" and bourgeois, under the patronage of the State. It is a "right to full development" for a privileged minority.

But such a monopoly cannot be maintained without it being protected by a monopolist legislation and coercion, organised by the State—with the result that the claims of these individualists necessarily leads them to a return to the idea of the State and authority that they themselves have criticised so well. Their position is thus the same as that of [Herbert] Spencer or the "Manchester school" of economists who also begin with a severe criticism of the State but end by recognising its functions in full in order to maintain the monopoly of property, which the State is always the true protector.

XI

ANARCHY (CONTINUED)

Socialist Ideas in the International–
Authoritarian Communists and Mutualists

WE HAVE INDICATED THE GROWTH OF THE ANARCHIST IDEA FROM THE
French Revolution and Godwin to Proudhon. Its next flourishing was
achieved within the great International Workers' Association, which inspired the workers with so much hope and the bourgeoisie with so much
terror in the years 1868–1870, just before the Franco-Prussian War.

That this Association was not founded by Marx, as Marxists claim, is
obvious. It was the outcome of the meeting, in 1862, in London of a delegation of French workers, who had come to visit the second International
Exhibition, and representatives of English Trade Unions who were joined
by some English radicals to receive the delegation. The links established
during this visit were strengthened in 1863 on the occasion of a meeting
in sympathy for Poland[9] and the Association was finally established the
following year.[10]

---

9   The plight of Poland and the cause of Polish Independence were leading concerns for
    many socialists and radicals in the nineteenth century. Poland had been partitioned
    between the Russian Empire, the Kingdom of Prussia, and Habsburg Austria at the
    end of the eighteenth century. The support for Polish Independence was particularly
    strong in French radical circles with the notable exception of Proudhon who pointed
    out that those seeking independence were the nobility who had no desire to emanci-
    pate their peasants. Bakunin was initially a firm supporter of Polish Independence but
    his experience of a failed uprising made him recognise, as Proudhon had concluded,
    the need to combine political revolt with social revolution. (Editor)

10 I find in the minutes of the Council meetings of the "International Workers Union" in

Already in 1830 Robert Owen had tried to organise an "International Union of All Trades" at the same time as founding in England the "Grand National Trades Union."[11]

But the idea had soon to be abandoned because of the savage prosecutions that the English Government directed against the National Union. However, the idea was not lost. It smouldered under the ashes in England; it found supporters in France; and, after the defeat of the Revolution of 1848, it was carried by French refugees to the United States and spread there in a paper, *L'International* [*The International*].

In 1862, the French workers who came to London, being mostly Proudhonian "Mutualists," and the English Trade Unionists belonging mainly to the school of Robert Owen, English "Owenism" thus joined hands with French "Mutualism"—and the result was the creation of a strong international workers organisation to fight the bosses on the economic field and to break, once and for all, with all purely political radical parties.[12]

In Marx and others this union of the two main socialist workers currents of the time found the support of the debris from the secret political

---

London, 13 and 20 March 1878, the traces of an interesting debate. Eccarius, a founder of the International, wanted the suppression in an Appeal of the Council a sentence which stated that the International had its origin during the 1862 World Exhibition and that it should be replaced with the words "inspired by this necessity, the French and English workers, united by their sympathy for Poland, in 1863 struck an alliance with social as well as political goals and the result of this alliance was the foundation of the International Workers Association in September 1864." This resulted in a very lively discussion the following week, on 20 March, during which Jung, who had witnessed the founding of the International and was an active member of its General Council confirmed that indeed the International Workers Association had its origin at the 1862 Exhibition.

11   The Grand National Consolidated Trades Union of 1834 was an early attempt by British workers form a national union confederation. There had been several attempts to form one in the 1820s and the short-lived National Association for the Protection of Labour was established in 1830. In 1833, Robert Owen returned from the United States and argued for a guild-based system of co-operative production. He was able to gain the support of the Builders' Union which called for a Grand National Guild to take over the entire building trade. In February 1834, a conference was held in London which founded the Grand National Consolidated Trades Union. This, unlike other organisations founded by Owen, was open only to trade unionists and, as a result, initially he did not join it. Its foundation coincided with a period of industrial unrest and corresponding repression by the State (most famously, the Tolpuddle Martyrs). The Union did not survive to the end of the year. (Editor)

12   See W. Tcherkesoff, *Précurseurs de l'Internationale* [*Forerunners of the International*], Bruxelles, 1899.

organisation of the Communists, which represented what was still preserved of the secret societies of Blanqui and Barbès which, like the German communist secret societies, had their origin in the conspiracy of Babeuf.

The reader has seen in a previous chapter (chapter V) that the years 1856–1862 were marked by a wonderful development in the natural sciences and philosophy. These were also the years of a general political awakening of radical ideas in Europe and America. These two movements also awakened the masses of workers who were beginning to understand that the task of preparing the proletarian revolution was their responsibility. The International Exhibition of 1862 which was portrayed as a great celebration of the world's industry would become a new point of departure in the struggles of Labour for its emancipation; and now the International [Workers'] Association, by openly announcing its break with the old political parties and the resolve of the workers to take into their own hands their liberation, necessarily produced a profound impression.

Also the International began to spread rapidly in the Latin countries. Its fighting strength soon became threatening [to the bourgeoisie]; and as for ideas, the congresses of its Federations and its annual congress of the entire Association provided the workers an opportunity to discuss what the social revolution should consist of and how they could achieve it. Thus they simulated the creative power of the working masses in search for new forms of organisation [*groupement*] for production, consumption and exchange.

Everywhere it was expected that a great European revolution would break out soon. Yet there was no even remotely definite idea concerning the *political forms* that the revolution might take nor on the first steps it would have to make. On the contrary, several opposing currents of socialist thought met and clashed within the International.

The dominant idea of the Association was *the direct struggle of Labour against Capital on the economic field*—that is to say, the emancipation of Labour, not by legislation which the bourgeoisie consent to, but by the workers themselves wrestling concessions from the bosses and someday forcing them to permanently capitulate.

But *how* the liberation of the workers from the capitalist yoke would be accomplished? *What form* the new organisation of production and exchange would take? On this the socialists were just as divided in 1864–1870 as they were twenty years before, when in 1848 the representatives of the different socialist schools met in the Constituent Assembly of the Republic sitting in Paris.[13]

---

13   It is worth noting that Proudhon was an elected member of this body and argued for

Like their French predecessors of 1848, whose various aspirations were summarised so well by Considerant in his book *Le Socialisme devant le Vieux Monde*,[14] the socialists of the International did not rally under the banner of one single doctrine. They wavered between several solutions and no solution was sufficiently right, nor obvious enough, to rally minds; especially as the most advanced had not yet broken with respect for Capital and Authority.

So let us take a look at the various currents.

There was, first, the direct legacy of the Jacobinism of the Great [French] Revolution—the conspiracy of Babeuf [in 1795]—that is to say, the secret societies of the French Communists (the Blanquists) and the German Communists (the *Communist-League*[15]). Both lived upon the traditions of the fierce Jacobinism of 1793. We know that in 1848 they dreamt of someday seizing political power in the State by means of a conspiracy—*perhaps with the assistance of a dictator*—and of establishing, on the model of the Jacobin societies of 1793 (but this time in favour of the workers), "the dictatorship of the proletariat." This dictatorship, they thought, would impose communism by means of legislation.

To remain a proprietor would be rendered so onerous by means of all kinds of restrictive laws and taxes that the property-owners would be happy to rid themselves of their properties and hand them to the State. Then "armies of labourers" would be sent to cultivate the fields: and industrial production, also carried out for the State, would be organised on the same semi-military basis.[16]

---

his social, political, and economic reforms like other socialists. His *Confessions of a Revolutionary* recounts his experiences which reaffirmed his anti-statists ideas (extracts can be found in *Property is Theft!*. (Editor)

14   Victor Prosper Considerant published *Le socialisme devant le vieux monde, ou, Le vivant devant les morts* [*Socialism Before the Old World, or the living to the dead*] in Paris during 1848. It has never been translated into English. (Editor)

15   The Communist League (*Bund der Kommunisten*) was founded in 1847 in London by a merger of the League of the Just and the Communist Correspondence Committee (headed by Marx and Engels). It is considered the first Marxist political party and Marx and Engels wrote the *Communist Manifesto* for it. Ineffective during the 1848 German revolution, it was formally disbanded after the 1852 Cologne Communist Trial. (Editor)

16   It is interesting to note that similar ideas about State agriculture carried on by "armies of labourers," which was widespread at the time, were also advocated by Napoleon III—when he was a pretender to the Presidency of the Republic—in a pamphlet, *L'extinction du paupérisme* [Published in 1844, *The Extinction of the Pauperism* was a

The same ideals were widespread at the time of the foundation of the International, and they even continued to circulate much later: in France, amongst the Blanquists, and in Germany, amongst the Lassalleans and Social Democrats.

On the other hand, the workers of the school of Robert Owen were diametrically opposed to those Jacobin ideas. They absolutely refused to resort to the force of government and above all counted upon the action of trade unions to [both] make the revolution and establish a socialist society. The English Owenites did not want communism; but, as with the French Fourierists, they attached a great importance to freely formed and federated communities and groups which they emphasised possess in common the land and factories as well as stores for what was produced by their members. They would work either jointly or separately, according to the needs of production, and the remuneration for labour within the group as well as exchange between communities would be made in *labour notes*. These would represent the amount of hours of work given by each to communal cultivation or in the workshops and factories of the community. Or else, they would be paid by the community for the goods manufactured individually and brought to the communal exchange stores.

The same idea of remuneration by labour notes was accepted, as we have seen, by Proudhon and the Mutualists. They also rejected the intervention of State force in the society which would arise from the revolution. They declared that what today represents functions of the State in economic matters would be rendered unnecessary, all exchanges taking place by means of Banks of the People and Clearing Houses while education, sanitary arrangements, essential services [*les entreprises nécessaires*], the means of communication, etc. would be placed in the hands of independent communes.[17]

---

study of the causes of poverty in the French industrial working class, with proposals to eliminate it. It was written in prison after a failed (and farcical) attempted coup in 1840 and was influenced by Saint-Simonist ideas. It was widely circulated in France and played an important part in his electoral success during the 1848 Presidential election. (Editor)].

17 As Proudhon put it, "the initiative of communes and departments as to works that operate within their jurisdiction" and "the initiative of the workers companies as to carrying the works out" is "a consequence of the democratic principle and the free contract." In addition, "contrary as is the supremacy of the State to democratic principles in the matter of public works, it is also incompatible with the rights of workers created by the Revolution." So "it becomes necessary for the workers to form themselves into democratic societies" for "railroads" and "the construction and support of roads, bridges and harbours, and the work of afforestation, clearing, drainage, &c., in a word, all that we are in the habit of considering in the domain of the State" ("General Idea of

The same idea of labour notes, substituted for money in all exchanges, but alongside the idea of the *State becoming the owner of all land, mines, railways, and factories,* was propagated by two remarkable writers (stubbornly ignored by socialists today) Pecqueur and Vidal, who gave their system the name *Collectivism.* Vidal was the secretary of the Luxembourg Commission [in 1848] and at the same time Pecqueur wrote an entire treatise on this subject. He developed his system in detail—even in the shape of the laws which, according to him, it would be sufficient for the [National] Assembly to vote for to complete the social revolution.

By the time of the foundation of the International the names of Vidal and Pecqueur seemed to be entirely forgotten, even by their contemporaries, but their ideas were very widespread and they were soon propagated, like a new discovery, under the names of "scientific Socialism," "Marxism," and "Collectivism."

Socialist Ideas in the International–Saint-Simonism

Alongside these various schools that have just been mentioned, there were also the ideas of the Saint-Simonist school. After having a strong hold on minds before 1848, they still exerted a profound influence on the socialist conceptions of the members of the International.

A large number of brilliant writers and thinkers, politicians, historians and industrialists had developed in the thirties and forties under the influence of Saint-Simon. It suffices to mention here Auguste Comte in philosophy, Augustin Thierry amongst the historians, and Sismondi amongst the economists. All of the social reformers of the time were influenced by this school.

The progress accomplished in humanity, they said, had consisted thus far in transforming slavery into serfdom, and serfdom into wage-labour. But the time had arrived when it would become necessary to abolish in its turn wage-labour. And with wage-labour, individual property of what is needed to produce will disappear in turn. We must not see in this change anything impossible, they added, as property and authority have undergone many modifications in history. New modifications are imperative today, they will necessarily be accomplished.

The abolition of private property, said the Saint-Simonists, could be done gradually, by a series of measures (of which the Great [French] Revolution, remember had already taken the initiative). These measures would enable the State to appropriate—for example, by means of strong inheritance taxes—an ever increasing portion of the properties transmitted

---

the Revolution," *Property is Theft!*, 594–595). (Editor)

from one generation to another. Individual inheritance would thus be reduced and eventually disappear since the rich themselves would realise the advantages in abandoning the privileges belonging to a civilisation on its way out. So the voluntary relinquishing of property by the wealthy and the legal suppression of inheritance were to establish the Saint-Simonist State as the universal proprietor of land and industry, the supreme regulator of labour, absolute manager and director of the three functions: Art, Science and Industry.[18]

Everyone, being a worker in one of these branches, would thus be an *employee* [*fonctionnaire*] of the Saint-Simonist State, whose government would be composed of a hierarchy of the "best men"—the best in science, in the arts, in industry.

The distribution of products produced would be made in this system according to the expression: *To each according to his capacity, to each capacity according to its works.*

Apart from these predictions about the future, the Saint-Simonist school and positive philosophy, which derives its origin from it, gave the nineteenth century some very remarkable historical works in which the origins of authority, private property and the State were discussed in a truly scientific manner. These works retain to this day all their value.

At the same time, the Saint-Simonists subjected to severe criticism the classical school of political economy of Adam Smith and [David] Ricardo, which was later known as the "Manchester school" which preached "non-intervention of the State."

But while they thus fought the principle of industrial individualism and competition, the Saint-Simonists fell into the same error that they had combatted in the beginning, when they criticised the military State and its hierarchical classes. They ended by recognising the same omnipotence of the State and they based their system—as had been already noticed by Considerant—on inequality and authority as well as on a hierarchy of administrators. They even came to give to their governmental hierarchy the character of a priesthood.

Thus the Saint-Simonists differed from the communists [of their time] by the purely individual share that they allocated to each [person] from the mass of goods produced by the community. Despite the excellent work that several of them had produced in political economy, they had not yet managed to conceive the production of wealth as *a social fact*—a global fact. If they had done so, they would have necessarily been led to understand that

---

18   This can be found in Victor Considerant, *Le Socialisme devant le Vieux Monde*, 1848, an *excellent* account of the various schools. [Kropotkin is referring to *Le Socialisme devant le Vieux Monde* (Paris: Librairie Phalanstérienne, 1848), 36. (Editor)]

it is physically impossible to determine with justice the share to be apportioned to each producer out of the total wealth produced.

On this point, there was a profound difference between the communists and the Saint-Simonists. But there was one point on which both were agreed. Both ignored the individual and his rights. All that the communists conceded him was the right to elect his administrators and rulers—which the Saint-Simonists only accept with reluctance. Originally, they did not even recognise the right of election. But under communism, as under Saint-Simonism, the individual remained an employee [*fonctionnaire*] of the State.

With Cabet, the author of *Voyage to Icaria* and founder of a communist colony in America, Jacobin communism and the suppression of individuality reached their fullest expression.

Thus in the Cabet's *Voyage* we see authority, the State, everywhere, even in the kitchen of every household. Not content with providing a "Cook's Guide" to every family, the Republic of Icaria draws up a list of approved foodstuffs, makes its farmers and workers produce them and distributes them; "and as a person," Cabet tells us, "cannot have other foodstuffs than that which it distributes, you understand that no one can consume any other foodstuffs than those which it approves of." (*Voyage en Icarie*, 5th edition, 1848, p. 52)

The committee goes so far as to regulate the number of meals, their times, their duration, the number of dishes, their type and their order of service. As for clothing, they are all ordered by the Committee, on a template schema, the uniform everybody wears indicating the conditions and positions of the individual. The workers, always making the same things, are a regiment—"so much order and discipline prevail!" exclaimed Cabet.[19]

Needless to say that no one can publish anything except with approval of the Republic—and that after examination and authorisation, duly received, to be an author.

It is doubtful whether Cabet's utopia *in its entirety* had many followers in the International but the *spirit* of this utopia remained. It is absolutely certain—and we felt it strongly in the discussions that we engage in with authoritarians, especially with the German communists—that even the regulation that has just been quoted and which seems to us so absurd today, was still looked upon then as an expression of wisdom. Our criticisms were answered by these words of Cabet:

"Without doubt the Community necessarily imposes constraints and fetters; for its principle mission is to produce wealth and happiness; and for it to avoid duplication and waste, economise and increase agricultural and

---

19   *Voyage to Icaria*, 5th edition (Paris: Bureau du Populaire, 1848), 60. (Editor)

industrial production, it is absolutely necessary that *Society assigns, arranges and directs all*. It must *submit all wills and actions to its rule, to its order, to its discipline*. The good citizen must even abstain from all that has not been ordered."[20] (*Voyage to Icaria*, 5th edition, p. 403)

And, what is worse, it still retained with the authoritarians this belief, as stated by Cabet, that, after all, "the Community is no more impossible with a Monarch than with a republican President."[21] It was this idea which paved the way for the coup d'état of Napoleon III and which enabled the authoritarian socialists to so easily "leave alone" the bourgeois reaction.

Finally we must mention the school of Louis Blanc who at the time of the founding of the International had numerous followers in France and Germany where it was represented by a solid body of Lassalleans. These socialists, just as statist as the preceding ones, considered that the transfer of industrial property [currently] in the hands of Capital into those of Labour could be accomplished if a government, born of a revolution and inspired by socialist ideas, aided the workers to organise themselves, on a vast scale, co-operative workers associations to which the government would lend the necessary capital. These associations are united together in an extensive system of national production. Equal remuneration of all could be accepted as a transitional form—the ultimate goal being to arrive one day at the distribution of products according to the needs of each producer.

It was, as can be seen—as very well said by Considerant—"a communist Saint-Simonism" placed under the control of a democratic State.

Based on a large system of national credit which would lend money at a very low rate of interest and thus be placed in a position to compete with the production of the capitalists; supported in addition by orders [for goods and services] from the State, these workers associations would soon drive out capitalist industry and replace it.

They would also know to spread to agriculture. This economic, socialist goal—and not merely the democratic ideal of bourgeois politicians—workers were never to lose sight of.

All these ideas developed by socialist propaganda before 1848, by the revolution of February and June 1848, with various modifications in the details, were widespread in the International [Workers'] Association. Differences of opinions were strong, but the supporters of these schools

---

20 Emphasis is Kropotkin's. The last sentence is a paraphrase of a sentence on the next page: "*Liberty* is therefore only the right to do anything that that is not forbidden by *Nature, Reason* and *Society*, and to abstain from anything that is not ordered by them" (*Voyage to Icaria*, 404). (Editor)

21 Ibid., v–vi. (Editor)

were in agreement, as we have just seen, in recognising as the basis for the next revolution *a strong government* which would hold in its hands the entire economic life of the nation. They agreed on recognising the centralised and hierarchical organisation of the State.

Fortunately, alongside these Jacobin ideas there were also, to counterbalance them, the ideas of the Fourierists, which we will now analyse.

XII

ANARCHY (CONTINUED)

Socialist Ideas in the International–Fourierism

FOURIER, CONTEMPORARY OF THE GREAT [FRENCH] REVOLUTION, WAS NO longer alive when the International was founded. But his views had been popularised so well by his followers—especially by Considerant who had given them a certain scientific authority—that, consciously or not, the most enlightened minds of the International were under the influence of Fourierism.[22]

---

22   It is known from the work of our friend Tcherkesoff [in his *Pages of Socialist History: Teaching and Acts of Social Democracy* (New York: C.B. Cooper, 1902)] that it was from Considerant's manifesto, entitled *Principes du Socialisme: Manifeste de la Démocratie au Dix-Neuvièm Siècle*, published in 1847, that Marx and Engels borrowed the economic principles they expounded in their *Communist Manifesto*. It suffices to read the two manifestos to be convinced that not only the economic ideas but even the form must have been borrowed by Marx and Engels from Considerant.

As to the practical programme of action of the *Communist Manifesto* of Marx and Engels, it was, as Professor Ander has demonstrated, that of the programme of the secret organisations of the French and German communists which continued the work of the secret societies of Babeuf and Buonarroti.

[Considerant transformed *La Phalange*, a review he had launched in 1836, into a daily newspaper entitled *La Démocratie pacifique* (*The Peaceful Democracy*) in 1843. Its first issue contained a "manifesto of peaceful democracy" which proclaimed the need to struggle for the right to work, the organisation of industry on the basis of the association of capital, labour, and talent, universal suffrage, and so on. This manifesto

However, it should be noted that to understand the influence of Fourierism in those years that the dominant idea of Fourier was not that of the association of Capital, Labour and Talent for the *production* of wealth that is always found placed at the forefront in the history books about socialism. Its principal aim was to *put an end to individual commerce* that is carried out for *profits*, and which necessarily leads to considerable shady speculations. To achieve this he proposed to create a *free national organisation for the exchange of all products*. It was, as can be seen, reviving the idea that the Great [French] Revolution tried to achieve in 1793–1794, after the people of Paris had expelled the Girondins from the Convention and the *law of the maximum* had been approved.

To use Considerant's words from his *Socialisme devant le Vieux Monde* (a work we strongly recommend to modern socialists), Fourier saw the means of putting an end to all the infamies of present exploitation in *"the bringing into direct relation the producer and the consumer*, by organising intermediary *communal agencies*—depositaries, not the owners, of the produce, taking it directly from the source of production and delivering it directly for consumption."

Prices, under these conditions, would no longer be subject to speculation. They would be increased only "by straightforward transportation, maintenance and administration costs, which would form an almost imperceptible surcharge."[23]

Fourier, placed by his parents into a commercial firm, had already in his childhood developed a dedicated hatred of commerce, whose frauds he saw close up. Thereupon he took an oath to fight it. Much later, during the Great [French] Revolution, he could see close up the atrocious speculations that were conducted on the sale of the national goods as well as the rising prices of all produce during the war.[24] He had to see that neither the Jacobin Convention nor the Terror could control these speculations; and could understand how the absence of a *socialised exchange* paralysed even the effects of an economic revolution accomplished by the expropriation of

---

was reprinted in 1847 as a pamphlet (Kropotkin had 1848 as its publication date, which has been corrected). It was translated into English by Joan Roelofs: Victor Considerant, *Principles of Socialism: Manifesto of 19th Century Democracy* (Washington, D.C.: Maisonneuve Press, 2006). (Editor)]

23   Both the passages Kropotkin is quoting are from *Le Socialisme devant le Vieux Monde*, 39. (Editor)

24   The *biens nationaux* were properties confiscated during the French Revolution from the Catholic Church, the monarchy, émigrés, and suspected counter-revolutionaries. The word *biens* means "goods," both in the sense of "objects" and in the sense of "benefits" and so literally means both "national things" and "benefits for the nation." In short, "things for the good of the nation." (Editor)

the property of the Church and nobility in favour of democracy. Thereupon he had to foresee the necessity for the *nationalisation of trade* and appreciate the attempt made in this direction by the *sans-culottes* in 1793 and 1794. He became its apostle.[25]

The free Community, depository of produce, must provide, in his opinion, the solution of the great problem of the exchange and distribution of essential products. But the community would not be the owner [of the stored produce] as today are merchants or even current co-operatives. It would only be a depositary. It would be an agency, receiving the products for storage for distribution, but not imposing any tribute on the consumers nor speculating on price fluctuations.

Tackling the social problem by consumption and exchange is what makes Fourier the deepest socialist thinker.

But Fourier did not stop there. He extended his idea. He supposed that all the families of a rural or industrial, preferably mixed, community constitute a *phalanx*. They would put in common their land, their livestock, their tools and [their] machines, and they would cultivate their land, or pursue their industry, as if the land, the machines, etc., were their common property—while taking, however, an exact account of what each member had contributed to the common capital.

Two paramount principles, he said, must be respected in the phalanx. First, there must be no *disagreeable labour*. All work must be organised, distributed, and diversified so that it is *always attractive*. And then, [second,] no form of constraint could be accepted in a society organised on the principle of free association, no form of constraint could be tolerated, and none would be needed.

With some intelligent attention to the needs of every member of the phalanx and a little tolerance for the particularities of the various personalities

---

25 They were unaware of it in the International, but we know today that L'Ange from Lyons, struck by the miseries of his town during the Revolution, had already published a plan of "voluntary Association" encompassing the entire nation. This Association would have 30,000 granaries of abundance set up in every commune which would eliminate *private property and private commerce in items of primary necessity* and establish the exchange of products at their true value. (See the analysis of the pamphlets by L'Ange, first given by Michelet, then by [Jean] Jaurès and recently by Hubert Bourgin in his volume: *Fourier*, Paris, 1905). Did this plan of L'Ange inspire Fourier who reflected on the same subject? We do not know for sure; but Fourier evidently knows the great plan of the *sans-culottes* of 1793–1794—to nationalise trade—and he had to be inspired by it. As Michelet said in one of his handwritten notes quoted by Jaurès: "What made Fourier? Neither [L']Ange, nor Babeuf: *Lyons, sole predecessor of Fourier.*" We can say today: "*Lyons and the Revolution of 1793–94.*"

[*caractères*], and combining agricultural, industrial, intellectual, and artistic work, the members of the phalanx would soon recognise that even the passions of men, which, in the current [social] organisation very often represent an evil and a danger and, for this reason, always serve as an excuse for the use of force—the same passions can be a source of progress. It is sufficient to recognise them and find their social applications. New enterprises, dangerous adventures, social activities, the need for change, etc., would give them the necessary outlets.

It is true that Fourier still paid tribute to statist ideas. Thus he admitted that in order to *trial* his Association—to attempt "a simple harmony" which would be the precursor of "true harmony"—"a prince could intervene." "To the chief of France can be reserved the honour of extracting the human race from social chaos, of being the founder of Harmony and the liberator of the globe," he said in one of his early writings;[26] and he repeated the same ideas in 1808, in his *Théorie des quatre mouvements*.[27] Later, he even went so far as to appeal to Louis-Philippe for this purpose (Charles Pellarin, *Fourier: sa vie, sa théorie*, 4th edition, p. 114). But it was always only for attempting the preliminary trial.

As for "true harmony," "universal harmony," it had no government. Nor could this harmony be introduced "piece by piece." The transformation had to be social, political, economic and moral all at once. And when Fourier came to the critique of the State, he was as pitiless as we are today. "Political disorder," he said, "is at once the consequence and the expression of social disorder. Inequality is translated into inequity. The State, in the name of which power acts, is resolutely, *by origin and principle, the servant and protector of the privileged classes against the others.*"[28] And so on.

In the "harmonic society," which will arise from the full application of his principles, all constraint must be excluded.[29]

---

26   "Universal Harmony," *The Utopian Vision of Charles Fourier: Selected Texts on Work, Love, and Passionate Attraction* (Boston: Jonathan Cape, 1971), 82. (Editor)

27   *The Theory of the Four Movements* (Cambridge: Cambridge University Press, 1996). (Editor)

28   Kropotkin is quoting (with added emphasis) Hubert Bourgin's summary of Fourier's ideas on the subject: *Fourier: contribution à l'étude du socialisme francais* (Paris: Sociêtê Nouvelle de Librairie et d'Edition, 1905), 208. (Editor)

29   Even when Fourier makes restrictions, or speaks with a striking inconsistency of "distinctions" and "grades to conquer" to stimulate passion for work, or else obedience to the laws and rules in experiments relating to the trial of his theory, the general idea of his system is the entire freedom of the individual in the harmonious society of the future. Freedom, he said, consists of "being able to perform the acts to which our affinities call us." [Kropotkin is quoting Pellarin, 241] "If there are people who flatter

Writing immediately after the defeat of the Great [French] Revolution, Fourier was inevitably inclined toward peaceful solutions. He insisted upon the necessity of recognising the principle of *association* between Capital, Labour, and Talent. Accordingly, the value of each product procured in the phalanx was to be divided into three parts, one of which (half or seven-twelfths) would remunerate Labour, another (three-twelfths) would go to Capital, and the third (two or three-twelfths) to Talent.

However, most of those who held Fourierist ideas in the International attached no importance to this aspect of his system. They understood the influence of the time when Fourier wrote. In contrast, they mostly retained the following essential features of the Fourierist teaching:

1. The free Community, that is to say, a *small*, independent, territorial agglomeration becomes the basis, the unit, of the new socialist society.
2. The Community is the depositary of all that is produced in the vicinity, and the intermediary for all exchanges. It also represents the association of consumers, and very probably it will also, in the majority of cases, be the *unit of production* (which, moreover, may also be a professional grouping, or even a federation of producer groups).
3. These Communities freely federate between themselves to constitute the Federation, the Region, the Nation.
4. Work must be rendered attractive. Without this, it would still be slavery. And as long as this is not done, no solution of the social question is possible. Work must also be, and it can be, much more productive than it is today.
5. To maintain harmony in a community like this, no constraint is necessary. The influence of public opinion will suffice.

As for the distribution of products, or consumption, opinions were still very divided.

Since the founding of the International, the socialist idea had made progress and, first at the Brussels Congress in 1868 and then at Basle in 1869, the International declared itself by a large majority for *collective* ownership of arable land, forests, railways, canals, telegraphs, etc., of the mines and also machines. Having accepted collective ownership and expropriation to achieve this, the anti-statists of the International took the name of *collectivists*[30] to be clearly distinguished from the statist and centralising

---

themselves on bending human nature to the demands of current society, and who study it for that purpose, we are not amongst them," added his pupil Pellarin (p. 222).

30   In the words of Bakunin: "I hate Communism because it is the negation of liberty

communism of Marx and Engels and their followers and from that of the French communists who had remained in the authoritarian tradition of Babeuf and Cabet.[31]

We find in the pamphlet *Idées sur l'organisation sociale*[32] published in 1876 by James Guillaume who himself took an active part in the propaganda for collectivism, as well as in his essential work *L'Internationale: Documents et souvenirs* [*The International: Documents and Memories*] (4 volumes, published in Paris in 1905–1910) and, finally, in his article on "Collectivisme de l'Internationale," recently written for the *Encyclopédie syndicaliste*, all the details of the precise meaning attributed to the word "collectivism" by the most active members of the federalist International— Varlin, Guillaume, De Paepe, Bakunin and their friends. They indicated by this term "Collectivism" a *non-authoritarian, federalist* or *anarchist, Communism*. By calling themselves collectivists, they affirmed themselves above all anti-authoritarian: they did not want to prejudge the form that consumption would take in a society that had accomplished expropriation. The key was, for them, not to claim to lock society into a rigid framework: they wanted to reserve for the advanced groups the greatest possible latitude on this point.

---

and because for me humanity is unthinkable without liberty. I am not a Communist, because Communism concentrates and swallows up in itself for the benefit of the State all the forces of society, because it inevitably leads to the concentration of property in the hands of the State. [. . .] I want to see society and collective or social property organised from below upwards, by way of free associations, not from above downwards, by means of any kind of authority whatsoever. [. . .] That is the sense in which I am a Collectivist and not a Communist" (quoted by K.J. Kenafick, *Michael Bakunin and Karl Marx*, 67–68). (Editor)

31   At that time the social-democrats had not yet put forward their system of *State collectivism*: many of them were still *authoritarian-communists*. And they had, so it appears, completely forgotten the very precise meaning of *State-Capitalism* and *remuneration according to the hours of work* which had been given to the word "collectivism" before and during the revolution of 1848, first by C. Pecqueur in 1839 (*Économie sociale: Des intérêts du commerce, de l'industrie et de l'agriculture, et de la civilisation en général sous l'influence des applications de la vapeur*) and especially in 1842 (*Théorie nouvelle de l'économie sociale et politique: études sur l'organisation des sociétés*) and then by F. Vidal, secretary of the workers Luxembourg Commission, in a very remarkable work *Vivre en travaillant! Projets, voies et moyens de réformes sociales* published in Paris at the end of June 1848.

32   James Guillaume's *Idées sur l'organisation sociale* (*Ideas on Social Organisation*) can be found (entitled "On Building the New Social Order") in *Bakunin on Anarchism* (Montreal: Black Rose Books, 1980) and, slightly abridged, in Daniel Guérin's anthology *No Gods, No Masters* (Oakland/Edinburgh: AK Press, 2005). (Editor)

Unfortunately, the ideas raised in the International on collective property had not yet had time to spread amongst the working masses when the Franco-Prussian war broke out just ten months after the Basle Congress. This meant that no serious attempt in this direction was made during the Paris Commune. And after the crushing of France and the Commune, the federalist International had to concentrate all its efforts on maintaining its fundamental idea—the anti-authoritarian organisation of the workers forces *for the purpose of the direct struggle of Labour against Capital* to achieve the *social* revolution. Inevitably, questions about the future had to be neglected and if the idea of collectivism, understood as anarchist-communism, continued to be propagated by a few, it clashed, on the one hand, with the Statist-collectivist concepts developed by the Marxists once they began to abandon the ideas of the *Communist Manifesto* and, on the other, with the authoritarian-communism of the Blanquists and to the widespread prejudices against communism in general that had been established in the working masses of the Latin countries since 1848, under the influence of the powerful critique of authoritarian-communism which had been made by Proudhon. This resistance was so strong that in Spain, for example, where the federalist International was in close relations with a vast federation of workers trade unions, they interpreted collectivism then and much later as a simple affirmation of collective ownership and they added "and anarchy" (*anarquía y colectivismo*) to affirm the anti-statist idea without prejudging the mode of consumption—communist or otherwise—that would be accepted by each separate group of producers and consumers.

Finally, as regards the means of passing from the present society to a socialist society, the workers of the International attached no importance to what Fourier had said. They felt that a revolutionary situation was developing, and they saw coming a deeper and broader revolution than even that of 1848. And then, they said, they would do everything in their power to dispossess, without waiting for the orders of the government, Capital of the monopolies which it had appropriated.

The Impetus Given by the Commune-Bakunin

From the quick overview given in the preceding chapters, we have seen the terrain upon which the anarchist idea was to develop within the International.

It was, as we have seen, a mixture of the ideas of centralist and authoritarian Jacobinism with the ideas of local independence and federation. Both—as we now know—had their origin in the Great French Revolution. For if the centralist ideas were descended in a direct line from the Jacobinism of 1793, those of local independent action represented, on the other hand, the legacy of the powerful and constructive revolutionary action of the sections of Paris and the Communes of 1793–1794.

It must be said, however, that the first of these two currents, the Jacobin current, was without doubt the more powerful. The bourgeois intellectuals who entered the International were very often Jacobins in spirit and the workers were subject to their influence.

It required an event of such serious significance as the Paris Commune to give a new direction to revolutionary thought amongst the working masses of Europe and America.

In July 1870 began the terrible Franco-Prussian War into which Napoleon III and his advisers threw themselves to save the Empire from imminent Republican revolution. The war brought a crushing defeat, the collapse of the Empire, the Provisional Government of Thiers and Gambetta, and the Commune of Paris [in 1871] as well as attempts of the same kind in Saint-Étienne, Narbonne and other cities in the South [of France] and, later in Spain—in Barcelona and Cartagena [during 1873].[33]

For the International—for those, at least, who could think and learn from events—these communal uprisings were a revelation. Made under the red flag of the social revolution, which the workers in Paris defended to the death at their barricades, these uprisings indicated what should be, what would likely be in the Latin nations, the *political* form of the next revolution.

Not the Democratic Republic, as was thought in 1848, but THE COMMUNE—*free, independent and, very probably, communist.*

It goes without saying that the Paris Commune had experienced the confusion which then prevailed in minds concerning the economic and political measures that should be taken during a popular revolution to ensure its triumph. The same confusion that we have just seen in the International reigned in the Commune.

Jacobins and communalists—that is to say, *government* centralists and *federalists*—were both represented in the uprising in Paris and they soon found themselves within conflict in the Commune. The most combative element

---

33   A reference to the revolutionary events following the creation of the Republic in Spain in 1873. After the Catalan federalist republican Francisco Pi y Margall (1824–1901) became President, the more militant elements of the Federalist camp (called the Intransigents) launched various insurrections across the country. On 12 July 1873, armed Cantonalists (as the Intransigents and their allies were known) seized the municipal government of Cartegena and declared it independent. Similar revolts occurred throughout the south of Spain. In Barcelona, the members of the International tried (but failed) to produce a similar revolt but successfully organised a general strike. The military crushed all the various revolts. (Editor)

was amongst the Jacobins and the Blanquists. But Blanqui was in prison and amongst the Blanquist leaders—bourgeois for the most part—there was not much left of the communist ideas of their Babouvist predecessors. The economic question, for them, was a matter that would be dealt with later, after the triumph of the Commune, and this idea having prevailed at first the popular communist view did not have the time to develop. Still less had it the time to assert itself during the short life of the Paris Commune.

Under these conditions, defeat was swift and the ferocious vengeance of the frightened bourgeois proved, once more, that the triumph of a popular Commune was materially impossible if a parallel development of conquests in the economic field does not impassion the mass of the people for the Commune.

To achieve a political revolution it is necessary to know how to carry out at the same time the economic revolution.

But at the same time, the Paris Commune provided another valuable lesson. It clarified, in the Latin nations, the ideas of revolutionary proletarians.

The free Commune—that is the *political* form that the *social* revolution must take. Let the whole nation, let all the neighbouring nations, be against this course of action—but once the inhabitants of a town and of a given territory have decided that they want to communalise the consumption of items necessary for the satisfaction of their needs, and the exchange of these products and their production, *they must achieve that themselves, locally.* And if they do, if they put their energies at the service of such a great cause, they will find in their commune a strength they would never find if they tried to bring with them the whole nation with its backward, hostile or indifferent parts. It is better to fight those openly than having to drag them behind you, like so many balls chained to the feet of the Revolution.

More than that. We were able to understand that if no central government was needed to control the free communes—if national government is rejected and if national unity is obtained by the free federation of communes—then a central *municipal* government becomes equally useless and noxious. The questions to be decided upon in the commune are in fact much less complicated, and the interests of citizens less varied and less contradictory, than they are within a nation. The federative principle must therefore be sufficient to establish agreement between the different producer, consumer and other groups within the commune.

The Paris Commune answers a question that had tormented every true revolutionary. Twice France had tried to achieve a revolution in the socialist sense by seeking to impose it by a central government: in 1793–1794, when it tried, after the downfall of the Girondins, to introduce *"l'égalité de fait"*—real, economic equality—by means of severe legislative measures and in 1848 when it tried to bestow, through its National Assembly, a "Democratic Socialist Republic."

And twice it failed. Now life itself showed us a new solution—the free Commune which must itself accomplish the revolution, in its own territory, at the same time as it liberates itself from the centralised State. And this new idea reinforced the ideal of ANARCHY.

We understood then that there was in Proudhon's *General Idea of the Revolution in the Nineteenth Century* a deeply *practical* idea: the idea of Anarchy.[34] And in the Latin countries the thought of advanced men began working in this direction.

Alas, only in the Latin countries: in France, in Spain, in Italy, in French-speaking Switzerland and in the Walloon part of Belgium. The Germans, in contrast, drew from their victory over France a completely different lesson; they came to the worship of statist centralisation. They still remained mired in the Robespierrist phase. They still worshipped the Jacobin Club such as described by (contrary to reality) the Jacobin historians.

The centralised State, hostile even to tendencies of national independence of its different parts; a strong hierarchical centralisation and a strong government—these were the conclusions drawn by German socialists and radicals. They did not even want to understand that the victory they had accomplished over France was only a victory of big battalions—of universal obligatory military service over the system of recruitment still in force in France in 1870—a victory achieved primarily over the rottenness of the Second Empire when it was already being threatened by a revolution which would have benefited all of humanity, if it had not been not prevented by the German invasion.[35]

As such, in the Latin countries, the Paris Commune gave a boost to the idea of Anarchy. On the other hand, the authoritarian tendencies of the General Council of the International, asserting itself more and more and

---

34   Proudhon's *General Idea of the Revolution in the Nineteenth Century* was translated in 1923 by John Beverly Robinson and published by Freedom Press. It was reprinted with an introduction by Graham Purchase by Pluto Press in 1989. Extracts are included in *Property is Theft!*. (Editor)

35   Following the Napoleonic Wars, the restored Bourbon monarchy returned to its traditional reliance on long service volunteers. Numbers were increased by limited conscription by lot, from which the middle and upper classes could purchase exemptions. Such conscripts served the comparatively long period of seven years. This unequal system was still in place at the start of the Franco-Prussian War of 1870, which broke out before planned reforms could be implemented. The Prussian system of universal compulsory military service could mobilise some million troops in comparison to France's 288,000. (Editor)

threatening to undermine the strength of the association, reinforced the anarchist current. Led by Marx and Engels, who found support amongst the French Blanquist refugees who fled to London after the Commune, the General Council took advantage of the powers it had been given to make a *coup d'état* in the International. It replaced in the programme of action of the Association the direct struggle of Labour against Capital by agitation in bourgeois parliaments.

This *coup d'état* killed the International but it also opened eyes. It showed even the most gullible how absurd it was to entrust their affairs to a government even if it were as democratically elected as was the General Council of the International. In this way was provoked the autonomist revolt of the Spanish, Italian, Jura, and Belgian Walloon Federations, as well as a section of the English, against the authority of the General Council.[36]

In Michael Bakunin the anarchist tendency which was growing within the International found a powerful and inspired champion; and around Bakunin and his Jura friends gathered a small circle of young Italians and Spaniards who further developed his ideas.

Taking advantage of his vast knowledge of history and philosophy, Bakunin established the principles of modern Anarchy in a series of powerful pamphlets, newspaper articles and letters.

He boldly proclaimed the idea of the complete abolition of the State, with all its organisation, ideals and tendencies. The State had been a historical necessity in the past—an institution that developed the authority acquired by the religious caste. But now the complete destruction of the State is, in its turn, a historical necessity since the State is the negation of liberty and equality, and since it is known that it corrupts what it undertakes even when it undertakes to put into practice an idea for the general interest.

Every nation, however small it may be, every region, every commune must be absolutely free to organise itself as it sees fit, as long as it does not threaten its neighbours. "Federalism" and "autonomy" are not enough. These are just words always covering the authority of the centralised State. Complete independence of the Commune, the Federation of free Communes, and the social revolution within the Commune, that is to say trade unions [*les groupements corporative*] for production replacing the statist organisation of the society that exists today—that is, demonstrated Bakunin, the ideal which emerges before our civilisation from the mists

---

36 For more details of this *coup d'état* and its consequences, it is necessary to consult the excellent historical work of James Guillaume, *L'Internationale: Documents et Souvenirs (1864–1878)*, 4 vol., Paris, 1905–1910, chez P.-V. Stock, éditeur.

of the past.[37] The individual understands that he will be truly free only in proportion to the freedom of all others around him.

With these views, Bakunin was also an ardent propagandist of the social revolution, the imminent arrival of which most socialists then expected, and which he summoned in his letters and writings with words of fire.

---

37   The term "corporative" (*corporatif*) was originally the French word for craft guild and was popular in the nineteenth century French labour movement to refer to the associations which would replace wage-labour. For more discussion, see William H. Sewell, *Work and Revolution in France: The language of labor from the old regime to 1848* (Cambridge: Cambridge University Press, 1980). It should be not confused with capitalist corporations or corporatism as can be seen from Bakunin's description:

> The organisation of the trade sections, their federation in the International, and their representation by the Chambers of Labour, not only create a great academy, in which the workers of the International, combining theory and practice, can and must study economic science, they also bear in themselves the living germs of *the new social order*, which is to replace the bourgeois world. They are creating not only the ideas but also the facts of the future itself (Quoted in Rudolf Rocker, *Anarcho-Syndicalism*, 50).

The "Chambers of Labour" (*chambres de travail*) had been created in the Belgium section of the International and were local federations of trade unions (like trade councils in Britain). Bakunin's vision also predicted the workers' councils (*soviets*) of the Russian Revolutions: "The future organisation of society must proceed from the bottom up only, through free association or federations of the workers, into their associations to begin with, then into communes, regions, nations and, finally, into a great international and universal federation" (Bakunin, *No Gods, No Masters*, 208). (Editor)

XIII

ANARCHY (CONTINUED)

The Anarchist Concept as it Appears Today

IF, BEFORE 1848 AND LATER ON UNTIL THE INTERNATIONAL, THE REVOLT against the State, represented mainly by young bourgeois, took the character of a revolt of the individual against society and its moral conventions, henceforth, amongst the workers this revolt took a more profound character. It became the search for a form of society, free from the oppression and exploitation which currently occur with the help of the State.

International Workers' Association, in the idea of the workers who founded it, had to be, as we have seen, a vast federation of workers groups representing the seeds of a society regenerated by social revolution: a society where the current machinery of government and capitalist exploitation would disappear to make way for the new links which would arise between federations of producers and consumers.

Under these conditions, the anarchist ideal could no longer be *individual:* it became *social.*[38]

As the workers of the two worlds [that is, Europe and America] began to know each other directly and entered into direct relations across borders,

---

38 The word Kropotkin uses (*sociétaire*) has a wider meaning than merely "social." It literally refers to a member of a co-operative association and so Kropotkin is signifying a social organisation which is marked by active participation of its members in its affairs. In other words, anarchy now became *associational* both in *theory* (as had it been with Proudhon) and in *practice* (with its links to the militant labour movement). (Editor)

they developed a better understanding of the causes of the social problem and gained awareness of their own forces.

They foresaw that if the people regained possession of the land and if industrial workers took possession of the mills and factories and made themselves managers of production and directed them towards the production of what is necessary for life of the nation, we would achieve without difficulty an ample supply for all the needs of society. Recent progress in science and technology guaranteed this. And then the producers of different nations would know how to establish between themselves international exchange [of products] on an equitable basis. It was obvious for those who knew at first hand the factory, mill, mine, agriculture, commerce.

At the same time, an ever increasing number of workers perceived that the State, with its hierarchy of functionaries and the weight of its historical traditions, could only delay the dawning of a new society freed from monopolies and exploitation.

Developed in the course of history to establish and maintain the monopoly of land ownership in favour of one class—which, for that reason, became the ruling class par excellence—what means can the State provide to abolish this monopoly that the working class could not find in its own strength and groups? Then perfected during the course of the nineteenth century to ensure the monopoly of industrial property, trade, and banking to new enriched classes, to which the State was supplying "arms" cheaply by stripping the land from the village communes and crushing the cultivators by tax—what advantages could the State provide for abolishing these same privileges? Could its governmental machine, developed for the creation and upholding of these privileges, now be used to abolish them? Would not the new function require new organs? And these new organs would they not have to be created by the workers themselves, in *their* unions, *their* federations, completely outside the State?

From the moment the monopolies formed and solidified by the State have ceased to exist, the State no longer has any reason for being. *New* forms of groups must arise once relations between men are no longer relations of exploited and exploiter. *Life would be simplified* as soon as the mechanism that existed to enable the rich to exploit the labour of the poor ceased to be required.

The idea of independent Communes for the *territorial* groupings, and vast federations of trade unions for groupings *by social functions*—the two interwoven and providing support to each to meet the needs of society— allowed the anarchists to conceptualise in a real, concrete, way the possible organisation of a liberated society.[39] They had only to add groupings

---

39   Kropotkin, like the libertarians within the International, saw the economic bodies of

by personal affinities—groupings without number, infinitely varied, long-lasting or fleeting, emerging according to the needs of the moment for all possible purposes—groupings that we already see arising in today's society, outside of political and vocational groups.

These three kinds of groupings, covering each other like a network, would thus allow the satisfaction of all social needs: consumption, production and exchange, communications, sanitary arrangements, education, mutual protection against aggression, mutual aid, territorial defence; the satisfaction, finally, of scientific, artistic, literacy, entertainment needs. Everything always full of life and always ready to respond with new adaptations to the new needs and the new influences of the social and intellectual environment.

If a society of this kind developed on a territory sufficiently large and sufficiently populous enough to allow the necessary variety of tastes and needs, we would soon see that constraint by authority, whatever it may be, would be unnecessary. Unnecessary for maintaining the economic life of society, it would likewise be [unnecessary] for preventing most anti-social acts.[40]

Indeed, the most serious obstacle to the development and retention of the existing state of moral standards, necessary for life in society, lies above all in the absence of social equality in the State. Without equality—"without de facto equality," as was said in 1793—it is absolutely impossible for the sense of *justice* to become widespread. *Justice can only be egalitarian*; and sentiments of equality are denied today, at every step, at every moment, in our societies stratified into classes. It takes the *practice* of equality for the sentiment of justice towards all to enter into customs, habits. And that is what will happen in a society of equals.

Then, the need for constraint or rather the desire to resort to constraint would no longer be felt. We would be convinced that freedom of the

---

a free society being created in and by the struggle against capital such as unions. Thus, in an article written in 1881, he argued that anarchists must "bring the contribution of their energy to the workers' organisation and work to build up a force that will crush capital, come the day of revolution: the revolutionary trades association. Trades sections, federations embracing all the workers in the same trade, federation of all the trades of the locality, of the region [...] that is how they constitute the structures of the revolutionary army" ("The Workers' Movement in Spain," *Direct Struggle Against Capital*, 299). (Editor)

40 In contrast to those who portray him (like anarchists in general) as viewing an anarchist society as one of complete harmony without anti-social acts, Kropotkin shows here that he did not expect a free society to be without clashes between individuals. Rather, he argued that statist societies would produce far more anti-social acts than a free one and, moreover, that the State does *not* stop or deter them. (Editor)

individual does not need to be limited, as it is today, sometimes by the fear of legal or mystical punishment, sometimes by obedience to individuals accepted as superiors, or to metaphysical entities created by fear or ignorance—which leads, in today's society, to intellectual servitude, to the depression of personal initiative, to the lowering of moral standards, to the arresting of progress.

In an egalitarian environment man could in all confidence be guided by his own reason which, developed in this environment, would *necessarily* be imprinted by the sociable customs of that environment. And he could reach the full development of all his faculties—the full development of his *individuality*; whereas the individualism advocated today by the bourgeoisie as a way "for superior natures" to reach the full development of the human being, is merely a trick. The individualism they advocate is, on the contrary, the greatest obstacle to the development of any outstanding individuality.

Within a society that pursues *individual enrichment* and which, for this very reason, is condemned to poverty as a whole, the most gifted man is reduced to a bitter struggle just to obtain the means necessary to maintain his existence. As for the very small number of those who manage to conquer in addition some [of the] leisure necessary for the free development of individuality, society today only guarantees them that on one condition: *to submit to the yoke of the laws and the conventions of bourgeois mediocrity*; to never shake the kingdom of mediocrity by a criticism too penetrating, or by acts of revolt.

Only those who offer no threat to bourgeois society are allowed the "full development of their individuality," those who are interesting to it without ever being dangerous to it.

Anarchists, as we have said, base their predictions of the future on the observed facts.

Indeed, when we analyse the tendencies that dominate in civilised societies since the end of the eighteenth century, we have to note that the centralist and authoritarian tendency is still very strong in bourgeois circles and amongst those workers who have received a bourgeois education and tend to become bourgeois in their turn. But the anti-authoritarian, anti-centralist and anti-militarist tendency and the idea of free agreement also emerge very strongly in labour circles as well as in the circles of the free spirits in the intellectual classes of the bourgeoisie.

Indeed, as I have shown elsewhere (*Conquest of Bread, Mutual Aid*) there exists today a strong tendency to form freely, outside the State and the Churches, thousands and thousands of groupings to satisfy all sorts of needs: economic (groupings for railways, workers unions, syndicates of employers, co-operation for agriculture and export, etc.), political, intellectual, artistic, educational, recreation, propaganda and so on. What was formerly portrayed as indisputably functions of the State or the Church return today to the domain of the action of free groupings. This trend is visibly growing. It is sufficient that the breath of freedom has limited the jealous power of the Church and the State for these voluntary organisations to arise by the thousands. And we can predict that as soon as some new limitation of the power of these two ancient enemies of freedom is imposed on them, the free groupings will extend their spheres of activity further.

The future and progress are in this direction, and anarchy summarises both.

The Negation of the State

We must acknowledge that in their economic ideas, anarchists suffer the effect of the chaotic state in which all political economy is still in. As amongst the statist-socialists, we can distinguish amongst them various currents of opinion on this subject.

In agreement with those socialists who have remained socialists, the anarchists recognise that the current system of individual ownership of the land and of all that is required to produce, along with the current system of production for profit which is its consequence, are an *evil*; that our societies must abolish it, on pain of falling like so many ancient civilisations have already fallen.

But as to the means by which this change could be accomplished, the anarchists completely differ from all the factions of the statist-socialists in that they deny that we can find a solution to the social problem in the *State-Capitalist* taking ownership of production or, at least, its principle branches. The postal service or the railways in the hands of the current State, directed by the ministries appointed by Parliament [*la Chambre*], is not the ideal that we seek. We only see in that a new form of wage-labour and exploitation. We do not even believe that it is a path towards the abolition of wage-labour and exploitation, or even a transitional form in the evolution towards this aim.

Also, as long as socialism was understood in its wide and true sense—the abolition of the exploitation of Labour by Capital—the anarchists were, in this, in agreement with what were then the socialists. They differed only in the anti-authoritarian form of society that they wanted to see emerge from the social revolution, the coming of which both predicted and desired.

But they had to part completely with them when a large fraction, if not the majority, of the State socialists supported the idea that it was not a matter of immediately *abolishing* capitalist exploitation; that for our generation and for the phase of economic development we are going through today there can only be the question *of mitigating* exploitation, by imposing on the capitalists certain legal limitations.

To this, the anarchists could not consent. We maintain that if we want to one day achieve the abolition of capitalist exploitation we must, *starting today*, already direct our efforts towards its abolition. Starting today we must aim for the direct transfer of everything that is used in production—mines, factories, means of communication, and above all the means of existence of the producer—from the hands of individual Capital into those of communities of producers. Aim—and act accordingly.

Furthermore, we must take great care not to transfer these means of subsistence and production into the hands *of the current bourgeois State*. While the socialist political parties demand all across Europe the taking of possession of the railways, land, iron and coal mines and (in Switzerland, for example) the banks and the monopoly of [selling] alcohol *by the bourgeois State, as it is today*—we see in this taking possession of the common riches by the bourgeois State one of the greatest obstacles to that day when the social wealth passes into the hands *of the workers,* [*as both*] *producers and consumers*. We see in that the means of strengthening the capitalist, of augmenting his might against the rebel worker. This is also already seen amongst intelligent capitalists themselves. Their capital invested in railways, for example, is safer when the railways are a State property, operated in a military fashion by the State. For anyone who has a mind accustomed to reflecting on social facts as a whole there is no shadow of doubt on this point, which can be considered a social axiom: "We cannot prepare a social change without already taking the first steps in the same direction as the desired change; we are lead astray if we do not follow this path." In fact, we move away from that moment when the producers and consumers themselves will be the masters of production and exchange if we start by transferring production and exchange into the hands of parliaments, ministries, current functionaries who, inevitably, are today the instruments of big Capital, since all States depend on it.

We will not manage to destroy the monopolies created in the past by creating a new monopoly—always for the profit of the old monopolists.

Nor can we forget that the Church and the State were the political force to which the privileged classes, when they were just beginning to form, resorted to in order to become entrenched [*établies*] classes, armed by the law to have privileges and rights over other men; that the State is the institution that served to establish mutual insurance for the enjoyment of those rights. But, because of this very reason, neither the Church nor the State can today become the force which will be used to demolish these privileges. Neither one nor the other can be a form of the organisation that emerges when these privileges are abolished. History teaches us, on the contrary, that whenever a new economic form emerges in the life of a nation—when serfdom, for example, came to replace slavery, and later on wage-labour for serfdom—a new form of political grouping always had to develop.

Just as the Church can never be utilised to free man from his submission to ancient superstitions or to give him a new freely agreed ethics; just as the sentiments of equality, solidarity and unity of all men, which penetrate into all religions, will one day take a very different form than those that were taught by the various Churches, where they seized them to exploit them for the benefit of the clergy; likewise economic emancipation will be accomplished by smashing the old political forms represented by the State. Man will be forced to find new forms of organisation for the social functions that the State apportioned between its functionaries. And nothing will be done as long as this is not done.

Anarchy works to facilitate the blossoming of these new forms of social life. And this blossoming will take place, as it always has in the past, during great upheavals of liberation by the constructive force of the masses, aided [this time] by modern knowledge.

This is why anarchists refuse to accept the role of legislators or any other function in the State. We know that social revolution does not proceed by means of *laws*. For laws, even if they were passed by a Constituent Assembly under pressure from the street (and again: how would they be passed when it would be case of reconciling the most contrary interests?)—the laws, even after they were passed, are simply a pledge to work in a certain direction, an invitation to those on the ground to use their energy and their inventive, organisational, constructive spirit. But for that we must still have there on the ground forces ready and capable of transforming the phrases, the *wishes* of a law into the facts of real life.

This is also why a great number of anarchists, since the beginnings of the International to the present, have taken an active part in the workers organisations formed for the direct struggle of Labour against Capital.[41] This struggle, while serving far more powerfully than any indirect action to secure some improvements in the life of the worker and opening up the eyes of the workers to the evil done to society by capitalist organisation and by the State that upholds it, this struggle also awakes in the worker thoughts concerning the forms of consumption, production and direct exchange between those concerned, without the intervention of the capitalist and the State.

With regard to the form of the *remuneration of labour* in a society freed from Capital and State, as we have said, opinions amongst anarchists still remain divided.

---

41   The 1912 British edition adds: "and its protector—the State." (Editor)

All are agreed in rejecting the new form of wage-labour which would arise if the State took possession of the means of production and exchange, as it has already taken possession of the railways, the post office, education, social security [*l'assurance mutuelle*], and defence of the territory. New powers, industrial powers, added to those which it [already] possesses (taxes, defence of the territory, subsidised religions, etc.) would create a new, formidable instrument of tyranny.

The majority of anarchists today thus support the *communist-anarchist* solution. We begin to realise that the only form of communism possible in a civilised society is the anarchist communist form. Egalitarian in its essence, communism is a negation of all authority. Furthermore, an anarchist society of some size would not be possible if it did not begin by guaranteeing for all some minimum of well-being, produced in common.

Communism and Anarchy are thus two conceptions that necessarily complement each other.

But alongside the main communist current, there continues to be a current which sees in Anarchy a rehabilitation of *individualism*, and we shall say a few words on this current to finish.

The Individualist Current

The individualist current seems to be a survival of the past when, the means of production not yet reaching the efficiency that science and technical progress gives them today, communism was synonymous with a common poverty and mutual subjugation.

Barely sixty years ago, a modest wellbeing and some leisure were possible, indeed, only for a very small number of people who exploited the labour of others; and this is why all those who held on to some economic independence looked with dread at the day when they could no longer belong to the privileged minority. Indeed, it must not be forgotten that at that time Proudhon estimated the total production of France as being five cents per person per day.[42]

However today this obstacle no longer exists. With the immense productivity of human labour that we have in agriculture as in industry (see on this *Fields, Factories and Workshops*), it is certain that a very high degree of wellbeing for all could easily be obtained in a few years by communist labour intelligently organised, while not asking from everyone more than

---

42   A reference to Proudhon's *System of Economic Contradictions* in which he denounced that 7,500,000 men in France were estimated to have just five cents a day to live on (*Système des contradictions économiques ou Philosophie de la misère*, I [Paris: Guillaumin, 1846], 159). (Editor)

four or five hours of work per day. That would leave us at least five more hours of complete leisure.

Therefore this objection to communism exists no more.

In any event, today the individualist current is divided into two main branches. There are first of all the pure individualists, in the sense of Stirner, who have recently found a support in the artistic beauty of the writings of Nietzsche. But we will not dwell on them [here]. We have already said in a previous chapter how metaphysical and remote from real life is this "assertion of the individual"; how it offends the sentiments of equality—basis of all liberation—because you cannot free yourself as long as you want to dominate someone; and how close it brings those who profess themselves "individualists" to the minorities of nobles, priests, bourgeois, functionaries, etc. who also believe themselves "superiors" to the masses, and to whom we owe State, Church, Laws, Police, Militarism, and every age-old oppression.

The other branch of the "individualist-anarchists" comprises the mutualists, in the sense of Proudhon. They seek the solution of the social problem in a free, voluntary organisation, which would introduce the exchange of goods valued in labour notes [*bons de travail*].[43] These "notes" would represent the number of hours necessary in a given industrial situation [*un état donné de l'industrie*] to produce a particular product, or else the number of hours given by such-and-such an individual to functions with recognised public utility.

In reality, this system is not individualist any more. It represents a compromise between communism and individualism. Individualism in the remuneration of the producer—communism in the ownership of what is used to produce.[44]

Well, it is this same dualism that raises, in our view, an insurmountable obstacle to ensuring that the system could be introduced. It is impossible for a society to organise itself on two contradictory principles on this

---

43   Kropotkin here is repeating the common, but mistaken, opinion that Proudhon advocated "labour notes." This false notion was invented by Marx in *The Poverty of Philosophy* and flew in the face of what Proudhon actually argued in *System of Economic Contradictions*, namely: *"Products are bought only with products"* (Ibid., 246). In terms of the individualist anarchists, only Josiah Warren and Stephen Pearl Andrews advocated pricing commodities by time. See the introduction for further discussion. (Editor)

44   This reflects Proudhon's arguments in *What is Property?* that his system was a "synthesis" between "property" and "community" in which "the right to product is exclusive" but "the right to means is common" (*Property is Theft!*, 130, 112). For further discussion, see Introduction to that volume. (Editor)

point: the placing in common of what was produced until a certain day, and individualism for what will be produced [after that date]: not for the production of items of luxury, for which tastes and demand vary infinitely, but even for the strictly necessary, concerning which a certain consistency of opinion is established in every society.

It should not be forgotten, either, the immense variety of machines and methods used to produce in different places in a large society and in a developing industry. This means that with such-and-such a machine a given amount of work produces two or three times more than this other machine. So, for example, in the modern weaving industry, looms are so different in their qualities that the number of looms that one man can supervise varies from three to twenty (Northrop looms). Neither should it be forgotten the differences in muscle and brain energy needed for different workers in different branches of production. And if we take these facts into consideration, one begins to wonder whether the hour of work can ever be taken as an acceptable measure for the *market exchange* of products.

We can understand existing *commercial* exchange but we cannot comprehend a market exchange based on an evaluation—the hour of work—*that is no longer commercial* as soon as the labour force ceases to be treated as merchandise. The hour of work could be used to establish the equivalence of products (or rather to *roughly* estimate them) only in a society which has *already* accepted the communist principle for most products of prime necessity.

And if, as a concession to the idea of individualist remuneration, we introduced, in addition to the "simple" hour of work, a different payment for "skilled" work, which requires training, or if you resorted to "opportunity for advancement" in the hierarchy of the officials of industry, we would thus reinstate the distinctive features of modern wage-labour, with the same vices that we know and which make us seek ways to abolish it.

However, it must not be forgotten that the ideas of the mutualists have had some success in agriculture in the United States where this system continues, it seems, to function in some organisations of farmers.

Coming close to the mutualists, there are still the American individualist-anarchists who were represented in the fifties of the nineteenth century by S.P. Andrews, by W. Greene, later on by Lysander Spooner, and who are represented today by Benjamin Tucker, who published for many years the newspaper *Liberty.*

Their ideas are related to Proudhon's, but also to Herbert Spencer's. They start from the assertion that the only obligatory law for the anarchist is to look after his own affairs himself; that, consequently, each individual and each group have the *right* to act as they wish—even to oppress all humanity, if they have the strength. If these principles, says Tucker, received a general application, they would offer no danger since the powers of each individual would be limited by the equal rights of all the others.

But to reason that way is to pay, it seems to us, too large a tribute to metaphysics and to make imaginary assumptions. To say that someone has the right to oppress all humanity, if he has the strength, and that the rights of the individual are limited by the equal rights of others, is to lapse completely into the dialectic. Furthermore, for those of us who remain in the realm of reality, it is absolutely impossible to conceive a society, or even a simple agglomeration of men doing the least of things in common, in which the affairs of each would not concern many, if not all, of the others. Still less is it possible for us to imagine a society in which the continual contact between its members would not establish an interest of each one towards the others and not render it practically impossible to act without considering the consequences of his actions for society.

This is why Tucker, like Spencer, after having made an excellent critique of the State and a vigorous defence of the rights of the individual, but also recognising individual ownership of land, comes to reconstitute the State, to prevent the individualist citizens from harming one another. It is true that Tucker only recognises that the State has the right to *defend* its members but this right and this function are sufficient to constitute the State, with its current rights.[45] Indeed, if we examine the history of the State institution, we find that it is precisely under the pretext of defending the rights of the individual that the State was constituted. Its laws, its functionaries, charged with protecting the injured individual; its hierarchy, established to ensure the enforcement of laws; its universities, created to study the sources of the law; and its church to sanctify the idea; its ranks to maintain "order," and its compulsory military service; its monopolies, finally, its vices, its tyranny—everything flows from this first admission: the protection of the rights of the individual injured by another individual.

These brief remarks explain why the systems of individualist anarchy, if they find adherents amongst the "intellectuals" of the bourgeoisie, are not encountered much in the mass of workers. Be that as it may, all recognise the importance of the criticism made by the individualist anarchist in preventing their communist colleagues lapsing into centralism and bureaucracy, and always bringing thought back to the free individual— the primary source of any free society. The tendency to relapse into the

---

45   Tucker's position of landownership is somewhat contradictory insofar as he argued
      for "occupancy and use" for agricultural land and housing but supported wage-labour
      for workplaces. The latter would see the recreation of a State to defend the employer
      against the strikes of those who toil for him. See the introduction for further discus-
      sion. (Editor)

errors of the past exists only too well, we know, even amongst advanced revolutionaries.

We can therefore see that at this moment anarchist-communism is the solution which is gaining most ground amongst the workers—especially the Latin workers—who are interested in the questions of revolutionary action in a more or less near future and who lose faith in the kindness of the State.

The labour movement, which permits the workers to sense their solidarity outside the futile agitations of political parties, to gauge their forces and their capabilities in a more effective way than in the fleeting mechanism of elections, contributes greatly to preparing these [anarchist] ideas. So it is no exaggeration to predict that when serious movements commence amongst the workers of the towns and countryside attempts will be made in the anarchist direction and that those attempts will without doubt be more profound that those began by the French people in 1793 and 1794.

XIV

SOME CONCLUSIONS OF ANARCHY

AFTER SHOWING THE ORIGINS OF ANARCHY AND ITS PRINCIPLES, WE WILL now provide some examples that will allow us to better define the place occupied by our ideas in the contemporary scientific and social movement.

So, when we are spoken to about Law, with a capital letter, when we are told: "The Law is the objectification of Truth," or else: "The laws of development of the Law are the laws of development of the human spirit," or again: "The Law and Morality are identical and differ only formerly," we listen to these grandiose assertions with as little reverence as Mephistopheles did in Goethe's *Faust*.[46] We know that those who wrote these phrases believed they were being profound, spent some effort of thought before arriving here [at these words]. But we also know that these thinkers were on the wrong path; and we see in their grandiose phrases unconscious attempts at generalisations made, however, on altogether insufficient bases, further obscured by words to hypnotise people.

In the past, we endeavoured to give the Law a divine origin; later on, we sought to give it a metaphysical basis; but today we can already study the

---

46 Goethe's play *Faust* is based on a classic German legend. Faust is scholar who is high-ly successful yet dissatisfied with his life, which leads him to make a pact with the Devil via the demon Mephistopheles, exchanging his soul for unlimited knowledge and worldly pleasures. (Editor)

origin of conceptions of the Law, and their [historical] development, just as we would study the development of weaving or how bees make honey. And, benefiting from the works produced by the anthropological school, we study social customs and conceptions of law, beginning with the most primitive savages, to follow their successive evolution in the codes of different historical periods to the present.

Thus we come to this conclusion, already mentioned on one of the previous pages: All laws, we say, had *a double origin,* and it is precisely this double origin and it is exactly this which distinguishes them from customs, established by [common] practice, which represent the principles of morality existing in a particular society at a particular period. Law confirms these customs: it crystallises them but at the same time it takes advantage of them to introduce, usually in a concealed form, some new institution in the interest of the minority of rulers and armed men. For example, it introduces or it sanctifies slavery, or else division into castes, or else the authority of the father in the family, or the priest or the military authority; or, finally, it smuggles in serfdom, and, later on, subjugation to the State. In this way they have always succeeded in imposing a yoke on men without them being aware of it—a yoke which they could only throw off later by bloody revolutions.

And so things go at all times, up to the present day. We see it even in current so-called labour legislation by which, alongside "protection of labour," which represents the stated aim of these laws, they quietly introduce the idea of a *compulsory* arbitration by the State in case of a strike (compulsory arbitration—what a contradiction!), or else they smuggle in the principle of a compulsory working day of at least so many hours. They open the door to the military working of railways in the event of a strike, they give legal approval to the dispossession of the peasants in Ireland from whom a previous law had taken the land.[47] Or else, they introduce insurance against sickness, old age, and even unemployment and they thus give to the State the right and the duty to control every day of the worker, the right to force him never to take a day on holiday without the authorisation of the State, of the functionary.

And this will continue as long as *one part* of society makes laws for the whole of society, always increasing for that very reason the power of the State which constitutes the principal support of capitalism. This will continue as long as *laws* are made.

We understand therefore why anarchists have always, since Godwin, denied all written *laws,* despite the fact that, more than all the legislators,

---

47   The 1912 British edition adds: "by imposing high prices for the redemption of the land." (Editor)

the anarchist aspires to justice, which, for them, is equivalent to *equality*, and is impossible without it.

When the objection is raised against us that by rejecting the Law we likewise reject by that all morality, as we do not recognise the "categorical imperative" of which Kant spoke to us—we reply that the very language of this objection is incomprehensible and absolutely foreign to us.[48] It is as foreign and incomprehensible to us to the same degree as it would be to any naturalist who studies morality. This is why, before entering into discussion, we ask our interlocutors this question: "But, actually tell us, what do you mean by your categorical imperative? Can you not translate your assertions into a comprehensible language—as, for example, Laplace did when he found a way of expressing the formulas of higher mathematics inwords that everyone understood? All great scientists do so; why do you not do the same?"

In fact, what do we mean when we speak of the "universal law" or "categorical imperative"?—That all men accept this idea: "Do not do to others what you do not want them to do to you"?—If it is that, then very well. Let us study (as [Francis] Hutchinson and Adam Smith have already done) where these conceptions have come from and how they have developed.

Then let us study to what degree the idea of justice implies that of equality. This is a very important question, as only those who consider *others* as *an equal* can apply the rule: "Do not do to *others* what you do not want them to do to you." A serf-owner and a slave-merchant obviously could not recognise "the universal law" and the "categorical imperative" as regards the serf and negro, as they do not recognise them as their equal. And if our observation is correct, let us see if it is not absurd to want to instil morality while instilling ideas of inequality?

Finally, let us analyse, as [Jean-Marie] Guyau did, "self-sacrifice." And let us see what has contributed most in history to the development of moral sentiments in man—even if only the sentiments expressed in the egalitarian thought concerning his neighbour? Only after having made these three different studies can we deduce which social conditions and which institutions promise the best results for the future. Then we will learn how much religion has contributed to it? How much have economic and political inequalities established by laws? How much have law, punishment, prison? How much have the judge, the jailer, the executioner?

---

48   I take here an objection which is not invented but which I borrow from a recent correspondence with a German doctor. Kant said that the moral law is summarised in this expression: "Always treat others in such a way that your rule of conduct can become a universal law." This, he said, is a "categorical imperative"—a law innate in man.

Let us study all this in detail, separately, and then we can fruitfully discuss morality and moralisation by the law, by the tribunal, and by the commissioner of the police. But the grand words that only serve to hide the superficiality of our half-knowledge—let us set them aside. They were, perhaps, inevitable at one time; as for being useful, it is doubtful that they had ever been that; but now, since we are in a position to approach the study of the most difficult social questions in the same manner as that of the gardener and the botanist studying the most favourable conditions for the growth of a plant—let us do so!

The same applies for economic questions. So, when an economist comes and says to us: "In an absolutely open market the value of goods is measured by the quantity of work socially necessary to produce those goods" (see Ricardo, Proudhon, Marx, and so many others), we do *not* accept this assertion as an article of faith for the reason that it was stated by a particular authority, or because it seems "devilishly socialist" to say that labour is the true measure of market values. "It is possible," we say, "that it is true. But do you not notice that, in making this assertion, you maintain for that very reason that the value and the quantity of necessary labour are *proportional,* just as the velocity of a falling body is proportional to the number of seconds that the fall lasts? You thus affirm a certain *quantitative relationship* between these two quantities; so—did you make measurements, *quantitatively measured* observations, which ALONE could have confirmed your assertion concerning the quantities?"

"To say that in *general* exchange value grows if the amount of necessary labour is greater, you can do that. This is what Adam Smith had initially concluded. But to say that *therefore* these quantities are *proportional,* that one is the *measure* of the *other*—that is making a gross error. As gross as to say, for example, that the amount of rain that will fall tomorrow will be proportional to the amount of millimetres that the barometer has fallen below the average established for this place and this season. The first person to notice that there was a certain correlation between the low level of the barometer and the amount of rain falling; he who first recognised that a stone falling from a great height acquires a greater velocity than another stone which fell only a metre in height—these made scientific discoveries (this is what, indeed, Admin Smith did for value). But the man who would come after them to assert that the quantity of rain fallen *is measured* by the quantity by which the barometer has fallen below its average, or else that the distance traversed by a falling stone is proportional to the duration of its fall and is measured by it—this person would be talking nonsense. It would prove moreover that the *method* of *scientific* research is absolutely foreign to him and that his work *would not be scientific*—even if it is full of words borrowed from the jargon of the sciences."

Note, moreover, that if we used as an excuse our lack of precise data to establish by exact measurements the *value* of such-and-such commodity and the quantity of *labour* necessary to produce it, this would be no excuse at all. We know in the exact sciences thousands of similar cases—of correlations in which we see that two quantities depend on each other and if one of them grows so does the other. Thus, for example, the rate of growth of a plant depends, amongst other things, on the quantity of heat and light received by the plant; or else, the recoil of a canon increases when we increase the quantity of powder burnt in the charge.

But which scientist worthy of the name would have the absurd notion of asserting—without having *measured their relationships in bulk*—that *consequently* the speed of growth of the plant and the quantity of light received by it, or the recoil of the gun and the charge of powder that had just been burned, *are proportional quantities*: that one increases twice, thrice, ten times if the other increased in the same proportion—in other words, that the one is *the measure* of the other, as is said, since Ricardo, for value and labour?

Or else, who thereby, after having made the hypothesis, the assumption, that a relation of this kind exists between these two quantities would dare to present this hypothesis as a *law*? It is only economists or jurists—people who have no notion of what is meant by "law" in the natural sciences—who utter such assertions.

Generally, the relation between two quantities is extremely complex—which is also the case for *value* and *labour*. Strictly the exchange value and the quantity of labour *are not* proportional to one another: the one *never measures* the other. This is what Adam Smith had already noted. After having said that the exchange value of every article was measured by the quantity of labour necessary to produce this article, he had to add (after a study of market values) that if this were so under the regime of primitive exchange, *this was no longer the case under the capitalist system*.[49] Which is

---

49 "In that early and rude state of society which precedes both the accumulation of stock and the appropriation of land, the proportion between the quantities of labour necessary for acquiring different objects seems to be the only circumstance which can afford any rule for exchanging them for one another [...] the whole produce of labour belongs to the labourer; and the quantity of labour commonly employed in acquiring or producing any commodity, is the only circumstance which can regulate the quantity of labour which it ought commonly to purchase, command, or exchange for. [...] As soon as stock has accumulated in the hands of particular persons [...] something must be given for the profits of the undertaker of the work who hazards his stock in this adventure. The value which the workmen add to the materials, therefore, resolves itself in this case into two parts, of which the one pays their wages, the other the profits of their

completely true. The capitalist system *of forced labour* and *exchange for profit* destroys these simple relations and introduces several new factors which alter the relations between labour and exchange value. To ignore these is to no longer practice political economy. It is to confuse ideas and prevent the development of economic *science*.

The same remark which we have just made concerning value applies to almost all the economic assertions that pass today as established truths— especially amongst the socialists who like to be called scientific—and which are represented, with a priceless naivety, as natural laws. Not only are most of these alleged laws incorrect; but we also affirm that those who believe in them will soon discover that themselves if they only managed to understand the necessity of verifying their quantitative affirmations by quantitative research.

Moreover, all political economy appears to us anarchists in a different light than that given to it by economists—those of the bourgeois camp as well as the social-democrats. The scientific, inductive method, being absolutely foreign to them both, they by no means realise what a "law of nature" is despite their marked predilection for this expression. They do not notice that every law of nature has a *conditional* character. They always express themselves thusly: "*If* such conditions occur in nature, the results will be this or that.—*If* a straight line intersects another straight line so as to form equal angles on both sides at the point of intersection, the consequences will be as follows.—*If* only the movements which exist in interstellar space act on two bodies and if there are no other bodies acting upon them at a distance which is not infinite, then the centres of gravity of the two bodies will move towards each other at such a speed (this is the law of gravitation)."

And so on. Always an *if*, always *a condition*.

Consequently, all the so-called laws and theories of political economy are in reality only assertions having the following character: "If we accept that there is always in a given country a considerable number of people who cannot exist one month, or even fifteen days, without accepting the

---

employer upon the whole stock of materials and wages which he advanced. [...] In this state of things, the whole produce of labour does not always belong to the labourer. He must in most cases share it with the owner of the stock which employs him. Neither is the quantity of labour commonly employed in acquiring or producing any commodity, the only circumstance which can regulate the quantity which it ought commonly to purchase, command, or exchange for. An additional quantity, it is evident, must be due for the profits of the stock which advanced the wages and furnished the materials of that labour" (Adam Smith, *The Wealth of Nations*, Volume I [Chicago: University of Chicago, 1976], 53–55). (Editor)

work conditions which the State wishes to impose upon them (in the form of taxes), or which will be offered to them by those whom the State recognises as owners of the land, the factories, the railways, etc.—such and such consequences will follow."

So far, political economy has always been an enumeration of what happens under such conditions—without enumerating and analysing the conditions themselves, without examining *how* these conditions act in each particular case or what maintains these conditions. Even when these conditions were mentioned somewhere, it was to forget them the next moment. But the economists did not confine themselves to this forgetfulness. They represented *the facts which occur as a result of these conditions as fatal, immutable laws.*

As for socialist political economy, it is true that it criticises some of these conclusions [of bourgeois economics], or else it explains certain of them differently; but it commits the same forgetfulness all the time, and in any case it has not yet marked a path that was proper to it. It remains in the old framework, it is stuck in the same ruts. The most it has done (by Marx) is to take the *definitions* of metaphysical and bourgeois political economy and say: "You can see that even accepting your definitions, we can prove that the capitalist exploits the worker!" Which sounds good, perhaps, in a pamphlet but it has nothing to do with science.[50]

In general, we think that the *science* of political economy must be built differently. It must be treated *as a natural science* and it must set itself a different goal. It must occupy, in relation to human societies, a position analogous to that occupied by physiology with regard to plants and animals.[51] It must become *a physiology of society*. It must set itself the aim of studying the ever-increasing *needs* of society and the various *means* used to satisfy them. It must analyse these means to see to what extent they were formerly and are today appropriate to that end; and then—as the ultimate goal of all science is prediction, the application to practical life ([Francis] Bacon had already said this, long since)—it must study the means of better satisfying the totality of modern needs: the means of obtaining with the least expenditure of energy (with *economy*) the best results for humanity in general.

We can, therefore, understand why we draw conclusions so different in certain respects from those arrived at by most economists, both bourgeois

---

50   An initial attempt in this direct was made by F. Vidal in his book *De la répartition des richesses, ou de la Justice distributive* [*On the distribution of wealth, or distributive Justice*], Paris, 1846.

51   Physiology is the scientific study of the normal function in living systems. Its focus is determining how organism, organ systems, organs, cells, and biomolecules carry out the chemical or physical functions that exist in a living system. (Editor)

and social-democratic; why we do not concede the title of "laws" to certain correlations indicated by them; why our *exposition* of socialism differs from theirs; and why we deduce from the study of the tendencies and directions of development which we currently observe in economic life conclusions so different from theirs as to what is desirable and possible; in other words, why we come to libertarian communism, while they arrive at statist capitalism and collectivist wage-labour [*salariat collectiviste*].

It may be that we are wrong and that they are in the right. It is possible. But if we wish to verify who is wrong and who is right, this cannot be done either by means of Byzantine commentaries on what a writer has said or meant or by lecturing us about the trilogy of Hegel nor, above all, by continuing the use of the dialectical method.

This can only be done by starting to study economic relations as we study the facts of the natural sciences. [52]

---

52   The following few extracts from a letter that I received from a renowned biologist, a professor in Belgium, will allow me to better explain what has just been said:

"As I progress in the reading of *Fields, Factories, and Workshops*" (*Fields, Factories, and Workshops* appeared in French, published by Stock, in 1910, the professor wrote to me,) "I become more and more convinced that henceforward the study of economic and social questions is only accessible to those who have studied the natural sciences and *who are penetrated by the spirit of these sciences*. Those who have received classical education exclusively are no longer able to understand the present movement of ideas and are equally incapable of studying a host of specific questions.

".... The idea of integration of labour and of *the division of labour in time* [the idea that it would be useful for society that everyone could work in agriculture, industry, and intellectual tasks in order to vary his work and to fully develop his individuality—Kropotkin's note], is destined to become one of the cornerstones of economic science. There is a host of biological facts which concur with the idea I have just highlighted and which show that there is a law of nature [in other words, that in nature an economy of forces is often obtained by this means—Kropotkin's note]. If we examine the vital functions of any being during the different periods of its existence, or even during the different seasons, and in some cases during different times of the day, we find the application of the division of labour in time, which is inseparably connected with division of labour between the organs (the law of Adam Smith).

"Men of science who do not know the natural sciences are incapable of understanding the true scope of a LAW of nature; they are blinded

By always using the same method, Anarchy also arrives at conclusions which are specifically its own with regards to the political forms of society, and especially the State. The anarchist does not let himself be cowed by metaphysical assertions such as: "The State is the affirmation of the idea of supreme Justice in Society"; or else "the State is the instrument and the bearer of Progress," or even "Without the State, no Society." True to his method, the anarchist started to study the State with exactly the same dispositions of mind as a naturalist who proposes to study the societies of ants or bees, or those of birds which nest on the shores of lakes in the regions of the North. We have seen, from the short summary which has just been given in chapters X to XII, to which conclusions we have come to in light of these studies with regard to the political forms of the past and their probable and desirable evolution in the future.

Let us just add that for *our* European civilisation (the civilisation of the last fifteen centuries, to which we belong) the State is a form of social life which developed only in the sixteenth century—and this under the influence of a series of causes which will be found mentioned later in the study *The State: Its Historic Role*. Before this period, from the fall of the Roman Empire, the State—in its Roman form—did not exist. If it exists despite everything in school history books, it is a product of the imagination of historians who wanted to trace the genealogical tree of royalty in France to the chiefs of the Merovingian bands, in Russia to Rurik, etc. In actual history, the modern State was reconstructed only upon the ruins of the Medieval cities.

In addition, the State, as a political and military power, along with modern governmental Justice, the Church, and Capitalism appear in our eyes as institutions which are impossible to separate from each other. In

---

by the word *law,* and they imagine that a law, such as that of Adam Smith, has a fatal force from which it is impossible to escape. When they are shown the *other side* of this law, the deplorable results from the point of view of the development and happiness of the human individual, they respond: *this is an inexorable law,* and sometimes this response is given in a sharp tone, which indicates the feeling of a kind of infallibility. The naturalist knows that science can annul the harmful effects of a *law*: that very often the man who wishes to go against nature achieves success.

"Gravity causes objects to *fall*: this same gravity makes a balloon *rise*. To US it seems so simple; the economists of the classical school seem to have great trouble understanding the impact of a similar observation.

"The law of *division of labour in time* will become the corrective of the law of Adam Smith, and permit the integration of individual work."

history these four institutions developed while supporting and reinforcing each other.

They are bound together—not as mere coincidences. They are linked together by the bonds of cause and effect.

The State is, in short, a mutual insurance company formed by the landlord, the military, the judge, and the priest[53] in order to assure each of them authority over the people and the exploitation of [their] poverty.

Such was the origin of the State; such was its history, such is still its essence today.

To therefore imagine the abolition of capitalism while keeping the State and with the aid of the State—which was created in order to aid the development of capitalism and always grows, and is reinforced, hand in hand with it—this is as false, in our opinion, as to want to achieve the emancipation of the workers by means of the Church or by way of Caesarism. Certainly, there were many dreamers in the thirties, forties and even fifties of the nineteenth century who dreamt of a socialist caesarism: the tradition has held on since Babeuf until the present. But to feed these same illusions when we have entered the twentieth century is really too naïve.

A new form of political organisation must necessarily correspond to a new form of economic organisation; and require a new form of political structure; and, whether the change is made abruptly by a revolution or slowly by way of a gradual evolution, the two changes, political and economic, must go together, hand in hand. Each step towards economic emancipation, each real victory over Capital, will also be a victory over Authority: a step towards political liberation: it will be liberation from the yoke of the State by the free agreement—*territorial, professional* and *functional*—of all the interested parties.[54]

---

53   The 1912 British edition adds: "and later on the capitalist." (Editor)

54   The 1912 British edition adds: "And each step made towards taking from the State any one of its powers and attributes will be helping the masses to win a victory over Capitalism." (Editor)

XV

THE MEANS OF ACTION

IT IS OBVIOUS THAT IF ANARCHY THUS PARTS EQUALLY FROM ACADEMIC science as well as from its social-democratic colleagues in its methods of investigation and in its fundamental principles, it must also part from these by its means of action.

With our judgements on Right, Law and the State, we cannot see a guarantee of progress and even less a path towards the social revolution in an ever greater submission of the individual to the State. To say, as is often said by superficial critics of [current] society, that modern capitalism has its origin in "the anarchy of production,"[55] in "the doctrine of non-intervention of the State," which, so they claim, has practiced *laissez faire* and *laissez passer* and let it pass, [or] repeat it, we cannot since we know that it is not true. We are

---

55 A reference to Marxists who denounced capitalism for its lack of planning which leads gluts and scarcity in specific markets before leading to a general economic crisis. This is because each company produces for itself, not knowing whether their product will actually sell the expected amount at the expected price. Thus, to quote Engels, "the contradiction between socialised production and capitalistic appropriation now presents itself as *an antagonism between the organisation of production in the individual workshop and the anarchy of production in society generally*" (*Marx-Engels Collected Works*, Volume 24 [London: Lawrence & Wishat, 1989] 24: 313). (Editor)

fully aware that governments, while giving full liberty to the capitalists to enrich themselves by the labour of workers reduced to misery, have never, nowhere during the course of the nineteenth century given to workers the liberty to "do as they wished."[56] *Never, nowhere, has the formula "laissez faire, laissez passer" been applied*—why say the contrary?

In France, even under the terrible "revolutionary"—that is to say Jacobin—Convention, proclaimed death for strikes, for coalitions, and the formation of a State within the State! Must we talk, after that, of the Empire, the restored royalty, or even of the bourgeois republic?

In England, in 1813, they still hanged for striking and in 1834 workers were transported to Australia for having dared to form [a branch of] the Union of Trades of Robert Owen.[57] In the sixties strikers were still sent to hard labour under the well-known pretext of defending liberty of labour. And even now, in 1903, in England a trade union had to pay a Company 1,275,000 francs in damages from *dissuading* workers from going into the factory during a strike (for *picketing*). What about France, where permission to form a trade union was only granted in 1884, after the anarchist agitation in Lyon and that of the miners in Montceau-les-Mines! What about Belgium, Switzerland (remember the Airolo massacre![58]), and above all Germany and Russia?[59]

Furthermore, we need to remember how every State reduces the worker of the fields and towns to misery by means of *taxes* and by the *monopolies* it creates, in order to deliver him bound hand and foot to the manufacturer! Is it necessary to recount how, in England, they once curbed, and they further curb, the communal possession of the land by allowing the local lord

---

56   The French terms *laissez faire* ("let it be") and *laissez passer* ("let it go") are key parts of the doctrine of classical liberalism and refer to the doctrine that opposes governmental regulation of, or interference in, the economy beyond the minimum necessary for it to operate according to its own economic laws. As it includes defence of private property and the power that goes with it, this "minimum" can mean—as Kropotkin notes—substantial State power and action directed against working class rebels. (Editor)

57   A reference to the Tolpuddle Martyrs who were the six labourers in Dorset who attempted to affiliate with the Grand National and were convicted of swearing unlawful oaths and sentenced to transportation to Australia for seven years. (Editor)

58   Kropotkin is referring to the killing of four workers, and the wounding of thirteen, in 1875 when the Swiss Army crushed a strike by workers building the Gotthard rail tunnel. It should also be noted that around two hundred workers were killed building the tunnel (significantly, the exact number is not known). (Editor)

59   The British 1912 edition adds: "and the United States, where State intervention in favour of capitalist misrule was still worse?" (Editor)

(formally he was nothing but a judge: never a *landowner*) to enclose the lands of the community and to seize it for themselves for that very reason? Or else recount how, *at this very moment*, the land *is being stripped* from the Russian peasant communes by the government of Nicholas II?

Finally, is it necessary to speak of how all States today, without exception, establish immense monopolies of all kinds, not to mention those monopolies created in conquered lands such as Egypt, Tonkin, or the Transvaal? What use is there in speaking of *primitive accumulation*, as Marx did, as if it were a thing of the past when every year new monopolies are established by every parliament in the sphere of railways, trams, gas, water pipes, electricity, schools, etc., etc., without end!

In short, never, in any State, neither for one year nor even for an hour, has the system of *laissez-faire* existed. The State has always been at all times, and still is, the support, the buttress and *also the creator*, direct and indirect, of capital. Therefore, if it is permissible for bourgeois economists to assert that the system of "non-intervention" exists—since they seek to prove that the misery of the masses is a law of nature—how can socialists speak this language to the workers! *The freedom to resist exploitation, thus far, has never existed anywhere.* It was necessary, everywhere, to conquer it step by step, by countless struggles and sacrifices. "Non-intervention" and even more than "non-intervention"—aid, support, protection—has always existed only for the exploiters.

And *it could not be otherwise.*[60]

Socialism, we have said, in whatever form it may arise during the events leading up to communism will therefore have to find its own form of political relations. *It cannot* utilise the old political forms, [just] as it cannot utilise religious hierarchy and its teachings, or imperial or dictatorial forms and their theories. In one way or another it will have to become *more popular*, closer to the assembly [*forum*], than representative government. It must be less dependent on *representation* and become more *self-government*,[61] more *government of each by themselves*. This is what the proletariat of Paris sought to do in 1871; it is what the Sections of the Paris Commune and many smaller towns attempted to do in 1793–1794.

---

60 The British 1912 edition added: "To do so was one of the functions—the chief mission—of the State." The following paragraph was also included: "The State was established for the precise purpose of imposing the rule of the landowners, the employers of industry, the warrior class, and the clergy upon the peasants on the land and the artisans in the city. And the rich perfectly well know that if the machinery of the State ceased to protect them, their power over the labouring classes would be gone immediately." (Editor)

61 Self-government is in English in the original French text. (Editor)

When we observe the actual political life of France and England, as well as in the United States, we see germinating there a very distinct tendency to establish independent, but linked together, urban and rural municipalities for thousands and thousands of diverse needs by federative treaties, each concluded for a particular, specific, purpose. And these municipalities tend more and more to become producers of the commodities required to satisfy the needs of all their inhabitants. To communal trams are added communal water, often brought from afar by several federated towns, gas, light, power for factories, even communal coal mines, communal dairies for pure milk, the communal herd of goats for those suffering from tuberculosis (at Torquay), communal hot water mains, the communal kitchen garden, etc., etc.[62]

Of course, it is not the Emperor of Germany nor the Jacobins [recently] installed in power who govern Switzerland who work towards that goal: these, eyes turned towards the past, are seeking instead to centralise everything in the hands of the State and to destroy any trace of territorial or functional independence.[63]

It is the *progressive* part of European and American societies that must be considered. And in these we find a marked tendency to organise *outside the State* and to replace it more and more by appropriating, firstly, the functions which the State continues, it is true, to regard as its own but which it never knew how to satisfy properly.

The mission of the Church was to keep the people in an intellectual

---

62   Elected town councils in England and Wales were created by the 1835 Municipal Corporations Act and in Scotland by the 1833 Burgh Reform Act. In the last decades of the nineteenth century, these local authorities, acting on their own initiative, pioneered welfare provision (such as building houses, parks, hospitals, museums, libraries, swimming pools, playing fields, etc.) as well as providing public transport, energy, and other services. Kropotkin discussed this in an article entitled "Municipal Socialism" in the December 1902 issue of *Freedom* (and reprinted in *Act For Yourselves: Articles from FREEDOM 1886–1907* [London: Freedom Press, 1988]). The later part of the twentieth century saw the gradual but relentless encroachment of central government on the autonomy of local government. This centralisation of power accelerated under the neo-liberal regime of Thatcher who centralised power to stop local councils defending society from her pro-capitalist "reforms" (premised on the market being best placed to provide—for a profit to the shareholders, of course!—services for the people—and if people could not afford it, then it just showed they did not need it). (Editor)

63   The imperialists do the same in England. In 1902 they abolished *school boards*, or agencies elected by universal suffrage without distinction of sex which existed expressly to organise primary schools in each locality. Introduced around 1870, these agencies had rendered immense services to secular education.

slavery. The mission of the State was to keep it, half starved, in economic slavery. We are now trying to shake off both yokes.

Knowing this, we cannot consider every increasing submission to the State as a guarantee of progress. Institutions do not change their character at the whim of theorists. Hence we seek progress in the liberation, as complete as possible, of the individual: in the broadest possible development of the initiative of the individual and of the group and, at the same time, in the limitation of the powers of the State—not in their extension.

We represent the way forward as a series of steps—firstly, towards the abolition of the governmental authority which has imposed itself upon society, especially in the sixteenth century,[64] and has only continued to expend its powers since; and then—towards the widest possible development of the element of *agreement*, of *temporary contract*, at the same time as the independence of all groupings which will be created for a given goal and which, by their federations, will end by encompassing all society. By this we represent the structure of society as something which is never definitely constituted but which is always filled with life and, consequently, always changing form according to the needs of each moment.

This way of conceiving progress, as well as our conception of what is desirable for the future (everything that will contribute to increasing the amount of happiness of all) necessarily leads us to develop for the struggle our own tactics, which consist in developing the greatest possible amount of *individual initiative* in each group and in each individual—unity in action being obtained by unity of purpose and by the force of persuasion which every idea possesses when it has been freely expressed, seriously discussed and found just.

This perspective puts its stamp on all the tactics of the anarchists and on the inner life of each of their groups.

We affirm, then, that to work for the advent of a State-Capitalism, centralised in the hands of a government which has therefore become omnipotent, is to work *against* the already pronounced current of progress which seeks the new forms of organisation of society outside of the State.

We see in the incapacity of the statist socialist to understand the true historical problem of socialism a gross error of judgement—a survival of absolutist and religious prejudices, and we fight against it. To tell the workers that they will be able to introduce the socialist system *while retaining the machine of the State* and only changing the men in power; to prevent,

---

64   In *The State: Its Historic Role* (Parts VI and VII) Kropotkin argues that it was during the sixteenth century that the nascent State successfully waged war on the communes, guilds, and federations of the Middle Ages. (Editor)

instead of aiding, the mind of the workers progressing towards *the search for new forms of life* that would be *their* own—that is in our eyes a historic mistake which borders on the criminal.

Finally, since we are a revolutionary party, we above all seek the genesis and the development of previous revolutions and try to rid history of the false statist interpretations which have always been given to it. In the histories of the different revolutions, written to this day, we do not yet see *the people*, we do not learn anything about *the genesis of the revolution*. The phrases to which they are wont to repeat in the introduction [of such a book] on the desperate state of the people on the eve of its uprising do not even tell us how, in the midst of this despair, the hope of a possible improvement, of new times, emerged? Where did the spirit of revolt come from? That is why, after reading these histories, we refer to the primary sources in order to find some information on the progress of the wakening within the people as well as the part of the people in the revolutions.

Thus, for example, we understand the Great French Revolution quite differently from how Louis Blanc saw it, who represented it mainly as a great political movement carried out by the Jacobin Club. We see in it, above all, a great *popular* movement, and we especially note the role of the rural peasant movement ("every village had its Robespierre," as was rightly said by the Abbot Grégoire, the spokesman of the Committee on the Jacquerie, to the historian Schlosser[65]), a movement whose aim was the abolition of the survivals of feudal servitude and the regaining by the peasants of the lands taken by all kinds of vultures from the village communes—in which, it must be noted in passing, the peasants succeeded, especially in the East of France.

A revolutionary situation having been created by the uprisings of the peasants which continued for four years, there also developed at the same time, especially in the towns, a tendency towards communist equality;[66] and,

---

65   F.C. Schlosser, *History of the Eighteenth Century and of the Nineteenth Century Till the Overthrow of the French Empire* (London: Chapman and Hall, 1845) 6: 428; "The report of the Feudal Committee, made by Abbe Grégoire in February 1790, stated, in fact, that the peasant insurrection was still going on and that it had gained in strength since the month of January. It was spreading from the East to the West" (Peter Kropotkin, *The Great French Revolution*, 200). (Editor)

66   The 1912 British edition added: "We study the movement towards Communism which began to develop amongst the poorest part of the population in 1793–1794, and the admirable forms of voluntary popular organisation for a variety of functions, economic and political, that they worked out in the 'Sections' of the great cities and some of the small municipalities." (Editor)

in addition, we see the growing power of the bourgeoisie which shrewdly worked to establish its authority in the place of the authority of the royalty and nobility which it demolished systematically. To this end the bourgeois struggled bitterly, cruelly if need be, in order to establish a powerful, centralised State, which absorbed everything and secured their property (in part, on the assets they had just acquired during the Revolution) along with their full freedom to exploit the poor and speculate on the national wealth, without any legal restriction.

Indeed, the bourgeoisie obtained this authority, this right of exploitation, this *one-sided laissez-faire*; and it created its political form to maintain it—representative government in the centralised State.

In this statist centralisation, created by the Jacobins, Napoleon I found the ground already prepared for the Empire.

Similarly, fifty years later, Napoleon III found in the dreams of a centralised democratic republic which developed in France after [the revolution of] 1848 the ready-made elements for the Second Empire. And France still suffers from this centralised force, which for seventy years killed all local life, every endeavour, whether local, whether outside the capabilities of the State (professional, union, private association, commune, etc. endeavours). The first attempt to break this State yoke—an attempt which opened up a new historical era—was only made in 1871 by the Parisian proletariat.

We go even further. We affirm that as long as the statist socialists do not abandon their dream of socialising the instruments of labour in the hands of a centralised State, the inevitable result of their attempts at State Capitalism and the socialist State will be the failure of their dreams and military dictatorship.

Without entering here into the analysis of the various revolutionary movements, which confirm our perspective, it is sufficient to say that we understand the future social revolution not as a Jacobin dictatorship, nor as a transformation of social institutions accomplished by a Convention, a parliament, or a dictator. Never has a revolution been made in this way; and if the actual workers' uprising took this form, it would be doomed to perish without having a lasting result.

On the contrary, we understand the revolution as a widely spread popular movement and during which, in every town and village in the region seized by the insurrectionary spirit, the popular masses set themselves to the work of reconstructing society. The people—the peasants and the town workers—must *themselves begin the constructive work, building, on more or less broadly communist principles, without waiting for blueprints and orders from above.* Above all, they must arrange to feed and house everyone and them to promptly produce what is needed to feed, house, and clothe everyone.[67]

As for government, whether it be established by force or by election, whether it be the "dictatorship of the proletariat" as was said in the [eighteen-] forties in France and as is still said in Germany, or else whether it be a "provisional government," acclaimed or elected, or a "convention"—we do not place any hope in this government. We say in advance that it cannot do anything.

Not because that is our personal preference but because all history is there to show us that whenever men are thrown into a government by the revolutionary upsurge they have never lived up to their position. They cannot. Because isolated men [in the State[68]]—be they ever-so intelligent and ever-so devoted—are sure to fail in the task of reconstructing society on new principles. This requires the *collective spirit of the masses working on concrete things*: the ploughed field, the inhabited house, the running factory, the railway, the carriages of such-and-such line, the steamboat.[69]

Isolated men can discover the legal expression, the phrase, for a destruction of the old social forms when this destruction is in the process of being

---

67   The 1912 British edition adds this paragraph: "They may not be—they are sure not to be—the *majority* of the nation. But if they are a respectably numerous minority of cities and villages scattered over the country, starting life on their own new Socialist lines, they will be able to win the right, to pursue their own course. In all probability they will draw towards them a notable portion of the land, as was the case in France in 1793–1794." (Editor)

68   A key aspect of Kropotkin's critique of revolutionaries seizing State power was that it isolated them from the masses and he pointed to the Paris Commune as evidence of this process. See, for example, "Revolutionary Government" and "The Paris Commune" (both in *Words of a Rebel* and *Direct Struggle Against Capital*. (Editor)

69   In the great strike which broke out in Siberia on the immense Trans-Siberian line immediately after the war with Japan, we have a striking example of what the collective spirit of the masses, set in motion by events, can achieve if it works on the very things needing reform. It is known that all the working staff on this immense line, from the Ural mountains to Harbin, over a distance of more than 6,500 kilometres, went on strike in 1905. The strikers informed the commander-in-chief of the army, old Lenevitch, telling him that they would do *all* they could to bring home the regiments quickly, if the general wished to come to an agreement with the Strike Committee on the number of men, horses, baggage, that would be moving. General Linevitch agreed. And the result was that during the ten weeks that the strike lasted, the transportation was done with more order, with fewer accidents, and with much more speed than it had been done before. It was a true popular movement—workers and soldiers, all discipline disappearing, collaborating in this immense movement of hundreds of thousands of men.

accomplished. At the most, they can widen this destructive work a little and extend over a whole territory what is being done in only a part of the country. But to impose the destruction by a law, that is absolutely impossible—as it was proven, amongst other things, by all the history of the revolution of 1789–1794.[70]

As for the *new* forms of life which will begin to germinate in a revolution on the ruins of the previous forms—no government will ever be able to find *their* expression *as long as these forms do not establish themselves in the work of reconstruction by the masses being done at a thousand points simultaneously.* Who had guessed, who could have guessed, before 1789, the part played by the municipalities, the commune of Paris and its section in the revolutionary events of 1789–1794. We cannot legislate the future. All that can be done is foresee the essential tendencies and clear the way for them. That is what we are trying to do.

It is evident that by understanding the problem of the social revolution in this way, Anarchy cannot let itself be seduced by a programme that makes its aim: "The conquest of power in the current State."

We know that this conquest is not possible by peaceful means. The bourgeoisie will not give up its power without a struggle. It will not let itself be dispossessed without resisting. But as the socialists become a party of government and share power with the bourgeoisie, their socialism will necessarily fade: this is what has already happened. Otherwise the bourgeoisie, who are much more powerful numerically and intellectually than is suggested in the socialist press, would not recognise their right to share its power.

In addition, we also know that if an insurrection succeeded in giving France, or England, or Germany a provisional socialist government, it, without the spontaneous constructive activity of the people, would be absolutely powerless and would soon become a hindrance to the Revolution. It would be the stepping-stone for a dictator, representing the reaction.

In studying the preparatory periods of revolutions, we come to the conclusion that no revolution has had its origin in the resistance or attack of a parliament, or any other representative assembly. *All revolutions began within the people.* And no revolution has ever appeared, armed from head to foot like Minerva rising from the head of Jupiter.[71] All had, in addition to their

---

70   The 1912 British edition adds: "Many thousands of the *laws* passed by the revolutionary Convention had not even been put into force when reaction came and flung those laws into the waste paper basket." (Editor)

71   Minerva was the Roman goddess of wisdom and sponsor of arts, trade, and strategy. After impregnating the Titaness Metis, Jupiter (King and Father of the gods) recalled a

period of incubation, their period of evolution during which the popular masses, after having formulated very modest demands at the beginning, were penetrated little by little, and even rather slowly, by an increasingly revolutionary spirit. They grew bolder, they grew more daring, they gained *confidence* and, emerging from their lethargy of despair, gradually widened their programme. It took time for their "humble remonstrances" at the beginning to become revolutionary demands.

In fact, it took France four years, from 1789 to 1793, to just create a republican minority powerful enough to impose itself.

As to the period of incubation, this is how we understand it: First, isolated individuals, profoundly disgusted by what they saw around them, rebelled separately. Many of them perished, without any visible result; but the indifference of society was shaken by these lost sentinels.

The most satisfied and narrow-minded were forced to ask: "For what cause do these youths, honest and full of strength, give their lives?" It was no longer possible to remain indifferent; it was necessary to declare for or against. The mind worked.

Little by little, small groups of men were also penetrated by the same spirit of revolt. They also rebelled, sometimes with hope of a partial success—that of winning, for example, a strike and obtaining bread for their children or of getting rid of some hated functionary—but also very often without any hope of success: rebelled simply because it was impossible for them to wait any longer. Not one, two, or ten such revolts, but hundreds of insurrections preceded each Revolution.[72] There is a limit to all patience. We see it so well in the United States at this moment.

The *pacific* abolition of serfdom in Russia is sometimes cited; but it is forgotten, or it is unknown, that a long series of peasant insurrections preceded and brought about this emancipation. These disturbances began in the fifties—perhaps as an echo of 1848, or the disturbances of 1846 in

---

prophecy that his own child would overthrow him. Fearing that their child would grow stronger than he and rule the Heavens in his place, Jupiter swallowed Metis whole. The Titaness forged weapons and armour for her child while within the father-god. The constant pounding and ringing gave him a headache and to relieve the pain, Vulcan used a hammer to split Jupiter's head from which the adult Minerva emerged bearing her mother's weapons and armour. (Editor)

72   The British 1912 edition adds: "*This again was unavoidable.* Without such insurrections, no revolution has ever broken out. Without the menace contained in such revolts, no serious concession has ever been wrung by the people from the governing classes. Without such risings, the social mind was never able to get rid of its deep-rooted prejudices, nor to embolden itself sufficiently to conceive *hope.* And *hope*—the hope of an improvement—was always the mainspring of revolutions." (Editor)

Galicia[73]—and every year they spread further in Russia, while becoming increasingly serious and taking a bitter aspect hitherto unknown. This lasted until 1857, when Alexander II at last issued his letter to the nobility of the Lithuanian provinces containing a promise of liberation to the serfs. The words of Herzen: "Better to give freedom from above than wait for it to come from below"—words repeated by Alexander II before the slaver nobility of Moscow in 1856—were no empty threat: they reflected the reality [of the situation].

It was the same, even more so, at the approach of every revolution. It may also be said, as a general rule, that the character of each *revolution* was determined by the character and purpose of the insurrections that preceded it. More than that. It can be established as a historical fact that no serious political revolution could be accomplished if—the revolution already begun—it did not continue in a great number of local *insurrections* and if the unrest did not take on the character of *insurrections*, instead of taking that of *individual* [acts of] revenge, as was the case in Russia during the years 1906 and 1907.

Consequently, to expect that a *social* revolution will come without being preceded by insurrections that determine the spirit of the coming revolution is to cherish an absurd, childish hope. Seeking to prevent these insurrections by saying that a general uprising is being prepared is already criminal. But to seek to persuade workers that they will obtain all the benefits of a social revolution by limiting themselves to electoral agitation and spew all their bile upon acts of partial insurrection when they occur in historically revolutionary nations is to be yourself an obstacle to the spirit of revolution and all progress—an obstacle just as baneful as the Christian church has always been.[74]

---

73   This was a two-month uprising in Central-Eastern Europe of Galician peasants from February to March 1846 against serfdom, directed against manorial property and oppression (for example, the manorial prisons). While brutally put down by Austrian troops, serfdom, with *corvée* labour, was abolished in 1848. (Editor)

74   A reference to Marxists who opposed all partial revolts (sometimes including strikes) in favour of waiting to secure a majority in the Parliament. This perspective can be traced back to Marx and Engels with the former, for example, opposing in 1870 the kind of uprisings which produced the Paris Commune. (Editor)

XVI

CONCLUSION

WITHOUT GOING INTO FURTHER DEVELOPMENTS OF THE PRINCIPLES OF Anarchy and the anarchist programme of action—what has been said will probably suffice to indicate the place of Anarchy amidst the current knowledge of humanity.

Anarchy represents an attempt to apply the generalisations obtained by the inductive method of the natural sciences to the evaluation of human institutions. It is also an attempt to predict, on the basis of that evaluation, the march of humanity towards liberty, equality, and fraternity, in order to obtain the greatest possible sum of happiness for each of the units in human societies.

Anarchy is the inevitable result of the intellectual movement in the natural sciences which began towards the end of the eighteenth century, was retarded by the triumphant reaction in Europe after the defeat of the French Revolution, and recommenced anew in the full blossoming of its forces since the end of the [eighteen-]fifties. The roots of Anarchy are in the naturalist philosophy of the eighteenth century. But it could not acquire its full foundations until the revival of science which took place at the beginning of the second half of the nineteenth century and which gave new life to the study of institutions and human societies on a naturalist basis.

The purported "scientific laws" with which the German metaphysicians of the 1820s and 1830s were content find no place in the anarchist conception. It recognises no other method of research than the scientific method. And it applies this method to all the sciences generally known under the name of the humanitarian [or social] sciences.

Taking advantage of this method, as well as of recent research made under the impetus of this method, Anarchy attempts to construct all the sciences concerning man, and revise current notions about law, justice, etc. on the data already obtained by ethnological research and extending them further. Building on the work of its predecessors in the eighteenth century, Anarchy has sided with the individual against the State; with society against the authority which, by virtue of historical conditions, dominates it. Benefiting from the historical materials accumulated by modern science, Anarchy has demonstrated that State authority, whose oppression grows more and more in our days, is in reality only a harmful and unnecessary superstructure which, for us Europeans, only dates from the fifteenth and sixteenth centuries: a superstructure built in the interests of capitalism and which was already, in antiquity, the cause of the fall of Rome and Greece, as well as all the other centres of civilisation in the East and in Egypt.

The authority which was formed in the course of history to unite in a common interest lord, judge, soldier, and priest, and which during the whole course of history was an obstacle to the attempts of man to create for himself a life somewhat secure and free—this authority cannot become a weapon of liberation, no more than caesarism, imperialism or the Church can become instruments of social revolution.

In political economy, Anarchy has come to the conclusion that the actual evil lies not in that the capitalist appropriates the "surplus value" or net profit but in the fact that this net profit or surplus value is possible. The "surplus-value" exists only because millions of men do not have enough to eat unless they sell their strength and intellect at a price that will make the net profit or surplus value possible. This is why we consider that in political economy it is necessary above all to study the subject of consumption and that in a Revolution the first duty will be to remodel consumption, so that shelter, food, and clothing are guaranteed for all. Our forefathers of 1793–1794 understood this well.

As for "production," it should be organised so that the primary needs of all society should be satisfied from the outset and as quickly as possible. This is also why Anarchy cannot see in the coming revolution a mere substitution of "labour notes" for gold coins or a replacement of the current capitalists by the State [as sole] capitalist. It sees this as a first step towards *libertarian Communism*, [communism] without the State.

Is Anarchy right in its conclusions? The answer will be given to us by, on the one hand, a scientific criticism of its foundations and, on the other, practical life. But there is one point on which without doubt Anarchy is absolutely in the right. It is when it considers the study of social institutions as a matter of the natural sciences; when it parts forever with metaphysics; and when it takes for its method of reasoning the method that has served to establish all modern science and the materialist philosophy of our time. It is this [method] that will make the errors into which anarchists may have fallen in their conclusions all the more easily recognised. But to verify our conclusions is only possible by the scientific, inductive-deductive, method—the method on which every science is built and that developed every scientific conception of the universe.

In the following studies, on anarchist-communism and the historical development of the State and its current form, the reader will be able to see what we base our negative attitude towards the State on, and what are the ideas that make us conceive of the possibility of a society which, whilst accepting communism as its basis for economic organisation, at the same time would renounce the organisation of hierarchical centralisation which is termed "State."[75]

---

75 In addition to the already mentioned works on the history of the development of Anarchy, consult the excellent *Bibliographie de l'Anarchie*, by Mr. Nettlau, which is a part of *Bibliothèque des Temps nouveaux*, published by Elisée Reclus in 1897, Brussels and Paris (P.-V. Stock). The reader will find in there, in addition to lists of works, a *well-thought out* bibliography of various anarchist works and publications.

II

COMMUNISM AND ANARCHY

I

ANARCHIST COMMUNISM

When, at two congresses of the International [Workers' Association], one held in Florence in 1876 by the Italian Federation and the other in Chaux-de-Fonds in 1880 by the Jura Federation, the Italian and Jura anarchists decided to declare themselves "anarchist-communists," this decision caused a considerable sensation in the socialist world. Some saw in this declaration of principles a serious step forward. Others considered it absurd, saying that it contained an obvious contradiction.

It is true, as my friend James Guillaume points out to me, that the term anarchist or non-authoritarian communism, had already been used in 1870 in the Locle newspaper *Progrès* [*Progress*] in a letter from [Eugène] Varlin, quoted with approval by James Guillaume.[1] In fact, several anarchists had already, towards the end of 1869, agreed to conduct propaganda for this idea and in 1876 a distribution of the products of labour based on this idea of anti-authoritarian communism was recognised as feasible and recommended in a brochure by James Guillaume, *Idée sur l'organisation sociale*

---

1   "The principles that we must strive to uphold are those of the almost unanimous delegates of the International at the Congress of Basel [in 1869], that is to say collectivism or non-authoritarian communism" (James Guillaume, *L'internationale: documents et souvenirs* [Paris: Société nouvelle de librairie et d'édition,1905] I: 258). (Editor)

[*Ideas on Social Organisation*] (see above, [Part I, Chapter XII]). But, for the reasons already mentioned above, the idea did not spread as much as expected, and within the reformers and revolutionaries who remained under the influence of the Jacobin idea, the dominant conception of communism was of authoritarian communism as had been conceived by Cabet in his *Voyage to Icaria*—a conception which logically ended up in State communism. The State, represented by one or more parliaments, would undertake, it was said, to organise production. Then, it would deliver, by its administrative organs, either to the industrial groups or to the Municipalities, what was allocated to them to live, produce and enjoy themselves.

For production, therefore, something similar to what exists today in the State railway network and in the postal service was dreamt of. What is already happening for the transport of freight and passengers would be done, it was said, for the production of all wealth and for all services of general interest. They would start by socialising, in addition to the railway, the mines, then the big factories, and we would extend this system little by little to all the vast network of factories, flour mills, bakeries, supply shops and so on. There would be "squads" of ploughmen farming the land, miners working the mines, weavers operating the looms, bakers baking bread, etc. on behalf of the State—just as there are today legions of railway or postal employees. They even liked to stress, in the literature of the [eighteen-]forties, this word "squads"—the Germans made of it "armies"[2]—to emphasise the disciplined nature of the workers employed in such industry and commanded by a hierarchy of "work managers."

And as for consumption—they were outlining roughly as it is today in the barracks. No isolated households: the common meal would be introduced to economise on cooking costs, and phalansteries or hotel-houses to save on construction costs. It is true that the soldier is badly fed today and brutalised by his chiefs; but nothing prevents, it was said, to feed well the citizens lodged [*encasernés*] in the "common houses" or in the "communist

---

2   An obvious reference to point eight of the *Communist Manifesto*'s ten point list of measures "to centralise all instruments of production into the hands of the State": "Equal liability of all to work. Establishment of industrial armies, especially for agriculture." Other measures included: "Centralisation of credit in the hands of the State, by means of a national bank with State capital and an exclusive monopoly"; "Centralisation of the means of communication and transport in the hands of the State"; and "Extension of factories and instruments of production owned by the State" (*Marx-Engels Collected Works* [London: Lawrence & Wishat, 1976] 6: 504–505). It should also be mentioned that the Bolsheviks introduced the "militarisation of labour" during the Russian Civil War, as defended by (for example) Trotsky in *Terrorism and Communism: a reply to Karl Kautsky* (Ann Arbor: University of Michigan Press, 1961). (Editor)

cities." And citizens having freely elected their leaders, their treasurers, their officers, nothing will prevent them considering these leaders—commanders today and soldiers tomorrow—as *servants* of the Republic. "The Servant State" was indeed Louis Blanc's favourite phrase—and also Proudhon's *bête noire* who, more than once, cheered up the readers of *Voice of the People* with his sarcastic remarks towards this new democratic label of the State.[3]

The communism of the forties was full of these statist ideas, that Proudhon fought to the death before and after 1848; and the criticism he subjected it to, in 1846, in [*System of*] *Economic Contradictions* (second volume: "Community"), later in the *Voice of the People*, and at every opportunity in his subsequent writings, must have greatly contributed, without doubt, to discrediting this type of communism in France.[4] Indeed, we know that most of the French who took part in the foundation of the International and were active at its beginning were mutualists; they absolutely rejected communism. But State communism was taken up by German socialists stressing the discipline side; it was preached by them as a "scientific" discovery, belonging to them, and at the time we are talking about when communism was spoken of we almost always heard about State communism as it was preached by the German successors of the French communists of 1848.

So, when two anarchist federations of the International declared themselves "anarchist-communists," this declaration—especially when it was made by the Jura Federation, [which was] better known in France—was considered by a great number of our friends as a serious step forward. "Anarchist communism"—or "libertarian communism," as it was named originally in France[5]—gained many supporters and, circumstances helping,

---

3   *Œuvres complètes: Mélanges, Articles de journaux*, third volume, Paris 1871. Many admirable pages can be found there on the State and Anarchy which it would be very useful to reproduce for a wide audience.

4   A few of the articles from Proudhon's polemic with Louis Blanc and Pierre Leroux in *Voice of the People* are contained in *Property is Theft!*, "Resistance to the Revolution," "Letter to Pierre Leroux," and "In Connection with Louis Blanc." Another has been published elsewhere: "Regarding Louis Blanc: The Present Utility and Future Possibility of the State," *Anarcho-Syndicalist Review* 66. (Editor)

5   A reference to the coining of the term "libertarian" (*libertaire*) by early French communist-anarchist Joseph Déjacque (1821–1864) in 1857 in a letter to Proudhon challenging his sexism and his support for individual ownership of the products of labour. The following year he started the newspaper *La Libertaire, Journal du Mouvement Social* in New York which lasted until 1861. The next recorded use of the term was when "libertarian communism" was used at a French regional anarchist Congress at Le Havre (16–22 November 1880). January the following year saw a French manifesto

it is from this era that the success of the anarchist idea amongst French workers mostly dates.

Indeed, these two words, communism and anarchy, put together represented a whole program. They announced a new concept of communism, entirely different from the one that had circulated until then. They together summed up a vast problem—*the* problem, shall we say, of humanity: the one that man has always tried to solve whilst outlining his institutions, since the communist tribe until our current societies.

How, indeed, do we unify the efforts of all in order to guarantee to all the greatest sum of wellbeing—and at the same time maintain, by extending them further, the conquests of individual freedom gained until now?

How to organise labour in common and still leave complete freedom to produce and for all initiatives?

Such has always been the problem of humanity since its beginnings. A huge problem which today calls on all intellects, on all wills, on all types [of people], in order to be solved, not on paper, but in life and by the very life of societies. The mere fact of saying these words, "*anarchist* communism," entails not only a new goal but also a new method of solving the social problem—bottom up, by the spontaneous action of the whole people.

It imposes on us all a labour of thought and study to see if this goal and this anarchist method to solve the social question—new for modern revolutionaries, however old for humanity—are good, feasible, and practical. That is what has been widely done since then.

Furthermore, the declaration anarchist-communist also raised formidable objections. On one hand, the opponents of anarchy—that is to say Louis Blanc's German successors, who persevered after him with his phrase of the "servant State" and [its role as the] "initiator of progress," did not fail to redouble their attacks against those who denied the State in all its possible forms. They first started by dismissing communism as an old idea [*vieillerie*] and they preached under the name of "collectivism" and "scientific socialism" the "labour notes" of Robert Owen and Proudhon, and the *individual* remuneration of producers who became "all public employees." As for us, they remarked that communism and anarchy "scream at finding themselves together." Since by communism they meant the authoritarian communism of Cabet—the only one they could conceive—it is quite obvious that their communism, which implies *archy* (power, government), and *an-archy* (no power, no government) are diametrically opposed to one

---

issued on "Libertarian or Anarchist Communism" (Max Nettlau, *A Short History of Anarchism*, 75–76, 145). (Editor)

another. One is the negation of the other, and nobody had considered har-
nessing them to the same cart. As for the matter of knowing whether authoritarian communism is the *only* possible form of communism, it was
not even touched upon by the opponents belonging to this school. They
thought this was an axiom.

Far more serious were the objections raised on the side of the anarchists
themselves. Here initially was repeated, without suspecting it, the objections that Proudhon had opposed, in the name of individual freedom, to
communism. And these objections, although [over] fifty years old, have lost
nothing of their value.

Proudhon indeed spoke *in the name of the individual*, watchful [*jaloux*]
to save all his freedom, to preserve the independence of his own home,
of his work, of his initiative, of his studies, of the luxury he can provide
himself without exploiting anyone, of the struggles that he wishes to undertake—his whole life, in a word. And this question of the rights of the
individual arises today with the same force as in the time of [*System of*]
Economic Contradictions.

Perhaps with even more force, as the State has immensely expanded its
encroachments on individual freedom by compulsory military service, by its
armies numbering millions of men and billions of taxes, by the school, by its
"protection" of the sciences and arts, embellished with police and Jesuitical
surveillance, and finally by the colossal development of officialdom.

Well, the anarchist of today repeats all these arguments. He speaks in
the name of the rebel individual throughout the ages, against the institutions of more or less partial but always authoritarian communism where
humanity stopped several times in the course of its long and painful history.

These objections cannot be treated lightly. They are no longer the disputes of advocates [of ideas]. They had to be posed, moreover, in one form
or another by the anarchist-communist himself, as well as by the individualist. Especially since the question raised by these objections goes right back
into this other far greater question—whether life in society is a means of
emancipation for the individual, or a cause of enslavement? If it leads to an
extension of individual freedom and to an expansion of the individual, or
to his diminishing? It is the fundamental question of all sociology, and, as
such, it deserves to be discussed thoroughly.

It is not, then, only a matter of abstract science. Tomorrow we may be
called upon to participate in the social revolution. To think we only have
to demolish and let others—who?—take care of the building would be
a bad joke.

Who, then, would the builders-rebuilders be, if not ourselves? Because,
while we can demolish a house without building another one in its stead,
we cannot do that with [social] institutions. When we demolish one, we

throw up at the very time of the demolition the foundations of what will develop later in its place. Indeed, if the people begin to evict the owners of the house, the land, the factory, it will not be to leave them empty, it will be to immediately occupy them in one way or another. And it will build, by this very fact, a new society.

Let us, then, try to indicate some essential aspects of this vast question.

II

AUTHORITARIAN COMMUNISM–
COMMUNIST COMMUNITIES

THE IMPORTANCE OF THE QUESTION WE HAVE JUST RAISED IS TOO OBVIOUS to be discussed. Many anarchists, including the communists, and thinkers in general while recognising the immense advantages which communism can offer to society also see in this form of social organisation a danger to the liberty and free development of the individual. Furthermore, as a whole, this question merges with that other problem, so vast, which our century has posed to its fullest extent: the question of the Individual and Society.

The problem has been obscured in various ways. For the most part, when we spoke of communism, we thought of the more or less Christian and monastic and always authoritarian communism which was preached in the first half of the nineteenth century, especially by Cabet and communist secret societies, and which was put into practise in certain communities in America. These, taking the family as a model, sought to constitute "the great communist family," "to reform man," and for this end they imposed, in addition to working in common, cohabiting closely as family, [physical] remoteness from present civilisation, isolation, the interference of the "brothers" and "sisters" in the whole psychological life of each member.

Furthermore, sufficient distinction was not made between the few isolated communities, founded on many occasions during the last three or
four centuries, and the federated and populous communes which might
emerge in a society on its way to accomplishing the social revolution: between communities founded by groups of intellectuals and city workers,
unable to struggle against all the harsh difficulties of the life of the agricultural pioneer in the virgin lands of America, and communities of the same
kind, also founded in America, but of farmers: German peasants, like those
of the Anama, or Slavic peasants, like the Doukhobors.

It would therefore be necessary, in the interest of the discussion, to consider separately:

1. production and consumption in common: its advantages and
   disadvantages;
2. cohabitation—is it necessary to model it on the current family?
3. the isolated communities of our times;
4. the federated communes of the future.

And finally, as a conclusion: does communism necessarily entail the diminishing of the individual? In other words: the individual in a communist society.

An immense movement of ideas took place during the nineteenth century under the name of socialism in general, beginning with the conspiracy of Babeuf, with Fourier, St. Simon, Robert Owen and Proudhon who
formulated the main currents of socialism, and then by the numerous
French ([Victor] Considerant, Pierre Leroux, Louis Blanc), German (Marx,
Engels), Russian (Chernyshevsky, Bakunin), etc., continuators who worked
either to popularise the ideas of the founders of modern socialism or to
underpin them on a scientific basis.

These ideas, in clarifying themselves, gave birth to two principal currents: authoritarian communism and anarchist communism, as well as a
number of intermediate schools seeking compromises [between the two],
such as State-capitalism, collectivism, co-operation; while, in the working
masses, they gave birth to a formidable workers movement which sought
to group the whole mass of workers by trades for the direct struggle against
capital, and which becomes increasingly international.

Several key points have been gained through this immense movement
of ideas and this action, and they have already largely penetrated into the
public conscience. These are:

[1] the abolition of wage-labour—the current form of ancient serfdom;

[2] the abolition of individual appropriation of all that is needed for production, the social organisation of the exchange of products;

[3] and, finally, the emancipation of the individual and of society in general from the political machine, from the State, which is used to maintain economic servitude.

On these three points agreement is close enough to be settled; for even those who advocate "labour notes" [*bon de travail*] or else tell us (like [Paul] Brousse) "all functionaries!" that is to say, "all employees of the State or the Municipality," admit that they advocate these palliatives *only because they do not see the immediate possibility of communism.* They accept, they say, this compromise as a stop-gap. And as for the State, the very people who remain staunch supporters of the State, of authority, even of dictatorship, tell us that when the *classes* we have today cease to exist, the State will have to disappear with them. Such was, at least, the opinion of the chiefs of the Marxist school.[6]

We can therefore say, without exaggerating the importance of our section of the socialist movement—the anarchist section—that in spite of the differences that arise between the various socialist sections and which are above all accentuated by the difference in the more or less revolutionary means of action accepted by each of them—we can say that all, by the words of their thinkers, acknowledge libertarian communism as the goal. The rest, by their own admission, would only be intermediate stages.

Well, any discussion of the stages to be traversed is futile if it is not based on the study of the *tendencies* that are emerging in modern society. And of these various tendencies, two especially deserve our attention.

One is that we are beginning to glimpse that in modern societies it is becoming increasingly difficult to determine the share that belongs to each [person] in production. Industry and agriculture have become so complicated today, so interwoven, all industries are so dependent on each other that the system of payment to the producer-worker by the results of his labour becomes increasingly impossible.

---

6   A reference to the famous expression by Engels (sometimes rendered as the State "*withers away*") from his 1880 pamphlet *Socialism: Utopian and Scientific*: "When, at last, it becomes the real representative of the whole of society, it renders itself unnecessary. As soon as there is no longer any social class to be held in subjection [...] a special repressive force, a State, is no longer necessary. [...] State interference in social relations becomes, in one domain after another, superfluous, and then dies out of itself; [...] The State is not 'abolished'. *It dies out*" (*Marx-Engels Collected Works*, Volume 24, 321). (Editor)

Formerly, when there was only one way to make shoes, to sew cloth, to forge nails, to mow a meadow and so on, it could be thought that if this worker produced more shoes, cloth, nails, or mowed more grass than another we rewarded the diligence or the knowledge of the worker by paying him a higher wage in proportion to the results he had obtained.

But today, when the productivity of labour depends mainly on machines and the organisation of work in each enterprise, it becomes less and less possible to grade the wage according to the results obtained by each worker. That is why the more an industry develops, the more payment by the piece disappears to be replaced by wages at so much a day. This, moreover, tends to become equalised.

Current bourgeois society certainly remains divided into classes and we have a whole class of bourgeois whose remuneration grows in inverse proportion to the work they do: the less they work, the more they are paid. On the other hand, within the working class itself we see four great divisions: women, agricultural labourers, workers who do unskilled labour, and finally those who have a more or less specialised trade. These divisions represent four degrees of exploitation which are only the results of the bourgeois organisation of production.

But in a society of equals, where all can learn a trade and where the exploitation of the peasant by the industrialist, and woman by man, will cease, these divisions between workers will have to disappear. Even today, wages within each of these divisions tend to equalise. This is what made them say, with reason, that the working day of a road-worker is *worth* that of a jeweller and what made Robert Owen conceive of his *labour notes*, paid to everyone who gave so many *hours of work* to the production of the articles accepted as necessary. In the Paris Commune of 1871 we also saw the salary of the administrators of the Commune limited to a uniform rate of fifteen francs a day.

However, if we consider all attempts at socialisation we see that apart from the association of a few thousand farmers in the United States, the labour note has not spread during the three-quarters of a century since Owen's attempt to apply it. And we have highlighted the reasons for this elsewhere (*The Conquest of Bread; The Wage System; Modern Science and Anarchy*).[7]

In contrast, we have seen many attempts at partial socialisation in the direction of communism occurring. Hundreds of communities—all more or less communist—have been founded over the past century almost

---

7   The pamphlet *The Wages System* (*Le Salariat*, 1889) was included as a chapter in the *Conquest of Bread* (*La Conquête du pain*, 1892) however both works circulated at the same time in most languages—with the former usually appearing first. *The Wage System* is included in *Direct Struggle Against Capital*. (Editor)

everywhere and at this very moment we know of more than a hundred—all more or less prosperous.

Setting aside the question of religion and its role in the organisation of communist communities, it would suffice to mention the history of the Doukhobors in Canada to show the *economic* superiority of communist labour compared to individual labour. Arriving penniless in Canada and forced to inhabit a part of the province of Alberta which was still unin-habited and cold; their wives, for lack of horses, hitched twenty or thirty of themselves to the plough whilst all the middle-aged men worked on the railroad and paid all their wages to the community—the six to seven thousand Doukhobors knew how, in seven or eight years, to achieve pros-perity by organising their agriculture and their lives with the aid of modern machinery, with American harvesters and balers, threshers and communal steam mills.[8]

Here we have a federation of about twenty communist villages, where each family lives in its house while the work in fields, etc., is done in com-mon and each family takes from the communal stores what it needs to live. This organisation, which has been maintained for some years by the religious idea of the community, is certainly not our ideal; but we must however recognise that from an *economic* point of view the immense supe-riority of communist work to individual work and the absolute possibility of adapting this work to the modern demands of agriculture with the aid of machines are fully proven.

Alongside these attempts at agrarian communism we can also indicate a number of attempts at *partial communism, for consumption only*, which we can see in the numerous attempts at socialisation emerging within bour-geois society, either between individuals or in the socialisation of munici-pal matters.

Hotels, ocean liners, boarding houses, are all attempts undertaken in this direction by the bourgeoisie. In exchange for an amount of so much per day, you have the choice of the ten or fifty dishes placed at your dis-posal at the hotel or on the ship, and no one controls the amount you can eat. This organisation even extends internationally, and before leaving Paris or London you can get coupons [*bons*] (at a rate of 10 francs per day) which enable you to stay at will in hundreds of hotels in France,

---

8   They have just bought, moreover, land on the shores of the Pacific in the British Columbia province of Canada where they established their *fruit-growing* colony—which these vegetarians much missed in the province of Alberta, where apple, pear, cherry, etc., trees do not provide any fruit—the flowers being killed by frosts in the month of May.

Germany, Switzerland, etc., all belonging to an international league of hotels.

The bourgeoisie understand very well the advantages of partial communism combined with the almost unlimited freedom of the individual *in respect to consumption*; and in all these institutions for a price of so-much per day they will take care of all your needs for lodging and food, except for those of extra luxury (wine, specially luxurious rooms) which are charged separately.

Insurance against fire (especially in villages where a certain equality of conditions permits an equal premium for all the inhabitants), against accidents, against burglars, that arrangement by which English fishermen supply you once a week, at the rate of two or three francs, with all the fish that a small family can consume; the clubs to pay the doctor, [which are] so widespread amongst English workers; the countless societies for insurance in the case of illness, etc., etc., all this immense series of institutions, born during the course of the nineteenth century, belong in the same category of an approximation towards partial communism, for a certain part of consumption.

Finally, we have a vast series of municipal institutions—water, gas, electricity, worker housing, trams with uniform fares, energy supplies [*force motrice*], etc.—in which similar attempts at the socialisation of consumption are applied on a scale which expands more every day. And what is very important is that these institutions for more or less communist consumption necessarily lead the towns to the municipal organisation of production (gas, electric power, dairies). Better than that. We will see in a few years in England the town itself owning and operating its coal mines in order to obtain light and electricity without paying a tribute to the owners of the coal mines. In Manchester it was already resolved in principle when a trust of the main mining companies raised the price of coal immensely during the Boer War. One or two towns in central England already have their own mines.

All this is certainly not yet communism. Far from it. But the principle which prevails in many of these institutions already contains part of the communist principle: *for a contribution of so much per year or per day* (in money today, in labour tomorrow) *you have the right to satisfy such-and-such category of your needs—luxury excepted.*

These rough drafts of communism lack many things to be [completely] communist, of which two are especially essential: First, the fixed payment is made in money instead of being done by labour; and second, the consumers have no voice in the administration of the enterprise. However, if the idea, if the tendency, of these institutions were well understood, there would be no difficulty, *even today*, in starting by private or co-operative [*sociétaire*] initiative a community in which the first point, *payment by labour*, could be introduced.

Thus, let us suppose a territory of 500 hectares. Two hundred maisonettes, each surrounded by a garden or a vegetable plot of a quarter hectare, are built on this land. The enterprise provides each family that occupies one of these houses a choice of what they want from fifty dishes per day; or else it supplies bread, vegetables, meat, coffee as demanded for cooking at home. And, in return, it asks either yearly payment in money or *your choice of so many hours of work* in one of the branches of work within the establishment: [such as] agriculture, cattle raising, cooking, cleaning.

This could done tomorrow if we wished; and it is astonishing that such a farm-hotel-garden has not yet been founded by some enterprising hotelier.

III

SMALL COMMUNIST COMMUNITIES— CAUSES OF THEIR FAILURES

IT MAY PERHAPS BE OBJECTED THAT IT IS HERE, BY INTRODUCING WORK IN common, that communists have generally failed. And yet this objection cannot be sustained. The causes of failure have always been elsewhere.

First, almost all the communities were founded as a result of a surge of quasi-religious enthusiasm. They asked men to be "pioneers of humanity," to submit to the regulations of a meticulous morality, to be completely remade by communist life, to give all their time, both the hours of work and of leisure, to the community, to live entirely for the community. It was foolish.

It was acting as monks do and demanding of men—without any need— to be what they are not. It is only very recently that communities have been founded by anarchist workers without any pretensions of this kind, for a purely economic purpose—that of escaping from employer exploitation.

The other mistake was to model the community on the family and to want to make it "the great family." For that they lived under one roof, always forced at every moment to be in the company of the same "brothers and sisters." But since two [real] brothers, sons of the same parents, often find it difficult to live in the same house, and family life is not successful for everyone, it was a fundamental error to impose on all "the great family" instead of seeking, on the contrary, to guarantee as far as possible the freedom and the home [life] of everyone.

A first condition for the success of a community would be to abandon the idea of a phalanstery and live in separate houses as is done in England.

Besides, a *small* community cannot last. The "brothers and sisters," forced into continual contact, amidst the scarcity of new impressions, end up detesting each other. But if it is enough for two people to become rivals, or simply cannot abide each other, for their quarrel to bring about the dissolution of a community, it would be strange if small communities could survive for a long time, especially since the communities founded up to now isolated themselves from the wider world. It can be predicted beforehand that a close association of ten, twenty, or a hundred people will only last three or four years. It would even be regrettable if it lasted longer; since this would only prove either that all had let themselves be subjugated by one individual or that all had lost their individuality. And since it is *certain* that in three, four or five years a part of the members of a community would wish to leave, it would be necessary to have at least ten or more federated communities so that those who, for one reason or another, wish to leave such-and-such community can enter another community and that other people from other groups can replace them. Otherwise the communist hive must necessarily perish or fall (as it almost always happens) into the hands of a single individual—generally the "brother" more cunning than the rest.

Lastly, all the communities founded up until now isolated themselves from society. But struggle, a life of struggle, is far more urgently needed by an active man than a well-supplied table. This need to see the world, to plunge into its currents, to fight its battles, to suffer its hardships is all the more pressing for the younger generation. That is why young people, as soon as they reach eighteen or twenty, necessarily leave a community which is not part of the rest of society.

Indeed, imagine yourself at the age of sixteen to twenty shut away in a communist community somewhere in Texas, Canada or Brazil. Books, newspapers, pictures tell you of these great and beautiful cities where intense living flows into the streets, theatres, meetings like a raging torrent. "There is life," you say to yourself: "Here is death, worse than death—stupor!—Poverty? Hunger? Well, I want poverty, hunger, provided that it is struggle and not the moral and intellectual stupor that is worse than death!" And you leave the community—and you are right.

We understand, therefore, what a mistake the Icarians and other communists committed founding their communities in the North American prairies. It would have been better to pay the rent for land in Europe than go away into the desert—unless you dream, like the communists of the

Anama, the Shakers and the Doukhobors, of the foundation of a *new religious empire*. For *social* reformers, we need struggle, proximity to intellectual centres, continual contact with the society that we seek to reform—and the inspiration of science, art, progress which is not obtained from books alone.

Needless to say that the government of the community was always the most serious stumbling block for all the practical communists. Indeed, you must read *Voyage to Icaria* by Cabet to understand how detestable, impossible, were the communities founded by the Icarians. Cabet demanded the complete annihilation of the human personality before the high-priest founder. You understand the hatred that Proudhon dedicated to this whole sect! It deserved it.

Beside this we see that those communists who have had very little authority in their communities, or have had none at all (like "Young Icaria"), have even managed the best. This is understandable. Political hatreds are always violent. We can live in a city next to our political adversaries if we are not forced to rub shoulders with them at every moment. But how is life possible if we are forced, [as] in a small community, to see each other every day, every hour? The political struggle enters the workshop, the working area, the place of rest, and life becomes impossible.

In contrast, it has been proved time and time again that communist work, *communist production*, succeeds marvellously. In no commercial enterprise has the increase in value given to the land by labour been as large as it has been in *each* of the communities founded either in America or in Europe.

We have already seen that in large communities, like that of the seven thousand Doukhobors in Canada, economic success was complete and rapid. But the same economic success was also seen in a tiny community of seven or eight anarchist workers near Newcastle. They also started without a penny, renting a three-hectare farm (we in London made a contribution in order to buy them a cow which would give milk to the children of the small colony); nevertheless, in three or four years they were able to give to their three hectares a very high increase in value by combining intensive gardening and greenhouse cultivation. They came from Newcastle to admire their remarkable success. (Their magnificent tomato crops, grown in a greenhouse, were purchased by the Sunderland Co-operative).

If this little community had to disband after three or four years, it was because this is *the inevitable fate* of any small agglomeration maintained by the enthusiasm of a few individuals. But it was not economic failure which led them to disband. It was personal reasons—inevitable in such a small circle, condemned to permanent cohabitation.

And yet, if we had three or four federated anarchist communities the departure of the founder would not have led to the disappearance of the community: there would only have been an exchange of personnel.

Of course, there have been many cases of management mistakes as there also are in capitalist enterprises; but since it is known that the proportion of *commercial* bankruptcies is about four out of five in the first five years after their establishment, it must be admitted that nothing similar to this enormous proportion of failures is to be found in communist communities. So, when the bourgeois press tries to be witty and speaks of offering anarchists an island on which to establish their commune—building on experience, we are ready to accept this proposal on the sole condition that this island is, for example, the Isle de France[9] and that upon evaluation of social capital we receive our share of it. But since we know that neither the Isle de France nor our share of social wealth will be given to us to make a genuine experiment in communism, we will work so that the people take them one great day by the social revolution. Paris in 1871, and Barcelona, were not very far from that—and ideas have progressed since then.[10]

Above all the progress is in that we understand that an isolated *town* proclaiming itself a commune would find it difficult to survive. The attempt should consequently begin on a *territory*—that of, for example, one of the States in the American West, [like] Idaho or Ohio—as some socialists in the United States suggest—and they are absolutely right. Indeed, it is on a fairly large territory, *including town and countryside*—and not within a town or village alone—that we will embark one day towards the communist future.

We have so often demonstrated that statist communism is impossible, that it would be pointless to dwell on this subject. Besides, the proof is in the fact that the statists themselves, the proponents of the socialist State, no longer believe in it themselves. None amongst them think any more about the programme of Jacobin communism written by Cabet in his *Voyage to Icaria*. Marx's communist *Manifesto* is already an anachronism for the Marxists. Most statist-socialists are occupied today with the conquering of a share of power in *the current State*—the bourgeois State—and do not even trouble themselves to clarify what they mean by a socialist State which would nevertheless not be *the State as sole-capitalist* and *All employees of the State*. When we tell them that this is what they want, they get annoyed; but they do not explain what other form of [social] organisation they intend to establish.[11] Since they do not believe in the possibility of an *imminent*

---

9   That is, Île-de-France (literally, "Island of France"), the province of France centred on Paris and the surrounding districts. (Editor)

10   A reference to the Paris Commune and the general strike called by the Spanish section of the International in July 1873. (Editor)

11   Lenin was more forthcoming in *State and Revolution*: "*All* citizens are transformed into hired employees of the state [...] *All* citizens become employees and workers of

social revolution, their aim is simply to become part of the government in the current bourgeois State. They leave it to the future to determine where this will lead.

As for those who have tried to sketch the future socialist State, when we reproach them of wanting to kill all freedom by concentrating production into the hands of functionaries of the State, they reply that all they want are bureaus of statistics. But this is mere playing with words. Besides, it is known today that the only valid statistics are those recorded by the individual himself, giving his age, sex, occupation, social position, the list of what he sold or bought, the list of his needs.

The questions posed to individuals in recent serious investigations were usually developed by individual volunteers or by scientific societies, and the role of statistical bureaus is reduced today to distributing questionnaires, classifying the [returned] forms and totalling them by means of adding machines. To so reduce the State, government, to this role and say that by government *it is meant only this* signifies (when it is said sincerely) nothing else but an honourable retreat. Indeed, it must be admitted that the Jacobins of thirty years ago have retreated immensely from their ideal of dictatorship and socialist centralisation. None would dare say today that the production and consumption of potatoes or rice must be regulated by the parliament of the *Volksstaat* (People's State) as was said in German socialist newspapers thirty years ago.

---

a single country-wide state 'syndicate'. [...] The whole of society will have become a single office and a single factory, with equality of labour and pay" (*Collected Works* Vol. 25 [Moscow: Progress Publishers, 1964], 473–474). (Editor)

IV

DOES COMMUNISM IMPLY THE DIMINISHING OF THE INDIVIDUAL?

THE COMMUNIST STATE BEING A UTOPIA THAT ITS OWN SUPPORTERS ARE beginning to abandon, it is pointless to dwell on it further: it is time to proceed further. What is much more important to examine, in fact, is the question of whether anarchist communism does not also result in a diminishing of individual freedom.

The fact is that in all discussions on freedom our ideas are obscured by the survivals of the centuries of serfdom and religious oppression we have experienced.

Economists have represented as a state of freedom the forced contract agreed by the worker under the threat of hunger with the boss. Politicians, on the other hand, have described as a state of freedom the present situation in which the citizen becomes a serf and a taxpayer of the State. The falseness of these assertions is therefore obvious.

Indeed, how can we describe as a state of freedom that of the citizens of a modern State, who may be called upon tomorrow to go to Africa to shoot at point-blank range harmless Kabyles for the sole purpose of opening a new field of speculations for bankers and the plundering of the Kabyles' land for European adventurers? Indeed, how can we believe ourselves free when each one of us is forced to give certainly well over a month of work every year to maintain a horde of rulers, whose sole purpose is that of preventing the ideas of social progress from emerging, the exploited from managing to free themselves from their exploiters, the masses, held in ignorance by the Church and the State, succeeding in learning something about the origin of their serfdom?

Representing this servitude as Freedom therefore becomes more and more difficult. However, the most advanced moralists, such as [John Stuart] Mill and his numerous students, in defining liberty as the right to do everything except infringing on the equal liberty of others have not given a correct definition to the word freedom. Ignoring that the word "right" is a very confused legacy from the past which says nothing or says too much, Mill's definition has enabled [Herbert] Spencer, along with a countless number of writers and even some individualist anarchists, to reconstruct courts and legal punishments, up to the death penalty—that is to say, inevitably, in the final analysis, the State which they themselves had admirably criticised.

Let us see, what is Freedom?

Putting aside all unconscious actions and considering solely reflective actions (the only ones that the law, religions and penal systems seek to influence), every action of this kind is preceded by some discussion in the human brain. "I shall go out, take a walk," thinks such-and-such a man... "But no, I have an appointment with a friend," or else "I promised to finish some work"; or else: "My wife and children will be sad to be left alone," or else again: "I shall lose my job if I do not go to work."

The last thought implies, as we can see, the fear of punishment while in the first two the man has only to deal with himself, with his habits of loyalty, his sympathies. And there lies all the difference. We say that a man who is forced to make this final thought "I renounce such-and-such pleasure in light of such-and-such punishment" is not a free man. And we affirm that humanity *can* and *must* liberate itself from the fear of punishment, that it *can* constitute an anarchist society in which the fear of punishment and even the displeasure of being rebuked shall disappear. It is towards this ideal that we go.

But we also know that we cannot and must not free ourselves from our sympathies (the pain of causing sorrow to those we love, or those who do not want to upset or even to disappoint), nor above all [from] our habits of loyalty (keeping promises). *From these two relationships, man is never free,* and [so] the "absolute" individualism which we have heard a lot about recently, especially since Nietzsche, is an absurdity, an impossibility.

Robinson [Crusoe] on his island was not *absolutely free*, in the sense given to that word in discussions.[12] When he began [to build] his boat and

12   *Robinson Crusoe* is a novel by Daniel Defoe (c. 1660–1731), published in 1719. It

cultivate his garden, or when he started to make provisions for the winter, he was already captured, entangled by his work. If he felt lazy and would have preferred to remain lying in his cave, he hesitated for a moment and ended up going to start work. But as soon as he had a dog as a companion, as soon as he had two or three goats and, above all, after he had met Friday, he had *obligations*. He had to consider the *interests of others*, he was no longer that *perfect individualist* about whom they love talking to us.

From the day a man loves a woman or has children, either raised by himself or entrusted to others (society), from the day that he has just one domestic animal—perhaps even a vegetable garden which requires to be watered at certain hours—he is no longer the imaginary "I-could-not-care-less," "the egoist," the individualist," who is sometimes presented to us as the archetype of the free man. This kind [of person] cannot be the dominant type, not on Robinson's island let alone in society *whatever [kind] it is*. It may occur in an exceptional situation, it indeed arises in the form of the rebel against a cruel and hypocritical society like ours; but it will never become the general type, or even a desirable type. Man takes *and will always take* into consideration the interests of other men—ever more, as they establish closer relations of mutual interest between themselves and these others themselves more clearly affirm their feelings, their desires, their rights to equality, to respect.

Thus we find no other definition of freedom than this one: *the possibility of acting without being influenced in the decisions being made by the fear of punishment by society* (bodily constraint, the threat of hunger or even censure, except when it comes from a friend).

Understanding freedom in this way—and we doubt that a broader and at the same time concrete definition of freedom can be found—we can certainly say that communism *can* diminish, even kill, all individual liberty. This has, indeed, been preached under the pretext of bringing happiness to humanity and in many communist communities it has been attempted. *But it can also enlarge this liberty to its utmost limits—impossible to reach by individualist work unless you have others to exploit and consider these others as inferior.*

All depends on the fundamental ideas by which we wish to associate. *It is not the communist form of association which brings about servitude: it is the*

---

is presented as the autobiography of the title character, who becomes a castaway and spends twenty-seven years alone on a remote tropical desert island. The story is thought to be based on the life of Alexander Selkirk (1676–1721), a Scottish castaway who lived for four years on a Pacific island. The first edition credited the work's protagonist as its author, leading many readers to believe he was a real person and the book a recounting of actual events. (Editor)

ideas of individual freedom which we bring into the association which determine its more or less libertarian character.

This is true for any form of association. The cohabitation of two individuals in the same house can lead to the enslavement of one to the will of the other as it can bring freedom for both. Likewise in the family. Likewise when two people garden together or produce a newspaper. Likewise for any association, however large or small it may be. Likewise for any social institution. Thus, in the tenth, eleventh and twelfth centuries, we find communes of equals, of equally free men, anxious to maintain this freedom and this equality—and four hundred years later we see the same commune calling for the dictatorship of a priest, a warlord [*condottier*], a king. The communal institutions remained; but the *idea* of Roman law, of the State, had gained the upper hand whilst those of equality, of freedom, of arbitration in disputes and of federation at all levels had disappeared—and it is servitude, decline.

In today's society, where no one is allowed to use the field, the factory, the instruments of labour, unless he acknowledge himself the inferior, the subject of some Sir—servitude, submission, lack of freedom, the practice of the whip are *imposed* by the very form of society. By contrast, in a communist society which recognises the right of everyone, on an egalitarian basis, to all the instruments of labour and to all the means of existence that society possesses, the only men on their knees in front of others are those who are by their nature voluntary serfs. Each being equal to everyone else as far as the right to well-being is concerned, he does not have to kneel before the will and arrogance of others and so secures equality in all personal relationships with his co-members.

Indeed, the more we reflect on this subject, the more we see that of all the institutions, of all the forms of social grouping that have been tried until now, it is still communism that guarantees the most freedom for the individual—provided that the guiding idea of the commune is egalitarian Freedom, the absence of authority, Anarchy.

Communism, an economic institution, is capable of assuming all forms, either of freedom or of oppression. It can produce a convent in which all implicitly obey their superior; and it can be an absolutely free organisation, leaving to the individual all his freedom—an association which lasts only as long as the associates wish to remain together, imposing nothing on anybody; watchful, on the contrary, to intervene to defend the freedom of the individual, to enlarge it, to extend it in all directions. It can be authoritarian (in which case the community soon perishes) or it can be anarchist.

The State, on the contrary, cannot take this or that form at will. Those who think they can do so give the word "State" an arbitrary meaning, contrary to the origin, to the entire history, of the institution. The State is the perfect example of a hierarchical institution, developed over centuries to subject all individuals and all of their possible groupings to the central will.

The State is necessarily hierarchical, authoritarian—or it ceases to be the State.[13]

There is also another point of the utmost importance, which is recommended especially to the attention of every libertarian spirit. We finally realise now that without communism man will never be able to reach that full development of individuality which is, perhaps, the most powerful desire of every thinking being. It is highly probably that this essential point would have been recognised for some time if we had not always confused *individuation*—that is to say, the complete development of individuality—with *individualism*. Now, individualism—it is high time to understand this—is nothing but the *Every man for himself, and the Devil take the hindmost* of the bourgeoisie, who believed to find in it the means of freeing himself from society by imposing on workers economic serfdom under the protection of the State but now notices that he himself has also become a serf of the State.

Communism guarantees economic freedom better than any other form of grouping because, better than any other form of production, it can guarantee to all well-being and even luxury by only asking man for a few hours of work per day instead of the whole day. Now, *to have ten or eleven hours of leisure per day out of the sixteen during which we lead a conscious life* (eight hours for sleep), *is already enlarging the freedom of the individual* to a

---

13   Louis Blanc having opposed the MASTER STATE to the SERVANT STATE, Proudhon replied with these lines which we could say were written yesterday: "The State, says Louis Blanc, has so far been the master and tyrant of citizens; henceforth it must be their servant. The relationship has changed: therein lies the whole revolution—As if, in all eras, the apologists of monarchy had not claimed, too, that royalty was the *servant* of the people, that *kings were made for the people, not the people for kings*, and other fables that the people have refuted. We know today what this servitude of the State, this devotion of the government to freedom, means. Did not [Napoleon] Bonaparte call himself the servant of the Revolution? What services he rendered to it!... So much for the *servant State* that was the Louis Blanc's response to my first query. As for the question of knowing how the State can really and effectively become a *servant*; how, being a servant, it can still be the State, Louis Blanc does not explain: he keeps a prudent silence" (*Mélanges: Articles de journaux*, 3rd volume, p. 43. See also further, p. 53, the passage where he demonstrates that "what we call in politics *Authority* is analogous and equivalent to what we call, in political economy, *Property*: that these two ideas are appropriate to each other and identical; that to attack one is to attack the other; that one is meaningless without the other; that if you eliminate the first, we must also eliminate the second, and *vice versa*").

point which for thousands of years has been one of the ideals of humanity. Previously, this was not the case and, consequently, any aspiration towards luxury, wealth, progress was excluded from a communist society. But today, with modern means of production with machinery, this *can* be done. In a communist society, man could have at least ten hours of leisure. *And this is already freeing man from the heaviest burdens of servitude which weighs him down. It is an increase of liberty.*

Recognising all as equals and renouncing the government of man by man is again expanding the freedom of the individual to a point which no other form of grouping has ever admitted, even as a dream. It becomes possible only after the first step has been taken: when man has his existence guaranteed and is not forced to sell his strength and intellect to whoever wants to give him a pittance to exploit him.

Lastly, recognising that the basis of all progress is variety of occupations and organising in such a way so that man is not only absolutely free during his hours of leisure but also that he can vary his work, and that from child-hood education prepares him for this variety—this is easy to achieve under a communist regime—is again to free the individual; it is to open the doors wide for his complete development in every direction.[14]

For the rest, everything depends upon the ideas with which the commune is founded. We know of a religious community in which a man, if he felt unhappy and betrayed his sadness on his face, saw himself accosted by a "brother" who told him: "Are you sad? Look merry all the same, otherwise you will sadden the brothers and sisters." And we know of a community of seven people one of whose members called for the appointment of four committees—gardening, supplies, housekeeping, and exportation—with absolute rights for the chairman of each committee.

Communes have certainly been founded, or invaded after their foundation, by "criminals of authority" (a special type, recommended for the attention of the pupils of Mr. Lombroso) and a number of communities were founded by maniacs of the absorption of the individual by society. But it is not the communist institution which produced them: it is Christianity (eminently authoritarian in its essence) and Roman law, the State. It is the statist education of these men, accustomed to thinking that no society is possible without lictors[15] and judges; and this idea remains a permanent threat to all freedom. As for the fundamental idea of communism, which is to consume and produce without counting the exact share of each [individual], it represents, on the contrary, an idea of freedom, of liberation.

---

14   On this see *Fields, Factories and Workshops*, Paris 1910.

15   A *lictor* in Ancient Rome was an attendant to the chief magistrates whose duties included carrying out sentences issued against criminals. (Editor)

We can therefore draw the following conclusions.

So far attempts at communism have failed because:

1. They were based on a religious impulse instead of seeing in the commune simply a method of economic consumption and production;
2. They withdrew themselves from society;
3. They were imbued with an authoritarian spirit;
4. They were isolated instead of federated;
5. They demanded from the founders an amount of labour that left them no leisure;
6. They were modelled on the patriarchal, authoritarian family instead of proposing, on the contrary, the goal of the fullest possible liberation of the individual.

Communism, being an eminently economic institution, in no way prejudges the amount of liberty guaranteed to the individual, to the initiator, to the rebel against crystallising customs. The commune *may* be authoritarian, which inevitably leads to its death, and it *may* be libertarian, which led, in the twelfth century even under the partial communism of the young cities of that age, to the creation of a new civilisation full of vigour, a resurgence of Europe.

But the only form of communism which can last is one where, given the existing close contact between citizens, every effort is made to extend the freedom of the individual in all different directions.

Under these conditions, under the influence of this idea, the freedom of the individual, increased by all the leisure attained, would not be diminished any more than it is today by municipal gas, home deliveries of food by large shops, modern hotels, or by the fact that during work hours we are side by side with thousands of [other] workers.

With Anarchy as an end and as a means, communism becomes possible. Without it, it inevitably becomes servitude and, therefore, it cannot last.

III

THE STATE: ITS HISTORIC ROLE

THE STATE
ITS HISTORIC ROLE

I

BY TAKING THE *STATE AND ITS HISTORIC ROLE* AS THE SUBJECT FOR THIS STUDY, I believe I am responding to a deeply felt need at the present time: that of exploring the very concept of the State, of studying its essence, its past role and the part it may be called upon to play in the future.

It is above all on the question of the State that socialists are divided. Two main currents emerge in all of the factions that exist amongst us which correspond to different temperaments, different ways of thinking and above all in the degree of confidence in the forthcoming revolution.

There are those, on the one hand, who hope to accomplish the social revolution through the State: to preserve most of its powers, to even extend them, to use them for the revolution. And there are those who, like us, see in the State, not only in its present form but in its very essence and in all the forms that it may take, an obstacle to the social revolution: the greatest hindrance to the birth of a society based on equality and freedom, the historic form developed to prevent this blossoming. They work to abolish the State, not to reform it.

The division, as we see, is deep. It corresponds with two divergent currents which are encountered in all the philosophy, literature and action of our time. And if the prevailing notions on the State remain as obscure as they are today, it will be, without a doubt, upon this question that the most obstinate struggles will be waged when—soon, hopefully—communist ideas seek their practical realisation in the life of societies.

It is therefore important, after having so often criticised the current State, to seek the reason for its emergence, to go deeper into the role it has played in the past, to compare it with the institutions that it has replaced.

Let us first agree on what we mean by the term "State."

There is, as is well-known, the German school which likes to confuse *the State* with *Society*. This confusion is to be found amongst the best German thinkers and many of the French who cannot conceive of society without statist concentration: and this is why anarchists are usually reproached for wanting to "destroy society," of preaching the return to "the permanent war of each against all."

However, to think that way is to completely ignore the advances made in the domain of history during the past thirty years; it is to ignore [the fact] that man lived in societies for thousands of years before he knew of the State; it is to forget that for the European nations the State is of recent origin—that it barely dates from the sixteenth century; it is, finally, to disregard that the most glorious periods of humanity were those in which liberties and local life were not yet destroyed by the State, and in which large numbers of men lived in communes and free federations.

The State is only one of the forms taken by society during the course of history. How can we confuse the permanent and the accidental?

In addition, some have also confused *State* with *Government*. Since there can be no State without government, it has sometimes been said that it is the absence of government, not the abolition of the State, that must be aimed for.

However, it seems to me that in the State and government we have two concepts of a different order. The idea of the State implies something quite different from the idea of government. It not only includes the existence of a power placed above society, but also of a *territorial concentration* and a *concentration of many functions in the life of societies in the hands of a few*. It implies some new relationships between members of society which did not exist before the formation of the State. A whole mechanism of legislation and of policing is developed to subject some classes to the domination of other classes.

This distinction, which at first sight might not be obvious, emerges especially when we study the origins of the State.

Moreover, there is only one way of really understanding the State: it is to study its historic development, and this is what we shall try to do.

The Roman Empire was a State in the real sense of the word. To this day it remains the ideal of the jurist.

Its organs covered a vast domain with a tight network. Everything flowed towards Rome: economic life, military life, judicial reports, wealth, education and even religion. From Rome came the laws, the magistrates, the legions to defend the territory, the prefects,[1] the gods. The whole life of the Empire went back to the Senate—later to Caesar, the omnipotent, omniscient, god of the Empire. Every province, every district had its Capitol in miniature, its small portion of Roman sovereignty to direct every aspect of its life. A single law, the law imposed by Rome, prevailed in the Empire; and this empire did not represent a confederation of fellow citizens: it was simply a herd of *subjects*.

Even now, the jurist and the authoritarian still admire the unity of that Empire, the unitarian spirit of its laws, the beauty—they say—[and] the harmony of that organisation.

But the disintegration from within, hastened by the barbarian invasion; the extinction of local life, which could no longer resist the attacks from outside nor the gangrene spreading from the centre, the domination by the rich who had appropriated the land [for themselves] and the misery of those who cultivated it—all these causes tore the Empire apart, and on its ruins a new civilisation developed which is ours today.

And if, leaving aside the civilisation of antiquity, we study the origins and developments of this young barbarian civilisation until the times when, in its turn, it gave birth to our modern States, we will be able to grasp the essence of the State. We shall grasp it better than had we embarked on the study of the Roman Empire, or that of Alexander of Macedonia, or even the despotic monarchies of the East.

By taking these powerful barbarian demolishers of the Roman Empire as our point of departure, we can trace the evolution of our entire civilisation from its beginnings to the State phase.

II

Most philosophers of the eighteenth century had a very elementary idea of the origin of societies.

At first, they said, men lived in small, isolated families and perpetual war between these families characterised the normal situation. But one fine day, realising at last the inconveniences of their endless struggles, men decided to put themselves into society. A social contract was concluded between the scattered families who willingly submitted themselves to an authority which—need I say?—became the starting-point and the initiator of all progress. Is it necessary to add, since we have already been told at school, that our present governments have so far maintained their

---

1   Prefects (Latin: *Praefectus*) were military or civil officials in the Roman Empire whose authority was conferred by a higher authority. (Editor)

noble role as the salt of the earth, the peacemakers and civilisers of the human race?

Conceived at the time when we knew little about the origins of man, this idea dominated the eighteenth century; and it must be said that in the hands of the Encyclopaedists and of Rousseau the idea of the "social contract" became a weapon against the divine rights of royalty. Nevertheless, despite the services it rendered in the past, this theory must be acknowledged as false.

The fact is that all animals, except some carnivores and birds of prey, and some species that are disappearing, live in societies. In the struggle for life, it is the sociable species which prevail over those that are not. In each category of animals they are at the top of the ladder and there can be no doubt that the first human-like beings were already living in societies.

Man did not create society; society existed before man.

We now also know—anthropology has convincingly demonstrated it—that the point of departure for humanity was not the family but the clan, the tribe. The patriarchal family as we know it, or as it is depicted in Hebrew traditions, only appeared much later. Man spent tens of thousands of years in the clan or tribal phase—let us call it the primitive or, if you wish, the savage tribe—and man had already developed a whole series of institutions, habits and customs many of which preceded the institutions of the patriarchal family.

In these tribes the separate family no more existed than it exists amongst so many other sociable mammals. Division within the tribe was rather by generations; and from a far distant age, going right back to the dawn of the human race, limitations had been established to prevent sexual relations [les rapports de marriage] between different generations, which were allowed [between those] in the same generation. We can still find traces of that period in some contemporary tribes and in the language, customs and superstitions of peoples much more advanced in civilisation.

The whole tribe hunted or gathered in common and, their hunger satisfied, they devoted themselves passionately to their dramatised dances. To this day we still find tribes who are very close to this primitive phase pushed to the peripheries of the large continents, or to mountainous regions, the least accessible [parts] of our globe.

The accumulation of private property could not take place there, since anything that had belonged to a particular member of the tribe was destroyed or burned where his body was buried. This is still done, even in England, by the Gypsies, and funeral rites of the "civilised" still bear the imprint [of this custom]: the Chinese burn paper models of the dead person's possessions, and at the military leader's funeral his horse, his sword and decorations accompany him to his grave. The meaning of the institution is lost: but the form has survived.

Far from expressing contempt for human life, these primitive people hated murder and blood. To spill blood was considered so serious that every drop spilled—not only human blood but also that of certain animals—required that the aggressor should lose an equal amount of his own blood.

Furthermore, a murder within the tribe is something *quite unknown*; for example, among the Inuits or Eskimos—those survivors of the Stone Age who inhabit the Arctic regions—amongst the Aleutians, etc., we definitely know that there has not been a single murder *within the tribe* for fifty, sixty or more years.

But when tribes of different origin, colour, and language met in their migrations, it often ended in war. It is true that, even then, men sought to pacify these encounters. As Maine, Post and E. Nys have so well demonstrated, tradition was already developing the seeds of what later became international law. For instance, a village could not be attacked without warning the inhabitants. Never would anyone dare to kill on the path used by women to reach the spring. And to make peace it was often necessary to balance the numbers of men killed on both sides.

However, all these precautions and many others besides were not enough: solidarity did not extend beyond the clan or tribe; quarrels arose between people of different clans and tribes, and these quarrels would end in violence and even murder.

Accordingly, a general law began to be developed between the clans and tribes. "Your members have wounded or killed one of ours; we have a right therefore to kill one of you or to inflict an identical wound on one of you"—it did not matter who, since the tribe was always responsible for the acts of its members. The well-known verses of the Bible: "Blood for blood, an eye for an eye, a tooth for a tooth, a wound for a wound, a life for a life"—but no more!—as Koenigswarter noted so well, derive their origin from this. It was their concept of justice... and we have no reason to feel superior since the principle of "a life for a life" which prevails in our [legal] codes is only one of many survivals [from the past].

As you can see, a whole series of institutions, and many others I shall not mention, as well as a complete code of tribal morality was already developed during this primitive phase. And to keep this nucleus of sociable customs alive, habit, custom, and tradition were enough. There was no authority to impose it.

Primitive people had, without doubt, temporary leaders. The sorcerer, the rainmaker—the scholars of the time—sought to benefit from what they knew or believed they knew about nature to dominate their fellow men.

Similarly, he who could more easily memorise the proverbs and songs in which tradition was embodied gained influence. At popular festivals he would recite these proverbs and songs in which were passed on the decisions taken on such-and-such an occasion by the people's assembly in such-and-such a controversy. In many tribes this is still done. And from that age onwards, these "educated" [people] sought to ensure domination by passing on their knowledge only to the chosen few, the initiated. All religions, and even the arts and crafts, began with "mysteries"; and modern research shows us the important role secret societies of the initiates play to maintain certain traditional practices in primitive clans. Already the seeds of authority are present there.

It goes without saying that the brave, the audacious, and above all, the wise also became temporary leaders in the conflicts with other tribes or during migrations. But the alliance between the bearer of the "law" (those who knew by heart tradition and past decisions), the military chief and the sorcerer did not exist; the *State* was no more part of these tribes than it is in a society of bees or ants, or amongst our contemporaries the Patagonians and Eskimos.

This phase nevertheless lasted for thousands and thousands of years and the barbarians who overran the Roman Empire had also gone through it. They had barely emerged from it.

In the early centuries of our era there were widespread migrations of the tribes and confederations of tribes that inhabited Central and Northern Asia. Influxes of tribes, driven by more or less civilised peoples, came down from the high plateaux of Asia—probably driven by the rapid desiccation of these plateaux[2]—spread all over Europe, each driving the other and mixing together in their rush towards the West.

During these migrations, when so many tribes of different origins were mixed, the primitive tribe which still existed amongst most of the savage inhabitants of Europe was bound to disintegrate. The tribe was based on a common origin and the worship of common ancestors; but to which common origin could these agglomerations [of people] appeal when they emerged from the confusion of the migrations, the drives, the inter-tribal wars, during which here and there we can already see the emergence of the patriarchal family—the nucleus deriving from the monopolisation of some of the women conquered or abducted from other nearby tribes?

The old ties were broken, and to avoid dispersal (which happened, in fact, to many tribes, now lost to history) new [social] ties had to emerge.

---

2   The reasons which lead me to this hypothesis are put forward in a paper, *Desiccation of Eur-Asia*, written for the Research Department of the Geographical Society of London, and published in the *Geographical Journal* of the society, June 1904 [vol. 23, no. 6, pp. 722–734].

And they arose. They were found in the communal possession *of the land*—of the territory on which each agglomeration had finally settled.[3]

The common possession of a certain territory—of this small valley, of those hills—became the basis for a new understanding. The ancestor gods had lost all meaning; then local gods, of that valley, river, forest, came to provide religious blessing to the new agglomerations, replacing the gods of the primitive tribe. Later Christianity, always ready to accommodate itself to pagan survivals [from the past], made them local saints.

Henceforth, the village commune consisting entirely or partly of distinct families—all united, however, by the common possession of the land—became the essential common bond for centuries to come.

Over vast areas of eastern Europe, Asia and Africa it still exists. The barbarians—Scandinavians, Germans, Slavs, etc.—who destroyed the Roman Empire lived under this kind of organisation. And by studying the barbarian codes of that period, as well as the confederations of village communes that exist today amongst the Kabyles, Mongols, Hindus, Africans, etc., it has been possible to reconstruct in its entirety this form of society which signifies the starting point of our present civilisation.

Let us take a look at this institution.

III

The village commune consisted, as it still does, of distinct families. But the families of the same village owned the land in common. They considered it as their common heritage and apportioned it according to the size of each family—their needs and their strengths. Hundreds of millions of men still live in this way in Eastern Europe, India, Java, etc. It is the same system that has been established in our time freely in Siberia by Russian peasants once the State gave them a chance to occupy the vast Siberian territory in their own way.

Today the cultivation of the land in a village community is carried out by each household independently. Since all the arable land is distributed between the households (and redistributed when necessary) each cultivates its field as best it can. But originally the land was also worked in common and this custom is still carried on in many places—at least on a part of the land. As to the clearing of woodland and the thinning of forests, the construction of bridges, the building of small forts and towers for use as places

---

3   Readers interested in this subject as well as in the communal and free cities phases, will find further details and the necessary information on the literature of the subject in my *Mutual Aid*, Paris (Hachette), 1900.

of refuge in the event of invasion—all that was done in common, just as hundreds of millions of peasants still do where the village commune has resisted the encroachments of the State. But "consumption," to use a modern expression, was already taking place by families, each of which having its cattle, its vegetable garden and its provisions. The means for [both] hoarding and for passing down by inheritance accumulated goods had already been introduced.

In all its affairs the village commune was sovereign. Local custom was law and the plenary assembly of all the heads of family, men and women, was the judge, the only judge, in civil and criminal matters. When one of the inhabitants had lodged a complaint against another by sticking his knife in the ground at the place where the commune normally gathered, the commune had to "find the sentence" according to local custom once the *fact* of an offence had been established by the juries of the two parties in dispute.

If I were to recount all the interesting aspects of this phase, I would not have the space in which to do so. I must therefore refer the reader to *Mutual Aid*. Suffice it to mention here that *all* the institutions which States later seized for the benefit of minorities, all the notions of law that exist in our codes (mutilated for the advantage of minorities) and all the forms of judicial procedure, in so far as they offer guarantees to the individual, originated in the village commune. So when we imagine that we have made a great advance by introducing, for example, the jury, we have only returned to the institution of the so-called "barbarians" after having changed it to the advantage of the ruling classes. Roman law merely superimposed itself onto customary law.

The sense of national unity was developing at the same time through large free federations of village communes.

The village commune, based on the possession and very often on the cultivation of the land in common, sovereign [both] as judge and legislator of customary law, satisfied most of the needs of social existence [*l'être social*].

But not for all its needs: there were still others to be satisfied. But the spirit of the time was not to appeal to a government as soon as a new need made itself felt. It was, on the contrary, to take the initiative yourself to unite, to join forces, to federate; to create an agreement, large or small, numerous or restricted, which fulfilled the new need. And society then was literally covered, like a network, with sworn brotherhoods; of guilds for mutual support, of "con-jurations," within the village and outwith the village, in the federation.

We can observe this phase and spirit at work even today, amongst many barbarian federations which have remained outside the modern States which are modelled on the Roman or rather Byzantine type.

Thus, to take one example amongst many, the Kabyles have maintained their village commune, with the powers I have just mentioned: land in common, communal tribunal, etc. But man feels the need for action beyond the narrow confines of his hamlet. Some rove the world, seeking adventures as merchants. Others devote themselves to some trade—or "art." And these merchants, these artisans, unite into "brotherhoods," even though they belong to different villages, tribes or confederations. It is necessary to unite for mutual assistance on distant journeys, it is necessary for the mutual exchange of the mysteries of the trade—and they come together. They swear brotherhood and practice it in a way that strikes the European: real brotherhood, and not just in words.

But then, misfortune can happen to anyone. Who knows whether tomorrow, perhaps, in a brawl a normally gentle and quiet man may exceed the established limits of decorum and sociability? Who knows if he might not resort to blows and inflict wounds? It will then be necessary to pay heavy compensation to the insulted or wounded; it will be necessary for him to defend himself before the village assembly and to reconstruct the facts, on the testimony of six, ten, or twelve "sworn brothers" ["*conjurés*"]. All the more reason to enter a brotherhood.

Besides, man feels the need to engage in politics, to intrigue perhaps, to propagate a particular moral opinion or a particular custom. There is, finally, external peace to be safeguarded; alliances with other tribes to be concluded; federations to be constituted far and wide; ideas on intertribal law to be spread. Well then, to satisfy all these needs of an emotional or intellectual nature the Kabyles, the Mongols, the Malays do not appeal to a government; they do not have one. Men of customary law and individual initiative, they have not been impaired from acting for themselves by the corruption of a government and a Church. They unite spontaneously. They form sworn brotherhoods, political and religious societies, associations of crafts [*unions de métiers*]—guilds, as they were called in the Middle Ages, *çofs* as they are called today by the Kabyles. And these *çofs* extend beyond the boundaries of the hamlet; they radiate far into the desert and into foreign cities; and brotherhood is practised in these associations. To refuse help to a member of his *cof*—even at the risk of losing all his possessions and his life—is to commit an act of treason towards the "brotherhood"; it is to be treated as the murderer of the "brother."

What we find today among the Kabyles, Mongols, Malays, etc., was the very essence of life of the barbarians in Europe from the fifth to the twelfth and even until the fifteenth century. Under the name of *guilds, friendships, brotherhoods, universitas,*[4] etc., associations multiplied: for mutual defence, to

---

4   The word *universitas* originally applied to the scholastic guilds, a corporation organised

avenge affronts suffered by some member of the association and to express solidarity, to replace "eye for an eye" vengeance by compensation, followed by acceptance of the aggressor into the brotherhood; for the exercise of crafts, for aid in case of illness, for defence of the territory; to prevent encroachments of the emerging authority; for commerce, for the practice of "good neigh-bourliness"; for propaganda—in a word, for all that Europeans, educated by the Rome of the Caesars and the Popes, nowadays demand from the State. It is even very doubtful whether there was a single man in that period, free or serf—except those who had been expelled by their own brotherhoods—who did not belong to a brotherhood or some guild, in addition to his commune.

The Scandinavian *Sagas* extol their exploits; the devotion of sworn brothers is the theme of the most beautiful poems. Naturally, the Church and emerging kings, representatives of the Byzantine (or Roman) law which [also] reappeared, hurled their denunciations and their decrees against these brotherhoods; but fortunately they remained a dead letter.

The whole history of the period loses its meaning, it becomes absolutely incomprehensible, if we do not take into account those brotherhoods, these unions of brothers and sisters, which sprung up everywhere to meet the many needs of the economic and personal lives of man.

To fully grasp the immense progress achieved by this double institution of village communes and freely sworn brotherhoods—outside any Roman, Christian, or Statist influence—take Europe as it was at the time of the bar-barian invasion and compare it to what it became in the tenth and eleventh centuries. The wild forest is conquered, colonised; villages cover the coun-try and they are surrounded by fields and hedges, protected by small forts, connected to each other by paths crossing forests and marshes.

In these villages you find the seeds of the industrial arts and you discov-er a whole network of institutions for maintaining internal and external peace. In the event of murder or injury the villagers no longer seek, as previously in the tribe, to slay or to inflict an equivalent wound on the ag-gressor, or one of his kin or his fellow villagers [*co-villageois*]. Rather it is the brigand-lords who still adhere to that principle (hence their endless wars); whereas between villagers *compensation*, fixed by arbiters, becomes the rule; after which peace is re-established and the aggressor is often, if not always, adopted by the family who was wronged by his aggression.

Arbitration for all disputes becomes a deeply rooted institution, a daily practice—in spite of and against the bishops and the emerging kinglets

---

for the purposes of higher learning. The word "university" is derived from the Latin *universitas magistrorum et scholarium* which roughly means "community of teachers and scholars." These medieval universities were established across Europe between the eleventh and fourteenth centuries. (Editor)

who would like every difference to be laid before them, or their agents, in order to benefit from the *fred*—a fine once levied by the village on the violators of the public peace in every dispute and which the kings and bishops now appropriated.

Finally hundreds of villages are already united in powerful federations, sworn to internal peace, who consider their territory as a common heritage and are united for mutual defence. These were the seeds of European *nations*. And to this day we can still study these federations in action amongst Mongolian, Turko-Finnish[5] and Malayan tribes.

Yet black clouds are gathering on the horizon. Other associations, those of dominant minorities, are also formed and they seek slowly to transform these free men into serfs, into subjects. Rome is dead; but its tradition is reborn and the Christian church, haunted by the visions of Eastern theocracies, gives its powerful support to the new powers that seek to establish themselves.

Far from being the bloodthirsty beast that some wished to make him [in order] to prove the necessity to dominate him, man has always loved quiet, peace. Quarrelsome rather than fierce, he prefers his cattle, his land, and his hut to the profession of soldier. This is why, no sooner had the great migrations of barbarians slowed down, no sooner had the hordes and the tribes more or less settled themselves in their respective territories, we see the defence of the territory against new waves of emigrants entrusted to the care of someone who engages a small band of adventurers—hardened warriors or brigands—to follow him while the great mass rears its cattle or works the land. And this defender soon begins to accumulate wealth; he gives horses and iron (then very expensive) to the destitute settler who has neither horse nor plough, and enslaves him. He also starts to seize the beginnings of military power.

Moreover, little by little, tradition, which is the law, is forgotten by most. In each village there are hardly any elders who have been able to remember the verses and songs in which are recounted the "precedents" of which customary law is composed, and who recites them on the days of great festivals before the commune. And, little by little, a few families make it their speciality, transmitted from father to son, of remembering these songs and verses, to "preserve the law" in its purity. Villagers would go to them to adjudicate on complicated disputes, especially when two villages or two confederations could not agree to accept the decisions of the arbiters taken from their midst.

---

5   A somewhat dated reference to the Khazars, Magyars, and other a multi-ethnic conglomerates of semi-nomadic Turkic peoples who lived in an area extending from Eastern Europe to Central Asia. (Editor)

Princely or royal authority is already germinating in these families, and the more I study the institutions of that period the more I see that knowledge of the customary law did much more to establish that authority than the power of the sword. Man let himself be enslaved much more by his desire to "punish" the aggressor according to "the law" than by direct military conquest.

And, gradually, the first "concentration of powers," the first mutual insurance for domination—that of the judge and the military chief—is made against the village community. A single man assumes these two functions. He surrounds himself with armed men to implement judicial decisions; he fortifies himself in his small tower; he accumulates in his family the riches of the time—bread, cattle, iron—and little by little imposes his domination on the peasants in the vicinity.

The scholar of the period, that is to say the sorcerer or the priest, are not long in lending support to him, to share domination; or, by joining force and knowledge of customary law to his feared wizard power, the priest takes it for himself. Hence, the temporal authority of the bishops in the ninth, tenth, and eleventh centuries.

I would need a lecture [in itself] rather than a chapter to thoroughly deal with this subject, so full of new lessons, and to recount how free men gradually became serfs, forced to work for the lord of the manor, secular or clerical; how authority was slowly, hesitantly [*par tâtonnement*] constituted over villages and boroughs; how the peasants joined together, rebelled, fought to oppose this growing domination; and how they were defeated in those struggles against the stout walls of the castle, against the men clad in iron who defended them.

It is enough for me to say that around the tenth and eleventh centuries Europe seemed to be moving towards the constitution of barbarian kingdoms like those we find today in the heart of Africa or those theocracies we know from Eastern history. This could not happen in a day; but the seeds of those petty royalties and of those petty theocracies were already there; they asserted themselves more and more.

Fortunately the "barbarian" spirit—Scandinavian, Saxon, Celt, German, Slav—which had driven men for seven or eight centuries to seek the satisfaction of their needs through individual initiative and the free agreement of brotherhoods and guilds—fortunately this spirit still lived in the villages and boroughs. The barbarians allowed themselves to be enslaved, they laboured for the master, but their spirit of free action and free agreement had not yet been corrupted. Their brotherhoods were more alive than ever, and the crusades had only succeeded in arousing and developing them in the West.

Then the revolution of the urban commune, resulting from the union of the village commune and the sworn brotherhood of the artisan and the merchant—a revolution which had been long prepared by the federal spirit of the time—exploded in the eleventh and twelfth centuries with a striking unity [*ensemble frappant*] across Europe. It had already began in the Italian communes during the tenth century.

This revolution, which most university historians prefer to ignore or to underestimate, saved Europe from the disaster which threatened it. It stopped the development of theocratic and despotic kingdoms in which our civilisation would probably have ended up sinking after a few centuries of pompous self-fulfilment, as the civilisations of Mesopotamia, Assyria and Babylon sank. It opened a new phase of life—the phase of free communes.

IV

It is easy to understand why modern historians, trained in the Roman spirit and seeking to trace all institutions back to Rome, have so much difficulty understanding the communalist movement of the eleventh and twelfth centuries. The virile affirmation of the individual which succeeded in constituting society by the free federation of men, villages and cities was the complete negation of the unitarian and centralising Roman spirit by which they seek to explain history in our university education. Nor is it connected to any historical personality or with any central institution.

It is a natural development, belonging, like the tribe and the village commune, to a certain phase in human evolution, and not to any particular nation or region.

This is the reason why university science does not grasp it and why Augustin Thierry and Sismondi, who had understood the spirit of the period, had no continuators in France, where Luchaire is today still the only one to have taken up—more or less—the tradition of the great historian of the Merovingian and communalist periods. This is even why, in England and Germany, the revival of studies into this period and a vague understanding of its spirit are of very recent origin.

The commune of the Middle Ages, the free city, derives its origin, on the one hand, to the village commune and, on the other, to those thousands of brotherhoods and guilds that were formed in that period outwith the territorial union. A federation between these two kinds of unions, it asserted itself under the protection of its fortified enclosing walls and turrets.

In many regions it was a peaceful development. Elsewhere—and this is the rule for Western Europe—it was the result of a revolution. When the inhabitants of a particular borough felt sufficiently protected by their walls, they made a "conjuration." They mutually swore an oath to drop all pending matters concerning insults, violence [*les batteries*] or injuries and swore for the disputes that would arise in the future never to have recourse to any judge other than the syndics which they would nominate themselves. In every good-neighbourliness or craft guild, in every sworn brotherhood, it had long been regular practice. In every village community such had been the practice in the past, before the bishop and the kinglet had succeeded in introducing, and later imposing upon it, their judge.

Now, the hamlets and parishes which made up the borough, as well as the guilds and brotherhoods which had developed there, regarded themselves as a single *amitas*, nominated their judges and swore permanent union between all these groups.

A charter was quickly drafted and accepted. If necessary, they sent for a copy of the charter of a neighbouring small commune (today we know of hundreds of these charters) and the commune was formed. The bishop or the prince, who had been up to then the judge in the commune and had often become more or less the master, had thus only to acknowledge the *fait accompli*—or fight the young conjuration with arms. Often the king—that is to say the prince who sought to secure his superiority over the other princes and whose coffers were always empty—"granted" the charter for a fee. He thus renounced his intention of imposing *his* judge on the commune while ensuring his prominence as regards the other feudal lords. But this was by no means the rule: hundreds of communes lived without any ratification other than their goodwill, their ramparts and their spears.

In a hundred years, this movement spread, with a striking unity, throughout Europe—by imitation, note it well, covering Scotland, France, the Netherlands, Scandinavia, Germany, Italy, Poland and Russia. And when we now compare the charters and the internal organisation of the French, English, Scottish, Dutch, Scandinavian, German, Polish, Russian, Swiss, Italian and Spanish communes, we are struck by the close similarity of these charters and the organisation that grew up sheltered by these "social contracts." What a striking lesson for the Romanists and the Hegelians who know of no other means than servitude before the law to achieve similarity in institutions!

From the Atlantic to the middle course of the Volga, and from Norway to Sicily, Europe was covered with such communes—some becoming populous cities such as Florence, Venice, Amiens, Nuremberg or Novgorod, others remaining boroughs of a hundred or even twenty families, and yet treated as equals by their more prosperous sisters.

Organisms full of vigour, communes obviously differed in their evolution. The geographical location, the nature of external commerce, the resistance to be overcome from outside, gave each commune its [own] history. But for all the principle is the same. Pskov in Russia and Bruges in

Flanders, a Scottish town of three hundred inhabitants and wealthy Venice with its islands, a borough in the north of France or Poland and Florence the Beautiful represent the same *amitas*: the same fellowship of the village communes and guilds, associated within the boundaries of the walls. Their constitution, in its general features, is the same.

Generally, the town whose walls grew longer and thicker with the population and which flanked itself with higher and higher towers, each raised by this neighbourhood [*quartier*] or that guild and bearing its individual stamp—generally, I say, the town was divided into four, five or six sections, or districts, which radiated from the citadel or the cathedral towards the walls. By preference these sectors were each inhabited by an "art" or craft while the new crafts—the "young arts"—occupied the suburbs which were soon enclosed by a new fortified wall.

The *street*, or the parish, represented the territorial unit, which corresponded to the earlier village community. Each street, or parish, had its popular assembly, its forum, its popular tribunal, its priest, its militia, its banner and often its seal, symbol of its sovereignty. Federated with other streets it nevertheless retained its independence.

The professional unit, which often merged with the neighbourhood [*quartier*] or district, was the guild—the craft association [*l'union de metier*]. The latter also had its saints, its assembly, its forum, its judges. It had its funds, its land holdings, its militia and its banner. It also had its seal, emblem of its *sovereignty*. In the event of war, if it judged it appropriate, its militia joined with the other guilds and planted its banner alongside the large banner, or the *carrosse*, of the city.

The city, in short, was the union of the neighbourhoods [*quartiers*], streets, parishes and guilds, and had its plenary assembly in the grand forum, its grand belfry,[6] its elected judges, its banner to rally the militias of the guilds and neighbourhoods. It dealt with other cities as sovereign, federated with whom it wished, concluded alliances nationwide or even outwith its own nation. Thus the English "Cinque Ports" around Dover were federated with French and Dutch ports on the other side of the Channel;[7]

6   In the cities of the Middle Ages the belfry was the symbol of communal freedoms obtained from the local feudal lord. As well as housing the bell which called the people to communal deliberations or to signal the approach of an enemy, it also held the communal charters which confirmed in writing the commune's freedoms (and the commitment of the local lord to respect them). (Editor)

7   The Confederation of Cinque Ports was a series of coastal towns in Kent and Sussex (Hastings, New Romney, Hythe, Dover, Sandwich) originally formed for military and trade purposes. The name is Norman French, meaning "five ports." (Editor)

the Russian Novgorod was the ally of the Germanic-Scandinavian Hansa, and so on. In its external relations each city possessed all the attributes of the modern State and from that period was constituted, by free contracts, what was later known as international law, placed under the sanction of the public opinion of all the cities, and later more often violated than respected by States.

How often would a city, unable "to find the sentence" in a particularly complicated case, send someone to "seek the sentence" in a neighbouring city! How many times did the prevailing spirit of that period—arbitration, rather than the authority of the judge—express itself by two communes taking a third as arbitrator!

The crafts did the same. They handled their commercial and craft arrangements independently [par-dessus] of their cities and made their treaties without regard of nationality. And when, in our ignorance, we boast of our international congresses of workers, we forget that in the fifteenth century international congresses of crafts, even of apprentices, were already being held.

Lastly, the city either defended itself against aggressors and itself waged fierce wars against the feudal lords in the vicinity by naming each year one or rather two military commanders for its militias; or it accepted a "military defender"—a prince or a duke which it selected for one year and dismissed at will. For the maintenance of his soldiers, he would generally be given the proceeds from judicial fines; but he was forbidden to interfere in the affairs of the city.[8]

Or else, too weak to free itself entirely from its neighbours the feudal vultures, it kept as a more or less permanent military defender its bishop or a particular prince—Guelph or Ghibelline in Italy, the Rurik family in Russia, or Algirdas in Lithuania—but was jealously vigilant in preventing the authority of the bishop or the prince extending beyond the men encamped in the castle. It even forbade him to enter the town without permission. To this day the King of England cannot enter the City of London without the permission of its Lord Mayor.

The economic life of the cities in the Middle Ages deserves to be recounted in detail but I am forced to overlook it here and refer the reader to what I have said in *Mutual Aid* basing myself on a vast body of modern historical research. It will suffice to simply note that internal commerce was always dealt with by the guilds—not by individual artisans—prices being set by mutual agreement. Furthermore, at the beginning of this period external commerce was dealt with *exclusively by the city*. Only later did it

---

8   In Russia, we know of hundreds of these annual contracts concluded between the cities (their *vétche*, or *forum*) and princes.

become the monopoly of the Merchants' Guild and, later still, of isolated individuals. Finally, they never worked on Sunday, nor on Saturday afternoon (bath day). The supply of the main staples was always handled by the city, and this custom was preserved for wheat in some Swiss towns until the middle of the nineteenth century.

In short it is shown by a huge mass of documents of all kinds that humanity has never known, neither before nor after, a period of relative well-being equally assured to all as existed in the cities of the Middle Ages. The present poverty, insecurity and over-work were unknown.

V

With these elements—freedom, organisation from the simple to the complex, production and exchange by the crafts (guilds), foreign trade handled by the whole city and not by individuals, and the purchase of provisions by the city to supply them to the citizens at cost price—with these elements the towns of the Middle Ages during the first two centuries of their free existence became centres of well-being for all the inhabitants, centres of opulence and civilisation, as has never been seen since.

We have but to consult the documents which enable us to establish the rate of remuneration for labour compared to the cost of commodities— [Thorold] Rogers has done this for England and a great number of German writers for Germany—and we see that the labour of the artisan and even of a simple day-labourer was at that time remunerated at a rate that is not reached in our time, not even by the working class elite. The account books of the colleges of the University of Oxford (which have been kept for seven centuries since the twelfth century) and of certain English estates, [as well as] those of a large number of German and Swiss towns, are there to bear witness.

When we consider, in addition, the artistic finish and the amount of decorative work the worker then put equally into the beautiful works of art he produced and into the simplest items of domestic life—a gate, a candlestick, a piece of pottery—and we see that during his work he did not know the rush, the overwork of our time; that he could forge, sculpt, weave, embroider with leisure—as only a very small number of worker-artists amongst us can do today.

And let us finally browse through the donations made to the churches and the communal houses of the parish, the guild or the city, whether in works of art—in decorative panels, sculptures, wrought or cast metal—or in money, and we realise the degree of well-being these cities were able to achieve; we can also sense the spirit of research and invention which prevailed there, the air of freedom which inspired their works, the feeling of fraternal solidarity which was established in these guilds, where men of the same trade were linked not merely by the commercial and technical side of the trade but by ties of sociability, of brotherhood. Was it not, in fact, the law of the guild that two brothers had to attend the bedside of each sick brother—a custom which certainly required devotion in those times of contagious diseases and plagues—to follow him to the grave, to take care of his widow and children?

The abject poverty, the debasement, the uncertain future for the many, and the isolation of poverty, which characterise our modern cities, were absolutely unknown in those "free oases, arising in the twelfth century amidst the feudal forest."

In those cities, sheltered by the conquered liberties, under the impetus of the spirit of free agreement and of free initiative, a whole new civilisation grew up and reached such a blossoming that we have not seen its like in history to the present day.

All modern industry comes to us from these cities. In three centuries, industries and the arts reached such perfection that our century has only been able to surpass them in speed of production but rarely in quality and very rarely in the beauty of the product. All the arts we seek in vain to revive now—the beauty of Raphael, the strength and boldness of Michelangelo, the art and science of Leonardo da Vinci, the poetry and language of Dante, the architecture, finally, to which we owe the cathedrals of Laon, Rheims, Cologne, Pisa, Florence—as Victor Hugo so well put it "the people was the builder"[9]—the treasures of the beauty of Florence and Venice, the town halls of Bremen and Prague, the towers of Nuremberg and Pisa, and so on *ad infinitum*—all this was the product of that period.

Do you wish to measure the progress of that civilisation at a glance? Compare the dome of St. Mark in Venice with the rustic arch of the Normans; the paintings of Raphael with the embroidery of the Bayeux Tapestries; the mathematical and physics instruments and the clocks of Nuremberg with the hour-glasses of the preceding centuries; the rich language of Dante with the barbaric Latin of the tenth century. A new world was born between the two!

Never, with the exception of that other glorious period—again of free cities—of ancient Greece, had humanity made such a leap forward. Never, in two or three centuries, had man undergone a change so profound nor so extended his power over the forces of nature.

---

9   A slight paraphrase ("le peuple en fut le maçon") of Victor Hugo's 1831 novel *Notre-Dame de Paris* (translated as *The Hunchback of Notre-Dame*): "Le temps est l'architecte, le peuple est le maçon" ("The time is the architect, the people is the builder"). (Editor)

Perhaps you are thinking of the civilisation of our century whose progress we are constantly praising? But in each of its manifestations it is only the daughter of the civilisation that grew up within the free communes. All the great discoveries made by modern science—the compass, the clock, the watch, printing, maritime discoveries, gunpowder, the laws of gravitation, atmospheric pressure of which the steam engine was only a development, the rudiments of chemistry, the scientific method already indicated by Roger Bacon and practiced in Italian universities—where did all these come from if not the free cities, in the civilisation which was developed under the shelter of communal liberties?

But it may be said that I forget the conflicts, the internal struggles, with which the history of these communes is filled, the turmoil of the streets, the bitter battles against the lords, the insurrections of the "young arts" against the "old arts," the bloodshed and reprisals of these struggles.

Well, no, I forget nothing. But like Leo and Botta—the two historians of medieval Italy—like Sismondi, like Ferrari, Gino Capponi and so many others, I see that these struggles were the very guarantee of a free life in the free city. I perceive a renewal, a new impetus towards progress after each of those struggles. After having recounted in detail these struggles and conflicts, and having also measured the immensity of the progress achieved while these struggles bloodied the streets—the well-being assured to all the inhabitants, the civilisation renewed—Leo and Botta concluded with this thought, [which is] so right which often comes to my mind; I would like to see it engraved in the minds of every modern revolutionary:

"A commune," they said, "only presents the image of a moral whole, is only universal in its manner of being, like the human mind itself, *only when it has admitted conflict, opposition*."[10]

Yes, conflict, freely debated, without any external power, the State, coming to throw its immense weight into the balance in favour of one of the forces engaged in the struggle.

Like those two authors, I also believe that we have often caused "much more evil by *imposing* peace, because we linked together opposites in wanting to create a general political order and sacrificed individualities and small organisms, in order to absorb them in a vast body without colour and without life."[11]

---

10   Kropotkin's emphasis, Henri Leo and Carlo Botta, *Histoire d'Italie, depuis les premiers temps jusqu'a nos jours* (Paris: Béthune et Plon, 1844) I: 462. (Editor)

11   This is a slight paraphrase of Henri Leo and Carlo Botta: "more harm was done by peace through war, because we linked together opposites in seeking to create a general political order and sacrificed individualities and small ways of living [*les petits*

That is why the communes—so long as they did not themselves seek to become States and to impose around them "submission in a vast body without colour and without life"—that is why they grew and emerged rejuvenated from every struggle, flourishing with the clash of weapons in the streets; whereas two centuries later this same civilisation collapsed at the sound of wars fathered by States.

In the commune, struggle was for the conquest and upholding of the liberty of the individual, for the federative principle, for the right to unite and to act; whereas the wars of the States were intended to extinguish these liberties, to subjugate the individual, to annihilate free agreement, to unite men in the same servitude in relation to the king, the judge, the priest—the State.

Therein lies all the difference. There are struggles and conflicts that destroy. And there are those which hurl humanity forward.

VI

During the course of the sixteenth century the modern barbarians destroyed all this civilisation of the cities of the Middle Ages. These barbarians did not succeed in annihilating it, but they succeeded in halting its progress for at least two or three centuries. They threw it in a new direction, in which humanity struggles with difficulty at the moment, not knowing how to escape.

They subjugated the individual. They stripped him of all his liberties, and required him to forget all his associations based on free agreement and free initiative. Their aim was to level the whole of society to an identical submission to the master. They destroyed all ties between men, declaring that the State and the Church, alone, must henceforth form the association between their subjects; that the Church and the State alone have the task of watching over the industrial, commercial, judicial, artistic, personal [*passionnels*] interests for which men of the twelfth century were accustomed to unite directly.

And who are these barbarians? It is the State: the Triple Alliance, finally constituted, of the military chief, the Roman judge, and the priest—the three forming a mutual insurance for domination—the three, united in one power which will command in the name of the interests of society—and will crush that society.

---

existences], in order to absorb them in a vast body without colour and without life" (*Histoire d'Italie, depuis les premiers temps jusqu'a nos jours* [Paris: Béthune et Plon, 1844] I: 751). (Editor)

We ask ourselves, naturally, how were these new barbarians able to over-come the communes, once so powerful? Where did they find the strength for conquest?

They found this force, first of all, in the village. Just as the communes of Ancient Greece were unable to abolish slavery and perished because of that—so the communes of the Middle Ages did not know how to free the peasant from serfdom along with the town-dweller.

It is true that almost everywhere the town-dweller—an artisan-farmer himself—had at the time of his emancipation sought to rouse the country-side to help him gain their freedom. For two centuries, the townspeople in Italy, Spain, and Germany had sustained a bitter war against the feudal lords. Feats of heroism and perseverance were displayed by the burghers in this war on the castles. They bled themselves white to become masters of the castles of feudalism and to fell the feudal forest that surrounded them.

But they were only partially successful. War-weary, they finally made peace over the heads of the peasant. To buy peace, they handed him over to the lord as long as he lived outside the territory conquered by the com-mune. In Italy and Germany they ended up accepting the lord as fellow burgher [*combourgeois*], on condition that he came to live in the commune. Elsewhere, they ended by sharing his domination over the peasant. And the lord took his revenge on the "low people" of the towns, whom he hated and despised, bathing the streets in blood by conflicts and the practice of retaliation [*talion*] of the noble families, who did not bring their differences before the syndics and the communal judges but settled them by the sword in the street, hurling one part of community [*communaux*] against another.

The lord also demoralised the commune with his largesse, his intrigues, his lordly way of life and by his education received at the court of the bish-op or the king. He convinced it to embrace his struggles. And the burgher ended by imitating the lord: he became lord in his turn, also enriching himself by distant commerce or from the labour of the serfs confined in the villages.

After which the peasant gave the emerging kings, emperors, tsars and the popes his assistance when they began building their kingdoms and sub-jecting the towns. Where the peasant did not march under their orders, he did not oppose them.

It is in the countryside, in a fortified castle situated in the middle of ru-ral communities that royalty was slowly established. In the twelfth century, it existed in name only, and we know today what to think of the bandits, chiefs of small bands of brigands, who adorned themselves with that name: a name which—as Augustin Thierry has so well demonstrated—did not mean very much at the time, when there were "the king (the superior, the senior) of the basoche,"[12] "the king of the nets" (amongst fishermen), "the king of the beggars."

Slowly, gropingly, a baron better placed in a region, more powerful or more cunning than the others, succeeded, here and there, in raising himself above his fellows. The Church hastened to support him. And by force, guile, money, sword and poison if need be, one of these feudal barons grew [in power] at the expense of the others. But royal authority never succeeded in constituting itself in any of the free cities, which had their noisy forum, their Tarpeian Rock[13] or their river for the tyrants: it arose in the towns which had grown in the heart of the countryside.

After having sought in vain to establish this authority in Rheims, or in Laon, it was in Paris—an agglomeration of villages and boroughs surrounded by a rich countryside which had not yet known the life of free cities; it was in Westminster, at the gates of the populous City of London; it was in the Kremlin, built in the centre of rich villages on the banks of the Moskva [river], after having failed in Suzdal and in Vladimir—but never in Novgorod, Pskov, Nuremberg, Laon or Florence—that royal authority was consolidated.

The peasants of the surrounding area supplied the emerging monarchies with food, horses and men, and commerce—royal and not communal in this case—increased their wealth. The Church swaddled them with its care. It protected them, came to their aid with its coffers, invented the local saint and his miracles for them. It enveloped with its worship Notre Dame of Paris or the Image of the Virgin of Iberia in Moscow.[14] And while the civilisation of the free cities, freed from the bishops, seized its youthful elan, the Church worked hard to reconstitute its authority by means of the rising royalty, swaddled by its care, its incense, and its coins, the royal cradle of

---

12   The *basoche* was the guild of the legal clerks of the court system from the Middle Ages until the French Revolution. The word derives from the Latin *basilica*, the kind of building in which the legal trade was practiced in the Middle Ages. (Editor)

13   The Tarpeian Rock was a steep cliff of the southern summit of the Capitoline Hill, overlooking the Roman Forum in Ancient Rome, it was used during the Roman Republic as an execution site for murderers, traitors, etc. (Editor)

14   The Panagia Portaitissa is an Eastern Orthodox icon of the Virgin Mary which, according to the Sacred Tradition of the Eastern Orthodox Church, was painted by Luke the Evangelist and to which numerous miracles have been attributed. In 1648, Patriarch Nikon of Moscow, while he was still Archimandrite of Novospassky Monastery, commissioned an exact copy of it to be made and sent to Russia. Almost immediately upon its arrival, the icon had numerous miracles attributed to it by the faithful. The Iverskaya Chapel was built in 1669 to enshrine the icon next to the Kremlin walls in Moscow. (Editor)

the one it had finally chosen to rebuild with him, through him, its ecclesiastical authority. In Paris, Moscow, Madrid and Prague you see it leaning over the cradle of royalty, a lighted torch in its hand, the executioner by its side.

Fierce in its work, strong in its statist education, leaning on the man of will or cunning it took from any class of society, made for intrigue and versed in Roman and Byzantine law—you can see it relentlessly marching towards its ideal: the Hebrew king, absolute but obedient to the high priest—the secular arm at the orders of the ecclesiastical power.

In the sixteenth century this slow labour of the two conspirators is already in full force. A king already dominates the other barons, his rivals, and this power will soon fall upon the free cities to crush them in their turn.

Besides, the towns of the sixteenth century were no longer what they had been in the twelfth, thirteenth and fourteenth centuries.

Born of the libertarian revolution, they did not have the courage or the strength to spread their ideas of equality to the neighbouring countryside, not even to those who had later settled within their walls, [those] sanctuaries of freedom, to create industrial crafts there.

In every town is found a distinction between the old families who had made the revolution of the twelfth century, or simply "the families," and those who were established later in the city. The old "merchant guild" would not hear of accepting the newcomers. It refused to incorporate the "young arts" for [the purposes of] commerce. And, from the simple steward of the city that it once was when it carried out external trade for the whole city, it became the middleman who enriches itself on its own behalf through distant commerce. It imported Eastern ostentation, it became moneylender to the city and, later, joins with the burgher-lord [*seigneur combourgeois*] and the priest against the "lower classes"; or else it sought support from the emerging king to maintain its right to enrichment, its commercial monopoly. Becoming personal, commerce destroys the free city.

The guilds of the old crafts which at the beginning formed the city and its government also did not wish to recognise the same rights to the young guilds, established later by new crafts. These must conquer their rights by a revolution. And that is what they do everywhere. But if in certain cities this revolution becomes the starting point for a renewal of all the ways of life and all the arts (this is so clearly seen in Florence), in other cities it ends in the victory of the *popolo grasso* over the *popolo basso*[15]—by a crushing [of the rebellion], by mass deportations, by executions, especially when the lords and priests interfere.

---

15   Italian for "common people" and "fat people," respectively. During the Middle Ages in Italy, the wealthy and influential members of society were called *Popolo Grosse*, which literally meant "fat people." (Editor)

And, needless to say, the king will use as a pretext the defence of the "lower people" in order to crush the "fat people" and to subjugate them both after he has made himself master of the city!

And then the cities had to die since *even men's ideas had changed*. The teaching of canonic law and Roman law had modified the mind-set [of the people].

The European of the twelfth century was fundamentally a federalist. As a man of free initiative, of free agreement, of desired and freely entered associations, he saw in himself the point of departure for the whole of society. He did not seek safety through obedience nor did he ask for a saviour for society. The idea of Christian and Roman discipline was unknown to him.

But under the influence of the Christian church—always in love with authority, always longing [*jalousie*] to impose its dominion over the souls and above all the labour of the faithful; and on the other hand, under the influence of Roman law which, from the twelfth century onwards, had already appeared at the courts of powerful lords, kings and popes, and soon became the favourite [subject of] study in the universities—under the influence of these two teachings which are so much in accord, though originally bitter enemies, minds became corrupted as the priest and the jurist triumphed.

Man fell in love with authority. A revolution of the lower crafts is accomplished in a commune, the commune calls for a saviour. It gives itself a dictator, a municipal Caesar; it grants him full powers to exterminate the opposition party. And he takes advantage of this, using all the refinements in cruelty suggested to him by the Church or by examples borrowed from the despotic kingdoms of the East.

The Church without doubt supports him. Had it not always dreamt of the biblical king who will kneel before the high priest and be his docile instrument? Has it not always hated with all its might those ideas of rationalism which breathed in the free towns during the first Renaissance, that of the twelfth century? Did it not curse those "pagan" ideas which brought man back to nature under the influence of the rediscovery of Greek civilisation? And, later, did it not get the princes to stifle these ideas which, in the name of primitive Christianity, raised men against the pope, the priest and religion in general? Fire, the [breaking] wheel and the gallows—those weapons so dear at all times to the Church—were used against the heretics. Whatever the instrument: pope, king or dictator—it matters little to it as long as fire, the wheel and the gallows operate against its enemies.

And under this double teaching of the Roman jurist and the priest, the federalist spirit which had made the free commune, the spirit of initiative and free agreement was dying to make way for the spirit of discipline, for pyramidal authoritarian organisation. Both the rich and the commoners demanded a saviour.

And when the saviour appeared; when the king, enriched far from the turmoil of the forum in some town of his creation, supported by the wealthy Church and followed by conquered nobles and their peasants, knocked at the gates of the cities, promising the "lower classes" his lofty protection against the rich and the submissive rich his protection against the rebellious poor—the towns, already gnawed away by the blight of authority, lacked the strength to resist him.

The great invasions of Europe by waves of peoples once more coming from the East aided the rising royalty in this work of the concentration of powers.

The Mongols had conquered and devastated Eastern Europe in the thirteenth century, and soon an empire was founded there, in Moscow, under the protection of the Tartar khans and the Russian Christian Church. The Turks had come to settle in Europe and pushed as far as Vienna, devastating everything in their path. Thereupon, powerful States were formed in Poland, Bohemia, Hungary, in Central Europe, to resist these two invasions. While at the other end [of Europe], the war of extermination waged against the Moors in Spain allowed another powerful empire to constitute itself in Castile and Aragon, supported by the Roman Church and the Inquisition—by the sword and the stake.

These invasions and wars inevitably led Europe to enter a new phase—that of military States.

Since the communes themselves were becoming small States, these little States inevitably had to be swallowed up by the large ones.

VII

The victory of the State over the communes of the Middle Ages and the federalist institutions of the time was nevertheless not immediate. There was a period when it was threatened to the point of being in doubt.

An immense popular movement—religious in its form and expressions but eminently egalitarian and communist in its aspirations—arose in the towns and countryside of Central Europe.

Already, in the fourteenth century (in 1358 in France and in 1381 in England) two similar great movements had taken place. The two powerful uprisings of the Jacquerie and of Wat Tyler had shaken society to its very foundations. Both, though, had been principally directed against the nobles and, though both had been defeated, they had broken feudal power. The uprising of peasants in England had put an end to serfdom and the Jacquerie in France had so severely checked serfdom in its development that henceforth the institution simply vegetated, without ever reaching the power that it was to achieve later in Germany and Eastern Europe.

Now, in the sixteenth century, a similar movement took place in Central Europe. Under the name of the Hussite uprising in Bohemia, Anabaptism in Germany, Switzerland and in the Low Countries, it was—besides the revolt against the lord—a comprehensive revolt against the State and Church, against Roman and canon law, in the name of primitive Christianity.[16]

Long misrepresented by statist and ecclesiastical historians, this movement is just beginning to be understood today.

The absolute freedom of the individual, who must only obey the commands of his conscience, and communism were the watchwords of this uprising. And it was only later, after the State and Church had succeeded in exterminating its most ardent champions and misappropriated it for their own benefit, that this movement, diminished [in scope] and deprived of its revolutionary character, became the Lutheran Reformation.

With Luther the movement was welcomed by the princes; but it had begun as communist anarchism, preached and put into practice in some places. And if we disregard the religious phrasing which was a tribute to the times, we find in it the very essence of the current of ideas which we represent today: the negation of laws—laws of the State or allegedly divine [in origin]—the conscience of the individual being his one and only law; the commune, absolute master of its destiny, taking back from the lords communal lands and refusing any personal or money fee to the State;[17] communism in a word, and equality put into practice. So when Denck, one of the philosophers of the Anabaptist movement, was asked if he nevertheless did not acknowledge the authority of the Bible, he replied that the only rule of conduct which each individual finds *for himself* in the Bible was obligatory for him. And yet these same, so vague, phrases—derived from ecclesiastical jargon—this authority of "the book," from which is so easily borrowed arguments for and against communism, for and against authority, and so undecided when it is a question of clearly affirming freedom—did not this religious tendency already contain the seeds of the certain defeat of the uprising?

---

16   The "times of troubles" in Russia at the beginning of the seventeenth century represent a similar movement, directed against serfdom and the State but without a religious basis.

17   Medieval serfs did not receive land as a free gift and to use it they owed certain duties to their lord. These took the form of personal services (such as working on the lord's fields for two or three days each week) or paying a fee for certain activities (such as being obligated to use the lord's mill to ground their wheat). They were also expected to provide such personal services in labour as well as taxes to the monarchy. (Editor)

Born in the towns, the movement soon spread to the countryside. The peasants refused to obey anybody and, fixing an old shoe on a pike by way of a flag, reclaimed the land from the lords, broke the bonds of serfdom, drove away the priests and judges and formed themselves into free communes. And it was only by the stake, the wheel and the gallows, it was only by massacring more than a hundred thousand peasants in a few years that royal or imperial power, allied with that of the papal or the reformed Church—Luther encouraging the massacre of the peasants even more vehemently than the Pope—put an end to those uprisings which had threatened for a time the formation of the emerging States.

Born from popular Anabaptism, the Lutheran Reformation, supported by the State, massacred the people and crushed the movement from which it had drawn its strength at its origin. Then the remnants of the popular wave sought refuge in the communities of the "Moravian Brothers," who, in turn, were destroyed a century later by the Church and the State. Those of them who were not exterminated sought sanctuary, some in south-eastern Russia (the Mennonite community who have since emigrated to Canada), and others to Greenland where they could continue to live to this day in communities refusing all service to the State.

Henceforth the State was assured of its existence. The jurist, the priest and the war-lord, constituted in a joint alliance around the thrones, could pursue their work of annihilation.

What lies, amassed by statist historians in the pay of the State, on that period!

Indeed, have we not all learned at school for instance that the State rendered the great service of forming, on the ruins of feudal society, the national unions previously made impossible by the rivalries between cities? Having learned this at school, almost all of us have continued to believe this into middle age.

And yet we learn today that, in spite of all the rivalries, the medieval cities had already worked for four centuries to establish these unions by desired, freely agreed federation and had succeeded.

The Lombardy union, for example, encompassed the cities of Northern Italy, with its federal treasury in Milan. Other federations such as the Tuscany union, the Rhineland union (which included sixty towns), the federations of Westphalia, of Bohemia, of Serbia, of Poland, of Russian towns covered Europe. At the same time, the commercial union of the Hanse included Scandinavian, German, Polish, and Russian towns throughout the Baltic basin. There were already all the elements as well as the fact itself of freely formed large human agglomerations.

Do you want the living proof of these groupings? You have it in Switzerland! There the union initially asserted itself between the village communes (the Old Cantons), just as it was formed in France at the same time in Laon. And since in Switzerland the separation between town and village had not been as deep as [in those places] where the towns were engaged in large-scale distant commerce, the towns gave assistance to the peasant insurrection of the sixteenth century and then the union included towns and villages to constitute a federation which continues to this day.

But the State, by its very nature, cannot tolerate free federation: it represents that horror of all jurists, "a State within the State." The State does not recognise a freely agreed union operating within it; it knows only *subjects*. Only it and its sister, the Church, arrogate the right to serve as the link between men.

Consequently, the State must, inevitably, destroy cities based on the direct union between citizens. It must abolish all association within the city, abolish the city itself, and destroy all direct association between the cities. For the federal principle it must substitute the principle of submission, of discipline. That is its essence. Without this principle it ceases to be a State.

And the sixteenth century—a century of carnage and wars—is fully summed up by this struggle of the rising State against the free towns and their federations. The towns were besieged, stormed, sacked, their inhabitants decimated or deported.

The State eventually wins total victory. And these are the consequences:

In the sixteenth century Europe was covered with rich cities, whose artisans, masons, weavers and engravers produced marvels of art; their universities laid the foundations of modern empirical science, their caravans roamed the continents, their vessels ploughed the rivers and seas.

What remained two centuries later? Towns that had as many as fifty to a hundred thousand inhabitants and which had possessed (as was the case in Florence) more schools and, in the communal hospitals, more beds per person than there are now possessed in the towns best equipped in this respect—became rotten boroughs.[18] Their populations massacred or deported, the State and Church seized their wealth. Industry dies under the strict supervision of the employees of the State. Commerce is dead. Even the roads which had once linked these cities together became impassable in the seventeenth century.

---

18   The term *rotten borough* came into use in eighteenth century Britain and was used to mean a parliamentary borough with a tiny electorate. This meant that the electorate could not vote as they pleased due to dependency on and pressure by the local landlord, when the electorate was not reduced to just him. Usually these boroughs were once more populous and important and so the word "rotten" had the connotation of corruption as well as that of long-term decline. (Editor)

The State is war. And wars devastated Europe, completing the ruin of the towns which the State had not yet directly destroyed.

The towns crushed, at least the villages gained something from the concentration of State control? Of course not! Read what the historians tell us of life in the countryside in Scotland, in Tuscany, in Germany during the sixteenth century and compare their accounts with those of the misery in England in the years before 1648, in France under the "Sun King" Louis XIV, in Germany, in Italy, everywhere, after a century of statist domination.

Misery—everywhere. All are unanimous in recognising it, in reporting it. Where serfdom had been abolished, it is reconstituted under a thousand new forms; and where it had not yet been destroyed, it was shaped under the protection of the State into a savage institution bearing all the characteristics of ancient slavery or worse. In Russia it was the rising State of the Romanovs that introduced serfdom and soon gave it the form of slavery.

But could anything else come out of statist misery, since its first concern, after [crushing] the towns, was to annihilate the village commune, destroy all the ties that existed between the peasants, to deliver their lands to plundering by the rich, to subjugate them, every individual, to the functionary, the priest, the lord?

VIII

To annihilate the independence of the cities; to pillage the rich guilds of merchants and artisans; to centralise in its hands the external commerce of the cities, and ruin it; to seize the internal administration of the guilds and subject internal commerce as well as the manufacture of anything, down to the smallest detail, to [the control of] a host of functionaries—and in this way kill industry and the crafts; to seize the local militias and the whole of the municipal administration, to crush the weak for the benefit of the strong by taxation, and ruining countries by wars—such was the role of the emerging State in the sixteenth and seventeenth centuries in relation to urban agglomerates.

The same tactic [was used], obviously, for the villages, for the peasants. As soon as the State felt strong enough, it hastened to destroy the commune in the village, to ruin the peasants in its clutches, and to plunder the common lands.

Historians and economists in the pay of the State teach us, of course, that the village commune having become an outdated form of land possession—a form which hindered the progress of agriculture—had to disappear under "the action of natural economic forces." The bourgeois politicians and economists keep repeating this to the present day; and there are even revolutionaries and socialists—those who claim to be scientific—who recite this commonplace fable [*fable convenue*], taught at school.

Well, never has a more odious lie been asserted in science. A conscious lie, for history abounds with documents to prove for those who want to know—for France, it would almost be enough to [just] consult Dalloz— that the village commune was initially deprived of all its powers by the State; its independence, its juridical and legislative powers; and then its lands were either simply stolen by the rich under the protection of the State, or directly confiscated by the State.

In France the pillage started as early as the sixteenth century, and followed its course at a faster pace in the following century. From 1659 the State took the communes under its lofty tutelage, and we have only to consult Louis XIV's edict of 1667 to discover the scale of the plunder of communal properties at that time.[19] "Each has put up with it according to his propriety ... they have divided them ... to strip the communes they used fictitious debts," said the "Sun King" in that edict ... and two years later he confiscated all the income of the communes for his own benefit. This is called a "natural death" in the language which claims to be scientific.

In the following century, it is estimated that half, at least, of communal land was simply appropriated by the nobility and the clergy under the patronage of the State. And yet the commune continued to exist until 1787. The village assembly gathered under the elm [tree], apportioned the lands, distributed the [demands for] taxes—you can find the evidence in Babeau (*Le village sous l'ancien régime* [*The Village Under the Ancien Régime*]). Turgot, in the province in which he was the Intendant,[20] had already found the village assemblies "too noisy" and under his administration they were abolished, replaced by assemblies elected from amongst the village big-wigs. And on the eve of the Revolution, in 1787, the State generalised that measure. The *mir* was abolished and the affairs of the commune thus fell into the hands of a few syndics, elected by the richest bourgeois and peasants.

The Constituent Assembly was quick in confirming this law, in December 1789, and the bourgeois then replaced the lords in stripping the communes of what remained of their communal lands. It then needed Jacquerie after Jacquerie to force the Convention, in 1793, to confirm

---

19   *Edit du Roi, portant règlement général sur les Communes et Communaux des Paroisses et Communautés d'Habitants,* issued in April, 1667. Contained in Le Gras de Gallon, *Conférence de l'ordonnance de Louis XIV du mois d'août 1669, sur le fait des Euaux et Forests,* Volume 2 (Paris, 1725), 258–261. (Editor)

20   An Intendant was a royal civil servant in the pre-revolution Monarchy and was considered a symbol of royal centralisation and absolutism. Turgot was the Intendant of Limoges between 1761 and 1774. (Editor)

what the rebellious peasants had just achieved in eastern France. That is to say, the Convention ordered the return of the communal lands to the peasants—something which, moreover, only took place *where it was already achieved by revolutionary action*. It is time to understand that this is the fate of all revolutionary laws. They only come into effect when the fact is already accomplished.

But while recognising the right of the communes to the lands that had been taken away from them since 1669, the law had to add its bourgeois venom. Its intention was that the communal lands should be divided in equal parts only between "citizens"—that is to say amongst the village bourgeoisie.[21] By a stroke of the pen it wanted to dispossess the "inhabitants" and the mass of the impoverished peasants, who were most in need of these lands. Thereupon, fortunately, there were new Jacqueries and in July 1793 the Convention authorised the division of the land by head, between all the inhabitants—something, again, which was only done here and there, but which served as a pretext for a new pillage of communal lands.[22]

Were these measures not already enough to cause what these gentlemen call "the natural death" of the commune? And yet the commune still lived. Then, on 24 August 1794, the reaction coming to power struck the major blow. The State confiscated all the lands of the communes and used them as a fund to guarantee the national debt, putting them up for auction and delivering them to its creatures, the Thermidorians.

On the 2 Prairial Year V,[23] after three years of scrambling [for the spoils], this law was happily repealed. But, at the same time, the communes were abolished and replaced by cantonal councils, so that the State could more easily pack them with its creatures. This lasted until 1801 when the village communes were reintroduced; but then the government itself undertook to appoint the mayors and syndics in each of the 36,000 communes! And this absurdity lasted until the Revolution of July 1830; after which the law of 1789 was reintroduced. And, in the meantime, the communal lands were again confiscated entirely by the State in 1813 and pillaged anew for three years. What remained was not returned to the communes until 1816.

---

21 Kropotkin discusses the desire by the bourgeois to limit political involvement to "active" citizens (defined by a having a certain amount of wealth) and exclude "passive" citizens (that is, the working classes) in chapter LIX of *The Great French Revolution*. (Editor)

22 Kropotkin discusses the fate of the communal lands in chapters XLVIII and XLIX of *The Great French Revolution*. (Editor)

23 Kropotkin is using the French Revolutionary Calendar for the 21st of May, 1797. (Editor)

Do you think that was the end?—Not at all! Each new regime saw in the communal lands a means of rewarding its henchmen. Thus, from 1830, on three different occasions—the first in 1837 and the last under Napoleon III—laws were enacted to *force* the peasants to divide what remained of their communal forests and pastures, and three times the State was obliged to annul those laws on account of the resistance of the peasants. All the same, Napoleon III took advantage of it to seize a few large estates and to make presents of them to his creatures.

Such are the facts. And this is what these gentlemen call, in "scientific" language, the natural death of communal ownership "under the influence of economic laws." We might as well call the massacre of a hundred thousand soldiers on the battlefield a natural death!

Well, what was done in France was done in Belgium, in England, in Germany, in Austria—everywhere in Europe, except in the Slav countries.[24]

But no matter! The periods of increased pillaging of the communes are similar throughout western Europe. Only the methods vary. Thus in England they did not dare to proceed by general measures; they preferred to pass through Parliament some thousands of separate Enclosure Acts (acts of "demarcation") by which, in every particular case, Parliament sanctioned the confiscation—*it does so to this day*—and gave the lord the right to keep the communal lands that he had enclosed by a fence [*ceintes d'un enclose*]. And while nature had hitherto followed the narrow furrows by which the communal fields were temporarily divided between the various families of a village in England, and that we have in the works of a certain Marshall[25] clear descriptions of this form of possession at the beginning of the nineteenth century, while the communal household was still retained in some municipalities up to the present,[26] there is no lack of scholars (such as Seebohm, worthy emulator of Fustel de Coulanges) to maintain and teach that the commune never existed in England as anything other than a form of serfdom!

In Belgium, in Germany, in Italy, in Spain we find the same methods [at work]. And, in one way or another, the individual appropriation of the

---

24   It is already being done in Russia, the government having authorised the pillaging of communal lands by the law of 1906 and encouraged this pillage through its functionaries.

25   "Marshall's works, which passed unnoticed until Nasse and Sir Henry Maine drew attention to them, leave no doubt as to the village-community system having been widely spread, in nearly all English counties, at the beginning of the nineteenth century" (Kropotkin, *Mutual Aid*, 190). (Editor)

26   See Dr. Gilbert Slater, "The Inclosure of Common Fields" in the *Geographical Journal* of the Geographical Society of London, with plans and maps, January 1907. Later published in volume form.

formally communal lands was almost completed in Western Europe by the fifties of the nineteenth century. The peasants have retained only scraps of their communal lands.

This is the way that this mutual insurance between the lord, the priest, the soldier and the judge which has the name "the State" behaved towards the peasants, in order to strip them of their last guarantee against destitution and economic servitude.

But while it was approving and organising this pillage could the State respect the institution of the commune as an organ of local life?

Obviously not.

To admit that citizens could constitute between themselves a federation which appropriates some of the functions of the State would have been a contradiction in principle. The State demands from its subjects direct personal submission without intermediaries; it wants equality in servitude; it cannot allow "the State within the State."

Also, as soon as the State began to form itself in the sixteenth century, it worked to destroy all the ties of association which existed between citizens, whether in the town or the village. If it tolerated, under the name of municipal institutions, some remnants of autonomy—never of independence—it was only for a fiscal purpose, to correspondingly reduce the central budget; or else, to enable the big-wigs of the province to get rich at the expense of the people, as was the case in England, [quite] legally until recent years, and in institutions and customs to this day.

This is understandable. Local life is [based on] customary right whereas the centralisation of powers is [a matter of] Roman law. The two cannot live side by side; one must destroy the other.

That is why under the French regime in Algeria when a Kabyle *djemmah*—a village commune—wants to plead for its lands each inhabitant of the commune must lodge a separate complaint with the courts, which will judge fifty or two hundred separate cases rather than accept the collective complaint of the commune. The Jacobin code developed in the Code Napoleon hardly knows customary law: it prefers Roman law, or rather Byzantine law.

That is why, still in France, when the wind blows down a tree onto the national road, or a peasant who does not want to do the *corvée* labour himself to repair a communal road prefers to pay two or three francs to a stone breaker [to do it]—it is necessary that twelve to fifteen employees of the Ministries of the Interior and of Finance be set into motion and that *more than fifty documents* pass between these austere functionaries before the tree can be sold or before the peasant receives permission to pay two or three francs to the municipal treasury.

You doubt it, perhaps? Well, you will find these fifty documents, listed and duly numbered by M. Tricoche, in the *Journal des Economistes* (April, 1893).

That was, of course, under the Third Republic, for I do not speak of the barbaric procedures of the Ancien Régime which was satisfied with five or at the most six documents. Also, the scholars will tell you that in this barbaric time, control by the State was a sham.

And if it were only that! It would be, after all, only some twenty thousand functionaries too many, and another billion added to the budget. A mere trifle for the lovers of "order" and alignment!

But there is worse at the bottom of all this. There is the *principle* that destroys everything.

The peasants of a village have a thousand common interests: interests of household, of neighbourhood, of continuous relationships. They are inevitably led to unite for a thousand different things. But the State does not want, cannot allow that they are united! Since it gives them the school and the priest, the gendarme, and the judge—that should be enough for them. And if other interests arise—they can be dealt with through the channels of State and Church!

Thus until 1883 villagers in France were strictly prohibited from combining, if only for bulk-buying chemical fertilisers or irrigating of their meadows. It was not until 1883–1886 that the Republic decided to grant the peasants this right by voting in the law on trade unions, which was hedged in with strong provisos and restrictions.

And we, stupefied by State education, we rejoice in the sudden advances achieved by agricultural unions without blushing at the thought that this right which has been denied the peasants until now in the Middle Ages belonged without question to every man—free or serf. Slaves that we are, we already view this as a "conquest for democracy."

This is the state of stupefaction we have reached with our false education, tainted by the State, and our Statist prejudices!

IX

"If you have common interests in the town and the village then ask the State and the Church to deal with them. But it is forbidden for you to combine directly to deal with them yourselves!" Such is the concept that echoes across Europe since the sixteenth century.

"All alliances and covines of masons and carpenters, and congregations, chapters, ordinances and oaths betwixt them made, or to be made, shall be from henceforth void and wholly annulled" reads an edict by Edward III,

King of England, at the end of the fourteenth century.[27] But it was necessary to defeat the towns and of the popular insurrections of which we have
spoken for the State to dare to lay its hands on all the institutions—guilds,
brotherhoods, etc.—which bound the artisans together and dissolve them,
to destroy them.

This is what is seen so clearly in England, where we have a mass of
documents [available] to follow this movement step by step. Little by little
the State lays its hands on all the guilds and brotherhoods. It tights its grip
on them, abolishes their conjurations, their syndics (which it replaces by
its functionaries), their tribunals, their feasts; and at the beginning of the
sixteenth century, under Henry VIII, the State confiscates without any kind

---

27   This Act of Edward III was issued in 1360 and continued as follows: "so that every
     mason and carpenter, of what condition that he be, shall be compelled by his master
     to whom he serveth to do every work that to him pertaineth to do." In addition, the
     Ordinance of Labourers imposed in 1349 was followed by the *Statue of Labourers* in
     1351 (the latter was confirmed fifteen years later, in 1368). Both were ultimately vain
     attempts to aid landlords and masters facing labour shortages caused by the Black
     Death by freezing wages at the level they were before the plague by prohibiting increas-
     es in wages to a maximum (that paid in 1346) as well as the movement of workers from
     their home areas in search of better conditions:

     > "[I]t was ordained by our lord king [...] against the malice of servants
     > who were idle and not willing to serve after the pestilence without
     > excessive wages, that such manner of servants, men as well as women,
     > should be bound to serve, receiving the customary salary and wages
     > in the places where they are bound to serve [...] and that the same
     > servants refusing to serve in such a manner should be punished by
     > imprisonment of their bodies [...] servants having no regard to the
     > ordinance but to their ease and singular covetousness, do withdraw
     > themselves from serving great men and others, unless they have livery
     > and wages double or treble of what they were wont [...] to the great
     > damage of the great men and impoverishment of all the commonality;
     > whereof the commonality prays remedy. Wherefore in the parliament
     > by the assent of the prelates, earls, barons, and those of the common-
     > ality assembled there, in order to refrain the malice of the servants."
     > (*Statue of Labourers*)

     They also mandated that all able-bodied men and women under 60 must work and
     imposed harsh penalties to those who remained idle. Both laws were very unpopular
     and were contributing factors to subsequent social unrest in England, most notably the
     Peasants' Revolt of 1381. (Editor)

of procedure all that the guilds possess. The heir of the great protestant king completes his work.[28]

It is daylight robbery, without apologies, as Thorold Rogers said so well. And it is again this theft that the so-called scientific economists represent as the "natural" death of the guilds under the influence of "economic laws"!

Indeed, could the State tolerate the guild, the trade corporation, with its tribunal, its militia, its treasury, its sworn organisation? It was "the State within the State"! The real State *had* to destroy it and this it did everywhere: in England, in France, in Germany, in Bohemia, and in Russia, retaining only the appearance as an instrument of the tax collector, as part of its vast administrative machine.

And—is it any wonder that the guilds, master craftsmen and jurandes,[29] deprived of all that hitherto had been their lives, placed under [the control of] royal functionaries, became mere cogs in the [machinery of] administration, that by the eighteenth century they were no more than an obstruction, a hindrance, to the development of industries, whereas previously they were life itself for four centuries. The State had killed them.

But it was not enough for the State to abolish all the workings of the inner life of the sworn brotherhoods of the crafts which hindered it by placing themselves between it and its subjects. It was not enough for it to confiscate their funds and their properties. It had to seize their functions as well as their money.

In a city of the Middle Ages when there was a conflict of interests within a trade or two different guilds were in disagreement, there was no other recourse than the city. They had to come to an agreement, to arrive at some kind of compromise, since all were mutually bound together in the city. And this never failed to be done—by arbitration, by appeal to another city if need be.

---

28   A reference to an Act passed in the last year of the reign of Henry VIII seizing all the funds of the guilds (used for the welfare of its members and their families) and other properties. The confiscation of guild land (whose revenue was used to generate these funds and to provide interest-free loans) was planned by Henry VIII but carried out when his son Edward VI (1537–1553) assumed the throne in 1547. Henry's daughter, Elizabeth (1533–1603), continued the long sorry history of State action against labour by enacting the *Statute of Artificers* of 1563 which sought to fix prices, impose maximum wages, restrict workers' freedom of movement as well as transferring to the newly forming English State functions previously held by the craft guilds. Local magistrates regulated wages while workers required permission to move employers. The Statute was abolished in 1813. (Editor)

29   The *jurande* was a guild body made up of its *juré*, members of the guild elected (usually for one year) to represent it and defend its interests. (Editor)

Henceforth the State was the sole judge. At times all the local, insignificant disputes in small towns with a few hundred inhabitants were piled up in the form of documents in the offices of the king or of parliament. The English parliament was literally inundated by thousands of these minor local squabbles. It then took thousands of functionaries in the capital—most of them corruptible—to read, classify, evaluate all these, to pronounce on the smallest detail: [for example] to regulate the manner in which a horseshoe had to be forged, how to bleach linen, to salt herrings, to make a barrel and so on *ad infinitum*, and the flood [of issues] always rose!

But this was not all. Before long the State laid its hands on the export trade. It saw a source of enrichment—and seized it. Formerly, when a dispute arose between two towns over the value of exported cloth, or the quality of wool, or the capacity of herring barrels, the towns themselves would remonstrate with each other. If the dispute dragged on, a third city was approached to judge it as arbitrator (this was constantly seen). Or else a congress of the guilds of the weavers or coopers was convened to resolve on an international level the quality and value of cloth or the capacity of barrels.

Henceforth it was the State in London or in Paris which undertook to settle all these disputes. Through its functionaries it regulated the capacity of barrels, defined the quality of cloth, specified and ordered the number of threads and their thickness in the warp and the weave, meddled by its ordinances with the smallest details of every industry.

You can guess with what result. Industry was dying in the eighteenth century under this supervision.

What had become, indeed, of the art of Benvenuto Cellini under the tutelage of the State?—It disappeared! And the architecture of those guilds of masons and carpenters whose works of art we still admire? Just look at the hideous monuments of the statist period and at a glance you will judge that architecture was dead, so dead that it has not yet recovered from the blows dealt to it by the State.

What became of the textiles of Bruges, the cloth from Holland? Where were those blacksmiths, so skilled in handling iron and who, in every European town, knew how to make this thankless metal lend itself to [the creation of] the most exquisite designs? Where were those turners, those watchmakers, those fitters who had made Nuremberg one of the glories of the Middle Ages for precision instruments? Talk to James Watt who, two centuries later, spent thirty years looking in vain for a worker who knew how to produce a more or less circular cylinder for his steam engine. So his machine remained in draft form for three decades for the lack of workers to construct it.

Such was the work of the State in the industrial field. All it could do was to tighten the screw on the worker, depopulate the countryside, sow misery in the towns, reduce millions of people to starvation, impose industrial serfdom.

And it is these pathetic remains of the old guilds, these organisms battered and crushed [*pressurés*] by the State, these useless cogs of the bureaucracy, which the ever "scientific" economists have in their ignorance confused with the guilds of the Middle Ages. What the Great [French] Revolution swept away as harmful to industry was not the guild, nor even the craft association [*l'union de metier*]; it was a useless and harmful cog in the statist machine.

But what the Revolution took great care not to sweep away was the power of the State over industry, over the factory serf.

Do you remember the discussion which took place at the Convention—at the terrible Convention—regarding a strike? To the grievances of the strikers, the Convention replied:

"The State alone has the duty to watch over the interests of all citizens. By striking, you are forming a coalition, you are creating a State within the State. So death!"

In this reply only the bourgeois nature of the Revolution has been seen. But does it not have a much deeper meaning? Does it not sum up the attitude of the State towards society as a whole, which found its complete and logical expression in the Jacobinism of 1793? "You have a complaint? Lodge any complaint with the State! It alone has the mission to redress the grievances of its subjects. As for you uniting to defend yourselves—never!" It was in this sense that the Republic was called one and *indivisible*.

Does not the modern Jacobin socialist think the same? Did not the Convention express the essence of Jacobin thought with the ruthless logic typical of it?

In this reply of the Convention was summed up the attitude of all States in regard to all coalitions and all private societies, whatever their aim.

As for the strike, it is still the case that in Russia striking is considered a crime of high treason. To a great extent [this applies] also in Germany, where Wilhelm said to the miners: "Appeal to me; but if you ever presume to act for yourselves you will know the sabres of my soldiers."

It is still almost always the case in France. And it is with such a struggle in England[—]after having struggled for a century by [means of] secret societies, by the dagger for traitors and for the masters, by explosive powder under machines (as late as 1860), by sand poured into grease-boxes [i.e., sabotage] and so on[—]that English workers are beginning to win the right to strike, and will soon have it in full—if they do not fall into the traps already set for them by the State, in seeking to impose compulsory arbitration in return for the eight hour law.[30]

More than a century of terrible struggles! And what misery, with workers dying in prison, transported to Australia, shot, hanged, to regain the right to combine, which—I never tire of repeating this—every man, free or serf, practised freely so long as the State did not lay [*imposé*] its heavy hand on societies.

But what! Was it only the worker who was treated in this way?

Let us merely recall the struggles that the bourgeoisie had to wage against the State to win the right to form commercial societies—a right which the State only began to concede when it discovered a convenient means of creating monopolies for the benefit of its creatures and to fill its coffers. Think of the struggles to dare to write, to speak, or even to think otherwise than [the way] the State decrees through the Academy, the University and the Church! Of the struggles that must be waged to this day in order to be able to teach children to read—a right which the State reserves [for itself] but does not use! Of the struggles to even secure the right to have fun together! Not to mention those which would have to be waged in order to dare to choose your judge and your laws—something which was formerly an everyday practice—nor the struggles that will be needed before that book of infamous punishments known as the Penal Code, invented by the spirit of the inquisition and of the despotic empires of the East, is thrown into the fire!

Observe next taxation—an institution of purely statist origin—this formidable weapon used by the State, in Europe as in the young societies of the two Americas, to keep the masses under its heel, to favour its minions, to ruin the majority for the benefit of the rulers and to maintain the old divisions and the old castes.

Then take the wars, without which States cannot be established nor maintained, wars which become disastrous, inevitable, as soon as it is admitted that a particular region—because it is part of a State—has interests opposed to those of its neighbours who form part of another State. Think of past wars and of those that subjugated people will have to wage

---

30   During the 1890s, when Kropotkin was initially writing, there had been massive movements across the industrialised world for an eight-hour workday. He was very impressed by this strike wave and urged anarchists to take part. However, in 1907, he lamented how this promising movement was side-tracked into electing Socialist politicians who promised to legislate an eight-hour day and, of course, never did (see, respectively, "1st May 1891" and "1886–1907: Glimpses into the Labour Movement in this Country," *Direct Struggle Against Capital*). (Editor)

to conquer the right to breathe freely; of the wars for markets; of the wars to create colonial empires. And in France we unfortunately know only too well that every war, victorious or not, is followed by slavery.

And finally, what is worse than all that has just been enumerated is that the education we all receive from the State, at school and after, has so corrupted our minds that the very notion of freedom ends up going astray, disguising itself as servitude.

It is a sad sight to see those who believe they are revolutionaries bestow their hatred on the anarchist—because his concepts of freedom go beyond their petty and narrow notions of freedom learned in the state-controlled school. And yet, this spectacle is a reality.

It is because the spirit of voluntary servitude was, and still is, always cleverly cultivated in the minds of the young in order to perpetuate the enslavement of the subject to the State.

Libertarian philosophy is stifled by the Roman and Catholic pseudo-philosophy of the State. History is corrupted from the very first page, where it lies when speaking of the Merovingian and Carolingian monarchies, to the last page where it glorifies Jacobinism and refuses to recognise the role of the people in creating [social] institutions. The natural sciences are perverted, [in order] to be placed at the service of the double idol: Church-State. The psychology of the individual, and even more that of societies, is falsified in each of their assertions to justify the triple alliance of soldier, priest and judge. Finally, morality, after having preached for centuries obedience to the Church or the book, is today emancipated only to then preach servility to the State: "No direct moral obligations towards your neighbour, nor even the feeling of solidarity; all your obligations are to the State," we are told, we are taught, in this new cult of the old Roman and Caesarean divinity. "The neighbour, the comrade, the companion—forget them. You will only know them through the intermediary of some organ of your State. And every one of you will make a virtue of being equally enslaved to it."

And the glorification of the State and discipline, for which the University and the Church, the press and the political parties work, is propagated so successfully that even revolutionaries dare not face this fetish.

The modern radical is a centralising statist, an extreme Jacobin. And the socialist falls into step.[31] Like the Florentines at the end of the fifteenth

---

31 As expressed, for example, by Marx in 1850: "The workers [...] must not only strive for a single and indivisible German republic, but also within this republic for the most determined centralisation of power in the hands of the State authority. They must not allow themselves to be misguided by the democratic talk of freedom for the communities, of self-government, etc. [...] the path of revolutionary activity [...] can

century who knew no better than to call on the dictatorship of the State to save themselves from the Patricians—the socialists only know to call upon the same gods, the dictatorship of the State, to save themselves from the horrors of the economic regime created by this same State!

X

If we go a little deeper into these diverse categories of facts, which I have scarcely touched upon in this short overview, it will be understood why— seeing the State as was in history and as it is in its very essence today—and convinced that a social institution cannot lend itself to *all* desired goals since, like every organ, it developed through the function it performed for a definite purpose, not for all possible purposes—it will be understood, I say, why we reach the conclusion of the abolition of the State.

We see in it the institution, developed during the history of human societies to prevent the direct association between men, to impede the development of local and individual initiative, to crush existing liberties, to prevent their new blossoming—all this [in order] to subjugate the masses to minorities.

And we know that an institution which has a long history dating back several thousand years cannot lend itself to a function opposed to that for which and by which it was developed during the course of history.

To this absolutely unshakeable argument for anyone who has reflected on history—what response do we get?

We are answered with an almost childish argument.

"The State is there," we are told. "It exists, it represents a powerful ready-made organisation. Why not use it instead of destroying it? It works for evil [ends]—that is true; but that is because it is in the hands of the exploiters. Taken over by the people, why would it not be used for a better purpose, for the good of the people?"

Always the same dream—that of the Marquis de Posa, in Schiller's drama, trying to make absolutism an instrument of emancipation;[32] or else

---

proceed with full force only from the centre. [...] As in France in 1793 so today in Germany, it is the task of the really revolutionary party to carry through the strictest centralisation." (*Marx-Engels Collected Works*, Volume 10 [London: Lawrence & Wishart, 1978], 285). (Editor)

32 The Marquis de Posa is a character from Schiller's 1787 play *Don Carlos* (addressing the revolt of the Netherlands against Spanish rule in the sixteenth century) whose famous speech to the King of Spain proclaims Schiller's belief in personal freedom and democracy, but ends in a prostrate plea to the King: "A single word of yours can suddenly / Create the world anew. Give us the freedom / To think." (Editor)

the dream of the gentle Abbe Pierre, in Zola's *Rome*, wanting to make the Church the lever for socialism![33]

How sad it is to have to answer such arguments! For those who think this way either do not have a clue as to the true historic role of the State or else they understand the *social* revolution in a form so trivial, so anodyne that it has nothing in common with socialist aspirations.

Take a concrete example, France.

All those who think must have noticed this striking fact, that the Third Republic, in spite of its republican form of government, remained monarchist in its essence. We have all reproached it for not having republicanised France—I am not saying doing nothing for the *social* revolution, but of not having even introduced customs—just the *republican* spirit. For the little that has been done for the past twenty-five years to democratise customs, or to spread a little education, has been done everywhere, in all the European monarchies, under the same pressure of the times we are going through.

So where does the strange anomaly of a republic which remained monarchical come from?

It comes from the fact that France remained a State, at the same point that it was thirty years ago. Those holding power have changed the name; but all this immense ministerial scaffolding, all this centralised organisation of bureaucrats, all this imitation of the Rome of the Caesars which has been developed in France, all this formidable organisation to ensure and extend the exploitation of the masses in favour of a few privileged groups that is the essence of the State-institution—all that remained. And these cogs [of the bureaucratic machine] continue, as in the past, to exchange their fifty documents when the wind has blown down a tree onto a national highway, and to pour the millions deducted from the nation into the coffers of the privileged. The [official] stamp on the documents has changed; but the State, its spirit, its organs, its territorial centralisation, its centralisation of functions, its favouritism, its role as creator of monopolies, have remained. Like an octopus, they expand [their grip] on the country day-by-day.

The republicans—I speak of the sincere ones—had fuelled the illusion

---

33   Abbé Pierre Froment is the hero of Zola's *Three Cities Trilogy*, of which *Rome* (1896) is the second book. In these works, Zola discusses Catholicism with the hero writing a book to create his "dream of resuscitating a Christian and evangelical Rome, which should assure the happiness of the world" based on "a Christian love for the lowly and the wretched." He visits Rome and meets with Pope, who promptly rejects the Abbé's vision of a return "to the spirit of primitive Christianity" and places his work on the index of forbidden books. It ends with denunciations of the Catholic Church and a panegyric to science as sovereign and sweeping all before it. (Editor)

that we could "utilise the organisation of the State" to produce a change in the republican sense and these are the results. Whereas it was necessary to break the old organisation, *smash the State* and rebuild a new organisation starting with the very foundations of society—the liberated village commune, federalism, groupings from simple to complex, the free workers union—they thought of using the "organisation that already existed." And not having understood that we cannot make a historical institution go in the direction that we wish to point it—in the opposite direction to the one it has taken for centuries—they were swallowed up by the institution.

And yet, in this case it was not even a question of changing all the economic relations in society! It was only a question of merely reforming certain aspects of the political relations between men.

But after such a complete failure, in the face of such a sorry experience, they still insist in telling us that the conquest of powers in the State by the people will be sufficient to accomplish the social revolution! That the old machine, the old organisation, slowly developed in the course of history to crush freedom, to crush the individual, to establish oppression on a legal basis, to create monopolists, to lead minds astray by accustoming them to servitude—will lend itself perfectly to new functions: that it will become the instrument, the framework, to germinate a new life, to establish freedom and equality on economic foundations, to eradicate monopolies, to awaken society and march to the conquest of a future of freedom and equality!

What a sad, what a tragic error!

To give full scope to socialism involves rebuilding from the bottom to the top a society currently based on the narrow individualism of the shop-keeper. It is a question not only—as has sometimes been said by those indulging in vague metaphysics—of giving the worker "the whole product of his labour"; whereas it is a question of completely reconstructing all relationships, from those which exist today between each individual and his churchwarden or his station-master to those which exist between crafts, hamlets, cities and regions. In every street and hamlet, in every group of men gathered around a factory or along a railway line, it is necessary to awaken the creative, constructive, organisational spirit in order to rebuild all [aspects of] life—in the factory, in the village, in the shop, in production, in distribution [*approvisionnement*]. All the relations between individuals and human agglomerations must be rebuilt, from the very day, from the very moment when we lay hands [*touchera*] on the current commercial or administrative organisation.

And they want this immense task, which requires the free exercise of the popular genius, to be carried out within the framework of the State, within the organisation's pyramidal ladder that makes the essence of the State!

They want the State, whose very reason for existing—as we have seen—is the crushing of the individual, the hatred of initiative, the triumph of *one* idea which must inevitably be that of mediocrity, to become the lever to accomplish this immense transformation!… They want to direct [*gouverner*] the renewal of a society by means of decrees and electoral majorities…

What childishness!

Throughout the history of our civilisation, two traditions, two opposing tendencies, have existed: the roman tradition and the popular tradition; the imperial tradition and the federalist tradition; the authoritarian tradition and the libertarian tradition.

And once more, on the eve of the social revolution, these two traditions come face to face.

Between these two currents, always living, always in conflict within humanity—the current of the people and the current of minorities thirsting for political and religious domination—we have made our choice.

We continue the one which drove men in the twelfth century to organise on the basis of free agreement, the free initiative of the individual, the free federation of the interested parties. And we leave others to cling to the imperial, Roman and canonical tradition.

History has not been an uninterrupted evolution. On several occasions, [social] evolution has stopped in one region, to start again elsewhere. Egypt, the Middle East, the shores of the Mediterranean, Central Europe were, in turn, the scene of historical development. And every time this evolution begins first with the phase of the primitive tribe, then followed by the village commune; then by the free city, and finally to die in the State phase.

In Egypt, civilisation begins with the primitive tribe. It reaches the village commune, later to the period of free cities; later still, to the State which, after a period of flourishing, brings—death.

Evolution begins again in Assyria, in Persia, in Palestine. It again passes through the same phases: the tribe, the village commune, the free city, the all-powerful State—death!

A new civilisation then begins in Greece. Still by the tribe. Slowly it reaches the village commune, then the republican cities. In these cities civilisation reaches its highest peaks. But the East brings its poisonous breath, its traditions of despotism. Wars and conquests create the Empire of Alexander of Macedonia. The State is established, it grows, it kills all civilisation and then—it is death!

Rome in its turn begins civilisation again. It is still the primitive tribe that we find at its origins; then the village commune; then the city. At this phase it reaches the peak of its civilisation. But the State, the Empire comes and then—death!

On the ruins of the Roman Empire, Celtic, Germanic, Slavic, Scandinavian tribes start civilisation afresh. Slowly the primitive tribe develops its institutions to reach the village commune. It stays in this phase until the twelfth century. Then arises the republican city and this brings the blossoming of the human spirit, expressed by the architectural monuments, the magnificent development of the arts, the discoveries that laid the foundations of natural sciences... But then comes the State...

Death?

Yes, death—or else renewal! Either the State forever, crushing individual and local life, seizing all areas of human activity, bringing its wars and its internal struggles for the possession of power, its superficial revolutions which only change tyrants and, inevitably, at the end of this evolution—death! Or, States smashed to pieces and a new life starting again in thousands and thousands of centres, on the enduring principle of the initiative of the individual and of groups, on that of free agreement.

Choose!

IV

THE MODERN STATE

I

THE ESSENTIAL PRINCIPLE OF MODERN SOCIETIES

WHAT IS IMPORTANT TO US IS TO ANALYSE THE DISTINCTIVE FEATURES OF society and the modern State in order to determine where we are going, what is attained today, and what we hope to conquer in the future.

The current society is certainly not the outcome of any principle, logically developed to be applied to the thousand needs of [human] life. Like any living organism it represents, on the contrary, a very intricate outcome of thousands of struggles and thousands of compromises, of survivals of the past and of longings for a better future.

The theocratic spirit of high antiquity, slavery, imperialism, serfdom, the medieval commune, ancient prejudices, and the modern spirit—all these are found more or less represented, with all nuances, in all imaginable forms of mitigation [in modern societies]. Shadows of the past and outlines of the future; customs and conceptions dating from the Stone Age and tendencies towards a future which is scarcely emerging on the horizon—all these are found in continual struggle, in every individual, in every social stratum, in every generation, as in society as a whole.

However, if we consider the great struggles, the great popular revolutions which took place in Europe and America since the twelfth century, we see a principle emerging. All the uprisings were directed at the abolition of what had survived of ancient slavery in its mitigated form—serfdom. All had the aim of freeing either villagers or townspeople, or both, from the *obligatory labour* that was imposed upon them by law in favour of particular masters. To recognise the right of man to dispose of his own person and to work as he pleases and for as long as he pleases, without anyone having the right to *compel* him—in other words, *to liberate the person* of the peasant and the artisan, such was the objective of all the popular revolutions: the great uprisings of the communes in the twelfth century; the peasant wars in the fifteenth and sixteenth centuries in Bohemia, Germany, and the Netherlands, the revolutions of 1381 and 1648 in England, and, finally the Great Revolution [of 1789–1793] in France.

It is true that this goal was only partially attained. As the individual freed himself and he conquered his personal liberty, new economic conditions were imposed upon him to paralyse his liberty, to forge new chains, to bring him back under the yoke by the threat of starvation. We have seen a recent example of this when the Russian serfs, liberated in 1861, were forced to buy back the land they had cultivated for centuries, which brought ruin and misery, so their enslavement was recreated. What was done in Russia today was also done, in one way or another, everywhere in Western Europe. Physical compulsion disappeared, new forms of constraint were established. Personal serfdom abolished, servitude reappeared in a new form—the economic form.

And yet, despite all that, the dominant principle of modern societies is that of individual freedom, proclaimed, at least in theory, for everyone. By law, work is no longer obligatory for anyone. A caste of slaves, forced to toil for their masters, does not exist; and, at least in Europe, there are no more serfs obliged to give to their master three days' work a week in return for [the use of] a plot of land to which they remain bound all their life. Everyone is free to work if he wants, as long as he wants, and at what he wants.

That is—in theory, at least—the dominant principle of current society.

However, we know—and socialists of every shade [of opinion] never cease demonstrating it every day—to what extent this freedom is illusory. Millions and millions of men, women, and children are constantly forced by the threat of hunger to alienate their liberty, to give their labour to a master under the conditions that he wishes to impose upon them. And we know—and we try to clearly prove it to the masses—that, in the form of land-rent [*rente*], house-rent and interest generally paid to the capitalist,[1]

---

1   The word *rente* (rent) in French includes all forms of property income as well as the economic rent associated with land use. Also, the version published in *Freedom* in 1914 added "profit" to this list of property-income exploited from the worker. (Editor)

the worker and the peasant continue to give, to several masters instead of one, the same three days a week; very often even more than the three days, just to obtain the right to cultivate the land or to even have a roof over their head [*de vivre sous un abri*].

We also know that if one day an economist took the trouble to practice [real] political economy and calculate all that the various masters (boss, landlord, middle-men, shareholders and so on, in addition to the State) levy directly or indirectly on the wages of the worker, we would be amazed at the meagre share left for him to pay all the other workers whose products he consumes: to pay the labour of the peasant who has grown the wheat he eats, the bricklayer who built the house he lives in, those who made his furniture, his clothes, and so on. We would be struck to see how little goes to all the workers who produce what this other worker consumes compared to the immense part which goes to the barons of modern feudalism.

However, this dispossession of the worker is no longer done by one master lawfully imposed on the person of each worker. There is for that an entire mechanism, extremely complicated—impersonal and irresponsible. As in past centuries, the worker gives a considerable part of his work to the privileged; but he no longer does it under the whip of a master. The compulsion is no longer a bodily constraint. He will be thrown onto the street, forced to live in a slum, to never have enough to eat, to see his children perish from starvation, to beg in his old age; but he will not be put on a bench in a police-station in order to be administered a beating for a badly sewn coat or a badly cultivated field, as was done during our lifetime in Eastern Europe and formerly practiced across Europe.

Under the present regime, often more ferocious and pitiless than the former, man retains, nevertheless, a feeling of personal liberty. We know that for the proletarian this feeling is almost an illusion. Yet we must recognise that all modern progress and all our hopes for the future are still based on this feeling of freedom, however limited it may be in reality.

The most destitute of tramps, in his moments of darkest misery, will not exchange his stone bed under the arch of a bridge for the bowl of soup which would be guaranteed to him every day along with the chain of the slave. Better yet. This feeling, this principle of individual liberty, is so dear to modern man that continually we see whole groups of workers accepting months of misery and marching against bayonets merely to maintain some acquired rights.

Indeed, the most obstinate strikes and the most desperate popular revolts today stem from questions of liberty, of acquired rights, rather than from questions of wages.

The right and liberty of a man to work on what he wants and as much as he wants, thus remains *the principle* of modern societies. And the strongest accusation we raise against current society is to prove that this freedom, so dear to the workers, is continually rendered illusionary by the necessity of selling his [labour] forces to a capitalist; that the modern State is the most powerful weapon for maintaining the workers in this necessity by means of the privileges and monopolies which it continually bestows upon one class of citizens to the detriment of the worker. We begin to understand, in fact, that the principle on which all are agreed is continually evaded by a series of monopolies; that he who owns nothing becomes again the serf of those who do own, since he is forced to accept the terms of the master of the land or the factory in order to work; since he pays to the rich—to all the rich— an immense tribute, thanks to the monopolies established in their favour. These monopolies are attacked by the people, not [only] for the idleness they allow the privileged classes but above all for the domination which they assured them over the working class.

The great criticism that we direct at modern society is not that it has taken the wrong path by proclaiming that henceforth everyone will work as he wants and as long as he wants; but in having created conditions of ownership that *do not permit the worker to work as he wants and for as long as he wants*. We describe this society as cruel because, after having proclaimed the principle of individual liberty, it has placed the worker of the fields and industry in conditions which nullify this principle; because it reduces the worker to a state of disguised serfdom—to the state of a man which misery forces to toil to enrich the masters and to perpetuate his own condition of inferiority. He must forge his own chains.

Well, if that is true; if this principle, "You will work at what you want and as long as you want," is really dear to modern man; if every form of obligatory and servile work repels him; if his individual liberty trumps all else—then the activity [*conduite*] of the revolutionary is indicated.

He will reject all forms of a disguised serfdom. He will work to ensure that this freedom is no longer just a word. He will seek to know what prevents the worker from really being the sole master of his [mental] abilities and his arms; and he will work to abolish these barriers—by force if necessary—while at the same time taking care not to introduce other barriers which, while perhaps procuring an increase in well-being, would once more cause man to lose his freedom.

Let us then analyse those obstacles which, in current society, reduce the freedom of the worker and enslave him.

II

SERFS OF THE STATE

NOBODY CAN BE FORCED BY LAW TO WORK FOR OTHERS. SUCH IS, WE SAY, the principle of modern societies, conquered by a series of revolutions. And those of us who have known serfdom in the first half of the last century [in Russia], or else have only seen its remnants (in England, for example they had been preserved until 1848 in the form of the forced labour of children who were removed by law from their impoverished parents, if they were in the Workhouse, and transported to the cotton factories in the North), those amongst us who have known the mark etched by these institutions upon the whole of society will understand with a single word the importance of the change produced by the definite abolition of legal servitude.

But if the legal obligation to work for others no longer exists between individuals, the State thus far has retained the right to impose obligatory work on its subjects. More than that. As the relations of master and serf disappeared from society, the State more and more extended its right to the forced labour of citizens; so much so that the powers of the modern State would make the jurists who tried to establish royal power in the fifteenth and sixteenth centuries blush with envy.

Today, for example, the State imposes compulsory education on all citizens. An excellent thing in principle, so long as we consider it from the point of view of the *right* of the child to go to school even though their parents seek to keep them at home or send them to the factory or to an ignorant sister [from a convent]. But in reality—what has become of the information given today in primary schools? A whole body of doctrines is instilled, created to secure the rights of the State over the citizen; to justify the monopolies that the State bestows on whole groups of citizens; to proclaim sacrosanct the right of the rich to exploit the poor and [thus] become rich thanks to this poverty; to teach children that vengeance [*vindicte*], [when] carried out by society, is supreme justice and that conquerors were the greatest men of humanity.[2] Worse than that! State-controlled teaching—a worthy heir to instruction by the Jesuits—is the perfect means of killing any spirit of initiative and independence and to teach the child servility of thought and action.

And when the child has grown, the State will force him to do compulsory military service and it will command him, in addition, to do various [kinds of] labour for the municipality and the State in the case of an emergency. Finally, by means of taxes, it will oblige every citizen to perform a formidable amount of work for the State as well as for the protected of the State—while making him believe that it is he who voluntarily establishes it himself and who disposes, through his representatives, the sums of money which flow into the coffers of the State.

Once again a new principle has been proclaimed. Personal servitude no longer exists. There are no more serfs of the State as there were in past centuries even in France and England. A king can no longer order ten or twenty thousand of his subjects to come build fortresses for him or build the gardens and palaces of Versailles in spite of the "prodigious morality amongst the workers, whose bodies are carried away every night in carts," as Madame de Sévigné wrote.[3] The palaces of Windsor, Versailles and Peterhof are no longer built by means of *corvée* labour.[4] It is by means of taxes, under the pretext of productive works and under the pretext of protecting the liberty of the citizens and increasing their wealth, that the State demands all these services from its subjects.

---

2   See, for example, Kropotkin's pamphlet *L'Organisation de la Vindicte appelée Justice* (Paris: Au Bureau des "Temps Nouveaux," 1901), translated as *Organised Vengeance called 'Justice'* (London: Freedom Press, 1902). (Editor)

3   In a letter dated 12 October 1678: "The prodigious morality amongst the workers, whose bodies are carried away every night in carts, as if from a charity-hospital. One hides the grim convoys so as not to terrify the worksite" (*Lettres de Madame de Sévigné de sa famille et de ses amis*, Volume II [Lavigne/Chamerot: Paris 1836], 31). (Editor)

4   These are the main royal palaces and associated gardens of the royalty of England, France, and Russia, respectively. (Editor)

We are the first to applaud the abolition of the principle of serfdom and to indicate its importance for the general advancement of the ideas of liberation. To be [physically] brought from Nancy or Lyons to Versailles to build palaces for the amusement of the king's favourites was far harder than paying so much in taxes—so many days of labour—even though these taxes would also be spent on unnecessary works or even on works harmful to the nation. We are grateful, and more than grateful, to the men of 1793 for having freed Europe from *corvée* labour.

But it is nevertheless true that in proportion as the liberation from personal servitude of man to man was achieved during the course of the nineteenth century, servitude towards the State was always growing. From decade to decade the work demanded by the State from each citizen grew in number, in variety, in quantity. Towards the end of the nineteenth century we even see the State regaining its right to *corvée* labour. It imposes, for example, on railway workers (a recent law in Italy) compulsory work in the event of a strike—*corvée* labour, because it is *corvée* labour—for the benefit of the big companies that own the railways. From the railway to the mine, and from the mine to the factory, there is but a step. And once the pretext of *public safety*, or even only of necessity or *public utility*, has been recognised—there is no longer any limit to the powers of the State.

If the miners or the railway employees have not yet been treated as guilty of high treason every time they went on strike[5] and not hung high for that, it was only because the need has not yet been felt. It is more convenient to take advantage of some threatening gestures by a few strikers to shoot the crowd at point blank range and to send the ringleaders to hard labour. This is commonly done today, in a republic as in a monarchy.

Until now "voluntary servitude" has sufficed. But on the day when the need, or rather the fear of this need, was felt in Italy, Parliament did not hesitate for a moment to pass a law to this effect although the Italian railways still remain in the hands of private companies. For "oneself"—in the name of "public safety"—the State will certainly not hesitate to do, with even more severity, what it already once did for its favourite, the big companies. It did it well in Russia. In Spain, it went as far as torture to protect the monopolists. Indeed, since the terrible tortures practiced in Montjuich in 1896, torture has returned to Spain, [as] an institution for the benefit of the current protected of the State, wealthy financiers.[6]

---

5   The 1914 *Freedom* version adds: "(in Russia it has already been done, in 1906, while a new law treats as felony all strikes in 'establishments of public utility')." (Editor)

6   A reference to the torturing of suspects following the wholesale arrest of hundreds of anarchists after a bomb was thrown into the procession on Corpus Christi Day in Barcelona in 1896, avoiding various members of the ruling class at the front but

In fact, we are heading so far down this path, driven by what those favoured by the government whispered to it, and the second half of the nineteenth century has gone so far towards centralisation, that, if we are not careful, we shall soon see the discontented, the strikers—no longer shot as fermenters of revolt and looting but guillotined and transported to the pestilent swamps of some colony for simply neglecting a *public service*.

They do it in the army—they will do it in the mines. The Conservatives are already loudly demanding it in England.

For we must not be mistaken. Two great movements, two great currents of ideas and action characterised the nineteenth century. On the one hand, we saw a sustained struggle against all the vestiges of the former servitude. Not only did the armies of the First Republic abolish serfdom as they marched victoriously through Europe; but when these armies were driven out of the lands they had liberated and serfdom was restored there, it could no longer maintain itself for long. The inspiration of the revolution of 1848 definitely carried with it Western Europe; It [serfdom] had to die even in Russia in 1861 and seventeen years later in the Balkan peninsula.

More than that. In every nation man worked to claim his rights to personal freedom. He emancipated himself from prejudices concerning royalty, the nobility, and the upper classes and by a thousand small acts of revolt performed in every corner of Europe he affirmed, by the very use he made of it, his right to be recognised as a free man.

Moreover, the whole intellectual movement of the century—poetry, fiction, drama, when they ceased being a mere amusement for the leisured class [*les oisifs*]—bore this character. Taking France, think of Victor Hugo, of Eugène Sue in his *Mystères du Peuple* [*Mysteries of the People*], of Alexandre Dumas—the father, of course—of George Sand, etc.; then of the great conspirators, Barbès and Blanqui, of historians like Sismondi and Augustin Thierry. And we see that they have all expressed in literature the movement which has taken place in every corner of France, in every family, in every conscious individual to free the individual from the habits and customs of an era of personal servitude. And what has been done in France has been done everywhere, more or less, always to free men,

---

killing seven working class people and a soldier at its rear (so suggesting the act of an *agent provocateur*). Those arrested were subjected to terrible treatment in the prison of Montjuich, from which several died, while five anarchists were officially executed (eighteen were condemned to long imprisonment and acquitted prisoners were deported to a Spanish prison colony in the western Sahara). The actual bomb thrower was never found. Kropotkin dates this 1901 (when prisoners were released) and this has been corrected. (Editor)

women and children from the customs and ideas which centuries of servitude had established.

But alongside this great liberating movement, another which unfortunately also had its origins in the Great [French] Revolution, was going on at the same time. This one had for its purpose to develop the omnipotence of the State in the name of that vague and ambiguous term, which opened the door to all ambitions and treachery—the *public good.*[7]

Coming from the time when the Church sought to conquer souls to lead them to salvation, bequeathed to our civilisation by the Roman Empire and Roman Law, this idea of the omnipotence of the State has silently made tremendous progress during the last half of the century that has just ended.

Just compare compulsory military service as it exists today with the forms it had taken in past centuries—and you will be terrified by the ground gained by this servitude towards the State under the pretext of equality.

Never did the serf of the Middle Ages let himself be deprived of his human rights to the same degree as modern man, who voluntarily abdicates them through a spirit of voluntary servitude. At the age of twenty—that is to say at the age which has the most thirst and need for freedom, of the "abuses" even of freedom—the young man lets himself be imprisoned for two or three years in a barracks [conscripted into the armed forces], where he ruins his physical, intellectual and moral health. Why?... To learn a trade which the Swiss learn in six weeks and the Boers learned, better than the European armies, by clearing the land and crossing their grasslands on horseback.

Not only does he risk his life but he goes further in his voluntary servitude than the serf. He lets his commanders control his love-life, he leaves the woman he loves, he makes a vow of celibacy and he glorifies obeying like an automaton his commanders of whom he can judge neither the knowledge, nor the military talent, nor even the integrity. What serf of the Middle Ages, apart from the stable boy who followed the armies with the baggage, ever agreed to march to war under the conditions imposed today upon the modern serf stupefied by the ideas of discipline? Worse! The serfs of the twentieth century undergo even the horrors, the abominations of the punishment battalion in Africa—the Biribi—without rebelling.

When at that time did the serf—peasant or artisan—renounce his right to oppose his secret leagues to those of his Lords and to defend by arms the right to join together? Was there an epoch in the Middle Ages so dark that the people of the cities renounced their right to judge the judges and to throw them into the water on the day when they did not approve of their

---

7   Kropotkin clarifies his meaning in the 1914 *Freedom* version by immediately adding: "*organised, not by the nation itself in each town and village, but by its chosen so-called representatives.*" (Editor)

judgments? And when then, even during the darkest periods of the old oppression, did we see the State having the real possibility of perverting all teaching, from primary education to the University, through its system of schools? Machiavelli had long dreamt of it, but his dream was not achieved until the nineteenth century!

We therefore have had an immense *progressive* movement working during the first half of the [last] century to completely liberate the individual and his thought; and an immense *regressive* movement which imposed itself on the former during the whole of the second half of the century to re-establish the servitude of old for the benefit of the State—and to increase it, to portray it as *voluntary*. It is the salient characteristic of the period.

But this only relates to direct servitude. As for indirect servitude, obtained by means of taxation and capitalist monopoly [and] less visible at first sight, it grows every day. It becomes so threatening that it is time to seriously study it.

III

TAXATION: A MEANS OF CREATING THE POWERS OF THE STATE

IF THE STATE, BY MILITARY SERVICE, BY THE EDUCATION WHICH IT DIRECTS in the interests of the rich classes, by the Church, and by its thousands of functionaries, already exercises a formidable power over its subjects—this power is further increased tenfold by means of taxation.

An innocuous instrument in its infancy, welcomed and called for by taxpayers themselves when it was introduced to replace *corvée* labour, taxation has today become, in addition to a very heavy burden, a formidable weapon, a power all the greater because it disguises itself under a thousand [different] aspects, capable of directing the whole economic and political life of societies in the interest of the rulers and the rich. For those who are in power now use it not only for carving out [high] salaries but above all to make and unmake fortunes, to accumulate immense wealth in the hands of a privileged few, to establish monopolies, to ruin the people and enslave them to the rich—and all this without the taxpayer even suspecting the power they have given to their rulers.

"What is more just, though, than taxation?" the defenders of the State will no doubt tell us. "Look," they will say, "a bridge built by the inhabitants of a town. The river, swollen by the rains, will carry it away if it is not repaired at once. Is it not natural and right to call upon all the inhabitants of the town to repair this bridge? And as the great majority have their own work to do—is it not be reasonable to replace their personal labour, their inexperienced *corvée* labour, with a payment which will make it possible to call upon specialist workers and engineers?"

"Or else," they say, "here. A ford that becomes impassable in certain seasons. Why should the inhabitants of the neighbouring towns not tax themselves to build a bridge? Why should they not pay [so much] per head instead of all coming with a spade in their hands to repair this embankment? To shore-up this route? Or again, why build a granary into which each inhabitant will have to pour so much wheat a year to avert food shortages instead of entrusting the State to take care of food in case of scarcity in return of a trivial tax?"

All this seems so natural, so just, so reasonable, that even the most stubborn would have nothing to say about it—even more so provided that a certain equality of conditions prevails in the town.

And, providing multiple examples of this kind, the economists and the defenders of the State in general hasten to conclude that taxation is justifiable, desirable from every point of view and… "Long live taxation!"

Well, all this reasoning is false. For if certain communal taxes really have their origin in *communal labour, done together*—taxation or rather the formidable and manifold taxes that we pay to the State have a very different origin—*conquest*.

It was on the *conquered* peoples that the monarchs of the East and later on the Emperors of Rome levied *corvée labour*. The Roman citizen was exempt; he dumped it on the peoples under its domination. Until the Great [French] Revolution—partly to the present day—the supposed descendants of the conquering race (Roman, German, or Norman), that is to say the so-called "nobles," were exempted from taxation. The peasant, the black bone conquered by the white bone, alone figured on the list of those subject to "*corvée* labour and taxation" ["*corvéables et taillables*"].[8] The lands of the nobles and the "ennobled" paid nothing [in France] until 1789. And up to the present day the stupendously rich English landowners pay next to nothing for their immense estates and keep them uncultivated until their value has increased tenfold.

Thus the taxes we are now paying to the State come from conquest,

---

8   A reference to the pre-modern Kazakhstan (the Kazakh khanate) in which the Kazakh aristocracy (called the white bone—*ak suiuk*) traced their descent from Genghis Khan and had special rights and privileges. The general population of Kazakh was known as black bone (*kara suiuk*). (Editor)

serfdom—never from freely agreed communal labour. Indeed, when the State overwhelmed the people with *corvée* labours in the sixteenth, seventeenth and eighteenth centuries, it was not a question of those works which the hamlets or villages undertook by the free consent of their inhabitants. Communal works continued to be carried out by the inhabitants of the communes. But alongside this work hundreds of thousands of peasants were brought under military escort from remote villages to build a national road or a fortress; to transport the provisions needed to supply an army; to follow, with their exhausted horses, the nobles setting off to the conquest of new castles. Others toiled in the mines and factories of the State; others again, under the whips of functionaries, obeyed the criminal whimsies of the masters, digging the ponds of the royal castles, or building palaces for kings, lords and their courtesans while the women and children of these *corvée* labourers fed upon the weeds of the uncultivated fields, begged on the roads, or, starving, fell under the bullets of soldiers when attempting to plunder the convoys of exported wheat.

Corvée labour, imposed first upon the conquered races (as the French, the English, the Germans now impose it upon the blacks of Africa) and later on upon all the peasants; such was the origin—the true origin—of the taxes which we today pay to the State. Will we be surprised then that it has retained to our days the stamp of its origin?

It was an immense relief for the countryside when, at the approach of the Great [French] Revolution, the corvées labour for the State were replaced by a kind of fee—taxation paid in money. When the Revolution, at last bringing a ray of light into the cottages, abolished part of the salt tax[9] and land tax[10] which weighed directly on the poorest and when the idea of a

---

9   The *gabelle* was originally imposed in the fourteenth century and denoted any tax on the sale of agricultural and industrial commodities. In the fifteenth century the *gabelle* began to mean specifically the salt tax, that is, a tax on consumption of salt and the nobility, the clergy, and certain other privileged persons were exempt. It was one of the most hated and grossly unequal forms of indirect taxation and was forcefully expressed in the lists of grievances drawn up for the Estates-General of 1789 on the eve of the revolution. It was abolished in March 1790. (Editor)

10   The *tailles* was a direct land tax on the French peasantry and non-nobles, imposed on each household and based on how much land it held. Originally an "exceptional" tax (i.e., imposed and collected in times of need, as the king was expected to survive on the revenues of the "domaine royal," or lands that belonged to him directly), it became permanent in 1439. The total amount of the *taille* was set by the French king from year to year, and this amount was then apportioned among the various provinces for collection. The clergy, nobles, officers of the crown, and magistrates were exempt from the tax. (Editor)

more equitable (and also more beneficial to the State) tax began to appear, there was, we are told, a general contentment in the country. Especially amongst the peasants more or less enriched by trade and lending at interest.

But until the present taxation has remained faithful to its original source. In the hands of the bourgeois which has seized power, it has never ceased to grow and never ceased being employed mainly for the benefit of the bourgeoisie. By means of taxation, the gang of rulers—the State, representing the quadruple alliance of the king, the Church, the judge, and the lord-soldier—has never ceased to extend its powers and to treat the people like a conquered race. And today, by means of this invaluable instrument which strikes without us directly feeling the blows, we have become almost as enslaved by the State as our fathers formally were by their landlords and masters.

How much work does each of us give to the State? No economist has ever sought to estimate the number of working days that the worker in the fields and factories gives each year to this Babylonian idol. We would search the textbooks of political economy in vain to find an approximate estimate of what the man who produces wealth gives of his labour to the State. A simple estimation based on the budget of the State, the nation, the provinces, and the municipalities (which also contribute to the expenditure of the State) would say nothing; because it would be necessary to estimate not what is in the coffers of the treasury but what the payment of each Franc paid to the Treasury represents of the real expenditures made by the taxpayer. All we can say is that the amount of work the producer gives each year to the State is immense. It must reach, and for certain categories [of worker] exceed, the three days of work a week that the serf once gave to his lord.

And note well that, whatever may be done to overhaul the basis of tax assessment, it is always the worker who bears the entire burden. Every centime paid to the Treasury is ultimately paid by the worker, the producer.

The State may well trim to a certain extent the revenue of the rich. But it is also necessary for the rich to have an income that this income is made, produced by someone—and that can only be done by he who produces something by his labour. The State demands from the rich its share of the spoils; but where do these spoils come from, which ultimately represents so much sold wheat, iron, porcelain or cloth—all the result of the labour of the producer? Apart from the wealth that comes from abroad and which represents the exploitation of other workers—the inhabitants of Russia, the East, Argentina, Africa—it is still the workers of the country itself who must give so many days of their labour to pay tax, as well as to enrich the rich.

If the tax levied by the State—compared to its immense expenditures—seems to be a little less heavy in England than in the other countries of

Europe, it is for two reasons. One is that Parliament, half composed of landowners, favours them by allowing them to levy an immense tribute on the residents of the towns and countryside and pay only a small tax; and the other—the main one—is that of all the European countries England is the one which levies most upon the labour of the workers of other nations.[11]

We are sometimes told that a progressive tax on income would, according to our rulers, strike the rich for the benefit of the poor. This was indeed the idea of the Great [French] Revolution, when it introduced this form of taxation. But today all that we obtain by slightly progressive taxation is to trim a little of the revenue of the rich; we take a little more than before from what he has taken away from the worker. But that is all. It is always the worker who pays, and who generally pays *more* than what the State takes from the rich.

Thus we were able to see for ourselves in Bromley how immediately after the tax on inhabited houses in our municipality was increased by around five francs per year on all worker housing—(a half-house, as they say in England)—the rent went up by the amount of 60 centimes per week, or about 30 francs a year. The owner of the building immediately dumped the increase on his tenants and he took advantage of the blow to augment his exploitation.

As for indirect taxes, we not only know that it is the objects consumed by everyone that are especially hit by taxation (the others yield little) but also

---

11   The sums levied by the English on the capital they have lent to other nations are variously estimated. It is only known that more than two and a half billions (100 million pounds sterling) represents the English revenue on the sums they have lent only to various *States* and *railway* companies. If we add to this the interest levied each year on the sums which the English lent to foreign *cities*, then to the various maritime and other *shipping* companies (everywhere, but especially in America), *lighthouses*, underwater *cables*, *telegraphs*, *banks* in Asia, Africa, America and Australia (this revenue is immense) and, finally, what was placed in a thousand *industries* of all the countries of the world, the English statisticians reach the minimum figure of seven and a half billion francs a year. The net profit which England makes on all her experts (less than a billion and a half) is so small in comparison with the income obtained by cutting share coupons with a pair of scissors that we can say that the principal industry of England is the trading of capital. It has become what Holland was at the beginning of the seventeenth century—the principal moneylender of the world. France follows it closely; Belgium in proportion to its population. Indeed, according to the assessment of Alfred Neymarck, France holds 25 to 30 billion foreign securities, which would already give an annual income of one billion to a billion and a half only on the securities officially listed on the Paris Stock Exchange.

that any increase of a few centimes on the tax upon beverages, or coffee, or wheat results in a much higher increase in the prices paid by the consumer.

It is evident, moreover, that only he who *produces, who creates wealth by his labour,* can *pay* taxes. The rest is only a division of the spoils taken away from he who produces—a division which for the worker always amounts to an increase in exploitation.

So we can say that, apart from the taxes levied upon the riches made abroad,[12] the billions paid each year to the public Treasury—in France, for example—are levied almost entirely on the labour of the ten million workers possessed by France.

Here the worker pays as a consumer of drinks, sugar, matches, petrol; there, it is he who, when paying his rent, pays the Treasury the tax which the State has levied on the owner of the house. Here again, by buying his bread he pays the property taxes, the rent for the land, the rent and taxes of the bakery, the [costs of governmental] overseeing, the [expenditure of the] Ministry of Finance, and so on. There, finally, by buying a dress, she pays taxes on imported cotton, the monopoly created by protectionism. By buying his coal, when travelling by train, he pays the monopolies of the mines and of the railways, created by the State in favour of capitalists, the owners of the mines and the railway lines—in short, it is always he who pays all the aftereffects of the taxes that the State, the province, the municipality levy on the soil and its products, the raw material, the factory, the revenue of the employer, the privilege of education—everything, everything that the municipality, the province and the State see coming into their coffers.

How many days of labour a year do all these taxes represent? Is it not very probable that, having added them all together we would find that the modern worker toils more for the State than the serf formerly worked for his master?

But if it were only that!

But the reality is that taxation gives rulers the means of rendering exploitation even more intense, of holding the people in misery, to create legally, without speaking of theft or of [massive frauds like] the Panamas, fortunes which capital could never have accumulated alone.

---

12   The 1914 *Freedom* version adds: "derived from the exploitation of foreign workers by means of interest on foreign loans." (Editor)

IV

TAXATION: A MEANS OF ENRICHING THE WEALTHY

TAXATION IS SO CONVENIENT! THE NAÏVE—THE "DEAR CITIZENS" OF ELECTION times—have been brought up to see in taxation the means of accomplishing the great civilising works useful for the nation; and they accept all sorts of taxes so easily! But the rulers know perfectly well that taxation offers them the most convenient means of making great futures at the expense of the small; to impoverish the masses and enrich the few; to better deliver the peasant and the proletarian to the manufacturer and to the speculator; to encourage one industry at the expense of another, and all industries in general at the expense of agriculture, and especially the peasant or the whole nation.

If tomorrow they dared to vote in the Chamber 50,000,000 francs for the benefit of the landowners (as [Lord] Salisbury did in England in 1900 to reward his Conservative voters[13]), all of France would cry out as

---

13 A reference to the 1896 Agricultural Relief Bill introduced under the Conservative Prime Minister Lord Salisbury, which halved the local tax burden of landowners. Ostensibly aiming to offset the effects of the depression in farming by reducing local taxation on the agrarian economy, it granted assistance directly to landowners, so

one man; the Ministry would be immediately toppled [*par terre*]. Well, by means of taxation the same fifty millions from the pockets of the poor are placed in those of the rich without them noticing the filching. No one cries out—and the same end is attained marvellously. So much so that this function of taxation goes unnoticed by those who make the study of taxes their speciality.

It is so simple! It is enough, for example, to burden the peasant, his horse and his cart, or else his windows, with a few additional centimes [in taxes] to thereby ruin tens of thousands of farming households. Those who already hardly succeeded in making both ends meet, those who already the slightest shock could ruin and relegate to the ranks of the proletariat were crushed this time by the slight increase in taxation. They sell their plots and go to the cities, offering their arms to the owners of the factories. Others sell their horse and start working hard with the spade, hoping to recover. But a new increase in taxes, which is undoubtedly done in a few years, brings the final blow: they become proletarians in their turn.

This proletarianisation of the weak by the State, by the rulers, is done continuously, year after year, without making anyone cry out, except the ruined whose voice does not reach the general public. This has been seen on a grand scale during the last forty years in Russia, especially in central Russia, where the dream of the bigwig industrialists of creating a proletariat has been realised by means of taxation—whereas a law which would have sought to ruin a few millions of peasants by a single strike of the pen would have made everyone cry out, even in Russia under absolute government. Taxation has accomplished quietly what the legislator did not dare to do openly.

And the economists who bestow upon themselves the title "scientific"— to then speak to us about the "established" laws of economic development, of "capitalist fatalism," and its "self-negation" when a simple study of taxation would alone explain a good half of what they attribute to the supposed inevitability of economic laws. It is that the ruin and expropriation of the peasant—such as was done in England during the seventeenth century and which Marx had described as "primitive capitalist accumulation"— continues to this day, year after year, by the means of this so convenient instrument—taxation.

Far from growing according to immanent laws of internal growth, the strength of capital would be badly paralysed in its expansion if it had not the State in its service which, on the one hand, creates new monopolies

---

failing the tenant farmers who were bearing the brunt of the decline in agricultural prices. It was denounced by opponents as a "dole" to the landlords. (Editor)

(mines, railways, water supply, telephones, measures against workers associations, action against strikers, privileged education, etc., etc.) and, on the other hand, builds fortunes and ruins the masses of workers by means of taxation.

If capitalism has helped to create the modern State, it is also—let us not forget—the modern State that creates and nourishes capitalism.

Adam Smith had already indicated, more than a century ago, this power of taxation;[14] but the study whose outlines he had indicated was not continued and today to show this power of taxation we must gather our examples from everywhere.

So let us take the taxation of land which is one of the most powerful weapons in the hands of the State. The eighth report of the State Bureau of Labor [of Illinois] offers a wealth of evidence to show how—even in a democratic State—the fortunes of millionaires were made simply by the way the State struck the land and building in Chicago.

This great city has grown by leaps and bounds, reaching 1.5 million inhabitants in fifty years. Well, by imposing taxes on built property while only imposing it slightly on undeveloped property, even in the most central streets of the city, the State created the fortunes of millionaires. Plots of land on such-and-such a great street worth fifty years ago six thousand francs for a tenth of a hectare have now reached the value of five million to six million francs.

It is obvious however that if the tax had been "metric," that is to say so much by the square metre whether built-upon or undeveloped—well yes if the land had been municipalised, such fortunes would never have accumulated. The city would have benefited from the increase in its population, reducing accordingly the taxes on the houses inhabited by workers. Now, on the contrary, since it is the six- and ten-storey houses inhabited by the workers which bear the bulk of the taxes, it is the worker who is forced to work to enable the rich to become even richer; and, on the other hand, he is forced to live in unhealthy slums which, as is well known, arrest even the intellectual development of the class that inhabits these slums and delivers it all the better to the manufacturer. The *Eighth Biennial Report of the Bureau of Labor Statistics of Illinois Taxation*, 1894, is full of striking information on this subject.

Or else let us take the English arsenal of Woolwich. Formerly, the land on which Woolwich grew up on was only a warren, inhabited only by rabbits.

---

14   Adam Smith discusses taxation in Volume II, Book V, Chapter II of *The Wealth of Nations* (Chicago: University of Chicago, 1976). (Editor)

Since the State built its great arsenal there, where 20,000 men work in State factories manufacturing devices of destruction, Woolwich and its neighbouring communities have become a populous city.[15]

One day, in June 1899, a member of Parliament asked the government to increase the wages of the workers. "What is the point?" replied the economist-Minister Goschen, "It will all be absorbed by the landlords!... During the last ten years wages have risen by twenty percent; but in the meantime the rents of the workers rose by fifty per cent. The increase of wages (I quote verbally) had the effect of sending a larger sum into the pockets of the landlords" (millionaires already). The minister's argument was evidently specious; but the fact that millionaires absorb most of the wage increases is worth addressing. It is perfectly true.

In addition, the inhabitants of Woolwich, like those of any other great city, are continually summoned to [pay] double and triple taxes to drain, channel [the sewer system], pave [the streets of] the city, which once polluted has now become healthy. And, thanks to the system of taxation on land and property in force, all this mass of money went to enrich the landlords by the same amount. "The landlord is everywhere in the habit of selling back to the citizens in detail what they have already paid for in common," said, quite rightly, the journal of the Woolwich Co-operators, *Comradeship*.[16]

Or else, a steam ferry has to be taken to cross the Thames and to connect Woolwich with London. Initially, it was a monopoly which parliament created in favour of a capitalist, authorising him to establish a link by steam ferry. Then, after a while, as the monopolist charged too much for the crossing, the municipality bought-back from the monopolist the right to maintain this ferry. The whole cost to the taxpayers was 5.5 million francs in eight years. But then, a small plot of land near the ferry rose in value to seventy-five thousand francs, which is obviously pocketed by the landowner. And as this plot will continue to rise in value, here is a new monopoly established, a new capitalist added to the legions of others already created by the English State.[17]

---

15 The 1914 version in *Freedom* immediately adds the following paragraph: "But who has profited chiefly by that growth? Owing to taxation as it exists in this country, it was the landlord! Not the workers who built the Arsenal and for years were putting its machinery into action—but the local landlords!" (Editor)

16 Frederick Verinder, "Taxation of Land Values," Part II, *Comradeship* No. 11 (February 1900), 16. Kropotkin paraphrases this passage to clarify for his French readers: "These sell back in detail to the taxpayers the profits they have pocketed from the sanitary improvements, paid for by these same taxpayers." The journal subsequently published a letter from Kropotkin (No 13, April 1900) entitled "Prince Kropotkin on Land Monopoly and Co-Operation" which covers many of the points he raises here. (Editor)

17 The 1914 *Freedom* version expands slightly:

But what! The workers in the Woolwich State factories eventually form a union and, through [their] struggles, they succeeded in securing their wages at a higher level than in other factories of the same kind. They also founded a [consumers'] co-operative and so cut their living expenses by a quarter—and "the best of the harvest" goes to the lords![18] When one of these gentlemen decides to sell a plot of his land, his agent announces to us in the local newspapers (this is verbatim): "The high wages paid by the Arsenal to workers, thanks to their unions, as well as the existence in Woolwich of a prosperous co-operative [society] render this land eminently suitable for building of worker's dwellings." Which means: "You can pay dearly for this plot, gentlemen builders of workers' houses. You will easily recoup on the rents." And they pay, they buy to build, to be repaid later on by the worker.[19]

Or, speaking still of Woolwich, one day a steam ferry was running across the Thames, in order to connect Woolwich with London. Of course, the Government, to begin with, made of the ferry a monopoly in favour of a railway company. Later on, as the company charged too much for the crossing, and the "dear citizen" grumbled, the municipality bought the ferry right back from the company, the whole costing the town about £220,000 in eight years.

But then it appeared that a free ferry was a new handsome gift made to the landlords. The value of land in Woolwich went up by leaps. A tiny bit of land situated close by the ferry rose at once in value fully £3,000, which, of course, was a gift of the town to the owner of that piece of the land. And as the land in Woolwich will continue to rise in value (every war scare contributing to raise the value of land round the big Arsenal), we have here a new monopoly, and numbers of new capitalists added to the legions of others by the State, with the aid of the working people's money.

It then adds this paragraph: "You see now for what the State exists, and why it is so dear to all those who are capitalists or expect to become either capitalists or members of the capitalist-making machinery." (Editor)

18 The 1914 *Freedom* version has: "But lo! thanks to our laws, they who profit most from both the Union and the Co-operative are again—the landlords?" (Editor)

19 The 1914 *Freedom* version has:

In other words, this means: "You can pay, gentlemen builders, a high price for this land. It is most suitable for workers' houses. With the higher wages obtained by the workers, and their economies, you will be able to get higher rents." And the "gentleman builder" pays the landlord

But that is not all. A few enthusiasts, with untold sorrows and immense work, succeeded in founding in this same Woolwich a sort of co-operative city of working class maisonettes. The land was bought by a co-operative; it was drained, [the sewers] channelled, and the streets build in co-operation; then the plots were sold to workers who, always thanks to the co-operative, could build their maisonettes cheaply.[20] The founders [of the scheme] congratulated themselves on its success and enquired about the terms under which they could buy a hectare of land to enlarge their co-operative city. They had paid the rate of 37,500 francs per hectare (£500 per acre) for theirs; now they are asked for 75,000 francs for the next hectare... Why? "But, gentlemen, your city is going so well that it has doubled the value of this land."

Absolutely! Since the State has constituted and maintains the monopoly of land in favour of Mr. So-and-So, they have [simply] toiled to enrich this gentleman and to render the extension of their worker city impossible.

"Long live the State."

"Work for us, poor creature who thinks you can improve your lot by co-operatives without daring to touch at the same time, property, taxation, and the State!"[21]

But, without going to Chicago or Woolwich, do we not see in every great city how the State, merely by imposing a heavier tax on the six-storey house inhabited by workers than upon the private mansion of the rich, establishes a formidable privilege in favour of the latter? It allows him to pocket the increase in value given to his property by the growth and beautification of the city—especially by the house with six floors where the misery which beautifies the city for a beggar's wage throngs.

Or else, we are surprised that the cities grow so rapidly to the detriment of the countryside. And we do not want to see that the entire financial policy of the nineteenth century was to burden the farmer—the real producer, since he managed to obtain three, four and ten times more produce from the soil than before—to the benefit of the cities, that is to say the bankers, the lawyers, the merchants, and all the pack of sensualists [*jouisseurs*] and rulers.

And do not tell us that the creation of monopolies in favour of the rich is not the essence of the modern State and the sympathies which it finds

---

a higher price—and extorts higher rents from the worker. Don't you admire that mechanism? If not—never talk of Aesthetics! (Editor)

20   The 1914 *Freedom* version adds: "True, the scheme was not exactly what they intended it to be at the outset: their Communist tendencies were lost amidst mercantile considerations." (Editor)

21   The 1914 *Freedom* version adds this paragraph: "Keep them up—and remain their slave!" (Editor)

amongst the rich and educated who have passed through the schools of the State. Here is an excellent recent example of the use of taxes in Africa.

We know that the principal objective of the war of England against the Boers was to abolish the Boer law which prevented blacks being forced to work in the gold mines. The English companies founded for the exploitation of these mines did not make the profits they had been expected to. Well, here is what Earl Grey said to parliament: "They must dismiss from their minds the idea of developing their mines with white labour. Means had to be sought to induce the natives to seek, spontaneously, employment at the mines... an incentive to labour must be provided by imposition of a hut-tax of at least £1, in conformity to the practice of Basutoland; and also by the establishment of a small labour-tax, which these able-bodied natives should be required to pay who are unable to show a certificate for four months' work." (Hobson, *The War in South Africa*, p. 234).[22]

So here is serfdom which they did not dare to introduce openly but which was introduced *by taxation*. Assume every miserable hut struck with 25 francs [that is, £1] of tax and serfdom is made. And Rudd, the agent of Rhodes, dots the i's [and crosses the t's] by writing: "If under the cry of civilisation we in Egypt lately mowed down 10,000 or 20,000 Dervishes with Maxims, surely it cannot be considered a hardship to compel the natives in South Africa *to give three months in the year to do a little honest work*." Always two or three days a week! There is no escape. As for paying for the "honest work," Rudd bluntly stated: 60 to 70 francs per month is "morbid sentimentality." Quarter that would be amply sufficient (*Ibid.*, p. 235).[23] That way, the black will not enrich themselves and will remain a serf. They must *take* from him, by tax, what he earns as wages; he must be prevented from giving himself rest.

And indeed, since the English have become the masters of the Transvaal and of the "blacks," the extraction of gold rose from 313 million francs to 875 million [per annum]. Nearly 200,000 "blacks" are now forced to toil in the mines to enrich the companies that were the primary causes of the war.[24]

But what the English did in Africa to reduce blacks to poverty and to impose forced labour on them, the State did for three centuries in Europe

22   J. A. Hobson, *The War in South Africa: Its Causes and Effects* (London: James Hisbet & Co., 1900). Kropotkin's paraphrased translation has been replaced with the original quote. (Editor)

23   Kropotkin's emphasis and, again, the original text of the book has been reproduced. (Editor)

24   This footnote was added to the 1914 *Freedom* version: "These lines were written two years ago; the figures have increased since. As to how the imported Hindus, and the British workers too, are treated—we saw it lately. Slavery breeds slavery." (Editor)

in relation to the peasants; and it does it again to impose the same forced labour onto the workers of the towns.

And academics speak to us about the "immutable laws" of Political Economy!

Remaining still in the domain of recent history, we might tell of another blow made by means of taxation. We could entitle it: "How the British Government took 4.6 million francs from the Nation to give them to the Big Tea Merchants—a Farce in one Act." On Saturday, 3 March 1900, it was learned in London that the government was going to increase by two pence (twenty centimes) per pound (per 450 grams) the customs duty on tea. Immediately, on Saturday and Monday, twenty-two million pounds of tea which were in customs in London awaiting payment of the tax were taken out by the merchants by paying the *previous* duty; and, Tuesday, the price of tea in all the shops in London was raised by two pence [per pound]. If we count only the twenty-two million pounds removed on Saturday and Monday, this would already make a *net* profit of 44 million pennies, or 4,583,000 francs taken from the pockets of the taxpayers and given to the tea merchants. But the same manoeuvre was carried out in all the other customs, in Liverpool, in Scotland, etc. without counting the tea which had been taken out of the customs before notification of the tax increase. It will no doubt be about ten million *given* by the State to these gentlemen.

The same goes for tobacco, beer, spirits, wine—and here are the wealthy enriched by about 25 million [francs] taken from the poor. And, "Long live Taxation! Long live the State!"

And you, children of the poor, thus learn in the primary school (the children of the rich learn something else at university), learn that taxation has been created to relieve the poor dear peasants from *corvée* labours, replacing them with a small annual payment to the coffers of the State. And tell your mother, bent under the weight of years of work and domestic toil [*d'économie domestique*] that they teach you there a great and beautiful science—Political Economy…

Take, indeed, education. We have come a long way since the time when the community itself found a house for the school as well as the teacher and where the wise man, the physician, the philosopher, surrounded himself with voluntary pupils to transmit to them the secrets of his science or his philosophy. Today, we have so-called free education provided at our expense by the State; we have secondary schools, universities, academies, subsidised scientific societies, scientific missions—what have you.

Since the State asks no better than to always extend the sphere of its power and that the citizens demand nothing better than to be exempted from thinking about matters of general interest—to "emancipate" themselves from their fellow citizens by abandoning common matters to a third party—everything works out perfectly. "Education," says the State, "delighted, ladies and gentlemen, to give it to your children! To lighten your cares, we will even *forbid* you from meddling with education. We will write all the programmes—and no criticism, please! First, we will stupefy your children by the study of dead languages and the virtues of Roman Law. That will make them pliable and submissive. Then, to deprive them of any inclination to revolt, we shall teach them the virtues of the State and of governments as well as contempt for the governed. We will make them believe that they, having learned Latin, become the salt of the earth, the leaven of progress, that without them humanity would perish. This will flatter you; as for them, they will swallow it up marvellously and become as vain as hell. That is what we need. We will teach them that the misery of the masses is a "law of nature" and they will be delighted to learn it and to repeat it. However, changing the teaching according to the varying tastes of the times, we will tell them that sometimes this is the will of God, sometimes that it is an "iron law" which causes the worker to be impoverished as soon as he begins to enrich himself, since he has forgotten in his well-being to have children.[25] All education will have the purpose of making your children believe that there is no salvation outside the providential State! And you will applaud, will you not?"

"Then, after having made the people pay for the cost of all education—primary, secondary, university and academic—we will arrange ourselves in such a way as to keep the best portions of the budgetary pie for the sons of the bourgeois.[26] And this great fellow, the people, boasting of their universities and their scholars, will not even perceive how we will construct government as a monopoly for those who can afford the luxury of colleges and universities

---

25 A reference to Thomas Malthus and his "law of population" and the related "iron law of wages." Malthus blamed the poverty of his time on the tendency of population (that is to say, numbers of working class people) to exceed food supplies rather than an unjust economic system as the radicals he attacked (like William Godwin) were arguing. His assertions were well received—for obvious reasons—by the ruling class of his and subsequent times while radicals and socialists viewed them as apologetics. Proudhon wrote against Malthus on many occasions, most famously in his article "The Malthusians" (included in *Property is Theft!*) as did Kropotkin (see, for example *Anarchist Communism: Its Basis and Principles* (London: Freedom Press, 1891) and *Fields, Factories and Workshops; or, Industry combined with agriculture and brain work with manual work* (New York: T. Nelson and Sons, 1912). (Editor)

26 The 1914 *Freedom* version adds: "And the workmen will not even notice that: they will have learned that they are 'the Unfit.'" (Editor)

for their children. If we told them point blank: You will be governed, judged, accused and defended, educated and stupefied by the rich, in the interest of the rich—they would without doubt revolt. It is obvious! But with taxation and a few nice, very "liberal" laws stating to the people, for example, that they must have undergone twenty examinations to be admitted to the high office of judge or minister—the fellow will find that very good!"

And this is how, one thing leading to another, the government of the people by the landlords and the wealthy bourgeois, against which the people once revolted when they saw it face-on, is reconstituted in another form under the disguise of taxation with the consent and almost the applause of the people!

We need not talk about taxation for the military because everyone should already know what to expect on that. When, then, was the permanent army not the means of keeping the people in bondage? And when did a regular army succeed in conquering a country if it met a people in arms?[27]

But take any tax—direct or indirect: on land, on income, or on consumption, for contracting debts of the State or under the pretext of paying them (because they never are); take the tax for war or public education, analyse it, see to what it ultimately leads you, and you will be struck by the immense force, by the omnipotence which we have given to our rulers.

Taxation is the most convenient form for the rich to keep the people in misery. It is also the means for ruining entire groups of farmers and industrial workers as they manage through an incredible series of efforts to increase ever-so-slightly their well-being. It is at the same time the most convenient instrument for making government the eternal monopoly of the rich. Finally, it allows, under different pretexts, the forging of the weapons which will one day be used to crush the people if they revolt.

An octopus with a thousand heads and a thousand suckers, like the sea monsters of the old tales, it makes it possible to envelop all society and to channel all individual efforts so as to make them result in the enrichment and governmental monopoly of the privileged classes.

And so long as the State, armed with taxation, continues to exist, the liberation of the proletarian cannot be accomplished in any way, neither by the path of reforms nor even by revolution. For if the revolution does not crush this octopus, if it does not destroy its head and cut off its arms and suckers, it will be strangled by the beast. The revolution itself will be placed at the service of monopoly, as was the [French] revolution of 1793.

---

27   The 1914 *Freedom* version has a different paragraph: "We need not talk about the taxation for military purposes. By this time every one ought to understand what armies and navies are kept for. Evidently not for the defence of the country, but for the conquest of new markets and new territory, to exploit them in the interest of the few." (Editor)

V

MONOPOLIES

Let us continue to examine how the modern State, that which established itself in Europe after the sixteenth century and later in the young republics of the two Americas, works to enslave the individual. After having accepted the personal emancipation of a few strata of society that had broken the yoke of serfdom in the free cities, it applied itself, as we have seen, to maintaining serfdom for the peasants as long as possible, and to re-establish economic servitude for all under a new form, bringing its subjects under the yoke of its functionaries and a whole new class of privileged bureaucrats, the Church, the landlords, merchants, and capitalists. And we have just seen how the State wielded taxation for this purpose.

We are now going to take a look at another weapon which the State knew so well how to use—the creation of privileges and monopolies to the benefit of some of its subjects to the detriment of others. Here we see the State in its true function, fulfilling its true mission. It applied itself to this from its beginnings: it is even this which enabled it to form and group under its protection the lord, the soldier, the priest and the judge. The sovereign was recognised at this price. To this mission it remains faithful to this day; and if it failed, if it ceased to be a mutual insurance [company] between the privileged, that would be the death of the institution—of the historical growth which has taken a form determined by this end and which we call State.

It is striking, indeed, to note to what extent the creation of monopolies for the benefit of those who already possessed these [privileges] from birth or else those with theocratic or military power was the very essence of the [social] organisation that started to develop in Europe in the sixteenth century, replacing that of the free cities of the Middle Ages.

We can take any nation: France, England, the German, Italian or Slavic States—everywhere we find in the emerging State the same character. This is why we need only look at the development of monopolies in a single nation—England, for example, where this development has been studied best—to understand and grasp this essential role of the State in all modern nations.[28] None offers the least exception.

It is very clear, indeed, how the establishment of the emerging State in England since the end of the sixteenth century and the establishment of monopolies in favour of the privileged went hand in hand.[29]

Even before the reign of Elizabeth, when the English State was still in its infancy, the Tudor kings always created monopolies for their favourites. Under Elizabeth, when maritime commerce began to develop and a whole series of new industries were introduced in England, this tendency became even more marked. Each new industry was erected as a monopoly, either in favour of foreigners who paid the Queen or in favour of Courtiers whom they made a point of rewarding.[30]

The exploitation of the alum deposits in Yorkshire, salt, tin mines, the coal mines around Newcastle, the glass industry, the improved manufacture of soap, pins, and so on—all these were set up as monopolies which prevented the development of industries and tended to kill the small industrialists. For example, to protect the Courtiers to whom the soap monopoly had been granted, they went so far as to forbid individuals from making soap for their laundry at home.

---

28 We have for England the work of Professor Hermann Levy, *Monopole, Kartelle und Trusts*, published in 1909, and translated into English as *Monopoly and Competition* (London, 1911). It has this advantage that the author does not even deal with the role of the State: it is the economic causes of monopolies that concerns him. Therefore there is no bias against the State.

29 See G. Unwin's *Industrial Organisation* [*in the Sixteenth and Seventeenth Centuries*] (Oxford, 1904), H. Price's *English Patents of Monopolies* (Boston, 1906), W. Cunningham's *The Growth of English Industry* [*and Commerce in Modern Times: The Mercantile System* (1882)], and especially the works of Hermann Levy and Macrosty.

30 The 1914 *Freedom* version immediately adds: "for their services (against the nation)." (Editor)

Under James I[31] the creation of "concessions" and of patents continued to increase until 1624 when finally, at the approach of the Revolution, a law was passed against monopolies. But this law was a two-faced law: it condemned the monopolies and at the same time not only retained those that existed but authorised new and very important ones. Besides, it was violated as soon as it was passed. They benefited from one of its paragraphs which assisted the old corporations of the towns in establishing monopolies in a certain town initially and later to extend them to entire regions. From 1630 to 1650, the government also took advantage of "patents" to establish new monopolies.[32]

It took the Revolution of 1688 to put an end to this orgy of monopolies.[33] And it was not until 1689, when a new Parliament (which represented an alliance between the commercial and industrial bourgeoisie and the landed aristocracy against royal absolutism and the *camarilla*[34]) began to function, that measures were taken against the creation of new monopolies

---

31   The French edition has "James II" but this must be a typographical error as shown by the 1914 Freedom version having James I. (Editor)

32   The term patent originates from the Latin *patere* ("to lay open") but, in this context, it is a shortened version of the term *letters patent*. This was a royal decree granting exclusive rights to a person or corporation. By the sixteenth century, the English Crown would habitually abuse the granting of letters patent for monopolies. After public outcry, King James I of England (James VI of Scotland) was forced to revoke all existing monopolies and declare that they were only to be used for "projects of new invention." This was incorporated into the Statute of Monopolies (1624) in which Parliament restricted the Crown's power so that the King could only issue *letters patent* to the inventors or introducers of original inventions for a fixed number of years. The Statute became the foundation for later developments in patent law in England and elsewhere. (Editor)

33   A reference to the so-called "Glorious Revolution" of 1688 in which a few English parliamentarians appealed to the Dutch William III, Prince of Orange, to invade the United Kingdom to replace the Catholic King James II (James VII of Scotland) who was asserting his divine right to rule. William and his wife Anne (daughter of James) became joint monarchs but subject to Parliament (albeit one elected by only the wealthiest). This ended absolute monarchy in the United Kingdom and its replacement by a constitutional one. Compared to the civil wars of two decades previously, the invasion was relatively bloodless—at least in England. In the 1914 *Freedom* version Kropotkin dates the revolution as being from 1648 to 1688. (Editor)

34   A *camarilla* is a group of courtiers or favourites who surround a monarch and influence from behind the scenes. The term derives from the Spanish word *camarilla* meaning "little chamber" or private cabinet of the king and was first used to describe the circle of cronies around King Ferdinand VII who reigned Spain from 1814 to 1833. (Editor)

by the royalty. The economic historians even say that for nearly a century after 1689 the English parliament was watchful [*jaloux*] of not allowing the creation of industrial monopolies that would have favoured certain manufacturers over others.

It must indeed be recognised that the Revolution and the coming to power of the bourgeoisie had this consequence and that in this way great industries, such as cotton, wool, iron, coal, etc., could develop without being hindered by monopolists. They could even develop into *national* industries, in which a mass of small entrepreneurs could take part. This enabled thousands of workers in the small workshops to contribute the thousand improvements without which these industries could never have advanced.

But meanwhile the statist bureaucracy was forming and strengthening. Governmental centralisation which is the essence of every State made its way—and soon the creation of new monopolies in new spheres recommenced, this time on a far larger scale than in the times of the Tudors. Then, the art [of monopolising] was in its infancy. Now, the State was mature.

If Parliament was prevented to a certain extent by the representatives of the local bourgeoisie from interfering in England even in emerging industries and from favouring some at the expense of others, it carried its monopolist activity to the colonies. Here it acted on a grand scale. The [East] India Company,[35] the Hudson Bay Company in Canada[36] became fantastically wealthy kingdoms, given to groups of private individuals. Later on, concessions of territories in America, of gold-fields in Australia, privileges for navigation, and the seizure of new branches of business, became in the hands of the State the means of granting to its favourites [*protégés*] fabulous incomes. Colossal fortunes were amassed in this way.

---

35   The East India Company was an English joint-stock company formed to pursue trade with the East Indies but ended up trading mainly with the Indian subcontinent and China. The company eventually accounted for half of the world's trade, particularly in basic commodities. It received a Royal Charter from Queen Elizabeth I in 1600 and wealthy merchants and aristocrats owned its shares. It eventually came to rule large areas of India with its own private armies, exercising military power and assuming administrative functions. Following the Indian Rebellion of 1857, the British Crown assumed direct control of India in the form of the new British Raj. (Editor)

36   The Hudson's Bay Company was incorporated by English royal charter in 1670 controlled the fur trade throughout much of the English controlled North America for several centuries and it functioned as the de facto government in parts of North America. In the late nineteenth century, with its signing of the Deed of Surrender, its vast territory became the largest portion of the newly formed Dominion of Canada, in which the company was the largest private landowner. (Editor)

True to its double composition, of bourgeois in the House of Commons and of landed aristocracy in the House of Lords, the English Parliament[37] first applied itself throughout the eighteenth century to proletarianising the peasants and delivering the cultivators of the soil, bound feet and hands, to the landowners. By means of acts of "demarcation" (*Enclosure Acts*), by which Parliament declared the communal lands the private property of the lord, as soon as the lord had surrounded them with any fence,[38] nearly 3,000,000 hectares of communal land passed from the hands of the communes to those of the lords between 1709 and 1869.[39] Overall, the result of monopolist legislation by the English Parliament is that a *third* of all the cultivatable land of England now belongs to 523 families.

Demarcation [of boundaries] was an act of open robbery but in the eighteenth century the State, which had been renovated by the Revolution [of 1688], already felt strong enough to defy discontent and possibly the insurrections of the peasants. Had it not for that the support of the bourgeoisie?

For if Parliament thus endowed the lords with estates, it also favoured the bourgeois industrialists. By driving the peasants out of the villages into the towns, it gave the industrialists the "hands" of hungry peasants. In addition, by virtue of Parliament's interpretation of the Poor Law, the agents of the cotton manufacturers roamed the workhouses, that is to say the prisons in which proletarians without work were confined with their families; and from these prisons they carried away carts full of children who, under the name of *workhouse apprentices*, had to work fourteen or sixteen hours a day in the cotton factories. Many a town in Lancashire has a population which bears to this day the stamp of its origin [in this practice]. The impoverished blood of these hungry children, brought from the *workhouses* of the South,

---

37   The 1914 *Freedom* version adds: "the British Parliament had other ways to exploit the nation than to favour a few factory-owners at the expense of the others. It had all the rural population to re-enslave. So it did it." (Editor)

38   The 1914 *Freedom* version adds: "Parliament robbed the peasants [...] Historically, he [the lord] had not the slightest shadow of right to these lands: they belonged to the village community. All that he might have claimed was the right of pasture on an equal footing with all the commoners, whenever that right was granted him by the community. He was the magistrate of the locality and the head of the militias but not the owner of the land. And yet Parliament, by an act of sheer robbery, gave him the communal land." (Editor)

39   On the evils caused by demarcation, excellent information can be found, with supporting maps, in a recent work on this subject by Dr. Gilbert Slater, *The English Peasantry and the Enclosure of Common Fields* (London, 1907). On the agrarian question in general and the plunder of the nation by legislators, see the work of Alfred Russel Wallace, the follower of Darwin, *Land Nationalisation; its Necessity and its Aims* [1906].

and made to work [in the factories] under the whip of the foremen to enrich the bourgeois of the midlands, often from the age of seven, is still seen in the stunted and anaemic population of these small towns [of Lancashire and Yorkshire]. This lasted until the nineteenth century.

Finally, Parliament always crushed by its legislation the national industries in the colonies to aid infant industries [in mainland Britain]. Thus the textile industry of India, which had attained such a high degree of artistic perfection, was killed. They delivered this rich market to English rubbish. The weaving of cloth in Ireland was killed in the same way in favour of the cotton-works of Manchester.

We thus see that the bourgeois Parliament, anxious to enrich its customers by the development of large national industries, during the eighteenth century opposed that individual industrialists or distinct branches of English industry should be favoured at the expense of the others—it made up for this by the proletarianisation of the great mass of the agricultural population and the colonies which it delivered to most ignoble exploitation by powerful monopolists. At the same time, if it could, it maintained and favoured in England even the mining monopolies established in the preceding century, such as that of the Newcastle mine-owners which lasted until 1844 or else that of the copper mines which lasted until 1820.[40]

---

40   The 1914 *Freedom* version adds the following paragraph: "And in the meantime new branches of monopolies, far more profitable than the old ones, began to be created by the same legislators." (Editor)

VI

MONOPOLIES IN THE NINETEENTH CENTURY

AS OF THE FIRST HALF OF THE NINETEENTH CENTURY NEW MONOPOLIES began to be emerge under the protection of the Law before which the old ones were merely children's toys.

Initially, the attentions of business tycoons were on the railways and the main lines of ocean navigation subsidised by the State. Colossal fortunes were made in a few decades in England and in France with the help of "concessions" received by individuals and companies for the construction of railway lines, generally with the guarantee a certain [minimum] revenue.

To this were added the great metallurgical and mining companies for supplying the railways with rails, iron or steel bridges, rolling stock, and fuel—all realising fabulous profits and immense speculations on the acquired lands. Big companies for the construction of iron ships, and especially for production of iron, steel, copper for war material as well as for this same material—warships, cannons, guns, swords, etc.; the large canal enterprises (Suez, Panama, etc.) and finally what was called "the development" of countries backward in industry followed closely. Millionaires were thus created by steam, by half-starved workers, who were pitilessly shot or transported to forced labour as soon as they made the slightest attempt at revolt.

The construction of a vast network of railways in Russia (begun in the [eighteen-]sixties), in the peninsulas of Europe, in the United States, in Mexico, in the republics of South America—all these were sources of unheard-of riches, accumulated by a real robbery under the protection of the State. What misery it once was, when a feudal baron plundered some merchant caravan passing near his castle! Here, they were hundreds of millions of human flocks being fleeced by business tycoons with the open connivance of States, of governments—autocratic, parliamentarian or republican.

But that is not all.[41] Soon they were joined by the construction of ships for the merchant navy subsidised by the various States, subsidised shipping lines, submarine cables, and [transcontinental] telegraphs; the boring of isthmus and tunnels, the beautification of cities inaugurated under Napoleon III, and finally—dominating all this like the Eiffel Tower dominates the neighbouring houses [in Paris]—the borrowing of the States and the subsidised banks!

All these dances of the billions became material for "concessions." Finance, commerce, war, armaments, education—all were used to create monopolies, to manufacture billionaires.[42]

And let no one try to excuse these monopolies and concessions by saying that in this way they succeeded, nevertheless, in carrying out a mass of useful initiatives. Because for every million of capital usefully employed in these enterprises the founders of these Companies added three, four, five, sometimes ten millions to the burden of public debt. We need only recall Panama, where millions were devoured to "float" the Companies and only a tenth of the money paid by the shareholders went to the real work of piercing the isthmus. But what was done in Panama was done with all companies, without exception, in America, in the Republic of the United States, as in the European monarchies. "Nearly all our railroad companies and other incorporations are loaded down in this way," said Henry George in *Progress and Poverty*. "When one dollar's worth of capital has been really used, certificates for two, three, four, five, or even ten have been issued, *and upon this fictitious amount interest or dividends are paid*."[43]

---

41   The 1914 *Freedom* version adds: "New sources of enrichment, for the privileged ones were soon discovered." (Editor)

42   The 1914 *Freedom* version has a different paragraph here: "All these new perfected instruments of robbery were now brought into the monopolies market and sold by the minions of the State. Hordes of millionaires and multi-millionaires were created." (Editor)

43   Kropotkin's emphasis; Henry George, *Poverty and Progress* (William Reeves: London, 1884), 145. Kropotkin's translation has been replaced with the original text. (Editor)

And if it were only that![44] When these great companies are formed, their power over human agglomerations is such that it can only be compared to that of the brigands who once held the roads and levied a tribute upon every traveller whether he was on foot or the head of a merchant caravan.[45] And for every millionaire who emerges with the aid of the State there are millions that pour down in the ministries.

The pillage of national wealth which has been done and is still being done with the consent and with aid of the State—especially where there are still natural resources to grab—is simply sickening. We must look at, for example, the great Trans-Canadian [railway] to get an idea of this pillage authorised by the State. All the best land on the shores of the Great Lakes in North America or in the big cities along rivers belongs to the company [the Canadian Pacific Railway] that received the privilege of building this line. A strip of land seven and a half kilometres wide on each side along its entire

---

44   The 1914 *Freedom* version has the following slightly different paragraph:

> The worse is, that once these big companies had been formed, their power over human agglomerations became such that it could only be compared with the power exercised in the medieval age by feudal barons, who levied a tribute upon everyone who passed on the high road in the vicinity of their castles. And while millionaires were thus created by the State, millions and millions flowed into the pockets of the functionaries in the Ministries. (Editor)

45   Henry George, in *Protection and Free Trade*, gave the following example of an iron mine in the State of Michigan. The owners had bought it by paying for the land 15 fr. per hectare. They assigned the right to extract the ore to a certain Colby for the payment of 2 fr. per tonne of ore mined. Colby assigned this right to Morse and Co. for 2 francs 62 c. per tonne, which Morse sold to Sellwood for 4 fr. 37 [c.] per tonne. Sellwood did not extract it himself but had it done by an entrepreneur that he paid 0 fr 62 ½ c. per tonne and for which extraction by the tonne was all-inclusive (wages, machinery, supervision administration, 0 fr 50 c.); which gave a net profit of 0 fr. 12 ½ c. As it was possible to extract 1,200 tonnes a day, this gave a net revenue: 150 fr per day to the entrepreneur who had the extraction done; 450 fr. for Sellwood; 8,400 fr. for Morse and Co.; 750 [fr.] for Colby and 2,400 fr. for the owners; or a net income of 12,150 fr. per day in addition to the cost of labour and the profits realised by the work entrepreneur. It was the price of the monopoly, guaranteed by the State—the surcharge paid by the consumer for leaving to the State the right to establish monopolies. This example is a small picture of what has been done on a large scale in all concessions: for railways, canals, ships, rolling stock, armaments, etc.

length was given [by the Canadian Federal Parliament] to the capitalists who undertook to build the Trans-Canadian;[46] and when this, advancing towards the west, crossed unproductive plateaus, the equivalent of this strip of land was allocated a bit everywhere, where there were fertile lands which would soon reach a high value. Where the State still distributed land to new settlers free of charge, the land was allocated to the Trans-Canadian was divided into lots of one square mile, placed like the black squares on a chessboard in the midst of the lands which the State gave to the settlers. With the result that today, the squares belonging to the State and given to the emigrants being all inhabited, the land given to the capitalists of the Trans-Canadian is worth hundreds of millions of dollars. And as to the capital that the Company was supposed to have spent to build the line, it represents according to all three or four times the sum that was actually spent.

It is absolutely the same wherever we look, so much so it becomes difficult to name a single big fortune due solely to industry, without the aid of any monopoly of governmental origin. In the United Sates, as Henry George had already noted, it is absolutely impossible.

Thus the immense fortune of the Rothschilds owes its origin entirely to the loans made by the founder banker of the family to kings, to fight either other kings or their own subjects.

The no less colossal fortune of the Dukes of Westminster is entirely due to the fact that their ancestors obtained from the whims [bon plaisir] of kings the lands upon which a great part of London is now built; and this fortune is maintained solely because the English Parliament, contrary to all justice, does not want to raise the question of the blatant appropriation of the land of the English nation by the lords.

As for the fortunes of the big American billionaires—the Astors, the Vanderbilts, the Rockefellers, [the Carnegies[47]], the trusts of oil, steel, railways, and even matches, etc.—all have their origin in monopolies created by the State.

In a word, if someone one day made a list of the riches that were seized by the financiers and business tycoons with the aid of privileges and monopolies established by States; if someone succeeded in evaluating the riches that were thus withdrawn from the public wealth by all governments—parliamentarian, monarchist and republican—to give them to individuals in exchange for more or less disguised brides—the workers would be amazed, outraged. These are incredible figures, hardly conceivable for those who live on their meagre wages.

---

46   The 1914 *Freedom* version adds: "in addition to all the profits they would draw from the railway." (Editor)

47   Added in the 1914 *Freedom* version. (Editor)

Alongside these figures—a product of pillage—those spoken to us by the anointed treatises of political economy are trifles, crumbs. When the economists want us to believe that at the origin of Capital the poor would find behind the hoarded money the privations of the bosses from the profits of their industrial establishments, either these gentlemen are ignorant or else they knowing say what is not true.[48] The rapine, the appropriation, the plunder of national wealth with the aid of the State by "interesting" the powerful—this is the real source of the immense fortunes accumulated each year by the lords and the bourgeois.

Perhaps it will be said: "But you are talking of the monopolisation of the riches in virgin countries, newly conquered by the industrial civilisation of the nineteenth century." And it will be added: "This is not the case for the older countries, so to speak, in their political life, such as England or France."

Well, it is absolutely the same in the countries most advanced in their political life. The rulers of these States continually find new opportunities to deprive the citizens for the benefit of their favourites [protégés]. Was "Panama," which served to enrich so many business tycoons, not purely French? Was it not an application of the *Enrich yourselves!* attributed to Guizot; and alongside Panama, which ended in a scandal, have there not been hundreds of others which flourish to this day? We have only to think of Morocco, the Tripoli adventure, that of the Yalou in Korea, the plunder of Persia, etc.[49] These acts of high fraud are still occurring every day and they will only end after the social revolution.

Capital and Sate are two parallel growths which would be impossible the one without the other and which, for this reason, must always be combated together—both at once. The State would never have been able to

---

48   The 1914 *Freedom* version states:

> By the side of these colossal legal robberies, the fortunes that are as-
> cribed by the economists to the moral virtues of the capitalists are a
> mere trifle. When the economists tell us that at the origin of Capital
> the worker would find the pence and shillings carefully put aside, at
> the cost of hard privation, by the masters of the factories—these econo-
> mists are either ignoramuses who repeat parrot-like the fables they were
> taught at the University, or they consciously tell what they themselves
> know to be lies. (Editor)

49   References to various imperialist acts: the annexation of the Touat-Gourara-Tidikelt
regions in Morocco by France in 1901; the annexation of Tropoli in Libya by Italy in
1911; the annexation of Taiwan (1895) and Korea (1910) by Japan; the division of
Persia (modern-day Iran) between Britain and Russia (1907). (Editor)

form and acquire the power which it possesses today—not even that which it possessed in the Rome of the emperors, in the Egypt of the Pharaohs, in Assyria, etc.—if it had not favoured, as it did, the growth of landed and industrial capital and the exploitation first of the tribes of pastoral people, then peasant farmers and later still workers of industry. It was by protecting with its whip and its sword those to whom it gave the possibility of monopolising the soil and of getting hold of (first by pillage, and later by the forced labour of the conquered) some tools either for the cultivation of the soil or for obtaining industrial products; it was by forcing those who possessed nothing to work for those who owned (land, iron, slaves) that little by little was formed this formidable organisation that is called State. And if capitalism would never have reached its present form without the watchful, thoughtful and continuous aid of the State, the State in its turn would never have reached this formidable strength, this power of absorption, the possibility of holding in its hands the whole life of every citizen it has today, if it had not consciously worked with patience and method to constitute Capital. Without the help of Capital, royal power would never even have managed to free itself from the Church and without the help of the capitalist it would never have been able to lay hands on the whole existence of modern man, from his first days at school to his grave.

That is why, when it is said that Capitalism dates from the fifteenth or sixteenth century, this statement can be considered as having some utility—*as long as it serves to affirm the parallelism* of the development of the State and Capital. But the fact is that exploitation of the capitalist already existed where there were the first seeds of individual ownership of the soil, where the [exclusive] right of such-and-such individuals to graze livestock on such-and-such land, and later the possibility of cultivating such-and-such land by forced or hired labour had been established. At this very moment, we can see Capital already achieving its pernicious work amongst the Mongol pastoral peoples (the Mongols, the Buryats) who are just emerging from the tribal phase. It is sufficient, indeed, for commerce to leave the tribal phase (during which nothing could be sold by a member of the tribe to another member), it is enough that trade becomes *individual,* so that capitalism already appears. And as soon as the State (coming from outside or developed within such-and-such a tribe) puts it hands on the tribe by taxation and its functionaries, as it does with the Mongolian tribes, the proletariat and capitalism are already born, and they necessarily begin their evolution. It is precisely to deliver the Kabyles, the Moroccans, the Arabs of Tripolitania, the Egyptian fellahs,[50] the Persians, etc. into the grip of

50   A fellah is a farmer or agricultural labourer in the Middle East and North Africa (the word derives from the Arabic word for "ploughman" or "tiller"). The 1914 *Freedom*

the capitalists imported from Europe and to the indigenous exploiters that the European States are making their conquests in Africa and Asia. And in these countries, recently conquered, we can see on the spot how the State and Capital are intimately linked, how one produces the other, how they mutually determine their parallel evolution.

versions adds "the Hottentots, the Somalis" to the list of tribal peoples being colonised by Western Imperial Powers. (Editor)

VII

MONOPOLIES IN CONSTITUTIONAL ENGLAND–IN GERMANY–KINGS OF THE ERA

THE ECONOMISTS WHO HAVE RECENTLY STUDIED THE DEVELOPMENT OF monopolies in various States made this remark that in England—not only in the eighteenth century, as we have just seen, but also in the nineteenth century—the creation of monopolies in *national industries* and also of these combinations between bosses to raise the prices of their products that we call *cartels* or *trusts* has not reached the extent it has recently taken in Germany.

However, this fact is explained not by the virtues of the political organisation of the English State—which is just as monopolist as the others—but, as these same economists point out, by the island location of England which allows the cheap import of goods (even bulky goods with low prices) and the free trade that results from it.

Furthermore, having conquered colonies as rich as India and having colonised (always thanks to its maritime location) territories like North America and Australia, the English State found such numerous and such immense opportunities in these countries to create monopolies of a colossal stature that it directed its principal activity there.

Without these two reasons, it would be the same in England as elsewhere. In fact, Adam Smith had already pointed out that three bosses never meet without conspiring amongst themselves against their workers— and, obviously, also against consumers.[51] The tendency to form combinations of bosses—*cartels* and *trusts*—has always existed and we find in

---

51 Given how often Adam Smith's name is used to bolster the position of those with economic power, it is useful to quote *The Wealth of Nations* (Chicago: University of Chicago, 1976):

> The workmen desire to get as much, the masters to give as little as possible. The former are disposed to combine in order to raise, the latter in order to lower the wages of labour [...] The masters, being fewer in number, can combine much more easily; and the law, besides, authorises, or at least does not prohibit their combinations, while it prohibits those of the workmen. [...] We rarely hear, it has been said, of the combinations of masters, though frequently of those of workmen. But whoever imagines, upon this account that masters rarely combine, is as ignorant of the world as of the subject. Masters are always and every where in a sort of tacit, but constant and uniform combination, not to raise the wages of labour above their actual rate [...] We seldom, indeed, hear of this combination, because it is the usual, and one may say, the natural state of things. (Volume I, 74–75)
>
> People of the same trade seldom meet together, even for merriment and diversion, but the conversation ends in a conspiracy against the public, or in some contrivance to raise prices. (Volume I, 144)
>
> Merchants and master manufacturers are [...] the two classes of people who commonly employ the largest capitals [...] The interest of the dealers, however, in any particular branch of trade or manufactures, is always in some respects different from, and even opposite to, that of the public. To widen the market and to narrow the competition, is always the interest of the dealers. To widen the market may frequently be agreeable enough to the interest of the public; but to narrow the competition must always be against it, and can serve only to enable the dealers, by raising their profits above what they naturally would be, to levy, for their own benefit, an absurd tax upon the rest of their fellow-citizens. The proposal of any new law or regulation of commerce which comes from this order [...] comes from an order of men whose interest is never exactly the same with that of the public, who have generally an interest to deceive and even to oppress the public, and who accordingly have, upon many occasions, both deceived and oppressed it. (Volume I, 278)

Macrosty's book a number of facts that show how the bosses conspired against consumers.[52]

The English parliament, like all other governments, favoured these bosses' conspiracies; the law only struck agreements between workers, which it punished as conspiracies against the security of the State.

But there was, besides this, the free trade which was introduced in the forties [of the nineteenth century] and the low prices of imports by sea which quite often thwarted the conspiracies of the bosses. Being the first to create big industry at home which little feared foreign competition and demanded the free import of raw materials; having given at the same time two-thirds of its land to a handful of lords who drove the peasants off their estates; and thus forced to live on imported wheat, barley, oats and meat, England was *forced* to maintain free trade.[53]

But free trade also allowed the import of manufactured goods. And then—it has been ably recounted by Hermann Levy—each time a combination between bosses was formed to increase prices, either of sewing thread, or cement, or glassware, we imported these goods from abroad. Inferior for the most part in quality, they nevertheless competed when the inferior quality was not considered important. In this way the plans of the bosses who had devised a *cartel* or a kind of *trust* were frustrated. But— what struggles to maintain free trade which was by no means to the taste of the great landowning lords and their farmers.

However, starting around the years 1886–1895 the creation of large cartels or trusts of bosses monopolising certain industries began to occur in England as elsewhere. And the cause—we learn today—is that bosses' syndicates began to be organised *internationally* so as to include entrepreneurs of the same industries in the protectionist countries as well as those in England.[54] In this way, the privilege established in Germany or in Russia in

---

These, and others like them, are the passages Kropotkin had in mind. (Editor)

52   Presumably a reference to Henry Macrosty's book *The Trust Movement in British Industry: A Study of Business Organisation* (London: Longman, Green & Co.: 1907). (Editor)

53   We even import food for the little livestock we raise in England: oil-cakes, hay, various meal; and as for meat, English peasants only started eating beef and mutton when we started, in the sixties, to import meat from America, and later from Australia and New Zealand. Until then, meat was an unattainable luxury for the peasants.

54   These syndicates, which include in addition to English manufacturers, the main manufacturers of sewing thread, glass, cement, etc. in the protectionist nations prevent foreign competition from lowering prices in England. Previously, German or Russian manufacturers of these same products, after having sold a certain quantity of them at home at a high price (thanks to the customs tariff), could send a part to England once the main English manufacturers of these products had come to an agreement

favour of German or Russian manufacturers spreads to the countries of free trade. The effect of these international syndicates is being felt everywhere. They contribute to a high degree to price increases. They raise not only—it must be noted—the prices of these specific goods targeted by the syndicate *but those of all goods.*

Need we add that these syndicates or *trusts* enjoy under a thousand relationships (banks, etc.) the high protection of the States whereas workers international unions are outlawed by these same governments. Thus the French government banned the International and the Belgian and German governments immediately deport the agitator from England encouraging the organisation of an international workers trade union. But we have never seen an agent of the *trusts* expelled from anywhere.[55]

To return to the English parliament, it has never failed in the mission of all governments of ancient and modern States: that of promoting the exploitation of the poor by the rich. In the nineteenth century, as before, it never failed to create monopolies as soon as the opportunity presented itself. Thus Professor Levy, who wants to show how England is superior to Germany in this respect, nevertheless is forced to recognise that the English parliament did not fail to take advantage of any lack of opportunities for foreign import in order to foster monopolies.

---

amongst themselves and had formed a syndicate to raise prices. Today, entering into an *international bosses syndicate*, the big German and Russian manufacturers commit not to do that.

55 Concerning this modern growth of international *cartels*, let me summarise what Mr. André Morizet has related in the *Guerre Sociale* [*Social War*] of 6 February 1912 on the international agreement that exists for the supply of armour-plating. It originally contained ten participants, including Krupp, Schneider, Maxim, Carnegie, etc., divided into four groups: English, German, French and American. These ten participants made arrangements amongst themselves to distribute government orders without competing. The participant to which the order was entrusted tendered a certain agreed price and the other members of the cartel bid slightly higher prices. Furthermore there was a *pool*—a fund consisting of payments of so much percent on each order which was used to equalise the profits of the various orders. Since 1899, three more large companies were admitted to this cartel in order to avoid competition. We can understand the immense strength this syndicate has. Not only does it offer the means to plunder the coffers of the State and to realise immense profits but it has every interest in urging all States, large and small, to build battleships. That is why we see, at this moment, a real fever to build *Dreadnoughts* and *Super-Dreadnoughts*. Bankers, interested in this syndicate, ask no better than to lend the necessary money to States, whatever their public debts already are—"Long live the State!"

Thus the monopoly of Newcastle coal merchants on the London market was assisted by the law until 1830 and the cartel of these merchants was broken only in 1844 during the strong Chartist agitation of the time. As recently as 1870–1880 these coalitions of shipping companies, the *Shipping rings* which we have heard so much about, were formed—fostered, it goes without saying, by the State.

But if there was only that! All that could be monopolised was monopolised by the English parliament.

As soon as we started to light the towns with gas, to bring pure water from afar, to channel the sewers, to build tramways, and finally, just recently, to install telephones, the English parliament never failed to set up these public services as monopolies in favour of privileged companies. So that today, for example, people living in the towns of Kent and several other counties have to pay preposterous prices for water and it is impossible for them to bring and distribute the needed household water by themselves: parliament granted this privilege to companies. Elsewhere it is the gas, elsewhere the trams, and everywhere, until 1 January 1912, it was the monopoly on telephones.

The first telephones were introduced in England by several private companies. And the State, parliament, obviously hastened to grant them the monopoly to install telephones in such-and-such towns, such-and-such regions, for thirty-one years. Soon most of these companies were amalgamated into a single powerful national company and then it was a scandalous monopoly. With its master-lines and its "concessions," the National Telephone Company charged English people five to ten times more for the telephone service than was paid elsewhere in Europe. And as the Company, armed with its monopoly, was making a *net* profit *of twenty-seven million* per year (official figures) on an annual expenditure of seventy-five million, it certainly did not press itself to increase the number of its stations, preferring to pay large dividends to its shareholders and to increase its reserve fund (having already reached more than one hundred million in fifteen years). This increased the "value" of this company and, consequently, the amount that the State would have to pay it to repurchase its privilege if it were forced to do so before the thirty-one years had passed. This situation had as a result that the private telephone, which had become so common on the continent, was in England only for the merchants and the rich. It was only on 1 January 1912 that the telephone system of the monopolist Company was repurchased by the post and telegraph administration after having enriched the monopolists by several hundred millions.[56]

---

56 The National Telephone Company (NTC) was a British telephone company from 1881 until 1911 that brought together smaller local companies in the early years of the

This is how we create an increasingly large and phenomenally wealthy bourgeoisie in a nation where half of the adult men wage-earners, more than four million men, earn *less* than thirty-four francs per week and more than three million—less than twenty-five francs. Now, thirty-four francs per week in England with the current prices of foodstuffs is hardly the *bare minimum* for a family of two adults and two children to live and pay [the rent on] their dwelling at the rate of five francs per week. The scrupulous studies of Professor Bowley and of [Benjamin] Rowntree in York, complemented by those of Chiozza Money, have fully established it.

If such was the creation of monopolies in a country of free trade, what to say about the protectionist countries where not only the competition of foreign products is rendered impossible but where the great iron industries, railway manufacturing, sugar, etc., always hard-pressed to find money, are continually subsidised by the State? Germany, France, Russia, the United States are the true breeding-grounds of monopolies and syndicates of bosses protected by the State. These organisations, very numerous and sometimes very powerful, have the potential to raise the prices of their products in appalling proportion.

Ores—almost all ores—metals, raw sugar and sugar refineries, ethanol for industry and a number of specialised industries (nails, pottery, etc.), tobacco, oil refining and so on—all this is formed into monopolies, cartels, or trusts—always thanks to the intervention of the State, and very often under its protection.

One of the best examples of this last kind is offered by the German sugar syndicates. The production of sugar being an industry subject to supervision by the State and to some extent in its management, 450 sugar refineries met under the patronage of the State to exploit the public. This exploitation lasted until the Brussels conference which limited a little the interested protection of the German and Russian governments in the sugar industry—to protect the English refiners.[57]

---

telephone. As it had become a monopoly, it was nationalised by the coalition Liberal and Labour government under the Telephone Transfer Act 1911 and taken over by the General Post Office (GPO) in 1912. It remained nationalised until it was re-privatised in 1984 (then called British Telecommunications). Perhaps needless to say, shares were priced lower than the market rate (by the end of the day it was floated on the stock-market, shares had risen by a third) meaning that the government had sold off public assets too cheaply and so giving investors millions in profits. (Editor)

57   A reference to the 1902 Brussels Sugar Convention. in which Britain and nine other nations attempted to stabilise world sugar prices by setting up a commission to investigate export bounties and decide on penalties. It created intergovernmental regulation

The same thing happens in Germany in several other industries, such as the brandy syndicate, the Westphalian coal syndicate, the protected syndicate of Steingut Fabriker pottery, the Union of manufacturers of nails made with German wire, etc., etc., without speaking of the shipping lines, the railways, the industries for war material and so on, nor of the monopolistic syndicates for the extraction of ores in Brazil, and so many others.

You can go to America—we find the same thing there. Not only in the times of colonisation and at the beginnings of modern industry but today still, every day, in every American town scandalous monopolies are formed. Everywhere it is the same tendency to favour and to strengthen, under the protection of the State, the exploitation of the poor by the propertied and the crafty. Each new advance of civilisation brings new monopolies, new methods of exploitation fostered by the State in America as in the old States of Europe.

Aristocracy and democracy, placed within the framework of the State, act the same. Both, having come to power, are equally enemies of the simplest justice towards the producer of all wealth—the worker.[58]

And if it were only the vile exploitation to which entire populations are delivered by States to enrich a certain number of industrialists, companies or bankers! If it were only that! But the evil is infinitely deeper. It is that the big railway, steel, coal, oil, copper, etc. companies, the big banking companies and the big financiers become a formidable *political* power in all modern States. We only have to think of the way in which bankers and large financiers dominate governments in matters of war. Thus, we know that the personal sympathies for Germany, not only of Alexander II but also of Queen Victoria, influenced Russian politics and English politics in 1870 and contributed to the crushing of France. We then saw how much the personal sympathies of King Edward VII mattered in the Franco-English

---

of the sugar trade in the name of eliminating anti-competitive practices. Member States agreed to liberalise trade by levying countervailing duties against the state-subsidised beet sugar that has been responsible for a spiral of over-production. It is seen as one of the influences in modern multilateral trade agreements and institutions. (Editor)

58 Delaisi gave an excellent example of a syndicate—that of Saint-Aubin—born under Louis XV which has always managed to prosper by seeking its shareholders in the high spheres of the rulers. Picking its shareholders and protectors firstly in the Court of the King, then in the imperial nobility of Napoleon I, then in the high aristocracy of the Restoration and finally in the republican bourgeoisie and changing its sphere of exploitation according to the times, this syndicate prospers still under the protection of the Legitimists, Bonapartists and Republicans associated for exploitation. The form of the State changes; but since its substance is the same the monopoly and the trust remain always there and the exploitation of the poor for the profit of the rich continues.

agreement.[59] But there would be no exaggeration to say that predilections of the Rothschild family, the interests of the high bank in Paris and the Catholic bank of Rome are much more powerful than the predilections and interests of queens and kings. We know, for example, that the attitude of the United States towards Cuba and Spain depended much more on the monopolist senators in the sugar industry than on the sympathies of the American statesmen towards the Cuban insurgents.[60]

---

59   A reference to the *Entente Cordiale*, a series of agreements signed on 8 April 1904 between the United Kingdom and the French Third Republic. Beyond the immediate concerns of colonial expansion addressed by the agreement (such as granting freedom of action to the UK in Egypt and to France in Morocco), the agreement marked the end of almost a thousand years of intermittent conflict between the two States and their predecessors. It also strengthened both powers against various rivals (most obviously, Germany) and was invoked when war finally broke out in 1914. (Editor)

60   A reference to the Spanish–American War of 1898 when an internal explosion of the *USS Maine* in Havana harbor in Cuba lead the United States to intervene in the Cuban War of Independence (1895–1898). After a short war, Spain was defeated and lost its empire. The U.S. annexed the former Spanish colonies of Puerto Rico, the Philippines and Guam, while in Cuba American forces did not allow armed rebels to enter the capital city of Santiago and left the old Spanish civil authorities in charge of the municipal offices. U.S. military occupation of Cuba lasted until 1902, while its new constitution saw the U.S. retain the right to intervene in Cuban affairs and to supervise its finances and foreign relations. During the occupation, Americans began taking over railroad, mine, sugar properties (for example, United Fruit moving into the Cuban sugar industry, buying 1,900,000 acres of land for about twenty cents an acre) and the American Tobacco Company arrived. By 1901, an estimated 80 percent (at least) of the export of Cuba's minerals were in American hands, mostly Bethlehem Steel (see chapter 12 of Howard Zinn's *A People's History of the United States* [Essex: Longman, 1996] for more details). (Editor)

VIII

WAR

Industrial Rivalries

As long ago as 1882, when England, Germany, Austria, and Romania, taking advantage of the isolation of France, leagued themselves against Russia and a terrible European war was about to break out, we showed in *Le Révolté* what were the real motives for rivalry between States and the wars that would result.[61]

The cause of modern wars is always competition for markets and the right to exploit nations backward in industry. In Europe we no longer fight for the honour of kings. Armies are pitted against each other so that the revenues of Your Most Powerful Rothschild or Schneider, the Most Worshipful Company of Anzin or the most Holy Catholic Bank of Rome may remain unimpaired. Kings no longer count.

In fact, all wars waged in Europe during the last hundred and fifty years were wars for commercial interests, rights of exploitation.

Towards the end of the eighteenth century great industry and world commerce, supported by a navy and colonies in America (Canada) and Asia (in

---

61 The book references 1883 but the original article has 1882 ("La Guerre," *Les Temps Nouveaux*, 2 March 1912). In 1882 Kropotkin wrote the pamphlet *La Guerre* (Geneva: Le Révolté, 1882) which was later included in *Words of a Rebel* (1885). Moreover, in 1883 he was a prisoner in France and so did not contribute to the anarchist press until he was freed in 1886. So while he may be referring to an article published in *Le Révolté* written by another anarchist, it seems far more likely that this is a typographical error by the printer. As such, the date has been changed to 1882. (Editor)

India), began to develop in France. Thereupon England, which had already crushed its competitors in Spain and Holland, anxious to keep for itself alone the monopoly of maritime commerce, of sea-power, and of a colonial empire, took advantage of the revolution in France to begin a whole series of wars against it. Since then it understood what [riches] the monopolised outlet for her growing industry would bring it.

Finding itself rich enough to pay for the armies of Prussia, Austria, and Russia, it waged during a quarter of a century a succession of terrible and disastrous wars against France. France had to bleed itself dry to sustain these wars; and only at this price was it able to uphold its right to remain a "great power." That is to say, it retained its right not to submit to all the conditions that the English monopolists wished to impose upon it to the advantage of their commerce. It retained its right to have a navy and military ports. Frustrated in its plans for expansion in North America (it had lost Canada) and in India (it had to abandon its colonies), it obtained in return permission to create a colonial empire in Africa—on condition that it did not touch Egypt—and to enrich its monopolists by pillaging the Arabs in Algeria.

Later on, in the second half of the nineteenth century, it was the turn of Germany. When serfdom was abolished as a consequence of the uprisings in 1848, and the abolition of communal property forced young peasants in mass to leave the country for the town, where they offered their "idle hands" at starvation wages to the entrepreneurs of industry—great industry began to flourish in various German States. German industrialists soon realised that if the people were given a good practical education they would quickly catch up with great industrial countries like France and England—on condition, needless to say, of procuring for Germany advantageous outlets beyond its frontiers. They knew what Proudhon had so well demonstrated:[62] that the industrialist can only succeed in substantially enriching himself if a large portion of his products is exported to countries where it can be sold at prices they could never obtain in the country of origin.

So in all the social strata of Germany, that of the exploited as well as of the exploiters, there was a passionate desire to unify Germany at any price: to build a powerful empire capable of supporting an immense army, a strong navy, and capable of conquering ports in the North Sea, in the Adriatic, and—one day—in Africa and the East—an empire which could dictate economic law in Europe.

---

62   Kropotkin is undoubtedly referring to Proudhon's chapter on "Free Trade" in his 1846 work *System of Economic Contradictions*. Sadly, as with most of its second volume, this discussion has not been translated into English. (Editor)

For this [to succeed], it was evidently necessary to break the strength of France, which would have opposed it and which then had, or seemed to have, the power to prevent it.

Hence—the terrible war of 1870, with all its sad consequences for universal progress which we suffer from even today.

By this war and this victory over France, a German Empire, that dream of radicals, socialists and, in part, German conservatives since 1848, was at last constituted and soon made itself felt and its political power and its right to dictate the law in Europe recognised.

Germany, on entering a striking period of youthful activity, indeed quickly succeeded in increasing its industrial productivity by double, treble, tenfold and at this moment the German bourgeoisie covets new sources of enrichment throughout the plains of Poland, the steppes of Hungary, the plateaus of Africa, and especially around the railway line to Bagdad—in the rich valleys of Asia Minor which can provide German capitalists with a hardworking population to exploit under one of the most beautiful skies in the world; perhaps, one day, also Egypt.

Therefore, it is ports for export and especially military ports in the Mediterranean Adriatic and in the Adriatic of the Indian Ocean—the Persian Gulf—as well as on the African coast in Beira, and later in the Pacific Ocean, that these German colonial tycoons wish to conquer. Their faithful servant, the German Empire with its armies and battleships, is at their service.

But everywhere these new conquerors encountered a formidable rival, the English who bar their way.

Jealous of keeping its supremacy on the seas, jealous above all of holding its colonies for exploitation by its [own] monopolists; frightened by the success of German Empire's colonial policy and the rapid development of its navy, England redoubled its efforts to have a fleet capable of definitely crushing the German fleet. It also looks everywhere for allies to weaken the military power of Germany on land. And when the English press sows alarm and terror by pretending to fear a German invasion, it knows very well that danger does not lie there. What it needs is the power to launch the regular army to where Germany, in accord with Turkey, might attack some colony of the British Empire (Egypt, for instance). And for that it must be able to retain at home a strong "territorial" army that can drown in blood, if necessary, any workers' revolt. It is for this reason, predominantly, that military science is taught to young bourgeois, grouped in squads of "scouts."[63]

---

63   The British Boy Scouts organised strike-breaking during the 1926 General Strike, for example. For further discussion of its imperialist and militarist origins, see Brain

The English bourgeoisie of today wants to act towards Germany as it twice acted towards Russia in order to halt, for fifty years or more, the development of that country's sea-power: once in 1855, with the help of Turkey, France, and Piedmont; and again in 1904 by hurling Japan against the Russian fleet and against its military port in the Pacific.[64]

That is why for the past two years we have been living on the alert, expecting a colossal European war to break out at any time.

Besides, we must not forget that the industrial wave, in rolling from West to East, has also invaded Italy, Austria and Russia. And these States are in their turn asserting their "right"—the right of their monopolists to the feeding frenzy in Africa and Asia.

Russian brigandage in Persia, Italian brigandage against the desert Arabs around Tripoli, and French brigandage in Morocco are the consequences.

The *consortium* of brigands, at the service of the monopolists who govern Europe, has "allowed" France to seize Morocco, as it "allowed" England to seize Egypt. It has "allowed" Italy to seize a part of the Ottoman Empire to prevent it being seized by Germany, and it has allowed Russia to take Northern Persia so that England might seize a substantial strip of land on the shores of the Persian Gulf before the German railway reached it!

And for this the Italians disgracefully massacre harmless Arabs, the French massacre Moors, and the hired assassins of the Tsar hang Persian patriots who endeavour to regenerate their country by a little political liberty.

Zola was right to say: "What scoundrels respectable people are!"[65]

High Finance

All States, we said, as soon as great industry develops itself in the nation, are made to seek war. They are driven by their industrialists, and even by workers, to conquer new markets—new sources of easy riches.

Morris, "The Truth about Baden-Powell and the Boy Scouts," *Ecology and Anarchism: Essays and Reviews on Contemporary Thought* (Malvern Wells: Images Publishing Ltd, 1996). For its founder's praise for fascism, see Christopher Hitchens, "Young Men in Shorts," *The Atlantic Magazine*, June 2004. (Editor)

64 A reference to the Crimean War (1853–1856) and the Russo-Japanese war (1904–1905), respectively. During the latter conflict, Kropotkin refused to take sides. See "La Guerre Russo-Japonaise," *Les Temps Nouveaux*, 5th March 1904. (Editor)

65 The final words of Zola's 1873 novel *Le Ventre de Paris*. This work has been translated at least three times under different titles: *Fat and Thin* (188), *Savage Paris* (1955) and *The Belly of Paris* (2007). (Editor)

But there is more. In every State there exists today a class—a clique, rather—infinitely more powerful even than entrepreneurs of industry and which, too, pushes for war. It is high finance, the big bankers, who intervene in international relations and who foment wars.

This is done today in a very simple manner.

Towards the end of the Middle Ages most of the major city-republics of Italy had ended up by getting into debt. When their period of decay had begun, owing to their wish to conquer rich markets in the East and the conquest of such markets bringing endless wars between the city-republics, these cities began to incur immense debts to their own guilds of big merchants.

The same phenomenon occurs today for States, with bankers' syndicates very willing to lend against a mortgage on their future income.

Naturally, it is mainly on the small States that this is practised. Bankers lend them money at seven, eight, ten percent, knowing that they can "realise" the loan only at seventy or eighty percent. So that, after deducting the "commissions" to banks and middlemen—which amount to ten to twenty and sometimes up to thirty percent—the State does not even receive three-quarters of the amount inscribed in its ledger.

On these amounts, swollen in this way, the indebted State must now pay both interest and depreciation. And when it does not do so at the appointed time, the bankers ask for nothing better than to add the arrears of interest and depreciation to the principal of the loan. The worse the finances of the debtor State grow, the more reckless the expenditure of its leaders—and the more willingly are new loans offered to it. Whereupon the bankers, setting themselves up as a "consortium" one day, lay hands on certain taxes, certain duties, certain railway lines.

This was how the big financiers ruined and later annexed Egypt by England. The more foolish the expenditure of the Khedive, the more they encouraged him. It was annexation by small doses.[66]

It is the same way that they ruined Turkey to take its provinces little by little. It was also the same thing, we are told, for Greece, that a group of financiers pushed for war against Turkey to seize part of defeated Greece's revenues.

---

66   The term Khedive is a title equivalent to viceroy. It was first used by Muhammad Ali Pasha (1769–1849), vassal of the Ottoman Empire and governor of Egypt and Sudan. In 1882, a rebellion saw Egypt in the hands of nationalists opposed to European domination of the country, leading to a British naval bombardment of Alexandria and then to the landing of a British expeditionary force. British troops defeated the Egyptian Army, restoring the government of the Khedive and international controls which had been in place to streamline Egyptian financing. The first period of British rule (1882–1914) is often called the "veiled protectorate." (Editor)

And that is how Japan was exploited by high finance in England and the United States before and during its wars against China and Russia.

As for China, for several years it has been partitioned by a syndicate representing the great banks of England, France, Germany and the United States. And since the Revolution in China,[67] Russia and Japan demand to be allowed to join this syndicate. They want to profit by it to extend not only their spheres of exploitation but also their territories. The partitioning of China, prepared by bankers, is thus the order of the day.

In short, there is in the lending States a complete organisation in which rulers, bankers, promoters of companies,[68] tycoons and all the shady gentlemen Zola has so well described in *L'Argent* lend a hand to exploit whole States.[69]

Where the naive believe they have discovered deep political reasons, or national hatreds, there are only plots hatched by the buccaneers of finance. They exploit everything: political and economic rivalries, national enmities, diplomatic traditions and religious conflicts.

In all the wars of the last quarter of a century we find the hand of high finance. The conquest of Egypt and the Transvaal, the annexation of Tripoli, the occupation of Morocco, the partition of Persia, the massacres in Manchuria, the massacres and international looting in China during the Boxer riots, the wars of Japan—everywhere we find great banks. Everywhere high finance has had a decisive voice. And if up till now a great European war has not yet broken out, it is because high finance hesitates. It does not quite know which way the scales will fall for the millions that will be brought into play: it does not know on which horse to put their millions.

As for the hundreds of thousands of human lives that war would cost— what has finance to do with them? The mind of the financier reasons with columns of figures which balance each other. The rest is not his domain: he does not even possess the imagination to bring human lives into his calculations.

---

67   The Xinhai Revolution, also known as the Revolution of 1911, overthrew China's last imperial dynasty (the Qing dynasty) and established the Republic of China. It consisted of many revolts and uprisings and its success in 1912 marked the end of two thousand years of imperial rule. (Editor)

68   That is, someone who solicits people to invest money in a company or corporation (usually when it is being formed). (Editor)

69   Zola's *L'Agrent* (*Money*) was published as a novel in 1891 and focuses on the financial world of the Second French Empire as embodied in the Paris *Bourse* (Stock Exchange). He aimed to show the terrible effects of speculation and fraud in company promotion on society as well as the impotency of contemporary regulation and laws. (Editor)

What a despicable world would be unveiled if only somebody took the trouble to study high finance behind the scenes! We can guess it sufficiently, if only from the small corner of the veil lifted by "Lysis" in his articles in *La Revue* (published in 1908 in a volume entitled *Contre l'Oligarchie Financière en France* [*Against the Financial Oligarchy in France* (Paris: Bureaux de "La Revue," 1908)]).

From this work we can, in fact, see how four or five big banks—Crédit Lyonnais, Société Générale, Comptoir National d'Escompte, and Crédit Industriel et Commercial—have a monopoly of large financial operations in France.

The bulk—nearly eight-tenths—of French savings, amounting every year to about two thousand million [of francs], is poured into these great banks; and when foreign States, great and small, railway companies, towns, industrial companies from the five parts of the globe present themselves in Paris to secure a loan, they address themselves to these four or five great banking companies. These banks have a monopoly on foreign loans and have at their disposal the necessary machinery to boost them.

It is evident that it was not the skill of the directors of these banks that created their lucrative position. It was *the State*, the French Government in the first place, that protected and favoured these banks and created for them a privileged position, which soon became a monopoly. And then the other States, the borrowing States, strengthened this monopoly. Thus Crédit Lyonnais, which monopolises Russian loans, owes this privileged position to the financial agents of the Russian government and to the Tsar's finance ministers.

The business transacted by these four or five companies amounts to thousands of millions. Thus, in two years, 1906 and 1907, they distributed in various loans seven and a half thousand million—7,500 million, including 5,500 million in foreign loans ("Lysis," p. 101). And when we learn that the "commission" of these companies for organising a foreign loan is five per cent for the "syndicate of middle-men [*apporteurs*]" (those who "arrange" new loans), five per cent. for the underwriting syndicate, and from seven to ten per cent for the syndicate, or rather trust, of the four or five banks we have just named, we see what immense sums go to these monopolists.

Thus, a single middle-man who "arranged" the loan of 1,250 million contracted by the Russian government in 1906 to crush the revolution thereby received—"Lysis" tells us—a commission of twelve million!

We can therefore understand the secret influence on international politics exercised by the big directors of these financial companies, with their mysterious accounts and with the plenary powers that certain directors exact and obtain from their shareholders—because they must be discreet when paying twelve million to Monsieur So-and-So, 250,000 francs to a certain minister, and so many millions, as well as awards, to the press! There is not, says "Lysis," a single major newspaper in France that is not paid by the banks. This is understandable. We can easily guess how much money it was necessary to distribute to the press when a series of Russian loans (State, railway, land bank loans) were being prepared during the years 1906 and 1907. How many pen-pushers [*plumitifs*] waxed fat on the loans can be seen from the book by "Lysis." What a windfall, in fact! The government of a great State beleaguered! A revolution to crush! This does not happen every day!

Well, everybody is more or less aware of that. There is not a single politician who does not know the ins-and-outs of all this jiggery-pokery, and who does not hear mentioned the names of the women and men who "received" large sums after each loan, great or small, Russian or Brazilian.

And everyone, if he has only the slightest knowledge of business, also knows very well how all this organisation of high finance is a product of the State—*an essential attribute of the State*.

And it would be this State—the State which is so careful not to diminish its powers or reduce its functions—which in the mind of statist reformers should become the instrument for the emancipation of the masses?! What nonsense!

Whether it is stupidity, ignorance, or deceit which makes them assert this, it is equally unpardonable in people who believe themselves called to direct the fate of nations.

IX

WAR AND INDUSTRY

Let us now go a little deeper and see how the State has created a whole class of men in modern industry directly interested in turning nations into military camps, ready to hurl themselves at one another.

There are now, indeed, immense industries that employ millions of men and which exist for the sole purpose of producing war material: which makes the owners of these factories and their financial backers have every interest to prepare for war and to fan the fear that wars are always ready to break out.

It is not a matter of the small fry—the manufacturers of low-quality firearms, shoddy swords, and revolvers that always misfire, as we have in Birmingham, Liège, etc. These barely matter, although the trade in these weapons, carried on by exporters who speculate in "colonial" wars, has already attained some importance. So we know that English merchants supplied weapons to the Matabele when they were preparing to rise against the English, who were imposing serfdom upon them.[70] Later on, French man-

---

70 In 1891 the British government granted a royal charter to the British South Africa Company (BSAC) over Matabeleland and Mashonaland (in modern Zimbabwe), so becoming British protectorates and ruled by the company. This lead to mass colonisation with the British controlling labour as well as mineral resources. The First

ufacturers, and even well-known English manufacturers, made fortunes by
sending firearms, cannons, and ammunition to the Boers. And even now they
talk of quantities of weapons imported by English merchants into Arabia—
which will cause tribal uprisings, the plunder of a few merchants and English
intervention, to "restore order" and make some new "annexation."

Besides, these little facts no longer count. It is well known what bourgeois "patriotism" is worth and far more serious events have been witnessed
recently. Thus, during the last war between Russia and Japan, English gold
was supplied to the Japanese so that they might destroy Russia's emerging
sea-power in the Pacific Ocean, which England had taken umbrage to. But
at the same time the English coal companies sold 300,000 tons of coal
at a very high price to Russia to enable it to send Rojdestvensky's fleet
to the East. Two birds were killed with one stone: the coal companies in
Wales made a great deal of money and the financiers of Lombard Street
(the centre of financial operations in London) placed their money at nine
or ten percent in the Japanese loan, and mortgaged a substantial part of the
income of their "dear allies"!

These are but only a few facts amongst thousands of others of the same
kind. We would learn fine things about all this world of our rulers if the
bourgeoisie did not know how to keep their secrets! So let us move on to
another category of facts.

We know that all the great States have favoured, alongside their [own] ar-
senals, the creation of huge private factories that manufacture cannons,
battleships, warships of smaller size, shells, gunpowder, cartridges, etc.
Immense amounts are spent by all States to obtain these auxiliary factories,
where the most skilled workers and engineers are concentrated.

Now, it is obvious that it is in the direct interest of the capitalists who
have invested their capital in these enterprises to constantly maintain rumours of war, to incessantly press [the need] for armaments, to sow panic
if need be. Indeed, that is what they do.

And if the chances of a European war sometimes grow less, if the gentlemen of the government—though themselves interested as shareholders

---

Matabele War (1893–1894) pitted the BSAC against the Ndebele Kingdom. While
the Ndebele did have riflemen alongside spearmen, they were no match for the company's Maxim machine guns which, according to one eyewitness, "mow[ed] them down
literally like grass." Defeat lead to increased colonisation with the company officially
naming the land Rhodesia—after its founder and head, Cecil Rhodes—in 1895. The
Second Matabele War or Matabeleland Rebellion (1896–1897) saw the Ndebele un-
successfully revolt against the authority of the BSAC. The company ruled until the
1920s. (Editor)

in the great factories of this kind (Anzin, Krupp, Armstrong, etc.) as well as the great railway companies, coal mines, etc.—if the rulers sometimes require coaxing in order to make them sound the war-trumpet, they are compelled to do so by chauvinistic opinion fabricated by newspapers, or even by fermenting insurrections [to justify invention and annexation].

Indeed, is there not that prostitute—the big press—to prepare minds for new wars, to hasten those that are likely [to break out] or, at least, force governments to double, to treble their armaments? Thus, did we not see in England, during the ten years preceding the Boer War, the big press, and especially its assistants in the illustrated press, skilfully prepare minds for the necessity of a war "to arouse patriotism"? To this end no stone was left unturned. With much bluster they published novels about the next war in which we were told how the English, beaten at first, made a supreme effort and ended by destroying the German fleet and establishing themselves in Rotterdam. A lord spent a great deal of money to stage a patriotic play across England. It was too stupid to break even but it was necessary for those gentlemen who intrigued with Rhodes in Africa in order to seize the Transvaal gold fields and force the blacks to work in them.

Forgetting everything, they even went so far as to revive the cult—yes, *cult*—of England's sworn enemy, Napoleon I. And since then work in this direction has never ceased. In 1905 they almost succeeded in driving France, governed at that time by Clemenceau and Delcassé, into a war against Germany—the Minister for Foreign Affairs of the Conservative Government, Lord Lansdowne, having promised to support the French armies by sending an English army corps to the continent! Delcassé, attaching undue importance to this ridiculous proposal, very nearly launched France into a disastrous war.

In general, the more we advance with our statist bourgeois civilisation, the more the press, ceasing to be the expression of what is called public opinion, applies itself to manufacturing that opinion by the most infamous means. The press, in all great States, is already [just] two or three syndicates of financial tycoons; which manufacture the opinion needed in the interests of their businesses. The big newspapers belong to them and the rest are of no account.

But this is not all: the gangrene goes even deeper.

Modern wars are no longer just the massacre of hundreds of thousands of men in every battle—a massacre which those who have not followed the details of the great battles during the war in Manchuria and the horrific details of the siege and defence of Port Arthur have absolutely no idea. And yet the three great historical battles—Gravelotte, Potomac, Borodino (Moscow)—which lasted three days each and in which ninety to hundred and ten thousand men were killed and wounded on both sides, these were child's play in comparison to modern warfare![71]

Great battles are now fought on a front of fifty, sixty kilometres; they last not three days, but seven days (Liaoyang), ten days (Mukden);[72] and the losses are one hundred, one hundred and fifty thousand men *on each side*.

The devastation caused by shells fired with precision from a distance of five, six, seven kilometres by batteries placed in a position which cannot be discovered [by the enemy] as they use smokeless powder is unimaginable. It is no longer chance. The key positions occupied by the enemy are divided on a map into squares and the fire from all the batteries is concentrated on each square successively in order to destroy everything that is there.

When the fire from several hundred cannons is concentrated on a square kilometre, as is done today, there is no area of ten square metres that has not been struck by a shell, not a bush that has not been cut down by the howling monsters sent from nobody knows where. Seven or eight days of this terrible fire drives the soldiers to madness; and when the attacking columns—after having been repelled eight to ten times, but gaining a few more metres every time—finally reach the enemy's trenches, a hand-to-hand struggle begins. After throwing hand-grenades and pieces of pyroxyline at each other (two pieces of pyroxyline tied together with a string were used by the Japanese as a sling[73]), Russian and Japanese soldiers rolled in the trenches of Port Arthur like wild beasts, striking each other with their rifle-butts, knives, tearing each other's flesh with their teeth...

The western workers still have no idea about this terrible return to the most dreadful savagery that is modern warfare, and the bourgeois who do know are careful not to tell them.

But modern wars are not just the slaughter, the madness of massacre, the return to savagery. They are also the destruction of human labour on a colossal scale; and we continually feel the effect of this destruction *in time of peace* by an increase in the misery amongst the poor, parallel to the enrichment of the wealthy.

---

71   The Battle of Gravelotte on 18 August 1870 was the largest battle during the Franco-Prussian War; there were numerous battles during the American Civil War (1861–1865) in and around the Potomac River and its tributaries; The Battle of Borodino (near Moscow) was fought on 7 September 1812 during the French invasion of Russia. (Editor)

72   Two major land battles of the Russo-Japanese war of 1904–1905. (Editor)

73   A highly flammable nitrocellulose (a pulpy or cotton-like polymer derived from cellulose treated with nitric and sulphuric acids) used in making plastics, lacquers and explosives. (Editor)

Every war is the destruction of a formidable [amount of] material, which includes not only the war material itself but also things most necessary for everyday life, to society as a whole: bread, meat, vegetables, foodstuffs of all kind, draught animals, leather, coal, metal, clothing. All this represents the useful work of millions of men over decades; and all this will be wasted, burnt or scrapped in a few months. But that is already wasted even now, in anticipation of war.

And as this war material, these metals, these provisions must be prepared beforehand, the mere possibility of a new war in the near future brings about in all our industries shocks and crises that affect us all. You, me, we all feel the effects in every detail of our life. The bread we eat, the coal we burn, the railway ticket we buy, the price of everything depends on the rumours spread by speculators, on the likelihood of war [breaking out] in the near future.

Industrial crises due to expectations of war

The necessity for preparing in advance a formidable [amount of] war material and a mass of provisions of every kind, necessarily produces in all industries shocks and crises from which everyone, and especially workers, suffers to a terrible extent. Indeed, this was seen quite recently in the United States.

Everyone, no doubt, remembers the terrible industrial crisis that ravaged the United States during the past three or four years. In part, it is still continuing. Well, the origin of this crisis—whatever may have been said by "learned" economists who know the writings of their predecessors but ignore real life—the true origin of this crisis lay in the excessive production of the main industries which was carried on for several years in anticipation of a great war in Europe and also war between the United States and Japan. Those who pushed [the idea of] these wars knew very well the effect these predictions would have on American industries. For two or three years, indeed, there was a feverish activity in metal production, coal mining and the manufacturing of railway equipment, material for clothing, preserved foodstuffs.

The extraction of iron ore and manufacture of steel in the United States reached quite unexpected proportions during those years. It is above all steel that is consumed during modern wars and the United States produced it in fantastic amounts, as well as metals, such as nickel and manganese, required to manufacture the kinds of steel needed for war materials. It was in the supplies of iron, copper, lead and nickel that there was most speculation.

It was the same with supplies of wheat, preserved meat, fish and vegetables. Cottons, cloth and leather followed closely. And since every great industry gives rise to a number of smaller ones around it, the fever for production far in excess of the demand spread more and more. The lenders of money (or rather credit) who fuelled this production, profited by this fever—this goes without saying—even more than the chiefs of industry.

And then, at a stroke, production suddenly stopped without anyone being able to appeal to a single one of the causes which preceding crises had been attributed to. The truth is that from the day when European high finance was sure that Japan, ruined by the war in Manchuria, would not dare to attack the United States and that none of the European nations felt sufficiently sure of victory to unsheathe the sword, European capitalists refused [to provide] new credit to the American money-lenders who fuelled over-production as well as to the Japanese "nationalists."

"No more war in the short term!"—and steel mills, cooper mines, blast furnaces, shipyards, tanneries, speculators on commodities, all suddenly reduced their operations, their orders, their purchases.

It was then worse than a crisis: it was a disaster! Millions of working men and women were thrown onto the street in the most abject misery. Great and small factories closed, the contagion spread like an epidemic, sowing terror all around.

No one can describe the sufferings of millions (men, women and children), the broken lives, during this crisis while immense fortunes were being made in anticipation of the mangled flesh and piles of human corpses about to be heaped up in the great battles!

That is war; that is how the State enriches the wealthy, keeps the poor in misery and year by year makes them more enslaved to the rich.

Now a crisis similar to that in the United States will in all likelihood occur in Europe, and especially in England, as a result of the same causes.

Everybody was astonished around the middle of 1911 by the sudden and completely unexpected increase in English exports. Nothing in the economic world predicted it. No explanation has been given for it—precisely because the only possible explanation is that immense orders came from the continent in anticipation of a war between England and Germany. As we know, this war failed to break out in July 1911 but if it had started, France and Russia, Austria and Italy would have been forced to take part.

It is evident that the great financiers, who fuelled by their credit the speculators in metals, foodstuffs, cloth, leather, etc., had been warned of the threatening turn in the relations between the two maritime rivals. They knew how both governments were accelerating their military preparations and they hastened to make orders which increased English exports in 1911 beyond measure.[74]

---

74 Some figures will better indicate these shocks. Between 1900 and 1904 English

But it is also to the same cause that we owe this recent extraordinary rise in prices of all foodstuffs without exception, although neither the yield of last year's harvest nor the quantities of all kinds of goods accumulation in warehouses justified this increase. The fact is, moreover, that the rise in prices affected *all* goods not just provisions and demand continued to grow whilst nothing explained this exaggerated demand apart from the expectations of war.

And now it will suffice for the great colonial speculators of England and Germany to come to an arrangement concerning their share in the partition of East Africa and that they agree on "the spheres of influence" in Asia and in Africa—that is to say, on the next conquests—for the same sudden stoppage of industries that the United States suffered to occur in Europe.

In fact, this stoppage was already starting to be felt at the beginning of 1912. That is why in England the coal companies and "the Cotton Lords" proved so intransigent towards their workers and drove them to strike. They expected a reduction of orders, they already had too many goods in [their] inventories, too much coal piled up around their mines.

When we closely analyse these facts of the activity of modern States, we understand the extent to which the whole life of our civilised societies depends—not on the *facts* of economic development in nations but on *the way in which various circles of privileged people, more or less favoured by the State, react to these facts.*

Thus it is evident that the entry into the economic arena of such a powerful producer as modern Germany, with its schools, its technical education widely spread amongst its people, its youthful spirit, and the organisational capacities of its people, changed relations between nations. A new adjustment of forces had to happen. But, given the specific organisation of modern States, the adjustment of *economic* forces is hindered by another factor

---

exports were normal. For products of English origin, they stood at between seven and seven-and-a-half thousand million francs. In 1904 they began to talk of a great war; the United States pushed its production, and English exports rose in four years from 7,525 to 10,650 million. This lasted two years. But the much-desired war did not come and there was a sudden halt: the crisis of which we have spoken broke out in the United States, and exports of English produce fell to 9,495 million. However, 1910 arrived and the predictions of a great European war were set to come true. And in 1911 English exports rose to an absolutely unexpected height which they had never even remotely approached before and which nobody could explain. They were 11,350 million! Coal, steel, good fast ships, battleships, cartridges, cloth, linen, footwear— everything was in demanded, exported in bulk. Fortunes were visibly amassed. We are going to slaughter each other—what a godsend!

of *political* origin: the privileges, the monopolies formed and maintained by the State.

Fundamentally, in modern States—specifically formed to establish privileges in favour of the rich at the expense of the poor—it is always high finance which lays down the law in all political considerations. "What will Baron Rothschild say?" or else "What will the syndicate of great bankers in Paris, in Vienna, in London say?" has become the dominant element in political issues and relations between nations. It is the approval or disapproval of finance that makes and breaks ministries across Europe (in England there is also the approval of the official Church and of the brewers to consider; but the Church and the brewers are always in agreement with high finance, which is careful not to touch their income). And—as a Minister is after all a man who values his office, its power, and the opportunities of enrichment they offer him—it follows that questions of international relations are today reduced in the final analysis to knowing whether the favoured monopolists of a particular State will take this or that attitude towards the favourites of the same calibre in another State.

Thus, the *state of [economic] forces* involved is given by the technical development of the various nations at a certain point in history. But the *use* which will be made of these forces depends entirely on the level of subservience to their government and the statist form of organisation to which people have let themselves be reduced to. The forces which could have provided harmony, well-being, and a new flowering of a libertarian civilisation if they had free play in society—*when implemented within the framework of the State*, that is to say, an organisation specifically developed to enrich the wealthy and to absorb all advances for the benefit of the privileged classes—these same forces become an instrument of oppression, privilege and endless wars. They accelerate the enrichment of the privileged, they increase the misery and subjugation of the poor.

This is why economists who continue to consider economic forces alone, without analysing the statist framework within which they operate today, without taking into account statist ideology, nor the forces that each State necessarily places at the service of the wealthy in order to enrich them at the expense of the poor—this is why these economists remain completely outside the realities of the economic and social world.

X

THE ESSENTIAL CHARACTERISTICS OF THE STATE

WE HAVE BRIEFLY REVIEWED SOME OF THE ESSENTIAL FUNCTIONS OF THE State, its legislation on property, taxes, the formation of monopolies and finally defence—in other words, the right of war.

And we noticed this fact, significant to the highest degree, that in each of these functions the State always pursued, and still pursues, the same goal: to deliver the mass of the population it controls to groups of exploiters, to ensure to them the right of exploitation, to extend it. It is with this aim that the State was formed—it is what makes up its essential mission to the present.

The legislation of States on the right of ownership has never had, anywhere, the aim to ensure to each the fruits of his labour as academic science on Law proclaims. On the contrary, the State law has always aimed, it still does, to *dispossess* the great mass of the nation of a large part of the fruits of its labour, to the advantage of a privileged few. To keep the masses in a state close to poverty and to deliver them: in antiquity—to the lord and the priesthood, during the Middle Ages—to the lord, the priest and the merchant, and today—to the industrial and financial entrepreneur in addition to the previous three: such was the essential function of all States, theocratic, oligarchic or democratic.

Tax, as we have seen, is an instrument of a formidable power that the State wields to this end. This instrument allows the rulers to continue the expropriation of the poor in favour of the rich—the perfected expropriation which, without it being any less efficient, is not obvious. It allows them to artificially maintain poverty despite the immense growth in the productivity of human labour—without resorting for that [task] to the brutal forms of direct appropriation which were used in the past. What the feudal lord did, when he was extorting his serfs under the protection of the State, the State does now under an "acceptable" form by means of tax—but always in favour of some rich person, and by also sharing a part of the loot between the rich and its numerous functionaries.

We then saw how the State wields and still wields industrial, commercial and financial monopoly; and how it allows groups of entrepreneurs and business tycoons to quickly accumulate immense fortunes, by appropriating the product of the labour of the subjects of the State. And we showed how it is that all the new sources of enrichment offered to civilised nations, either as a consequence of technical and scientific progress or by the conquest of industrially backward countries, find themselves monopolised by a small minority of privileged people. This allows the State to enrich its coffers and to always extend its remits and power.

Finally, we saw what a terrible weapon to perpetuate social inequalities, monopolies and privileges of all sorts represents this other remit of the State: the maintaining of armies and the right of war. Under cover of patriotism, defence of the homeland, the State uses the army and wars for the same goal. Throughout history, since antiquity to the present day, conquests were always conducted to deliver new populations to be exploited by classes favoured by the State. It is the same today: every war is waged to profit bankers, speculators, and the privileged. And in peacetime, the fabulous sums allocated to armaments, as well as loans by States, allow the rulers to create immense fortunes and new exploiters, chosen [from] amongst their favourites.

In this deep-rooted tendency to enrich some groups of citizens at the expense of the labour and sacrifices of the entire nation resides the very essence of this form of centralised political organisation which is called *State* and which only developed in Europe, amongst the peoples which had demolished the Roman Empire, after the period of the free cities—that is to say, in the sixteenth and seventeenth centuries.

Note well that this is not in any way about what is called "abuse of power," such as the atrocities continuously committed by all governments towards their subjects or conquered nations, as soon as it is a question of protecting people of the privileged class. We are not talking for the moment of the banditry of functionaries, the illegal extortions carried out by all rulers, the insults and suffering they lavish on the governed, nor the national hatred that they spread and uphold. In this respect, it suffices to note that "power" and "abuse of power" necessarily go hand in hand, and that functionaries have inevitably established a solidarity [amongst themselves] which allows them to forget what they like to call "the sad necessities of the exercise of power."

Therefore we do not stop at these "sad necessities." We restrict ourselves to considering the very essence of the organisation which was formed on several occasions in human societies and which, each time that it was re-born, always carried the same characteristic of mutual insurance between the church, the soldier and the lord, to live at the expense of the labour of the masses. Modern times only offer this difference: the wealthy commercial bourgeois, industrialists and moneylenders, and a horde of functionaries came to join the preceding trinity.

It is in the interest of the privileged—not of the nation—that the State took the land away from the peasants to give to groups of monopolisers, and that it drove a good part of the farmers away from the villages. And, that once masses of out of work proletarians started to accumulate in the cities, State legislation delivered these hungry proletarians to the favourites of royalty, to the industrial bourgeois, and later to moneylenders, to business tycoons, to big finance. All this teeming mass was put at the service of the government's minions.

Later, when the privileged classes, who had developed with great skill and wisdom this political form—the State—began to notice that the exploited masses were trying to throw off the yoke, they knew how to find a new way to broaden the basis of their exploitation. Conquest had been, since the beginning of time, a means of enrichment not for the conquering *nations* (to those was given "the glory"), but for the ruling classes of these nations—just think about the riches delivered by Napoleon I to his generals and to his "military nobility!" Also, when technical discoveries and advances in navigation allowed States to maintain big standing armies and a powerful navy—the ruling classes knew how to use this navy and these armies to conquer "colonies." It is in this way that Dutch, English, French, Belgian, German and even Russian bourgeoisies applied themselves in turn to the conquest of industrially backward nations—which now leads to the partition of Africa and Asia between them.

These States, that is to say, these bourgeoisies—because the workers gain nothing, except a few crumbs fallen from the table of the rich—these bourgeoisies thus end up becoming simultaneously masters and exploiters of vast populations, in addition to their "dear" fellow countrymen. As for the workers, they are won over in turn by promises of easy prey made by their masters. In the meantime they ask for customs "protection" against foreign competition and, duly prepared by a criminal press in the pay of capitalists, they are ready to pounce on their neighbours to fight over the pickings, instead of rebelling against their compatriot exploiters and their all powerful weapon, the State.

CAN THE STATE BE USED FOR THE EMANCIPATION OF THE WORKERS?

THAT IS WHAT ANCIENT AND MODERN HISTORY SHOWS US. AND YET, following an error of judgment which truly becomes tragic, while the State that provides the most terrible weapons to impoverish the peasant and the worker and to enrich by their labour the lord, the priest, the bourgeois, the financier and all the privileged gangsters of the rulers—it is to this same State, to the bourgeois State, to the exploiter State and guardian of the exploiters—that radical democrats and socialists ask to protect them against the monopolist exploiters! And when we say that it is the abolition of the State that we have to aim for, we are told: "Let us first abolish classes, and when this has been done, then we can place the State into a museum of antiquities, together with the stone axe and the spindle!"[75]

---

75   A reference to the famous 1884 work by Engels, *Origins of the Family, Private Property, and the State*, which argues: "The state, then, has not existed from eternity. There have been societies that managed without it, that had no idea of the state and state authority. At a certain stage of economic development, which was necessarily bound up with the split of society into classes, the state became a necessity owing to this split. We are now rapidly approaching a stage in the development of production at which the existence of

By this quip they evaded, in the fifties of the last century, the discussion that Proudhon called for on the necessity of abolishing the State institution and the means of achieving this. And it is still being repeated today. "Let us seize power in the State"—the current bourgeois State, of course—"and then we will make the social revolution"—such is the slogan today.[76]

Proudhon's idea had been to invite the workers to pose this question: "How could society organise itself without resorting to the State institution, developed during the darkest times of humanity to keep the masses in economic and intellectual poverty and to exploit their labour?" And he was answered with a paradox, a sophism.

Indeed, how can we talk about abolishing classes without touching the institution which was the instrument for establishing them and which remains the instrument which perpetuates them? But instead of going deeper into this question—*the* question placed before us by all modern evolution—what do we do?

Is not the first question that the social reformer should ask himself this one: "The State, which was developed in the history of civilisations to give a legal character to the exploitation of the masses by the privileged classes, *can* it be the instrument of their liberation?"

Furthermore, are not other groupings than the State already emerging in the evolution of modern societies—groups which can bring to society co-ordination, harmony of individual efforts and become the instrument of the liberation of the masses, without resorting to the submission of all to the pyramidal hierarchy of the State? The commune, for example, groupings by

---

these classes not only will have ceased to be a necessity, but will become a positive hindrance to production. They will fall as inevitably as they arose at an earlier stage. Along with them the state will inevitably fall. Society, which will reorganise production on the basis of a free and equal association of the producers, will put the whole machinery of state where it will then belong: into the museum of antiquities, by the side of the spinning-wheel and the bronze axe" (*Marx-Engels Collected Works*, Volume 26 [London: Lawrence & Wishat, 1990], 272). (Editor)

76   A reference to, for example, Engels's arguments from 1883 that while he and Marx saw the State's "gradual dissolution and ultimate disappearance," the proletariat "will first have to possess itself of the organised political force of the State and with its aid stamp out the resistance of the Capitalist class and re-organise society." The anarchists "reverse the matter" by advocating revolution "has to begin by abolishing the political organisation of the State." For Marxists "the only organisation the victorious working class finds ready-made for use, is that of the State. It may require adaptation to the new functions. But to destroy that at such a moment, would be to destroy the only organism by means of which the working class can exert its newly conquered power" (*Marx-Engels Collected Works*, Volume 47 [London: Lawrence & Wishat, 1993], 10). (Editor)

trades and by professions in addition to groupings by neighbourhoods and sections, which preceded the State in the free cities [of the Middle Ages]; the thousand societies that spring up today for the satisfaction of a thousand social needs: the federative principle that we see applied in modern groupings—do not these forms of organisation of society offer a field of activity which promises much more for our goals of emancipation than the efforts expended to make the State and its centralisation even more powerful than they already are?

Is this not the essential question that the social reformer should ask before choosing his course of action?

Well, instead of going deeper into this question, the democrats, radicals, as well as socialists, only know, only want one thing, the State! Not the future State, "the people's State" of their dreams of yesteryear, but well and truly the current bourgeois State, the State nothing more and nothing less. This must seize, they say, all the life of society: economic, educational, intellectual activities and organising: industry, exchange, instruction, jurisdiction, administration—*everything* that fills our social life!

To workers who want their emancipation, they say: "Just let us worm ourselves into the powers of the current political form, developed by the nobles, the bourgeois, the capitalists to exploit you!" They say that, while we know very well by all the teachings of history that a new *economic* form of society has never been able to develop without a new *political* form being developed at the same time, developed by those who were seeking their emancipation.

Serfdom—and absolute royalty; corporative organisation—and the free cities, the republics of the twelfth to fifteenth centuries; merchant domination—and these same republics under the *podestas* and the *condottieri*;[77] imperialism—and the military States of the seventeenth and eighteenth centuries; the reign of the bourgeoisie—and representative government, are not all these forms going hand in hand striking evidence [of this]?

In order to develop itself as it has developed today and to maintain its power, despite all the progress of science and the democratic spirit, the bourgeoisie developed with much shrewdness representative government during the course of the nineteenth century.

And the spokespersons of the modern proletariat are so timid that they do not even dare to tackle the problem raised by the 1848 revolution—the problem of knowing what new political form the modern proletariat must

---

77   *Podesta* were high officials (usually chief magistrate of a city state) in many Italian cities beginning in the later Middle Ages; *Condottieri* were the leaders of the professional military free companies (or mercenaries) contracted by the Italian city-states and the Papacy from the late Middle Ages and throughout the Renaissance. (Editor)

and can develop to achieve its emancipation? How will it seek to organise the two essential functions of any society: the social production of everything necessary to live and the social consumption of these products? How will it guarantee to everyone, not in words but in reality, the entire product of his labour by guaranteeing him *well-being* in exchange for his work? What form will "the organisation of labour" take as it cannot be accomplished by the State and must be the work of the workers themselves?

That is what the French proletarian, educated in the past by 1793 and 1848, asked their intellectual leaders.

But did they [their leaders] know how to answer them? They only knew how to keep on repeating this old formula, which said nothing, which evaded the answer: "Seize power in the bourgeois State, use this power to widen the functions of the modern State—and the problem of your emancipation will be solved!"

Once again the proletarian received lead instead of bread! This time from those to whom it had given its trust—and its blood!

To ask an institution which represents a historical growth that it serves to destroy the privileges that it strove to develop is to acknowledge you are incapable of understanding what a historical growth is in the life of societies. It is to ignore this general rule of all organic nature, that new functions require new organs, and that they need to develop them themselves. It is to acknowledge that you are too lazy and too timid in spirit to think in a new direction, imposed by a new evolution.

The whole of history is there to prove this truth, that each time that new social strata started to demonstrate an activity and an intelligence which met their own needs, each time that they attempted to display a creative force in the domain of an economic production which furthered their interests and those of society in general—*they knew how to find new forms of political organisation*; and these new political forms allowed the new strata to imprint their individuality on the era they were inaugurating. Can a *social* revolution be an exception to the rule? Can it do without this creative activity?

Thus the revolt of the communes in the twelfth century (in the eleventh century in Italy) and the abolition of serfdom in these communes which freed themselves from the bishop, the feudal baron, and the king mark the advent in history of a new class. And this class—as we saw in our previous study—while working towards its emancipation, soon created a whole new civilisation at the same time as the institutions which allowed it to develop.

The artisan takes the place of the villein.[78] He becomes a free man and, under the protection of the walls of his commune, he gives an invigorating impetus to the technical "arts" and science which soon, with Galileo, opens a new era for the emancipated human spirit. Helped by thinkers and artists who were only too pleased to display their intellectuality in the new paths of intellectual freedom, man rediscovers the exact sciences and the philosophy of Ancient Greece, forgotten in the darkness of the Roman Empire and of the barbarian era which finished the work of breaking up this Empire. It creates the magnificent architecture that we do not know how to equal; it discovers the means and acquires the necessary audacity to develop distant navigation. It opens the Renaissance era, with its humanist programme.

Well, could our ancestors ever have accomplished all these wonders if they had timidly clung to the institutions that existed in Europe from the fifth to the twelfth century? Remnants of Caesarist forms from the Roman Empire, mixed with theocratic forms imported from the East, these dying institutions from a slave past choked the invigorating federative and respectful of individuality spirit that the so-called Scandinavian, Gaul, Saxon and Slavic "barbarians" had brought with them. Was it to this rottenness that the man who was trying to emancipate himself had to cling to, like the spokespersons of the working masses do today?[79]

Obviously not!—Likewise the citizens of the liberated cities immediately tried, from the first day, to create by their "conspiracies," that is to say by their mutual oaths, new institutions within their fortified cities. It is to the parish, recognised as an independent unit, *sovereign*; to the street and to the "neighbourhood," or to the "section" (federations of streets), and on the

---

78 A villein in the feudal era denoted a peasant (tenant farmer) who was legally tied to a lord of the manor. A villein could not leave the land without the landowner's consent. In the medieval social hierarchy, villeins were below a free peasant (or "freeman") and above a slave. The majority of medieval European peasants were villeins. (Editor)

79 Asked about Marx's comments in *The Civil War in France* on the need of smashing the state-machine, Engels explained: "It is simply a question of showing that the victorious proletariat must first reshape the old, bureaucratic, administratively centralised state machine before they can use it for their own purposes; whereas, since 1848, *all* bourgeois republicans, so long as they were in opposition, have heaped abuse on that machine but, no sooner in office, have taken it over intact and made use of it, partly against reaction but to an even greater extent against the proletariat" (*Marx-Engels Collected Works*, Volume 47, 74). Later he reiterated this position: "A republic, in relation to the proletariat, differs from a monarchy only in that it is the *ready-made* political form for the future rule of the proletariat. You [in France] have the advantage of us in that it is already in being" (*Marx-Engels Collected Works*, Volume 50, 276). (Editor)

other hand to the guild, just as independent; and finally to the organised and *sovereign* "arts" (each consequently having its "justice," its banner and its militia) and finally to the *forum*, to the popular assembly representing the federation of parishes and guilds, that they looked to for the organisation of the various elements of the city. A series of institutions, absolutely contrary to the spirit of the Roman State and to the theocratic State of the East, were thus developed during the course of the three or four centuries that followed.

Who then—unless he prefers to ignore the life of the free Communes of this era, as do our statists (worthy pupils of the mind-numbing schools of the State)—who could therefore doubt for a moment that it was *these new institutions*, derived from the federative principle and respectful of individuality, which allowed the Communes of the Middle ages to develop, in the midst of the darkness of that era, the rich civilisation, the arts and science that we find in the fifteenth century?

XII

THE MODERN CONSTITUTIONAL STATE

IT WAS THE SAME FOR THE INDUSTRIAL AND MERCHANT BOURGEOISIE. IN accordance with the causes that we indicated in the study on the historical role of the State (Moorish, Turkish and Mongol invasions, and causes of the internal decadence in the Communes), the royal military State had managed to develop in Europe in the course of the sixteenth, seventeenth and eighteenth centuries on the ruins of the free Communes. But after over two centuries of this regime, the industrial and intellectual bourgeoisie, in England first at the onset of 1648 and one hundred and forty years later in France, made a new step forward. It understood that it would be absolutely impossible to achieve intellectual, commercial, industrial development—its overall [*mondial*] development that it already foresaw—if the human herds remained under the rule of a bureaucracy grown up around the palace where a Louis XIV could say "The State, it is me!" Since Montesquieu, the thinkers of the bourgeoisie—and there were some distinguished ones—understood that industry, commerce, education, science, technology, arts, social morality never could achieve the development they were capable of, and that the masses would never get out of the dreadful poverty in which they had been left engulfed, as long as the fate of the people remained in the hands of a clique and of the clergy: as long as the State—master of past and future privileges—remained in the hands of the Church and of the Court, with its favourites and its preferences.

Also, as soon as their forces allowed it, what did the English and French bourgeoisies do? Did they limit themselves to a simple change of dynasty, of rulers? Were they content to replace the king in a State of royal creation? Obviously not!

Their men of action preferred to lead the masses into profound economic revolutions than to stay forever in the stagnant swamp of an absolute royalty. And the political institutions which had developed under the royal absolution were changed from top to bottom by these revolutions.

They believed at first that it would suffice to reduce royalty and its entourage to zero and to transfer power from the hands of individuals from the royal palace and the Church into those of the representatives of what they called the Third Estate.[80] But they soon realised that this would not be enough to completely demolish the old regime: to change the structure of society from top to bottom [was needed]. And when they saw the huge forces of the royalty stand before them, which did not by any means acknowledge itself deposed, they did not hesitate to unleash the passion, the fury of the destitute against the nobles and priests, and to take their properties, the main source of their power.

"And yet," we will doubtless be told, "they did not seek to demolish the State. They opposed this with all their vigour when they realised that the people wanted to go further and destroy the State, to put in its place federated Communes and Sections and a whole new economic organisation!"

That is true. But the English bourgeoisie and the French bourgeoisie were in no way seeking to destroy institutions that would allow them to create privileges in *their* favour. They only wanted to substitute themselves for the nobility and the clergy and enjoy the privileges. Consequently the bourgeois certainly could not aim at the destruction of the State. The institution which had served to enrich the Church and nobility had to remain. It now had to allow the bourgeoisie to enrich themselves in turn—by opening, it is true, new channels of enrichment by the development of industries and sciences, by spreading knowledge, by introducing free labour[81]—but

---

80   A reference to the estates of the realm which existed in pre-revolutionary France and other Christian European nations from the medieval period to early modern Europe. The social hierarchy under the *Ancien Régime* was based on a three-estate system under the monarchy: clergy (the First Estate), nobles (the Second Estate), and everyone else (the Third Estate). It is estimated that ninety-eight per cent of the population made up this last category and it included bourgeoisie, wage-workers, and peasants. (Editor)

81   The term free labour [*le travail affranchi*] refers to the abolition of the unfree labour associated with serfdom such as the certain number of days *corvée* labour provided to

still using the nation's labour [*la travail national*] to enrich, above all, themselves as the noblemen and the Church had enriched themselves until then.

Becoming heir to the established privileges, the bourgeoisie obviously did not seek to demolish the State. On the contrary, they worked to increase its power, to augment its functions, knowing that it could be they and their children who would above all furnish the functionaries and henceforth benefit from the privileges.

It was only the people, or rather a part of the popular masses—those that Desmoulins called "the beyond Marat"—who wanted emancipation without trying to subject any strata of society to its exploitation or its rule. These started in fact to lay the foundations of a new political organisation, which had to substitute itself to that of the State. It was the *Commune*. And as this decentralisation was still not sufficient, even in the big towns, it was pushed further, to the *Section*.

We see, in fact, a striking phenomenon taking place during the revolution, from 1789. Since the National Assembly was inevitably composed of representatives of the past, opposed to the Revolution becoming deeper and, above all, that the popular masses could really gain their freedom—it was the Communes which pushed forward. A municipal revolution, as Michelet and Aulard pointed out so well, was achieved from 1789. And since a revolution is not made by decrees, since it is on the ground that the balance of power in society must be overturned, it was the thousands of urban and village "municipalities" which undertook to carry out in the localities the abolition of feudal rights. Before the Assembly decided to proclaim it *in principle* on 4 August 1789 and well before proclaiming it de facto four years later, after having expelled the Girondins, the municipalities in some parts of France were already acting in this manner.

But the municipalities, and especially the advanced sections of large towns, did not limit themselves to this. When the National Assembly decided to proclaim the confiscation of the property of the clergy and the sale of these assets, the State had no mechanism to carry this decision out. Well, it was the Communes, and in the large towns—the Sections, which volunteered to carry out the immense revolutionary transfer of fortunes. They alone were capable of doing it, *and they accomplished it de facto*.

But where we can see even better the constructive spirit of the people, *outside the State*, is when the war started in 1792. When the armed struggle became a matter of life or death for the Revolution, when France was invaded by foreigners invited by royalty and it had to *do the impossible*: with neither army nor republican officers, it had to drive these foreigners from the land—it was the sections and the Communes which undertook

---

landlords or the monarchical State by their subjects. (Editor)

to accomplish this huge task for which the State did not even have the necessary mechanism: to enlist volunteers, that is to say, *to choose men*, to decide who amongst those who presented themselves to give shoes, bread, rifle, lead and powder—because at the moment of reckoning the republican *was lacking everything*: bread as much as lead, musket as much as shoes and clothes.

In fact, who will know how to sort the men who volunteer? Who will ensure that the volunteer, after having received "sword, lead, bread," will not throw away the rifle at the first opportunity or will not join the royalist packs? Who will find leathers and cloth? Sow clothes, scrape caves to get saltpetre?[82] Who, finally, will tell the volunteer, when he is at the border, the truth about the progress of the Revolution in his native town and about the intrigues of the counter-revolutionaries? Who will inspire in him the burning zeal without which the impossible cannot be done, nor victories won? It was the sections and the communes who accomplished all this immense work. The statist historians could ignore it but the French people preserved the memory of it: it is they who taught it to us!

Would the Bastille and the Tuileries have ever been taken without this effort of the people—the unknowns?[83] Would the republicans have driven out the enemy and abolished royalty and feudalism if they had not understood—without perhaps expressing it in these words that come from our pen—that *for a new phase of social life we need an organisation which will help make it blossom?* And if they had not found this organisation in the Commune, in their devotion, in the activity of their revolutionary Sections, almost independent of the Commune and linked to each other by temporary Committees, created whenever events indicated the need for it?

---

82   Saltpetre is a chemical compound (potassium nitrate) and one of the major components of gunpowder. A major natural source of it is deposits crystallising on cave walls. (Editor)

83   Kropotkin is referring to two popular insurrections in Paris during the French Revolution. The storming of the Bastille (a medieval fortress and prison) on 14 July 1789 began the French Revolution with the destruction of a symbol of the power and abuses of the monarchy by the mass action of the people. The storming of the Tuileries Palace on the 10 August 1792 resulted in the fall of the French monarchy six weeks later and the increase of *sans-culotte* influence in Paris. See chapters XII and XXXIII of Kropotkin's *The Great French Revolution*. (Editor)

XIII

IS IT SENSIBLE TO STRENGTHEN THE CURRENT STATE?

IT IS THEREFORE ESSENTIAL THAT TO FREE THEMSELVES THE MASSES WHO produce everything without being allowed to control the consumption of what they produce, find the means which enable them to display their creative forces and to develop themselves new, egalitarian, forms of consumption and of production.

The State and national representation cannot find these forms. It is the very *life* of the consumer and of the producer, his intellect, his organising spirit which must find them and improve them by applying them to the daily needs of life.

It is the same for forms of political organisation. In order to free themselves from the exploitation they are subjected to under the supervision of the State, the masses cannot remain under the domination of the forms which prevent the blossoming of popular initiative. These were developed by governments to perpetuate the servitude of the people, to *prevent it from letting its creative force blossom* and to develop institutions of egalitarian mutual aid. New forms must be found to serve the opposite goal.

But if we recognise that in order to be able to reshape the forms of consumption and production the class of producers will have to reshape the political forms of the organisation of society, we see at once how wrong it is to arm the *current bourgeois State* with the immense force which the management of economic monopolies—industrial and commercial exchange—gives it in addition to the political monopolies it already possesses.

Let us not talk about an imaginary State in which a government, composed of angels descended from the heavens for the needs of the discussion, would be the enemy of the powers we would have armed it with. To entertain such utopias is to lead the revolution to rocks where it will inevitably flounder. We must take the *current bourgeois State as it is*—and wonder if it is sensible to arm *this institution* with a more and more formidable power?

Is it sensible to give the institution which currently exists to hold the worker in servitude—because who would doubt that such is today the main function of the State?—is it sensible to strengthen it by giving it the ownership of a vast railway network? To give it the monopoly of alcoholic beverages, tobacco, sugar, etc., as well as that of credit and banking—in addition to that of justice, public education, territorial defence, and colonial banditry?

To hope that the oppressive mechanism, thus reinforced, becomes an instrument of revolution, is that not to ignore what history teaches us about what a creature of habit [*l'esprit routinier*] all bureaucracy is and about the strength of resistance of institutions? Is it not to make precisely the mistake we reproach [other] revolutionaries for—that of imagining that it is enough to expel a king to have a republic or name a socialist dictator to have collectivism?

Besides, did we not notice very recently—in 1905 and 1906 in Russia—the danger of arming a reactionary State with the power that railways and all sorts of monopolies gives it?

Whereas the government of Louis XVI, seeing itself facing bankruptcy, had to capitulate before the bourgeoisie who wanted the constitution; whereas the Manchu dynasty was forced to abdicate,[84] unable to borrow millions to fight republicans—the Romanov dynasty, beleaguered by the revolution which had triumphed in 1905, found it easy to borrow 1,200 million from France in 1906. And when members of the Russian Duma issued a manifesto to tell foreign financiers "Do not lend anything, the Russian State is going bankrupt!"—these financiers, better informed, replied: "But since you handed over 60,000 kilometres of railway tracks, bought-out the companies that built them, since you gave it the huge

---

84   The Manchu, or Qing, was the last imperial dynasty of China and ruled from 1644 until overthrown in 1912 by the Chinese revolution that started in 1911. (Editor)

monopoly on drinks, we do not fear bankruptcy. It is not a Louis XVI monarchy which owned nothing!"

And they lent the twelve hundred million.

Well, it is to increase the capital owned by the modern bourgeois States that the radicals and socialists are working today. They did not even bother to discuss—like English co-operators asked me one day—if there were no way to hand over the railways *directly* to the railway-workers' trade-unions, to free the enterprise from the yoke of the capitalist, instead of creating a new capitalist, even more dangerous than the bourgeois companies, the State.[85]

But no! The so-called statist intellectuals learned nothing in school other than faith in a saviour State, the omnipotent State; and they never even wanted to listen to those who were shouting at them "reckless-people" as they marched onwards, hypnotised by the State-capitalist and Vidal's statist-collectivism, that they had resurrected under the name of "scientific socialism"!

The result we can see, not only in moments of crisis as in Russia, but in Europe every day. There, where railways are a public service of the State, all the government has to do if it feels threatened by a strike is to issue a two-line decree to "mobilise" all the railway workers.[86] As a result striking becomes an act of rebellion. To shoot the striking railway workers is no longer an act of deference towards the plutocracy; it becomes an act of devotion to the motherland.[87]

---

85 Kropotkin mentioned this letter in his article "Syndicalisme et parlementairisme" ["Trade Unionism and Parliamentarism"], *Les Temps Nouveaux* (13 October 1906), which argued "all the workers, engineers, stokers, etc., *managing that industry themselves* [...] *This is the future*. For it is not going to be the ministers but rather the workers themselves who will see to the honest management of industry." The task was "to build up a force capable of imposing better working conditions on the bosses, but also—indeed primarily—to create among the working classes the union structures that might some day replace the bosses and take into their own hands the production and management of every industry." This article is included in *Direct Struggle Against Capital*. (Editor)

86 Kropotkin discusses this with regards to Holland in "Le Gréve Générale en Hollande" ["The General Strike in Holland"], *Les Temps Nouveaux*, 11 April 1903. (Editor)

87 Kropotkin is referring to, amongst other events, the 1910 French railway strike. This started on 10 October 1910 on the Paris-Nord system. The following day, the strike committee called for a general railway strike and on the 12th, the Western division came out. The Prime Minister, Aristide Briand (a former socialist and advocate of the general strike), arrested the strike committee and conscripted the railway workers into the army. Martial law was thereby established for any striker who refused to work

It is the same thing for coalmines, large munitions factories, steel re-fineries, and even for food. And in this way a whole new mentality is in the process of being formed in society—not only amongst the bourgeois, but also amongst the workers. The exploitation of labour, far from being restricted, is placed under the permanent protection of the law. It becomes an institution, just like the State itself. It becomes a part of the *Constitution*, just like serfdom was in France until the Great Revolution or the division into classes of peasants, artisans, merchants with their established duties towards the two classes—that of the nobles and of clergy—that we still see in Russia.

"*The duty to be exploited!*"—That is where we are heading with this State-capitalist idea.

---

would be immediately court-martialled like any solider who refused to follow orders (an act which could result in being shot). The strike ended on 18 October. (Editor)

XIV

CONCLUSIONS

WE CLEARLY SEE, FROM THE ABOVE, HOW WRONG IT IS TO SEE IN THE STATE [only] a hierarchical organisation of functionaries, elected or appointed to administer the various branches of social life and harmonise their action, and think it will be enough to change their personnel to make the machine go in any direction.

If the historical function—social and political—of the State had been limited to that, it would not have destroyed, as it did, every freedom of local institutions; it would not have centralised everything, justice, education, religions, arts, sciences, army, etc., in its ministries; it would not have wielded tax, as it has done, in the interest of the rich and to always hold the poor below "the poverty line," as the young English economists say; it would not have wielded, as it has done, monopoly, to allow the rich to absorb the entire increase of wealth due to the progress of technology and science.

It is because the State is much more than the organisation of an administration with a view to establishing "harmony" in society, as they say in the universities. It is an organisation, developed and slowly perfected over the course of three centuries, to uphold the rights acquired by certain classes to benefit from the labour of the working masses; to expand these rights and create new ones, which lead to new subjugations [*inféodations*] of the citizens, impoverished by legislation, towards groups of individuals showered with favours from the governmental hierarchy. Such is the true essence of the State. All the rest are only words that the State itself taught to the people and which is repeated by apathy without closer analysis of them: words just as deceitful as those taught by the Church to cover its thirst for power, enrichment and more power!

It is high time, however, to submit these words to a serious criticism and to wonder where the infatuation of the radicals of the nineteenth century and their socialist continuators for an omnipotent State came from? We would then see that it above all came from the misconception that is usually made about the Jacobins of the Great [French] Revolution—of the legend that is created, or rather was created, around the Jacobin club. Because it is to this Club and its branches in the provinces that bourgeois historians of the Revolution (except Michelet) attributed all the glory of the great principles expressed by the Revolution and the terrible struggles that it had to sustain against royalty and royalists.

It is time to classify this legend in its true place, amongst the other legends of the Church and the State. We are already gradually beginning to know the truth about the Revolution and we start to notice that the Jacobin club was the club—not of the people but of the bourgeoisie which had come into power and wealth; not of the Revolution, but of those who knew how to take advantage of it. At none of the great moments of upheaval was it at the forefront of the Revolution: it always limited itself to channelling the threatening upsurges, to make them return to the frameworks of the State and—to smother them by killing the bold elements which were going beyond the views of the bourgeoisie that it represented.

Nursery for functionaries, which it provided in [large] numbers after each new step forward made by the Revolution (10 August, 31 May),[88] the Jacobin club was *the bulwark of the bourgeoisie coming to power against the egalitarian tendencies of the people.* It is precisely for that—for having known how to prevent the people from taking the communist and egalitarian path—it is so glorified by most historians.

It must be said that this Club had a well-defined ideal: it was the omnipotent State, which did not tolerate within itself any local power, such

---

88   Kropotkin is referring to two popular insurrections in Paris which are defining events in the history of the French Revolution. The storming of the Tuileries Palace and the Insurrection of 31 May to 2 June 1793 resulted in the fall of the Girondinists in the National Convention under pressure of the Parisian *sans-culottes*. Both mass uprisings pushed the revolution in a more radical direction. See chapters XXXIII and XLVI of Kropotkin's *The Great French Revolution* for details. (Editor)

as a sovereign Commune, any professional power, such as trade unions, no will except that of the Jacobins of the Convention—which necessarily, inevitably, led to the dictatorship of the police of the Committee of General Security, and necessarily again to the consular dictatorship, [then] to the Empire.[89] That is why the Jacobins broke the strength of the Communes and especially the Paris Commune and its sections (after having transformed them into simple policing bodies [*bureaux de police*], placed under the orders of the Committee of Security). That is why they waged war on the Church—while seeking to maintain a clergy and a religion; that is why they did not accept the slightest provincial independence, nor the slightest functional independence in the organisation of the crafts, in education, in scientific researches, in Art.

"The State, it is I!" of Louis XIV was only a child's toy in relation to the "State, it is us" of the Jacobins. It was the absorption of the whole national life, concentrated into a pyramid of functionaries. And this whole was to be used to enrich a certain class of citizens and at the same time maintain all the rest—that is to say, the whole nation except the privileged—in poverty. A poverty that would not be absolute destitution, begging, as it was the case under the old regime—starving beggars are not the workers needed by the bourgeois—but a poverty that forces man to sell his working strength to whoever wants to exploit it, and sell it at a price that only allows man *by exception* to get out of this state of wage-earning proletarian.

There is the ideal of the Jacobin State. Read all the literature of the time—except the writings of those called the Enraged, the Anarchists, and who were guillotined or otherwise eliminated for that reason—and you will see that this is precisely the Jacobin ideal.[90]

---

89 The Committee of General Security was a French parliamentary committee that acted as police agency during the French Revolution. Along with the Committee of Public Safety, it oversaw the Reign of Terror as well as supervising the local police committees in charge of investigating reports of treason and had the authority to refer suspects to the Revolutionary Tribunal and so execution by guillotine. By 1794 the Committee became part of the opposition to Robespierre and was involved in the Thermidor coup which saw a five-member committee called the Directory become the government of France. This, in turn, was overthrown by Napoleon Bonaparte in the Coup of 18 Brumaire (8–9 November 1799) and was replaced by the Consulate headed by Napoleon as First Consul. Napoleon did not declare himself head of state until May 1804 when the Senate passed a bill introducing the French Empire, with Napoleon as Emperor. The coronation ceremony took place on 2 December 1804, when Napoleon crowned himself as Emperor of the French, establishing the Empire. (Editor)

90 Kropotkin discusses both "les Enragés" and "les Anarchistes" of this time (and their fate) in his *Great French Revolution*—see, for example, chapters LX and CLI. (Editor)

But then, we are led to wonder, how it is possible that the socialists of the second half of the nineteenth century adopted the ideal of the *Jacobin State* when this ideal had been designed from the viewpoint of the bourgeois, in direct opposition to the egalitarian and communist tendencies of the people which had arisen during the Revolution?[91] Here is the explanation to which my studies of this subject led me and that I believe to be true.

The link between the Jacobin Club of 1793 and the statist socialist militants—Louis Blanc, Vidal, Lassalle, the Marxists—is, in my opinion, the conspiracy of Babeuf. It is not in vain that it is, so to speak, canonised by the State socialists.

Now Babeuf—direct and pure descendant of the Jacobin Club of 1793—had conceived this idea that a revolutionary surprise attack, prepared by a conspiracy, could create a *communist dictatorship* in France. But once—true Jacobin—he had conceived the communist revolution as something which could be done by decrees, he came to two other conclusions: *democracy first* would prepare communism; and then a single individual, a dictator, *provided that he had the strength of will to save the world*, will introduce communism![92]

In this conception, passed on like a tradition by secret societies during the entire nineteenth century, lies the key to the riddle which allows to this day socialists to work towards creating an omnipotent State. The belief—because it is, after all, only an article of messianic faith—that one day a man will appear who will have "the strength of will to save the world" by communism and who, attaining "the dictatorship of the proletariat," will achieve communism by his decrees, silently persisted during the entire nineteenth century. Indeed, we can see, twenty-five years apart, the faith in the "caesarism" of Napoleon III in France, and the leader of the German revolutionary socialists, Lassalle, after his conversations with Bismarck on a unified Germany writing that socialism will be introduced in Germany by a royal dynasty, but probably not by that of the Hohenzollern.

Faith in the Messiah, always! The faith which made Louis Napoleon popular after the massacres of June 1848[93]—that same faith in the om-

---

91   Compare with Lenin: "A Jacobin who wholly identifies himself with the *organisation* of the proletariat—a proletariat *conscious* of its class interests—is a *revolutionary* Social Democrat." (*Collected Works* [Moscow: Progress Publishers, 1961]7: 383) (Editor)

92   Cf. my work, *The Great French Revolution*, ch. LVIII.

93   The June Days uprising (*les journées de Juin*) occurred between 23–26 June 1848 in response to plans to close the National Workshops, created by the Second Republic in order to provide work for the unemployed. The National Guard, led by General Louis Eugène Cavaignac, quelled the protests with over 10,000 people killed or injured and

nipotence of a dictatorship, *combined with the fear of great popular upris-ings*[94]—here, is the explanation of this tragic contradiction that the modern developments of statist-socialism offer us. If the representatives of this doctrine ask, on one hand, emancipation of the worker from bourgeois exploitation, and if, on the other hand, they work to strength the State that represents the true creator and defender of the bourgeoisie—it is obviously that they still have faith in finding their Napoleon, their Bismarck, their Lord Beaconsfield who one day will use the unified strength of the State to work against its mission, against its entire machinery and all its traditions.

* * *

Those who want to meditate on the ideas outlined in these two studies on the historic State and the modern State will understand one of the essential elements of Anarchy. He will understand why anarchists refuse to support the State in any way and [refuse to] become part of the machinery of State. He will see why, taking advantage of the marked tendency of the time to establish thousands of groups which seek to substitute themselves for the State in all the functions that the State had monopolised—anarchists work so that the masses of the workers of the soil and of factory endeavour *to form organisations full of vitality in this direction*, rather than applying their strengths and intelligence to strengthen the bourgeois State.

He will also understand why and how anarchists aim at the destruction of the State by undermining wherever they can the idea of territorial centralisation and centralisation of functions, by opposing to it the independence of each locality and of each grouping formed for a social function; and why they seek union in action: not in pyramidal hierarchy, not in the orders of the central Committee of a secret organisation, but in the free group, federative, from the simple to the complex.

And he will understand that the seeds of the new life will be found

---

4,000 later deported to Algeria. It marked the end of the hopes of a "Democratic and Social Republic" (République démocratique et sociale) and the victory of the liberals over the Radical Republicans and Socialists. (Editor)

94   The need for popular uprisings was the major theme of Kropotkin's article "Insurrections et revolution" ["Insurrections and Revolution"], *Les Temps Nouveaux* (6 August 1910). "If the Revolution is ever to be feasible," Kropotkin argued, "local insurrections are called for. Indeed, huge numbers of them. [...] The whole of history is there for proof. And if the careerist leaders of the proletarian movement today—be they intellectuals or workers—preach the opposite, it is because they want no truck with revolution at all. *They fear it.*" This article is included in *Direct Struggle Against Capital*. (Editor)

in these free groups, respectful of human individuality, when the spirit of voluntary servitude and messianic faith will have given way to the spirit of independence, voluntary solidarity and the analysis of historical and social facts, finally freed from authoritarian and semi-religious prejudices that school and bourgeois statist literature instil in us.

He will also see, in the mists of a not very far future, what man will be able to reach one day when weary of his servitude he will seek his liberation in the free action of free men who act in solidarity for a common aim: to mutually guarantee by their collective labour a certain minimum of well-being in order to allow the individual to work on the complete development of his faculties, his individuality, and thereby achieve his *individuation*, of which we have heard so much about recently.

And he will finally understand, that individuation, that is to say, the fullest possible development of individuality, does not consist—as taught by the bourgeois and their mediocrities—in removing from the creative activity of man his social tendencies and his instincts of solidarity, to keep only the narrow and absurd individualism of the bourgeoisie which recommends that society be forgotten and the worship of the individual isolated from society. He will understand, on the contrary, that it is precisely *social inclinations* and *collective creation*, when they are given their free rein, which allow the individual to reach his full development and to soar to [great] heights, where, so far, only the great geniuses knew how to rise in a few beautiful creations of Art.

PART V

APPENDICES

I

EXPLANATORY NOTES

(Biographies of the some of the authors and some of the technical terms mentioned in this book)
[We have supplemented Kropotkin's original notes with text enclosed by square brackets as per all editorial additions. We have also corrected any minor errors (incorrect dates, etc.).
(Editor)]

[**Adler**, Georg (1863–1908), German economist and associate professor of political science at the University of Kiel. Author of various works on socialism and socialists.]

[**Alexander of Macedonia** (356BCE–323BCE), king of the Ancient Greek kingdom of Macedonia, commonly known as Alexander the Great.]

[**Alexander II** of Russia (1818–1881), Emperor (or Tsar) of Russia from 1885 until his assassination by Populists in 1881. Initially viewed himself as a reforming Emperor, with his most significant change being the emancipation of the serfs in 1861, but he became increasingly reactionary. In his youth, Kropotkin was his page in the Royal Court and saw his decline first hand.]

[**Algirdas** (c. 1296–1377), monarch of medieval Lithuania. Ruled from 1345 to 1377, creating an empire stretching from the present Baltic States to the Black Sea and to within fifty miles of Moscow.]

[The **Amana** Colony was formed of seven villages in east-central Iowa, United States. It was founded by German Pietists after being persecuted in their homeland by the government and Lutheran Church. Calling themselves the Community of True Inspiration, they initially settled in New York near Buffalo but, seeking more isolated surroundings, they moved to Iowa in 1856 where they lived a communal life based on an almost completely self-sufficient economy until the mid-1930s.]

Anabaptism, a religious movement at the time of the Reformation. It was directed against the authority of the Catholic Church but it went much further [than Luther]. The Anabaptists demanded the complete freedom of the individual in religious and moral matters, and in the social domain they preached equality and the absence of private property. They rejected all forms of coercion, that is to say the oath, seigneurial justice, military service, and obedience to the government, which they considered contrary to the principles of Christianity. Generally, historians only pay attention to this movement after it became the object of prosecution in Zwickau during 1520. However, it originated in the movement of [John] *Wycliff* and the *Lollards* in England (in the fourteenth century),[1] and in the movement of the *Hussites* in Bohemia (at the end of the fourteenth century). Long before Luther had nailed his "Theses" on the Reformation to the door of the church of Wittenberg, a revolt was already germinating in the minds of artisan townsfolk and peasants who had heard discussion on the Bible; and it was directed against the State and the Law, always favourable to the lords. The Anabaptists were the left wing of the movement, while the Lutherans represented the moderate fraction favoured by the princes and the lords. During the Great Peasant War (1525)[2] and

---

1   John Wycliffe (c.1320–1384) was an English scholastic philosopher, theologian, Biblical translator, reformer, and seminary professor at Oxford. He was an influential dissident within the Roman Catholic priesthood during the fourteenth century and attacked the privileged status of the clergy as well as the luxury and pomp of local parishes and their ceremonies. Wycliffe was also an advocate for translation of the Bible into everyday language rather than Latin and completed a translation into Middle English in 1382 (this is now known as Wycliffe's Bible). Wycliffe's followers were known as Lollards and existed from the mid-fourteenth century to the English Reformation in the sixteenth century. (Editor)

2   The German Peasant War was a widespread popular revolt in the German-speaking areas of Central Europe from 1524 to 1525. The war consisted, like the preceding Hussite Wars, of a series of both economic and religious revolts in which peasants

in the town of Münster,[3] with *John of Leiden*[4] and *Thomas Münzter*,[5] the Anabaptists entered into open revolt. Both of these movements were drowned in blood and it is estimated that tens of thousands of Anabaptists (up to 100,000 according to some historians) were massacred or burned [at the stake]. Later on, the movement transferred to England, where it took more peaceful forms. It was also continued in Austria (the Moravian brothers), in Russia by the Mennonites, and even in Greenland, always taking more or less communist forms. (See the German works of Keller, Hase, and Cornelius;[6] and an excellent summary, in English, by Richard Heath,[7]*Anabaptism* [*from its rise at Zwickau to its fall at Münster 1521– 1536*], 1895).

[The **Ancien Régime** (French for "Former Regime") refers to the monarchy abolished by the Great French Revolution of 1789–1793. This aristocratic

---

and farmers, often supported by Protestant clergy, took the lead. It began with separate insurrections, beginning in the southwestern part of what is now Germany and neighbouring Alsace, and spread in subsequent insurrections to the central and eastern areas of Germany and present-day Austria. It was Europe's largest and most widespread popular uprising prior to the French Revolution of 1789. The aristocracy slaughtered up to 100,000 of the 300,000 poorly armed peasants and farmers. (Editor)

3   The Münster Rebellion (1534–1535) was an attempt by radical Anabaptists to establish a commune based on their principles in the German city of Münster. The city was under Anabaptist rule from February 1534, when the city hall was seized, until its fall in June 1535. (Editor)

4   John of Leiden (1509–1536), was an Anabaptist leader from Leiden in the Holy Roman Empire's County of Holland. In 1533 he moved to Münster (in North-Rhine-Westphalia, Germany) where he became an influential prophet and a leader of the Münster Rebellion. He was tortured and executed when the insurrection was suppressed after a siege of the fortified city. (Editor)

5   Thomas Müntzer (1489–1525) was a radical German preacher and theologian of the early Reformation whose opposition to both Luther and the Roman Catholic Church led to his open defiance of late-feudal authority in central Germany. Müntzer was foremost amongst those reformers who took issue with Luther's compromises with feudal authority and became a leader of the German peasant uprising of 1525. He was captured after the battle of Frankenhausen, tortured and then executed. (Editor)

6   German historians: Ludwig Keller (1849–1915), *Geschichte der Wiedertäufer und ihres Reichs zu Münster* (*History of the Anabaptists and their realm in Münster*), 1880; Johann Hast (1808–1852), *Geschichte der Wiedertäufer* (*History of the Anabaptists*), 1836; Carl Adolf Cornelius (1819–1903), *Geschichte des münsterischen Aufruhrs* (*History of the Münster Uprising*), 2 volumes, 1855 and 1860. (Editor)

7   Richard Health (1831–1912) was a British Historian. (Editor)

political system was established in the Kingdom of France from approximately the fifteenth century until the latter part of the eighteenth century. Its Kings aimed to create a centralised State based on the notion of "absolute monarchy" and the monarch's divine right to rule.]

[**Andler**, Charles Philippe Théodore (1866–1933), French Germanist and philosopher. Works include *Les origines du socialisme d'état en Allemagne* (*The origins of state socialism in Germany*), 1897.]

[**Andrews**, Stephen Pearl (1812–1886) American individualist anarchist. Converted to individualism by Josiah Warren, in 1851 they established Modern Times in Brentwood, New York, which lasted until 1864. Andrews, like Warren, argued that to be paid "justly" was to be paid according to the "Cost Principle" (individuals being paid according to the amount of labour they exert) and so advocated payment and pricing by labour notes whose unit ("the Labor Dollar") was defined as "*a day's work of eight hours* [...] *of the average degree of severity or intensity.*" His works include: *Cost the Limit of Price*, 1851; *The Constitution of Government in the Sovereignty of the Individual*, 1851; *The Science of Society*, 1851; *The Sovereignty of the Individual*, 1853; *The Labor Dollar*, 1881; *The New Civilization*, 1885.]

Anthropology, a science which studies man: his physical constitution in different climates, his races, his physical growth, and the development of his institutions and of his social, moral, and religious conceptions. Institutions and social, moral, and religious conceptions are often considered as part of *Ethnology*. By the *Anthropological School* we mean all the work done in the second half of the nineteenth century to study the origins and development of conceptions and social institutions from the point of view of the natural sciences.

[The **Anzin** Mining Company was a large French mining company.]

[**Aristippus** of Cyrene (c. 435BCE– c. 356 BCE), founder of the Cyrenaic school of philosophy. He was a pupil of Socrates but adopted a very different philosophical outlook and advocated a hedonistic lifestyle. Although many of the sensationalistic stories about him are probably false, they depict a man who is willing to engage in activity that is shocking, undignified, and callous for the sake of his own pleasure and who displays disdain for conventional standards as being mere societal prejudices. Aristippus, however, thought that his willingness to do anything whatsoever for the sake of pleasure, his total flexibility, brought him a kind of freedom for his disregard of social conventions made him master of himself.]

[**Armstrong** Whitworth & Co Ltd was a major British manufacturing company of the early years of the twentieth century, engaged in the construction of armaments, ships, locomotives, automobiles and aircraft.]

[**Astor**, John Jacob (1763–1848), German-American businessman, merchant, real estate mogul and investor. He mainly made his fortune in the fur trade and by investing in real estate in or around New York City. The first multi-millionaire in the United States.]

[**Augustus** (63BCE–14 CE), founder of the Roman Principate and considered the first Roman emperor. He ruled the Roman Empire from 27BCE until his death.]

[**Aulard**, François Victor Alphonse (1849–1928), French historian. Principal work: *Histoire politique de la Révolution française: origines et développement de la démocratie et de la république: 1789–1804*, 1901.]

[**Babeau**, Albert (1835–1914), French historian, specialist on society under the Ancien Régime.]

Babeuf, François-Noël (1764–1797), French Communist; took part in the Great Revolution; published *Le Tribun du Peuple* [*The Tribune of the People*], in which he preached social revolution. Founded with [Philippe] Buonarroti, Sylvain Maréchal, Darthé and several others,[8] a secret society whose aim was to seize power and establish a Directorate which would introduce communism on a national basis. The conspiracy was discovered and Babeuf, along with Darthé, was guillotined. (See *Conspiration de l'Egalité, dite de Babeuf* [*History of Babeuf's 'Conspiracy of Equals'*] by Buonarroti, 2 vols, Brussels, 1828).

[**Babouvist**, supporter or follower of François-Noël Babeuf or his ideas.]

Bacon, Francis (1561–1626), great English philosopher; considered as the father of the *inductive method* because, faced with the scholastics and metaphysics which prevailed until then, he demonstrated that research and discovery will only progress when the human mind was accustomed to understanding that *observation* and free and methodical *experimental* research

---

8   Sylvain Maréchal (1750–1803) was a French writer, poet, philosopher, and political theorist, a precursor of utopian socialism and communism who wrote the *Manifeste des Égaux* (*Manifesto of the Equals*), 1801; Augustin Alexandre Darthé (1769–1797) was a French revolutionary. (Editor)

provided the only means of discovering natural laws, of comprehending the true causes of phenomena and being able to predict them. Scholastic erudition, which juggled with words, had to be abandoned and true knowledge could be obtained only by *induction*, that is to say by the meticulous study of the separate facts on which generalisations are constructed on the basis of a great number of comparisons and exclusions, and thus finding that which is common, general, to these observed facts; then to verify these *inductions* by submitting them to verification against new masses of facts, taken from observation and experiments. This was the fundamental idea of all the works of Bacon which makes it possible to regard him as the father of the natural sciences as they were developed over the course of the nineteenth century. It is to this method that modern science owes all its great discoveries.

[**Bacon**, Roger (c. 1220–1292), English philosopher and Franciscan friar. He placed considerable emphasis on the study of nature through empirical methods.]

Bain, Alexander (1818–1903), one of the principal Scottish[9] representatives of the system of philosophy which seeks its basis not in abstract metaphysical speculations but in the facts of the natural sciences and which studies the powers of the human mind and the degree of certainty of our judgements based mainly on physiology and physical psychology. Principal works: *Mind and Body* [1872], *The Senses and the Intellect* [1855], *Logic* [1870: in 2 volumes, *Deduction* and *Induction*].

Bakunin, Michael (1814–1876), Russian political writer, revolutionary, and an indefatigable agitator. Took part in the revolutionary movements of his time in Germany, Switzerland, France, Italy, Austria and Poland as well as in the Dresden revolution of 1849. Condemned to death for participating in this, he was extradited by Saxony to Austria, and by that to Nicholas I in 1852.[10] After a two year imprisonment in an Austrian fortress, where he was shackled and riveted to the wall, and six years in the fortress of St. Petersburg, he was not released until after the death of Nicolas in 1856. Exiled after that to Siberia, he escaped in 1861 and joined his close friend Alexander Herzen in London. Became a member of the International [Workers' Association] wherein he was for a time the lifeblood of the Jura Federation, composed of socialists of French-speaking

---

9   Kropotkin had Bain listed as "English" even though he was born and bred in Aberdeen. (Editor)

10   Nicholas I (1796–1855) was the Emperor of Russia from 1825 until 1855. (Editor)

Switzerland, and who, in agreement with the Spanish, Italian and Eastern and Central Belgium federations, represented, in opposition to the General Council of the International (led by Marx), the ideas of federalism, hostility to the State, and direct action in the struggle against capital; which led to the rupture of these federations with the General Council, which was transferred by the Marxists in 1872 to New York where it died.

The Latin federations, which concluded a federative alliance between themselves, continued to sustain the life of the International until 1878 after which the International, fiercely prosecuted by governments, had to disappear—the Latin federations gave rise to, on the one hand, the modern anarchist movement and, on the other, the syndicalist movement. Principal works: *God and the State*; *Statism and Anarchy*, and many pamphlets. His *Oeuvres* are now published in Paris by James Guillaume. His detailed *Biographie* was written by Max Nettlau in three large handwritten volumes deposited in the principal libraries. A short abridgment has been produced by the author (*Michael Bakunin. Eine biographische Skizze*, Berlin 1901).[11]

[**Barbès**, Armand Sigismond Auguste (1809–1870), French revolutionary. He formed a republican secret society, the *Société des Saisons*, with Louis-Auguste Blanqui in 1838. Organised a *coup d'état* in 1839 against the July Monarchy and took an active part in the 1848 revolution.]

[**Basch**, Victor-Guillaume (1863–1944), French socialist, politician and professor of Germanistics and philosophy at the Sorbonne.]

[**Bayle**, Pierre (1647–1706), French philosopher and writer. Principal work: *Dictionnaire Historique et Critique* (*Historical and Critical Dictionary*), 1697.]

[**Beaconsfield**, Lord (1804–1881), better known as Benjamin Disraeli (1st Earl of Beaconsfield). British Conservative politician and writer who was

---

11   *God and the State* (New York: Dover, 1970) and *Statism and Anarchy* (Cambridge: Cambridge University Press, 1990). Anthologies of Bakunin's work include: *Bakunin: Selected Texts 1868–1875* (London: The Merlin Press Ltd, 2016), *The Basic Bakunin* (Buffalo, NY: Prometheus Books, 1994), *Bakunin on Anarchism* (Montréal: Black Rose Books, 1980), *Michael Bakunin: Selected Writings* (London: Jonathan Cape, 1973), and *The Political Philosophy of Bakunin* (New York: The Free Press, 1953). The best biography is Mark Leier's *Bakunin: The Creative Passion* (New York: Thomas Dunne Books, 2006), while *Bakunin: The Philosophy of Freedom* (Montréal: Black Rose Books, 1993) by Brian Morris is an excellent summary of his both life and ideas. (Editor)

Prime Minister twice. Combined limited social reform at home with imperialist adventures aboard.]

Bentham, Jeremy (1748–1832), English political writer, granted French cit-
izenship by the Convention for his work on reforming legislation. Founder
of the English philosophical school of *Utilitarianism* which recognises that
the aim of society must be the well-being of the greatest number and that
the purpose of morals must aim at demonstrating to the individual that
the social interest coincides with the personal interest. Most of his works
are translated into French. *Œuvres completes* published in 1845 in Brussels.

Bernard, Claude (1818–1878), French physiologist. Noteworthy not only
for his discoveries in physiology but especially for the materialist spirit in which his works were conceived wherein he sought to interpret all
the processes of physiological and psychical life by physical and chemical
processes. His *Leçons de physiologie expérimentale* [*Lessons in Experimental
Physiology*], 1855, and his works on the effects of toxic materials, 1857,
and especially on the physiology of the nervous system, 1858, are epoch
making in science.

Berthelot, Marcelin (1827–1907), French chemist, opened a new field for
chemistry by his remarkable syntheses of organic bodies, that is to say, by
producing in the laboratory, by combining in different proportions hydrogen, oxygen, carbon, nitrogen, etc., various substances which enter into the
composition of living beings, or are produced by their organs (hydrocarbons,
sugars, alcohols, ethers, fatty substances, etc.). All his work was a beautiful
illustration of the unity of physical forces which represents the greatest conquest of science in the nineteenth century and of that other conquest of the
same period—the transformation of heat into work. Thus Berthelot was
able to nourish boundless hopes concerning the powers of science to ensure the well-being of humanity and to remain true, in his philosophy and
in its application to life, to the best traditions of the Encyclopaedists. He
published nearly 1,200 essays. His Principal Works are: *Organic Chemistry
Based on Synthesis*, 1860; *Lectures on the General Methods of Synthesis*, 1864;
Lectures on Isomery, 1865; *Chemical Synthesis*, 1875.

[The **Biribi** was the military prisons and disciplinary service in French-
controlled North Africa. It was exposed by Lucien Descaves (1861–1949),
a French novelist, in a book of the same name—*Biribi* (1890)—which
drew upon the author's harrowing experiences in army disciplinary companies in Tunisia.]

[**Bismark**, Otto von (1815–1898), conservative German statesman who dominated European affairs from the 1860s to 1890. After a series of short victorious wars, he unified numerous States into the German Empire in 1871 and was its Chancellor until 1890. He implemented the world's first welfare State in the 1880s, working closely with big industry to make it acceptable to conservatives (partly to undermine support for socialists).]

Blanc, Louis (1811–1882), French socialist, political writer and historian. Published in 1840 his book *The Organisation of Labour* which made him a leader of a socialist school. The misery of the masses having its cause in the individualism of present society and bourgeois competition, he demanded the organisation of labour on the basis of solidarity and equal wages[12] which would enable everyone to satisfy all their needs and work according to their abilities. Appointed a member of the provisional government during the revolution of 24th February 1848, he founded a "Workers' Commission" which sat at the Luxembourg [Palace]. Prosecuted for the attempted uprising of 15th May [that year], he had to leave France and remained in exile until 1870. Principal works: *Organisation of Labour*, 1840; *History of the French Revolution*, in 12 volumes, 1847–1862; *History of Ten Years, 1830–40* [1841].

[**Blanqui**, Louis Auguste (1805–1881), French socialist revolutionary. He organised numerous conspiracies to overthrow the regime and thought that the revolution had to be carried out by a small group which would establish a temporary dictatorship. This would create the new social order after which power would be handed to the people. Blanqui's uncompromising politics and regular insurrections ensured that he spent half his life in prison.]

[**Blanquist**, supporter or follower of Blanqui or his ideas.]

[The Second **Boer War** was waged from 1899 to 1902 between the British Empire and the two independent Boer republics of the Orange Free State and the South African Republic. After a long hard-fought war, the two independent republics lost and were absorbed into the British Empire. This war cost around seventy-five thousand lives: twenty-two thousand British soldiers (7,792 battle casualties, the rest through disease), six to seven thousand Boer Commandos, twenty to twenty-eight thousand Boer civilians (mostly women and children due to disease in concentration camps) and an

---

12   The 1912 British Edition adds: "the first step being the socialisation of the instruments of production. He wanted, therefore, the 'Organisation of Labour,' the State helping in promoting social workshops." (Editor)

estimated twenty thousand black Africans. Kropotkin wrote three articles on this war: "British Workers and the War," *Freedom,* March–April 1900; "An Urgent Need: A Labor Convention," *Freedom,* September–October 1900; "One War Over—When is the Next?," *Freedom,* June 1902.]

[**Botta**, Carlo Giuseppe Guglielmo (1766–1837), Italian historian.]

[**Bourgin**, Hubert (1874–1955), French writer and member of the Socialist Party. His works include *Fourier: contribution à l'étude du socialisme francais* (Paris: Georges Bellais, 1905) and *Proudhon* (Paris: Georges Bellais, 1901).]

[**Bowley**, Arthur Lyon (1869–1957), English statistician and economist. His works include *Wages and Income in the United Kingdom Since 1860,* 1900.]

[**Bray**, John Francis (1809–1897), American-born English socialist. One of the "Ricardian socialists," he argued that the profits of the employers was caused by unequal exchange which ensured that workers were not paid the full value of their labour. The remedy was creating a centrally planned society based on equal exchange between producers. Principal works: *Labour's Wrongs and Labour's Remedy*, 1839; *Government and society considered in relation to first principles*, 1842.]

Brehons. Amongst all the free people who had not been conquered by the Roman Empire and had no written law during the first centuries of the Christian era—Gauls, Celts, Saxon, Scandinavian peoples, Slavs, Finns, etc.—the traditional law, that is to say the decisions taken previously by popular assemblies, was memorised—preferably by certain families or in certain fraternities or special guilds. It was their duty to recite the traditional [common] law before the people during the festivals which accompanied the great federal assemblies of large parts of these tribes. The law was often put in the shape of rhythmic phrases, or *triads,* to better facilitate memorisation. This custom still continues to exist amongst the nomadic peoples of Asia. In Ireland, those who were entrusted with the keeping of the law were called *Brehons,* and they combined this function with priestly functions. The collection of the Irish [common] laws compiled in the fifth century and known under the name of the *Senchus Mor* (*Great Antiquity*), is one of the most remarkable documents amongst similar collections. Some modern historians represent the Brehons and similar reciters of the law as *lawmakers*; but this was not correct. The lawmakers were the popular assemblies which created the precedents of the law by their decisions while the Irish *Brehons,* the Scandinavian *Knung, Knyazes* of the Russians, etc., were only those to whom it entrusted to hold the words of the law in its traditional form.

[**Brousse,** Paul (1844–1912), French socialist. Originally an anarchist active in the Jura Federation from 1873 to 1880, publishing an article in *L'Avant-Garde* which defined propaganda of the deed. Returning to France in 1880, he became progressively more reformist, joined the socialist party and become the leader of its ultra-reformist wing, the "possibilists."]

Büchner, Ludwig (1824–1899), German naturalist and materialist philosopher, was especially known for his popular work *Force and Matter*, 1855, which represents an attempt at atomist-materialist philosophy, based on the conquests of modern science. He became a passionate advocate of Darwinism, which he popularised in his books and published *Man and his Position in Nature* [*Der Mensch und seine Stellung in der Natur*], 1872, *Love and Love Relations in the Animal World* [*Liebe und Liebesleben in der Tierwelt*], 1879, which is an essay on the social life and social instincts of animals, and numerous studies on scientific popularisation. By all his works he powerfully contributed to the propagation of the dynamic conception of nature.

Buffon, Georges-Louis (1707–1788), French naturalist, founder of comparative anatomy, made the first attempt to construct a system of all of nature in which theology played no part and wrote a complete course of zoology. Principal work: *Histoire naturelle* [*Natural History*], 1749–1788, the first volume of which contain a general overview of nature ([and it was] prosecuted by the Church).

Buonarroti, Filippo [Philippe] (1761–1837), Italian lawyer. Influenced by Rousseau, he spread revolutionary propaganda and was expelled from Tuscany, Corsica, and Sardinia. Joined in 1796 the authoritarian-communist conspiracy of Babeuf, which he later recounted in a book *La conspiration de Babeuf* [*History of Babeuf's 'Conspiracy of Equals'*], 1828; in the thirties and forties [of the nineteenth century] was one of the principal organisers of secret societies of communists [in France and Italy].

Burnouf, Émile (1821–1907), French Hellenist.[13] Produced in 1872 an important work on the science of religions based on rationalist basis [translated into English as *The Science of Religions*, fourth edition, 1885].

---

13   A person who studies or admires Greek civilisation. (Editor)

Byelaeff, [Ivan Dmitrievich] (1810–1873), Russian historian; has described better than any other historian, in four volumes entitled *Tales from Russian History* (in Russian), the inner life of the Russian republics of the Middle Ages—Novgorod and Pskov. Writes, at the approach of the liberation of the serfs, an excellent *History of the Peasants in Russia* and also published a large work on the Russian Annals.

Cabet, Etienne (1788–1856), French Communist who developed his ideas in his journal, *Le Populaire*, and published anonymously in 1840 his principal work, *Voyage en Icarie* [*Voyage to Icaria*], in which he developed an authoritarian communist ideal. Republished since in several editions of which those of 1842 and afterwards contain an analysis of the socialist predecessors of Cabet. In 1848 he tried to put his ideas into practice in Texas, then in the State of Illinois, but failed. However, the colony Young Icaria continued to exist into the nineties of the nineteenth century. (See also the works of Jules Prudhommeaux).[14]

[**Caesarism, Caesarist,** autocratic rule by a popular dictator or emperor, derived from Julius Caesar (100BCE–44BCE) and his desire to declare himself emperor of Rome (for which he was assassinated in the Roman Senate on the Ides of March). That is, military or imperial dictatorship led by a charismatic strongman whose rule is based upon a cult of personality. Both Napoleon Bonaparte and Benito Mussolini represented Caesarism.]

[**Capponi, Gino** (1792–1876), Italian statesman and historian.]

[**Carnegie**, Andrew (1835–1919), Scottish-American industrialist. He led the expansion of the American steel industry in the late nineteenth century (first breaking, by force, the trade unions at Homestead) and swiftly became one of the richest Americans ever. He combined a desire for world peace with making profits from State orders for armour-plate for battleships. Became a philanthropist in his final years.]

[The **Catholic Bank of Rome**, or the *Bank of the Holy Spirit* (Italian: *Il Banco di Santo Spirito*) was founded by Pope Paul V (1550–1621) in the first year of his papacy (1605) and was the first national bank in Europe (as the bank of the Papal States).]

---

14   A reference to two books by French historian, peace activist, and advocate of cooperation Jules Prudhommeaux (1869–1948): *Histoire de la Communauté Icarienne* (Nîmes: Imprimerie coopérative La Laborieuse, 1906) and *Étienne Cabet et les origines du communisme Icarien* (Nîmes: Imprimerie coopérative La Laborieuse, 1907). (Editor)

[**Cellini**, Benvenuto (1500–1571), Italian goldsmith, sculptor, draftsman, soldier, musician, artist, writer, and poet.]

[**Chartism** was a working class movement for political reform in Britain between 1838 and 1848. It took its name from the *People's Charter* of 1838 which called for six basic democratic reforms of the State. Starting as a petition movement which tried to mobilise "moral force," it soon attracted men who advocated "physical force" in the form of insurrection.]

[**Chelcicky**, Peter (c.1390–c.1460), Christian spiritual leader and author in fifteenth century Bohemia (in the modern Czech Republic). He was one of the most influential thinkers of the Bohemian Reformation and critiqued the immorality and violence of the contemporary church and State. He taught that the believer should not accept government office, nor even appeal to its authority, for to take part in government was sinful. An advocate of non-violence, he was a communalist in the original Christian sense and thought that there must be complete equality in the Christian community.]

[**Chernyshevsky**, Nikolay Gavrilovich (1828–1889) Russian revolutionary democrat, materialist philosopher, critic, and socialist. Founder of Russian populism, he agitated for the revolutionary overthrow of the autocracy and the creation of a socialist society based on the peasant commune. In 1862 he was arrested and wrote *What Is to Be Done?* (1863) in prison. This was an inspiration to many later Russian revolutionaries who sought to emulate its hero Rakhmetov and his complete dedication to the revolution.]

Clausius, Rudolf (1822–1888), German physicist, renowned for his work on optics, electricity, and especially the mechanical theory of heat, considered as a state of matter in motion, and of which he discovered one of the fundamental laws [namely, the second law of thermodynamics]. Principal work: *Treatise on the Mechanical Theory of Heat*, 2 vols. [1867].

[**Clemenceau**, Georges Benjamin (1841–1929), French politician and journalist. A leader of the Radical Party, he played a central role in the politics of the Third Republic. Was Prime Minister twice (1906–1909 and 1917–1920).]

Comte, Auguste (1798–1857), founder of Positivism. His principal works are: *Course of Positive Philosophy*, 1830–1842 in 6 vols., a monumental work representing an attempt to construct a synthetic philosophy of our knowledge from the purely scientific point of view. His second great work,

System of Positive Politics or Treatise on Sociology, 1851–1856, 4 vols., is an application of positive philosophy to human relations within society; but it also aims, contrary to the very essence of positive philosophy, to establish a religion whose object of worship would be "Humanity."

The word "positive" originally had the following meaning for Comte: It established that all human knowledge begins with *theological* conceptions (thus, for example, man sees in thunder the voice of an angry god); later it consists of *metaphysical* conceptions which sees in all physical facts an abstract, imaginary force placed outside of natural facts ("vital force," "the soul of Nature," etc.); and finally science reaches *positive knowledge* which is not concerned with "final causes" nor with "substances" but seeks only to establish the laws according to which such-and-such facts are invariably followed by such-and-such consequences—that is to say, to establish the *relations* between phenomena and their *necessary sequence*. The affirmations of positive philosophy are based on experience alone; it is necessary to reject wanting to know what is outside of experience. Positive philosophy is the synthesis of these six principal sciences: mathematics, astronomy, physics, chemistry, biology, sociology. It rejects all supernatural belief. Comte's work exerted a profound influence on all the science and philosophy of the second half of the nineteenth century. The principal followers of Comte were Littré and J. S. Mill (see these two entries).

Considerant, Victor (1802–1893), French socialist writer, follower and continuator of Fourier. Edited *La Phalange* [*The Phalanx*] in 1837 and *LaDémocratie Pacifique* [*Peaceful Democracy*] in 1845. Tried to establish a phalanstery in Texas. Developed the ideas of Fourier in a series of works of great value, of which the chief are: *Destinée sociale* [*Social Destiny*], 1834; *Théorie de l'éducation naturelle et attrayante* [*Theory of Natural and Attractive Education*], 1835; *Bases de la politique positive: manifeste de l'école sociétaire, fondée par Fourier* [*Bases of Positive Politics: Manifesto of the social school founded by Fourier*], 1835; *Principes du Socialisme: Manifeste de la Démocratie pacifique* [*Principles of Socialism: Manifesto of the Peaceful Democracy*] first appeared in 1843, prosecuted and published in a second edition in 1847; served, as W. Tcherkesoff has shown, as the basis for the *Communist Manifesto* of Marx and Engels; *Le Socialisme devant le Vieux Monde* [*Socialism Before the Old World*], 1848, a survey of the different socialist schools.

[*Corvée* **labour** was a form of unpaid, unfree labour usually associated with medieval and early modern Europe. It was owed by a serf to their feudal lord or to royalty. When imposed by a State for the purposes of public works, it was termed statue labour. It was usually intermittent in nature and for limited periods of time—such as a certain number of days' work a year.]

[**Cunningham**, William (1849–1919), Scottish economist and economic historian. Principal works: *Growth of English Industry and Commerce in Modern Times: The Mercantile System*, 1882; *The Use and Abuse of Money*, 1891; *The Rise and Decline of the Free Trade Movement*, 1905.]

[**Cuvier**, Jean Léopold Nicolas Frédéric (1769–1832), French naturalist and zoologist. Known as Georges Cuvier, he was a major figure in the natural sciences in the early nineteenth century and was instrumental in establishing the fields of comparative anatomy and palaeontology through his work in comparing living animals with fossils. Cuvier believed there was no evidence for, and strongly opposed, the pre-Darwinian theory of evolution proposed by Jean-Baptiste de Lamarck.]

[**d'Alembert**, Jean-Baptiste le Rond (1717–1783), French mathematician, mechanician, physicist, philosopher and music theorist. Until 1759 he was also co-editor with Denis Diderot of the *Encyclopédie*.]

[**da Vinci**, Leonardo (1452–1519), Italian polymath. His areas of interest included invention, painting, sculpting, architecture, science, music, mathematics, engineering, literature, anatomy, geology, astronomy, botany, writing, history and cartography.]

[**Dalloz**, Victor Alexis Désiré (1795–1869), French jurist, politician and publisher. He edited a journal dedicated to the study of judicial decisions and in 1832 he published the *Répertoire de jurisprudence générale du royaume*, an index, summary and reference of all contemporary judicial decisions. He also helped found the legal publishing house Dalloz.]

[**Dante** (c.1265–1321), major Italian poet of the Late Middle Ages.]

Darwin, Charles (1809–1882), English naturalist who accomplished a true revolution in ideas through his work *On the Origin of Species by Means of Natural Selection, or the Preservation of Favoured Races in the Struggle for Life* published in 1859, followed by *The Descent of Man, and Selection in Relation to Sex*, 1871, *The Variation of Animals and Plants Under Domestication*, 1868, etc. The transmutation or transformation of species under the influence of the environment as well as the use and non-use of organs under new conditions of existence had already been indicated by Buffon. It was proclaimed and defended by Jean Lamarck in 1809 and later found an adherent in Isidore Geoffroy Saint-Hilaire.[15] Darwin explained the natural descent of species by natural selection which must occur during the struggle for existence carried out by each species against the adverse circumstances of the climate, etc., against other enemy species and even within the same species. All the species of plants and animals which now inhabit the Earth descend from some extremely simple primordial forms by means of an evolution due to natural selection. The importance of Darwin's work, supported by thirty years of research, diverse observations and experimentation was swiftly recognised by scientists. In spite of opposition from academies, universities, and churches, "the struggle for existence" was more readily accepted by current society than the direct action of the environment and the formation of species under the influences of the surroundings with which Lamarck was concerned. On the other hand, Darwin himself as he proceeded in his researches hastened to recognise the importance of the Lamarckian factor (in *Variation*, etc.) and he endeavoured to mitigate (*Descent of Man*) the exaggerated notion that his vulgarisers had attached to "the struggle for existence."[16]

[**de Paepe**, César (1841–1890), Belgium medical doctor and a prominent member of the International Workers' Association. Influenced by Proudhon, he extended his ideas into the labour movement by arguing that unions were required both for the current struggle within capitalism and the structure of a socialist society. He played a key part in the Collectivist victory over the right-wing mutualists at the 1868 Brussels conference. Initially siding with its libertarian (federalist) wing in the 1872 split with Marx, he later moved towards a social democratic position.]

[**Delaisi**, Francis (1873–1947), French anarchist, syndicalist, journalist and economist.]

[**Delcassé**, Théophile (1852–1923), French politician.]

[**Denck**, Hans (c.1495–1527), German theologian and Anabaptist leader during the Reformation.]

[**Desmoulins**, Camille (1760–1794), French journalist and politician who

---

15   Isidore Geoffroy Saint-Hilaire (1805–1861) was a French zoologist and an authority on deviation from normal structure. (Editor)

16   Kropotkin discusses Lamarckian tendencies of Darwin in his essay "The Theory of Evolution and Mutual Aid," *The Nineteenth Century and Later*, January 1910 (this is included in Peter Kropotkin, *Evolution and Environment*). (Editor)

played an important role in the French Revolution.]

Diderot, Denis (1713–1784), French philosopher. After having been prosecuted for his *Pensées philosophiques* [*Philosophical Thoughts*], 1746, and imprisoned for his *Lettres sur les aveugles* [*Letters on the Blind*],1749, he conceived the project of the *Encyclopaedia*, an immense work for its time, which he nevertheless succeeds in completing in twenty-one years (1751–1772) with the assistance of D'Alembert, Holbach, etc., despite the opposition and intrigues of the clergy and the civil authorities.[17]

[The **Doukhobors** ("Spirit-Warriors of Christ") are a Spiritual Christian religious group of Russian origin. As well as pacifism, the Doukhobors embraced vegetarianism and lived communally. In the 1880s they became aware of Leo Tolstoy (1828–1910) and his radical Christian philosophy which they found very similar to their traditional teachings. Seven and a half thousand emigrated to Canada in 1899 because of their opposition to the tyranny and oppression of the Tzarist regime, their pacifist beliefs and desire to avoid government interference in their way of life. Quakers and Tolstoyans covered most of the costs of passage for the emigrants, with Tolstoy giving 30,000 roubles of his royalties to the emigration fund. Kropotkin also helped the emigrants. Interestingly, given Kropotkin's arguments on the role of the State in enforcing capitalist property rights, the community's aversion towards private ownership of land meant they initially registered their land in the name of the community. However, in 1906, the new Minister of Interior insisted that the land be registered in the name of individual owners. This led to more than a third of Doukhobor lands returning to the hands of Crown the following year.]

[**Dumas**, Alexandre (1802–1870), French writer.]

[**Eccarius**, Johann Georg (1818–1889), German tailor, socialist, and labour activist. He was a member of the League of the Just and later of the League of Communists before becoming General Secretary of the International Workers' Association in 1867.]

---

17 In his essay on "Anarchism" for the eleventh edition of the *Encyclopaedia Britannica*, Kropotkin refers the *Supplement to the Voyage of Bougainville* as the work most expressing Diderot's anarchistic tendencies. For more discussion of the *Supplement*, see Peter G. Stillman "Diderot's *Supplément au voyage de Bougainville*: steps towards an anarchist utopia," *Anarchism and Utopianism* (Manchester and New York: Manchester University Press, 2009), Laurence Davis and Ruth Kinna (eds.). (Editor)

[**Edward III** (1312–1377) ruled England from 1327 until his death. He is noted for his military success and for restoring royal authority, transforming his Kingdom into one of the most formidable military powers in Europe.]

[**Edward VII** (1841–1910) King of the British Empire from 1901 until his death.]

[**Elizabeth I** (1533–1603), Queen of England and Ireland from 1558 until her death.]

[**Elliot**, Hugh Samuel Roger (1881–1930), British biologist and psychologist.]

Encyclopaedists (The), initiators of and contributors to the great French Encyclopaedia (see Diderot). Its contributors included D'Alembert, Buffon, Condillac, Helvetius, d'Holbach, Mably, Turgot, etc.[18] The importance of this work was mainly due to the fact that it not only represented an attempt to summarise all the knowledge of the time and to treat the natural sciences, mathematics, history, art and literature with the same objectivity but also because the *Encyclopaedia* became the organ for all the irreligious [rationalist] thought of France in the eighteenth century. This is why the name Encyclopaedistis often given to those who share the philosophical ideas of the *Encyclopaedia*.

[**Engels**, Friedrich (1820–1895), German philosopher, socialist, journalist, and capitalist. Close friend of Karl Marx with whom he founded Marxism. In 1848, he co-authored *The Manifesto of the Communist Party* with Marx and supported him financially while he wrote *Capital*. After Marx's death, he popularised his ideas as well as editing and publishing the second and third volumes of *Capital*. Principal works: *The Condition of the Working Class in England*, 1844; *The Peasant War in Germany*, 1850; *Herr Eugen Dühring's Revolution in Science*, 1878; *Socialism: Utopian and Scientific*, 1880; *The Origin of the Family, Private Property and the State*, 1884.]

[The **English Revolution**, usually known as the English Civil War, was a series of armed conflicts between the Parliamentarians and Royalists over

---

18   Étienne Bonnot de Condillac (1714–1780) was a French philosopher and epistemologist who studied psychology and the philosophy of the mind; Claude Adrien Helvétius (1715–1771) was a French philosopher and intellectual; Paul-Henri Thiry, Baron d'Holbach (1723–1789) was a French-German author and philosopher; Gabriel Bonnot de Mably (1709–1785) was a French philosopher, historian, and writer;. (Editor)

how England would be governed: whether by the divine right of Kings or by politicians elected under a restricted or wider franchise. The First Civil War (1642–1646) saw victory for Parliament and the imprisonment of the King, Charles I (1600–1649). The Second English Civil War (1648–1649) began when Charles organised a series of Royalist uprisings across England along a Scottish invasion and ended when the Parliamentarians under Oliver Cromwell (1599–1658) defeated the Royalists and Scots at the Battle of Preston. The activities of the King caused Parliament to debate whether to return him to power, with moderates willing to negotiate with him. This resulted in the Army marching on Parliament and conducting "Pride's Purge" (named after the commanding officer of the operation, Thomas Pride) in December 1648. Troops arrested forty-five Members of Parliament and kept 146 out of the chamber, leaving the Rump Parliament of seventy-five Members to set up, in the name of the people of England, a High Court of Justice for the trial of Charles I for treason. He was beheaded in 1649 as a "tyrant, traitor, murderer and public enemy" and the monarchy was replaced with, initially, the Commonwealth of England (1649–1653) and then the Protectorate (1653–1659) under Cromwell's personal rule.[19] Charles II (1630–1685) returned to the throne in 1660. The wars established the predominance of Parliament in constitutional matters and that a Monarch cannot govern without Parliament's consent although both notions were only legally established by the so-called "Glorious Revolution" of 1688 which established a constitutional monarchy. Kropotkin contrasts the English and French revolution in Chapter XIV of *The Great French Revolution*.]

Fechner, Gustav (1801–1887), German physiologist and philosopher. Although a metaphysician and a follower of Schelling, he nevertheless began to study psychology on purely physiological and experimental ground. Matter and Mind are for him of the same nature and only represent two different ways in which human intellect conceives the same phenomena. Their laws are the same. His *Elements of Psychophysics*, published in 1860, was epoch-making.

---

19   Also of note during the civil war were the Levellers, a republican and democratic movement dedicated to levelling out social and political inequalities as well as popular sovereignty and extended suffrage. In contrast, Cromwell wished to govern with a plutocratic Parliament voted in by an electorate limited to those with significant property. He viewed the Levellers with concern and repressed them: by 1650, they were no longer a threat. Interestingly, the Levellers were referred to by a Cromwellian opponent as "Switzerising anarchists." (Editor)

[**Fénelon**, François, (1651–1715), French Roman Catholic archbishop, theologian, poet and writer. He today is remembered as a defender of human rights and the author of *The Adventures of Telemachus* (1699). This work although set in Ancient Greek mythology was immediately recognised as a scathing rebuke to the autocratic reign of Louis XIV. It also denounces war, luxury and selfishness while proclaiming the brotherhood of man, co-operation and a federation of nations.]

[**Ferrari**, Giuseppe (1811–1876), Italian historian and political philosopher.]

Fourier, François [Marie] Charles (1772–1837), with Saint-Simon and Robert Owen, one of the three principal founders of socialism. The essence of his theory is that the full and free development of human nature is the first condition for attaining happiness and virtue; while misery and crime are the two inevitable results of the unnatural coercion and obstacles which our [current] society imposes on satisfaction of needs. Hence results the necessity of a total reconstruction of society on new co-operative bases (for more details, see [Part I,] Chapter XII of this work). Principal works: *Traiteé des Quatre Mouvements* [*Theory of the Four Movements*], 1808; *Traité de l'Association domestique-agricole* [*Treatise on the Domestic-Agricultural Association*, 1822; *Le Nouveau Monde Industriel* [*The New Industrial World*], 1829. Expounded by Charles Pellarin. A community [*familistère*] was founded in Guise by Godin which implemented a part of Fourier's ideas.[20] An important [socialist] school which counted amongst its ranks [Victor] Considerant, Pierre Leroux and many other talented writers which was developed by his followers.

[**Foxwell**, Herbert Somerton (1849–1936), English neo-classical economist and long-time professor at University College London. His introduction to Anton Menger's *The Right to the Whole Produce of Labour* is 105 pages long compared to Wenger's original 180 pages (excluding his prefaces, appendix and extensive bibliography).]

---

20   Jean-Baptiste André Godin (1817–1888) was a French industrialist, writer, and social innovator. A manufacturer of cast-iron stoves, he was heavily influenced by Charles Fourier and created an industrial and residential community called the *Familistère* (Social Palace) within Guise, a town in northern France. Created between 1856 and 1859, Godin spent twenty years developing the *Familistère* before, in 1880, converting it as he had long intended into a co-operative society owned by its workers called *L'Association coopérative du Capital et du Travail* (The Co-operative Association of Capital and Labour). (Editor)

[**Fustel de Coulanges**, Numa Denis (1830–1889), French historian.]

[Galilei, **Galileo** (1564–1642), Italian polymath: astronomer, physicist, engineer, philosopher, and mathematician. He played a major role in the scientific revolution of the seventeenth century and was tried by the Inquisition for his astronomical theories (such as that the sun was at the centre of the solar system and the planets revolve around it).]

[**Garibaldi**, Giuseppe (1807–1882), Italian general, politician, and nationalist. He personally commanded and fought in many military campaigns that led eventually to Italian unification.]

[**George**, Henry (1839–1897), American social reformer, politician and political economist. The most influential proponent of the land value tax, which he called the "single tax." He argued that people should own what they create but that everything found in nature, most importantly the land, belongs equally to all of humanity. As the value of land was created by the community, its rent belonged to the community. Principal works: *Progress and Poverty*, 1879; *Protection or Free Trade*, 1886; *The Condition of Labor*, 1891.]

[The **Girondists** were a moderate republican political faction during the French Revolution. So-named because their most prominent exponents in the Legislative Assembly and the National Convention were deputies from the Gironde. Accused of federalism by the Jacobins and repressed during the Terror. Kropotkin discusses their ideas and claims they were federalists in Chapters XXXIX, XL and XLII of *The Great French Revolution*.]

Godwin, William (1756–1836), English political writer and historian. His principal work is *An Enquiry Concerning Political Justice and its Influence on Morals and Happiness*, two volumes, 1793. By "political" justice, Godwin understands a situation in which the life of society is influenced by the principles of morality and truth. He demonstrates in his work that every government by the very fact of its existence, by its very nature, hinders the development of public morals; so also private ownership; and he sees the day when each one, free from all constraint and acting by virtue of his own wishes, will act for the good of the community because he will be guided by the principles of reason. Having very nearly been sentenced to forced labour along with his friends accused of Jacobin republicanism, Godwin removed from the second edition of his work, published in 1898, the communist pages that were in the first edition.

[**Goethe**, Johann Wolfgang von (1749–1832), German writer, artist and politician.]

[**Goschen**, George Joachim (1831–1907), British statesman, political economist and merchant banker. Was Chancellor of the Exchequer between 1887 and 1892.]

[**Gould**, Jason "Jay" (1836–1892), leading American railroad developer and speculator. One of the ruthless robber-barons of the latter half of the nineteenth century and known for proclaiming, "I can hire half the working class to kill the other half."]

[**Gray**, John (1799–1883), British socialist economist. Associated with the co-operative movement of Robert Owen for a time, he is best known as being one of the "Ricardian socialists" and proposing a central bank which would issue labour notes to ensure that workers received the full product of their labour. Principal works: *Lectures on Human Happiness*, 1825; *The Social System: A Treatise on the Principle of Exchange*, 1831; *An Efficient Remedy for the Distress of Nations*, 1842; *The Currency Question*, 1847; *Lectures on the Nature and Use of Money*, 1848.]

[**Greene**, William Batchelder (1819–1878), American mutualist and individualist anarchist. Promotor of free banking and active in labour reform movements, elected vice-president of the New England Labor Reform League and president of the Massachusetts Labor Union. Principal works: *Equality*, 1849; *Mutual Banking*, 1850; *Socialistic, Mutualistic, and Financial Fragments*, 1875.]

[**Grégoire**, Henri (1750–1831), French Roman Catholic priest, constitutional bishop of Blois and a revolutionary politician. Often referred to as Abbé Grégoire, he was an ardent abolitionist and ardent republican supporting the motion for the abolition of the monarchy with the memorable phrase, "Kings are in morality what monsters are in the world of nature."]

[**Grey**, Albert, 4th Earl Grey (1851–1917), British nobleman and politician. A staunch imperialist, in 1894 Grey inherited his Earldom from his uncle and took his place in the House of Lords whilst undertaking business ventures around the British Empire. Worked with Cecil Rhodes when Rhodes was seeking a royal charter for the Rudd Concession and became an administrator in Rhodesia.]

Grove, [William Robert] (1811–1896), Welsh physicist,[21] published in 1846 a remarkable article on the "Correlation of Physical Forces," and in 1856 a book on the same subject to prove that sound, heat, light, electricity, and magnetism are not separate "substances" or entities, as had been said until then, but merely various forms of vibrations of molecules which can be transformed into one another. Mechanical movement can be transformed into sound, light, heat, electricity, and magnetism. And, on the other hand, light, and electricity can be transformed into heat, magnetism, sound, and mechanical motion. He also ventured to ask whether gravity was not a result of these various kinds of vibrations? All the mechanical progress achieved during the second half of the nineteenth century was a series of applications of this fundamental principle of physics: that of the transformation of the various physical forces.

[**Grün**, Karl Theodor Ferdinand (1817–1887), German journalist and socialist. He played a prominent role in radical political movements leading up to and in the Revolution of 1848 and was an important figure in the democratic and socialist movements in Germany. While in exile in France, he befriended Proudhon whose writings had greatly influenced him and whose ideas he helped popularise amongst German radicals. Published in 1845 a history of francophone socialism, *Die sozialen Bewegungen in Frankreich und Belgien*. He was also a target of Marx's criticism.]

[The **Guelphs** and **Ghibellines** were factions supporting the Pope and the Holy Roman Emperor, respectively, in the city-states of central and northern Italy between the twelfth and fourteenth centuries.]

[**Guillaume**, James (1844–1916), anarchist writer and activist. A leading member of the Jura Federation of the International Workers' Association and associate of Bakunin. He took an active role in the organising of the St. Imier congress in 1872 which launched the (majority) anti-authoritarian International. His pamphlet *Idées sur l'organisation sociale* (*Ideas on Social Organisation*) was written in 1874 but not published until two years later. His monumental four volume work on the First International—*L'Internationale: Documents et Souvenirs, (1864–1878)* (*The International: Documents and Memories (1864–1878)*), 1905–1910—has sadly never been translated into English.]

[**Guizot**, François Pierre Guillaume (1787–1874), French historian and politician. He was Prime Minister of France immediately before the 1848

---

21   Kropotkin had Grove as "English" and this has been corrected. (Editor)

revolution and during the revolution unswervingly supported restricting suffrage to propertied men, telling those who wanted the vote to "enrich yourselves" (*enrichissez-vous*) through hard work and thrift.]

[**Guyau**, Jean-Marie (1854–1888), French philosopher and poet. His works primarily analyse and respond to modern philosophy, especially moral philosophy and moral theory. Kropotkin discusses his ideas in Chapter XIII of *Ethics*. Principal work: *Esquisse d'une morale sans obligation ni sanction* (*Sketch of a Morality without obligation or punishment*), 1884.]

Haeckel, Ernst [Heinrich Philipp August] (born 1834 [and died 1919]), German biologist and philosopher. He became a devoted follower of Darwin and published three remarkable works: *General Morphology*, 1866; *History of Natural Creation*, 1868; *Anthropogeny: or, the Evolutionary History of Man* [1874]. Later, he became a defender of "Monism" as a link between religion and science and published two works on it which had many repercussions but which did not come to the conclusions that we would have expected from him.[22]

Heat. See below: **Mechanical Theory of Heat**.

Hegel, Georg Wilhelm [Friedrich] (1770–1831), German metaphysical philosopher who exerted a great influence in Germany in the first third of the nineteenth century. The idea, for him, is the universal principle which manifests itself through various forms of being. His system consisted of three major parts: the first comprised logic—the science of the "pure idea" [or the "Idea in itself" (*Ides an sich*)]. The second, the Philosophy of Nature, dealt with the idea "externalised" in the facts of Nature [that is, the Idea has taken the form of its contradiction, "Being" and so the "Idea out of itself" (*Idee ausser sich*)]; and in the third part, the philosophy of Spirit [the "Idea in and for itself" (*Idee an und für sich*)], Hegel indicated how the pure idea, after having "exteriorised" itself in Nature, returned to itself as Spirit, and thus attained its perfect realisation (thesis, antithesis, synthesis). Principal works: *Phenomenology of Spirit*, 1807; [*Science of*] *Logic*, 1812; [*Lectures on*

---

22   The 1912 British edition lists these two works as *Monism as a Link between Religion and Science* and *The Riddle of the Universe*. It also clarifies what was meant: "he cast aside the religious dualism which opposes the heavens to the earth, the soul to the body, and so on; but instead of coming to a purely dynamic conception of the universe, as might have been expected from his previous works, he came to the metaphysical (Hegelian) conception of the 'Spirit' being an emanation of 'Matter.'" (Editor)

the] *Philosophy of Law, History, Nature* (1821 and posthumous).[23]

Helmholtz, Hermann Ludwig [Ferdinard von] (1821–1894), German physiologist. Published in 1847 his remarkable work *On the Conservation of Force* which was one of the foundations of the scientific materialist philosophy of the mid-nineteenth century and [*Treatise on*] *Physiological Optics* in 1856–1866.

[**Henry VIII** (1491–1547), second Tudor monarch of England. His rule was marked by belief in the divine right of Kings and a corresponding increase in centralisation, autocracy and repression. As well as ruling by royal prerogative, he broke with the Pope and declared himself Supreme Head of the Church of England. As well as seizing control of the guilds and their resources, he seized the property of the Catholic Church.]

[**Hess,** Moses (1812–1875), German-French-Jewish philosopher and socialist. A friend of Karl Marx, with whom he worked on the newspaper *Rheinische Zeitung*. Hess also introduced Engels to the communism of the early 1840s.]

Herzen, Alexander (1812–1870), Russian political writer. After being prosecuted in Russia for his opinions, he went to Paris where [during the 1848 Revolution] he helped Proudhon found the newspaper *Le Peuple* [*The People*]. Expelled from France after 13 June 1849. After the defeat of the European revolution of 1848, he wrote a book of supreme beauty, *From the Other Shore*, which contained a critique of the revolution from the socialist point of view. Moving later to London, he founded there the first free Russian printing press and [in 1852] the newspaper *The Bell* [*Kólokol*], in collaboration with his close friend Ogarev and Turgenev and which exerted a profound influence in Russia for the emancipation of the serfs.[24]

---

23 The 1912 British Edition adds: "The evil which this philosophy has done in driving scientific research out of the sound ways it had opened by the end of the eighteenth century, and giving a new authority both to the Biblical interpretation of Nature and to the reign of sweeping generalisations based upon the use of metaphysical 'words' having a vague and floating sense—can be best appreciated when we see how all the discoveries which were already prepared by the end of the eighteenth century were delayed in appearing for half a century; and also when we see the influence of this philosophy in political matters—the Hegelians maintaining that 'all that exists is rational,' and thus excusing the worst forms of political and religious reaction." (Editor)

24 Nikolay Platonovich Ogarev (1813–1877) was a Russian poet, historian, and political activist. He was deeply critical of the limitations of the Emancipation reform of 1861,

He attacked with rare force serfdom and autocracy. His principal works, translated into [English,] French and German, are *From the Other Shore* [1850], *Letters from France and Italy* [1852] and his autobiography, *My Past and Thoughts* [1867] which, besides its political significance, is of great literary beauty.

Hobbes, Thomas (1588–1679), English philosopher and political writer. Markedly royalist at the approach of the revolution of 1648, he was forced to take refuge in France. His principal works are: *De Cive*, 1642; *Leviathan or The Matter, Forme and Power of a Common Wealth Ecclesiasticall*, 1651; *De Corpore Politico*, 1658–1659. Right, he said, is force: nothing is just nor unjust in itself. He depicted primitive men as being in continual war with each other and he saw the chief cause of the origin of the State in the fear that men had of one another and in their common misery. A strong authority was needed to secure peace and to improve the living standards of men. Consequently, he was a resolute proponent of the absolute right of the king and at the same time an enemy of the Church as a political authority. He was the first, amongst well-known philosophers, to preach a materialist conception [of the Universe], absolutely devoid of religion.

[**Hobson**, John Atkinson (1858–1940), English economist, social scientist and critic of imperialism. His works include: *Problems of Poverty*, 1891; *Evolution of Modern Capitalism*, 1894; *The War in South Africa: Its Causes and Effects*, 1900; *Imperialism: a Study*, 1902; *The Industrial System*, 1909; *Confessions of an Economic Heretic*, 1938.]

[**Hodgskin**, Thomas (1787–1869), English writer on political economy and critic of capitalism. During the debates on banning worker's "combinations" (unions), he supported the right to organise. He used Ricardo's labour theory of value to denounce the exploitation of workers by capitalists in a series of lectures later published as *Labour Defended Against the Claims of Capital*, 1825. Other works include *Popular Political Economy*, 1827, and *Natural and Artificial Right of Property Contrasted*, 1832.]

[The House of **Hohenzollern** was the hereditary Kings of Prussia after it was founded in 1701 and Emperors of Germany after its unification in

---

claiming that the serfs were not free but had simply exchanged one form of serfdom for another. Nicholas Turgenev (1789–1871) was a Russian writer and political activist. Kropotkin, unlike in the 1912 British edition, fails to mention that Bakunin also worked with Herzen on *The Bell* as well as being close friends. Kropotkin discusses all three in more detail in *Russian Literature: Ideals and Realities* (293–302). (Editor)

1871. Defeat in World War I led to the German Revolution of 1918 and the establishment of a republic.]

Holbach, Paul Henri (1723–1789), French philosopher who worked with the Encyclopaedists to develop an account of the sciences on an openly materialist basis. He did this in his essential work, *Système de la Nature* [*The System of Nature*], 1770. In his subsequent works he demonstrated that religion is not only useless but also harmful to the morality and happiness of a nation. See *Le Christianisme dévoilé* [*Christianity Unveiled*], 1755; *La morale universelle*, 1776; *La politique naturelle* [1773].

[**Hugo**, Victor Marie (1802–1885) French poet, novelist and dramatist. The most well-known French Romantic writer, he was a passionate supporter of republicanism. His works touch upon most of the political and social issues and artistic trends of his time.]

[The **Hussites** (from the Czech for "Chalice People") were a Christian movement in the Kingdom of Bohemia following the teachings of Jan Hus (c. 1369–1415), a Czech priest, philosopher and early Christian reformer who was one of the forerunners of the Protestant Reformation. This predominantly religious movement also raised social issues. It contained various fractions including the radical Taborites who during the Hussite Wars joined local peasants to create a communal society. They announced the Millennium of Christ and declared there would be no more servants and masters, all property would be held in common, and there would be no more taxation.]

[The **Hussite Wars** of 1419 to 1434 (also known as the Bohemian Wars or the Hussite Revolution) were fought between the Hussites and various monarchs who sought to enforce the authority of the Roman Catholic Church against the Hussites. These wars began when the death of King Wenceslaus (1361–1419) saw a revolution sweep over the country with churches and monasteries destroyed, and Church property seized. Pope Martin V (1369–1431) called upon Catholics of the West to take up arms against the Hussites and there followed twelve years of warfare during which the Hussites defeated five crusades proclaimed against them by the Pope (1420, 1421, 1422, 1427, and 1431). The fighting ended when the moderate faction of the Hussites defeated the radical Taborites and agreed to submit to the authority of the King of Bohemia and the Church in return to being allowed to practice their own rites.]

Hutcheson, Francis (1694–1746), one of the most prominent representatives of the School of Philosophy known as Scottish Philosophy. He demonstrated that if we can divide the motives of our actions into egotistic and altruistic motives, it is nevertheless the latter as well as the actions that flow from them which meet our approval. This is because we possess a "moral sentiment," which comes from our nature. Principal work: *An Inquiry into the Original of Our Ideas of Beauty and Virtue*, 1725.

Huxley, Thomas Henry (1825–1895), English biologist, author of an excellent work on the comparative anatomy of animals. Became a friend and passionate supporter of Darwin and distinguished himself above all by his bold theories on evolution and the animal origin of man (*Man's Place in Nature*, 1863).

[The **Icarians** were followers of the French utopian socialist Étienne Cabet. Cabet led his followers to America to establish communities based on his ideas in 1848. In the 1870s, the Icarian colonists near Corning, Iowa, split over allowing women the right to vote. Those opposed—following Cabet on this issue—were called Old Icarians (*vieux icariens*) while those in favour were Young Icarians (*jeunes icariens*). The former carried the day, resulting in the latter moving to a new site on the same property. The Old Icarian community was no longer viable and disbanded in 1878 while the Young Icarians survived until 1898. The Corning Icarian community was the longest-lived non-religious communal living experiment in American history.]

Induction, Inductive-Deductive Method, the method of the natural sciences to which we owe the immense progress of science as a whole in the nineteenth century. It consists of the following:

1. By observations and experiment we seek to acquire a knowledge of the facts which relate to the subject under study.
2. These facts are discussed, and we see if they lead (Latin verb, *inducere*) to a generalisation (that is to say, a general statement concerned a great number or broad division of the facts), or a hypothesis which makes it possible to unite or encompass the observed facts. (For example, after observing many facts about the movements of the planets, Kepler made a generalisation and a hypothesis assuming that all the planets move around the sun along ellipses with the Sun occupying one of the foci).
3. From the hypothesis made (or hypotheses made), we deduce consequences (deductions: from the verb *deducere*) which allow us to predict, to anticipate new facts; these must be correct, if the hypothesis is right.

4. These deductions are compared with the observed facts referred to in paragraph 1. If necessary, new observations or experiments are made to ascertain whether our hypothesis is in agreement with facts observed or obtained in the case of experiments. The hypothesis is either rejected or modified, until we find one which agrees with the present state of our knowledge. (Thus, from the hypothesis of Kepler, we deduce the positions which each of the planets must occupy at a given moment in its movement around the sun and compare the calculated positions with the real positions. Since they agree, the hypothesis is confirmed. In addition, we calculate the orbiting *speeds* of planets resulting from the hypothesis in order to compare them with the facts). As for any minor differences that are found, the causes are again investigated by the same inductive method

5. Finally, a *hypothesis* is considered as a *law* when it has been confirmed in a mass of cases and when we have found the why, the *cause*—that is to say, a fact even more general than the fact established by induction. (For the planets, Kepler's hypothesis was accepted as a law—a *permanent relationship*—when it was confirmed for centuries—and the even more general fact of universal gravitation provided it with a primary explanation).

This method is the method of all the exact sciences.

Jacobins, name given to the members of a political club (*Amis de la Constitution* [*Friends of the Constitution*]) which exerted a great influence during the [Great French] Revolution of 1789–1793. It contained all the advanced, republican and revolutionary elements of the bourgeoisie. It courageously struggled against royalty and later supported Robespierre, it [also] fought against the Cordeliers club (to which Danton belonged as well as more advanced elements, such as Hébert, Chaumette and prominent members of the Commune of Paris). It was closed by the reaction after the 9th Thermidor [27 July 1794]. Today, the name Jacobin is often given to the advocates of a powerful, centralised revolutionary government.

[**Jacquerie,** a peasant uprising. The term comes from a revolt by peasants in northern France in the early summer of 1358 during which the nobles derided the peasants as "Jacques" because of their padded tunic called a "Jacque."]

[**James I** (1566–1625), Stuart King of Scotland (as James VI) from 1567 and King of England and Ireland (as James I) from the union of the Scottish and English crowns in 1603 until his death.]

[**Jaurès**, Jean (1859–1914), French socialist and historian.]

Joule, James [Prescott] (1818–1889), English physicist who was the first to find the exact measure of the mechanical equivalent of heat. (See *Mechanical theory of heat, Mayer*))

[**Jung**, Hermann (1830–1901), Swiss watchmaker and active in the international working-class movement. He took part in the Revolution of 1848–1849 in Germany and then was a member of the General Council of the First International (1864–1872). He opposed the decisions of the Hague Congress in 1872.]

[**Jurist**, an expert or writer on law. Usually an eminent judge, lawyer or legal scholar.]

[**Kabyles**, a Berber ethnic group native to Kabylia in the north of Algeria, one hundred miles east of Algiers. Under the pretext of a slight to their consul, the French invaded and captured Algiers in 1830. Settlers benefited from the French government's confiscation of communal land from tribal peoples, with the Kabyle's land being stolen from 1857 onwards (despite vigorous resistance, which continued as late as Mokrani's rebellion in 1871). Repression included the deportation of resisters to the labour camps of New Caledonia where they joined exiled Communards from the Paris Commune. The Kabyles were left behind when the Communards were granted an amnesty in 1879 and they were not able to return to Algeria until after 1904. Kropotkin discusses their institutions in Chapter IV ("Mutual Aid Among the Barbarians") of *Mutual Aid*.]

Kant, Emmanuel (1724–1804), German philosopher who exercised and still exercises a great influence. In his earlier works he was chiefly concerned with the natural sciences; but his great fame is based on his system of *critical* philosophy which he expounded in his *Critique of Pure Reason* (1781). He posed the question of recognising the principles and limitations of human knowledge, and he reached this conclusion. There exists, he said, two worlds: (1) The world of physical phenomena which occur in space and time, and which we know *only* by our senses, which means (according to his teaching of "critical, transcendental idealism") that they are only *phenomena*, having no reality "in itself"; and (2) the world of innate ideas—"the thing in itself"—which exists only in time (not in space). In other words, we have a matter given by our senses and a form given by our understanding which cannot make us know the absolute truth. In order to perceive the world of "things in themselves" which is hidden behind the phenomena perceived by our senses, he studied the origin of moral ideas (*Critique of Practical Reason*, 1788). He shows in this work that our reason possesses the ability of posing laws to itself. It is the duty of man equipped with moral sense to obey the *categorical imperative* (imperative, resulting from the very essence of our mind), which prescribes us to treat others in such a way that our action can become a general law. From his idea of innate moral sense, he deduces by means of his metaphysics the idea of free will, of immortality, and of God. In his philosophy of law he showed that the absolute respect for moral liberty was to be the foundation of all life in society and in the State, and indicated the establishment of this ideal of freedom was the goal of future historical development.

[**Kepler**, Johannes (1571–1630) German mathematician and astronomer. A key figure in the seventeenth century scientific revolution, best known for his laws of planetary motion.]

[**Kessler**, Karl Fedorovich (1815–1881), German-Russian zoologist. He was one of the first zoologists to propose that mutual aid, rather than mutual struggle, was the main factor in the evolution of a species in 1879 when he read a paper entitled *On the Law of Mutual Aid* to members of the Society of Naturalists of St. Petersburg. Kropotkin refers to his work in *Mutual Aid* and his theory of co-operation, like Kropotkin's, aimed at supplementing rather than replacing the standard interpretation of Darwin's theory of evolution.]

[**Kirchhoff**, Gustav Robert (1824–1887), German physicist. He contributed to the understanding of electrical circuits, spectroscopy, and the emission of black-body radiation by heated objects.]

[**Knowles**, James Thomas (1831–1908), English architect as well as founder (in 1877) and editor of *The Nineteenth Century* (in 1901 the words *And After* were added to the title). The monthly journal was intended to publish debate by leading intellectuals and became very influential. Knowles was a personal friend of Kropotkin's and the journal published many articles by him on both anarchism and scientific issues.]

[**Koenigswarter**, Louis-Jean (1814–1878), French jurist and economist.]

Kostomaroff, Nicholas (1817–1885), Russian historian, founder of the Federalist school in [the study of] Russian history.

[The **Krupp** family, German dynasty from Essen famous for their production of steel, artillery, ammunition, and other armaments.]

[**L'Ange**, François-Joseph (1743–1793) utopian socialist and communalist propagandist in Lyons during the Great French Revolution. His ideas may have influenced Fourier who stayed in Lyons during the revolution: "Particularly interesting to the student of Fourier are the various utopian projects and the proposals for fixing the price of bread advanced between 1790 and 1793 by the quasi-socialist justice of the peace François-Joseph L'Ange. The central idea of L'Ange, who was a victim of the Terror in 1793, was that to avoid speculation in basic foodstuffs a national share-holding company should be formed through which each year the totality of French consumers would pay a fixed and determined price for the nation's entire harvest. Grain and other basic commodities would then be distributed through a network of associations or *centuries*, each consisting of a hundred families and each with its own warehouse, school, and assembly." (Jonathan Beecher, *Charles Fourier: The Visionary and His World* [Berkeley/London: University of California Press, 1986], 39). Kropotkin sketches his ideas in Chapter LIX of *The Great French Revolution*. See also Hubert Bourgin, *Fourier: Contribution a l'etude du socialisme francais* (Paris: Sociêtê Nouvelle de Librairie et d'Edition, 1905), 94–101; Félix Duhem, "François-Joseph L'Ange 1743–1793," *Annales historiques de la Révolution français* (January-March 1951), 38–47; and *Oeuvres* (edited by Paul Leutrat, Paris, 1968).]

Lamarck, Jean Baptiste (1744–1829), French naturalist. Laid the foundations for a new classification of plants and animals (*La flore française* [*French Flora*], 1778, and *Histoire naturelle des animaux sans vertèbres* [*Natural History of Animals without Vertebrae*], 1816–1822). In his *Philosophie Zoologique* [*Zoological Philosophy*] (1809), he formulated the idea of transformism, that is to say, of the continual variation of plant and animal species, and of their gradual evolution under the action of the environment and the use, or non-use, of specific organs which results from that. This idea met with strong opposition from official academic science, especially from Cuvier, so that academies and universities continued to preach the invariability of species ([a position] to which Comte also subscribed) until public opinion, aroused by the work of Darwin and the general awakening of the natural sciences in 1855–1862, forced scientists and universities to change their opinion.

[**Lanessan**, Jean-Marie Antoine Louis (1843–1919), French naturalist, physician and politician.]

[**Lankester**, Sir Edwin Ray (1847–1929), British zoologist.]

[**Lansdowne**, Lord (1845–1927), Henry Charles Keith Petty-Fitzmaurice, 5th Marquess of Lansdowne, British politician. He was the fifth Governor General of Canada, Viceroy of India, Secretary of State for War, and Secretary of State for Foreign Affairs (1900–1905).]

[**Lao Tzu**, legendary Chinese philosopher and writer. He is the reputed author of the *Tao Te Ching* and the founder of philosophical Taoism. Although now usually considered a legendary figure (he is a deity in religious Taoism and traditional Chinese religions), he is usually dated to around the sixth century BCE. On his libertarian ideas: Brain Morris, "Lao Tzu and Anarchism," *Ecology and Anarchism: Essays and Reviews on Contemporary Thought* (Malvern Wells: Images Publishing Ltd, 1996); John Clark, "Master Lao and the Anarchist Prince," *The Anarchist Moment: Reflections on Culture, Nature and Power* (Montréal-Buffalo: Black Rose Books, 1986).]

Laplace, Pierre (1719–1827), one of the greatest astronomers and mathematicians of all ages. His principal works are *Exposition du système du monde* [*Exposition of a System of the Universe*], 1796, in which he gave a mechanical explanation of the origin of our solar system; *Mécaniqne celeste* [*Treatise of Celestial Mechanics*], in five volumes 1799–1825, his masterpiece, in which he gave the mechanical explanation of the system of the universe by universal gravitation; *Théorie analytique des probabilités* [*Analytical Theory of Probabilities*], 1812, and a large number of essays. All his great works are a model of clear thought and lucidity.

[**Lassalle**, Ferdinand Johann Gottlieb (1825–1864), German State socialist. Helped create the General German Workers' Association in 1863 which aimed to win universal suffrage by peaceful and legal means as well as State aid for co-operatives. He was willing to work and compromise with the Imperial powers to achieve reforms. His followers merged the Association with the Marxist Social Democratic Workers Party to form the Socialist Workers Party of Germany in 1875, renamed to the Social Democratic Party of Germany in 1890.]

[**Lassalleans** were supporters of Ferdinand Lassalle or his ideas.]

Lavoisier, Antoine (1743–1794), great French chemist, was the first to discover that water is composed of the two gases oxygen and hydrogen. Worked hard to develop a theory of the phenomena of combustion, heat, and fermentation, and created in 1786 a new system of chemical nomenclature which contributed immensely to the development of chemistry.[25] Principal work *Traité élémentaire de chimie* [*Elementary Treatise on Chemistry*], 1789.

[**Lavrov**, Pyotr Lavrovich (1823–1900), Russian theorist of narodism (or Russian populism), philosopher, publicist and sociologist.]

[**Leo**, Heinrich (1799–1878), Prussian historian. Published a history of the Italian states in five volumes, 1829–1832.]

[**Leroux**, Pierre (1797–1871), French philosopher and follower of Saint-Simon. He introduced the term "socialism" into French political discourse in an 1834 essay entitled "Individualism and Socialism." The son of an artisan, he helped found *Le Globe*, the official organ of the Saint-Simonist community of which he was a prominent member. After the outbreak of the revolution of 1848 he was elected to the Constituent Assembly, and in late 1849 to the Legislative Assembly. At the turn of 1849 he, along with Louis Blanc, was involved in a polemic with Proudhon over the nature of socialism and the State (see, for example, "Letter to Pierre Leroux" in *Property is Theft!*).]

[**Levy**, Hermann (1797–1871), German economist.]

Lewes, George Henry (1817–1878), English physiologist, ardent disciple of Comte; was one of those who laid the foundations of a psychology based on the physiological study of the brain and nerve centres. Principal works: *Physiology of Common Life*, 1870; *The Problems of Life and Mind* [in five volumes],1877; *The Physical Basis of Mind*, 1877, He also wrote a *Biographical History of Philosophy*, 1845, a *Life of Goethe* [in 1855] and *Comte's Philosophy of the Sciences*, 1853.

Littré, Maximilian-Emile (1801–1884), French positivist, doctor, and publicist who later devoted himself to the in-depth study of languages and literature. One of the principal representatives of Comte's philosophy, which he did much to popularise by publishing *Revue positive* [*Positive Review*] and a series of articles and books on the subject. Author of the great *Dictionnaire de la langue française* [*Dictionary of the French Language*], a monumental book to which he devoted 30 years of work.

[**Lombroso**, Cesare (1835–1909) Italian criminologist. Argued that criminality was inherited and someone "born criminal" could be identified by

---

25   The 1912 British edition notes: "Was the first to prove the indestructibility of matter by experiment." (Editor)

physical defects such as a sloping forehead, ears of unusual size, asymmetry of the face or cranium, excessively long arms, etc. While popular for a time, his ideas were soon completely discredited (see Stephen Jay Gould, *The Mismeasure of Man* [London: Penguin Books, 1996]). Kropotkin mentions him because he dedicated a great deal of his research, study, and writing to the analysis of anarchists including such works as "The Physiognomy of the Anarchists" (*The Monist* I: 3) in 1890, "Anarchy and its Heroes" in 1897 and "A Paradoxical Anarchist" (*Popular Science Monthly*, volume 50) in January 1900. In one article, he asserted "that the anarchist movement is composed for the most part (except for a very few exceptions, like Reclus and Kropotkin) of criminals and madmen."]

Lomonosov, Michael (1711–1766), Russian writer of whom it was rightly said that he represented a university in himself. One of the creators of Russian science and literature. Wrote odes in verse, a Russian grammar (which had not existed until then), and a physical geography of the polar regions, wherein he had already expressed the mechanical theory of heat, as well as a large number of scientific articles.

[**Louis XIV** (1638–1715), King of France from 1643 until his death. Known as the Sun King (*le Roi-Soleil*) and believer in the divine right of kings, Louis accelerated the work of his predecessors in creating a centralised State, governed by him from the capital. He supposedly proclaimed "I am the state" ("L'état, c'est moi.").]

[**Louis XV** (1710–1774), King of France from 1715 until his death.]

[**Louis XVI** (1754–1793), King of France from 1774 to his death by guillotine in 1793.]

[**Louis Philippe** (1773–1850), King of the French from 1830 to 1848. He was proclaimed king after his cousin Charles X (1757–1836) was forced to abdicate in the wake of the July Revolution of 1830. His government, known as the July Monarchy, was dominated by members of the wealthy French elite and numerous former Napoleonic officials and abdicated after the outbreak of the French Revolution of 1848.]

[**Luchaire**, Denis Jean Achille (1846–1908), French historian and professor of medieval history at the Sorbonne.]

[**Luther**, Martin (1483–1546), German professor of theology, composer, priest, monk and a key figure in the Reformation.]

[The **Lutheran Reformation**, better known as the Protestant Reformation or simply as the **Reformation**, was a schism from the Roman Catholic Church initiated by Martin Luther and continued by John Calvin (1509–1564) and other early Protestant Reformers in sixteenth-century Europe. It is usually considered to have occurred between 1517 (with the *Ninety-five Theses* published by Martin Luther) and 1648 (when the Peace of Westphalia ended the Thirty Years' War).]

[The **Luxembourg Commission** was established by a decree of the provisional government of the Second Republic on 28 February 1848. It was an official commission of inquiry into the conditions of French workers in response to the radical upheavals of that year, convened at the Palais de Luxembourg and headed by Louis Blanc. An assembly of workers' delegates, it aimed to create workers associations to emancipate labour. While Proudhon was critical of some of its more centralised ideas, he worked with its members to create a Bank of the People in 1849 (see, for example, "Bank of the People," *Property is Theft!*).]

Lyell, Charles (1797–1875), Scottish geologist.[26] His work, *Principles of Geology*, 1838, beautifully written, greatly increased in subsequent editions and translated into many languages represents an epoch [making work] in geology. He demonstrated that the modifications of the earth's surface—which at the beginning of the nineteenth century were attributed ([by] Cuvier, L. von Buch) to sudden cataclysms which destroyed the plants and animals inhabiting the Earth after which a new "creation" of living beings took place—had been accomplished by the accumulation of the effects of slow physical changes occurring everywhere on the surface of the Earth before our very eyes. When Darwin published his work *On the Origin of the Species* in 1859, his friend Lyell eagerly supported it and published a second remarkable book, *The Antiquity of Man*, 1863, in which he accepted the fact of a *glacial period* which scholars persisted in denying up to them (attributing the deposits of this period of the "flood" mentioned in the biblical traditions). He thus confirmed the idea expressed in France by some pioneers (Boucher de Pertes[27]) that man existed on Earth at a time

---

26   Kropotkin lists Lyell as "English" in spite being born near Dundee. (Editor)

27   Jacques Boucher de Crèvecoeur de Perthes (1788–1868), sometimes known as Boucher de Perthes, was a French archaeologist notable for his discovery around 1830 of flint tools in the gravels of the Somme valley. In 1847 he commenced the publication of his monumental three volume work, *Antiquités celtiques et antédiluviennes*, in which he was the first to establish the existence of man in the Pleistocene or early Quaternary period. (Editor)

when Europe still had a glacial climate and was inhabited by mammoths, reindeers, cave bears, and other large animals accustomed to a very cold climate. This work, bold for its time and specially for England, exerted a profound influence on the development of modern science and helped to rid it of the obstacles imposed upon it by the churches.

[**Lysis**, pseudonym of financier and moderate socialist Eugène Letailleur (1869–1927) whose 1908 book *Contre l'Oligarchie Financière en France.* (*Against the Financial Oligarchy in France*) analysed finance capital and its wider impact on society.]

[**Machiavelli**, Niccolò di Bernardo dei (1469–1527), Italian historian, politician, diplomat, philosopher, and writer based in Florence during the Renaissance. He is most famous for writing *The Prince* which advocated the employment of immorality, cunning, and duplicity in statecraft.]

[**MacKay**, John Henry (1864–1933), German-raised individualist anarchist. The author of *The Anarchists* (1891), writer for Benjamin Tucker's *Liberty*, biographer of Max Stirner—*Max Stirner. Sein Leben und sein Werk*, 1898—and a key populariser of Stirner's ideas.]

[**Macrosty**, Henry William (1865–1941), civil servant and statistician. Reformist State socialist who served on the Fabian Society's executive from 1895 to 1907, he wrote extensively on monopolies and trusts. Principal works: *The growth of monopoly in English industry*, 1899; *Trusts and the State: A Sketch of Competition*, 1901; *The Trust Movement in British Industry: A Study of Business Organisation*, 1907.]

Maine, Henry Sumner (1822–1888), Scottish[28] jurist and explorer of the life and common law of the village commune. His work *Ancient Law*, published in 1861, caused a sensation in western Europe where, under the influence of Roman law, there was no interest in this subject. Other works: *Village-Communities in the East and West* [1871], *Lectures on the Early History of Institutions* [1875]. Academia in France continues, unfortunately, to ignore the work of the school of law created by Maine.

[**Marat**, Jean-Paul (1743–1793), radical journalist and politician during the French Revolution. His journalism was renowned for its fiery character and urging of basic reforms for the poor. He was a vigorous defender of the *sans-culottes* and was assassinated in his bathtub by Charlotte Corday, a

---

28   Again, Kropotkin has "English." (Editor)

Girondist sympathiser.]

[**Marr**, Friedrich Wilhelm Adolph, (1819–1904), German agitator, political journalist and publisher of the satirical magazine *Mephistopheles* (1847/48–1852). Part of the leftists of the radical-democratic "party," he was a delegate to the National Assembly in Frankfurt after the March Revolution of 1848.]

Marx, Karl (1818–1883), German economist, head of the school of modern social-democracy. Leaving Germany as a political refugee to France in the 1840s, he published in Paris with Ruge,[29] a review (two issues published) in which his socialist articles were soon noticed in radical and socialist circles. Expelled from France in 1844 and from Belgium in 1848, he initially returned to Germany (1848–1849), where he published the [newspaper] *Rheinische Zeitung*. With the reaction taking over, he quickly left Germany again and then, with Engels, settled in London. At the founding of the International [Workers' Association], in September 1864, he was invited to take part in the drafting of its Statutes and was nominated to be a member of the provisional General Council. He soon became the most influential member of the General Council of the Association, which sat in London. His principal works are: *The Poverty of Philosophy*, 1847, reply to Proudhon's *Philosophy of Poverty* ([*System of*] *Economic Contradictions*); *Communist Manifesto*, 1848 (on its probable origin, see W. Tcherkesoff's *Pages of Socialist History*, 1896, and Professor Andler's *Introduction historique et commentaires* (*Historical Introduction and Comments*), Paris, 1901); [*A Contribution to the*] *Critique of Political Economy*, 1857, and especially *Capital*, the first volume of which appeared in 1867; it was translated into French by J. Roy in 1872–1875, and was later followed by three other volumes, the second of which was already posthumous.[30] The first volume of *Capital*, which contains the well-known analysis of the genesis of capital [namely, Part 8: Primitive Accumulation], has become the foundation of the [economic] ideas of Social Democracy.

Maurer, Georg [Ludwig von] (1790–1872), founder in Germany of the

---

29   Arnold Ruge (1802–1880) was a German philosopher and political writer. In Paris, he briefly co-edited the *Deutsch–Französische Jahrbücher* with Karl Marx. Having little sympathy with Marx's socialist theories, they soon parted ways. (Editor)

30   Volumes 2 and 3 of *Capital* were published by Engels from notes left by Marx in 1885 and 1894, respectively. *Theories of Surplus Value* (known as the forth volume of *Capital*) was published in three books by leading German Marxist Karl Kautsky (1854–1938) between 1905 and 1910. (Editor)

school which carefully studied the village and urban commune and produced a large number of serious works on this subject. Principal works: *Einleitung zur Geschichte der Mark-, Hof-, Dorf- und Stadt-Verfaßung und der öffentlichen Gewalt* [*Introduction to the history of the mark-, household-, village- and city-Constitution and the public force*], 1854; and *Geschichte der Markenverfassung in Deutschland* [*History of the Organisation of the Mark in Germany*], 1856, followed by several others on the town and village. The mark being communal property of land.

[**Mayer**, Julius Robert (1814–1878), German physician and physicist. One of the founders of thermodynamics and developed in 1841 one of the original statements of the conservation of energy or what is now known as one of the first versions of the first law of thermodynamics, namely that "energy can be neither created nor destroyed."]

[**Maxim**, Hiram Stevens (1840–1916), American-born British inventor who created the Maxim Gun (called "the weapon most associated with the British imperial conquest"). He established the Maxim Gun Company which was taken over by Vickers, Sons and Company in 1897 to form Vickers, Sons, and Maxim.]

Mechanical Theory of Heat. This theory explains the various phenomena of heat by demonstrating that they are all the results of the vibrations of the molecules in the bodies whose temperature we see increase. When the sum of these invisible vibrations increases in a piece of iron, or in a liquid, or in some gas, we see the temperature of this gas, this liquid or that solid increase. Heat is only a mode of movement. This is why any friction produces heat. When powerful brakes stop the rotation of the wheels of a train, their movement turns into friction on the rails and reappears in the heating of the rails and wheels, and in the form of sparks which are iron particles heated and torn from the rails.

The exact quantity of movement necessary to raise the temperature of a litre of water by one degree centigrade is called "the *mechanical* equivalent of heat."

The mechanical theory of heat was already foreseen, and even partly formulated, in the eighteenth century. Later on, in the twenties of the nineteenth century, it was expressed by the engineer *Seguin* the elder, a man of great talent, whose ideas were not appreciated by his contemporaries.[31] The

31   In a note to the French translation of Grove's *The Correlation of Physical Forces*, Marc Séguin the elder pointed out that his uncle "the citizen Montgolfier" (*Journal des Mines*, vol. XIII, no. 73) had proclaimed in the year 1800 "that movement cannot be

German physician *Mayer* (1845) formulated the mechanical theory of heat in a precise and complete way, but he could not get it accepted by scientists either. *Joule* made exact experiments in 1856 to measure the mechanical equivalent of heat. It was only in 1860 that this theory, which represented the greatest conquest of science in the nineteenth century, was finally understood and generally accepted. Its applications in science and industry are countless.

[**Mendéléeff**, Dmitri (1834–1907), a remarkable Russian chemist, best known for his discovery of the "Periodic Law of Elements." It is known that all the bodies which we find on the earth's surface, whether living or dead matter, are composed of some eighty or ninety different bodies, which cannot be decomposed, and therefore are named *elements*. These enter among themselves into an infinite number of combinations. The *elements* Mendéléeff discovered, if we write them down in the order of the increasing complexity of their molecules, can be disposed in a table containing eight vertical columns and twelve horizontal lines. If such a table is made, it appears that all the elements placed in each column will have some chemical properties in common; so also all the elements inscribed in each horizontal row—the energy of the chemical properties increasing in each row as you go from Column 1 to Column 8. This suggests the idea (1) that the molecule of each element is probably a complex system of still smaller molecules (or rather atoms) in continual movement round each other—like the planet Jupiter or Saturn, with their several moons; and (2) that in the structure of these systems there is a certain *periodicity*, i.e., a repetition of some scheme of structure. This discovery has immensely helped the development of chemistry. His conception of the cosmic ether as matter, the atoms of which are in vibrations so rapid that they cannot be fixed and kept in more or less permanent chemical combinations, though yet less known, is equally important.][32]

[**Menger**, Anton (1841–1906), Austrian university professor, juridical expert and social theorist. The English-language translation of his principal work has the full title *The Right to the Whole Produce of Labour; the origin and development of the theory of labour's claim to the whole product of industry* (London: MacMillan and Co., 1899). It contains an extensive discussion of the ideas of such noted anarchists as Godwin and Proudhon; British socialist William Thompson and his contemporaries, as well as Karl Marx and other German socialists.]

---

destroyed or created, that force and heat are expressions, in different forms, of one and the same cause."

32   Entry from the 1912 British edition. (Editor)

[The **Merovingians** were a Salian Frankish dynasty that ruled the Franks for nearly 300 years in a region known as Francia in Latin, beginning in the middle of the fifth century. Their territory largely corresponded to ancient Gaul as well as the Roman provinces of Raetia, Germania Superior and the southern part of Germania.]

[**Michelangelo** di Lodovico Buonarroti Simoni (1475–1564), Italian sculptor, painter, architect, and poet of the High Renaissance who exerted an unparalleled influence on the development of Western art.]

[**Michelet**, Jules (1798–1874), French historian. Principal work: *Histoire de France* (1833–1867).]

Mill, John Stuart (1806–1878), English economist and philosopher. One of the most eminent representatives of "empiricism" (that is to say, research based on observation and experimentation) in his *A System of Logic* where he admirably developed the theory of inductive method (see entry above). Author of *Principles of Political Economy*, 1848; *On Liberty*, 1859; [*Considerations on*] *Representative Government* [1861] and *A System of Logic*, 1843.

Moleschott, Jacob (1822–1893), Dutch materialist physiologist. Wrote in German several popular works to spread materialist philosophy, amongst which *Kreisleuf des Lebens* (*The Cycle of Life*), had a great impact.

[**Money**, Leo George Chiozza (1870–1944), Italian-born British economist and Liberal politician. Noted for his 1905 work *Riches and Poverty*, an analysis of the distribution of wealth in the United Kingdom (revised in 1912).]

[**Morizet**, André (1876–1942), French socialist and founding member of the Communist Party, he re-joined the Socialist Party and was elected to the Senate from 1927 to 1942.]

[**Napoleon I** (1769–1821), French military and political leader. Napoleon Bonaparte rose to prominence during the latter stages of the French Revolution and its associated wars in Europe. He overthrew the French Directory, replacing it with the French Consulate on 9 November 1799 (18th *Brumaire*, Year VIII under the French Republican Calendar). Initially installing himself as First Consul, five years later the French Senate proclaimed him Emperor Napoleon I (1804–1815).]

[**Napoleon III** (1808–1873), the last monarch of France. Louis-Napoleon Bonaparte was the nephew of Napoleon Bonaparte and was elected President of the Second Republic in December 1848. He organised a coup on 2 December 1851 and disbanded the National Assembly. This was overwhelmingly approved in a plebiscite and one year later another plebiscite confirmed the creation of the Second Empire and his ascension to the throne as Napoleon III. His rule ended with France's defeat in Franco-Prussian war of 1871 and the declaration of the Third Republic.]

[**Nettlau**, Max Heinrich Hermann Reinhardt (1865–1944), German anarchist and historian. He wrote numerous biographies of famous anarchists, a seven volume history of anarchism and contributed to the anarchist press on a host of subjects beyond the merely historical or biographical. He is best-known in English for *A Short History of Anarchism* (London: Freedom Press, 1996).]

[**Neymarck**, Alfred (1848–1921), French economist and statistician. Founder and editor of the newspaper *Le Rentier* as well as president and laureate of the Statistical Society of Paris. Works include *La Statistique Internationale de Valeurs Mobilières*, 1911.]

[**Nicholas II** (1868–1918), last Tsar (Emperor) of Russia. He ruled from 1894 until his abdication in March 1917 as a result of the February Revolution. Due to anti-Semitic pogroms, the brutal repression of popular protests and strikes, the violent suppression of the 1905 Revolution and the execution of political opponents, he was known as Nicholas the Bloody.]

[**Nietzsche**, Friedrich Wilhelm (1844–1900), German philosopher, cultural critic, and poet. He attacked religion, morality, and contemporary culture. His philosophy was based on the idea of "life-affirmation," questioning of all doctrines that hamper the development of the individual. Morality was particularly attacked as it had a negative impact on the flourishing of what Nietzsche called "higher men" (as it allowed the "weak" to take power over the "strong"). The "higher man" (*Übermensch*) is solitary and deals with others only instrumentally, as means to an end. While denouncing the State, he wrote negatively of anarchists. In spite of this, Nietzsche was read with interest by a number of anarchists for his critique of conventional morality.]

[**Nihilism** was a Russian movement in the latter half of the nineteenth century which rejected all authority. Their name derives from the Latin *nihil* ("nothing"). It opposed the abusive nature of the Eastern Orthodox

Church, the Tsarist monarchy and the aristocracy. The movement took its name from the 1862 novel *Fathers and Sons* by the Russian author Ivan Turgenev (1818–1883) whose main character, Eugene Bazarov, described himself as a Nihilist. Bazarov is strident in his profession of faith in nothing but science and he "takes a negative attitude towards all the institutions of the present time and he throws overboard all the conventionalities and the petty lies of ordinary society life."[33] The movement later became the *Narodnik* movement (Russian Populists) which argued that the newly freed serfs had become wage-slaves and that the bourgeoisie had joined the land-owners in exploiting all toilers. Rejecting the Marxist view that capitalism needed to develop in Russia before socialism could be created, they viewed the village commune (the *mir*) as a key means of creating socialism.]

[**Nys**, Ernest (1851–1920), Belgian jurist and essayist. Principal works: *Les origines du droit international* (*The origins of International Law*), 1894; *Études de droit international et de droit politique* (*Studies in international law and political law*), 1896.]

Owen, Robert (1771–1858), the principal founder of English socialism and one of the principal promoters of the co-operative movement and of trade unionism, which from 1830–1831 he endeavoured to make national and even international. He tried to apply his principles in a co-operative factory and village [New Harmony, in Indiana, 1825], and published a mass of pro-paganda and popular books. His principal works are: [*A New View of Society*, 1814]; *Outline of the Rational System* [*of Society*], 1830; *The Book of the New Moral World* [1845], and *Revolution in the Mind and Practice of the Human Race* [1849]. He was, with Fourier and Saint-Simon, one of the three great founders of modern socialism, representing voluntary, non-statist socialism and exerted a profound influence on minds, especially in England, where his ideas inspired, to this day, a large number of radicals.[34]

[The **Panama** scandal involved abuses and corruption in the management of the *Compagnie Universelle du Canal Interocéanique*, formed in France in 1879 to dig the Panama Canal. The failure of the project ruined tens of thousands of small shareholders. A judicial examination into it re-vealed that the company, finding itself in financial difficulties, had bribed

---

33 Peter Kropotkin, *Russian Literature: Ideals and Realities*, 107. (Editor)

34 As may be expected, Kropotkin referred to "England" throughout this passage. However, Owen and had a wide influence across all of Britain. In addition, he began to apply his ideas when he was the part-owner and manager of the New Lanark mills in Scotland. (Editor)

influential officials, politicians and newspaper editors and it uncovered corruption deep within the bureaucracy of the French Third Republic. In spite of a public outcry, almost all of the officials entangled in the scandal escaped punishment, and only the minor defendants were convicted. The term "Panama" came to denote large-scale fraud and swindles.]

[The **Peasants' Revolt** began in May 1381 and was triggered by the imposition of a poll tax of twelve pence for every adult, regardless of wealth. The revolt was not only about taxation, as the peasants also sought increased liberty and other social reforms. Groups from across England converged on London where they attacked government targets, opened prisons, and destroyed legal records. King Richard II promised to implement all demands but after his officials murdered Wat Tyler during negotiations on June 15 he revoked all the concessions he had made. The wider revolt was suppressed and by November at least 1,500 people had been executed for treason or killed in battle.]

[**Pecqueur**, Constantin (1801–1887), French socialist and politician. First a follower of Saint-Simon and then Fourier, he developed his own theories based on State ownership of the means of production. During the 1848 Revolution he was an ally of Louis Blanc.]

[**Pellarin**, Charles (1804–1883), French naval doctor, utopian socialist, sociologist, anthropologist and journalist. Originally a follower of Saint-Simon, he joined the Fourierists and contributed to several of their journals (including *La Réforme Industrielle*, *Le Phalanstère* and *La Démocratie Pacifique*, edited by Victor Considerant). He wrote the first biography of Fourier, entitled *Fourier: Sa Vie et sa Théorie* (*Fourier: His life and his Theory*).]

[A **phalanstery** (*phalanstère*) was a self-contained structure which housed a co-operative community. The idea was developed in the early 1800s by Charles Fourier who envisioned a highly organised and regulated community living under one roof and working together for mutual benefit. A member's quality of life would vary with their work, "talent" and "capital" (amount invested). Everyone would work while a spirit of competition would exist in the shape of emulation.]

[**Post**, Albert Hermann (1839–1895), German jurist and judge. Considered a pioneer of the anthropology of laws.]

[**Price**, William Hyde (unknown), American academic and economist. Principal work: *The English patents of monopoly*, 1906.]

Proudhon, Pierre-Joseph (1809–1865), French socialist, the most powerful critic of the capitalist system and the State, as well as statist and authoritarian theories of communism and socialism. On his "mutualism" system, see [Part I,] Chapter X. Principal works: *Qu'est-ce que la propriété?* [*What is Property?*], 1840; *Système des contradictions économiques* [*System of Economic Contradictions*], 1846; *Confessions d'un révolutionnaire* [*Confessions of a Revolutionary*], 1849; *Idée générale de la révolution au XIXe siècle* [*General Idea of the Revolution in the Nineteenth Century*], 1851; *De la justice dans la Révolution et dans l'Église* [*On Justice in the Revolution and the Church*], 1858; *De la capacité politique des classes ouvrières* [*On the Political Capacity of the Working Class*], 1865.[35]

[**Rabelais**, François (unknown–1553), French Renaissance writer, humanist, physician, humanist, monk and Greek scholar. He wrote of the utopia *Abbey of Thélème* in the book *Pantagruel* (c. 1532), a monastic institution that is based on the principle "Do What Thou Wilt" and rejected poverty, celibacy and obedience.]

[**Raphael** (1483–1520), Italian painter and architect of the High Renaissance.]

[**Reclus**, Élisée-Jean-Jacques (1830–1905) renowned French geographer, writer and anarchist. An associate of Bakunin, he took an active role in the Paris Commune (for which he was exiled). He played an important role in the development of communist-anarchism and was as famous as Kropotkin within the movement.]

[The **Reformation**, see **Lutheran Reformation**.]

[**Rhodes**, Cecil John (1853–1902) British businessman, mining magnate and politician. An ardent believer in, and practitioner of, British imperialism, Rhodes and his British South Africa Company seized vast swathes of land to found the southern African territory of Rhodesia

---

35   Surprisingly little of Proudhon's extensive writings have been translated into English: the first two memoirs on property (*What is Property?* and *Letter to Blanqui*), volume 1 of *System of Economic Contradictions*, *General Idea of the Revolution* and Part 1 of *The Federative Principle*. Extracts from all these works, and many others, are included in *Property is Theft!*. His standard biography is George Woodcock's *Pierre-Joseph Proudhon: A Biography* (Montréal: Black Rose, 1987) while the best introduction to his ideas and their context is K. Steven Vincent's *Pierre-Joseph Proudhon and the Rise of French Republican Socialism* (Oxford: Oxford University Press, 1984). (Editor)

(now Zimbabwe and Zambia), which the company named after him in 1895.]

Ricardo, David (1772–1823), English economist of the school considered as "classical" by university science. Developed, after Adam Smith, the theory that the necessary quantity of labour is the measure of [exchange] the value [of a commodity] and a theory of ground rent to which the university economists attribute scientific value. Principal work: *On the Principles of Political Economy and Taxation* (1817).

[**Robespierre**, Maximilien François Marie Isidore de (1758–1794), French lawyer and politician. One of the best-known and most influential figures of the French Revolution, a bourgeois republican influenced by Rousseau and Montesquieu, he was a member of the Estates-General, the Constituent Assembly and the Jacobin Club. A member of the Committee of Public Safety during the Reign of Terror, for which he was arrested and executed.]

[**Rogers**, James Edwin Thorold (1823–1890), English economist, historian, and Liberal politician. Principal works: *Six Centuries of Work and Wages: The History of English Labour* in two volumes, 1884; *The Economic Interpretation of History*, 1888; *A history of agriculture and prices in England: from the year after the Oxford parliament (1259) to the commencement of the continental war (1793)* in seven volumes, 1866–1902.]

[The **Romanovs** ruled Russia from 1613 until the February Revolution of 1917.]

[**Rothschild**, Baron (1840–1915), patriarch of a famously wealthy British banking family and often used in socialist propaganda as a personification of the ruling class or the rich.]

Rousseau, Jean Jacques (1712–1778), French [speaking] philosopher and socialist writer.[36] One of the precursors of the Great [French] Revolution, whose democratic and deist ideas exercised a profound influence on the leading men of that period (Robespierre was above all amongst this number) as well as on the radical thinkers of the nineteenth century. Principal works: *D l'origine de l'inégalité parmi les hommes* [*Discourseon the Origin and Basis of Inequality Among Men*], 1754; *Emile*, 1762; *Le contrat social* [*The*

---

36   Rousseau, while living most of his life in France and having a deep influence there, was actually born in Geneva, part of French-speaking Switzerland. (Editor)

Social Contract], 1762; the novel *Nouvelle Héloïse* [*The New Heloise*], 1759; *Mes confessions* [*Confessions*], published after his death [written in 1770, published in 1782].

[**Rowntree**, Benjamin Seebohm (1871–1954), English sociological researcher, social reformer and industrialist. In 1901 produced the book *Poverty, A Study of Town Life*, widely considered a seminal work of sociology which details his investigation of poverty in York.]

[**Rudd**, Charles Dunell (1844–1916), main business associate of Cecil John Rhodes. He helped arrange the Rudd Concession granting exclusive mining rights in Matabeleland, Mashonaland and other adjoining territories in what is today Zimbabwe. This proved the foundation for the royal charter granted by Britain to Rhodes's British South Africa Company in 1889 and thereafter for the Pioneer Column's occupation of Mashonaland in 1890, which marked the beginning of white colonisation.]

[**Rurik** (c. 830–879) Varangian chieftain. He gained control of Ladoga in 862, built the Holmgard settlement near Novgorod, and founded the Rurik Dynasty which ruled Kievan Rus (and later the Grand Duchy of Moscow and Tsardom of Russia) until the seventeenth century.]

Saint-Simon [Henri Claude] (1760–1825), French socialist, one of the founders of modern socialism. His critique of the capitalist economic system was so penetrating and scientific that those who today call themselves "scientific socialists" [that is, Marxists] have not yet added anything to it, and we saw the best minds of the time in France endorse the "Saint-Simon school."[37] For the reforms he proposed see the text [Part I,] Chapter XIII. Principal works: [*Du*] *Système industriel* [*On the Industrial System*], 1821–1822; *Catéchisme des industriels* [*Catechism of the Industrialists*], 1823; *Opinions littéraires, philosophiques et industrielles* [*Literary, Philosophical and Industrial Opinions*], 1825.

[**Salisbury**, Lord (1830–1903), British Conservative statesman. Robert Arthur Talbot Gascoyne-Cecil, 3rd Marquess of Salisbury, was prime minister three times.]

[**Sand**, George (1804–1876), French novelist and memoirist. Pseudonym

---

37   The 1912 British edition adds he "inspired a great number of the best thinkers (Auguste Comte), historians (Augustin Thierry), economists (Sismondi), and industrial philanthropists of the nineteenth century." (Editor)

of Amantine-Lucile-Aurore Dupin.]

Schelling, Friedrich [Wilhelm Joseph] (1775–1854), German philosopher. Attempted to construct a system of the philosophy of nature which represented the identification of nature and mind, and gave a more real meaning to the metaphysical "words" of his predecessors; but did not succeed.

[**Schiller**, Johann Christoph Friedrich von (1759–1805), German Romantic poet, philosopher, historian and playwright. His philosophical work was concerned with human freedom, which also guided his historical researches and found its way into his dramas.]

[**Schlosser**, Friedrich Christoph (1776–1861), German historian.]

[**Schneider**, Adolphe (1802–1845) French financier, industrialist and industrialist in steel, railways, armaments and shipbuilding.]

[**Sechenov**, Ivan Mikhaylovich Sechenov (1829–1905), Russian physiologist.]

[**Seebohm** Frederic Arthur (1833–1912), British economic historian.]

Séguin, Marc (1786–1875), French engineer, inventor of the tubular boiler and originator of a conception of the physical forces which is now confirmed in part by the study of the vibrations of the ether.[38] See *Mechanical theory of heat.*

[**Madame Sévigné** (1626–1696), French aristocrat. Her full title was Marie de Rabutin-Chantal, marquise de Sévigné, and is remembered for her letter-writing.]

[**Shaman** is the name given to sorcerers by the different populations of Northern Asia. They are supposed to deal with the dark forces of Nature. By their incantations and dances they are supposed to conjure illness and all sorts of misfortunes.[39]]

---

38 Ether (or Aether) theories in physics propose the existence of a medium, the ether, a space-filling substance or field, thought to be necessary as a transmission medium for the propagation of certain forces (such as electromagnetic or gravitational forces). This had little in common with the ether of classical elements from which the name was borrowed. Such theories fell out of use in modern physics and astronomy with the rise of Einstein's special theory of relativity. (Editor)

39 From the 1912 British Edition. (Editor)

[**Sismondi**, Jean Charles Léonard de (1773–1842), Swiss historian and political economist. Best known for his works on French and Italian history as well as his economic ideas. As an economist, he was a pioneer in the study of economic cycles and represented a humanitarian protest against the dominant laissez-faire capitalist orthodoxy of his time, arguing that economic science studied the means of increasing wealth too much, and the use of wealth for producing happiness too little. His principal economic work was *Nouveaux principes d'économie politique* (*New Principles of Political Economy*), 1819. His principal historical works were the sixteen volume *Histoire des républiques italiennes du Moyen Âge* (*History of the Italian republics of the Middle Ages*), 1807–1818, and the twenty-nine volume *Histoire des Français* (*History of France*), 1821–1844.]

[**Slater**, Gilbert (1864–1938), English economist.]

Smith, Adam (1723–1790), Scottish economist and philosopher, a pupil of [Francis] Hutcheson; above all known as the founder of political economy on a scientific basis. In his *Theory of Moral Sentiments*, 1759, a remarkable work boycotted to this day by religious moralists, he established that the initial origin of the moral sentiments resides in *sympathy* for his fellow man, which is natural in man.[40] And in his *An Inquiry into the Nature and Causes of the Wealth of Nations*, published in 1776, and whose reputation soon spread to France (French translations appeared in 1788), he envisioned wealth as the result of labour and capital as accumulated labour, and he discussed the multiple obstacles then imposed by governments on the development of industries and commerce, and to the enrichment of nations. Through this work became the founder of the so-called liberal school in political economy.

Spencer, Herbert (1820–1903), English philosopher. Worked on the development of a general system of synthetic philosophy on a materialist basis, set out in the following series: *First Principles*, 1862; *Principles of Biology*, 1864; *Principles of Psychology*, 1855; *Principles of Sociology* (a first attempt, much more advanced than his subsequent works, appeared in 1854 under the title *Social Statics*, and the rest appeared at different periods), *The Data of Ethics*, 1879 [this was later included in *Principles of Ethics*, 1897]; *The Man versus the State*, 1884.

[**Spooner**, Lysander (1808–1887), American individualist anarchist, lawyer, political essayist, abolitionist, jurist. Advocate of "Natural Law" who

---

40 Kropotkin discusses Smith's work in Chapter VIII of *Ethics: Origin and Development* (New York: Benjamin Blom, 1968), 204–210. (Editor)

envisioned replacing capitalism with a self-employed society. Principal works: *The Unconstitutionality of Slavery*, 1845; *Poverty: Its Illegal Causes, and Legal Cure*, 1846; *An Essay on Trial by Jury*, 1852; *No Treason: The Constitution of No Authority*, 1870; *Natural Law, or the Science of Justice*, 1882; *A Letter to Grover Cleveland, on His False Inaugural Address, The Usurpations and Crimes of Lawmakers and Judges, and the Consequent Poverty, Ignorance, and Servitude of the People*, 1886]

[**Stirner**, Max (1806–1856), German philosopher and egoist. Stirner, whose real name was Johann Kaspar Schmidt, is often seen as one of the forerunners of nihilism, existentialism, psychoanalytic theory, and post-modernism. While never calling himself an anarchist, he is usually seen as an advocate of individualist anarchism. His main work, published in 1844, is *The Ego and Its Own* (*Der Einzige und sein Eigentum*, literally *The Unique and His Property*)[41] which, as well as having an immediate and destructive impact on contemporary left-Hegelianism in Germany, argued for an ego-ism which places the autonomous individual at the centre of everything. While he had no influence on anarchism until his work was rediscovered in the 1890s, it did have a significant role in the intellectual development of Karl Marx (whose *The German Ideology*—first published in 1932—con-tains a large section seeking to mock him). Other works include: *The False Principle of our Education*, 1842; *Art and Religion*, 1842; *Stirner's Critics*, 1845; *History of Reaction*, 1851.]

[**Sue**, Eugène (1804–1857), French novelist.]

[A **Syndic** (from the Latin *syndicus* for an advocate, representative) was an agent or delegate of a guild, university, or other body, entrusted with special functions or powers. In Europe during the Middle Ages and Renaissance, nearly all guilds had representative bodies the members of which were termed *syndici*.]

[**Tcherkesoff**, Warlaam (1846–1925), Georgian anarchist and journal-ist. Involved in both the anarchist communist movement and later in the Georgian national liberation movement. Born into the family of a Georgian Prince in Tbilisi, Georgia (then part of Imperial Russia), he joined the Russian socialist movement. Arrested twice between 1866 and 1869, he was impris-oned at the Peter and Paul Fortress before being exiled to Tomsk in 1874

---

41   The American individualist anarchist Steven T. Byington (1869–1957) who translated the work in 1907 decided to entitle Stirner's book *The Ego and Its Own* and it is by this it is best known in the English-speaking world. (Editor)

from which, two years later, he escaped to Western Europe. He criticised Marxism in works like *Concentration of Capital: A Marxian Fallacy*, 1911, and *Pages of Socialist History: Teachings and Acts of Social Democracy*, 1902.]

[**Tennyson**, Alfred, (1809–1892), English poet.]

[**Thermidor**. On 27 July 1794 (9 Thermidor Year II, according to the French Republican Calendar) members of the national bodies of the revolutionary government arrested and executed Maximilien Robespierre along with several other leading members of the Jacobin Club who had dominated the Committee of Public Safety. This coup d'état was triggered by a vote of the National Convention, so ending the most radical phase of the French Revolution. Thermidor has come to mean a retreat from more radical goals and strategies during a revolution. Kropotkin, in *The Great French Revolution*, noted how the so-called "radical" Jacobins had already sent the far-left to the guillotine.]

Thierry, Augustin (1795–1873), renowned French historian, Saint-Simonist, who was the first to study the true history of primitive institutions, free from statist ideas and royal dynasties whose jurists and historians, raised in the ideas of Roman law, sought to "embellish" the primitive periods of Gallic, German, Scandinavian, Slavic, etc. societies of the so-called barbarians towards and after the fall of the Roman Empire. His *Lettres sur l'histoire de France* [*Letters on the History of France*], 1820; his *Récits* [*des temps*] *mérovingiens* [*Stories of Merovingian Times*], 1840; and his *Histoire de la formation et des progrès du tiers-état* [*History of the Formation and Progress of the Third Estate*], 1853, opened a new path for the history of France and of Europe in general which unfortunately was not followed by Academic science.

[**Thompson**, William (1775–1833), Irish socialist and feminist writer whose ideas influenced the Co-operative, Trade Union and Chartist movements. Initially an advocate of the worker receiving the full product of their labour, he moved to defending distribution according to need (communism). Opposed Robert Owen's argument to wait for investment from wealthy benefactors or the government for large scale communities, arguing for independent small scale communities established by the workers' own resources. Principal works: *An Inquiry into the Principles of the Distribution of Wealth Most Conducive to Human Happiness; applied to the Newly Proposed System of Voluntary Equality of Wealth*, 1824; *Appeal of One Half the Human Race, Women, Against the Pretensions of the Other Half, Men, to Retain Them in Political, and thence in Civil and Domestic Slavery*, 1825; *Labour Rewarded. The Claims of Labour* *and Capital Conciliated: or, How to Secure to Labour the Whole Products of Its Exertions*, 1827; *Practical Directions for the Speedy and Economical Establishment of Communities on the Principles of Mutual Co-operation, United Possessions and Equality of Exertions and the Means of Enjoyments*, 1830.]

[**Tricoche**, George Nestler (1859–1938), French economist.]

[**Tucker**, Benjamin Ricketson (1854–1939), American individualist anarchist. Editor and publisher of *Liberty* (1881–1908), he denounced the "Four Monopolies" of capitalism and argued that a free market based on "occupancy and use" of land, mutual banking, without patents and tariffs would produce a society where labour would receive its full product (and so considered himself a socialist). Embraced Max Stirner's Egoism when this was rediscovered in the 1890s. Principal work: *Instead of a Book*, 1893 (reprinted with some changes and additions as *Individual Liberty*, 1926).]

[The **Tudor** dynasty was a royal house which ruled England and its colonies from 1485 until 1603. Its first monarch was Henry VII and its last Elizabeth. After Elizabeth died without children, the Stuart dynasty replaced the Tudors when James VI of Scotland became James I of England.]

[**Turgot**, Anne Robert Jacques (1727–1781), French economist and statesman. Appointed by Louis XVI as Controller-General of Finances, he sought to introduce various economic reforms of a liberal nature (such as a free market in grain) and replacing taxes in kind or in labour with taxes in money. His *Six Edicts* included the suppression of some of the *Corvée* labour due to the nobility as well as the jurandes and masters of the craft guilds. Opposition to his policies by the nobility lead to his fall.]

[**Tyler**, Wat (died 1381) a leader of the 1381 **Peasants' Revolt** in England. Nothing is known of his early life, he was killed by officers loyal to King Richard II during negotiations at Smithfield, London.]

[**Unitarian**, a regime that was centralised, indivisible and constituted into a homogeneous single unit (*unitaire*).]

[**Unwin**, George (1870–1925), English economic historian. Works include: *Industrial organisation in the sixteenth and seventeenth centuries*, 1904; *The gilds and companies of London*, 1908.]

[**Vanderbilt**, Cornelius (1794–1877), American business tycoon in railroads and shipping.]

[**Varlin**, Eugène (1839–1871), French mutualist, communard and a founder of the International Workers' Association. A bookbinder by trade, he was one of the pioneers of French syndicalism and an associate of Bakunin. He believed that trade unions should also be the means of organising production in a free society. Elected to the Paris Commune, he fought in its defence and was tortured and shot after he was captured in its final days.]

[**Victoria** (1819–1901), Queen of the British Empire from 1837 until her death.]

[**Vida**, Marco Girolamo (c. 1485–1566), Italian humanist, bishop and poet. His major work was the Latin epic poem *Christiados libri sex* (*The Christiad in Six Books*) whose first dialogue in *De Dignitate Rei Publicae* (*Dialogues on the Dignity of the Republic*) suggested that men in a state of nature had "no empires, no domination, no magistracies, no public council, in short there could not have been such and so profound desire of commanding" as there is now. His paean to "pristine liberty" accounts for some fifteen pages.]

[**Vidal**, François (1814–1872), French socialist. In his youth, he was fascinated by the ideas of Saint-Simon and Fourier and in 1846 Vidal published *De la répartition de richesses ou De la justice distributive en économie sociale* (*On the Distribution of Wealth, or the Distributive Justice of Social Economy*) which argued that colonies for the unemployed and labour associations should be set up with State help as a means for the gradual peaceful transition to socialism. During the Revolution of 1848, he was Louis Blanc's secretary in the Luxembourg Commission and elected to the National Assembly in 1850.]

Vogt, Karl (1817–1895), Swiss naturalist, professor of geology and zoology and politician. Took part in the Revolution of 1848 [in Germany]. His materialist works, especially *Köhlerglaube und Wissenschaft* (*A Pitman's Faith and Science*), published in 1854 or 1855, *Old and New from the Life of Animals and Men*, *Zoological Letters*, etc. had a great impact.

[**Voltaire** (1694–1778), French Enlightenment writer, historian and philosopher, *nom de plume* of François-Marie Arouet. Famous for his wit and for his advocacy of civil liberties, including freedom of religion, freedom of expression and separation of church and State. A prolific writer, Voltaire produced works in almost every literary form, including plays, poems, novels, essays and historical and scientific works.]

Wallace, Alfred Russel (born in 1823 [and died 1913]), English naturalist. Sent in 1858 (from Asia, where he made collections for natural history) an essay to the Linnean Society of London[42] in which he defended, independently of Darwin, the variability of species by means of natural selection in the struggle for existence. This essay was communicated to the Linnean Society at the same time as that of Darwin who, in 1844, had arrived at the same idea.[43] Principal Works: *Contributions to the Theory of Natural Selection*, 1855–1870; *The Malay Archipelago*, 1869; *Darwinism*, 1889. Returning to the ideas of Robert Owen, which he had professed in his youth, is now conducting a serious campaign for the nationalisation of the land.[44]

[**Warren**, Josiah (1798–1874), American Individualist Anarchist. While he never called himself an anarchist, he is usually considered the founder of individual anarchism in the United States. Originally a follower of Robert Owen, he joined New Harmony in Indiana but concluded that individualism ("sovereignty of the individual") was needed as the basis of co-operation and urged "cost the limit of price"—cost being determined by the labour-time used to produce a good (that is, Owen's "labour notes"). Put his theories to the test by establishing the "Time Store" (in Cincinnati) followed by "Utopia" (in Ohio) and "Modern Times" (Long Island). In 1833

---

42 The Linnean Society of London is a society dedicated to the study of natural history and taxonomy. It was founded in 1788 by botanist Sir James Edward Smith (1759–1828) and took its name from the Swedish naturalist Carl Linnaeus (1707–1778) who systematised biological classification through his binomial nomenclature (and so known as the "father of taxonomy"). (Editor)

43 Whilst collecting specimens and researching in the Malay Archipelago in 1857, Wallace started corresponding with Darwin and in March the following year sent his paper *On the Tendency of Varieties to Depart Indefinitely From the Original Type*. The paper dealt with environmental impacts and the resulting divergence (or evolution) of species—a theory similar to, but not the same as, Darwin's own "natural selection" (Wallace's theory developed around species adapting to environmental pressures to survive while Darwin's stressed the pressure of competition between the same, or similar, species). On 1 July 1858, a joint paper outlining each man's theory entitled *On the Tendency of Species to form Varieties; and on the Perpetuation of Varieties and Species by Natural Means of Selection* (Wallace and Darwin respectively) was read at the Linnean Society. Wallace's paper was subsequently published in the *Journal of the Proceedings of the Linnean Society: Zoology* ([August 1858] 3: 9), directly preceded by Charles Darwin's first published comments on the subject. (Editor)

44 See, for example, Greta Jones, "Alfred Russel Wallace, Robert Owen and the Theory of Natural Selection," *The British Journal for the History of Science* 35: 1 (March, 2002). (Editor)

he edited *The Peaceful Revolutionist*. Principal works: *Equitable Commerce*, 1852; *True Civilisation*, 1863.]

[**Weismann**, August Friedrich Leopold (1834–1914), German evolutionary biologist. His main contribution was the germ plasm theory according to which (in a multicellular organism) inheritance only takes place by means of the germ cells. Thus the relationship between the hereditary material (germ plasm) and the rest of the body was one-way: the germ-plasm formed the body, but the body did not influence the germ-plasm, except indirectly in its participation in a population subject to natural selection. This idea is central to the modern evolutionary synthesis (developed around 1930–1940) though it is not expressed in the same terms as it utilises genetics derived from the work of Gregor Mendel (1822–1884).]

[**Weitling**, Wilhelm (1808–1871), German journeyman tailor and an influential (authoritarian) communist. Both praised and attacked by Marx and Engels, called by the latter the "founder of German communism," Weitling joined the League of the Just in 1837. He took part in protests and street battles in 1839 with Parisian workers. When the League merged with Marx's Communist Correspondence Committee to form the Communist League, Weitling played an active part and clashed with him over policies during the revolutionary upheavals in Germany.]

[**Workhouses** in England and Wales were places where those unable to support themselves were offered accommodation and employment. It can be traced to the Poor Law Act of 1388, which attempted to address the labour shortages following the Black Death in England by restricting the movement of labourers and ultimately led to the State becoming responsible for the support of the poor. The system evolved in the seventeenth and eighteenth centuries to allow parishes to reduce the cost to taxpayers by obliging those seeking poor relief to enter a workhouse and undertake a set amount of work, usually for no pay, under strict discipline. The New Poor Law of 1834 attempted to discourage the provision of relief to anyone who refused to enter a workhouse. Some Poor Law authorities hoped to run workhouses at a profit by utilising the free labour of their inmates. Workhouses were only formally abolished in 1930.]

[**Wurtz**, Charles Adolphe (1817–1884), French chemist.]

[**Zeno** of Citium (c. 334BCE–c. 262BCE), founder of the Stoic school of philosophy. He taught in Athens from about 300BCE. Based on the moral ideas of the Cynics, Stoicism laid great emphasis on the goodness and peace of mind gained from living a life of virtue in accordance with nature. The most famous of his works was *The Republic* written in opposition to Plato's work of the same title. Although it has not survived, more is known about it than any of his other works and it outlined Zeno's vision of the ideal Stoic society built on egalitarian principles. According to Diogenes Laertius (a third century biographer of the Greek philosophers whose *Lives and Opinions of Eminent Philosophers* is a principal source for the history of Greek philosophy), Zeno argued "we should look upon all people in general to be our fellow-countryfolk and citizens, observing one manner of living and one kind of order, like a flock feeding together with equal right in one common pasture. This Zeno wrote, fancying to himself, as in a dream, a certain scheme of civil order, and the image of a philosophical commonwealth." He also "teaches that neither temples nor courts of law, nor gymnasia, ought to be erected in a city; moreover, that he writes thus about money: that he does not think that people ought to coin money either for purposes of trade, or of travelling" as well as "recognising no other form of marriage than the union of the man who lives freely with a consenting woman."]

[**Zola**, Émile François (1840–1902), French writer. A major figure in the political liberalisation of France, Zola was a novelist, playwright, journalist, the best-known practitioner of the literary school of naturalism, and an important contributor to the development of theatrical naturalism. He was a major figure in French radical politics and in the exoneration of the falsely accused and convicted Jewish army officer Alfred Dreyfus (1859–1935).]

II

HERBERT SPENCER: HIS PHILOSOPHY

HERBERT SPENCER, WHO WAS BORN IN 1820 AND DIED ON THE 8TH OF December 1903, was part of the brilliant group of scientists to which Darwin, Lyell, John S. Mill, Bain, Huxley, etc., belonged in England and which contributed so powerfully to the glorious awakening of the natural sciences and the triumph of the inductive method in the sixties of the nineteenth century. Spencer is, in addition, connected with such radicals as Carlyle, Ruskin, George Eliot, who under, the double influence of Robert Owen, the Fourierists and Saint-Simonists as well as the political radicalism of the "Chartists," imprinted a radical character, and somewhat socialist tone, to the movement of ideas in England during these same years of 1860–1870.[1]

Spencer initially began as a railway engineer; then, as a writer on economics; and it was then (1848–1852) that he became friends with the physiologist George Lewis and his companion, the author of *Felix Holt*,

---

1 Thomas Carlyle (1795–1881) was a Scottish philosopher, satirical writer, essayist, historian, and teacher; John Ruskin (1819–1900) was the leading English art critic, prominent social thinker, and philanthropist; George Eliot was the pen name of Mary Anne Evans (1819–1880), an English novelist, poet, journalist, translator and one of the leading writers of the Victorian era. (Editor)

Adam Bede and other radical novels, who wrote under the pseudonym of George Eliot.[2] This remarkable woman, not yet forgiven by English hypocrisy for having married Lewis openly without intervention of Church or State, exercised a profound influence on Spencer.

In 1850 he wrote his best work, *Social Statics: or, the Conditions essential to Human Happiness specified, and the first of them developed* [which was published in 1851].

At that time he did not yet have the strong respect for bourgeois property and the contempt for the vanquished in the struggle for existence that we see in his later works, and he bluntly pronounced himself in favour of land nationalisation. There is a breath of idealism in his *Social Statics*.

It is true that Spencer never accepted the State socialism of Louis Blanc or the statist collectivism of Vidal and Pecqueur and their German successors. He had already developed his anti-government views in 1842 under the title: *The Proper Sphere of Government*.[3] But he recognised that the land must belong to the nation and we find in [*Social*] *Statics* passages in which we feel the breath of communism.

Later he revised this work and weakened these passages. However, until his last days he maintained his rebellion against the monopolists of the land as well as against all kinds of economic, political, intellectual or religious oppression. He always protested against the "unprincipled" policy of the reactionaries. During the war against the Boers he openly spoke against English aggression and a few months before his death he still argued against the protectionism of the adventurer Chamberlain.[4] All his life he refused the titles of nobility and honours[5] that were offered to him, and if a university sent him an honorific title he did not even acknowledge receipt.

This explains the silence maintained about Spencer by the criminals of the upper classes [*haute pègre*].

---

2   George Henry Lewes (1817–1878) was an English philosopher and critic of literature and theatre. Although married to Agnes Jervis, he and George Eliot lived together for over 20 years. (Editor)

3   This was originally a series of twelve letters published in the journal, *The Nonconformist*, in 1842 before appearing in 1843 as the book *The Proper Sphere of Government*. (Editor)

4   Joseph Chamberlain (1836–1914) held the post of Secretary of State for the Colonies from 1895 to 1903, during which he sought to expand the British Empire. He sanctioned the conquest of the Ashanti, occupying Kumasi and annexing the territory to the Gold Coast as well as presiding over the Second Boer War. (Editor).

5   Kropotkin uses the term "crachats" or, literally, "spits" but was used in a popular sense to mean something which distinguished the higher ranks in the orders of knighthood. (Editor)

The principal service, however, rendered by Spencer is not to be found in his *Social Statics*. It was in the development of his *Synthetic Philosophy*, which may be considered, after the work of Auguste Comte, as the main philosophical work of the nineteenth century.

The philosophers of the eighteenth century, and especially the Encyclopaedists, had already tried to construct a synthetic philosophy of the universe. A summary of all that is essential in our knowledge of Nature and man: on the planets and the stars, on physical and chemical forces (or rather the physical and chemical *movements* of molecules), on the facts of plant and animal life, on psychology, on the life of human societies, on the development of their ideas, on their moral ideal: A *System of Nature*,[6] as Holbach had tried to do—from the falling stone to the dream of the poet, all understood as a material fact.

Later on, Auguste Comte continued the same work. He tried to construct a *positive philosophy* which was to summarise the essential facts of our knowledge of Nature, without any intervention of gods, occult forces, or metaphysical words, which always make a veiled allusion to supernatural forces.

The positive philosophy of Comte, whatever the Germans and English (who imagine or pretend that they have not suffered its influence) may say, imprinted its mark on the scientific thought of the nineteenth century. It provoked the awakening of the natural sciences in the sixties, of which we have spoken in [Chapter V of] *Modern Science and Anarchy*. It also inspired Mill, Huxley, Lewes, Bain, and many others and suggested to Spencer, likewise, the idea of constructing his synthetic philosophy. It gave him the method to use.

But Comte's philosophy—without mentioning his fundamental error, of which we have already discussed [in Chapter IV of *Modern Science and Anarchy*]—had a formidable gap. Comte was not a naturalist. Zoology and geology were foreign to him. Relying in this on [the opinion of] Cuvier, he denied the variability of species. This of course prevented him from conceiving *evolution, development,* as we understand them today.

Already in 1801 the great naturalist Lamarck, taking a step forward from the ideas of Buffon, had affirmed that the various species of plants and

---

6   Kropotkin wrote *Tableau de la Nature* rather than *Système de la Nature*. He appears to have confused Holbach's *Système de la nature ou des loix du monde physique & du monde moral* (*The System of Nature, or Laws of the Moral and Physical World*) with his *Tableau des Saints, ou Examen de l'esprit, de la conduite, des maximes & du mérite des personages que le christiannisme révère & propose pour modèles*, both published in 1770 (the former under the pseudonym of Mirabau). (Editor)

animals that now inhabit the earth had developed gradually; that they originated from other species of plants and animals which, under the influence of the environment they lived in, had always acquired new and novel forms. In a very dry climate, where evaporation is very great, the blades of leaves will change; the leaf will even disappear to give rise to a hard and dry thorn. An animal forced to traverse deserts will gradually acquire lighter proportions than one that lives in the mud of swamps. A buttercup which grows in a water covered meadow will have leaves different from those of a buttercup sprouting in a dry meadow.

Everything continually changes in nature; forms are not permanent and the plants and the animals which we find today are the product of *a slow adaptation* to conditions which, likewise, always change.

Yet the reaction that reigned after the Great [French] Revolution was such that these ideas of Lamarck were forgotten, boycotted. German metaphysics then dominated and, together with the cult of royalty, it reinstated the god of the Hebrews who at will stops the sun and ensures that not a single hair falls from a man's head without his consent; it revived the worship of an immortal soul of the universe, part [and parcel] of this god.

Nevertheless the idea of *natural development*, of *evolution* made its way. If our system of planets and our sun are the product of a slow development as Laplace and Kant had already proved them to be—why should not the clusters of nebulous matter that we see in the starry sky represent worlds as yet unformed? Is not the universe a realm of solar systems always in the process of evolution, which always begins again forever?

If Buffon and Lamarck had already guessed that the lion, the tiger, the giraffe are so well adapted to the environments they inhabit, it was because those surroundings have made them what they are—the facts which accumulated from all sides at the beginning of the century by distant travels brought new evidence every day in support of this idea. The variability of species became a proven fact. *Transformism* and, therefore, the always renewed *development* of new species imposed themselves [on men's minds].

At the same time geology established that thousands of centuries had passed before the first fish, then the first lizards, then the first birds, then mammals, and finally man, had made their appearance on earth. These ideas were very widespread in the first half of the century—only they did not dare to affirm them openly. Even in 1840, when Chambers put them into a system in his book *Vestiges of [the Natural History of] Creation*, which created a great sensation, he did not dare confess his name and hid his identity so well that for forty years no one could discover who was the author of that book.[7]

---

7   Robert Chambers (1802–1871) was a Scottish publisher, geologist, evolutionary thinker and writer. His *Vestiges of the Natural History of Creation* (1844) was published

So when metaphysicians tell us today that it was Hegel who discovered, or solely popularised, the idea of *change*, of *evolution*—these gentlemen only prove that the history of the natural sciences remains as unknown to them as the very language [*l'alphabet*] of these sciences and their method.

The idea of evolution had imposed itself in all the fields [of science]. It was therefore absolutely necessary to apply it to the interpretation of the whole system of Nature as well as to human institutions, to religions, to moral ideas. It was necessary—whilst maintaining the fundamental idea of Auguste Comte's positive philosophy—to extend it in such a way as to encompass the whole of all that lives and develops on earth.

It was to this [task] that Spencer dedicated himself.

Like Darwin, he was physically of the "weak." But by submitting rigorously to a particular [regime of] physical and intellectual hygiene, by conserving his strength, he managed to complete this formidable task.

He wrote, in fact, a complete system of synthetic philosophy which comprises, firstly, physical and chemical forces; then the life of the innumerable suns in the process of formation or in the process of decay which populate the universe; then the evolution of our solar system and of our planet. This forms the *First Principles* [1862].

Next comes the evolution of living beings on our globe, addressed in the *Principles of Biology* [in two volumes, 1864, 1867]. This is a very technical book in which Spencer, following the lines already indicated or dimly seen by the genius of Comte, put much original work and in which he shows how, by the action of chemical forces, life first appeared on our globe; how it began with small collections of microscopic cells and how all the immense variety of plants and animals, from the simplest to the most complex, gradually developed.[8] Here Spencer has in part anticipated Darwin; and if he was far from possessing Darwin's knowledge and from having studied every question as deeply as he had, he on the other hand sometimes reached broader and fairer general views than those of his great contemporary and master.

According to Spencer, new species of plants and animals originate *initially*, as Lamarck had stated, in the direct influence of the environment on

---

anonymously and brought together various ideas of stellar evolution with the progressive transmutation of species in an accessible narrative. Charles Darwin believed it prepared the public mind for the scientific theories of evolution by natural selection. (Editor)

8   A summary of some of this admirable work can be found, written in a simple style, in the charming little book of Edmond Perrier, *Les Colonie animales* [Edmond Perrier, *Les Colonies animales et la Formation des organismes* (Paris: G. Masson, 1881)—Jean Octave Edmond Perrier (1844–1921) was a French zoologist (Editor)].

individuals. This he called *direct adaptation*. Then, these new variations, produced either by the dryness or the dampness, by the cold or warmth of the climate, by the kind of nourishment, etc., etc.—if they are substantial enough to be useful in the struggle for existence—allow those individuals who possess them and who are, therefore, the best adapted to the environment to survive and to leave a healthier offspring. This survival of the "best adapted" is the *natural selection in the struggle for existence* indicated by Darwin. Spencer referred to it as *indirect adaptation*.

This *double* origin of species is also the point of view that prevails today in science. Darwin himself was eager to accept it.[9]

The next part of Spencer's philosophy is the *Principles of Psychology* [in two volumes, 1870, 1880]. Here he takes an entirely materialist point of view. He does not use the word "materialism." But, like Bain, he definitely leaves out all metaphysics. He lays the foundations of materialist psychology.

Then he gives us the *Principles of Sociology* [in three volumes, 1874–1875, 1879, 1885]—the foundations of the science of societies based, as Comte had foreseen, on the gradual development of customs and institutions.

And finally he gives us the *Principles of Ethics* [in two volumes, 1897], that is, of Morals. Two parts of this last volume [*division*]—*The Data of Ethics* [1879] and *Justice* [1891]—are fairly well known in France.

Thus we have a complete system of evolutionary philosophy.

In all its parts, Spencer's philosophy, including his *Principles of Ethics*, is absolutely free from any Christian influence. That is a lot. We appreciate the service rendered by Spencer when we think how much of what is written in our days on philosophy, and especially on moral questions, is still subject to the influence of Christianity.

Nobody before him had known how to produce an absolutely *agnostic*, non-Christian system of the universe, of organisms, of man, of human societies and their moral conceptions. For Spencer, Christianity is a religion like the others, having the same origin in the same fears and the same

---

9   Kropotkin was reflecting the scientific consensus of the time which (like, as Kropotkin demonstrated, Darwin himself) combined Darwinian natural selection and Lamarckian selection based on environmental pressures shaping the organisation. This perspective failed to survive developments in genetics in the 1930s. Nevertheless, as discussed in the introduction, the core of this position is reflected in on-going debates over the *nature* and *nurture*. In other words, the environment shapes how organisms develop and which traits they express and so Kropotkin's theories of mutual aid are not dependent on any Lamarckian elements of his (or Spencer's) theories—quite the reverse as mutual aid is strengthened by having a genetic basis. (Editor)

aspirations, which undoubtedly exerted an immense influence on humanity but which represents, for the philosopher, [only] a fact in the history of societies—just like our juridical conceptions and our institutions. Spencer also studies its natural origin and evolution. Even when he does speak of morals, he is interested rather in the origin and development of a given custom or a moral principle than in the founders of a given religion or moral teaching.

What Spencer lacks, however, is the spirit of attack, the fighting spirit. He builds his system of the universe, seen as a result of physical forces, but we would also like to see him directly demolish the superstitions that encumber the minds [of men] and prevent them from accepting this system. Spencer passes them in silence, or throws them, in passing, a word of contempt.

Spencer's style is sometimes heavy. Very often his proofs are insufficient to convince you (Darwin had already noticed this). Moreover, we feel the absence of the poet, of the artist, in him. But when you have read his works—if only abridged—you feel that you are entering into possession of a complete conception of the universe, of the whole of nature, in which there is no longer any place for the mysterious, the supernatural. You understand that you can alter it in many details but that an important point has been gained. An "absolute," a "substance" represented as a "divine spirit," seems to you so small, so fictitious, as soon as you can get a real, concrete, idea of the life of the universe, solar systems, planets, and those pretentious little beings—men!

Spencer does not rise high enough to give you great and beautiful overviews. Always too down to earth, he does not speak to the poetic elation that inspires us in the contemplation of the universe in its entirety. Unfortunately, the poetry of Nature, of the universe, does not exist in him. But he makes us understand how life was born on this planet by chemical and physical forces alone; how, by the action of the same forces, the simplest plants had to appear and how, after more and more complicated adaptations, much more complex plants had to develop. He shows you how the other branch [of life], that of animals, must also have appeared; how it too must have developed in order to reach man, to improve him in turn and one day to surpass him. He makes you sense why evolution has been until now a *progress*; why humanity can and must move towards higher and higher *goals*, as long as this evolution lasts.

In his *Principles of Sociology* Spencer unfolds in the same way the range of human institutions, beliefs, general ideas, civilisations, from the simplest to the most complex. In details he can obviously be wrong—he often is. Our conception of the evolution of society is already very different from his.

But Spencer familiarises us with the true method of interpreting social facts—the method of the inductive sciences which consists in seeking the explanation of all social facts in natural causes—initially the closest and simplest—and not in supernatural forces or hypotheses born of *verbal*, metaphysical analyses. If we are accustomed to this method, we indeed see that all our institutions, our economic relations, our languages, our religions, our music, our moral ideas, our poetry, etc., are explained by the same series of natural facts that explain the movements of suns and those of the dust that circulates in space, the colours of the rainbow and those of the butterfly, the forms of flowers and of animals, the customs of ants and those of elephants, of men.

It is true that Spencer does not highlight this unity of nature to us; he does not make us feel the beauty, the poetry, of this synthetic interpretation of the universe. For this he lacks the genius of Laplace, the poetic feeling of Humboldt, the beauty of style possessed by Elisée Reclus. These and many other qualities are lacking in him. But he makes us understand how the naturalist reasons, once he is freed of the religious and scholastic teaching by which they try to paralyse the mind.

Is Spencer himself—we are lead to wonder—entirely freed of this dead weight? Yes, almost; but not entirely.

In all sciences, when study has been pushed to its furthest, we reach a certain limit that we cannot *at a given moment* go beyond. This is precisely what makes science forever young; always attractive. What a delight it was amongst us when, towards the middle of the nineteenth century, such wonderful discoveries were made in astronomy, the physical sciences, the life sciences, psychology. What grand horizons opened before our eyes at that time, when the limits of science were suddenly widened! They were widened at that time, but eliminated? No; for immediately new limits were posed, new problems to solve arose on all sides.

Thus science continually pushes back its limits. Where it stopped twenty years ago we now have a conquered field. The limit has receded. But after having made great progress science now stops again to review all of its conquests, probe the new horizons opening before it, and accumulate new facts before taking a new surge and going on to new conquests.

Thus, fifty years ago we said: "Here is a group of phenomena—attractions and repulsions—which have something in common. Let us call them 'electric phenomena,' and call the cause of these facts whatever it may be, unknown for the moment, 'electricity.'" And when the impatient asked us: "What is this electricity?" we had the honesty to answer that we did not know anything about it—for the time being.

Today, a step forward is being made. We have found a point of similarity between sound, heat, light and electricity. When a bell rings it produces waves in the air, alternately compressed and stretched [*raréfié*], which follow one upon the other like waves on the surface of a pond.

These sound waves move in the air with a velocity of around 300 metres per second and they are propagated in a way that is so well known to us that we submit it to mathematical calculation. This has been known for a long time ago. But it has now been discovered that heat and light *and also electricity* are propagated in just the same way, but at a speed of 300,000 kilometres per second. It is certainly matter that is infinitely more rarefied than air that vibrates in the case of electrical phenomena; but electricity is due to vibrations quite similar to those produced in the air by a bell, and which we can submit to the same mathematical study.

Doubtless this is still not to know everything about electricity: the unknown surrounds us on all sides; but it is a first approximation. Knowing this, we will arrive at a second approximation which will interpret the facts even more accurately. And in the meantime, we are already talking from one continent to another without using a submarine cable; and we get the news of the day on board a vessel sailing full speed across the Ocean.

"But what is this vibrating matter?" you might perhaps ask. "I know nothing about it *for the moment*—any more than I knew anything about electricity or heat fifty years ago": that will be the response. And if you insist, if you ask: "Will we know something in fifty years?" nobody will be able to answer you.[10] All we can tell you is that one day we will know much more than we do now. How could we predict in 1860 that towards the end of the century we would be able to send electric vibrations from Ireland to New York when we did not even know that electricity consisted of vibrations analogous to light vibrations? Let us strive to teach less nonsense in our schools, let us strive to teach the natural sciences better, so as to develop audacity—always audacity—in young minds and time will tell!

This is all that science can tell you.

Well, Spencer said more, and that more was too much.

---

10   In fact, the study of the newly discovered gases—argon, neon, etc.—whose atoms are vibrating so quickly that it is extremely difficult to get them to chemically combine has already suggested to Mendéléeff that ether is only matter whose atoms are vibrating even faster than neon and argon—so fast that they cannot enter into any chemical combination and that they travel freely within interstellar spaces, in the midst of condensing atoms which form suns and planets from the gas and dust clusters which surround them.

He affirmed that beyond a certain limit lies not the *unknown*, which will perhaps be known within a hundred years—but the *unknowable*, which *cannot* be known by our intelligence; where-upon Frederic Harrison, an English Positivist, made this absolutely correct remark: "Well! You seem to know a good deal about this unknown of which you make an unknowable, since you can affirm that it *cannot* be known."[11]

Indeed, to state that this "beyond" of today's science is *unknowable* we must be sure that it differs *essentially* from all that we have come to know so far. But this is to know an immense amount about this unknowable. It is to affirm that it differs so much from all the mechanical, chemical, intellectual and emotional phenomena of which we know something that it will never be possible to bring it under any of these categories. To make such a statement about something that we say we know nothing about is obviously a blatant contradiction. It is to say at the same time: "I do not know anything about it," and: "I know enough to say that it does not resemble, either directly or indirectly, anything I know!"

If we know anything about the universe, its past existence and the laws of its development; if we are capable of establishing the relations that exist, say, between the distance separating us from the Milky Way and the movements of suns, as well as the molecules that vibrate in this space; if, in a word, the science of the universe is possible, it is because between this universe and our brain, our nervous system and our [bodily] structure [*organisation*] in general, there exists *similarity of structure*.

If our brain were composed of matter which differed essentially from those which compose the universe of suns, stars, plants and other animals; if the laws of molecular vibrations and chemical transformations differed for our brain and spinal cord from those existing outside our planet; if, lastly, light crossing the distance between the stars and my eye obeyed, on its way, other laws than those governing my eye, my visual nerves and my brain—we could never have been able to know anything true about the universe and the laws—the constant relationships that exist there; whereas we now know enough to *predict* a mass of things and to know that the *laws* themselves, which enable us to predict, are only relations grasped by our brain.

This is why not only is there a contradiction to declare the unknown as the unknowable; but we have every reason to believe, on the contrary, that there is *nothing in nature which fails to have an equivalent in our brain*—[*itself*] *part of this same nature*, composed of the same physical and chemical

---

11   Frederic Harrison (1831–1923) was a British jurist, historian, and radical influenced by Christian Socialism. Kropotkin is almost certainly paraphrasing Harrison's article "The Ghost of Religion" (*The Nineteenth Century*, March 1884). (Editor)

elements. Nothing which, consequently, *must* remain unknown forever, that is to say, cannot find its representation in our brain.

At bottom, to speak of the Unknowable is to always return, unwittingly, to the great *words* of religions and it is because the religious will not fail to exploit this error of Spencer that we allow ourselves to go into these somewhat arduous details. To admit Spencer's unknowable is always to suppose a force infinitely superior to those that act in our intelligence and which are expressed by the activity of our brain; whereas nothing, absolutely nothing, authorises us to suppose such a force. For the naturalist, the abstract, the absolute, the unknowable, is always the same hypothesis that Laplace found unnecessary for his System of the World,[12] and which we no longer need to explain not only the universe but also life on our planet in all its manifestations. It is a luxury, a useless superstructure, a survival [from the past].

Apart from the error concerning the Unknowable, Spencer's philosophy thus allows us to account for the whole range of physical, biological, psychological, historical and moral phenomena always by means of the same scientific inductive method.

By reading his works you see how all these facts, so varied and forming part of such diverse sciences, are connected; how all are manifestations of the same physical forces; and how we understand and judge them if we always follow the same methods of reasoning that we would use for physical facts.

Does it follow that all the judgments Spencer makes in conformity with this method are correct, true? That he has himself always perfectly applied the correct method? Certainly not! Whether it be a book by Spencer or by any other thinker, it is always up to us, to our own reason, to see whether the author concludes correctly, whether he always remains faithful to his method. And it is here that we see the scientific method in its best light.

It forces the author to state his facts and reasoning in such a way that you may judge them for yourself. It is not a god who speaks. It is your equal who reasons and who invites you to do the same.

Well, as long as Spencer discusses physics, chemistry, biology and even psychology (that is to say, our emotions, our ways of feeling, thinking and acting), his conclusions are almost always correct. But when he comes to Sociology and social Morals (Ethics) it becomes something completely different.

---

12   A reference to the frequently cited, but apparently apocryphal, interaction between Laplace and Napoleon I on the existence of God. Laplace presented Napoleon a copy of his work and was asked why he had written such large book on the system of the universe and had never once mentioned its Creator. To which Laplace replied: "I had no need of that hypothesis" ("Je n'avais pas besoin de cette hypothèse-là."). (Editor)

So far he has *searched*—and found. Here—we feel it at once—*he has ready-made ideas*; the ideas of bourgeois radicalism that he had developed in 1850 in his *Social Statics*, before he had begun to elaborate his philosophical system of nature. And he even revised these ideas in a more bourgeois direction.

It is evident that in every scientific study everyone has, at the start, some supposition—a hypothesis that he sets out to verify, either to prove or to reject it. And even in the natural sciences it happens that we are passionate about our hypothesis while others can clearly see its faults.

But it is worse in everything that deals with the life of societies. Everyone starting work in this area has already his *ideal* of society. He has already drawn from his life and experience a certain manner of judging the privileges of fortune and birth, which he accepts or rejects; he has his standard for the divisions of society; he undergoes thousands of influences from his environment. And as the sciences that deal with social facts are still in their infancy, and Spencer was the first after Comte to really apply a scientific method to social facts, it is very natural that he was unable to shake off the influence of the bourgeois ideas of his surroundings.

Thus it happens that we are continually astonished by Spencer's conclusions. As much as we admire his suggestions in the *Principles of Biology* we feel the narrowness of his views as soon as he speaks, for example, of the relations between Labour and Capital in society.

So, to mention only one example—a very important one, moreover—Spencer was raised in the bourgeois and religious idea of *just reward*. You have acted badly—we will punish you; you have been a very industrious engineer—and your employer will add a shilling a week to your wages. Spencer believes so any way. And thus this principle of "just" reward becomes for him a law of nature.

As for children, the young who have not learnt to feed themselves, reward in an animal species will not be proportionate to efforts, he says; it is inevitable. But "among adults there must be conformity to the *law* that benefits received *shall* be directly proportionate to merits possessed: merits being measured by power of self-sustentation."[13]

Further: "Such are the *laws* by conformity to which a species is maintained; and if we assume that the preservation of a particular species is a *desideratum*, there arises in it an *obligation* to conform to these laws, which we may call, according to the case in question, quasi-ethical or ethical."[14] (*Justice*, p. 4)

---

13   Kropotkin's emphasis; Herbert Spencer, *Justice: Being Part IV of the Principles of Ethics* (London/Edinburgh: Williams and Norgate, 1891), 6. (Editor)

14   Kropotkin's emphasis; Spencer, *Justice*, 7. (Editor)

As we can see, all this language, with its idea of reward, of law, of obligation, is no longer that of a naturalist. It is not an observer of nature who speaks; it is a writer in law, in political economy, who lectures you.

Now, the explanation of this fact is this: Spencer knows socialism. He rejects it, saying that if everyone were not rewarded strictly in proportion to his works, his merits, it would be the death of society. And to prove this principle—unassailable in his eyes—he tries to turn it into a law of Nature, which forces him to abandon the scientific method in this context. And this is what also makes us immediately notice his error.

The modern Science of Societies—Sociology—is no longer satisfied with uncovering in a certain manner the "laws of the Spirit" as the Hegelians did. Since Comte it has studied the various stages through which humanity has passed, from the savages of the Stone Age to the present, and it discovers in our modern institutions a mass of survivals [from the past]—institutions that even date from the Stone Age. Our religions, our codes, our burial customs, our great yearly feasts, our ceremonies are all full of them. And it is by investigating the *evolution*, the gradual development, of institutions and superstitions that we come to understand—let us say the word: to despise—our legal, statist, ritualistic and other institutions, and predict the future developments of our societies.

Spencer has done this work, but with that lack of comprehension of other institutions than those found in England that characterises the great majority of the English. Besides, he did not know men. He did not travel (he had only been once to the United States and once to Italy, where he felt quite unhappy in an environment that was not his usual English surroundings), and he never understood the institutions of non-political peoples.

This is why we continually encounter in his *Sociology* and *Ethics* absolutely false assertions, whether it be interpreting ancient customs or lifting the veil of the future.

If we have the right to reproach Spencer in the way we have—it must nevertheless be said that his concepts in sociology and ethics (social morals) are far more advanced than any found in the statist theories of society hitherto produced by all the writers of the bourgeois camp.

What he deduces from his learned analysis is that civilised societies are moving towards a complete liberation from all the theocratic, governmental, and military survivals [from the past] that exist amongst us to this day.

As far as the future can be predicted by studying the past, human societies, said Spencer, are moving towards a condition in which the belligerent and aggressive spirit, as well as the military structure that characterises the infancy of societies, will give place to an industrial spirit and an organisation based on reciprocity and voluntary co-operation. Therein, as the old warrior institutions—royalty, nobility, army, State—increasingly disappear, in turn, will grow the altruistic, community spirit. So much so that—and here Spencer is at one with the anarchists—society will reach a stage in which, without any external pressure, by virtue of established social habits, no one will act with the aim of enslaving others, but will, on the contrary, contribute to increasing the general good and guaranteeing the independence of all.

There, where all the statist theorists preached discipline, subordination, statist concentration, Spencer foresees the abolition of the State, the emancipation of the individual, complete freedom. And, although a bourgeois individualist himself, he does not stop at this stage of *individualism* that is the ideal of the present bourgeoisie: he sees *free co-operation* (what we call *communist free agreement*) extending to all branches of human activity, and bringing society *to the perfect development of the human personality*, with all its personal, individual traits—to INDIVIDUATION, to quote Spencer.

The land being common property and the whole revenue it gives going to society—not to the individual—Spencer thinks (and he is obviously wrong in this) that there will be no need to touch individual property in the domain of industry. Intelligent co-operation will suffice. It should be noted that by co-operation Spencer does not mean those companies of shareholders from the Fourth Estate [i.e., from the proletariat] which, today, are called co-operatives. He understands all combined efforts by individuals, whether to produce in common or to consume, without adding to these the ideas of profits and exploitation by the shareholders which are the essence of existing co-operative societies. He sees what amongst anarchists is called "a free environment."[15]

It will be a society, he says, "in which individual life will thus be pushed to its greatest extension compatible with life in society, *and social life will have no other aim than to maintain the most comprehensive sphere for individual life.*"[16] Thus he would go as far as *communist free agreement*, the aim

---

15   Kropotkin discusses Herbert Spencer's views on this subject more critically in "Co-operation: A Reply to Herbert Spencer" (*Freedom*, December 1896 and January 1897). (Editor)

16   Kropotkin appears to be summarising Spencer's ideas rather than providing an actual quote. As an example: "He will infer that the type of nature to which the highest social life affords a sphere such that every faculty has its due amount, and no more than the due amount, of function and accompanying gratification, is the type of nature toward which progress cannot cease till it is reached." (Herbert Spencer, *The Principles*

of which would be the widest development of *individual* life—the highest *individuation*, like he said in opposition to *individualism*—understanding by individuation the most complete development of all the faculties of everyone and not the stupid individualism of the bourgeoisie that preaches "every man for himself and the devil take the hindmost."

Only, as a true bourgeois, Spencer glimpsed at every corner the spectre of the "idler" who will no longer work if his existence is guaranteed in a communist society; everywhere he saw the *loafer* (homeless) who shivers at the door of a club while waiting for the bourgeois gentleman whom he will help into his carriage and of whom he would demand (oh, the rascal!) a penny or two. Thus, we sometimes have to rub our eyes [in disbelief] when reading Spencer, to wonder if it is really him, a man of such intelligence, who flings such quips at the tramp, grumbles at free education and against the obligation to give a copy of his works to the free library of the British Museum.

The narrow spirit of the bourgeoisie reappears amidst the highest conceptions—and in this Spencer is strikingly akin to Fourier who, likewise a man of genius, had similar reversions to the [mentality of the] shop-keeper in the middle of his finest insights. Nor should we forget the Collectivists who have the same fear of the "idler" veiled only by palaver and formulas!

But modify Spencer's conclusions where he sins only too obviously against what the study of man teaches us. Look deeper into his most bourgeois remark to reveal the true motive—which will always be the hatred of any imposition on the full and complete freedom of man, the desire to produce the greatest amount of initiative, freedom and confidence in his powers; correct the system where Spencer has insufficiently considered the consequences of modern capitalism; seek the real reason for his respect for property, which will always be, as with Proudhon, hatred of the State and fear of the convent and barracks. Make these corrections—and this is the beauty and advantage of all inductive, scientific, research, that its errors can be corrected without undermining the whole—and you will find in Spencer a social system greatly resembling that of the communist-anarchists.

If individualist anarchists, like Tucker, have accepted Spencer as is, with his bourgeois individualism for industrial property and his bourgeois "reward," they have accepted the letter of his system rather than the spirit. For it would have been enough to make the corrections authorised by Spencer

---

of Ethics 1: 186). Also see Spencer's 1893 "General Preface" (v–x) to this work. The version printed in *Freedom* has: "It will be a society, he says, 'in which individual life will be developed as far as it is compatible with life in society, *whilst social life will have no other aim than to offer the best sphere of development to the individual.*'" (Editor)

himself, by introducing his voluntary co-operation and his attack on individual appropriation of the land, in order to reach our conclusions. It was this which was noted—with regret, of course—by several big English newspapers in their obituary articles on Spencer. Spencer, they said, was getting too close to anarchist-communism. That is why he was so cordially hated in England.

Up to the present, in all the theories of Society which were presented to us by philosophers, the individual was sacrificed to the State. Comte, after Kant, and so many others, fell into the same error, and the German metaphysicians added to that in their ferocious worship of the State.

Spencer's system is the first that, on the one hand, frees itself of all religious superstition, from all metaphysical superstructure and, on the other, frankly and openly affirms the sovereignty of the individual. The State no longer takes precedence as the "aim of human evolution" (Hegelian style). On the contrary, it is the individual who is placed front and centre, and it is for him to choose the society he wants, for him to determine to what degree he will want to give himself to this society.

Spencer teaches us that it is his too great submission to the herd that we need to fight in man—not his spirit of independence; while all previous religions and social systems have specifically fought the spirit of independence, for fear of [it] making rebels.

Unfortunately, here again Spencer does not remain faithful to himself. He makes a revolutionary statement—and hastens to soften it by offering a compromise. And once on this road he is obliged to proceed from one concession to another; so that in the end he compromises all his work.

After having given the insolent title *The Man versus the State* to one of the parts of his *Sociology*, he nevertheless admits the *negative*, conservative, role for the State. So the State must not employ public funds to create a national library; it will not set up universities: this is not its business. But it will ensure that individuals are protected from one another. It will protect the rights of proprietors.

But, as it is necessary to have representatives to make laws, judges to explain these laws, and universities to teach the art of making laws and interpreting them—lo and behold, little by little, Spencer manages to reconstruct the State in its worst functions, up to the prison and the perfected guillotine.

Here again, here above all, he lacked boldness. The *middle ground* [*juste milieu*] holds him back. Perhaps he felt hindered by lack of knowledge, as he outlined his philosophy at a time when his knowledge was still limited and he was hampered all his life by his ignorance of languages other than English. Or was it his nature and education which did not allow him to take the leap that a philosopher of his immense intelligence should have taken?... Or was it the influence of the English surroundings—always "centre left" and never "Mountain"?...[17]

Here is a short sketch, the distinctive characteristics of Spencer.

To create a *synthetic* philosophy which provides a summary of human knowledge as a whole and which gives a material explanation for all the facts of nature as well as of the intellectual life of man and the life of societies—this is an immense work. Spencer partly achieved it.

But, while acknowledging the service he has rendered, it would be false to let ourselves be carried away by our admiration into believing that his work really contains the final results of science and of the inductive method applied to man. The fundamental idea of this work is right. But in its applications it was repeatedly flawed due to various causes. Some of them have just been indicated; others, such as the use of the fallacious method of analogies, and especially the exaggeration of the struggle for existence between individuals of the same species and the lack of attention given to mutual aid—another principle of Nature—are mentioned in the text of this book [in Chapter VI of *Modern Science and Anarchy*].

We cannot accept all of Spencer's conclusions. We must even correct most of them in his *Sociology*; as a Russian writer, Mikhailovsky, has done on a very important point—the theory of progress.[18] Here, we must remain more faithful to the scientific method; there, we must get rid of some prejudices; there again, conduct further study of some group of facts.

But above and beyond all this, there remains one fact of the greatest importance proved by Spencer.

From the moment that we seek to construct a synthetic philosophy of the universe, including the life of societies, we necessarily arrive not only at the negation of a force that governs the universe; not only at the negation of the immortal soul or any special vital force; but we also arrive at the overthrowing of this other fetish, the State—the government of

---

17   A reference to the far-left of the Jacobins in the Great French Revolution, named "The Mountain" because they sat in the highest seats in the French Parliament. (Editor)

18   Nikolai Konstantinovich Mikhailovsky (1842–1904) was a Russian literacy critic, sociologist, writer and a theoretician of *Narodnik* (Populist) movement. His critique of Spencer, entitled "Chto takoye Progress?" ("What is Progress?"), appeared in *Otechesvennye Zapisk*i (*Annals of the Fatherland*) in 1869–1870 (contained in abridged for in *Readings in Russian Philosophical Thought: Philosophy of History* [Ontario: Wilfrid Laurier University Press, 1977], edited by Louis Shein). For more on Mikhailovsky, see Andrzej Walicki, *A History of Russian Thought: From the Enlightenment to Marxism* (Stanford: Stanford University Press, 1979), 252–267. (Editor)

man by man. We manage to, as regards the future of civilised societies, foresee Anarchy.

In this sense, Herbert Spencer has certainly contributed to the growing anarchist philosophy of the century which we have just entered.

SUPPLEMENTARY MATERIAL

The following articles and pamphlets are related to and expand on the themes raised by Kropotkin in *Modern Science and Anarchy*. Most have been translated or appear in a full, unabridged, translation here for the first time. (Editor)

CHARLES DARWIN

This short obituary of Charles Darwin appears to be the first-time Kropotkin referred to evolutionary ideas within the anarchist press. It was originally published in *Le Révolté* (29 April 1882) and raises ideas that Kropotkin later returned to in *Mutual Aid* as well as *Modern Science and Anarchy*. This is the first time it has been translated. (Editor)

IN THE PERSON OF CHARLES DARWIN HUMANITY HAS JUST LOST A SCIENTIST who not only has given a truly scientific and rational direction to research on the laws of development of organised creatures but also has unwittingly powerfully contributed to demolishing religious prejudices and has exerted a vast influence on the development of the spirit of criticism and demolition of our century.

By his book *On the Origin of Species* and by a series of works that followed this book, Darwin has *proven*, established in a scientific manner, that the immense variety of animal and plant forms which we see on our planet was not the work of a creator who amused himself by creating a polyparium today, a fish tomorrow, a monkey or a man the day after tomorrow. He has demonstrated that all this variety of forms was the natural result of the action of physical forces, acting for thousands and millions of centuries first on simple cells, then on agglomerations of cells, then on planets and animals—simple at first and then more and more complicated over the course of centuries—diversifying according to the various climates and various environments in which they live and propagated.

He has proven that man, who has always sought to place himself outside and above the animal kingdom, has had absolutely the same origin as all other animals. The human species is only a species of sophisticated animals in the same way as the monkey, the horse, the dog, which are also sophisticated species in relation to their ancestors—this perfection being nothing but a more perfect adaptation to the environment and a development of the abilities and structure favourable to the struggle for existence. In a remote epoch, several hundreds of centuries ago, man and ape had as a common ancestor the same kind of animal which, developing in two different directions, has ended up with on one side the ape and on the other—man. Man and ape are thus first cousins, like the poodle and the Newfoundland dog, both derived from common ancestors: what [human] craft has done to produce these two races of dogs, natural development has done to produce these two species: man and ape.

Twenty years ago when atheists were discussing with believers, they were asked a question which was difficult for them to answer scientifically. It was explaining how animals and plants are so marvellously adapted to the environment in which they live. How it is that the heron is so wonderfully made for the marshes, the eagle for hunting, the camel for the desert, the fish for water, etc. Darwin showed that this structure, appropriate for the environment, is a consequence of "natural selection," assisted by "the struggle for existence." The very influence of the environment first produces certain changes in the structure [of the creature]; these changes are transmitted to the children and become more pronounced. The gazelle which is a little more agile than the others, the eagle whose eye is a little more keen, the camel [which is] a little more capable of enduring thirst, are more likely to survive in the struggle for existence and to leave offspring who, while inheriting their qualities, will develop them even more. If today the camel is so well made for the desert and the heron for the marsh, it is because all those who were born ill-adapted to the environment perished or were less likely to leave offspring, whereas the better adapted survived and left little ones that resembled them. The mind of a creator or of nature has nothing to do with it. It is a simple result of natural causes.

The bourgeoisie sought to make the "struggle for existence" an argument against socialism. This is understandable: it uses all available means. But—without entering into developments which the format of *Le Révolté* does not allow—it suffices to say that the facts established by Darwin are absolutely against the theories which the bourgeoisie wish to bolster. "The best adapted to the environment are those who survive the best in the struggle for existence," says science. But who is better suited to the environment: he who produces everything, he who invents, he who is capable of working with hands and head to provide himself with his existence and develop himself—the worker, in a word—or else that abject being who knows not how to produce, who despises labour, who only knows how to waste what others have produced?—he is condemned by nature to perish; and he will perish, he is already disappearing. That is what science says.

Furthermore, if Darwin has not said this himself others, applying his methods and developing his ideas, have proven that sociable species, in which all the individuals are supportive of each other, are those which prosper, develop, spread; whereas the species which live by banditry, like the falcon for example, are in decline over the whole surface of our globe. Solidarity and united work—that is what strengthens species in the struggle they have to sustain against the hostile forces of nature to maintain their existence, that is what science tells us. Far from justifying exploitation (they cannot even do that), the research of Darwin and his successors is, on the contrary, an excellent argument to prove that the best form of organisation of an animal society is the communist-anarchist organisation.

As a scientist and as an Englishman, Darwin did not himself reach the final implications of his studies. But others have developed his ideas and explained their true meaning; and his ideas have given a new impetus to the atheist movement. In Russia they have powerfully contributed (as far as a scientific idea can contribute) to the development of the revolutionary movement and the spirit of criticism of Nihilism.

Analysing the influence of Darwin on the development of the natural sciences is not our field. But we still have two facts to raise in our short note.

One concerns the detrimental influence on science of official "scientists." When Darwin published his book in 1859, all the scholars (with very few exceptions) were *against* him: all the public, the great mass, was *for* him. For ten, fifteen years, the scholars never ceased to say: "The hypotheses of Mr. Darwin are very spiritual, but they have no scientific basis." The academies refused to open their doors to them. But the masses, the public, the young people have *forced* the scholars to accept Darwin's ideas. Today it would be difficult to find ten scholars who doubt the correctness of these ideas.

Darwin was a hard worker and seeing the immensity of the research he did, it is clear that he had to dig all his whole life long to collect this formidable mass of facts on which he based his theories. And yet he took thirty years to gather them before publishing his work. In the future society, when everyone will have the education that Darwin had at the beginning of his studies and the leisure to devote himself to science, as soon as someone has conceived a hypothesis and it is a question of collecting the masses of facts to verify it—the same work will be done in a few years at most by collective efforts. In a communist society, thirty years would not have passed between the utterance of an idea and its scientific recognition by all the facts necessary to support it: it would be done in two or three years. And the idea, thrown into the world, would find millions of minds ready to seize it, to develop it and to make it bear fruit.

One further point. It is an old habit when we say: "Darwin's theory." It is always a language born of the regime of private property to designate theories by the name of an author. Indeed, it would be a great error to believe that it was Darwin's mind which discovered the beautiful theory of "natural selection." Like every great discovery, this theory was already in the air during the course of our century. The scientists of revolutionary France in the last century had foreseen it and at the very moment when Darwin published his book another scientist, [Alfred Russel] Wallace, published a work on the same subject while [Herbert] Spencer came to a similar conclusion. This amounts to Darwin [alone] having developed this theory in all its aspects, having debated the facts that appeared contradictory, having accumulated the great masses of facts that support it. But the theory of the origin of the species is not the work of an individual: it is the work of the nineteenth century.

ANARCHY: ITS PHILOSOPHY, ITS IDEAL

A lecture which was to be held on March 6th, 1896, in the

Tivoli-Vauxhall theatre in Paris

This was one of the two lectures, the other being *The State: Its Historic Role*, which Kropotkin was stopped by the French police from giving in Paris 1896. We have included it here because of its obvious links with the themes of *Modern Science and Anarchy*. Moreover, the most easily accessible version of this text (in the anthologies *Anarchism: A Collection of Revolutionary Writings* and *Fugitive Writings*) is substantially edited (without indicating) resulting in over a quarter of the original being removed. In addition, the original English-language translation (by Freedom Press in 1897) was slightly abridged. We have slightly revised the 1897 translation and any missing text has been restored. (Editor)

CITIZENS,[1]

It is not without a certain hesitation that I have decided to take the philosophy and ideal of Anarchy as the subject of this lecture.

---

1   Kropotkin, as would be expected in a lecture, starts with "Citoyennes et Citoyens" (literally, "Citizenesses and Citizens"). This welcome was not included in the 1897 British pamphlet. (Editor)

Those who are persuaded that anarchy is a collection of visions relating to the future, and an unconscious striving toward the destruction of all present civilisation, are still very numerous; and to clear the ground of such prejudices of our education as maintain this view we should have, perhaps, to enter into many details which it would be difficult to embody in a single lecture. Did not the Parisian press, only two or three years ago, maintain that the whole philosophy of the anarchist consisted of destruction, and that its only argument was violence?

Nevertheless anarchists have been spoken of so much lately, that part of the public has at last taken to reading and discussing our doctrines. Sometimes men have even given themselves the trouble to reflect, and at the present moment we have at least gained a point: it is willingly admitted that anarchists have an ideal. Their ideal is even found too beautiful, too lofty for a society not composed of superior beings.

But is it not pretentious on my part to speak of a philosophy, when, according to our critics, our ideas are but dim visions of a distant future? Can anarchy pretend to possess a philosophy, when it is denied that social-ism has one?

This is what I am about to answer with all possible precision and clear-ness, only asking you to excuse me beforehand if I repeat an example or two which I have already given at a London lecture, and which seem to be best fitted to explain what is meant by the philosophy of anarchy.[2]

* * *

You will not bear me any ill-will if I begin by taking a few elementary illustrations borrowed from natural sciences. Not for the purpose of de-ducing our social ideas from them—far from it; but simply the better to set off certain relations, which are easier grasped in phenomena verified by the exact sciences than in examples only taken from the complex facts of human societies.

Well, then, what especially strikes us at present in exact sciences, is the profound modification which they are undergoing now, in the whole of their conceptions and interpretations of the facts of the universe.

There was a time, you know, when man imagined the earth placed in the centre of the universe. Sun, moon, planets and stars seemed to roll round our globe; and this globe, inhabited by man, represented for him the centre of creation. He himself—the superior being on his planet—was the elected of his Creator. The sun, the moon, the stars were but made for him; toward

---

2   *Les Temps Nouveaux* [*New Times*], publication de la *Révolte*. Paris, 1894. [This pam-phlet has never been translated into English—Editor]

him was directed all the attention of a God, who watched the least of his actions, arrested the sun's course for him, wafted in the clouds, launching his showers or his thunder-bolts on fields and cities, to recompense the virtue or punish the crimes of mankind. For thousands of years man thus conceived the universe.

You know also what an immense change was produced in the sixteenth century in all conceptions of the civilised part of mankind, when it was demonstrated that, far from being the centre of the universe, the earth was only a grain of sand in the solar system—a ball, much smaller even than the other planets; that the sun itself—though immense in comparison to our little earth, was but a star among many other countless stars which we see shining in the skies and swarming in the milky-way. How small man appeared in comparison to this immensity without limits, how ridiculous his pretensions! All the philosophy of that epoch, all social and religious conceptions, felt the effects of this transformation in cosmogony. Natural science, whose present development we are so proud of, only dates from that time.

But a change, much more profound, and with far wider reaching results, is being effected at the present time in the whole of the sciences, and anarchy, you will see, is but one of the many manifestations of this evolution. It is only one of the branches of the developing new philosophy.[3]

* * *

Take any work on astronomy of the last century, or the beginning of ours. You will no longer find in it, it goes without saying, our tiny planet placed in the centre of the universe. But you will meet at every step the idea of a central luminary—the sun—which by its powerful attraction governs our planetary world. From this central body radiates a force guiding the course of the planets, and maintaining the harmony of the system. Issued from a central agglomeration, planets have, so to say, budded from it; they owe their birth to this agglomeration; they owe everything to the radiant star that represents it still: the rhythm of their movements, their orbits set at wisely regulated distances, the life that animates them and adorns their surfaces. And when any perturbation disturbs their course and makes them deviate from their orbits, the central body re-establishes order in the system; it assures and perpetuates its existence.

This conception, however, is also disappearing as the other one did. After having fixed all their attention on the sun and the large planets, astronomers are beginning to study now the infinitely small ones that people

3   This sentence was missing from the 1897 British pamphlet. (Editor)

the universe. And they discover that the interplanetary and interstellar spaces are peopled and crossed in all imaginable directions by little swarms of matter, invisible, infinitely small when taken separately, but all-powerful in their numbers. Among those masses, some, like the bolide[4] that fell in Spain some time ago, are still rather big; others weigh but a few ounces or grains, while around them is wafted dust, almost microscopic, filling up the spaces.

It is to this dust, to these infinitely tiny bodies that dash through space in all directions with giddy swiftness, that clash with one another, agglomerate, disintegrate, everywhere and always, it is to them that today astronomers look for an explanation of the origin of our solar system, the movements that animate its parts, and the harmony of their whole. Yet another step, and soon universal gravitation itself will be but the result of all the disordered and incoherent movements of these infinitely small bodies—of oscillations of atoms that manifest themselves in all possible directions.

Thus the centre, the origin of force, formerly transferred from the earth to the sun, now turns out to be scattered and disseminated: it is everywhere and nowhere. With the astronomer, we perceive that solar systems are the work of infinitely small bodies; that the power which was supposed to govern the system is itself but the result of the collisions among those infinitely tiny clusters of matter, that the harmony of stellar systems is harmony only because it is an adaptation, a resultant of all these numberless movements uniting, completing, equilibrating one another.

The whole aspect of the universe changes with this new conception. The idea of force governing the world, of pre-established law, preconceived harmony, disappears to make room for the harmony that Fourier had caught a glimpse of: the one which results from the disorderly and incoherent movements of numberless hosts of matter, each of which goes its own way and all of which hold each other in equilibrium.

* * *

If it were only astronomy that were undergoing this change! But no; the same modification takes place in the philosophy of all sciences without exception; those which study nature as well as those which study human relations.

In physical sciences, the entities of heat, magnetism and electricity disappear. When a physicist speaks today of a heated or electrified body, he no longer sees an inanimate mass, to which an unknown force should be added. He strives to recognise in this body and in the surrounding space, the

---

4   A large meteor that explodes in the atmosphere. (Editor)

course, the vibrations of infinitely small atoms which dash in all directions, vibrate, move, live and by their vibrations, their shocks, their life, produce the phenomena of heat, light, magnetism or electricity.

In sciences that deal with organic life, the notion of species and its variations is being substituted by a notion of the variations of the individual. The botanist and zoologist study the individual—his life, his adaptations to his surroundings. Changes produced in him by the action of drought or damp, heat or cold, abundance or poverty of nourishment, of his more or less sensitiveness to the action of exterior surroundings will originate species; and the variations of species are now for the biologist but resultants—a given sum of variations that have been produced in each individual separately. A species will be what the individuals are, each undergoing numberless influences from the surroundings in which they live, and to which they correspond each in his own way.

And when a physiologist speaks now of the life of a plant or of an animal, he sees rather an agglomeration, a colony of millions of separate individuals than an unified and indivisible personality. He speaks of a federation of digestive, sensual, nervous organs, all very intimately connected with one another, each feeling the consequence of the well-being or indisposition of each, but each living its own life. Each organ, each part of an organ in its turn is composed of independent cells which associate to struggle against conditions unfavourable to their existence. The individual is quite a world of federations, a whole *cosmos* in himself.

And in this world of aggregated beings the physiologist sees the autonomous cells of blood, of the tissues, of the nerve-centres; he recognises the millions of white corpuscles—the phagocytes—who wend their way to the parts of the body infected by microbes in order to give battle to the invaders. More than that: in each microscopic cell he discovers today a world of autonomous organisms, each of which lives its own life, looks for well-being for itself and attains it by grouping and associating itself with others. In short, each individual is a cosmos of organs, each organ is a cosmos of cells, each cell is a cosmos of infinitely small ones; and in this complex world, the well-being of the whole depends entirely on the sum of well-being enjoyed by each of the least microscopic particles of organised matter.

A whole revolution is thus produced in the philosophy of life.

* * *

But it is especially in psychology that this revolution leads to consequences of great importance.

Quite recently the psychologist spoke of man as an entire being, one and indivisible. Remaining faithful to religious tradition, he used to class men as good and bad, intelligent and stupid, egotists and altruists. Even with materialists of the eighteenth century, the idea of a soul, of an indivisible entity, was still upheld.

But what would we think today of a psychologist who would still speak like this! The modern psychologist sees in man a multitude of separate faculties, autonomous tendencies, equal among themselves, performing their functions independently, balancing, opposing one another continually. Taken as a whole, man is nothing but a resultant, always changeable, of all his divers faculties, of all his autonomous tendencies, of brain cells and nerve centres. All are related so closely to one another that they each react on all the others, but they lead their own life without being subordinated to a central organ—the soul.

* * *

Without entering into further details you thus see that a profound modification is being produced at this moment in the whole of natural sciences. Not that this analysis is extended to details formerly neglected. No! the facts are not new, but the way of looking at them is in course of evolution; and if we had to characterise this tendency in a few words, we might say that if formerly science strove to study the results and the great sums (integrals, as mathematicians say), today it strives to study the infinitely small ones—the individuals of which those sums are composed and in which it now recognises independence and individuality at the same time as this intimate aggregation.

As to the harmony that the human mind discovers in nature, and which harmony is, on the whole, but the verification of a certain stability of phenomena, the modern scientist no doubt recognises it more than ever. But he no longer tries to explain it by the action of laws conceived according to a certain plan pre-established by an intelligent will.

What used to be called "natural law" is nothing but a certain relation among phenomena which we dimly see, and each "law" takes a temporary character of causality; that is to say: *If* such a phenomenon is produced under such conditions, such another phenomenon will follow. No law placed outside the phenomena: each phenomenon governs that which follows it—not law.

Nothing preconceived in what we call harmony in nature. The chance of collisions and encounters has sufficed to establish it. Such a phenomenon will last for centuries because the adaption, the equilibrium it represents has taken centuries to be established; while such another will last but an instant if that form of momentary equilibrium was born in an instant. If the planets of our solar system do not collide with one another and do not destroy one another every day, if they last millions of years, it is because they represent an equilibrium that has taken millions of centuries to establish as a resultant of millions of blind forces. If continents are not continually destroyed by volcanic shocks, it is because they have taken thousands and thousands of centuries to build up, molecule by molecule, and to take their present shape. But lightning will only last an instant; because it represents a momentary rupture of the equilibrium, a sudden redistribution of forces.

Harmony thus appears as a temporary adjustment, established among all forces acting upon a given spot—a provisory adaptation; and that adjustment will only last under one condition: that of being continually modified; of representing every moment the resultant of all conflicting actions. Let but one of those forces be hampered in its action for some time and harmony disappears. Force will accumulate its effect; it *must* come to light, it *must* exercise its action, and if other forces hinder its manifestation it will not be annihilated by that, but will end by upsetting the present adjustment, by destroying harmony, in order to find a new form of equilibrium and to work to form a new adaptation. Such is the eruption of a volcano, whose imprisoned force ends by breaking the petrified lavas which hindered them to pour forth the gases, the molten lavas, and the incandescent ashes. Such, also, are the revolutions of mankind.

* * *

An analogous transformation is being produced at the same time in the sciences that deal with man.

Thus we see that history, after having been the history of kingdoms, tends to become the history of nations and then the study of individuals. The historian wants to know how the members, of which such a nation was composed, lived at such a time, what their beliefs were, their means of existence, what ideal of society was visible to them, and what means they possessed to march toward this ideal. And by the action of all those forces, formerly neglected, he interprets the great historical phenomena.

So the scholar who studies jurisprudence is no longer content with such or such a code. Like the ethnologist he wants to know the genesis of the institution that succeed one another; he follows their evolution through ages, and in this study he applies himself far less to written law than to local customs—to the "customary law" in which the constructive genius of the unknown masses has found expression in all times. A wholly new science is being elaborated in this direction and promises to upset established conceptions we learned at school, succeeding in interpreting history in the same manner as natural sciences interpret the phenomena of Nature.

And, finally, political economy, which was at the beginning a study of the wealth *of nations*, becomes today a study of the wealth *of individuals*. It cares less to know if such a nation has or has not a large foreign trade; it wants to be assured that bread is not wanting in the peasant's or worker's cottage. It knocks at all doors—at that of the palace as well as that of the hovel—and asks the rich as well as the poor: Up to what point are your needs satisfied both for necessaries and luxuries? And as it discovers that the most pressing needs of nine-tenths of each nation are not satisfied, it asks itself the question that a physiologist would ask himself about a plant or an animal: "Which are the means to satisfy the needs of all with the least loss of power? How can a society guarantee to each, and consequently to all, the greatest sum of satisfaction?" It is in this direction that economic science is being transformed; and after having been so long a simple statement of phenomena interpreted in the interest of a rich minority, it tends to become (or rather it elaborates the elements to become) a science in the true sense of the word—a physiology of human societies.

* * *

While a new philosophy—a new view of knowledge taken as a whole—is thus being worked out, we may observe that a different conception of society, very different from that which now prevails, is in process of formation. Under the name of anarchy, a new interpretation of the past and present life of society arises, giving at the same time a forecast as regards its future, both conceived in the same spirit as the above-mentioned interpretation in natural sciences. Anarchy, therefore, appears as a constituent part of the new philosophy, and that is why anarchists come in contact, on so many points, with the greatest thinkers and poets of the present day.

In fact, it is certain that in proportion as the human mind frees itself from ideas inculcated by minorities of priests, military chiefs and judges, all striving to establish their domination, and of scientists paid to perpetuate it, a conception of society arises, in which conception there is no longer room for those dominating minorities. A society entering into possession of the social capital accumulated by the labour of preceding generations, organising itself so as to make use of this capital in the interests of all, and constituting itself without reconstituting the power of the ruling minorities. It comprises in its midst an infinite variety of capacities, temperaments and individual energies: it excludes none. It even calls for struggles and contentions; because we know that periods of contests, so long as they were freely fought out, without the weight of constituted authority being thrown on the one side of the balance, were periods when human genius took its mightiest flight and achieved the greatest aims. Acknowledging, as a fact, the equal rights of all its members to the treasures accumulated in the past, it no longer recognises a division between exploited and exploiters, governed and governors, dominated and dominators, and it seeks to establish a certain harmonious compatibility in its midst—not by subjecting all its members to an authority that is fictitiously supposed to represent society, not by trying to establish uniformity, but by urging all men to develop free initiative, free action, free association.

It seeks the most complete development of individuality combined with the highest development of voluntary association in all its aspects, in all possible degrees, for all imaginable aims; ever changing, ever modified associations which carry in themselves the elements of their durability and constantly assume new forms, which answer best to the multiple aspirations of all. A society to which pre-established forms, crystallised by law, are repugnant; which looks for harmony in an ever-changing and fugitive equilibrium between a multitude of varied forces and influences of every kind, following their own course,—these forces promoting themselves the energies which are favourable to their march toward progress, toward the liberty of developing in broad daylight and counter-balancing one another.

This conception and ideal of society is certainly not new. On the contrary, when we analyse the history of popular institutions—the clan, the village community, the guild and even the urban commune of the Middle Ages in their first stages—we find the same popular tendency to constitute a society according to this idea; a tendency, however, always trammelled by domineering minorities. All popular movements bore this stamp more or less, and with the Anabaptists and their forerunners in the ninth century we already find the same ideas clearly expressed in the religious language which was in use at that time. Unfortunately, till the end of the last century, this ideal was always tainted by a theocratic spirit; and it is only nowadays that the conception of society deduced from the observation of social phenomena is rid of its swaddling-clothes.

It is only today that the ideal of a society where each governs himself according to his own will (which is evidently a result of the social influences borne by each) is affirmed in its economic, political and moral aspects at one and the same time, and that this ideal presents itself based on the necessity of communism, imposed on our modern societies by the eminently social character of our present production.

* * *

In fact, we know full well today that it is futile to speak of liberty as long as economic slavery exists.

"Speak not of liberty—poverty is slavery!" is not a vain formula; it has penetrated into the ideas of the great working-class masses; it filters through all the present literature; it even carries those along who live on the poverty of others, and takes from them the arrogance with which they formerly asserted their rights to exploitation.

Millions of socialists of both hemispheres already agree that the present form of capitalistic appropriation cannot last much longer. Capitalists themselves feel that it must go and dare not defend it with their former assurance. Their only argument is reduced to saying to us: "You have invented nothing better!" But as to denying the fatal consequences of the present forms of property, as to justifying their right to property, they cannot do it. They will practice this right as long as freedom of action is left to them, but without trying to base it on an idea.

This is easily understood.

For instance, take the town of Paris—a creation of so many centuries, a product of the genius of a whole nation, a result of the labour of twenty or thirty generations. How could one maintain to an inhabitant of that town who works every day to embellish it, to purify it, to nourish it, to make it a centre of thought and art—how could one assert before one who produces this wealth that the palaces adorning the streets of Paris belong in all justice to those who are the legal proprietors today, when we are all creating their value, which would be *nil* without us?

Such a fiction can be kept up for some time by the skill of the people's educators. The great battalions of workers may not even reflect about it; but from the moment a minority of thinking men agitate the question and submit it to all, there can be no doubt of the result. Popular opinion answers: "It is by spoliation that they hold these riches!"

Likewise, how can the peasant be made to believe that the bourgeois or manorial land belongs to the proprietor who has a legal claim, when a peasant can tell us the history of each bit of land for ten leagues around? Above all, how make him believe that it is useful for the nation that Mr. So-and-So keeps a piece of land for his park when so many neighbouring peasants would be only too glad to cultivate it?

And, lastly, how make the worker in a factory, or the miner in a mine, believe that factory and mine equitably belong to their present masters, when worker and even miner are beginning to see clearly through Panama scandals, bribery, French, Turkish or other railways, pillage of the State and legal theft, from which great commercial and industrial property are derived?

In fact the masses have never believed in sophisms taught by economists, uttered more to confirm exploiters in their rights than to convert the exploited! Peasants and workers, crushed by misery and finding no support in the well-to-do classes, have let things go, save from time to time when they have affirmed their rights by insurrection. And if workers ever thought that the day would come when personal appropriation of capital would profit all by turning it into a stock of wealth to be shared by all, this illusion is vanishing like so many others. The worker perceives that he has been disinherited, and that disinherited he will remain, unless he has recourse to strikes or revolts to tear from his masters the smallest part of riches built up by his own efforts; that is to say, in order to get that little, he already must impose on himself the pangs of hunger and face imprisonment, if not exposure to Imperial, Royal or Republican fusillades.

But a greater evil of the present system becomes more and more marked; namely, that in a system based on private appropriation, all that is necessary to life and to production—land, housing, food and tools—having once passed into the hands of a few, the production of necessities that would give well-being to all is continually hampered. The worker feels vaguely that our present technical power could give abundance to all, but he also perceives how the capitalistic system and the State hinder the conquest of this well-being in every way.

Far from producing more than is needed to assure material riches, we do not produce enough. When a peasant covets the parks and gardens of industrial filibusters and Panamists,[5] round which judges and police mount guard—when he dreams of covering them with crops which, he knows, would carry abundance to the villages whose inhabitants feed on bread hardly washed down with sloe wine—he understands this.

The miner, forced to be idle three days a week, thinks of the tons of coal he might extract, and which are sorely needed in poor households.

The worker whose factory is closed, and who tramps the streets in search of work, sees bricklayers out of work like himself, while one-fifth of the population of Paris live in insanitary hovels; he hears shoe-makers complain of want of work, while so many people need shoes—and so on.

In short, if certain economists delight in writing treatises on over-production, and in explaining each industrial crisis by this cause, they would be much at a loss if called upon to name a single article produced

---

5   A reference to the Panama scandals of 1892, associated with the failed French at-
     tempt to build the Panama Canal. Nearly a billion francs were lost when the French
     government took bribes to keep quiet about the financial troubles of the company
     trying to build the canal. Some 800,000 French people lost their investments and
     of the nine stock issues, a large amount raised was pocketed by financiers and politi-
     cians. It is regarded as one of the largest corruption scandals of the nineteenth century.
     Moreover, the death toll of the project was estimated at over 22,000 between 1881 and
     1889. (Editor)

by France in greater quantities than are necessary to satisfy the needs of the whole population. It is certainly not corn: the country is obliged to import it. It is not wine either: peasants drink but little wine, and substitute sloe wine in its stead, and the inhabitants of towns have to be content with adulterated stuff. It is evidently not houses: millions still live in cottages of the most wretched description, with one or two apertures. It is not even good or bad books, for they are still objects of luxury in the villages. Only one thing is produced in quantities greater than need-ed,—it is the budget-devouring individual; but such merchandise is not mentioned in lectures by political economists, although those individuals possess all the attributes of merchandise, being ever ready to sell them-selves to the highest bidder.

What economists call over-production is but a production that is above the purchasing power of the worker, who is reduced to poverty by Capital and State. Now, this sort of over-production remains fatally characteris-tic of the present capitalist production, because—Proudhon has already shown it[6]—workers cannot buy with their salaries what they have produced and at the same time copiously nourish the swarm of idlers who live upon their work.

The very essence of the present economic system is that the worker can never enjoy the well-being he has produced, and that the number of those who live at his expense will always augment. The more a country is advanced in industry, the more this number grows. Inevitably, industry is directed, and will have to be directed, not towards what is needed to satisfy the needs of all, but towards that which, at a given moment, brings in the greatest temporary profit to a few. Of necessity, the abundance of some will be based on the poverty of others, and the straitened circum-stances of the greater number will have to be maintained at all costs, that there may be hands to sell themselves for a part only of that which they are capable of producing; without which, private accumulation of capital is impossible!

These characteristics of our economic system are its very essence. Without them, it cannot exist; for, who would sell his labour power for less than it is capable of bringing in, if he were not forced thereto by the threat

---

6   A reference to Proudhon's argument first raised in *What is Property?* that workers "can-not repurchase their products; since, producing for a master who in one form or an-other makes a profit, they are obliged to pay more for their own labour than they get for it": "If the worker receives for his labour an average of three francs per day, his employer [...] must sell the day's labour of his employee, in the form of merchandise, for more than three francs. The worker cannot, then, repurchase that which he has produced for his master (*Property is Theft!*, 125). (Editor)

of hunger? And those essential traits of the system are also its most crushing condemnation.

* * *

As long as England and France were pioneers of industry, in the midst of nations backward in their technical development, and as long as neighbours purchased their wools, their cotton goods, their silks, their iron and machines, as well as a whole range of articles of luxury, at a price that allowed them to enrich themselves at the expense of their clients,—the worker could be buoyed up by hope that he, too, would be called upon to appropriate an ever and ever larger share of the booty to himself. But these conditions are disappearing. In their turn, the backward nations of thirty years ago have become great producers of cotton goods, wools, silks, machines and articles of luxury. In certain branches of industry they have even taken the lead, and not only do they struggle with the pioneers of industry and commerce in distant lands, but they even compete with those pioneers in their own countries. In a few years Germany, Switzerland, Italy, the United States, Russia and Japan have become great industrial countries. Mexico, the Indies, even Serbia, are on the march—and what will it be when China begins to imitate Japan in manufacturing for the world's market?

The result is, that industrial crises, the frequency and duration of which are always augmenting, have passed into a chronic state in many industries. Likewise, wars for Oriental and African markets have become the order of the day since several years; it is now twenty-five years that the sword of war has been suspended over European States. And if war has not burst forth, it is especially due to influential financiers who find it advantageous that States should become more and more indebted. But the day on which Money will find its interest in fomenting war, human flocks will be driven against other human flocks, and will butcher one another to settle the affairs of the world's master-financiers.

All is linked, all holds together under the present economic system, and all tends to make the fall of the industrial and mercantile system under which we live inevitable. Its duration is but a question of time that may already be counted by years and no longer by centuries. A question of time—and energetic attack on our part! Idlers do not make history: they suffer it!

* * *

That is why such powerful minorities constitute themselves in the midst of civilised nations, and loudly ask for the return to the community of all riches accumulated by the work of preceding generations. The holding in common of land, mines, factories, inhabited houses and means of transport is already the watch-word of these imposing fractions, and repression—the favourite weapon of the rich and powerful—can no longer do anything to arrest the triumphal march of the spirit of revolt. And if millions of workers do not rise to seize the land and factories from the monopolists by force, be sure it is not for want of desire. They but wait for a favourable opportunity—a chance, such as presented itself in 1848, when they will be able to start the destruction of the present economic system, with the hope of being supported by an international movement.

That time cannot be long in coming; for since the International was crushed by governments in 1872[7]—especially since then—it has made immense progress of which its most ardent partisans are hardly aware. It is, in fact, constituted—in ideas, in sentiments, in the establishment of constant intercommunication. It is true the French, English, Italian and German plutocrats are so many rivals, and at any moment can even cause nations to war with one another. Nevertheless, be sure when the communist and social revolution does take place in France, France will find the same sympathies as formerly among the nations of the world, including Germans, Italians and English. And when Germany, which, by the way, is nearer a revolution than is thought, will plant the flag—unfortunately a Jacobin one—of this revolution, when it will throw itself into the revolution with all the ardour of youth in an ascendant period, such as it is traversing today, it will find on this side of the Rhine all the sympathies and all the support of a nation that loves the audacity of revolutionists and hates the arrogance of plutocracy.

* * *

Diverse causes have up till now delayed the bursting forth of this inevitable revolution. The possibility of a great European war is no doubt partly answerable for it. But there is, it seems to me, another cause, a deeper-rooted one, to which I would call your attention. There is going on just now among the socialists—many signs lead us to believe it—a great transformation in ideas, like the one I sketched at the beginning of this lecture in speaking of general sciences. And the uncertainty of socialists themselves concerning the organisation of the society they are wishing for, paralyses their energy up to a certain point. At the beginning, in the forties, socialism presented itself as communism, as a republic one and indivisible, as a governmental

---

7   The International Workers' Association was banned in France in 1872 as part of the repression following the crushing of the Paris Commune. Kropotkin, along with 52 other comrades, was arrested in 1882 and imprisoned in 1883 for being a member of the International after a famous trial at Lyons. (Editor)

and Jacobin dictatorship, in its application to economics. Such was the ideal of that time. Religious and freethinking socialists were equally ready to submit to any strong government, even an imperial one, if that government would only remodel economic relations to the worker's advantage.

A profound revolution has since been accomplished, especially among Latin and English peoples. Governmental communism, like theocratic communism, is repugnant to the worker. And this repugnance gave rise to a new conception or doctrine—that of *collectivism*—in the International. This doctrine at first signified the collective possession of the instruments of production (not including what is necessary to live), and the right of each group to accept such method of remuneration, whether communistic or individualistic, as pleased its members. Little by little, however, this system was transformed into a sort of compromise between communistic and individualistic wage remuneration. Today the collectivist wants all that belongs to production to become common property, but that each should be individually remunerated by labour checks, according to the number of hours he has spent in production. These checks would serve to buy all merchandise in the socialist stores at cost price, which price would also be estimated in hours of labour.

But if you analyse this idea you will agree that its essence, as summed up by one of our friends, is reduced to this:

Partial communism in the possession of instruments of production and education; competition among individuals and groups for bread, housing and clothing;

Individualism for works of art and thought;

The social assistance for children, invalids and old people.

In a word—a struggle for the means of existence mitigated by charity. Always the Christian maxim: "Wound to heal afterwards!" And always the door open to inquisition, in order to know if you are a man who must be left to struggle, or a man the State must succour.

The idea of labour checks, you know, is old. It dates from Robert Owen; Proudhon commended it in 1848; Marxists have made "scientific socialism" of it today.

We must say, however, that this system seems to have little hold on the minds of the masses; it would seem they foresaw its drawbacks, not to say its impossibility.

Firstly, the duration of time given to any work does not give the measure of social utility of the work accomplished, and the theories of value that economists have endeavoured to base, from Adam Smith to Marx, only on the cost of production, valued in labour time, have not solved the question of value. As soon as there is exchange, the value of an article becomes a complex quantity, and depends also on the degree of satisfaction which it brings to the needs—not of the individual, as certain economists stated formerly, but of the whole of society, taken in its entirety. Value is a *social* fact. Being the result of an exchange, it has a double aspect: that of labour, and that of satisfaction of needs, both evidently conceived in their social and not individual aspect.

On the other hand, when we analyse the evils of the present economic system, we see—and the worker knows it full well—that their essence lies in the *forced* necessity of the worker to sell his labour power. Not having the wherewithal to live for the next fortnight, and being prevented by the State from using his labour power without selling it to someone, the worker sells himself to the one who undertakes to give him work; he renounces the benefits his labour might bring him in; he abandons the lion's share of what he produces to his employer; he even abdicates his liberty; he renounces his right to make his opinion heard on the utility of what he is about to produce and on the way of producing it.

Thus results the accumulation of capital, not in its faculty of absorbing surplus-value but in the forced position the worker is placed to sell his labour power: the seller being sure in advance that he will *not* receive all that his strength can produce, of being wounded in his interests, and of becoming the inferior of the buyer. Without this the capitalist would never have tried to buy him; which proves that to change the system it must be attacked in its essence: in its cause—sale and purchase—not in its effect—capitalism.

Workers themselves have a vague intuition of this, and we hear them say oftener and oftener that nothing will be done if the social revolution does not begin with the distribution of products, if it does not guarantee the necessities of life to all—that is to say, housing, food and clothing. And we know that to do this is quite possible, with the powerful means of production at our disposal. If the worker continues to be paid in wages, he necessarily will remain the slave or the subordinate of the one to whom he is forced to sell his labour force—be the buyer a private individual or the State.

In the popular mind—in that sum total of thousands of opinions crossing the human brain—it is felt that if the State were to be substituted for the employer, in his role of buyer and overseer of labour, it would still be an odious tyranny. A man of the people does not reason about abstractions, he thinks in concrete terms, and that is why he feels that the abstraction, the State, would for him assume the form of numberless functionaries, taken from among his factory and workshop comrades, and he knows what importance he can attach to their virtues: excellent comrades today, they become unbearable foremen tomorrow. And he looks for a social constitution that will eliminate the present evils without creating new ones.

That is why collectivism has never taken hold of the masses, who always come back to communism—but a communism more and more stripped of the Jacobin theocracy and authoritarianism of the forties—to free, anarchist, communism.

Nay more: in calling to mind all we have seen during this quarter of a century in the European socialist movement, I cannot help believing that modern socialism is forced to make a step towards libertarian communism; and that so long as that step is not taken, the incertitude in the popular mind that I have just pointed out will paralyze the efforts of *socialist* propaganda.

Socialists seem to me to be brought, by force of circumstances, to recognise that the material guarantee of existence of all the members of the community shall be *the first* act of the social revolution.

But they are also driven to take another step. They are obliged to recognise that this guarantee must come, not from the State, but independently of the State, and without its intervention.

* * *

We have already obtained the unanimous assent of those who have studied the subject, that a society, having recovered the possession of all riches accumulated in its midst, can liberally assure abundance to all in return for four or five hours effective and manual work a day, as far as regards production. If everybody, from childhood, learned whence came the bread he eats, the house he dwells in, the book he studies, and so on; and if each one accustomed himself to complete mental work by manual labour in some branch of manufacture,—society could easily perform this task, to say nothing of the further simplification of production which a more or less near future has in store for us.

In fact, it suffices to recall for a moment the present terrible waste, to conceive what a civilised society can produce with but a small quantity of labour if all share in it, and what grand works might be undertaken that are out of the question today. Unfortunately, the metaphysics called political economy has never troubled about that which should have been its essence—*economy* of labour.

There is no longer any doubt as regards the possibility of wealth in a communist society, armed with our present machinery and tools. Doubts only arise when the question at issue is, whether a society can exist in which man's actions are not subject to State control; whether, to reach well-being, it is not necessary for European communities to sacrifice the little personal liberty they have reconquered at the cost of so many sacrifices during this century?

A section of socialists believe that it is impossible to attain such a result without sacrificing personal liberty on the altar of the State. Another section, to which we belong, believes, on the contrary, that it is only by the abolition of the State, by the conquest of perfect liberty by the individual, by free agreement, association and absolute free federation that we can reach communism—the possession in common of our social inheritance, and the production in common of all riches.

That is the question outweighing all others at present, and socialism *must* solve it, on pain of seeing all its efforts endangered and all its ulterior development paralysed.

Let us, therefore, analyse it with all the attention it deserves.

* * *

If every socialist will carry his thoughts back to an earlier date, he will no doubt remember the host of prejudices aroused in him when, for the first time, he came to the idea that abolishing the capitalist system and private appropriation of land and capital had become an historical necessity.

The same feelings are today produced in the man who for the first time hears that the abolition of the State, its laws, its entire system of management, governmentalism and centralisation, also becomes an historical necessity: that the abolition of the one without the abolition of the other is materially impossible. Our whole education—made, be it noted, by Church and State, in the interests of both—revolts at this conception.

Is it less true for that? And shall we allow our belief in the State to survive the host of prejudices we have already sacrificed for our emancipation?

* * *

It is not my intention to criticise tonight the State. That has been done and redone so often, and I am obliged to put off to another lecture the analysis of the historical part played by the State.[8] A few general remarks will suffice.

To begin with, if man, since his origin, has always lived in societies, the State is but one of the forms of social life, quite recent as far as regards European societies. Men lived thousands of years before the first States were constituted; Greece and Rome existed for centuries before the Macedonian and Roman Empires were built up, and for us modern Europeans the centralised States date but from the sixteenth century. It was only then, after

---

8   A reference to *The State: Its Historic Role* (see Part III of *Modern Science and Anarchy*). (Editor)

the defeat of the free [medieval] communes had been completed that the mutual insurance company between military, judicial, landlord and capitalist authority which we call "State," could be fully established.

It was only in the sixteenth century that a mortal blow was dealt to ideas of local independence, to free union and organisation, to federation of all degrees among sovereign groups, possessing all functions now seized upon by the State. It was only then that the alliance between Church and the nascent power of Royalty put an end to an organisation, based on the principle of federation, which had existed from the ninth to the fifteenth century, and which had produced in Europe the great period of free cities of the middle ages, whose character has been so well understood in France by Sismondi and Augustin Thierry—two historians unfortunately too little read now-a-days.

We know well the means by which this association of the lord, priest, merchant, judge, soldier, and king founded its domination. It was by the annihilation of all free unions: of village communities, guilds, apprentice associations,[9] fraternities and medieval cities. It was by confiscating the land of the communes and the riches of the guilds; it was by the absolute and ferocious prohibition of all kinds of free agreement between men; it was by massacre, the wheel, the gibbet, the sword, and the fire that Church and State established their domination, and that they succeeded henceforth to reign over an incoherent agglomeration of subjects, who had no direct union any more among themselves.

* * *

It is now hardly thirty or forty years ago that we began to reconquer, by struggle, by revolt, the first steps of the right of association, that was freely practised by the artisans and the tillers of the soil through the whole of the middle ages.

And what is the tendency which already dominates the life of civilised nations? Is it not that of uniting, of associating, of forming a thousand free societies for the satisfaction of all the manifold needs of civilised man?[10]

And, already now, Europe is covered by thousands of voluntary associations for study and teaching, for industry, commerce, science, art, literature, exploitation, resistance to exploitation, amusement, serious work, gratification and self-denial, for all that makes up the life of an active and

---

9   Kropotkin lists guilds then *compagnonnages* which was an organisation of artisan apprentices who would travel around France ("*tour de France*") to work and study with various master-craftsmen in order to become one in turn. This was translated as "trades unions" which is somewhat misleading. (Editor)

10   This paragraph was not included in the 1897 British edition. (Editor)

thinking being. We see these societies rising in all nooks and corners of all domains: political, economic, artistic, intellectual. Some are as short-lived as roses, some hold their own since several decades, and all strive—while maintaining the independence of each group, circle, branch, or section—to federate, to unite, across frontiers as well as among each nation; to cover all the life of civilised men with a net, meshes of which are intersected and interwoven. Their numbers can already be reckoned by tens of thousands, they comprise millions of adherents—although less than fifty years have elapsed since Church and State began to tolerate a few of them—very few, indeed.

These societies already begin to encroach everywhere on the functions of the State, and strive to substitute free action of volunteers for that of a centralised State. In England we see arise insurance companies against theft; societies for coast defence, volunteer societies for land defence, which the State endeavours to get under its thumb, thereby making them instruments of domination, although their original aim was to do without the State. Were it not for Church and State, free societies would have already conquered the whole of the immense domain of education. And, in spite of all difficulties, they begin to invade this domain as well, and make their influence already felt.

And when we mark the progress already accomplished in that direction, in spite of and against the State, which tries by all means to maintain its supremacy of recent origin; when we see how voluntary societies invade everything and are only impeded in their development by the State, we are forced to recognise a powerful tendency, a latent force in modern society. And we ask ourselves this question: "If, five, ten, or twenty years hence—it matters little—the workers succeed by revolt in destroying the said mutual insurance society of landlords, bankers, priests, judges, and soldiers; if the people become masters of their destiny for a few months, and lay hands on the riches they have created, and which belong to them by right—will they really begin to reconstitute that blood-sucker, the State? Or will they not rather try to organise from the simple to the complex, according to mutual agreement and to the infinitely varied, ever-changing needs of each locality, in order to secure the possession of those riches for themselves, to mutually guarantee one another's life, and to produce what will be found necessary for life?"

Will they follow the dominant tendency of the century, towards decentralisation, home rule and free agreement; or will they march contrary to this tendency and strive to reconstitute demolished authority?

* * *

Educated men—"civilised," as Fourier used to say with disdain—tremble at the idea that society might someday be without judges, police, or gaolers…

But, frankly, do you need them as much as you have been told in musty books? Books written, be it noted, by scientists who generally know well what has been written before them, but, for the most part, absolutely ignore the people and their every-day life.

If we can wander, without fear, not only in the streets of Paris, which bristle with police, but especially in rustic walks where you rarely meet passers-by, is it to the police that we owe this security? or rather to the absence of people who care to rob or murder us? I am evidently not speaking of the one who carries millions about him. That one—a recent trial tells us—is soon robbed, by preference in places where there are as many policemen as lamp posts. No, I speak of the man who fears for his life and not for his purse filled with ill-gotten sovereigns. Are his fears real?

Besides, has not experience demonstrated quite recently that Jack the Ripper performed his exploits under the eye of the London police—a most active force—and that he only left off killing when the population of Whitechapel itself began to give chase to him?[11]

And in our every-day relations with our fellow-citizens, do you think that it is really judges, gaolers and police that hinder anti-social acts from multiplying? The judge, ever ferocious, because he is a maniac of law, the accuser, the informer, the police spy, all those interlopers that live from hand to mouth around the Law Courts, do they not scatter demoralisation far and wide into society? Read the trials, glance behind the scenes, push your analysis further than the exterior facade of law courts, and you will come out sickened.

Have not prisons—which kill all will and force of character in man, which enclose within their walls more vices than are met with on any other spot of the globe—always been universities of crime? Is not the court of a tribunal a school of ferocity? And so on.

When we ask for the abolition of the State and its organs we are always told that we dream of a society composed of men better than they are in reality. But no; a thousand times, no. All we ask is that men should not be made worse than they are, by such institutions!

* * *

---

11 Jack the Ripper was an unidentified serial killer who brutally murdered five women prostitutes in the largely impoverished areas in and around the Whitechapel district of London in August to November 1888. The murders were never solved and have become a source of much myth, folklore, and pseudo-history (and some genuine historical research). (Editor)

Once a German jurist of great renown, Jhering, wanted to sum up the scientific work of his life and write a treatise, in which he proposed to analyse the factors that preserve social life in society. *Purpose in Law* (*Der Zweck im Rechte*), such is the title of that book, which enjoys a well-deserved reputation.[12]

He made an elaborate plan of his treatise, and, with much erudition, discussed both coercive factors which are used to maintain society: wage-labour and the different forms of coercion which are sanctioned by law. At the end of his work he reserved two paragraphs only to mention the two non-coercive factors—the feeling of duty and the feeling of mutual sympathy—to which he attached little importance, as might be expected from a writer in law.

But what happened? As he went on analysing the coercive factors he realised their insufficiency. He consecrated a whole volume to their analysis, and the result was to lessen their importance! When he began the last two paragraphs, when he began to reflect upon the non-coercive factors of society, he perceived, on the contrary, their immense, outweighing importance; and instead of two paragraphs, he found himself obliged to write a second volume, twice as large as the first, on these two factors: voluntary restraint and mutual help; and yet, he analysed but an infinitesimal part of these latter—those which result from personal sympathy—and hardly touched free agreement, which results from social institutions.

Well, then, leave off repeating the formulas which you have learned at school; meditate on this subject; and the same thing that happened to Jhering will happen to you: you will recognise the infinitesimal importance of coercion, as compared to the voluntary assent, in society.

On the other hand, if by following the very old advice given by Bentham you begin to think of the fatal consequences—direct, and especially indirect—of legal coercion, like Tolstoy, like us, you will begin to hate the use of coercion, and you will begin to say that society possesses a thousand other means for preventing antisocial acts. If it neglects those means today, it is because, being educated by Church and State, our cowardice and apathy of spirit hinder us seeing clearly on this point. When a child has committed a fault, it is so easy to punish it: that puts and end to all discussions! It is so easy to hang a man—especially when there is an executioner who is paid so much for each execution—and it dispenses us from thinking of the cause of crimes.

* * *

---

12   Caspar Rudolph Ritter von Jhering (1818–1892) was a German jurist known as being a legal scholar and as the founder of a modern sociological and historical school of law. His two-volume *Der Zweck im Recht* appeared in 1877 and 1883. (Editor)

It is often said that anarchists live in a world of dreams to come, and do not see the things which happen today. We do see them only too well, and in their true colours, and that is what makes us carry the hatchet into the forest of prejudice that besets us.

Far from living in a world of visions and imagining men better than they are, we see them as they are; and that is why we affirm that the best of men is made essentially bad by the exercise of authority, and that the theory of the "balancing of powers" and "control of authorities" is a hypocritical formula, invented by those who have seized power, to make the "sovereign people," whom they despise, believe that the people themselves are governing. It is because we know men that we say to those who imagine that men would devour one another without those governors: You reason like the king, who, being sent across the frontier, called out, "What will become of my poor subjects without me?"

Ah, if men were those superior beings that the utopians of authority like to speak to us of, if we could close our eyes to reality, and live, like them, in a world of dreams and illusions as to the superiority of those who think themselves called to power, perhaps we also should do like them; perhaps we also should believe in the virtues of those who govern.

With virtuous masters, what dangers could slavery offer? Do you remember the Slave-owner of whom we heard so often, hardly thirty years ago? Was he not supposed to take paternal care of his slaves? "He alone," we were told, "could hinder these lazy, indolent, improvident children dying of hunger. How could he crush his slaves through hard labour, or mutilate them by blows, when his own interest lay in feeding them well, in taking care of them as much as of his own children! And then, did not 'the law' see to it that the least swerving of a slave-owner from the path of duty was punished?" How many times have we not been told so! But the reality was such that, having returned from a voyage to Brazil, Darwin was haunted all his life by the cries of agony of mutilated slaves, by the sobs of moaning women whose fingers were crushed in thumbscrews!

If the gentlemen in power were really so intelligent and so devoted to the public cause, as panegyrists of authority love to represent, what a pretty government and paternal utopia we should be able to construct! The employer would never be the tyrant of the worker; he would be the father! The factory would be a palace of delight, and never would masses of workers be doomed to physical deterioration. The State would not poison its workers by making matches with white phosphorus, for which it is so easy to substitute red phosphorus.[13] A judge would not have the

---

13 The making of matches is a State's monopoly in France. [Note added to the 1897 British pamphlet—Editor]

ferocity to condemn the wife and children of the one whom he sends to prison to suffer years of hunger and misery and to die some day of anaemia; never would a public prosecutor ask for the head of the accused for the unique pleasure of showing off his oratorical talent; and nowhere would we find a gaoler or an executioner to do the bidding of judges, who have not the courage to carry out their sentences themselves. What do I say! We should never have enough Plutarchs to praise the virtues of Members of Parliament who would all hold Panama cheques in horror![14] Biribi[15] would become an austere nursery of virtue, and permanent armies would be the joy of citizens, as soldiers would only take up arms to parade before nursemaids, and to carry bouquets of flowers on the point of their bayonets!

Oh, the beautiful utopia, the lovely Christmas dream we can make as soon as we admit that those who govern represent a superior caste, and have hardly any or no knowledge of simple mortals' weaknesses! It would then suffice to make them control one another in hierarchical fashion, to let them exchange fifty papers, at most, among different administrators, when the wind blows down a tree on the national road. Or, if need be, they would have only to be valued at their proper worth, during elections, by those same masses of mortals which are supposed to be endowed with all stupidity in their mutual relations but become wisdom itself when they have to elect their masters.

All the science of government, imagined by those who govern, is imbibed with these utopias. But we know men too well to dream such dreams.

---

14   A reference to the bribing of politicians during the Panama Scandals of 1892. (Editor)

15   *Biribi* is the name given in France to the *punishment battalions* in Algeria. Every young man who has been in prison before he begins his military service is sent to such a battalion. Many soldiers, for want of discipline, undergo the same punishment. The treatment in these places is so horrid that no Englishman would believe it possible. A very few years ago, the pear shaped hole in the ground, where men were left for weeks, and some were actually devoured by vermin, was an habitual punishment. At the present time it is quite habitual to let a man, handcuffed and chained, lay for a fortnight on the ground, covered by a bit of cloth, under the scorching sun of Algeria and through the bitterly cold nights, compelled to eat his food and to lap his water like a dog. Scores of the most terrible facts became known lately, since Georges Darien published his book *Biribi* (Paris, 1890, Savine publisher) based on actual experience, and full of the most horrible revelations. One of my Clairvaux companions had to spend two years of military service in such a battalion—his condemnation at Lyons, as the editor of an anarchist paper, being already a reason to be transported to Algeria. He fully confirmed, on his release, all that was written by Darien. [Note added by Kropotkin to the 1897 British pamphlet—Editor]

We have not two measures for the virtues of the governed and those of the governors; we know that we ourselves are not without faults and that the best of us would soon be corrupted by the exercise of power. We take men for what they are worth—and that is why we hate the government of man by man, and that we work with all our might—perhaps not strong enough—to put an end to it.

* * *

But it is not enough to destroy. We must also know how to build, and it is owing to not having thought about it that the masses have always been led astray in all their revolutions. After having demolished they abandoned the care of reconstruction to the bourgeoisie, who possessed a more or less precise conception of what they wished to realise, and who consequently reconstituted authority to their own advantage.

That is why anarchy, when it works to destroy authority in all its aspects, when it demands the abrogation of laws and the abolition of the mechanism that serves to impose them, when it refuses all hierarchical organisation and preaches free agreement—at the same time strives to maintain and enlarge the precious kernel of social customs without which no human or animal society can exist. Only, instead of demanding that those social customs should be maintained through the authority of a few, it demands it from the continued action of all.

Communist customs and institutions are of absolute necessity for society, not only to solve economic difficulties, but also to maintain and develop social customs that bring men in contact with one another; they must be looked to for establishing such relations between men that the interest of each should be the interest of all; and this alone can unite men instead of dividing them.

* * *

In fact, when we ask ourselves by what means a certain moral level can be maintained in a human or animal society, we find only three such means: the repression of anti-social acts; moral teaching; and the practice of mutual help itself. And as all three have already been put to the test of practice, we can judge them by their effects.

As to the impotence of repression—it is sufficiently demonstrated by the disorder of present society and by the necessity of a revolution that we all desire or feel inevitable. In the domain of economy, coercion has led us to industrial servitude; in the domain of politics—to the State, that is to say, to the destruction of all ties that formerly existed among citizens (the

Jacobins of 1793 even broke those which had resisted the monarchical State), and to the nation becoming nothing but an incoherent mass of obedient *subjects* of a central authority.[16]

Not only has a coercive system contributed and powerfully aided to create all the present economic, political and social evils, but it has given proof of its absolute impotence to raise the moral level of societies; it has not been even able to maintain it at the level it had already reached. If a benevolent fairy could only reveal to our eyes all the crimes that are committed every day, every minute, in a civilised society under cover of the unknown, or the protection of law itself,—society would shudder at that terrible state of affairs. The authors of the greatest political crimes, like those of Napoleon III's *coup d'état*, or the bloody week in May after the fall of the Commune of 1871, never are arraigned; and as a poet said; "the small miscreants are punished for the satisfaction of the great ones." More than that, when authority takes the moralisation of society in hand, by "punishing criminals" it only heaps up new crimes!

Practised for centuries, repression has so badly succeeded that it has but led us into a blind alley from which we can only issue by carrying torch and hatchet into the institutions of our authoritarian past.

* * *

Far be it from us not to recognise the importance of the second factor, moral teaching—especially that which is unconsciously transmitted in society and results from the whole of the ideas and comments emitted by each of us on facts and events of every-day life. But this force can only act on society under one condition, that of not being crossed by a mass of contradictory immoral teachings resulting from the practice of institutions.

In that case its influence is *nil* or baneful. Take Christian morality: what other teaching could have had more hold on minds than that spoken in the name of a crucified God, and could have acted with all its mystical force, all its poetry of martyrdom, its grandeur in forgiving executioners? And yet the institution was more powerful than the religion: soon Christianity—a revolt against imperial Rome—was conquered by that same Rome; it accepted its maxims, customs and language. The Christian church accepted the Roman law as its own, and as such—allied to the State—it became in history the most furious enemy of all semi-communist institutions, to which Christianity appealed at its origin.

Can we for a moment believe that moral teaching, patronised by circulars from ministers of public instruction, would have the creative force

---

16   The sentence in parenthesis was left out of the 1897 British edition. (Editor)

that Christianity has not had? And what could the verbal teaching of truly social men do, if it were counteracted by the whole teaching derived from institutions based, as our present institutions of property and State are, upon anti-social principles?

* * *

The third element alone remains—*the institution itself,* acting in such a way as to make social acts a state of habit and instinct. This element—history proves it—has never missed its aim, never has it acted as a double-bladed sword; and its influence has only been weakened when custom strove to become immovable, crystallised, to become in its turn a religion not to be questioned when it endeavoured to absorb the individual, taking all freedom of action from him and compelling him to revolt against that which had become, through its crystallisation, an enemy to progress.

In fact, all that was an element of progress in the past or an instrument of moral and intellectual improvement of the human race is due *to the practice of mutual aid,* to the customs that recognised the equality of men and brought them to ally, to unite, to associate for the purpose of producing and consuming, to unite for purpose of defence, to federate and to recognise no other judges in fighting out their differences than the arbitrators they took from their own midst.

Each time these institutions, issued from popular genius, when it had reconquered its liberty for a moment,—each time these institutions developed in a new direction, the moral level of society, its material well-being, its liberty, its intellectual progress, and the affirmation of individual originality made a step in advance. And, on the contrary, each time that in the course of history, whether following upon a foreign conquest, or whether by developing authoritarian prejudices men become more and more divided into governors and governed, exploiters and exploited, the moral level fell, the well-being of the masses decreased in order to insure riches to a few, and the spirit of the age declined.

History teaches us this, and from this lesson we have learned to have confidence in free communist institutions to raise the moral level of societies, debased by the practice of authority.

* * *

Today we live side by side without knowing one another. We come together at meetings on an election day: we listen to the lying or fanciful professions of faith of a candidate, and we return home. The State has the care of all questions of public interest; the State alone has the function of seeing that we do not harm the interests of our neighbour, and, if it fails in this, of punishing us in order to repair the evil.

Our neighbour may die of hunger or murder his children,—it is no business of ours; it is the business of the policeman. You hardly know one another, nothing unites you, everything tends to alienate you from one another, and finding no better way, you ask the Almighty (formerly it was a God, now it is the State) to do all that lies within his power to stop anti-social passions from reaching their highest climax.

In a communist society such estrangement, such confidence in an outside force could not exist. Communist organisation cannot be left to be constructed by legislative bodies called parliaments, municipal or communal councils. It must be the work of all, a natural growth, a product of the constructive genius of the great mass. Communism cannot be imposed from above; it could not live even for a few months if the constant and daily co-operation of all did not uphold it. It must be free.

It cannot exist without creating a continual contact between all for the thousands and thousands of common transactions; it cannot exist without creating local life, independent in the smallest unities—the block of houses, the street, the district, the commune. It would not answer its purpose if it did not cover society with a network of thousands of associations to satisfy its thousand needs: the necessaries of life, articles of luxury, of study, enjoyment, amusements. And such associations cannot remain narrow and local; they must necessarily tend (as is already the case with learned societies, cyclist clubs, humanitarian societies and the like) to become international.

And the sociable customs that communism—were it only partial at its origin—must inevitably engender in life, would already be a force incomparably more powerful to maintain and develop the kernel of sociable customs than all repressive machinery.

This, then, is the form—sociable institution—of which we ask the development of the spirit of harmony that Church and State had undertaken to impose on us—with the sad result we know only too well. And these remarks contain our answer to those who affirm that Communism and Anarchy cannot go together. They are, you see, a necessary complement to one another.

The most powerful development of individuality, or individual originality—as one of our comrades has so well said,—can only be produced when the first needs of food and shelter are satisfied; when the struggle for existence against the forces of nature has been simplified; when man's time is no longer taken up entirely by the meaner side of daily subsistence,—then only, his intelligence, his artistic taste, his inventive spirit, his genius, can develop freely and ever strive to greater achievements.

Communism is the best basis for individual development and freedom; not that individualism which drives man to the war of each against all— this is the only one known up till now,—but that which represents the full expansion of man's faculties, the superior development of what is original in him, the greatest fruitfulness of intelligence, feeling and will.

* * *

Such being our ideal, what does it matter to us that it cannot be realised at once!

Our first duty is to find out, by an analysis of society, its characteristic *tendencies* at a given moment of evolution and to state them clearly. Then, to act according to those tendencies in our relations with all those who think as we do. And, finally, from to-day and especially during a revolutionary period, work for the destruction of the institutions, as, well as the prejudices, that impede the development of such tendencies.

That is all we can do by peaceable or revolutionary methods, and we know that by favouring those tendencies we contribute to progress, while who resist them impede the march of progress.

Nevertheless, men often speak of stages to be travelled through, and they propose to work to reach what they consider to be the nearest station and only *then* to take the high road leading to what they recognise to be a still higher ideal.

But reasoning like this seems to me to misunderstand the true character of human progress and to make use of a badly chosen military comparison. Humanity is not a rolling ball, nor even a marching column. It is a whole that evolves simultaneously in the multitude of millions of which it is composed; and if you wish for a comparison, you must rather take it in the laws of organic evolution than in those of an inorganic moving body.

The fact is that each phase of development of a society is a resultant of all the activities of the intellects which compose that society; it bears the imprint of all those millions of wills. Consequently, whatever may be the stage of development that the twentieth century is preparing for us, this future state of society will show the effects of the awakening of libertarian ideas which is now taking place. And the depth with which this movement will be impressed upon the coming twentieth century institutions will depend upon the number of men who will have broken to-day with authoritarian prejudices, on the energy they will have used in attacking old institutions, on the impression they will make on the masses, on the clearness with which the ideal of a free society will have been impressed on the minds of the masses. But, to-day, we can say in full confidence, that in France the awakening of libertarian ideas had already put its stamp on society; and that the next revolution will not be the Jacobin revolution which it would have been had it burst out twenty years ago.

And as these ideas are neither the invention of a man nor a group, but result from the whole of the movement of ideas of the time, we can be sure that, whatever comes out of the next revolution, it will not be the dictatorial and centralised communism which was so much in vogue forty years ago, nor the authoritarian collectivism to which we were quite recently invited to ally ourselves, and which its advocates dare only defend very feebly at present.

The "first stage"—it is certain—will then be quite different from what was described under that name hardly twenty years ago.[17]

I have already mentioned that the great all-dominating question now is for the Socialist party, taken as a whole, to harmonise its ideal of society with the libertarian movement that germinates, in the spirit of the masses, in literature, in science, in philosophy. It is also, it is especially so, *to rouse within them the spirit of popular initiative* which has been lacking in previous revolutions.[18]

The pitfall into which all past revolutions have fallen was the absence of organising initiative among the popular masses. Admirable in intelligence when attacking, the people lacked initiative in contrasting the new system. Inevitably, it abandoned this to the educated classes, to the bourgeoisie who possessed its ideal of society and more or less knew what it wanted to emerge to its advantage during the turmoil.

In a revolution, demolishing is only part of the revolutionary's task. We must rebuild and reconstruction will be done either according to the formulas of the past, learned in books and which they will try to impose on the people or according to the popular genius which, spontaneously in every small village and in every urban centre, will set to work building the socialist society. But for that, it is necessary above all that there are men of initiative within it.

Yet it is precisely the workers' and peasants' initiative that all parties—the authoritarian socialist party included—have always stifled, wittingly or not, by party discipline. Committees, centres, ordering everything; local organs having but to obey, "so as not to put the unity of the organisation in danger." A whole teaching, in a word; a whole false history, written to serve that purpose, a whole incomprehensible pseudo-science of economics, elaborated to this end.

---

17   The 1897 British pamphlet adds: "The latest developments of the libertarian idea has already modified it beforehand in an anarchist sense." (Editor)

18   In the British pamphlet this sentence read: "It is also, it is especially so, to rouse the spirit of popular initiative" and the subsequent two paragraphs were left out. (Editor)

Well, then, those who will work to break up these superannuated tactics, those who will know how to rouse the spirit of initiative in individuals and in groups, those who will be able to create in their mutual relations a movement and a life based on the principles of free understanding—those that will understand that *variety, conflict even, is life, and that uniformity is death*—they will work, not for future centuries, but in good earnest for the next revolution, for our own times.

* * *

We need not fear the dangers and "abuses" of liberty. It is only those who do nothing who make no mistakes. As to those who only know how to obey, they make just as many, and more, mistakes than those who strike out their own path in trying to act in the direction their intelligence and their social education suggest to them. The ideal of liberty of the individual—if it is incorrectly understood owing to surroundings where the notion of solidarity is insufficiently accentuated by institutions—can certainly lead isolated men to acts that are repugnant to the social sentiments of humanity. Let us admit that it does happen: is it, however, a reason for throwing the principle of liberty overboard? Is it a reason for accepting the teaching of those masters who, in order to prevent "digressions," re-establish the censure of an enfranchised press and guillotine advanced parties to maintain uniformity and discipline—that which, when all is said, was in 1793 the best means of insuring the triumph of reaction?

The only thing to be done when we see anti-social acts committed in the name of liberty of the individual is to repudiate the principle of "each for himself and God for all," and to have the courage to say aloud in any one's presence what we think of such acts. This can perhaps bring about a conflict; but conflict is life itself. And from the conflict will arise an appreciation of those acts far more just than all those appreciations which could have been produced under the influence of old-established ideas.

When the moral level of a society descends to the point it has reached today we must expect beforehand that a revolt against such a society will sometimes assume forms that will make us shudder. No doubt, heads paraded on pikes disgust us; but the high and low gibbets of the old *régime* in France, and the iron cages Victor Hugo has told us of,[19] were they not the origin of this

---

19   Victor Marie Hugo (1802–1885) was a French poet, novelist, and dramatist of the
       Romantic movement. An active republican, he spoke in favour of many political caus-
       es including the abolition of the death penalty and prison reform. His disgust at the
       treatment of the poor, the conditions in French prison and in the corruptness of the
       French judicial system was made very clear in his novels, particularly *Les Miserables*

bloody exhibition? Let us hope that the coldblooded massacre of thirty-five thousand Parisians in May, 1871, after the fall of the Commune, and the bombardment of Paris by Thiers, will have passed over the French nation without leaving too great a fund of ferocity. Let us hope that. Let us also hope that the corruption of the swell mob, which is continually brought to light in recent trials, will not yet have ruined the heart of the nation. Let us hope it! Let us help that it be so! But if our hopes are not fulfilled—you, young socialists, will you then turn your backs on the people in revolt, because the ferocity of the rulers of today will have left its furrow in the people's minds; because the mud from above has splashed far and wide?

* * *

It is evident that so profound a revolution producing itself in people's minds cannot be confined to the domain of ideas without expanding to the sphere of action. As was so well expressed by the sympathetic young philosopher, too early snatched by death from our midst, Mark Guyau,[20] in one of the most beautiful books published for thirty years, there is no abyss between thought and action, at least for those who are not used to modern sophistry. Conception is already a beginning of action.

Consequently, the new ideas have provoked a multitude of acts of revolt in all countries, under all possible conditions: first, individual revolt against Capital and State; then collective revolt—strikes and working class insurrections—both preparing, in men's minds as in actions, a revolt of the masses, a revolution. In this, socialism and anarchism have only followed the course of evolution, which is always accomplished by *force-ideas* at the approach of great popular risings.

That is why it would be wrong to attribute the monopoly of acts of revolt to Anarchy. And, in fact, when we pass in review the acts of revolt of the last quarter of a century, we see them proceeding from all parties.

In all Europe we see a multitude of risings of working masses and peasants. Strikes, which were once "a war of folded arms," today easily turning

---

(1862). In that work it mentions that King Louis Philippe had "demolished the iron cage of Mont-Saint-Michel, built by Louis XI, and used by Louis XV." Le Mont-Saint-Michel is an island commune in Normandy, France. Inaccessible at low tide, it was an ideal location for military purposes and as a prison. After the Revolution, it was used to hold high-profile political prisoners but in 1836 many influential figures—including Hugo—launched a campaign to restore what was seen as a national architectural treasure. The prison was finally closed in 1863, and the mount was declared an historic monument in 1874. (Editor)

20   *La morale sans obligation ni sanction*, by M. Guyau.

to revolt, and sometimes taking—in the United States, in Belgium, in Andalusia—the proportions of vast insurrections. In the new and old worlds it is by the dozen that we count the risings of strikers having turned to revolts.

On the other hand, the individual act of revolt takes all possible characters, and all advanced parties contribute to it. We pass before us the rebel young woman Vera Zasulich shooting a satrap of Alexander II;[21] the Social Democrat Hödel and the Republican Nobiling shooting at the Emperor of Germany; the cooper Otero shooting at the King of Spain, and the religious Mazzinian, Passanante, striking at the King of Italy. We see agrarian murders in Ireland and explosions in London, organised by Irish Nationalists who have a horror of socialism and anarchism. We see a whole generation of young Russians—socialists, Constitutionalists and Jacobins—declare war to the knife against Alexander II, and pay for that revolt against autocracy by thirty-five executions and swarms of exiles. Numerous acts of personal revenge take place among Belgian, English and American miners; and it is only at the end of this long series that we see the anarchists appear with their acts of revolt in Spain and France.

And, during this same period, massacres, wholesale and retail, organised by *governments*, follow their regular course. To the applause of the European *bourgeoisie*, the Versailles Assembly causes thirty-five thousand Parisian workmen to be butchered—for the most part prisoners of the vanquished Commune. "Pinkerton thugs"—that private army of the rich American capitalists—massacre strikers according to the rules of that art. Priests incite an idiot to shoot at Louise Michel,[22] who—as a true anarchist—snatches her would-be murderer from his judges by pleading for him. Outside Europe the Indians of Canada are massacred and Riel is strangled,[23] the

---

21   Vera Ivanovna Zasulich (1849–1919) was a Russian Populist who tried to assassinate Colonel Fyodor Trepov in 1878 for his flogging of a political prisoner for not removing his cap in his presence. She used her trial to accuse the Trepov and Tsarist regime and was found not guilty by the jury. Going into exile before she could be re-arrested, she became a Marxist in 1883 while in exile in Switzerland. (Editor)

22   Louise Michel (1830–1905) was a French anarchist, Communard, and school teacher. An active participant in the Paris Commune of 1871, she was arrested and at her trial defied the court and dared the judges to sentence her to death. After spending twenty months in prison, she was sentenced to deportation in New Caledonia. After an amnesty was granted to the Communards, she returned to France in 1880 and became an active member of the anarchist movement. Instrumental in getting anarchists to embrace the black flag as their symbol, she raised it during a demonstration of unemployed workers in Paris on 9 March 1883. (Editor)

23   Louis David Riel (1844–1885) was a founder of the province of Manitoba and a leader

Matabele are exterminated,[24] Alexandria is bombarded,[25] without saying more of the butcheries in Madagascar, in Tonkin, in Turkoman's land everywhere, to which is given the name of war. And, finally, each year hundreds and even thousands of years of imprisonment are distributed among the rebellious workers of the two continents, and the wives and children, who are thus condemned to expiate the so-called crimes of their fathers, are doomed to the darkest misery.—The rebels are transported to Siberia, to Biribi, to Noumea and to Guiana; and in those places of exile the convicts are shot down like dogs for the least act of insubordination…

What a terrible indictment the balance sheet of the sufferings endured by workers and their friends, during this last quarter of a century, would be! What a multitude of horrible details that are unknown to the public at large and that would haunt you like a nightmare if I ventured to tell you them tonight! What a fit of passion each page would provoke if the martyrology of the modern forerunners of the great social revolution were written!— Well, then, we have lived through such a history, and each one of us has read whole pages from that book of blood and misery.

And, in the face of those sufferings, those executions, those Guianas, Siberias, Noumeas and Biribis, they have the insolence to reproach the rebel worker with want of respect for human life!!!

But the whole of our present life extinguishes the respect for human life! The judge who sentences to death, and his lieutenant, the executioner, who garrots in broad daylight in Madrid, or guillotines in the mists of Paris amid the jeers of the degraded members of high and low society; the general who massacres at Bac-leh, and the newspaper correspondent who strives

---

of the Métis people of the Canadian prairies. He led two resistance movements against the Canadian government in order to preserve Métis rights and culture as their homelands in the Northwest came progressively under the Canadian sphere of influence. The first was the Red River Rebellion of 1869–1870 which successfully negotiated the terms under which the modern province of Manitoba entered the Canadian Confederation. He was elected three times to the Canadian House of Commons, although he never took his seat. The second was the North-West Rebellion of 1885 which, although ultimately defeated, saw the land grants requested by the Saskatchewan Métis granted. Riel was arrested and convicted for high treason and hanged in the face of protests and popular appeals. (Editor)

24   A people of southern Africa driven out of the Transvaal by the Boers in 1837. Now known as the Ndebele, they live in Zimbabwe. (Editor)

25   The Bombardment of Alexandria in Egypt by the British Fleet took place on 11–13 July 1882 as part of the suppression of a nationalist revolt. The bombardment lasted ten-and-a-half hours and was followed by a full-scale invasion to restore the authority of the monarchy. Egypt remained under British occupation until 1956. (Editor)

to cover the assassins with glory; the employer who poisons his workmen with white lead, because—he answers—"it would cost so much more to substitute oxide of zinc for it;" the so-called English geographer who kills an old women lest she should awake a hostile village by her sobs, and the German geographer who causes the girl he had taken as a mistress to be hanged with her lover, the court-martial that is content with fifteen days arrest for the Biribi gaoler convicted of murder.... all, all, all in the present society teaches absolute contempt for human life—for that flesh that costs so little in the market! And those who garrot, assassinate, who kill depreciated human merchandise, they who have made a religion of the maxim that for the safety of the public you must garrot, shoot and kill, *they* complain that human life is not sufficiently respected!!!

No, citizens, as long as society accepts the law of retaliation, as long as religion and law, the barrack and the law-courts, the prison and industrial penal servitude, the press and the school continue to teach supreme contempt for the life of the individual,—do not ask the rebels against that society to respect it. It would be exacting a degree of gentleness and magnanimity from them, infinitely superior to that of the whole society.

If you wish, like us, that the entire liberty of the individual and, consequently, his life be respected, you are necessarily brought to repudiate the government of man by man, whatever shape it assumes; you are forced to accept the principles of Anarchy that you have spurned so long. You must then search with us the forms of society that can best realise that ideal and put an end to all the violence that rouses your indignation.

CO-OPERATION: A REPLY TO HERBERT SPENCER

Kropotkin discusses Herbert Spencer's views on co-operation in more detail. This writing deals with many of the issues he raises in *Modern Science and Anarchy* and originally appeared in *Freedom* (December 1896 and January 1897). Unusually, these articles did not appear in *Les Temps Nouveaux* and were specifically written for a British audience. (Editor)

I

HERBERT SPENCER HAS JUST BROUGHT OUT THE THIRD AND LAST VOLUME of his *Principles of Sociology,* and in one the closing chapters devoted to "Industrial Institutions," he evidently had to touch upon co-operation. So he did; and he came to a proposal concerning the mode of carrying on productive co-operation, which proposal he thought important enough to communicate in advance to the veteran co-operator, Mr. G. J. Holyoake.[1] It was published in the October issue of *Labour Co-Partnership.*[2]

---

1 George Jacob Holyoake (1817–1906) was a British secularist and leading member of the British co-operative movement. In 1842, he became the last person to be convicted for blasphemy in a public lecture and coined the term "secularism" in 1851 and "jingoism" in 1878. (Editor)

2 *Labour Co-Partnership* II: 189–190 (October 1896); subsequently published in Herbert Spencer, *The Principles of Sociology* (New York: Appleton and Company, 1898)

Coming as it does from the evolutionist philosopher, and representing what Herbert Spencer arrived at after so many years' work in Sociology, it deserves our full attention. It shows where a philosopher—well-meaning, but having spent his life amidst books, and imbued, moreover, with the religion of Wagedom and of "reward proportional to merit"[3]—could come to: what his last word of wisdom is.

Fully recognising the importance of labour co-partnerships, which represent a higher form of industrial organisation, Herbert Spencer proposes to substitute piece-work for time-wages in these co-partnerships; and to this change, if it only would take place, he attributes grand effects. At present time, he says, the workers and the employers in industrial co-partnerships have a prejudice against piece-work, and this prejudice is quite natural and justified when the head of the concern is a private employer (which he shows why). But in a co-partnership, where each worker receives a share of the profits, proportionately to his wages, all advantages are in favour of piece-work. Each worker being doubly interested in producing more, the productive power of the concern would be greatly increased, and the control and administration would be diminished. "Jealousies among the workers disappear. A cannot think his remuneration too low as compared with that of B, since each is now paid just as his work brings. Resentment against a foreman who ranks some above others no longer finds any place. Overlooking to check idleness becomes superfluous: the idling almost disappears, and another cause of dissension ceases." And so on. Then a further development is named: "Where the things are so large and perhaps complex (as in machinery) that an unaided man becomes incapable, work by the piece may be taken by groups of members." The Cornish miners do so. The work "is put up to auction and bid for by different gangs of men, who undertake the work as co-operative piece-work, at so much per fathom."

And then Spencer gives a full column to show the advantages of that sort of work... "The transition from the compulsory co-operation of militancy to the voluntary co-operation of industrialism is completed"... The day-wage worker is now coerced, "but under the arrangement described his activity becomes voluntary"... More than that—using Henry Maine's expression—"the transition from *status* (coercive State)[4] to contract reaches its limit"; coercion has vanished, and "the system of contract becomes

---

III: 569–574. (Editor)

3   Interestingly, Kropotkin does not make the obvious point that reward under capitalism is not related to merit—or how much labour a person can do hardly reflects their "merit." Presumably, he took these critiques of Spencer—and capitalism in general—as read. (Editor)

4   Kropotkin's explanatory note. (Editor)

unqualified" … "the entire organisation is based on contract, and each transaction is based on contract." Reward is proportionate to merit, both adjusting *themselves.*

The only regret of Herbert Spencer is that mankind has not attained that higher type of nature; that such high-type industrial institutions "are possible only with the best men"! But they will come. A few examples of the sort—and "admission into them would be the goal of working-class ambition." So far Spencer.

Now, it is always refreshing in our times, when the military utopias of German Socialism have such an ascendancy, to meet with a philosopher who seeks for a solution of the present miseries in free agreement, in each transaction being based on contract. At a time when we are told—and compelled to recognise under the penalty of ostracism—that the idea of social organisation is an "army" of workers severely "disciplined" and obeying the word of a "dictatorial chief,"[5] or of a group of chiefs, it is extremely satisfactory to see Spencer remaining true to the principle of free agreement, which he found to be the moving power of evolution at large, and which he now tries to apply even to the details of social organisation.

But Spencer seems not to know that what he advocates as the highest development of co-partnership is already practised, for hundreds of years since, by millions and millions of most ordinary men.[6] More than that. Just because these men know the institution of "co-operative piece-work" from a very long experience, they continually abandon in it the principle of "reward proportionate to merit"[7] within their own co-operations—probably because they have been convinced by experience of carrying this principle

---

5   It would be remiss not to mention Lenin's comments in early 1918: "Obedience, and unquestioning obedience at that, during work to the one-man decisions of Soviet directors, of the dictators elected or appointed by Soviet institutions, vested with dictatorial powers (as is demanded, for example, by the railway decree)" ("Six Theses on the Immediate Tasks of the Soviet Government," *Collected Works*, Volume 27 [Moscow: Progress Publishers, 1965], 316). (Editor)

6   To be fair to Spencer, unlike the extract published in *Labour Co-Partnership*, the chapter in his *The Principles of Sociology* does mention *artels* (*The Principles of Sociology*, Volume III [New York: Appleton and Company, 1898], 557–558). However, he does so essentially in passing and fails to discuss, unlike Kropotkin, what they mean as regards his thoughts on the capitalist present or a possible non-capitalist distant future. (Editor)

7   "One more aspect of the arrangement must be named. It conforms to the general law of species-life, and the law implied in our conception of justice—the law that reward shall be proportionate to merit."(Ibid., 573). (Editor)

through, and find that far from being *justice*, as Spencer believes, it is a crying *injustice*.

A few instances, all taken from Russia, where the subject has been best explored, will better explain this idea.[8]

Millions of acres of land are rented in Russia by village communities. Also meadows. When the community comes to mow a meadow, all men and women come out. It is a village *fête*. All mowers start in a row, and the ambition of every one of them is to leave the others behind: to do more work than the others. Women rack the cut grass and arrange it in heaps of equal size. In the evening, or next day, lots are cast, and each family takes one heap. The feeling of justice of the peasants does not admit that the tallest and strongest man should take more hay than the others. All have worked according to their forces—all are equally rewarded.

But a still higher form is also in existence: When scarcity prevails, the division of the produce is *according to the needs*. Although all have worked according to their forces, the division of the produce is made according to the numbers of "eaters" (of mouths) in each family. This form prevailed during the last famine, where relief was earned by village work, or received from outside. And, what was still more remarkable, the debt contracted in this last case had to be repaid by each family according to the numbers of "workers" (working units) in the family—not of its mouths. A family consisting of two workers and four children, for instance, received six parts of flour, but it had to repay only two parts.

This being the two highest forms of distribution of the produce, all possible and imaginable forms, in thousands of varieties, exist in both the village communities, and the fishing, wood-cutting, carrying, railway porters and industrial *artels*, which count hundreds of thousands and cover the whole life of the working part of the Russian nation.

Thus—to take but one instance—a railway and the wooden stations along it have to be built. If the contractor, or sub-contractor, cares in the least to have good work done, he treats, not with individual workers, but with *artels* (or gangs of from 50 to 250 men) of navvies and of carpenters. The bargain is certainly not so mechanical as an auction, because the qualities of the different bidding *artels* are taken into account. But once the work has been undertaken by a gang the contractor has nothing to do with the distribution of the earning. They will be distributed in this *artel* in one way,

---

8   Those who wish to know more about the subject ought to consult the article "*Artels*" (Russian name for such co-operations) in Meyer's or in Brockhaus's *Conversations-Lexikon*, where they will find the name of an elaborate German work on the subject. Some Russian works dealing with the subject are named in the article "Russia" in *Encyclopedia Britannica*.

in another *artel* in a different way—the ill ones always being provided for. The grouping of the *artel* being free, every member knows in advance now the distribution will take place in that gang.

One would spend his life in studying the different types of remuneration—piece work, day work, merit and no merit, in thousands of combinations which no genius could foretell or foresee, but which popular life works out on the spot, in accordance with the conditions of a given work. The same variety exists here as in the working out of animal species, and it is due to the same variety of causes.

And there is not one single branch of popular, agricultural, industrial, and commercial life in which like *artels* should not exist. Peasants form and dissolve them every day—for consumption and distribution. Fishing is done by *artels*, including sometimes a whole territory (the Ural Cossacks). The domestic trades (and they occupy 7,000,000 workers) are honey-combed with such co-operations. Nay, the railway porters, the privileged dock labourers who have permanent employment, the men who load and unload the goods on the exchanges (a highly privileged class), the carriers, the messengers in towns, and so on, are all organised in *artels*. In St. Petersburg you call an *artélstchik* of the Town Messengers' *Artel*, you give him a packet containing £1,000, and tell him to carry it to Mr. So-and-So—and usually no receipt is taken: the messenger belongs to an *artel*, and that is enough! In all private banks the keys and seals of the cash-boxes are in the hands of a special *artel*. And so on.

If Spencer knew man, we could take his words relative to the "higher type of institutions" which are "possible only with the best men" as highly complementary to the Russian nation. But the fact is that the Russian (especially the Great Russian) worker and peasant are imbued with that spirit and carry on the *artel* principle into every nook of their lives—not because they are the best men. They do so simply because the village community has not yet been wrecked by the State, and they carry on into industrial life the spirit of the institution which makes the essence of the agricultural life of the nation.[9]

Why, then, is the working part of the Russian nation, taken as a whole, even more miserable than the working parts of the West European nations?

To this we shall answer in our next number. But we can, already here, indicate our answer in a few words: "Simply because *the distribution of earnings*, amongst workers who produce for themselves and not for a capitalist, *is the least difficulty in the Social Question*. When Wagedom is not imposed from above, the workers find out, and work out, [a] thousand

---

9   Kropotkin discusses artels in more detail in "Co-operation in Russia," *The American Co-operative News* 2: 5 (November, 1897). (Editor)

new forms of sharing the earnings, more equitable than piece-wages or time-wages."

Like most middle-class writers who know little of the workers, Herbert Spencer, [in] spite of all the force of his genius, was dragged to inquire into "What is to be done to prevent workers from taking each other by the throat when they come to distribute the fruits of their labour? What is to be done to prevent idleness among them?" While the whole of the Social Question lies elsewhere—namely, in "How can the workers become enabled to produce for themselves?" When they will have *that*, they will find much better means of an equitable sharing of the fruits of their labour than those which any man of genius could find out for them in advance.

II

It was mentioned in the preceding article how widely distributed in Russia are such forms of co-operation and of sharing of earnings as, in Herbert Spencer's opinion, would imply a higher development of human nature. And it hardly need be added that for *consumption*, similar *artels* are of everyday occurrence in all branches of popular life. As soon as five, six, ten or twenty peasants come to St. Petersburg, or Moscow, or Odessa, to work in a factory or elsewhere, they hire lodgings in company, take their meals in common, and—if their trade allows it—they try to get work for the *artel*—not individually. Even the convicts on their way to Siberia, and in hard labour, live in an *artel* whose elected "elder" is the officially recognised representative of the convict *artel* in its relations with the authorities, food of the *artel*, conflicts with the authorities, work and so on.

That racial characteristics would be of no value to explain these facts Spencer will see at once, and he will understand, on the contrary, the importance of the *communal institutions* which exist in Russia for the maintenance of that spirit. The more so, as we see also in France that the peasants have been permitted to constitute the *syndicates agricoles*; not only do they largely use that right for a variety of purposes, but facts are known of their treating their *individually owned* plots of land as *common property* (for grazing and the like). To use the words of a recent official report, facts multiply of their putting their plots in common in order to redistribute them (*remuniements collectifs*).

Why then—it was asked at the end of the last article—do the Russian peasants, workers, artisans and so on, remain in such terrible poverty although they are so willing to associate, and associate in such an excellent way?

I might mention the ruin of the masses by *taxation*. But this is a very big subject, much neglected by modern economists,[10] which would require many developments. There is, however, another still more important reason. It is not enough to be imbued with the co-operative spirit; not enough to be capable of working out good forms of co-operation. Men must know *what to associate*, besides their hands and brains.

Spencer, like all middle-class theorists, sees the chief difficulty for the advent of a better state of affairs in the (presupposed) incapacity of the worker to understand his own interests. He is *sure* (that is a matter of religious faith with him) that if tomorrow the workers of such a factory, or mine, or railway, became owners of that factory, mine, or railway, they would quarrel, and the concern would perish in consequence of their incapacity to agree in the sharing of the profits.

Consequently, he cares little to find out such features in the actual life of mankind as would bring him to an opposite conclusion. Just as, in his great anthropological inquest, which has cost him and his contributors an incredible amount of labour and is now utterly valueless, because the real character of the savage and barbarian institutions does not appear from that preordained inquest, so also he shuts his eyes to the facts of real modern life which would bring him to conclusions different from those just mentioned.[11]

But the reality of modern life is this: As soon as the workers or the peasants, of any nationality, are brought by any circumstances to the common ownership of anything, and as soon as the State ceases to interfere by creating artificial differences of wealth and power among them, they admirably find out in a relatively short time the ways of managing that common property in the general interest.

Let me mention one or two examples out of thousands. There was in the Urals a royal ironworks, Votkinsk, which it was decided to abandon. The workers proposed to take it [over], as an *artel*. The State agreed, and gave to the *artel* some of those contracts which are given to various private ironworks. The *artel* prospers for several years since. Or else, in several places in Russia, where petty trades are much developed, the Ministry of War began a few years ago to give some of its contracts—on a pretty large scale—not to

---

10   Its importance has lately been brought into prominence in the twenty-second *Annual Report* of the Illinois Labor Bureau.

11   Every anthropologist knows how valueless is that immense work produced at Herbert Spencer's expense and at his instigation, and therefore will prefer Waitz's *Athropologie der Naturvölker*, which was compiled without preconceived ideas, or Post's *African Common Law*, and so on,—to say nothing of the original works, which are still better sources of information.

the sweaters, but to the artisans themselves, if they undertook it as *artels*.[12] In such cases, it made advances of money. A couple of months ago, the *Official Messenger* published the results—excellent on all accounts. Many Country Councils (zemstvos) have done the same, with excellent results.

Under the present conditions of capitalism—the English co-operators know it perfectly well—the chief difficulty is not so much in the organisation of production, not so much in finding an equitable way of sharing the earnings, but in the sale of the produce. When it comes to the market, the small concern is unavoidably crushed out of existence; it is killed by underselling and by thousands of wicked tricks of the other dealers. And this is why the English co-operators, who failed with their co-operative production when they had to find buyers in the commercial market, succeed now that they have made their own market—more honest than the usual commercial market—in their thousands of distributive co-operatives.

But this is only a small part of the difficulty. The other, much greater part, is—*what to associate*. At the present time, land, capital, knowledge, State and Municipal concessions, even education (how many children work in factories, mines, as newspaper sellers, and so on?)—all these are *constituted monopolies* in the hands of the rich. And, so long as these monopolies exist, all efforts of the co-operators are bound to remain extremely limited in scope. More than that. All their attempts are bound to remain *imbued with a narrow egotistic spirit which stands in direct contradiction to the spirit which Co-operation is intended to develop.* Started to counteract the narrow egotistic feeling of capitalism, brought to life with no other purpose but to break down and to crush out of existence that capitalistic spirit, Co-operation, under the present system of monopolies, becomes itself imbued with that same spirit of capitalist monopoly which it pretends to combat.

This is only normal and natural. And this is so evident, that as soon as a single of these monopolies is done away with, or is only limited in its application, the co-operative spirit grows in proportion. If that spirit, if that capacity for sharing the earnings is so immensely developed in Russia, or in some French villages, it is only because those Russian or French peasants

---

12   Interestingly, the Bolshevik regime also turned to the *artels* in order to supply the Red Army with personal equipment. The "run-down of large-scale industry and the bureaucratic methods applied to production orders and financial estimates made the whole system of supply based on *glavki* and *tsentry* [i.e., centralised state bodies] unreliable. The army started relying directly on *kustar'* [handicraft] output [...] *Artels* of production were the organisations to which military orders were sent [...] Kustar' activity developed to a large extent because it involved a smaller amount of bureaucratic procedure" (Silvana Malle, *The Economic Organization of War Communism, 1918–1921* [Cambridge: Cambridge University Press, 2002], 477–478). (Editor)

are—to some extent at least—freed from one of those monopolies, [the] land monopoly. They own land in common, and this alone is sufficient to develop among them the co-operative spirit which Spencer longs for and is ready to consider as a higher ideal to be reached in times to come by the human race. Take *one* of the monopolies away and the co-operative spirit develops much more than through half a century of practice in individually egoistic "Co-operation."

This is why Spencer would do infinitely more for human progress if, instead of directing his attention to the invention of panaceas for preventing workers from "jealousies" in the sharing of profits, he would inquire into the substance of institutions which breed jealousies, and of those which diminish them. While what he does now is to endeavour to conciliate two opposite currents of ideas and habits which exclude each other.

As to the still more limited panacea of piece-work, which he so warmly advocates and exaggerates in its consequences, it hardly need be criticised here, as the practical commonsense of several correspondents to *Labour Co-partnership* has sufficiently shown the utopian character of that panacea. One of the correspondents puts it especially clearly in its proper light, in this way. A thousand clothiers, he says, are holders of £1 shares and they start a coth factory. But, with the present cost of machinery, a capital of £1,000 is nothing, a trifle, which will not be enough to give work even to a hundred clothiers. Let us say, nevertheless, that they start a factory for a hundred men. They introduce, on Spencer's advice, piece-work; and by the exercise of much cleverness, ardour in work and so on, the production is increased so much that each of the hundred workers has to be paid £2 or £3 more. What will the shareholders say to that? Surely they will say: "Myself, I can hardly reach 26 shillings[13] in the factory which I work in. Why should I—employer of these hundred workers—be paid less than they are? They must not have more than 26 shillings." No fine reasoning will induce the capitalistically-reasoning shareholder to pay his worker more than he earns himself. And the utopia which was going to reform mankind and capitalism, fails to the ground.

We admire Spencer when he comes forward to claim the land of the country for all those who live and work on it. We admire him when he comes forward to claim the power of higher principles in politics. We admire him, also, when he appears as the champion of the Individual against the State (in theory, at least, though not in many of his practical reasonings). But he might leave the workers to find out for themselves how to come to an equitable distribution of what they have produced—when they, themselves, own the necessaries for production. Their systems will be more

---

13   Pre-decimalisation in 1971, there were 20 shillings in a British pound. (Editor)

equitable and more practical than whatever may be invented in his study by the evolutionist philosopher.

This, at any rate, he perfectly well knows himself: Great changes in society are not produced by small tricks. Great changes in mankind's moods of thought are not produced by such petty means as "Dutch auctions" and "piece-work wages," which are borrowed from the old mood of thought itself.

Herbert Spencer knows the value of *principles*—Need he be reminded of them?

LETTER TO COMRADESHIP

Kropotkin wrote this letter ("Prince Kropotkin on Land Monopoly and Co-Operation," *Comradeship*, No. 13, April 1900) in response to the two-part article on "Taxation of Land Values" which had appeared in *Comradeship* (No 10, January 1900; No 11, February 1900). As Kropotkin references the journal of the Woolwich Co-operative Society in "The Modern State," we have decided to include it.
February 22nd, 1900

DEAR —,

Be so kind as to express my very best thanks to the comrades who send me that excellent review, *Comradeship*. I usually read it through, beginning to end, with the greatest interest. The articles of F. Verinder struck me as especially good.[1] I was just hunting for more materials to show how the State, by means of mere taxation, created monopolies and fortunes, enriching the rich, and rendering life harder for the poor. I had been struck

---

1   Frederick Verinder (1858–1948) was a leading advocate of Henry George and his ideas on land nationalisation and land value taxation. He was Secretary of the English Land Restoration League and exchanged letters with Herbert Spencer on the latter's change of position on land nationalisation in *The Daily Chronicle* between August and October, 1894 which was subsequently issued as a pamphlet: *Mr. Herbert Spencer and the Land Restoration League*. (Editor)

by the remarks on this subject which I found in the eight annual report of the Labour Bureau of Illinois, but hunted for European data. Verinder's remarks supplied me with some of the necessary ones. His remarks, especially upon how even co-operation taken isolately—and even trade unionism—brings about the same result (p. 17 of No. 11), ought to be pondered over by every Co-operator, Trade Unionist, and Municipal Socialist.

Taken isolately, and without touching upon the fundamental laws of property in modern society, each of these currents works in the same way— *to increase the power and wealth of monopoly.*

One day, as I was staying at Blaydon with Mr. Joseph Cowen,[2] he took me to see an old co-operater of the village for a talk. "Yes, sir," said the old man, a miner, "formerly I used to get 18s. a week, now I have only 9s.; but with these 9s. I am as well off as I formerly was with 18s. The house belongs to me, as I bought it through the Co-operative Society, and all I buy at the co-operative stores is so much cheaper."

"But why do you get now only 9s. where you used to get 18s. formerly?"

"Well, we work only three days out of six: the price of coal having got down, we don't hurry to refill the stocks of coal."

And so the efforts of the co-operators—great, splendid efforts crowned with full success at Blaydon—have resulted under the present system of coalmines ownership and commercialism, altogether, to take, let us say, *some* worry off the mind of the worker; but, at the same time, in creating that colliery system which permits the owners to keep half of his men unemployed, or all of them half-employed, to raise the price of a first necessity—coal, and to have a reserve army of experienced hands for emergencies, which army costs him nothing, and the very possibility of which he owes to the co-operators.

I might quote many more examples. What is to conclude from them? Surely not against co-operation! But, that co-operation alone, trade unionism, and so called "Municipal Socialism," even when they have joined hands (which they ought to do, *without delay*[3]), still will only contribute to feed monopoly and capitalism so long as they don't make the next step—*anticipated by the immortal Robert Owen*—namely, attack also land and capitalist monopoly created by capital and State in their stronghold, the forms of property established by the State.

Yours fraternally,
P.K.

2   Joseph Cowen (1829–1900) was an English radical Liberal politician and journalist. (Editor)
3   Kropotkin discusses this need in his articles "The Trade Union Congress" in *Freedom* (October 1896) and "The Development of Trade-Unionism" in *Freedom* (March 1898), the latter is included in *Direct Struggle Against Capital*. (Editor)

ORGANISED VENGEANCE CALLED JUSTICE

This discussion of the origins of "Justice" was written in 1901
and published as a pamphlet (*L'Organisation de la Vindicte
appelée Justice* [Paris: Au Bureau des "Temps Nouveaux",
1901]) before being translated into English in a very abridged
form the following year (*Organised Vengeance called 'Justice'*
[London: Freedom Press, 1902]). This is a new translation
of the French original and is included for as well as being
considered as a supplement to *The State: Its Historic Role*
(which it mentions) it addresses how a libertarian society
would deal with anti-social acts. (Editor)

THE SAINT-SIMONIST ADOLPHE BLANQUI WAS PERFECTLY CORRECT TO
point out in his *The History of Political Economy* the importance which
economics forms have had in the history of humanity for determining the
political forms of society and even its concepts of right, morals and philosophy.[1] At that time, the liberals and radicals concentrated all their attention

---

1   Jérôme-Adolphe Blanqui (1798–1854) is better known as a leading French economist.
    His most important contributions were made in labour economics, economic history,
    and especially the history of economic thought, in which field his 1837 *treatise Histoire
    de l'économie politique en Europe depuis les anciens jusqu'à nos jours* (translated into

to the political regime and ignored the consequences of the bourgeois regime which was then being established on the ruins of the First Republic. It was therefore natural that, in order to emphasise the importance of the economic factor and to draw attention to a subject ignored by the best minds as well as to an immense socialist movement which was just beginning (his *History* is dated 1837), he even exaggerated the importance of the economic factor and sought to construct all of history upon economic relations. It was necessary, or in any case inevitable. This is repeated continually in the history of science. "With others," he said to himself, "lies the task of bringing out the importance of other factors: political forms of government, ideas on justice, theological conceptions, and the rest. Me, I must fully emphasise the importance of my subject. The importance of the others is already too well demonstrated."

It is well known to what exaggerations this idea was since taken by the German Social-Democratic school and it is known the efforts that we anarchists are making to draw attention and study to this other factor in the life of societies, the State.

It must be recognised, however, that we, while fighting for the abolition of the necessarily hierarchical, centralised, Jacobin and anti-libertarian by principle structure which has the name *State*—that we have also inevitably neglected to a certain extent in our criticism of current institutions so-called *Justice*. We have often spoken of it, anarchist journals are constantly criticising it, and yet we have not yet sufficiently undermined it in very its foundations.

This study was written to draw more attention to and to provoke discussion on this subject.

* * *

The study of the development of institutions necessarily leads to the conclusion that *State* and *Justice*—that is to say, the judge, the tribunal specifically instituted to establish justice in society—are two institutions which not only co-exist in history but are intrinsically linked together by the bonds of cause and effect. The institution of judges specially designated to apply the punishments of the law to those who have violated it necessarily brings about the establishment of the State. And whoever admits the necessity of the judge and tribunal specifically designated for this function, with all the system of laws and punishments which result from this, admits by this very fact the necessity of the State. It needs a body that enacts the laws, the

English in 1880 as *History of Political Economy in Europe*) was the first major work. The revolutionary Louis-Auguste Blanqui was his younger brother. (Editor)

uniformity of [legal] codes, the university to teach the interpretation and manufacturing of laws, a system of jails and executioners, the police and an army in the service of the State.

Indeed, the primitive tribe, always communist, knows no judge. Within the tribe, between members of the same tribe, theft, murder, assault *do not exist*. Custom is sufficient to prevent them. But in the extremely rare cases of someone breaking the sacred customs of the tribe, the whole tribe would stone or burn him [to death]. Each one would throw his stone at him, each one would bring his bundle of wood, in order that it would not be this or that person but the whole tribe that put him to death.

And if a man of another tribe has offended one of us, or has inflicted a wound, all our tribe *must* either kill the first person met from this other tribe or inflict upon anyone of that other tribe a wound of absolutely the same kind and size: not a grain of wheat (the millimetre of the time) wider or deeper.

This was their conception of justice.

* * *

Later on, in the village commune of the first centuries of our era, conceptions of justice changed. The idea of vengeance is little by little abandoned (very slowly, especially amongst farmers but surviving amongst warrior bands) and that of *compensation* for the wronged individual and family spreads. With the appearance of the separate, patriarchal and property-owning family (in livestock or slaves abducted from other tribes) compensation more and more takes the character of an evaluation of what the man who has been offended in some way, wounded or killed is "worth" (in possessions): so much for the slave, so much for the peasant, so much for the warrior chief or kinglet that a family has lost. This evaluation of men is the essence of the first barbarian codes.

The village commune gathers and it witnesses the *fact* of the affirmation of six or twelve jurors of each of the two parties who want to prevent brutal revenge occurring and prefer to pay and accept [instead] some compensation. The elders of the commune, or the *bards* who memorise the law (the evaluation of the men of different castes) in their songs, or else judges *invited* by the commune, determine the rate for the injury: so much an amount of livestock for such a wound or such a murder. For theft, it is simply the restoration of the stolen thing or its equivalent, plus a fine paid to the local gods or to the commune.

But little by little, in the midst of migration and conquests, the free communes of many tribes are enslaved, tribes and federations with different customs mix on the same territory, there are conquerors and conquered. And there is also the priest and the bishop—feared sorcerers—of the Christian religion who have settled amongst them. And little by little the bard, the invited judge, the elders who formally determined the rate of compensation are replaced by the judge sent by the bishop, the chief of the conqueror's military band, the lord or the kinglet. These, having learned something in the monasteries or at the court of the kings and taking inspiration from the example of the *Old Testament* will little by little become judges in the modern sense of the word. The fine which was formerly paid to the local gods—to the commune—now goes to the bishop, the kinglet, his lieutenant, or the lord. The fine becomes fundamental, while the compensation granted to the injured for the harm done them loses its importance with respect to the fine paid to this seed of the State. The idea of punishment starts to be introduced, then to dominate. The Christian Church especially does not wish to be content with compensation; it wants to punish, to impose its authority, to terrorise according to the model of its Hebrew predecessors. An injury to a man of the priesthood is no longer a mere wound: it is a crime of treason against god. In addition to compensation, punishment is required and the barbarity of the punishment increases. Secular power does the same.

* * *

In the tenth and eleventh centuries the revolution in the urban communes takes shape. They begin by driving out the judge of the bishop, of the lord, of the kinglet and they make their "conjuration." The burghers first swear to abandon all disputes arising from the law of retaliation. And when new disputes arise, never to seek the judge of the bishop or the lord but to go to the guild, the parish, or the commune. The syndics elected by the guild, the street, the parish, the commune or, in more severe cases, the guild, the parish, the commune gathered in full assembly will decide the compensation to be granted to the wronged party.

Furthermore, arbitration at all levels—between individuals, between guilds, between communes—reaches a really formidable expansion.

But, on the other hand, Christianity and the renewed study of Roman law also find their way into popular notions. The priest speaks only of the vengeance of a spiteful and vengeful god. His favourite argument (it is still the same in our day) is the eternal retribution that will be inflicted upon he who has sinned against the directives of the clergy. And, supported by the words of the gospels concerning those possessed by the devil, it sees a demonic spirit in every criminal and invents all kinds of tortures to drive the devil from the body of the "criminal." It burns him if necessary. And as, since its beginnings, the priest had concluded an alliance with the lord, and the priest himself is always a secular lord and the pope a king, the priest also denounces and pursues with his vengeance those who have broken the secular faith imposed by the warrior chief, the lord, the king, the priest-lord, the king-pope. The Pope himself, who is continually addressed as a supreme arbiter, surrounds himself with jurists versed in Roman Imperial and seigniorial law. Human common sense, knowledge of habits and customs, understanding of men, his equals—which previously were the qualities of the popular courts—are declared useless, harmful, fostering evil passions, inspirations of the devil, the rebellious spirit. "Precedent," the decision of such-and-such a judge, makes *law* and to give more control over the mind they seek the precedent in increasingly remote eras—in the decisions and laws of the Rome of the emperors and of the Hebrew Empire [of 1050–920 BCE].

Arbitration disappears more and more as the lord, prince, king, bishop, pope become more and more powerful and the alliance between temporal and clerical powers becomes more and more close. They no longer permit the arbitrator to intervene and demand by force that the parties in dispute appear before *their* lieutenants and judges. The compensation to the wronged party almost disappears entirely from "criminal" cases and is soon almost entirely replaced by *vengeance* wielded in the name of the Christian God or the Roman State. Under the influence of the East, punishments become more and more atrocious. The Church, and following it the temporal power, reach a refinement of cruelty in punishment which renders the reading or picturing of the punishments inflicted in the fifteenth and sixteenth centuries almost impossible for a modern reader.

* * *

The fundamental ideas on this essential, pivotal point of any human group have thus completely changed between the eleventh and sixteenth centuries. And when the State, by virtue of the causes we have sought to clarify in the study on *The State and its historic role*, when the State seizes the cities that have already renounced, *even in ideas*, the principles of federal arbitration and popular compensative justice (the essence of the commune of the twelfth century)—the conquest is relatively easy. The communes, under the influence of Christianity and Roman Law, had already become small States, they had already become statist in their dominant conceptions.

Certainly, it is extremely interesting to trace how the economic changes taking place during these five centuries, how distant commerce, exportation, creation of banks and of communal borrowing, wars, colonisation, and the seeds of production under the supervision of a capitalist entrepreneur, substitute themselves for communal production, consumption and commerce—it is very interesting, we say, to trace how these various and many economic factors influenced the dominant ideas of the century. Superb research in this direction has been disseminated by the historians of the communes in their works, along with a few analyses (more much difficult, yet always heterodox) on the influence of the dominant Christian and Roman ideas which are also disseminated in these works. But it would be just as false and anti-scientific to attribute an exaggerated and decisive influence to the first of these factors as it would be false in botany to say that the amount of heat received by a plant only or predominantly determines its growth, and to forget the influence of light or humidity. All the more false if were a case of specifying the factors which determine the variations in a given species.

* * *

This short historical sketch already reveals the extent to which the institution of societal vengeance, called justice, and the State are two interconnected, mutually supportive and historically inseparable institutions, each creating the other.

But a moment of quiet reflection is sufficient to understand how both are *logically inseparable*; how both have a common origin in the same circle of ideas about authority ensuring the safety of society and exercising vengeance on those who break the established precedents—the Law.

Give us judges, specially appointed by you or your rulers, to avenge ourselves against those who have broken the legal precedents gathered in the codes—or only to avenge Society in the name of the Law against violations of social customs—and the State is the logical consequence. And furthermore, retain the pyramidal, centralised institution meddling in the life of societies which we call the State—and you necessarily have judges appointed or approved by the State, supported by the executive power, to take revenge in the name of the State against those who have infringed its regulations.

* * *

Today we live in a time when a complete revision is to be made to all the foundations, to all the fundamental ideas on which modern society rests. We describe as legal theft or usurpation the property rights on land and social capital; we deny these rights. We describe as monopolies, established by a governing Mafia, the rights acquired by the shareholders of the railways, gas, etc. We describe as brigands the States that hurl themselves at each other with the aim of conquest.

And it now depends on ourselves whether we stop halfway and, paying tribute to our education of Christian and Roman vengeance, respect the bastard-child of these two currents of ideas—so-called justice—or bring the sharp axe of criticism to the institution that is the real basis of capitalism and the State.

Or else, instilled with prejudices of vengeance, of a vengeful God whose task we must lighten and of a State deified to the point of regarding it as the incarnation of justice, we will keep the institution—the secular arm of God—which we call Justice. We will give ourselves judges, appointed by ourselves or by our rulers, and we will say to them: "Ensure that the customs and judicial precedents known as the Law are respected. Strike, you incarnations of justice, those who have broken the social customs of the community. We will give you the necessary physical means of coercion as well as our moral support... Act."

Then the State—the force which is placed above Society and which inevitably seeks to centralise, to enlarge its powers—is constituted and will last until a new revolution comes to overthrow it.

The arbitrator could judge and be judged according to the understanding of justice in each separate case, his knowledge and understanding of existing human relationships, his conception of individual and social conscience. The judge appointed to adjudicate, specialised to punish, *must* have a code. Therefore we need a legislative machine, an organisation to create the code, to choose between the various precedents and to crystallise in the shape of law those of them that it finds useful to preserve. Direct government, that is to say the nation asked on how to formulate the mandatory precedent (the law), is obviously a chimera which even the supporters of direct government do not believe in. It *needs* indirect government, superior men, the *Uebermensch* (hero) of Nietzsche, appointed to *formulate* laws.

It also needs men to interpret the formulas of the laws, the university of the jurists. And these men will necessarily become maniacs of the verb and the letter; they will place upon society all the weight of the relics inherited from our ancestors. They will cry "Back!" when we want to move forward.

It needs, moreover, the lector armed with rods and axe—the executive power—force put to the service of the "Law," as the apologists would say of their own virtues. It needs the police, the spy, the agent provocateur and their helper, the prostitute; it needs the executioner; it needs the prison, the prison guard, prison labour and all the rest—all the unimaginable nastiness that surrounds and spreads from the universities of crime, the nurseries of anti-social tendencies that inevitably all prisons become.

And finally it needs the government to supervise, to organise, to rank the army of warders. It needs a formidable tax to maintain this machine, a law to make it work and again judges, police and prisons to enforce the prison legislation.

The judge brings with him the State and whoever wishes to study in history the growth of States will see what an immense, fundamental, paramount part the judge has played in the establishment of the modern centralised State.

* * *

Or else, after having revolutionised our ideas on so many fundamental points that were very sincerely believed to form the very basis of any society (property, the divine mission of kings, etc.), we will descend even further to the very foundations, to the origin of all oppressions. We will carry the torch of our critique to the enforcement of justice confided to a special caste, to the collection of ancient precedents: the Code.

We will then see that the Code (all codes) represents a compilation of precedents, formulas borrowed from notions of economic and intellectual servitude, absolutely repugnant to the conceptions which are emerging amongst us—socialists of all schools. They are crystallised formulas, "survivals," which our slave past wants to impose upon us to prevent our development. And we will repudiate the Code—all codes. It does not matter to us that they contain some affirmations of morality, the general idea of which we ourselves share. Once they impose *punishments* to maintain them, we do not want them—let alone the many servile assertions that each code mixes with its work of the moralisation of man by the whip. Every code is a crystallisation of the past, written to obstruct the growth of the future.

Continuing our criticism, we shall discover, without doubt, that every legal punishment is *a legalised vengeance, made compulsory*; and we will ask ourselves whether vengeance is necessary? Does it help to maintain social customs? Does it hinder the small minority of people who are inclined to violate them, to act contrary to customs? By proclaiming the *duty of vengeance*, does it not precisely serve to *maintain* in society anti-sociable habits? And when we ask whether the system of legal punishment, with the police, the false witness, the spy, the criminal education within prison, the maniac of the code and the rest, does not serve to pour into society a flood of intellectual and moral depravity far more dangerous than the anti-social actions of "criminals"—only when we have asked ourselves this question and have sought the answer in the study of current events, shall we see at once that there can be no hesitation on the answer to be given. We will then reject the system of punishments as we will have rejected codes.

Intellectually liberated from this "survival"—the worst—we can then study (without worrying about what the Church and the State did about it) what are the most practical means (considering men as what they are) to develop in them sociable feelings and to impede the development of anti-social sentiments.

Well! Whoever has done *this* study after getting rid of the judicial tradition will certainly not be able to reach a conclusion in favour of the judge and the prison system. He will look elsewhere.

He will see that arbitration by a third party, chosen by the parties in dispute, would be amply sufficient in the vast majority of cases. He will understand that the non-intervention of those who witness a fight or a conflict that is brewing is simply a bad habit we have acquired since we have the judge, the police, the priest and the State—that the active intervention of friends and neighbours would already prevent the vast majority of violent conflicts.

He will also understand that to give himself a police-force, gendarmes, executioners, prison-warders and judges, solely to carry out legal vengeance on this small minority of people who breach social customs or become aggressive instead of all taking care of themselves and each prepared to stop aggression or to mend its wrongs; that to act in this way is as unreasonable and uneconomic as leaving the task of managing industry to bosses instead of grouping together themselves to satisfy their needs. And if we believe that man can one day dispense with bosses, it is simply out of habit and laziness of thought that we have not yet succeeded in understanding that men who dispense with bosses will be intelligent enough to dispense with the bosses of morals—judges and police. Just as they will seek and find a way to satisfy their needs without bosses, they will be able to find the means (already amply indicated) of increasing human sociability and of preventing individuals too violent or anti-social *by nature* (do they even exist?) becoming a danger to society. Education, more or less guaranteed livelihood, closer contact between men, and above all the mitigation of sentences have already produced many striking changes in this direction. Would we in a collectivist or communist, socialist or anarchist society be less capable of pushing changes even further? Would we be inferior to our present rulers?

Conclusions

The organised public vengeance called Justice is a survival of a past of servitude, developed on the one hand in the interests of the privileged classes and on the other by the ideas of Roman law and those of divine wrath which make up the essence of Christianity just as much as its ideas of forgiveness and its denial of human revenge.

The organisation of societal revenge under the name of Justice corresponds in history with the State phase. Likewise, logically they are inseparable. The judge implies the centralised, Jacobin State; and the State implies the judge specially appointed to exercise legal vengeance on those who are guilty of anti-social acts.

Product of a past of economic, political and intellectual serfdom, this institution serves to perpetuate it. It serves to maintain in society the idea of compulsory revenge, made into a virtue. It serves as a school for anti-social passions in prisons. It pours into society a flood of depravity that ooze around the courts and jails through the police-officer, the executioner, the spy, the agent provocateur, the office of the private informer, etc.—this flood grows every day. The evil in any case exceeds the good that justice is supposed to accomplish by the threat of punishment.

A society which finds the organisation of economic life by the capitalist boss anti-economic and socially harmful would certainly also find that surrendering the development of sociable sentiments to an organisation of judicial vengeance is also anti-economic and anti-libertarian. It would understand that the Code is only a crystallisation, a deification of customs and conceptions of a past that all socialists reject. It can dispense with the judicial institution.

It would find the means to dispense with it in voluntary arbitration, in the closer ties which would arise between all citizens and the powerful educational means available to a society which would not abandon the care of its moral hygiene to the gendarme.

THE STATE: CREATOR OF MONOPOLIES

This short article returns to issues raised in *Modern Science and Anarchy* and was originally published in *Les Temps Nouveaux* (12 July 1913). This is the first time it has been translated.

(Editor)

IN THE CHAPTER "THE MODERN STATE" OF *MODERN SCIENCE AND ANARCHY*, I gave a number of facts proving to what extent the State, whatever its political form, has as its essence the establishment of monopolies to the advantage of certain of its subjects in order to always enrich the wealthy at the expense of the poor. But then recently a whole avalanche of revelations appeared which demonstrate beyond doubt this monopolist activity of the State. It is worthwhile to mention a few.

Thus we learn—printed in full in the official records of the English Parliament for 1899—that at that time out of the 44 people who were then members of the Conservative ministry, 25 were directors of 41 commercial and industrial companies. Of the nineteen ministers proper, eleven were in the same situation.

And these companies were not the paltry operations of some miserable coal mines or of some manufacturing factories: they were, on the contrary, important companies which had big dealings with the government. Thus, one of the ministers, Lord Balfour of Burleigh, was the direct of three companies including the Bank of Scotland, which had very serious dealings with the government; ten others were directors of railway companies and we can see from that the attentiveness of the government in strikes. Lord Selborne, the son-in-law of the Prime Minister and Under-Secretary of the Colonies, was a director of the "Pacific and Eastern" Company which received and still receives very large subsidies from the government. The Duke of Devonshire, chairman of the "Defence Committee of the Empire," was president of the great munitions factories in Barrow; one of the under-secretaries of State sat as the directory of a submarine telegraph company, and so on. And when they discussed it in Parliament, the Minister of Finance took to the floor to defend his colleagues. It was quite natural, he said. And it must be noted that it was a conservative government, composed of rich people, who took advantage of their positions to increase their fortunes.

Besides, to combine the functions of a Member of Parliament with those of the director of various companies is so common in England that a bank or industrial company is never formed without announcing that a number of its directors are a lord, a M.P. (Member of Parliament) or a clergyman. Otherwise no one would subscribe. I remember that in the late 1880s, when there was a new Parliament, the newspapers pointed out that in the Parliament that had just ended more than two-thirds of its members had been directors of companies. In the new Parliament, which contained many newcomers, directors accounted for only a third. It will take, the newspapers said, a few years to reach the level of the previous Parliament!

* * *

And yet, all this is nothing compared to what has just been revealed in America, in the United States. There everything is done bigger.

Thus, on June 20, the newspaper *New York World* began the publication, on four pages in small print, of the revelations of a certain Colonel Mulhall who, for ten years, was the paid agent of the National Association of American Manufacturers for "working" in their interests in the corridors of the legislative body of the United States. This gentleman recounts, with all the names and all the possible details supported by hundreds of letters and telegrams, personal accounts, etc., how he bought votes in the interest of his Association—especially during the Taft presidency when it was a question of American manufacturers preventing the reduction of custom duties on foreign goods and it was necessary to have his men on the committees that could predict in advance the cuts the Democrats would make when they came to power.

It is all an immense system of buying the members of legislative bodies, all this to create and sustain monopolies and thereby fulfils what constitutes the essential, fundamental, function of every State and especially of the modern State.

When will the proletarians, getting rid of the economist metaphysics which they have laboured to fill them, just simply shout out as their grandfathers did at the end of the eighteenth century: *Down with monopolies! String up the monopolists!*[2] Adding this time: *All the State to the rubbish dump!*

---

2   Literally: "*The monopolists to the lamp post!*" (*A la lanterne les monopoleurs*). This slogan gained special meaning in Paris during the early phase of the French Revolution in the summer of 1789. Lamp posts served as an instrument for mobs to hang officials and aristocrats from the lamp posts. In short, "la lanterne" became a symbol of popular justice in revolutionary France and "À la lanterne!" is mentioned in such emblematic songs as the *sans-culotte* version of *Ça Ira*—an unofficial anthem of revolutionaries—which proclaimed "les aristocrates à la lanterne!" ("aristocrats to the lamp-post!"). (Editor)

INDEX

A

Académie des Sciences, 98n7

Act of Edward III, 266–7, 267n27

adaptation/harmony/equilibrium, 457, 459

affinity groups, 164–5, 166–7

Alexander II of Russia, 195, 327, 371, 483

Alexander of Macedonia, 276, 371

Algirdas, 371–2

Amana Colony, 372

Anabaptism, 86, 258, 372

analogies, 114

anarchism: *agent provocateur*, 287n6; anti-State ideas and, 43, 50; authority and human nature, 471, 473; in Christianity, 86; as common people movement, 83–5, 134; "goodness," 12, 14–15, 17; from individual to social, 163; justice and equality, 176–7; labour goals, 163–4; legislators and, 169; liberalism and, 41; misrepresentation, 452, 471; need for scientific method, 53; origins of, 30–2, 32n84, 83–7, 86n1, 97, 136–7, 138; overview, 133–5, 197–9, 451–85; Paris Commune boosting, 160; social struggles and, 51; using tendencies in society, 15–16, 479; visualization of outcome, 130–2; Wolff critiques, 12–13, 14; workers encourage to adopt, 54

anarchism, individualistic, 33–6, 138–9, 171–3, 171n43, 441–2. *See also* individualism; Tucker, Benjamin

anarchist communism: addressing humanity's problem, 206; beginnings, 203, 203n1, 206–7; as common goal, 211; freedom and, 226; Hussite uprising, 258–9, 397; objections over, 206–7, 478; Spencer close to, 441–2. *See also* anarchism and communism

anarchism and communism: capitalist production, 185, 195n55; collectivism, 157; communism attack with war views, 58–9; dictatorship of communism, 51–2; insurrections (general), 195n74; labour and capital ideas, 167; State property, 168; workers' organizations, 54–5

anarchism and science: anarchism as subdivision of science, 130; dialectical method and, 127; evolution, 15; as mechanical

F

G

AK Press is small, in terms of staff and resources, but we also manage to be one of the world's most productive anarchist publishing houses. We publish close to twenty books every year, and distribute thousands of other titles published by like-minded independent presses and projects from around the globe. We're entirely worker-run and democratically managed. We operate without a corporate structure— no boss, no managers, no bullshit.

The Friends of AK program is a way you can directly contribute to the continued existence of AK Press, and ensure that we're able to keep publishing books like this one! Friends pay $25 a month directly into our publishing account ($30 for Canada, $35 for international), and receive a copy of every book AK Press publishes for the duration of their membership! Friends also receive a discount on anything they order from our website or buy at a table: 50% on AK titles, and 20% on everything else. We have a Friends of AK ebook program as well: $15 a month gets you an electronic copy of every book we publish for the duration of your membership. You can even sponsor a very discounted membership for someone in prison.

Email FRIENDSOFAK@AKPRESS.ORG for more info, or visit the Friends of AK Press website: HTTPS://WWW.AKPRESS.ORG/FRIENDS.HTML.

There are always great book projects in the works—so sign up now to become a Friend of AK Press, and let the presses roll!